SONCINO BOOKS OF THE BIBLE
EDITOR: REV. DR. A. COHEN, M.A., Ph.D., D.H.L.

Ezekiel

HEBREW TEXT & ENGLISH TRANSLATION
WITH AN INTRODUCTION
AND COMMENTARY

by
RABBI DR. S. FISCH, M.A.

*And they shall say: This land that was
desolate is become like the garden of Eden;
and the waste and desolate and ruined
cities are fortified and inhabited.*
EZEKIEL xxxvi. 35.

THE SONCINO PRESS
LONDON · NEW YORK

FIRST EDITION 1950
SECOND EDITION 1960
THIRD EDITION 1964
FOURTH EDITION 1966
FIFTH EDITION 1968
SIXTH EDITION 1970
SEVENTH EDITION 1972
EIGHTH EDITION 1976
NINTH EDITION 1978
TENTH EDITION 1985

PUBLISHERS' NOTE

*Thanks are due to the
Jewish Publication Society of America
for permission to use their very beautiful
English text of the Scriptures.*

MANUFACTURED IN THE UNITED STATES OF AMERICA

FOREWORD BY THE GENERAL EDITOR

IT has been said by a modern commentator that 'the Book of Ezekiel is generally considered to be one of the most difficult in the Bible ; it is certainly one of the most interesting.' No reader of the Book is likely to contest this judgment. The personality of Ezekiel, in particular, is a fascinating psychological problem. May this volume, which concludes the section of the prophets in THE SONCINO BOOKS OF THE BIBLE, help in the understanding of the man and his message!

The series is distinctive in the following respects :

(*i*) Each volume contains the Hebrew text and English translation together with the commentary. (*ii*) The exposition is designed primarily for the ordinary reader of the Bible rather than for the student, and aims at providing this class of reader with requisite direction for the understanding and appreciation of the Biblical Book. (*iii*) The commentary is invariably based upon the received Hebrew text. When this present difficulties, the most probable translation and interpretation are suggested, without resort to textual emendation. (*iv*) It offers a *Jewish* commentary. Without neglecting the valuable work of Christian expositors, it takes into account the exegesis of the Talmudical Rabbis as well as of the leading Jewish commentators.

All Biblical references are cited according to chapter and verse as in the Hebrew Bible. It is unfortunate that, unlike the American-Jewish translation, the English Authorized and Revised Versions, although made direct from the Hebrew text, did not conform to its chapter divisions. An undesirable complication was thereby introduced into Bible study. In the Hebrew the longer headings of the Psalms are counted as a separate verse ; consequently Ps. xxxiv. 12, e.g., corresponds to verse 11 in A.V. and R.V. It is also necessary to take into account a marginal note like that found against 1 Kings iv. 21, 'ch. v. 1 in Heb.', so that the Hebrew 1 Kings v. 14 tallies with iv. 34 in the English.

It is hoped that this Commentary, though more particularly planned for the needs of Jews, will prove helpful to all who desire a fuller knowledge of the Bible, irrespective of their creed.

A. COHEN

CONTENTS

INTRODUCTION

I. EZEKIEL: HIS LIFE AND PERSONALITY

(a) HIS LIFE

THE Book tells little of Ezekiel's personal life. He was the son of Buzi, born of the priestly family of Zadok. It is known from xxiv. 16ff. that he was married and his wife died suddenly. Carried away captive by the Babylonians from the Holy Land with king Jehoiachin, he lived in Tel-abib on the banks of the river Chebar (iii. 15), which seems to have been an area of settlement for the exiles.

Ezekiel received his prophetic call five years after he had arrived in Babylon (i. 2), but there is no indication given of the length of his ministry. His last prophecy was *in the five and twentieth year of our captivity* (xl. 1). This would extend his prophetic activities at least over a period of twenty years. Nor is there any authentic record as to the date of his death or the location of his grave. There is, however, a tradition that he died in Babylon during the reign of Nebuchadnezzar and was buried at Kefil, near Birs Nimrud, between the rivers Chebar and Euphrates. For centuries Mohammedans and Jews made pilgrimages to a magnificent tomb which exists there and to the nearby Synagogue named after him. Tradition also has it that king Jehoiachin, after he had been liberated by Evil-merodach, erected the mausoleum and the adjoining building. Over the grave there was, as late as the twelfth century, a lamp continually burning, and in the Synagogue ancient books and a Sepher Torah were preserved, alleged to have been written by Ezekiel, which were used for public reading of the Scriptures on the Day of Atonement (see Benjamin of Tudela, *Itinerary*, ed. Asher, i. 67).

(b) EZEKIEL THE PROPHET

Three distinct strains may be detected in his personality. He was, first of all, a prophet, indeed the outstanding prophetic figure during the exile. No definite proof exists that his prophetic mission had already begun in the Holy Land before he was carried off to Babylon. But since the Rabbis held that prophecy could not flourish outside the Holy Land, they believed that Ezekiel was already active as a prophet before his deportation (cf. M.K. 25a and Rashi *ad loc.*; Mechilta, Bo i; Targum to Ezek. i. 3). Two suggestions were made by Jehudah Halevi (*Kuzari*, II. 14) to account for Ezekiel's power of prophecy in a foreign land: his oracles related to the Holy Land, and he had lived there whence he derived his fitness for his prophetic calling. Whatever the reason, the fact remains that he was the only prophet whose sphere of activity lay outside the Land of Israel.

This is not the only exceptional characteristic of Ezekiel's prophetic career. Ezekiel is unique among the Hebrew prophets both in the nature of his vision and in his mode of expression. He is the only prophet who was addressed by the title *son of man*, the phrase occurring about a hundred times in the Book. The designation was intended to emphasize the mortal nature of man even when he had the privilege of beholding the vision of the Glory of God, and to check any tendency towards self-aggrandizement on his part. The term *son of man* indicates that whatever spiritual height a human being may reach, he remains just man (see on ii. 1).

Another phrase peculiar to Ezekiel is *the hand of the LORD came upon*, or a variant of the words (cf. i. 3, iii. 14, 22, viii. 1, xxxiii. 22, xxxvii. 1, xl. 1). Here, again, it was the awe-inspiring and overwhelming vision of the Divine Glory that rendered him temporarily incapable of receiving the communication from God, and he needed His aid to sustain him. The Rabbis declared that whatever Ezekiel beheld was also revealed to Isaiah, the difference being in their reception of their respective visions. Isaiah, they asserted, was like a city-dweller who saw the King often, while Ezekiel was like a villager who saw the King but rarely (Chag. 13b). In the

ix

Mechilta to Exod. xv. 2, there is a statement by R. Eliezer that at the miraculous crossing of the Red Sea, even a handmaid saw more of the Divine Glory than did Ezekiel and the other prophets. Nevertheless, Ezekiel's vision of the *Merkabah* was exceptionally vivid and terrifying.

He is further distinguished by his frequent use of simile and allegory, parable and symbol, and particularly by the performance of symbolical actions. These forms of his teaching, especially his symbolical acts, had the object of dispelling the people's illusory reliance upon the immunity of Jerusalem. The purpose was to demonstrate the final and irrevocable nature of the Divine judgment upon Israel (see further on this subject, Nachmanides on Gen. xii. 6).

On the question whether the prophet actually performed the symbolical actions in full sight of the people, or whether he described to them what was only a vision, there are varying views. It seems probable, as suggested by some authorities, that certain of them, such as his lying on his sides for a great number of days, were only in vision.

The style and diction of Ezekiel are also different from those of other prophets. While they clothed their utterances in highly poetic phrases, Ezekiel spoke mainly in prose, and even his poetic passages have not the lyrical and imaginative quality of the other prophets. The reason for his peculiar style may lie in the nature of his discourses. It messages were addressed to a people who had suffered the humiliating disaster of captivity, and in the circumstances only plain language was likely to achieve the purpose he had in view. He did not need to stir their imagination; his function was to give them positive directions (Malbim, Introduction to the Book).

Like all the prophets, Ezekiel lays his chief emphasis on the return of the people to the Torah as the eternal principle of Jewish life and to the covenant governing Israel's existence. All authentic prophecy is based upon the complete integrity of the Revelation on Sinai, with its basic teachings upon man's relationship to God and his fellows. All prophets paid due attention to both

aspects of human life and action, regulated by the ceremonial and ethical doctrines of Judaism.

Quite alien to the authentic Jewish outlook is the allegation of some critics that Ezekiel was unable to distinguish between the ritual and moral elements in religion, since he coupled high social morality with ritualistic demands, such as not eating the flesh with its blood and the desecration of the Sabbath (cf. Lofthouse, Introduction, p. 37; Wheeler Robinson, *Two Hebrew Prophets*, pp. 101f.). Ezekiel has even been accused of caring for nothing but the externals of religion. To this charge, Kirkpatrick (*The Doctrine of the Prophets*, p. 347) rightly retorts, 'Nothing can be more unfair than such an assertion.' The truth is that in Judaism the ethical and the 'religious' are inseparable. In conformity with this doctrine Ezekiel linked both together as equal essentials (cf. xxii. 1ff.). The basis of the ethical law is that man is made in the image of God, and it is the logical extension of the so-called ritual law which expresses man's reverence for the majesty of God.

(c) EZEKIEL THE PRIEST

Ezekiel, like his predecessor Jeremiah (according to Targum Yerushalmi quoted by Kimchi on i. 3, Buzi his father was identical with Jeremiah), belonged to the priesthood. It is doubtful whether he functioned as a priest in the Temple at Jerusalem before his exile, but it is reasonable to assume that he was trained in, and familiar with, the priestly duties.

His dual personality as prophet and priest is conspicuously reflected in his discourses. As a prophet he predicted the fall of Jerusalem and the ultimate restoration and regeneration of the people. As a priest he described the structure of the future Temple, and gave a minutely detailed account of the form of worship to be practised in it.

This mental precision is also evident in his prophecies relating to the fall of Jerusalem and the destruction of the heathen nations. The vision of the Temple of the future is a natural corollary to the prophecy concerning the final restoration of Israel. As Moses was shown a plan of the Tabernacle and king

David one of the Temple, which were to serve as models for the Sanctuaries to be subsequently built, so was Ezekiel shown a complete plan of the Sanctuary to be restored (cf. Jehudah Halevi, *Kuzari*, I. 99). That the discourses on the Temple, the order of service therein, and the division of the land among the people, refer to the Messianic age is evident from the fact that these immediately follow the prophecies dealing with the annihilation of Gog, which is to occur *in the end of days* (xxxviii. 16), after which peace and security would be established in Israel for ever.

A characteristic of Ezekiel is his concern with the ceremonial law. There are several traditional laws, not mentioned in the Pentateuch, which are recorded by him and so preserved for posterity. Talmudical references to them are found in Yoma 71b; M.K. 5a, 15b, 27b; Sanh. 81a, 83b.

The text of the concluding chapters, dealing with the Temple of the future, presents almost insurmountable difficulties. The types and number of sacrifices prescribed there differ from those mentioned in the Pentateuch; and there are many innovations which, according to the accepted law, are normally beyond the authority of a prophet to institute (Shab. 104a). With reference to these difficulties the Rabbis said that only Elijah, the prophet who is to herald the final redemption, will be able to explain them satisfactorily (Men. 45a).

(d) EZEKIEL THE MYSTIC ; THE MERKABAH

The most remarkable section of the Book is the opening chapter, in which the prophet tells of his experience by the banks of the river Chebar where he saw in the opened heavens the Divine Throne-Chariot. It gave rise to a system of esoteric thought known in Rabbinic literature as *Ma'aseh Merkabah*.

The origin of the term *Merkabah* in the mystical sense is generally attributed to Rabbinic sources. This is not correct. The word occurs in 1 Chron. xxviii. 18 as a designation for the cherubim, thus becoming a classical term in Talmudic gnosticism. The vision of the *Merkabah* by Ezekiel was not an entirely new

phenomenon in the revelation of God to man. God manifested Himself in a similar vision to Isaiah and perhaps to other prophets before him, and on mount Sinai all Israel beheld the Divine Presence (cf. Chag. 13b; Deut. Rabbah vii. 8; Pesikta Rabbathi, Parashath Hachodesh). What is new in Ezekiel's vision of the *Merkabah* is his bold and detailed description of it (cf. Maimonides, *Guide*, III. 6). Talmudic and Midrashic sources abound in evidence that mysticism was a branch of study among Jews at an early stage in their history, and Ezekiel's vision of the *Merkabah* served as an important element in this esoteric lore.

The occult doctrine was, however, reserved for men of the highest degree of mental and moral perfection. In the Mishnah (Chag. ii. 1), the law enacts that the account of the creation (*Ma'aseh Bereshith*) is not to be expounded in the presence of more than one person and the story of the *Merkabah* not even to one unless he be wise and of independent insight. According to Maimonides (Introduction to the *Guide*), the phrase *Ma'aseh Bereshith* in the Mishnah just quoted denotes natural science and *Ma'aseh Merkabah* metaphysics. Franck (*The Kabbalah*, p. 69) rightly arrives at the conclusion 'that a certain philosophy, a religious metaphysics was, so to speak, orally taught among some of the Tannaim, or the most ancient theologians of Judaism'.

In accordance with the Talmudic teaching (Chag. 13a) that less important parts of the *Merkabah* may be taught to men of high mental and moral standard, Maimonides expounded Ezekiel's vision in his *Guide* (III. 7), which he wrote primarily for his disciple R. Joseph ibn Aknin. But at the close of the chapter he reminded his pupil of the Talmudic restriction and requested him not to ask for a more detailed instruction (cf. also his Introduction). Referring to this exposition in the *Guide*, Malbim (Introduction to *Ezekiel*) remarked that, apart from the objections of Maimonides' critics to his interpretation, it was now out of date since the astronomical and philosophical principles upon which it was based had been abandoned. The

most remarkable passage in Maimonides' exposition is that in which he explains the closing clause, *This was the appearance of the likeness of the glory of the LORD* (i. 28). His comment is: '*The glory of the LORD* is different from "the Lord" Himself. All the figures in this vision refer to the glory of the Lord, i.e. to the chariot, and not to Him Who rides upon the chariot; for God cannot be compared to anything' (III. 7).

It is generally agreed that Jewish mysticism, from its beginning down to the later study of the Kabbalah, centred around the vision of the *Merkabah*. The most important tracts in the *Merkabah* literature are those called Hechaloth and the Books of Enoch. It is noteworthy that, commenting on *Ma'aseh ha-Merkabah u-Ma'aseh Bereshith* in Chag. 13a, Rashi remarked: 'These are the names of Baraithoth,' apparently referring to the Hechaloth tracts (cf. Midrash to *Proverbs*, ed. Buber, p. 34a, where an account of the principal subjects of *Merkabah* mysticism is given; Ginzberg, *Ginzë Schechter*, I, pp. 182ff.). It has been proved that the Books of Enoch were known to Jews and only neglected by them after Christianity had gained strength and used them as a support for its doctrines (cf. Jellinek, *Beth ha-Midrash*, IV, Introduction, pp. xi f.). Much of the Merkabah literature has not yet been published and important material on the subject is still extant in Hebrew MSS. (cf. Scholem, *Major Trends in Jewish Mysticism*, p. 44).

An attempt has been made to attribute to Midrashic sources a reinterpretation of the *Merkabah*. In support of this line of thought, Scholem (pp. 77f.) quotes the Midrashic passage in Gen. Rabbah lxxxii. 6: 'The patriarchs are the *Merkabah*.' To suggest that this dictum refers to the soul of man as being the *Merkabah* of Ezekiel's vision betrays a misunderstanding of Rabbinic idiom. What is intended is that as the *Ophannim*, *Chayyoth* and *Galgallim*, etc. ('wheels, living creatures and wheel-work') form the Divine Chariot in heaven, so were the patriarchs the Divine Chariot on earth, in that they brought the Glory of God down to the mundane sphere.

The *Merkabah* literature has left traces in the Jewish daily morning prayers, in the liturgy of the Festivals and, in particular, the liturgical poems of Eliezer Kalir. The famous *Merkabah* hymn, *Ha'adereth weha'emunah lechai olamim*, referred to as the 'Song of the Angels', which is to be found with several variations in the 'Greater Hechaloth' (Jellinek, *Beth ha-Midrash*, III, pp. 103f.), is recited by chasidic congregations every Sabbath in the morning ritual, and in all Synagogues on the Day of Atonement. Likewise, the first chapter of *Ezekiel* forms the *haphtarah* (lection from the prophets) on the first day of the Feast of Pentecost—a fitting theme for the anniversary of the revelation on Sinai.

II. EZEKIEL'S CALL AND ITS HISTORICAL BACKGROUND

The Hebrew prophet was originally called *roëh*, 'seer' (cf. 1 Sam. ix. 9) and at a later period was given the title of *nabi*, 'inspired speaker.' These designations do not signify two different types of prophets but are complementary. The term *roëh* indicates the power to behold visions, while the term *nabi* emphasizes the ability to convey the Divine message to the people by word of mouth. Both functions were necessary for the mission of the prophet. He was preacher, counsellor, sociologist, reformer and inspired critic of society. The prophet was, in the language of Scripture, a 'watchman' (iii. 17) to the people; or, as a modern historian expressed it, 'a storm-bird of world history.' He raised his voice of warning on the eve of critical events. When disaster befell and despair overwhelmed the people and threatened them with extinction, they turned to him for guidance, and the stern preacher became a sympathetic friend, comforting and directing them in their sorrows.

Aglow with the loftiest religious, ethical and political ideals, the prophets originated a style of oratory in which pathos and lyrical fervour, poetry and sober prose are found side by side. Their discourses, which were committed to writing by them or their disciples, are generally regarded as an incomparable spiritual treasury. Among the out-

standing of the prophets were Amos and Hosea in the Northern Kingdom, Isaiah, Micah and Jeremiah in Judea, and Ezekiel in Babylon.

The call Ezekiel received to take up his prophetic career in *the fifth year of king Jehoiachin's captivity* (i. 2), i.e. 593-2 B.C.E., came at a most crucial time in the nation's history. In that year a plot against the domination of the Babylonian invader was being prepared jointly by the patriots in Jerusalem and the exiles in Babylon. Ezekiel saw in this movement rebellion against God's judgment and therefore a threat to the nation's existence. Similarly, Jeremiah advised the exiles to submit to the king of Babylon (Jer. xxix. 5ff.). During the fateful years which preceded the destruction of Jerusalem, Ezekiel's addresses to his fellow-Jews were in the nature of exhortations against their dangerous policy and a prediction of the fate of the Holy City.

His orations were addressed to the people who were still left in Judea and to his fellow-exiles in Babylon, and the vision of the *Merkabah* in motion was a fitting introduction to his prophetic career. The main feature of the Divine Chariot drawn by the four-faced living creatures was its mobility. Hence Ezekiel saw *wheels* in his vision, which were not seen by Isaiah in his vision of the Divine Throne (Isa. vi). The sight of the departing *Merkabah* (chap. x) suggested to him the impending departure of the Divine Presence from the Temple in Jerusalem and the collapse of the Southern Kingdom.

III. THE BOOK

(a) ITS CONTENTS

Ezekiel is distinguished from the other prophetical Books in its methodical arrangement. It is divided into two equal sections of twenty-four chapters each. The first part deals with the siege and fall of Jerusalem and the destruction of the State, while the latter part is devoted to the regeneration of the people.

The two parts fall into several subdivisions. The first consists of (*i*) the revelation to Ezekiel and his appointment to the office of prophet (i-iii. 21).

(*ii*) The prophecies concerning the destruction of the national community (iii. 22-vii). (*iii*) The sins of Jerusalem and their sequel (viii-xii). (*iv*) The iniquities of Judah and the consequent punishment (xiii-xix). (*v*) Additional prophecies on the imminent fall of the State (xx-xxiv).

The latter section consists of three parts: (*i*) Prophecies on the annihilation of the heathen nations, the hostile neighbours of Judah (Ammon, Moab, Edom, Philistia, Tyre, Sidon and Egypt) (xxv-xxxii). These form an introduction to the concluding chapters which treat of the restoration of Israel, the destruction of those nations paving the way for the return of the exiled community to the Holy Land. (*ii*) Prophecies referring to the deliverance of Judah and Israel (xxxiii-xxxix). (*iii*) The plan and measurements of the future Temple and the new order in the restored Judah (xl-xlviii).

Another feature in the arrangement of the Book is that most of the prophecies are dated from Jehoiachin's captivity or from the reign of Zedekiah. The following are the dates which precede the prophecies: *the fifth year of king Jehoiachin's captivity* (i. 2); *the sixth year* (viii. 1); *the seventh year* (xx. 1); *the ninth year* (xxiv. 1); *the tenth year* (xxix. 1); *the eleventh year* (xxvi. 1, xxx. 20, xxxi. 1); *the twelfth year* (xxii. 1, 17, xxxiii. 21); *the five and twentieth year* (xl. 1); *the seven and twentieth year* (xxix. 17). This last date is reckoned from the reign of Nebuchadnezzar (see *ad loc.*).

(b) THE RABBIS AND THE BOOK

The Talmud reveals the fact that the Book of Ezekiel was at one time in danger of being suppressed and excluded from the Scriptural canon. In Shab. 13b the following passage occurs: 'Rab Judah said in the name of Rab: In truth, that man is to be remembered for blessing; his name is Chananiah son of Hezekiah. Had it not been for him, the Book of Ezekiel would have been withdrawn, because its words seem to contradict the teachings of the Torah. What did he do? Three hundred barrels of oil were provided for him (for lighting and food)

and he sat in an upper chamber where he reconciled all discrepancies.'

According to this passage, which is also repeated in other Talmudic sources, Chananiah, a Rabbi of the first century C.E., must have written an extensive commentary on *Ezekiel*. Of that commentary only a few fragments survive in the Talmud (cf. Men. 45a). Yet, despite this Rabbi's efforts at harmonization, many divergences were detected between the Book and the Mosaic code which baffled all attempts at reconciliation (cf. Introduction Ic).

(c) PLACE IN THE CANON

The Book of Ezekiel is now placed after *Isaiah* and *Jeremiah*, but in Talmudic times the order was *Jeremiah*, *Ezekiel* and *Isaiah*, the reason given in the Talmud (B.B. 14b) being that such was the natural order of the subject-matter. That means, *Jeremiah*, consisting mainly of predictions of national woe, follows *Kings*, which concludes with the account of the destruction of Jerusalem; and *Isaiah*, foretelling Israel's redemption, should follow *Ezekiel* which begins with forebodings of disaster and ends on a note of hope.

The Talmudic order, which is given as the undisputed opinion of the Rabbis, is also accepted by Maimonides in his Code (*Hilchoth Sepher Torah* vii. 15) and by the *Shulchan Aruch* (*Yoreh Deah* 283, 5). It has been conjectured that the Books were subsequently arranged in their existing order according to the criterion of their size.

(d) AUTHORSHIP AND COPY

There has never been doubt cast upon the unity of the Book. Not even the more advanced Biblical critics have suggested a Deutero- or Trito-Ezekiel. Nevertheless, some scholars of recent times, in spite of the straightforwardness and simplicity of *Ezekiel*, have advanced the theory that 'considerable additions have been made to his work' (cf. Wheeler Robinson, *Two Hebrew Prophets*, pp. 70ff.). The difficulties found in the text to support this theory are groundless and artificial. The methodical composition of the Book from beginning to end is evidence that it is the work of one man. The conservative scholar, Kirkpatrick, confirms the traditional view: 'The Book of Ezekiel bears the marks of careful plan and arrangement, and comes to us in all probability direct from the prophet himself. He speaks throughout in the first person' (*op. cit.* p. 336).

While Ezekiel is the author of the Book in its entirety, the final copy for inclusion in the canon was not written by him. In a Talmudic passage the statement is made, 'The men of the Great Synagogue wrote Ezekiel, the Twelve Prophets, Daniel and the Scroll of Esther' (B.B. 15a). The meaning is that these Books, though composed by their respective authors, were authoritatively revised and issued by the men of the Great Synagogue. One reason for this, stated by Rashi, was that the scene of the prophecies of *Ezekiel*, *Daniel* and *Esther* was 'outside the Holy Land.' Apparently, finality in connection with Holy Writ was not permitted in a foreign land; it was therefore necessary for the men of the Great Synagogue to give their approval to those exilic writings. As regards *The Twelve Prophets*, because they were small in size, the authors did not issue them as separate Books; but when the last prophets, Haggai, Zechariah and Malachi, themselves members of the Great Synagogue, decided to edit their prophecies, they included those of the other prophets in one scroll as a safeguard against their loss.

IV. THEOLOGICAL AND ETHICAL DOCTRINES

Divine Justice. In connection with his appointment as *watchman unto the house of Israel* (iii. 17ff.), Ezekiel referred to his duty to warn the renegade people before God laid *a stumblingblock before him*. Some non-Jewish commentators detect in the passage the ascription to God of an act which involves injustice. The objection vanishes in the light of Rabbinic interpretation. The Rabbis (Yoma 86b) applied the text to a person who had turned apostate inwardly but hypocritically still professed to be pious. Such hypocrisy would be exposed by

God Who would place a stumblingblock in the person's way which would cause him to commit his secret sins in public.

Divine Jealousy. The rendering of the noun *kin'ah* in relation to God by 'jealousy' has caused confusion among Biblical scholars. The truth is that the noun, when it relates to Divine disfavour, has nothing in common with jealousy. It is derived from the verb *kanah*, 'to acquire as one's own property', and denotes in the first instance the vindication of one's rights. The phrase *semel hakkin'ah hammakneh* (*the image of jealousy, which provoketh to jealousy*, viii. 3) has the meaning, 'the image of outraged authority, which provoketh Him to vindicate His exclusive rights' Likewise, the phrase *wenathatti kin'athi bach* (*and I will set My jealousy against thee*, xxiii. 25) should be understood as 'and I will set My violated rights against thee.'

The term *kin'ah*, describing God as being zealous for His violated rights, is used in *Ezekiel* and in other parts of the Bible only in respect of the cardinal sins of idolatry and immorality (cf. *The Soncino Chumash* on Num. xxv. 11). Attributing *kin'ah* to God is simply an expression of certain retribution for these offences which undermine the existence of human society. Ezekiel, in particular, laid stress on this doctrine in repeatedly employing the term *kin'ah* with reference to these sins.

Individual Responsibility. In chapters xviii and xxxiii the prophet deals at length with the doctrine of individual responsibility and moral freedom. His fellow-exiles, who apparently considered themselves better than their fathers, complained that they were being punished for the sins of their ancestors. His retort was that no man is penalized for the wrongs done by others; nor do the misdeeds or merits of others—not even those of the next-of-kin—determine his fate. The righteous will live and the wicked will perish.

There are two views on the originality of this doctrine. In the Talmud (Makk. 24a), R. Josë bar Chanina taught that this is one of the four adverse sentences which Moses pronounced upon Israel, but they were revoked by later prophets. Moses described God as *visiting the iniquity of the fathers upon the children* (Exod. xx. 5); Ezekiel annulled it and formulated the principle: *the soul that sinneth, it shall die* (xviii. 4). But another opinion is expressed in the Talmud (Ber. 7a), viz. that the text *visiting the iniquity of the fathers upon the children*, etc., is to be understood in the sense that only if the children are, like their fathers, haters of God, will they also suffer for the sins of their forebears. According to this latter view, there is no discrepancy between Moses and Ezekiel. The latter's doctrine of individual responsibility applies only to such children whose conduct is unlike that of their fathers (see on xviii. 2). In connection with this doctrine the prophet mentions the principle of free will. If an individual is not punished for his own sins after he had sincerely repented them, how much less should he be punished for the sins of others!

The Definition of Holiness. The fundamental principle of Ezekiel's vision of the restored Temple with all its implications is holiness, as indicated in xliv. 23, *They shall teach My people the difference between the holy and the common.* The correct understanding of the term 'holiness' sheds light on the regulations concerning the structure of the restored Temple and its ritual, which are aimed at separating that which is holy from that which is common.

On the text, *Ye shall be holy* (Lev. xix. 2), the Rabbis in the *Siphra* comment, 'Ye shall be restrained (*perushim*).' There is nothing mystical about this definition of 'holiness.' It denotes self-discipline and freeing oneself from base instincts, so as to gain a footing on a higher level of spiritual life. There are, of course, several degrees of holiness. On the highest and perfect level is God, since He is incorporeal and not subject to the laws of Nature. By virtue of his free will, man is able to rise to spiritual heights and become, to a certain degree, God-like. Such is the meaning of the injunction: *Ye shall be holy, for I the LORD your God am holy* (Lev. xix. 2).

It is this concept of the highest degree of holiness attributed to God that underlies all the regulations concerning the restored Temple and the regeneration of

Israel. The isolation of the Temple from the outside world, with its compartments within compartments as visualized by Ezekiel, and the exclusion of certain classes from its precincts—these features have the purpose of emphasizing the purely spiritual nature of the Divine worship which will be far removed from the material sphere.

Israel's Restoration. Like his predecessors, Ezekiel predicted not only the return from the Babylonian exile and the rebuilding of the Temple, but also the ultimate redemption and regeneration of Israel in a distant age in the future. The Messianic prophecies of Ezekiel resemble those of Isaiah. E.g. the passage, *Moreover I will take, even I, of the lofty top of the cedar, and will set it* (xvii. 22), is a parallel to *There shall come forth a shoot out of the stock of Jesse, and a twig shall grow forth out of his roots* (Isa. xi. 1). The declaration, *I will make with them a covenant of peace, and will cause evil beasts to cease out of the land; and they shall dwell safely in the wilderness, and sleep in the woods* (xxxiv. 25) is an echo of *The wolf shall dwell with the lamb,* etc. (Isa. xi. 6.)

An essential difference between the two is to be noted. Whereas Isaiah referred to a change in the natural instincts of the wild beast and universal peace for mankind, Ezekiel predicted the banishment of the beast of prey, and he is concerned only with the future peace of Israel. Only incidentally he *hints* at universal peace by declaring repeatedly that, as the sequel of Divine judgment on the nations and Israel's resultant salvation, God would be magnified and sanctified in the eyes of all peoples.

That he speaks chiefly of the peace and security of Israel is understandable when account is taken of the national temper in that period. The people had suffered the most humiliating defeat and lost all hope of rehabilitation. In addition to despair, they were deeply embittered against their enemies who gloated over their misfortunes. At such a time the prophet's mission was primarily to instil into the people a new spirit of confidence and faith in their future, and also to lessen their anguish by assuring them that their enemies would receive deserved punishment. This explains the inclusion in the Book of the prophecies concerning the destruction of the heathen peoples (xxv-xxxii), the abortive attack of Gog (xxxviii, xxxix), the vision of the dry bones (xxxvii. 1-14) indicating national revival, and finally the symbolical joining of the two sticks (xxxvii. 15ff.) predicting the reunion of Judah and Ephraim.

NOTE ON THE COMMENTARY

The commentary presented in this volume is largely based upon the classical Hebrew commentaries and Rabbinical expositions, combined with modern non-Jewish exegesis dealing with historical, geographical or archaeological matters. There are, in addition, numerous interpretations for which the writer alone is responsible. This commentary is not concerned with the far-fetched critical interpretations or emendations of the text. Rabbinic exposition, as presented in the following pages, will be found in repeated instances to remove difficulties for the solution of which the modern critic has had resort to textual alteration.

EZEKIEL

EZEKIEL

1. Now it came to pass in the thirtieth year, in the fourth month, in the fifth day of the month, as I

א וַיְהִי | בִּשְׁלֹשִׁים שָׁנָה
בָּרְבִיעִי בַּחֲמִשָּׁה לַחֹדֶשׁ וַאֲנִי

 v. 1. הפטרה ליום א׳ של שבועות

CHAPTER I

THE PROPHET'S VISION

EZEKIEL, who was among the Judeans taken into Babylonian captivity in the year 597 B.C.E., was the first prophet to live and prophesy in exile. His orations were addressed both to the people who were still left in Judea and to his fellow-captives in Babylon, and the vision of the Divine Chariot (*Merkabah*) was a fitting introduction to his prophetic career. The main feature of the *Merkabah* drawn by the four-faced *living creatures* was its mobility, and this explains the *wheels* in Ezekiel's vision. No wheels were seen by Isaiah in his vision of the Divine Throne (Isa. vi) or by any other prophet. In the vision of the departing *Merkabah* Ezekiel read the impending departure of the Divine Presence from the Temple in Jerusalem and the fall of Judea.

This, however, was not the first omen of the approaching disaster. Thirty years earlier (see on i. 1), the Book of the Law had been found in the Temple unfolded, according to tradition, at the passage: *The LORD will bring thee, and thy king whom thou shalt set over thee, unto a nation that thou hast not known* (Deut. xxviii. 36). The words were understood as a prediction of the fall of the Northern Kingdom and Judea. The affinity between the two occurrences—the vision of the departing *Merkabah* and the discovery of the Book of the Law—is obvious. Hence the linking of the two by the prophet dating the former from the latter.

The *Merkabah* as a source of Talmudic gnosticism, and later of Kabbalistic thought, is a subject on its own and is dealt with at greater length elsewhere. It need only be noted here that the *Ma'aseh Merkabah* ('The Work of the Chariot') has become the central theme for all Jewish esoteric literature and speculative theology. On the subject, cf. G. G. Scholem, *Major Trends in Jewish Mysticism*, pp. 39ff.

1-3 DATE AND PLACE OF THE VISION

1. *in the thirtieth year*. The vision of the *Merkabah* came to Ezekiel *in the thirtieth year* of the last Jubilee which occurred in the Land of Israel before the Babylonian exile. In that Jubilee year the Book of the Law was found in the Temple—an event interpreted as the first signal of the coming disaster (cf. 2 Kings xxii. 8-20). The vision of the departing *Merkabah* thirty years later was dated from the first omen (so the Targum) as giving the signal added confirmation. The vision in general, which was a foreboding of the departure of the Divine Presence from the Temple, was a fitting prelude to all the prophecies which follow (Kimchi). Many modern commentators interpret the phrase as the age of Ezekiel at the time, but this is very doubtful. Not only would the wording be unusual, but the impression to be derived from his status among the exiles is of an older man.

in the fourth month. viz. Tammuz, an ominous month, since in it the first breaches in Jerusalem's walls were made (Kimchi).

was among the captives by the river Chebar, that the heavens were opened, and I saw visions of God. 2. In the fifth day of the month, which was the fifth year of king Jehoiachin's captivity, 3. the word of the LORD came expressly unto Ezekiel the priest, the son of Buzi, in the land of the Chaldeans by the river Chebar; and the hand of the LORD was there upon him.

4. And I looked, and, behold, a stormy wind came out of the north,

בְּתוֹךְ־הַגּוֹלָה עַל־נְהַר כְּבָר
נִפְתְּחוּ הַשָּׁמַיִם וָאֶרְאֶה
מַרְאוֹת אֱלֹהִים: בַּחֲמִשָּׁה 2
לַחֹדֶשׁ הִיא הַשָּׁנָה הַחֲמִשִׁית
לְגָלוּת הַמֶּלֶךְ יוֹיָכִין: הָיֹה 3
הָיָה דְבַר־יְהֹוָה אֶל־
יְחֶזְקֵאל בֶּן־בּוּזִי הַכֹּהֵן
בְּאֶרֶץ כַּשְׂדִּים עַל־נְהַר כְּבָר
וַתְּהִי עָלָיו שָׁם יַד־יְהֹוָה:
וָאֵרֶא וְהִנֵּה רוּחַ סְעָרָה בָּאָה 4

the captives. lit. 'the captivity.' Lofthouse concludes from this term and the use of *among* that the exiles had by then formed themselves into a community.

the river Chebar. Some Rabbis identify *Chebar* with the Euphrates (Ber. R. xvi. 3). 'This was probably the artificial watercourse which started from the Euphrates above Babylon . . . The Sumerians called it *the Euphrates of Nippur* (*Purat Nippur*); the Babylonians and Jews, *the great river* (*naru kabari, nehar kebar;* its modern name among the Arabs is *the river Nile* (*Shatt en-Nil*). Recent excavations at Nippur have discovered abundant evidence of Jewish settlements in the neighbourhood, from the fifteenth century B.C.E., and perhaps earlier, down to the seventh century C.E.' (Cooke).

the heavens were opened. On the date mentioned Ezekiel experienced the vision which began with the opening of the heavens, comparable with the drawing of the stage curtain.

visions of God. The Hebrew may signify 'Divine visions,' i.e. concerning God or devised by Him.

2. *in the fifth day.* Verses 2f are in parenthesis.

the fifth year . . . captivity. i.e. in 593 or 592. The vision occurred at a most appropriate time, because in that year a plot against the Babylonian invader was being planned by patriots in Jerusalem and some exiles in Babylon. Ezekiel, like Jeremiah, saw in this movement a rebellion against God's judgment and therefore a threat to the national existence. During the critical years which preceded the fall of Jerusalem, his addresses were in the nature of exhortations against this dangerous policy and a prediction of the final fall of Jerusalem.

3. *the word of the LORD.* The reference is to the message in chapter ii which follows the vision of the *Merkabah.*

came expressly. lit. 'being was,' the verb being duplicated for the sake of emphasis. The phrase here denotes the solemnity of the experience.

the hand of the LORD. The spirit of prophecy overwhelmed the prophet like the grasp of a mighty hand (Rashi).

4-14   THE FOUR LIVING CREATURES
4. *a stormy wind came out of the north.* An indication of the forthcoming invasion of Judea by the Babylonians

a great cloud, with a fire flashing up, so that a brightness was round about it; and out of the midst thereof as the colour of electrum, out of the midst of the fire. 5. And out of the midst thereof came the likeness of four living creatures. And this was their appearance: they had the likeness of a man. 6. And every one had four faces, and every one of them had four wings. 7. And their feet were straight feet; and the sole of their feet was like the sole of a calf's foot; and they sparkled like the colour of burnished brass. 8. And they had the hands of a man under their

מִן־הַצָּפוֹן עָנָן גָּדוֹל וְאֵשׁ
מִתְלַקַּחַת וְנֹגַהּ לוֹ סָבִיב
וּמִתּוֹכָהּ כְּעֵין הַחַשְׁמַל מִתּוֹךְ
5 הָאֵשׁ: וּמִתּוֹכָהּ דְּמוּת אַרְבַּע
חַיּוֹת וְזֶה מַרְאֵיהֶן דְּמוּת אָדָם
6 לָהֵנָּה: וְאַרְבָּעָה פָנִים לְאֶחָת
וְאַרְבַּע כְּנָפַיִם לְאַחַת לָהֶם:
7 וְרַגְלֵיהֶם רֶגֶל יְשָׁרָה וְכַף
רַגְלֵיהֶם כְּכַף רֶגֶל עֵגֶל
וְנֹצְצִים כְּעֵין נְחֹשֶׁת קָלָל:
8 וִידֵי אָדָם מִתַּחַת כַּנְפֵיהֶם עַל

v. 8. וידי ק׳

whose empire extended to the land of the Chaldeans to the north of the Holy Land (cf. *Out of the north the evil shall break forth*, Jer. i. 14).

a great cloud. A portent of impending calamity.

a fire flashing up. Indicative of the burning of the Temple by the invading forces. The Hebrew phrase is literally 'a fire taking hold of itself,' i.e. a succession of outbursts of flame.

a brightness was round about it. The black cloud was lit up by the fire.

electrum. The Hebrew *chashmal* 'denotes some kind of bright metal; it is a foreign word, and most likely identical with Akkadian *esmaru*, polished bronze, and the Egyptian *chesmen* (?), bronze' (Cooke).

out of the midst of the fire. Explanatory of *out of the midst thereof.*

5. *out of the midst thereof.* Referring to *the fire* in the preceding verse.

they had the likeness of a man. The bodies of the *living creatures* stood upright and were shaped like the human

body, but some of the faces, as stated below, resembled those of various animals. The point that Ezekiel makes is that, despite their abnormal appearance, the supporters of the *Merkabah* were essentially human in form.

6. *every one had four faces.* Each of the four *living creatures* had the face of a man in front, of a lion on the right side, of an ox on the left side, and of an eagle behind. According to the Targum Jonathan, there were four faces in each direction, so that each creature had sixteen faces, and each of the faces had four wings. There were thus altogether sixty-four faces and 256 wings!

7. *straight feet.* *Feet* is here employed in the wider sense of 'legs.' By *straight* is meant that they had no joints. These were not necessary since the throne-bearers did not have to lie down or turn round (Rashi). No mention is made of the number of the feet.

a calf's foot. i.e. rounded, for turning smoothly in every direction (Lofthouse).

they sparkled. Descriptive of the *feet*, not the *living creatures* as a whole (cf. Dan. x. 6).

3

wings on their four sides; and as
for the faces and wings of them
four, 9. their wings were joined one
to another; they turned not when
they went; they went every one
straight forward. 10. As for the
likeness of their faces, they had the
face of a man; and they four had the
face of a lion on the right side;
and they four had the face of an ox
on the left side; they four had also
the face of an eagle. 11. Thus were
their faces; and their wings were
stretched upward; two wings of
every one were joined one to
another, and two covered their
bodies. 12. And they went every
one straight forward; whither the
spirit was to go, they went; they

אַרְבַּעַת רִבְעֵיהֶם וּפְנֵיהֶם
9 וְכַנְפֵיהֶםלְאַרְבַּעְתָּם: חֹבְרֹת
אִשָּׁה אֶל־־אֲחוֹתָהּ כַּנְפֵיהֶם
לֹא־יִסַּבּוּ בְלֶכְתָּן אִישׁ אֶל־
10 עֵבֶר פָּנָיו יֵלֵכוּ: וּדְמוּת
פְּנֵיהֶם פְּנֵי אָדָם וּפְנֵי אַרְיֵה
אֶל־־הַיָּמִין לְאַרְבַּעְתָּם
וּפְנֵי־־שׁוֹר מֵהַשְּׂמֹאול
לְאַרְבַּעְתָּן וּפְנֵי־־נֶשֶׁר
11 לְאַרְבַּעְתָּן: וּפְנֵיהֶםוְכַנְפֵיהֶם
פְּרֻדוֹת מִלְמָעְלָה לְאִישׁ
שְׁתַּיִם חֹבְרוֹת אִישׁ וּשְׁתַּיִם
12 מְכַסּוֹת אֵת גְּוִיֹּתֵיהֶנָה: וְאִישׁ
אֶל־עֵבֶר פָּנָיו יֵלֵכוּ אֶל אֲשֶׁר
יִהְיֶה־שָּׁמָּה הָרוּחַ לָלֶכֶת

v. 10. מלא ר

8. *as for the faces and wings of them four.*
The faces and wings of the four *living
creatures* were alike (Targum).

9. *their wings were joined one to another.*
Two of the four wings of each creature
were spread above the face and were
joined on both sides to the wings of its
neighbour, so that each face was hidden
by the wings (Rashi).

they turned not when they went. Each
creature having a face on each side, it
had no need to turn round when it
desired to alter its course; the face
towards the intended course moved
forward in that direction.

10. *as for the likeness of their faces.* See
on verse 6. Representations of the lion,
ox and eagle were common in Babylonian
sculpture, and so naturally appeared to

the mind of a Judean who was resident
in the country.

11. *and two covered their bodies.* Two
of the four wings attached to each
creature were not stretched upward but
covered its body. With this description
of the wings should be compared what
Isaiah saw in his vision (vi. 2). Lofthouse thinks that Ezekiel was influenced
by memories of king Solomon's Temple
(cf. 1 Kings vi. 23-28).

12. *they went every one straight forward.*
Wherever they proceeded, they always
moved forward, since each creature had
a face in the appropriate direction (see
on verse 9).

whither the spirit was to go, they went.
The *spirit* is the Divine will which
guided the movements of the creatures.

turned not when they went.   13. As
for the likeness of the living
creatures, their appearance was like
coals of fire, burning like the
appearance of torches; it flashed up
and   down   among   the   living
creatures; and there was brightness
to the fire, and out of the fire went
forth lightning.   14. And the living
creatures ran and returned as the
appearance of a flash of lightning.

15. Now as I beheld the living
creatures, behold one wheel at the
bottom hard by the living creatures,
at the four faces thereof. 16. The
appearance of the wheels and their
work was like unto the colour of a
beryl; and they four had one likeness; and their appearance and their
work was as it were a wheel within
a wheel. 17. When they went,
they went toward their four sides;

יֵלְכוּ לֹא יִסַּבּוּ בְּלֶכְתָּן׃

13 וּדְמוּת הַחַיּוֹת מַרְאֵיהֶם
כְּגַחֲלֵי־אֵשׁ בֹּעֲרוֹת כְּמַרְאֵה
הַלַּפִּדִים הִיא מִתְהַלֶּכֶת בֵּין
הַחַיּוֹת וְנֹגַהּ לָאֵשׁ וּמִן־הָאֵשׁ

14 יוֹצֵא בָרָק׃ וְהַחַיּוֹת רָצוֹא

15 וָשׁוֹב כְּמַרְאֵה הַבָּזָק׃ וָאֵרֶא
הַחַיּוֹת וְהִנֵּה אוֹפַן אֶחָד בָּאָרֶץ
אֵצֶל הַחַיּוֹת לְאַרְבַּעַת פָּנָיו׃

16 מַרְאֵה הָאוֹפַנִּים וּמַעֲשֵׂיהֶם
כְּעֵין תַּרְשִׁישׁ וּדְמוּת אֶחָד
לְאַרְבַּעְתָּן וּמַרְאֵיהֶם
וּמַעֲשֵׂיהֶם כַּאֲשֶׁר יִהְיֶה הָאוֹפַן

17 בְּתוֹךְ הָאוֹפָן׃ עַל־אַרְבַּעַת
רִבְעֵיהֶן בְּלֶכְתָּם יֵלֵכוּ לֹא

---

13. *like coals of fire.* A similar account
of God's manifestation is given in
Ps. xviii. 9.

there was brightness to the fire. This
abnormal fire was brighter than natural
fire (Rashi).

14. *ran and returned.* The creatures
were not stationary but galloped to and
fro with the speed of lightning. The
Hebrew word for *lightning* here is *bazak*,
another form of *barak*, the letters *z* and *r*
in Hebrew interchanging.

15-21   THE FOUR WHEELS

15. *at the four faces thereof.* To each
four-faced creature there was one wheel.
The Rabbis (Chag. 13b) identified the
wheel with the angel Sandalphon who
stands behind the *Merkabah* and forms
wreaths out of the prayers of the

righteous which he places before God.
In the Pseudepigraphic literature (Enoch
xli. 10, lxxi. 7), the *wheels* are represented
as angels, together with the Cherubim
and Seraphim, attendant upon God.

16. *the colour of a beryl.* lit. 'eye of
Tarshish,' i.e. Tartessus in Spain. The
stone was a species of chrysolite, perhaps
the topaz. It is mentioned again in
xxviii. 13. Kimchi explains that the
wheel resembled the beryl both in its
manifold colours (*appearance*) and in its
transparent quality (*work*).

as it were a wheel within a wheel. One
wheel was fixed into another crosswise, so
that in whatever direction the creature
turned the wheel revolved that way.

17. *they went toward their four sides.* The
wheels, too, were turned to the four

they turned not when they went. 18. As for their rings, they were high and they were dreadful; and they four had their rings full of eyes round about. 19. And when the living creatures went, the wheels went hard by them; and when the living creatures were lifted up from the bottom, the wheels were lifted up. 20. Whithersoever the spirit was to go, as the spirit was to go thither, so they went; and the wheels were lifted up beside them; for the spirit of the living creature was in the wheels. 21. When those went, these went, and when those stood, these stood; and when those were lifted up from the earth, the wheels were lifted up beside them; for the spirit of the living creature was in the wheels.

22. And over the heads of the living creatures there was the like-

18 יִסַּבּוּ בְּלֶכְתָּן: וְגַבֵּיהֶן וְגֹבַהּ
לָהֶם וְיִרְאָה לָהֶם וְגַבֹּתָם
מְלֵאֹת עֵינַיִם סָבִיב
19 לְאַרְבַּעְתָּן: וּבְלֶכֶת הַחַיּוֹת
יֵלְכוּ הָאוֹפַנִּים אֶצְלָם
וּבְהִנָּשֵׂא הַחַיּוֹת מֵעַל הָאָרֶץ
20 יִנָּשְׂאוּ הָאוֹפַנִּים: עַל אֲשֶׁר
יִהְיֶה־שָּׁם הָרוּחַ לָלֶכֶת יֵלֵכוּ
שָׁמָּה הָרוּחַ לָלֶכֶת וְהָאוֹפַנִּים
יִנָּשְׂאוּ לְעֻמָּתָם כִּי רוּחַ הַחַיָּה
21 בָּאוֹפַנִּים: בְּלֶכְתָּם יֵלֵכוּ
וּבְעָמְדָם יַעֲמֹדוּ וּבְהִנָּשְׂאָם
מֵעַל הָאָרֶץ יִנָּשְׂאוּ הָאוֹפַנִּים
לְעֻמָּתָם כִּי רוּחַ הַחַיָּה
22 בָּאוֹפַנִּים: וּדְמוּת עַל־—

squares formed by the creatures. This explains the reason for having *a wheel within a wheel* as stated in the preceding verse.

18. *they were high . . . dreadful*. lit. 'and height was to them and fear to them.' Ehrlich sees a play of words on *gobah* (height) and *gab* (ring) and interprets the former as 'power of raising itself,' as mentioned in the next verse.

dreadful. i.e. of awe-inspiring aspect.

had their rings full of eyes round about. The *rings* or felloes had eyes on each side, which directed the wheels on the route they were to go. 'The eye is the expression of life and intelligence (x. 12)' (Davidson).

19. The verse indicates that the wheel had no capacity for independent movement; it only moved with the creature.

20. *as the spirit was to go thither, so they went*. The creatures required no directing as to which route to take, because the will of God was known to them and the will of the creatures was known to the wheels. Both creatures and wheels moved as intended by the Divine Presence in the *Merkabah* (Rashi).

the living creature. The singular is used in the collective sense as in x. 20; or 'Ezekiel would naturally see only one at a time with any clearness' (Lofthouse).

21. *when those went, these went*. When the creatures moved the wheels moved with them. The repetition emphasizes the co-ordination between the creatures and the wheels.

22-28 THE DIVINE MANIFESTATION

22. *the likeness of a firmament*. Over the heads of the creatures appeared a

ness of a firmament, like the colour of the terrible ice, stretched forth over their heads above. 23. And under the firmament were their wings conformable the one to the other; this one of them had two which covered, and that one of them had two which covered, their bodies. 24. And when they went, I heard the noise of their wings like the noise of great waters, like the voice of the Almighty, a noise of tumult like the noise of a host; when they stood, they let down their wings. 25. For, when there was a voice above the firmament that was over their heads, as they stood, they let down their wings.

26. And above the firmament that was over their heads was the likeness of a throne, as the appearance of a sapphire stone; and upon the like-

רָאשֵׁי הַחַיָּה רָקִיעַ כְּעֵין הַקֶּרַח הַנּוֹרָא נָטוּי עַל־ 23 רָאשֵׁיהֶם מִלְמָעְלָה: וְתַחַת הָרָקִיעַ כַּנְפֵיהֶם יְשָׁרוֹת אִשָּׁה אֶל־אֲחוֹתָהּ לְאִישׁ שְׁתַּיִם מְכַסּוֹת לָהֵנָּה וּלְאִישׁ שְׁתַּיִם מְכַסּוֹת לָהֵנָּה אֵת גְּוִיֹּתֵיהֶם: 24 וָאֶשְׁמַע אֶת־קוֹל כַּנְפֵיהֶם כְּקוֹל מַיִם רַבִּים כְּקוֹל־שַׁדַּי בְּלֶכְתָּם קוֹל הֲמֻלָּה כְּקוֹל מַחֲנֶה בְּעָמְדָם תְּרַפֶּינָה 25 כַנְפֵיהֶן: וַיְהִי־קוֹל מֵעַל לָרָקִיעַ אֲשֶׁר עַל־רֹאשָׁם בְּעָמְדָם תְּרַפֶּינָה כַנְפֵיהֶן: 26 וּמִמַּעַל לָרָקִיעַ אֲשֶׁר עַל־רֹאשָׁם כְּמַרְאֵה אֶבֶן־סַפִּיר

kind of flooring upon which rested the throne of the glory of the Lord (verse 26). *like the colour of the terrible ice.* It was *terrible* by reason of its glittering brightness (Kimchi). The intention is possibly to suggest that the pale-bluish tint of the manifestation of God was *the like of a paved work of sapphire stone, and the like of the very heaven for clearness* (Exod. xxiv. 10).

23. *under the firmament were their wings.* Their outstretched wings did not extend to the sphere above the firmament, nor did they reach the firmament itself, but were beneath it. The wings were *conformable*, which means that they reached to a level height. *which covered.* lit. 'which covered them, viz. their bodies.' The phrase is re-

peated to make it clear that the description applies to each one of the creatures alike.

24. *like the voice of the Almighty.* Who spoke with a mighty voice on mount Sinai (cf. Deut. v. 19). Others explain the phrase as identical with *the voice of the LORD* (Ps. xxix. 3ff.), symbolic of thunder.

host. lit. 'camp' of soldiers (cf. Joel ii. 5).

25. *when there was a voice . . . they let down their wings.* This supplements the preceding verse: the creatures stood still and lowered their wings when the voice of God addressed to His prophets was heard above the firmament (Targum).

26. *a sapphire stone.* Cf. Exod. xxiv. 10 quoted in the note on verse 22.

ness of the throne was a likeness as the appearance of a man upon it above. 27. And I saw as the colour of electrum, as the appearance of fire round about enclosing it, from the appearance of his loins and upward; and from the appearance of his loins and downward I saw as it were the appearance of fire, and there was brightness round about him. 28. As the appearance of the bow that is in the cloud in the day of rain, so was the appearance of the brightness round about. This was the appearance of the likeness of the glory of the LORD. And when I saw it, I fell upon my face, and I heard a voice of one that spoke.

דְּמוּת כִּסֵּא וְעַל דְּמוּת הַכִּסֵּא
דְּמוּת כְּמַרְאֵה אָדָם עָלָיו
27 מִלְמָעְלָה: וָאֵרֶא | כְּעֵין
חַשְׁמַל כְּמַרְאֵה־אֵשׁ בֵּית־
לָהּ סָבִיב מִמַּרְאֵה מָתְנָיו
וּלְמַעְלָה וּמִמַּרְאֵה מָתְנָיו
וּלְמַטָּה רָאִיתִי כְּמַרְאֵה־אֵשׁ
28 וְנֹגַהּ לוֹ סָבִיב: כְּמַרְאֵה
הַקֶּשֶׁת אֲשֶׁר יִהְיֶה בֶעָנָן בְּיוֹם
הַגֶּשֶׁם כֵּן מַרְאֵה הַנֹּגַהּ סָבִיב
הוּא מַרְאֵה דְּמוּת כְּבוֹד־
יְהֹוָה וָאֶרְאֶה וָאֶפֹּל עַל־פָּנַי
וָאֶשְׁמַע קוֹל מְדַבֵּר:

v. 28. עד כאן

---

a likeness as the appearance of a man. Anthropomorphism is employed here by the prophet to portray the Divine Presence departing from the Temple in the *Merkabah* like an earthly king in his chariot setting out on a journey. That Ezekiel saw no actual human likeness on the throne is apparent from the verses that follow.

27. *I saw as the colour of electrum.* See on verse 4. Rashi observes: 'One is not allowed to reflect on this verse.' On this passage Maimonides made the following statement: 'It is also noteworthy that the likeness of man above the throne is divided, the upper part being like the colour of *chashmal*, the lower part like the appearance of fire . . Now consider how the sages clearly stated that the divided likeness of man does not represent God, Who is above the whole chariot, but represents a part of creation. The prophet likewise says *this was the*

appearance of the glory of the LORD; but *the glory of the LORD* is different from *the LORD* Himself. All the figures in this vision refer to the glory of the Lord, to the chariot, and not to Him Who rides upon the chariot; for God cannot be compared with anything' (*Guide*, III. 7).

his loins and upward. i.e. 'had the figure been really human' (Lofthouse).

about him. Relating to *the appearance of a man* (verse 26).

28. *as the appearance of the bow.* Just as the colours of the rainbow are not real but merely the effect of sunlight, so the likeness of the glory of the Lord as visualized by the prophet was only the reflection of the Divine light (Malbim).

I heard a voice of one that spoke. Lofthouse well remarks that 'the reticence at the end of the verse is specially noteworthy after the fullness of the preceding details.'

2 CHAPTER II ב

1. And He said unto me: 'Son of man, stand upon thy feet, and I will speak with thee.' 2. And spirit entered into me when He spoke unto me, and set me upon my feet; and I heard Him that spoke unto me.

3. And He said unto me: 'Son of man, I send thee to the children of Israel, to rebellious nations, that

1 וַיֹּאמֶר אֵלַי בֶּן־אָדָם עֲמֹד
עַל־רַגְלֶיךָ וַאֲדַבֵּר אֹתָךְ:
2 וַתָּבֹא בִי רוּחַ כַּאֲשֶׁר דִּבֶּר
אֵלַי וַתַּעֲמִדֵנִי עַל־רַגְלָי
וָאֶשְׁמַע אֵת מִדַּבֵּר אֵלָי:
3 וַיֹּאמֶר אֵלַי בֶּן־אָדָם שׁוֹלֵחַ
אֲנִי אוֹתְךָ אֶל־בְּנֵי יִשְׂרָאֵל
אֶל־גּוֹיִם הַמּוֹרְדִים אֲשֶׁר

CHAPTER II

1-7 THE MISSION OF EZEKIEL

1. son of man. This phrase, which frequently occurs in the Book as a designation of Ezekiel, is intended to emphasize that though he was privileged to witness the majestic, heavenly vision of the *Merkabah* he was nevertheless nothing more than a human being. A parallel occurs in Num. xii. 3 where Moses is described as *the man Moses*, although God had spoken with him *mouth to mouth, even manifestly* (verse 8). Likewise the narrative of Moses' appointment to his office as God's messenger in the deliverance of Israel and the greatest of the prophets is interrupted by a genealogical table (Exod. vi. 14-27), in order apparently to stress that, despite his exceptional eminence, he was born of a human father and mother. In later literature, e.g. the Book of Enoch (see on i. 15), the words are invested with a Messianic significance; but that is absent in the Bible.

stand upon thy feet. Awe-struck by the majestic sight of the Divine glory, the prophet had fallen upon his face (i. 28). He is now bidden to stand on his feet and be prepared to receive God's message.

2. *spirit entered into me . . . and I heard Him that spoke unto me.* While the prophet was lying prostrate on the ground his mind ceased functioning: all he heard was a voice speaking (i. 28). To render him fit for the reception of the Divine message, a spirit of strength and vitality set him on his feet and enabled him to understand the words uttered by the voice of God (Malbim).

that spoke unto me. The verb is not pointed *medabber* as in i. 28, but *mid-dabber*, i.e. the reflexive mood. It may be translated 'Who was addressing Himself unto me,' and convey the idea of intimate relationship.

3. *the children of Israel.* The mission of the prophet is to the whole nation, to his fellow-exiles in Babylon as well as to the people still living in the homeland.

rebellious. 'A very common phrase with Ezekiel. To him the constant tendency to rebel against Babylon, culminating in Zedekiah's desperate revolt, is typical of the whole attitude of Israel to God' (Lofthouse).

nations. This is a reference to the two tribes, Judah and Benjamin, who formed the Southern Kingdom. For an instance of Israel's tribes being called *nations*, cf. Gen. xxxv. 11 where the blessing of

9

have rebelled against Me; they and their fathers have transgressed against Me, even unto this very day; 4. and the children are brazen-faced and stiff-hearted, I do send thee unto them; and thou shalt say unto them: Thus saith the Lord GOD. 5. And they, whether they will hear, or whether they will forbear—for they are a rebellious house—yet shall know that there hath been a prophet among them.

6. And thou, son of man, be not afraid of them, neither be afraid of their words, though defiers and despisers be with thee, and thou dost dwell among scorpions; be not

מְרְדוּ־בִי הֵמָּה וַאֲבוֹתָם
פָּשְׁעוּ בִי עַד־עֶצֶם הַיּוֹם
4 הַזֶּה: וְהַבָּנִים קְשֵׁי פָנִים
וְחִזְקֵי־לֵב אֲנִי שׁוֹלֵחַ אוֹתְךָ
אֲלֵיהֶם וְאָמַרְתָּ אֲלֵיהֶם כֹּה
5 אָמַר אֲדֹנָי יֱהֹוִה: וְהֵמָּה אִם־
יִשְׁמְעוּ וְאִם־יֶחְדָּלוּ כִּי בֵּית
מְרִי הֵמָּה וְיָדְעוּ כִּי נָבִיא
6 הָיָה בְתוֹכָם: וְאַתָּה בֶן־אָדָם
אַל־תִּירָא מֵהֶם וּמִדִּבְרֵיהֶם
אַל־תִּירָא כִּי סָרָבִים
וְסַלּוֹנִים אוֹתְךָ וְאֶל־
עַקְרַבִּים אַתָּה יוֹשֵׁב

v. 5. קמץ בז״ק

Jacob foretells that he will become a company of nations.

they and their fathers. They were as sinful as their fathers and had not learnt from the experience of the past that the consequence of sin is retribution.

4. *the children are brazen-faced and stiff-hearted.* While their fathers were only transgressors against God, the present generation were even defying the exhortations of the prophet and clinging stubbornly to their hearts' dictates (Malbim).

thus saith the Lord GOD. The prophet was to preface his messages with this formula to impress upon the people the Divine origin of his communication.

5. *forbear.* lit. 'cease (to hear),' i.e. refuse to heed.

for they are a rebellious house. The words indicate that the second alternative will prove true; hence the force of what follows.

shall know that there hath been a prophet among them. Though Ezekiel may doubt whether his words would find a responsive heart among his rebellious people, he is nevertheless urged to deliver his message, which would have the value of convincing them of their guilt when his predictions of calamity came upon them.

6. *be not afraid of them, neither be afraid of their words.* Since the prophet's words were likely to arouse indignation among the people, he is assured that neither their hostile attitude nor their threats would harm him. Jeremiah was similarly encouraged at the beginning of his prophetic career (Jer. i. 8, 17).

defiers and despisers. A.V. and R.V. render 'briers and thorns.' The meaning of the second word (*sallonim*) seems to be established by its occurrence, though with a different vowel, in xxviii. 24, *a pricking brier* (*sillon*). As for the first word (*sarabim*), it is not found elsewhere in the Bible. In Rabbinic Hebrew it sometimes denotes

afraid of their words, nor be dismayed at their looks, for they are a rebellious house. 7. And thou shalt speak My words unto them, whether they will hear, or whether they will forbear; for they are most rebellious.

8. And thou, son of man, hear what I say unto thee: be not thou rebellious like that rebellious house; open thy mouth, and eat that which I give thee.' 9. And when I looked, behold, a hand was put forth unto me; and, lo, a roll of a book was therein; 10. and He spread it before

מִדִּבְרֵיהֶם אַל־תִּירָא
וּמִפְּנֵיהֶם אַל־תֵּחָת כִּי בֵּית
7 מְרִי הֵמָּה: וְדִבַּרְתָּ אֶת־
דְּבָרַי אֲלֵיהֶם אִם־יִשְׁמְעוּ
וְאִם־יֶחְדָּלוּ כִּי מְרִי הֵמָּה:
8 וְאַתָּה בֶן־אָדָם שְׁמַע אֵת
אֲשֶׁר־אֲנִי מְדַבֵּר אֵלֶיךָ אַל־
תְּהִי־מֶרִי כְּבֵית הַמֶּרִי פְּצֵה
פִיךָ וֶאֱכֹל אֵת אֲשֶׁר־אֲנִי נֹתֵן
9 אֵלֶיךָ: וָאֶרְאֶה וְהִנֵּה־יָד
שְׁלוּחָה אֵלָי וְהִנֵּה־בוֹ מְגִלַּת־
10 סֵפֶר: וַיִּפְרֹשׂ אוֹתָהּ לְפָנַי

קמץ בז״ק v. 6.

'rebelliousness.' Rashi (who, however, mentions that an early lexicographer, Dunash, defined it as 'thorns') and other Jewish commentators give it the sense of 'rebels.' Its meaning here cannot be determined with certainty, but the context appears to be in favour of A.V. and R.V. 'Briers and thorns,' among which *scorpions* lurk, is an expressive way of describing dangerous opponents. Ezekiel is exhorted to convey his message to the people without fear for his personal safety.

7. thou shalt speak My words unto them. The prophet is urged to speak *all* God's words and not omit any of them from fear (Malbim).

8-iii. 3 THE CHARGE TO THE PROPHET

The eating of the roll by Ezekiel was performed in a vision or is an allegory. Its symbolic meaning is a call to the prophet to 'digest,' as it were, the contents of the roll. He should make himself familiar with the writing on the roll by reading it as eagerly and attentively as one eats food to satisfy hunger.

8. be not thou rebellious. Like Moses, Jeremiah and Jonah, Ezekiel may have been reluctant to accept the dangerous task of bringing the Divine truth to a corrupt people, fearing their resentment and hostility, and also conscious of his inability to do justice to the mission committed to him. Hence the stern warning not to be like the rebellious nation and act disloyally against the Divine command.

open thy mouth, and eat. Kimchi interprets the eating of the scroll by the prophet as happening in a vision, while Rashi understands it as allegorical. Whichever it be, the symbolic meaning is clear. Ezekiel is instructed to 'devour' each word on the scroll and learn its contents by heart.

that which I give thee. This refers to the *roll* spoken of in the next verse.

9. a roll of a book. The Divine message was conveyed to the prophet in writing.

10. He spread it. As the scroll was rolled up, the hand which passed it to the prophet opened it to enable him to read what was written therein.

me, and it was written within and without; and there was written therein lamentations, and moaning, and woe.

וְהִיא כְתוּבָה פָּנִים וְאָחֹור
וְכָתוּב אֵלֶיהָ קִינִים וָהֶגֶה וָהִי׃

8   CHAPTER III   ג

1. And He said unto me: 'Son of man, eat that which thou findest; eat this roll, and go, speak unto the house of Israel.' 2. So I opened my mouth, and He caused me to eat that roll. 3. And He said unto me: 'Son of man, cause thy belly to eat, and fill thy bowels with this roll that I give thee.' Then did I eat it; and it was in my mouth as honey for sweetness.

4. And He said unto me: 'Son of

1 וַיֹּאמֶר אֵלַי בֶּן־אָדָם אֵת
אֲשֶׁר־תִּמְצָא אֱכֹול אֱכֹול
אֶת־הַמְּגִלָּה הַזֹּאת וְלֵךְ דַּבֵּר
2 אֶל־בֵּית יִשְׂרָאֵל׃ וָאֶפְתַּח
אֶת־פִּי וַיַּאֲכִלֵנִי אֵת הַמְּגִלָּה
3 הַזֹּאת׃ וַיֹּאמֶר אֵלַי בֶּן־אָדָם
בִּטְנְךָ תַאֲכֵל וּמֵעֶיךָ תְמַלֵּא
אֵת הַמְּגִלָּה הַזֹּאת אֲשֶׁר אֲנִי
נֹתֵן אֵלֶיךָ וָאֹכְלָה וַתְּהִי בְּפִי
4 כִּדְבַשׁ לְמָתֹוק׃ וַיֹּאמֶר אֵלַי

---

within and without. On both sides of the material.

there was written therein. Commenting on the singular form of *written* in the Hebrew, Ehrlich deduces that *lamentations,* etc. does not signify the contents but the superscription. *Therein,* lit. 'to it,' should accordingly be translated 'upon it.' Ezekiel did not at that moment read all that was inscribed on the scroll, but saw that it bore the heading *lamentations, and moaning, and woe.*

lamentations, etc. Only the message of the impending disaster, the first in his prophetic career, was revealed to Ezekiel in the scroll. His later message was one of comfort and encouragement.

CHAPTER III

1. *eat that which thou findest.* i.e. make thyself familiar with the whole of the contents on both sides of the scroll.

2. *I opened my mouth.* In obedience to the command in ii. 8.

He caused me to eat that roll. The prophet was in need of Divine help to preserve in his mind to the minutest detail a message of such unpleasantness (Malbim).

3. *cause thy belly to eat.* Swallow what has entered thy mouth.

it was in my mouth as honey for sweetness. He obeyed and mentally digested the ominous contents of the scroll, readily and gladly, as if they were of a delightful nature, because they emanated from God.

man, go, get thee unto the house of Israel, and speak with My words unto them. 5. For thou art not sent to a people of an unintelligible speech and of a slow tongue, but to the house of Israel; 6. not to many peoples of an unintelligible speech and of a slow tongue, whose words thou canst not understand. Surely, if I sent thee to them, they would hearken unto thee. 7. But the house of Israel will not consent to hearken unto thee; for they consent not to hearken unto Me; for all the house of Israel are of a hard forehead and of a stiff heart. 8. Behold, I have made thy face hard against their faces, and thy forehead hard against their foreheads. 9. As an

בֶּן־אָדָם לֶךְ־בֹּא אֶל־בֵּית יִשְׂרָאֵל וְדִבַּרְתָּ בִדְבָרַי
5 אֲלֵיהֶם: כִּי לֹא אֶל־עַם עִמְקֵי שָׂפָה וְכִבְדֵי לָשׁוֹן אַתָּה
6 שָׁלוּחַ אֶל־בֵּית יִשְׂרָאֵל: לֹא ׀ אֶל־עַמִּים רַבִּים עִמְקֵי שָׂפָה וְכִבְדֵי לָשׁוֹן אֲשֶׁר לֹא־תִשְׁמַע דִּבְרֵיהֶם אִם־לֹא אֲלֵיהֶם שְׁלַחְתִּיךָ הֵמָּה יִשְׁמְעוּ אֵלֶיךָ:
7 וּבֵית יִשְׂרָאֵל לֹא יֹאבוּ לִשְׁמֹעַ אֵלֶיךָ כִּי־אֵינָם אֹבִים לִשְׁמֹעַ אֵלָי כִּי כָּל־בֵּית יִשְׂרָאֵל חִזְקֵי־מֵצַח וּקְשֵׁי־לֵב הֵמָּה:
8 הִנֵּה נָתַתִּי אֶת־פָּנֶיךָ חֲזָקִים לְעֻמַּת פְּנֵיהֶם וְאֶת־מִצְחֲךָ
9 חָזָק לְעֻמַּת מִצְחָם: כְּשָׁמִיר

4-9 EZEKIEL ASSURED OF MORAL STRENGTH FOR HIS TASK

4. speak with My words unto them. The prophet was instructed to convey God's message to the people in the holy language in which he received it. Though the exiles were already using the Chaldaic language, they were still familiar with the Hebrew tongue (Malbim).

5. unintelligible speech . . . a slow tongue. lit. 'deep of lip and heavy of tongue.' The sacred language was understood by the exiles and would not sound to them like a foreign and unintelligible dialect.

6. surely, if I sent thee to them. Or possibly, 'even if I sent thee not to them

(directly), they would hearken unto thee,' should by some chance the prophet's message reach them. Here we have a thought which is not infrequently found in the prophetic literature, viz. that the Israelites are less loyal to God than heathen nations to their deities (cf. Jer. ii. 10f.), and these peoples would be more receptive of Divine communications if made to them.

7. for they consent not to hearken unto Me. The reason why they refuse to listen to the prophet is not personal antipathy to him, but because he is the mouthpiece of God (Kimchi).

8. I have made thy face hard. He is assured that God has endowed him with moral strength to withstand the opposition which he will encounter.

adamant harder than flint have I made thy forehead; fear them not, neither be dismayed at their looks, for they are a rebellious house.'

10. Moreover He said unto me: 'Son of man, all My words that I shall speak unto thee receive in thy heart, and hear with thine ears.

11. And go, get thee to them of the captivity, unto the children of thy people, and speak unto them, and tell them: Thus saith the Lord GOD; whether they will hear, or whether they will forbear.'

12. Then a spirit lifted me up, and I heard behind me the voice of a great rushing: 'Blessed be the glory

חֲזָק מִצֹּר נָתַתִּי מִצְחֶךָ לֹא־
תִירָא אוֹתָם וְלֹא־תֵחַת
מִפְּנֵיהֶם כִּי בֵּית מְרִי הֵמָּה:

10 וַיֹּאמֶר אֵלַי בֶּן־אָדָם אֶת־
כָּל־דְּבָרַי אֲשֶׁר אֲדַבֵּר אֵלֶיךָ
קַח בִּלְבָבְךָ וּבְאָזְנֶיךָ שְׁמָע:

11 וְלֵךְ בֹּא אֶל־הַגּוֹלָה אֶל־בְּנֵי
עַמֶּךָ וְדִבַּרְתָּ אֲלֵיהֶם וְאָמַרְתָּ
אֲלֵיהֶם כֹּה אָמַר אֲדֹנָי יֱהֹוִה
אִם־יִשְׁמְעוּ וְאִם־יֶחְדָּלוּ:

12 וַתִּשָּׂאֵנִי רוּחַ וָאֶשְׁמַע אַחֲרַי
קוֹל רַעַשׁ גָּדוֹל בָּרוּךְ כְּבוֹד־

9. *an adamant.* Hebrew *shamir*, the word for a substance of exceptional hardness. In Jer. xvii. 1 it is translated *diamond* and denotes the point of an engraving implement, and it also occurs figuratively to describe hardness of heart (Zech. vii. 12).

neither be dismayed . . . for they are a rebellious house. He need not feel inferior to his opponents; they are a sinful people and as such will not prevail against the messenger of God.

10-15 THE PROPHET ENTERS UPON HIS MISSION

His work begins with the exiled community among whom he is living; but before he sets out on his task, he experiences another vision to hearten him.

10. *receive in thy heart, and hear with thine ears.* i.e. take all the words to heart after attentively hearing them.

11. *thy people.* The phrase may be used here in a disparaging sense. Since they are *a rebellious house*, they are not described as 'My people.' Cf. Exod.

xxxii. 7 where the Israelites who worshipped the Golden Calf are called *thy* (Moses') *people.*

speak unto them, and tell them. He was to repeat his message again and again.

thus saith the Lord GOD. He must make clear to his audience that he is speaking in the name of God and not expressing his own thoughts.

whether they will forbear. See on ii. 5.

12. *a spirit lifted me up.* In his vision the prophet felt himself lifted up and carried away to the main colony of his fellow-captives

I heard behind me the voice of a great rushing. The loud sound of a rushing noise heard by the prophet was that of the *Merkabah* which was present in the vision, but withdrew as Ezekiel left on his mission (Malbim). 'The prophet had been in the presence of the theophany (i) during all that has hitherto been narrated (ii. 1-iii. 12), and thus when he was lifted up and carried away it seemed to him that he left the theophany *behind* him' (Davidson).

of the LORD from His place';
13. also the noise of the wings of
the living creatures as they touched
one another, and the noise of the
wheels beside them, even the noise
of a great rushing. 14. So a spirit
lifted me up, and took me away;
and I went in bitterness, in the heat
of my spirit, and the hand of the
LORD was strong upon me. 15. Then
I came to them of the captivity at
Tel-abib, that dwelt by the river
Chebar, and I sat where they sat;

13 יְהֹוָה מִמְּקוֹמוֹ: וְקוֹל | כַּנְפֵי
הַחַיּוֹת מַשִּׁיקוֹת אִשָּׁה אֶל־
אֲחוֹתָהּ וְקוֹל הָאוֹפַנִּים
לְעֻמָּתָם וְקוֹל רַעַשׁ גָּדוֹל:
14 וְרוּחַ נְשָׂאַתְנִי וַתִּקָּחֵנִי וָאֵלֵךְ
מַר בַּחֲמַת רוּחִי וְיַד־יְהֹוָה
15 עָלַי חָזָקָה: וָאָבוֹא אֶל־
הַגּוֹלָה תֵּל אָבִיב הַיֹּשְׁבִים
אֶל־נְהַר־כְּבָר וָאֵשֵׁר הֵמָּה
יוֹשְׁבִים שָׁם וָאֵשֵׁב שָׁם שִׁבְעַת

v. 15. ואשב ק

blessed be the glory of the LORD from His place. These words of praise were presumably uttered by the celestial beings and heard by the prophet as he turns away from the scene. Though the *Merkabah* is moving away—a foreboding of the departure of God's Presence from the Temple—*the glory of the LORD* yet remained in the place from which it is departing, since *His place* is universal (cf. Isa. vi. 3). Alternatively, as Malbim explains, *His place* may signify Jerusalem which continues to be the abode of the Divine glory.

13. *also the noise.* To be connected with *and I heard* in the preceding verse.

the wings of the living creatures, etc. The phrase *the voice of a great rushing* in the last verse is now defined as referring to the roaring noise made by the wings of the *living creatures* and the turning *wheels* as the *Merkabah* sets in motion.

14. *a spirit lifted me up.* The repetition of the phrase in verse 12 is due to the intervening description of *the noise of a great rushing.*

in bitterness. i.e. in distress. The prophet was deeply grieved to have to deliver so calamitous a message to his countrymen (Rashi).

in the heat of my spirit. Descriptive of the state of exaltation which he felt as the effect of the vision. It is less probably explained as 'righteous indignation against Israel.'

the hand of the LORD was strong upon me. The reluctance of the prophet to undertake his mission gave way to the overwhelming compulsion of the prophetic spirit (see on i. 3).

15. *Tel-abib.* Probably the principal settlement of the exiles. 'The name Tel-abib means "Hill of Corn Ears." The original name is much more probably *til-abubi* (Assyrian), a mound or heap produced by the action of storms. Sandhills of this kind were numerous in Babylonia, and formed barren spots where the conqueror might very well place his captives. The Hebrew ear then detected in the sound the more attractive meaning which it suggested in their own tongue, and modified the word accordingly' (Davidson).

and I sat where they sat. This is the rendering of the *kerë* (*waësheb*); the *kethib* (*waasher*) is adopted by R.V., 'and to where they dwelt,' which is, however, tautology.

and I remained there appalled among them seven days.

16. And it came to pass at the end of seven days, that the word of the LORD came unto me, saying: 17. 'Son of man, I have appointed thee a watchman unto the house of Israel; and when thou shalt hear a word at My mouth, thou shalt give them warning from Me. 18. When I say unto the wicked: Thou shalt surely die; and thou givest him not warning, nor speakest to warn the wicked from his wicked way, to save his life; the same wicked man shall die in his iniquity, but his blood will I require at thy hand. 19. Yet if thou warn the wicked, and he turn not from his wickedness, nor from his wicked way, he shall die in his

16 יָמִים מַשְׁמִים בְּתוֹכָם: וַיְהִי
מִקְצֵה שִׁבְעַת יָמִים • וַיְהִי
17 דְבַר־יְהֹוָה אֵלַי לֵאמֹר: בֶּן־
אָדָם צֹפֶה נְתַתִּיךָ לְבֵית
יִשְׂרָאֵל וְשָׁמַעְתָּ מִפִּי דָּבָר
18 וְהִזְהַרְתָּ אוֹתָם מִמֶּנִּי: בְּאָמְרִי
לָרָשָׁע מוֹת תָּמוּת וְלֹא
הִזְהַרְתּוֹ וְלֹא דִבַּרְתָּ לְהַזְהִיר
רָשָׁע מִדַּרְכּוֹ הָרְשָׁעָה לְחַיֹּתוֹ
הוּא רָשָׁע בַּעֲוֹנוֹ יָמוּת וְדָמוֹ
19 מִיָּדְךָ אֲבַקֵּשׁ: וְאַתָּה כִּי־
הִזְהַרְתָּ רָשָׁע וְלֹא־שָׁב
מֵרִשְׁעוֹ וּמִדַּרְכּוֹ הָרְשָׁעָה הוּא

v. 16. פסקא באמצע פסוק

I remained there appalled among them seven days. For seven days the prophet sat among his people silent and motionless, probably waiting for further instructions which he then received. The number *seven* plays a significant part throughout the Scriptures. In the view of Kimchi, this and the other incidents narrated to the end of chapter xi were not actually performed but were suggested to Ezekiel during his visionary state. Only then, as mentioned in xi. 25, he was allowed to speak to the people and tell them all his experiences.

16-21 HIS TASK IS TO ACT AS WATCHMAN

Ezekiel's function is now more precisely defined. His task was not only to preach and rebuke, but also to warn against the imminent danger of the fall of Jerusalem and the consequent suffering of the people. As a watchman on his tower warns the people of approaching danger, so was Ezekiel charged with the duty of calling the nation back to God lest they be overtaken by disaster. A fuller description of this phase in his career is found in chapter xxxiii.

16. M.T. makes a division between the two halves of the verse, the reason for which is uncertain.

17. *thou shalt give them warning from Me.* The watchman's duty is to try to prevent disaster by giving due warning; so will Ezekiel exhort his people to repent their sins in order to ward off the inevitable effects.

18. *when I say unto the wicked.* Not directly, but through a communication to Ezekiel which he should deliver to him.

his blood will I require at thy hand. The failure to save life corresponds to murder. The grave responsibility resting upon the prophet is made very clear in this verse. By keeping silent, he will share the punishment which the wicked man incurs.

iniquity; but thou hast delivered thy
soul. 20. Again, when a righteous
man doth turn from his righteousness, and commit iniquity, I will lay
a stumblingblock before him, he
shall die; because thou hast not
given him warning, he shall die in
his sin, and his righteous deeds
which he hath done shall not be
remembered; but his blood will
I require at thy hand. 21. Nevertheless if thou warn the righteous
man, that the righteous sin not, and
he doth not sin, he shall surely live,
because he took warning; and thou
hast delivered thy soul.'

22. And the hand of the LORD
came there upon me; and He said
unto me: 'Arise, go forth into the
plain, and I will there speak with
thee.' 23. Then I arose, and went
forth into the plain; and, behold,
the glory of the LORD stood there,

בַּעֲוֺנוֹ יָמוּת וְאַתָּה אֶת־נַפְשְׁךָ
20 הִצַּלְתָּ: וּבְשׁוּב צַדִּיק מִצִּדְקוֹ
וְעָשָׂה עָוֶל וְנָתַתִּי מִכְשׁוֹל
לְפָנָיו הוּא יָמוּת כִּי לֹא
הִזְהַרְתּוֹ בְּחַטָּאתוֹ יָמוּת וְלֹא
תִזָּכַרְן צִדְקֹתָו אֲשֶׁר עָשָׂה
21 וְדָמוֹ מִיָּדְךָ אֲבַקֵּשׁ: וְאַתָּה
כִּי הִזְהַרְתּוֹ צַדִּיק לְבִלְתִּי
חֲטֹא צַדִּיק וְהוּא לֹא־חָטָא
חָיוֹ יִחְיֶה כִּי נִזְהָר וְאַתָּה אֶת־
22 נַפְשְׁךָ הִצַּלְתָּ: וַתְּהִי עָלַי שָׁם
יַד־יְהֹוָה וַיֹּאמֶר אֵלַי קוּם צֵא
אֶל־הַבִּקְעָה וְשָׁם אֲדַבֵּר
23 אוֹתָךְ: וָאָקוּם וָאֵצֵא אֶל־
הַבִּקְעָה וְהִנֵּה־שָׁם כְּבוֹד־

v. 20. קמץ בז"ק v. 21. צדקותיו ק'

19. *but thou hast delivered thy soul.*
From the guilt of bloodshed. *Thy soul*
is the equivalent of 'thyself.'

20. *I will lay a stumblingblock before him.*
The Rabbis (Yoma 86b) understand the
verse to refer to a righteous man who has
turned apostate inwardly but hypocritically still professes to be pious.
Such hypocrisy would be exposed, for
God would put a stumblingblock in his
way which causes him to commit sin in
public.

*his righteous deeds . . . shall not be
remembered.* According to the Rabbis
(Kid. 40b), this applies to a man who
regrets his good deeds in the past.

22-27 A COMMAND TO REMAIN SILENT
Ezekiel is ordered by God to live in
solitude and not begin his duties as
watchman until all the prophecies necessary for his mission are revealed to him.
This section is to be regarded as an
introduction to chapters iv-xxiv.

22. *the hand of the LORD came there upon
me.* See on i. 3. Davidson remarks,
'It is probable that the prophet's retiring
to the plain was merely transacted in
vision. He felt himself transported away
from the presence of men to some lonely
retreat, and there the glory of the Lord
seemed again to stand before him.'
This interpretation agrees with the
opinion of Kimchi as quoted on iii. 15.

go forth into the plain. He was ordered
to leave Tel-abib for an uninhabited
place which was more suitable for the
appearance of the glory of the Lord.

as the glory which I saw by the river
Chebar; and I fell on my face.
24. Then spirit entered into me,
and set me upon my feet; and He
spoke with me, and said unto me:
'Go, shut thyself within thy house.
25. But thou, son of man, behold,
bands shall be put upon thee, and
thou shalt be bound with them, and
thou shalt not go out among them;
26. and I will make thy tongue
cleave to the roof of thy mouth,
that thou shalt be dumb, and shalt
not be to them a reprover; for they
are a rebellious house. 27. But
when I speak with thee, I will open
thy mouth, and thou shalt say unto
them: Thus saith the Lord GOD; he

יְהוָֹה עֹמֵד כַּכָּבוֹד אֲשֶׁר
רָאִיתִי עַל־נְהַר־כְּבָר וָאֶפֹּל
24 עַל־פָּנָי: וַתָּבֹא־בִי רוּחַ
וַתַּעֲמִדֵנִי עַל־רַגְלָי וַיְדַבֵּר
אֹתִי וַיֹּאמֶר אֵלַי בֹּא הִסָּגֵר
25 בְּתוֹךְ בֵּיתֶךָ: וְאַתָּה בֶן־אָדָם
הִנֵּה נָתְנוּ עָלֶיךָ עֲבוֹתִים
וַאֲסָרוּךָ בָּהֶם וְלֹא תֵצֵא
26 בְּתוֹכָם: וּלְשׁוֹנְךָ אַדְבִּיק
אֶל־חִכְּךָ וְנֶאֱלַמְתָּ וְלֹא־
תִהְיֶה לָהֶם לְאִישׁ מוֹכִיחַ כִּי
27 בֵּית מְרִי הֵמָּה: וּבְדַבְּרִי
אוֹתְךָ אֶפְתַּח אֶת־פִּיךָ
וְאָמַרְתָּ אֲלֵיהֶם כֹּה אָמַר אֲדֹנָי

23. *as the glory which I saw by the river Chebar.* He found himself again in the presence of the *Merkabah* which he saw on the occasion of his call to the prophetic office. The vision occurred to him on one more occasion (cf. viii. 2ff.).

I fell on my face. He prostrated himself in awe before the Divine manifestation.

24. *shut thyself within thy house.* The purpose of his retirement was to prevent him from reproving the people before he had received all God's instructions and beheld all the visions which are narrated up to the end of chapter xi (Kimchi).

25. *bands shall be put upon thee.* The Targum interprets this figuratively: the command to the prophet to confine himself to his house must be adhered to as though he were in fetters. Some modern commentators prefer the literal translation (so A.V., R.V.), 'they shall put bands upon thee and shall bind thee,'

and identify 'they' with *among them,* viz. the exiles were to do the fettering.

26. *I will make thy tongue cleave to the roof of thy mouth.* The meaning is, God forbids Ezekiel to converse with his fellow-captives; he is to act 'as though he were dumb. For the phraseology, cf. Ps. cxxxvii. 6. Evidently the time had not yet arrived when he was to address the community. We may dismiss the explanation that Ezekiel was suffering from mental or physical shock, since his silence was self-imposed at the command of God.

27. *when I speak with thee, I will open thy mouth.* Better, 'when I have spoken,' etc. Only after God had communicated to him all the prophecies and visions was he allowed to speak to the people. This happened when the vision finally departed, as stated in xi. 24f.

thus saith the Lord GOD, etc. See on ii. 4f.

that heareth, let him hear, and he that forbeareth, let him forbear; for they are a rebellious house.

יְהֹוָה הַשֹּׁמֵעַ ׀ יִשְׁמָ֔ע וְהֶחָדֵ֖ל ׀ יֶחְדָּ֑ל כִּ֛י בֵּ֥ית מְרִ֖י הֵֽמָּה׃

4   CHAPTER IV   ד

1. Thou also, son of man, take thee a tile, and lay it before thee, and trace upon it a city, even Jerusalem;

2. and lay siege against it, and build forts against it, and cast up a mound against it; set camps also against it, and set battering rams against it

1 וְאַתָּ֣ה בֶן־אָדָ֔ם קַח־לְךָ֙ לְבֵנָ֔ה וְנָתַתָּ֥ה אוֹתָ֖הּ לְפָנֶ֑יךָ וְחַקּוֹתָ֥ עָלֶ֛יהָ עִ֖יר אֶת־
2 יְרוּשָׁלָֽ͏ִם׃ וְנָתַתָּ֥ה עָלֶ֖יהָ מָצ֑וֹר וּבָנִ֤יתָ עָלֶ֙יהָ֙ דָּיֵ֔ק וְשָׁפַכְתָּ֥ עָלֶ֖יהָ סֹלְלָ֑ה וְנָתַתָּ֥ה עָלֶ֛יהָ מַחֲנ֖וֹת וְשִׂים־עָלֶ֥יהָ כָּרִ֖ים

v. 27. המ׳ בקמץ   v. 27. קמץ בז״ק

CHAPTER IV

THIS chapter and the first four verses of the next narrate four symbolic acts which, in a vision, Ezekiel was commanded to perform: iv. 1-3 relates to the siege of Jerusalem, 4-8 to the iniquity of Israel, 9-17 to the famine suffered during the siege, and v. 1-4 to the fate of the population in the doomed city.

1-3 SYMBOL OF THE SIEGE OF JERUSALEM

1. a tile. A slab of clay was the common material used for writing in Assyria and Babylonia. The inscription was engraved with a stylus while the clay was moist and it was then exposed to the sun for hardening. Very large numbers have been discovered during the last century and deciphered, some with designs of buildings on them.

2. lay siege against it. i.e. draw on the tile the plan of a siege.

forts. The Hebrew has the singular. It denotes a system of several towers used for attacking a besieged city. "Towers

of this kind, manned by archers, are seen on the Assyrian bas-reliefs' (Davidson). For the fulfilment of the prophecy, cf. 2 Kings xxv. 1 where the same Hebrew word is employed.

mound. A bank of soil raised to the level of the wall of the besieged city. It was used as an observation post and action station. 'The like can be seen in Assyrian representations of sieges, in the British Museum and elsewhere' (Lofthouse).

camps. Detachments of soldiers on all sides of the city.

battering rams. Josephus (*The Jewish War*, III. vii. 19) gives the following description of the battering ram as used by Vespasian against Jerusalem: 'This is a vast beam of wood like the mast of a ship; its forepart is armed with a thick piece of iron as the head of it, which is so carved as to be like the head of a ram, whence its name is taken. This ram is slung in the air by ropes passing over its middle, and is hung like the balance in a pair of scales from another beam, and braced by strong beams that pass on both sides of it in the nature of a cross. When

round about. 3. And take thou unto thee an iron griddle, and set it for a wall of iron between thee and the city; and set thy face toward it, and it shall be besieged, and thou shalt lay siege against it. This shall be a sign to the house of Israel.

4. Moreover lie thou upon thy left side, and lay the iniquity of the house of Israel upon it; according to the number of the days that thou shalt lie upon it, thou shalt bear their iniquity. 5. For I have appointed the years of their iniquity to be unto thee a number of days, even three hundred and ninety days; so shalt thou bear the iniquity of the

3 סָבִיב: וְאַתָּה קַח־לְךָ מַחֲבַת
בַּרְזֶל וְנָתַתָּה אוֹתָהּ קִיר בַּרְזֶל
בֵּינְךָ וּבֵין הָעִיר וַהֲכִינֹתָה
אֶת־פָּנֶיךָ אֵלֶיהָ וְהָיְתָה
בַמָּצוֹר וְצַרְתָּ עָלֶיהָ אוֹת הִיא
4 לְבֵית יִשְׂרָאֵל: וְאַתָּה שְׁכַב
עַל־צִדְּךָ הַשְּׂמָאלִי וְשַׂמְתָּ
אֶת־עֲוֹן בֵּית־יִשְׂרָאֵל עָלָיו
מִסְפַּר הַיָּמִים אֲשֶׁר תִּשְׁכַּב
5 עָלָיו תִּשָּׂא אֶת־עֲוֹנָם: וַאֲנִי
נָתַתִּי לְךָ אֶת־שְׁנֵי עֲוֹנָם
לְמִסְפַּר יָמִים שְׁלֹשׁ־מֵאוֹת
וְתִשְׁעִים יוֹם וְנָשָׂאתָ עֲוֹן בֵּית־

this ram is pulled backward by a great number of men with united force, and then thrust forward by the same men, it batters the walls with that iron part which is prominent.'

3. *griddle.* A kind of flat pan such as was used for baking a meal-offering (Lev. ii. 5). This was to represent *a wall of iron*, which Rashi and some moderns understand as the city wall upon which the population depended for safety, *iron* denoting the strength of the defence. 'It might, however, be a symbol of the implacable and iron severity of the siege, which itself but shows the inexorable grasp which the judgment of God had taken of the city' (Davidson).

set thy face toward it. i.e. assume the part of besieger.

thou shalt lay siege against it. Since the prophet was acting upon God's instruction, this was to indicate that He would be against Jerusalem in the contest (Metsudath David).

a sign to the house of Israel. The symbolic action of Ezekiel pointed to the forthcoming siege of Jerusalem.

4-6 SYMBOL OF THE PEOPLE'S SINS

The prophet now reverses his rôle. First he personified the enemy, now he represents the sinful nation which is to suffer calamity.

4. *lie thou upon thy left side.* The hardship which he suffered by lying on one side for a considerable time is emblematic of the iniquity of which the people was guilty. The *left side* is symbolic of Samaria and the Northern Kingdom of Israel whose territory was in the north (cf. xvi. 46).

the number of the days. Each day was to represent a year for the condemned nation.

5. *three hundred and ninety days.* The guilt of the Northern Kingdom extended

house of Israel. 6. And again, when thou hast accomplished these, thou shalt lie on thy right side, and shalt bear the iniquity of the house of Judah; forty days, each day for a year, have I appointed it unto thee. 7. And thou shalt set thy face toward the siege of Jerusalem, with thine arm uncovered; and thou shalt prophesy against it. 8. And, behold, I lay bands upon thee, and thou shalt not turn thee from one side to another, till thou hast accomplished the days of thy siege. 9. Take thou also unto thee wheat, and barley, and beans, and lentils,

6 יִשְׂרָאֵל ׃ וְכִלִּיתָ אֶת־אֵלֶּה
וְשָׁכַבְתָּ עַל־צִדְּךָ הַיְמָנִי
שֵׁנִית וְנָשָׂאתָ אֶת־עֲוֹן בֵּית־
יְהוּדָה אַרְבָּעִים יוֹם יוֹם לַשָּׁנָה
7 יוֹם לַשָּׁנָה נְתַתִּיו לָךְ ׃ וְאֶל־
מְצוֹר יְרוּשָׁלַ͏ִם תָּכִין פָּנֶיךָ
וּזְרֹעֲךָ חֲשׂוּפָה וְנִבֵּאתָ עָלֶיהָ ׃
8 וְהִנֵּה נָתַתִּי עָלֶיךָ עֲבוֹתִים
וְלֹא־תֵהָפֵךְ מִצִּדְּךָ אֶל־
צִדֶּךָ עַד־כַּלּוֹתְךָ יְמֵי
9 מְצוּרֶךָ ׃ וְאַתָּה קַח־לְךָ חִטִּין
וּשְׂעֹרִים וּפוֹל וַעֲדָשִׁים וְדֹחַן

הימני ק׳ v. 6.

over a period of 390 years (Seder Olam, Rashi and Ibn Ezra). Abarbanel, quoted by Malbim, reckons the period of Samaria's guilt from the time when the schism took place under Rehoboam (c. 932 B.C.E.) until the fall of Jerusalem. Corresponding to the 390 years of Israel's sinning, the prophet was ordered to lie on his left side the same number of days to atone for their iniquity.

6. *when thou hast accomplished these.* viz. the 390 days.

thou shalt lie on thy right side. The *right* indicates the south, i.e. the Kingdom of Judah which lay to the south or right.

forty days, each day for a year. Judah's corruption lasted forty years beginning soon after Samaria's fall. According to Malbim, the time is reckoned from the thirteenth year of the reign of Josiah (626 B.C.E.) when Jeremiah began his ministry (Jer. i. 2). Ibn Ezra suggests that the prophet's lying on his sides for a great number of days occurred in a vision.

7. *thou shalt set thy face toward the siege of Jerusalem.* The repetition of the phrase (cf. verse 3) has the intention of urging the prophet to fix his gaze upon the besieged city as drawn on the tile during the whole time he was lying on both sides (Rashi, Kimchi).

with thine arm uncovered. Like a warrior prepared for action (cf. Isa. lii. 10).

8. *I lay bands upon thee.* He was to lie completely still on his sides as though trussed and incapable of movement. The consequent discomfort symbolized the rigours of the siege.

thy siege. Some Hebrew MSS. read the plural, 'thy sieges,' referring both to Samaria and Jerusalem. Kimchi had the plural reading in his text.

9-17 SYMBOL OF FAMINE
DURING THE SIEGE

9. *take thou.* This was presumably to be done while Ezekiel was lying immobile on his side. If so, it is evident that it all happened in a vision in which such an inconsistency need not arouse surprise.

and millet, and spelt, and put them in one vessel, and make thee bread thereof; according to the number of the days that thou shalt lie upon thy side, even three hundred and ninety days, shalt thou eat thereof. 10. And thy food which thou shalt eat shall be by weight, twenty shekels a day; from time to time shalt thou eat it. 11. Thou shalt drink also water by measure, the sixth part of a hin; from time to time shalt thou drink. 12. And thou shalt eat it as barley cakes, and thou shalt bake it in their sight with dung that cometh out of man.'

וְכֻסְּמִים וְנָתַתָּה אוֹתָם בִּכְלִי
אֶחָד וְעָשִׂיתָ אוֹתָם לְךָ לְלֶחֶם
מִסְפַּר הַיָּמִים אֲשֶׁר־אַתָּה |
שׁוֹכֵב עַל־צִדְּךָ שְׁלֹשׁ־מֵאוֹת
וְתִשְׁעִים יוֹם תֹּאכְלֶנּוּ:
10 וּמַאֲכָלְךָ אֲשֶׁר תֹּאכְלֶנּוּ
בְּמִשְׁקוֹל עֶשְׂרִים שֶׁקֶל לַיּוֹם
11 מֵעֵת עַד־עֵת תֹּאכְלֶנּוּ: וּמַיִם
בִּמְשׂוּרָה תִשְׁתֶּה שִׁשִּׁית הַהִין
12 מֵעֵת עַד־עֵת תִּשְׁתֶּה: וְעֻגַת
שְׂעֹרִים תֹּאכְלֶנָּה וְהִיא בְּגֶלְלֵי
צֵאַת הָאָדָם תְּעֻגֶנָה לְעֵינֵיהֶם:

and make thee bread thereof. The bread made of such a strange mixture indicates the great scarcity during the siege. Instead of the normal wheaten bread, various kinds of cereals would have to be gathered and mixed to obtain the quantity required to make a loaf. It is improbable that the underlying idea is that the bread made from a mixture, against which the Torah raised objection (cf. Lev. xix. 19; Deut. xxii. 9), symbolized the uncleanness of the land in which the exiles were living.

upon thy side. i.e. upon each side. The bread of the mixed ingredients was to last for 390 days as stated in the verse and 40 days in addition, during which time he was ordered to lie on his two sides respectively (Kimchi). The modern view is that the inference to be drawn is that 390 is inclusive of the 40 days; but this is contrary to the explicit statement in verse 6.

10. *shall be by weight.* An indication of the great scarcity of food (cf. Lev. xxvi. 26).

twenty shekels a day. A shekel struck by a Maccabean king and still extant weighs 219 grains. Accordingly, Ezekiel's food for a whole day amounted to a little over nine ounces.

from time to time. The phrase is defined by the Rabbis as once in twenty-four hours.

11. *sixth part of a hin.* A *hin* was a liquid measure of about twelve pints, so that two pints of water was to be his daily ration, a very small quantity in a hot climate.

12. *as barley cakes.* Though mixed with inferior kinds of cereals, it was to be eaten with the same relish as when one eats barley bread.

in their sight. In the presence of the Israelites, so that they understand it as a sign of what is in store for them.

with dung that cometh out of man. 'It was customary in the east to use the dung of animals when perfectly dried as fuel. The hot ashes remaining from it

13. And the LORD said: 'Even thus shall the children of Israel eat their bread unclean, among the nations whither I will drive them.' 14. Then said I: 'Ah Lord GOD! behold, my soul hath not been polluted; for from my youth up even till now have I not eaten of that which dieth of itself, or is torn of beasts; neither came there abhorred flesh into my mouth.' 15. Then He said unto me: 'See, I have given thee cow's dung for man's dung, and thou shalt prepare thy bread thereon.' 16. Moreover He said unto me: 'Son of man, behold, I will break the staff of bread in Jerusalem, and they shall eat bread by weight, and with anxiety; and they shall drink water by measure, and in appalment;

13 וַיֹּאמֶר יְהֹוָה כָּכָה יֹאכְלוּ בְנֵי־
יִשְׂרָאֵל אֶת־לַחְמָם טָמֵא
בַּגּוֹיִם אֲשֶׁר אַדִּיחֵם שָׁם:
14 וָאֹמַר אֲהָהּ אֲדֹנָי יֱהֹוִה הִנֵּה
נַפְשִׁי לֹא מְטֻמָּאָה וּנְבֵלָה
וּטְרֵפָה לֹא־אָכַלְתִּי מִנְּעוּרַי
וְעַד־עַתָּה וְלֹא־בָא בְּפִי
15 בְּשַׂר פִּגּוּל: וַיֹּאמֶר אֵלַי רְאֵה
נָתַתִּי לְךָ אֶת־צְפוּעֵי הַבָּקָר
תַּחַת גֶּלְלֵי הָאָדָם וְעָשִׂיתָ אֶת־
16 לַחְמְךָ עֲלֵיהֶם: וַיֹּאמֶר אֵלַי
בֶּן־אָדָם הִנְנִי שֹׁבֵר מַטֵּה־
לֶחֶם בִּירוּשָׁלַ͏ִם וְאָכְלוּ־לֶחֶם
בְּמִשְׁקָל וּבִדְאָגָה וּמַיִם
בִּמְשׂוּרָה וּבְשִׁמָּמוֹן יִשְׁתּוּ:

צפיעי ק׳ v. 15.

being perfectly clean, and retaining their glow for a considerable time, were used for firing cakes upon or under . . . The material for firing which the prophet is commanded to use would certainly be unclean (Deut. xxiii. 13ff.) as well as loathsome' (Davidson).

13. *eat their bread unclean.* The meaning of the symbol is that the Israelites will eat unclean food in exile (cf. Hos. ix. 3). Perhaps *their bread unclean among the nations* denotes ritual as well as physical defilement, since foreign lands were regarded by the Israelites as unclean.

14. *my soul.* Equals 'I.'

that which dieth of itself. Such flesh was forbidden (Lev. xvii. 15; Deut. xiv. 21).

abhorred flesh. The Hebrew term *piggul* is applied to sacrificial flesh rendered unfit by disregard of the laws concerning sacrifices. It is also used in a wider sense of forbidden food (cf. Lev. vii. 18; Isa. lxv. 4).

15. *cow's dung.* The substitution was granted in response to the prophet's feeling of abhorrence. 'Dried cow-dung or camel-dung is still used for fuel by the Bedouin and fellahin' (Cooke).

16. *I will break the staff of bread.* This and the following verses explain the symbol of eating bread and drinking water by measure (verses 10f.). *Staff of bread* is a common expression in Scripture (e.g. v. 16; Lev. xxvi. 26; Ps. cv. 16), denoting man's reliance upon bread as his staple food.

23

17. that they may want bread and water, and be appalled one with another, and pine away in their iniquity.

לְמַ֣עַן יַחְסְר֗וּ לֶ֚חֶם וָמַ֔יִם וְנָשַׁ֖מּוּ אִ֣ישׁ וְאָחִ֑יו וְנָמַ֖קּוּ בַּעֲוֺנָֽם׃ ¹⁷

---

5   CHAPTER V   ה

1. And thou, son of man, take thee a sharp sword, as a barber's razor shalt thou take it unto thee, and cause it to pass upon thy head and upon thy beard; then take thee balances to weigh, and divide the hair. 2. A third part shalt thou burn in the fire in the midst of the city, when the days of the siege are fulfilled; and thou shalt take a third part, and smite it with the sword round about her; and a third part

וְאַתָּ֣ה בֶן־אָדָ֡ם קַח־לְךָ֣ | ¹
חֶ֣רֶב חַדָּ֗ה תַּ֚עַר הַגַּלָּבִים֙
תִּקָּחֶ֣נָּה לָּ֔ךְ וְהַעֲבַרְתָּ֥ עַל־
רֹאשְׁךָ֖ וְעַל־זְקָנֶ֑ךָ וְלָקַחְתָּ֥
לְךָ֛ מֹאזְנֵ֥י מִשְׁקָ֖ל וְחִלַּקְתָּֽם׃
שְׁלִשִׁ֗ית בָּא֤וּר תַּבְעִיר֙ בְּת֣וֹךְ ²
הָעִ֔יר כִּמְלֹ֖את יְמֵ֣י הַמָּצ֑וֹר
וְלָקַחְתָּ֣ אֶת־הַשְּׁלִשִׁית֮ תַּכֶּ֣ה
בַחֶרֶב֮ סְבִיבוֹתֶ֔יהָ וְהַשְּׁלִשִׁית֙

---

17. *one with another.* Everyone without exception (Kimchi).

CHAPTER V

1-4 THE NATION'S FATE

By means of another symbolic act Ezekiel was to indicate the impending destruction of the people by massacre and dispersion.

1. *a sharp sword, as a barber's razor.* Better, 'a sharp sword, i.e. a barber's razor.' The razor is described as a *sword,* emblematic of the invading army which Nebuchadnezzar would send against them. The same imagery had been previously used by Isaiah (vii. 20). 'The land is likened to a man; the enemy sweeps off the population clean as the razor does the hair of the body' (Davidson).

balances to weigh. The hair is to be divided into three equal parts. *Balances* may be a symbol of Divine justice.

2. *in the midst of the city.* Some suppose that the reference is to the plan of the city which was drawn on the tile (iv. 1). Others are of the opinion that the actual city of Jerusalem is intended. The action obviously takes place in a vision.

when the days of the siege are fulfilled. i.e. the 430 days during which the prophet was commanded to lie on his sides and play the rôle of besieger (iv. 4-8). The third of the prophet's hair burned in the midst of the city signifies that a third of the population will perish by fire, sword, famine and pestilence within the city during the siege.

round about her. viz. the city. This symbolizes the fate of those who seek to escape before and after the fall of the city, as, e.g. king Zedekiah and his retinue (cf. 2 Kings xxv. 4ff.).

thou shalt scatter to the wind, and I will draw out a sword after them. 3. Thou shalt also take thereof a few by number, and bind them in thy skirts. 4. And of them again shalt thou take, and cast them into the midst of the fire, and burn them in the fire; therefrom shall a fire come forth into all the house of Israel.

5. Thus saith the Lord GOD: This is Jerusalem! I have set her in the midst of the nations, and countries are round about her. 6. And she hath rebelled against Mine ordinances in doing wickedness more than the nations, and against My

תְּזָרֶה לָרוּחַ וְחֶרֶב אָרִיק
3 אַחֲרֵיהֶם: וְלָקַחְתָּ מִשָּׁם מְעַט
בְּמִסְפָּר וְצַרְתָּ אוֹתָם
4 בִּכְנָפֶיךָ: וּמֵהֶם עוֹד תִּקָּח
וְהִשְׁלַכְתָּ אוֹתָם אֶל־תּוֹךְ
הָאֵשׁ וְשָׂרַפְתָּ אֹתָם בָּאֵשׁ מִמֶּנּוּ
תֵצֵא־אֵשׁ אֶל־כָּל־בֵּית
5 יִשְׂרָאֵל: כֹּה אָמַר אֲדֹנָי יֱהֹוִה
זֹאת יְרוּשָׁלִַם בְּתוֹךְ הַגּוֹיִם
שַׂמְתִּיהָ וּסְבִיבוֹתֶיהָ אֲרָצוֹת:
6 וַתֶּמֶר אֶת־מִשְׁפָּטַי לְרִשְׁעָה
מִן־הַגּוֹיִם וְאֶת־חֻקּוֹתַי מִן־

קמץ בז״ק v. 4.

---

a third part thou shalt scatter to the wind. Signifying that a third of the population will be dispersed in foreign lands.

I will draw out a sword after them. They will not find peace in the lands of dispersion. The same fate is predicted by Jeremiah (ix. 15).

3. *thereof.* i.e. of the last third which was to be scattered to the wind.

bind them in thy skirts. A symbol that only a small remnant of the exiles in Babylon would survive and return to the Holy Land at the restoration.

4. *of them.* viz. of the hairs wrapped in his garment.

into the midst of the fire. Raging within the city. The intention is that even the remnant in exile would be subjected to calamity.

therefrom. i.e. from the fire which the prophet was commanded to make in the midst of the city. This fire will cause destruction to all the house of Israel, to those within the city and also to those who escaped or were exiled.

5-17 THE FOUR SYMBOLS EXPLAINED

5. *in the midst of the nations.* The Rabbis held Jerusalem to be located in the centre of the world, and the same thought was current in the Middle Ages. 'Following Ezekiel, Dante places Jerusalem at the centre of the world, with the Ganges as the extreme east and the pillars of Hercules as the extreme west' (Lofthouse). The prophet, however, is thinking less of geography and more of Jerusalem intended to be the radiating centre of the knowledge of God for all peoples. Her rejection of God was accordingly a serious hindrance to His cause and she must be punished *in the sight of the nations* (verse 8).

6. *in doing wickedness more than the nations.* Israel's guilt surpasses the wickedness committed by other peoples, because to him had been revealed God's *ordinances* and *statutes.* By the former, *mishpatim,* Jewish commentators understand commandments which concern the relationship between man and man, whereas the latter, *chukkim,* are the duties of man towards God.

statutes more than the countries that are round about her; for they have rejected Mine ordinances, and as for My statutes, they have not walked in them. 7. Therefore thus saith the Lord GOD: Because ye have outdone the nations that are round about you, in that ye have not walked in My statutes, neither have kept Mine ordinances, neither have done after the ordinances of the nations that are round about you; 8. therefore thus saith the Lord GOD: Behold, I, even I, am against thee, and I will execute judgments in the midst of thee in the sight of the nations. 9. And I will do in thee that which I have not done, and whereunto I will not do any more the like, because of all thine abominations. 10. Therefore the

הָאֲרָצוֹת אֲשֶׁר סְבִיבוֹתֶיהָ כִּי
בְמִשְׁפָּטַי מָאָסוּ וְחֻקּוֹתַי לֹא־
7 הָלְכוּ בָהֶם: לָכֵן כֹּה־אָמַר ׀
אֲדֹנָי יֱהֹוִה יַעַן הֲמָנְכֶם מִן־
הַגּוֹיִם אֲשֶׁר סְבִיבוֹתֵיכֶם
בְּחֻקּוֹתַי לֹא הֲלַכְתֶּם וְאֶת־
מִשְׁפָּטַי לֹא עֲשִׂיתֶם וּכְמִשְׁפְּטֵי
הַגּוֹיִם אֲשֶׁר סְבִיבוֹתֵיכֶם לֹא
8 עֲשִׂיתֶם: לָכֵן כֹּה אָמַר אֲדֹנָי
יֱהֹוִה הִנְנִי עָלַיִךְ גַּם־אָנִי
וְעָשִׂיתִי בְתוֹכֵךְ מִשְׁפָּטִים
9 לְעֵינֵי הַגּוֹיִם: וְעָשִׂיתִי בָךְ
אֵת אֲשֶׁר לֹא־עָשִׂיתִי וְאֵת
אֲשֶׁר־לֹא־אֶעֱשֶׂה כָמֹהוּ עוֹד
10 יַעַן כָּל־תּוֹעֲבֹתָיִךְ: לָכֵן

v. 6. קמץ בז״ק

---

7. *ye have outdone the nations.* The Hebrew word *hamanchem*, which occurs only here, is difficult and of uncertain meaning. A.V. has 'ye multiplied more than the nations'; R.V. 'ye are turbulent more than the nations.' It appears to be connected with the noun *hamon*, 'a tumultuous crowd,' and the meaning may be: 'ye are a worse crowd than the nations.' You have all the vices of the heathen nations and have not emulated their virtues.

neither have done after the ordinances of the nations. To reconcile the apparent contradiction between these words and the statement in xi. 12, *but have done after the ordinances of the nations,* the Talmud (Sanh. 39b) interprets the passage to mean: 'In your conduct you have not followed the example of the righteous Gentiles, but you have copied the evils of the corrupt peoples.' The phrase may, however, be explained in this sense: You have not fallen to the level of heathens but sunk even deeper in wickedness. Cf. the indictment in xvi. 47.

8. *even I.* lit. 'I also' on which Rashi comments: As you have betrayed Me, so will I betray you.

in the sight of the nations. Retribution will be exemplary to vindicate God's honour which Israel had publicly profaned.

9. *that which I have not done.* As the *abominations* are without precedent, so will be the manifestation of God's judgment.

fathers shall eat the sons in the midst of thee, and the sons shall eat their fathers; and I will execute judgments in thee, and the whole remnant of thee will I scatter unto all the winds. 11. Wherefore, as I live, saith the Lord GOD, surely, because thou hast defiled My sanctuary with all thy detestable things, and with all thine abominations, therefore will I also diminish thee; neither shall Mine eye spare, and I also will have no pity. 12. A third part of thee shall die with the pestilence, and with famine shall they be consumed in the midst of thee; and a third part shall fall by the sword round about thee; and a third part I will scatter unto all the winds, and will draw out a sword

אָבוֹת יֹאכְלוּ בָנִים בְּתוֹכֵךְ
וּבָנִים יֹאכְלוּ אֲבוֹתָם וְעָשִׂיתִי
בָךְ שְׁפָטִים וְזֵרִיתִי אֶת־כָּל־
11 שְׁאֵרִיתֵךְ לְכָל־רוּחַ: לָכֵן
חַי־אָנִי נְאֻם אֲדֹנָי יֱהֹוִה אִם־
לֹא יַעַן אֶת־מִקְדָּשִׁי טִמֵּאת
בְּכָל־שִׁקּוּצַיִךְ וּבְכָל־
תּוֹעֲבֹתָיִךְ וְגַם־אֲנִי אֶגְרַע
וְלֹא־תָחוֹס עֵינִי וְגַם־אֲנִי לֹא
12 אֶחְמוֹל: שְׁלִשָׁתֵיךְ בַּדֶּבֶר
יָמוּתוּ וּבָרָעָב יִכְלוּ בְתוֹכֵךְ
וְהַשְּׁלִשִׁית בַּחֶרֶב יִפְּלוּ
סְבִיבוֹתָיִךְ וְהַשְּׁלִישִׁית לְכָל־
רוּחַ אֱזָרֶה וְחֶרֶב אָרִיק

v. 11. למדנחאי אגדע כתיב v. 12. כצ״ל

10. *the fathers shall eat the sons*, etc. This frightful threat of what would happen during the siege of Jerusalem goes beyond Lev. xxvi. 29; Deut. xxviii. 53; Jer. xix. 9, in that the phrase *and the sons shall eat their fathers* is added. While Lam. iv. 10 records the flesh of children being devoured, nowhere is mention made of sons killing their parents during the extremities of famine. This part of the verse is the interpretation of the third of the hair being burned in the fire (verse 2).

I will execute judgments in thee. Part of the inhabitants will be destroyed by the invaders. This explains the symbol of a third of the hair being cut by the sword.

the whole remnant . . . all the winds. Explaining the symbol of the third part of the hair being scattered to the wind.

11. *thou hast defiled My sanctuary.* The verb is feminine and the subject is Jerusalem.

detestable things . . . abominations. A contemptuous reference to idolatry. It is recorded that king Manasseh defiled the Sanctuary by placing an idol within its precincts (2 Kings xxi. 7).

will I also diminish thee. The Hebrew text has nothing corresponding to *thee.* Kimchi understands the object to be 'thy honour': as thou, Jerusalem, hast impaired My honour by defiling the Temple, so will I impair thy honour in the eyes of the nations. Instead of *egra* (*I will diminish*) there is another reading in many MSS., *egda*, 'I will cut off' (thy seed; so the Targum).

12. *shall die with the pestilence.* The symbol of dividing the hair into three parts (verses 1-4) is more explicitly defined here after being generally explained in verse 10.

after them.   13. Thus shall Mine
anger spend itself, and I will satisfy
My fury upon them, and I will be
eased; and they shall know that
I the LORD have spoken in My zeal,
when I have spent My fury upon
them.   14. Moreover I will make
thee an amazement and a reproach,
among the nations that are round
about thee, in the sight of all that
pass by.   15. So it shall be a
reproach and a taunt, an instruction
and an astonishment, unto the
nations that are round about thee,
when I shall execute judgments in
thee in anger and in fury, and in
furious rebukes; I the LORD have
spoken it; 16. when I shall send
upon them the evil arrows of
famine, that are for destruction,
which I will send to destroy you; and
I will increase the famine upon you,
and will break your staff of bread;
17. and I will send upon you famine

13 אַחֲרֵיהֶם: וְכָלָה אַפִּי וַהֲנִחֹתִי
חֲמָתִי בָּם וְהִנֶּחָמְתִּי וְיָדְעוּ
כִּי־אֲנִי יְהֹוָה דִּבַּרְתִּי בְּקִנְאָתִי
14 בְּכַלּוֹתִי חֲמָתִי בָּם: וְאֶתְּנֵךְ
לְחָרְבָּה וּלְחֶרְפָּה בַּגּוֹיִם אֲשֶׁר
סְבִיבוֹתָיִךְ לְעֵינֵי כָּל־עוֹבֵר:
15 וְהָיְתָה חֶרְפָּה וּגְדוּפָה מוּסָר
וּמְשַׁמָּה לַגּוֹיִם אֲשֶׁר
סְבִיבוֹתָיִךְ בַּעֲשׂוֹתִי בָךְ
שְׁפָטִים בְּאַף וּבְחֵמָה
וּבְתֹכְחוֹת חֵמָה אֲנִי יְהֹוָה
16 דִּבַּרְתִּי: בְּשַׁלְּחִי אֶת־חִצֵּי
הָרָעָב הָרָעִים בָּהֶם אֲשֶׁר־
הָיוּ לְמַשְׁחִית אֲשֶׁר־אֲשַׁלַּח
אוֹתָם לְשַׁחֶתְכֶם וְרָעָב אֹסֵף
עֲלֵיכֶם וְשָׁבַרְתִּי לָכֶם מַטֵּה־
17 לָחֶם: וְשִׁלַּחְתִּי עֲלֵיכֶם רָעָב

13. *thus shall Mine anger*, etc.   Strongly
anthropomorphic language.

I will satisfy My fury.   More lit. 'I will
make My fury quiet'; the heat of the
Divine wrath will die down.   The phrase
is used again in xvi. 42, xxi. 22, xxiv. 13.

*they shall know that I the LORD have
spoken.*   When the punishment which is
predicted has been inflicted, they will
recognize that the calamity was the
decree of God and not due to chance.

14. *an amazement and a reproach.*   To
ape the manners of the surrounding
peoples Israel defied God; His retribution will have the effect of earning him
their contempt.

in the sight of all that pass by.   i.e. also
in the sight of passers-by (cf. Lam. ii. 15).

15. *it shall be.*   Better, 'she shall be';
the subject is Jerusalem.

an instruction.   i.e. a lesson of warning
(cf. xxiii. 48).

I the LORD have spoken it.   In Whose
power it is to carry out the threat.

16. *the evil arrows of famine.*   viz.
blasting, mildew, locusts, etc. (cf. Deut.
xxxii. 23f.).

I will increase the famine.   By with-
holding rain (Kimchi).

staff of bread.   See on iv. 16.

and evil beasts, and they shall bereave thee; and pestilence and blood shall pass through thee; and I will bring the sword upon thee. 1 the LORD have spoken it.'

וְהָיָה רָעָה וְשִׁכְּלָֽךְ וְדֶ֫בֶר וָדָם
יַעֲבָר־בָּ֑ךְ וְחֶ֫רֶב אָבִיא עָלַ֫יִךְ
אֲנִי יְהֹוָה דִּבַּֽרְתִּי׃

| 6 | CHAPTER VI | ו |

1. And the word of the LORD came unto me, saying: 2. 'Son of man, set thy face toward the mountains of Israel, and prophesy against them, 3. and say: Ye mountains of Israel, hear the word of the Lord GOD: Thus saith the Lord GOD concerning the mountains and concerning the hills, concerning the ravines and concerning the valleys: Behold, I, even I, will bring a sword upon you,

1 וַיְהִי דְבַר־יְהֹוָה אֵלַי לֵאמֹֽר׃
2 בֶּן־אָדָם שִׂים פָּנֶ֫יךָ אֶל־הָרֵי
יִשְׂרָאֵל וְהִנָּבֵא אֲלֵיהֶֽם׃
3 וְאָמַרְתָּ הָרֵי יִשְׂרָאֵל שִׁמְעוּ
דְּבַר־אֲדֹנָי יֱהֹוִה כֹּה־אָמַר
אֲדֹנָי יֱהֹוִה לֶהָרִים וְלַגְּבָעוֹת
לָאֲפִיקִים וְלַגֵּאָיוֹת הִנְנִי אֲנִי
מֵבִיא עֲלֵיכֶם חֶרֶב וְאִבַּדְתִּי

v. 3. ולגאיות ק׳

17. *evil beasts.* Cf. Lev. xxvi. 22; Deut. xxxii. 24.

they shall bereave thee. Famine and beasts of prey will work havoc particularly among the children whose power of resistance is less than that of adults (Kimchi).

blood. i.e. death by violence, bloodshed.

I the LORD have spoken it. As in verse 15.

CHAPTER VI

IN this chapter the prophet inveighs against the places of idolatrous worship which were located upon the mountains and in the valleys. These will be made desolate. The seats of idolatry, where carcasses and bones of animal sacrifices are strewn, will become the scene of slain Israelites. The remnant which will escape into foreign lands will eventually repent their sins and return to God.

1-10 ADDRESS TO THE MOUNTAINS IN THE LAND OF ISRAEL

2. *the mountains of Israel.* The seats of idolatrous worship. A similar prophecy occurs in xxxvi. 4ff.

3. *mountains . . . hills . . . ravines . . . valleys.* All these were scenes of idolatry. The latter two were chosen for pagan worship because of the leafy trees that flourished there near the streams which ran through them (cf. Deut. xii. 2).

a sword. The Hebrew noun *chereb* denotes any instrument designed to destroy materials (cf. Exod. xx. 22, *for if thou lift up thy tool (charbecha) upon it).* Both the idols and their worshippers, coupled together in the next verse, are doomed to destruction.

and I will destroy your high places.
4. And your altars shall become
desolate, and your sun-images shall
be broken; and I will cast down your
slain men before your idols. 5. And
I will lay the carcasses of the children
of Israel before their idols; and I
will scatter your bones round about
your altars. 6. In all your dwelling-
places the cities shall be laid waste,
and the high places shall be desolate;
that your altars may be laid waste

⁴ בָּמוֹתֵיכֶם: וְנָשַׁמּוּ
מִזְבְּחוֹתֵיכֶם וְנִשְׁבְּרוּ חַמָּנֵיכֶם
וְהִפַּלְתִּי חַלְלֵיכֶם לִפְנֵי
⁵ גִּלּוּלֵיכֶם: וְנָתַתִּי אֶת־פִּגְרֵי
בְּנֵי יִשְׂרָאֵל לִפְנֵי גִּלּוּלֵיהֶם
וְזֵרִיתִי אֶת־עַצְמוֹתֵיכֶם
⁶ סְבִיבוֹת מִזְבְּחוֹתֵיכֶם: בְּכֹל
מוֹשְׁבוֹתֵיכֶם הֶעָרִים
תֶּחֱרַבְנָה וְהַבָּמוֹת תִּישַׁמְנָה
לְמַעַן יֶחֶרְבוּ וְיֶאְשְׁמוּ

high places. Bamah means in the first instance 'a high place,' and in a wider sense a natural or artificial elevation used as an altar for the sacrificial worship of God or of idols. The attitude of the religious authorities towards the bamoth varied from time to time in accordance with the change of circumstances. According to Rabbinic tradition, they were allowed until the time of the erection of the Tabernacle in the wilderness, but forbidden during its existence for thirty-nine years. When the people of Israel entered Canaan and reached Gilgal, where they had a temporary Sanctuary for a period of fourteen years while engaged in conquering and distributing the land, the bamoth were again permitted. With the erection of the Sanctuary at Shiloh, which continued in existence for 369 years, they were again prohibited. After the destruction of the Sanctuary at Shiloh in the time of Eli, when the sacrificial worship was transferred first to Nob and after the destruction of Nob by Saul to Gibeon for fifty-seven years, bamoth were once more permitted; but with the erection of the Temple by Solomon they were finally forbidden (Mishnah Zeb. XIV. 4-8, T.B. Zeb. 118b). 'High Places have recently been discovered at Taanach, Gezer and Petra. Their general features were an altar, standing stones and asherah or sacred pole, laver, sacred cave, and depository for refuse' (Lofthouse).

4. sun-images. Set up to represent the sun-god and shaped as pillars or obelisks.

your slain men before your idols. The scene of guilt will be the scene of judgment.

5. I will lay the carcasses . . . before their idols. The dead bodies of the slain will lie unburied, in itself a serious indignity, before the objects of their adoration when the Israelites were alive, as evidence of the helplessness of the idols. A similar threat was made by Jeremiah (viii. 1f.).

I will scatter your bones round about your altars. Where once were found the remains of animal sacrifices will now be found the skeletons of the men who had brought the offerings.

6. the cities. Lofthouse points out that the word may signify quite small settlements. He quotes a remark made to the Egyptologist, Flinders Petrie, by an Arab who pointed to three tents in a valley and said, 'Behold the city of the sons of my tribe.'

and made desolate, and your idols
may be broken and cease, and your
sun-images may be hewn down, and
your works may be blotted out.
7. And the slain shall fall in the
midst of you, and ye shall know that
I am the LORD. 8. Yet will I leave
a remnant, in that ye shall have
some that escape the sword among
the nations, when ye shall be
scattered through the countries.
9. And they that escape of you shall
remember Me among the nations
whither they shall be carried captives, how that I have been anguished with their straying heart,
which hath departed from Me, and
with their eyes, which are gone
astray after their idols; and they
shall loathe themselves in their own
sight for the evils which they have
committed in all their abominations.
10. And they shall know that I am
the LORD; I have not said in vain
that I would do this evil unto them.

מִזְבְּחוֹתֵיכֶם וְנִשְׁבְּרוּ וְנִשְׁבַּתּוּ
גִּלּוּלֵיכֶם וְנִגְדְּעוּ חַמָּנֵיכֶם
7 וְנִמְחוּ מַעֲשֵׂיכֶם: וְנָפַל חָלָל
בְּתוֹכְכֶם וִידַעְתֶּם כִּי־אֲנִי
8 יְהֹוָה: וְהוֹתַרְתִּי בִּהְיוֹת לָכֶם
פְּלִיטֵי חֶרֶב בַּגּוֹיִם
9 בְּהִזָּרוֹתֵיכֶם בָּאֲרָצוֹת: וְזָכְרוּ
פְּלִיטֵיכֶם אוֹתִי בַּגּוֹיִם אֲשֶׁר
נִשְׁבּוּ־שָׁם אֲשֶׁר נִשְׁבַּרְתִּי אֶת־
לִבָּם הַזּוֹנֶה אֲשֶׁר־סָר מֵעָלַי
וְאֵת עֵינֵיהֶם הַזֹּנוֹת אַחֲרֵי
גִּלּוּלֵיהֶם וְנָקֹטוּ בִּפְנֵיהֶם אֶל־
הָרָעוֹת אֲשֶׁר עָשׂוּ לְכֹל
10 תּוֹעֲבֹתֵיהֶם: וְיָדְעוּ כִּי־אֲנִי
יְהֹוָה לֹא אֶל־חִנָּם דִּבַּרְתִּי
לַעֲשׂוֹת לָהֶם הָרָעָה הַזֹּאת:

your works. i.e. the idols. Cf. *neither
will we call any more the work of our hands
our gods* (Hos. xiv. 4).

7. *ye shall know that I am the LORD.*
The Sovereignty of God will be acknowledged when He has inflicted judgment
on those who worshipped false gods
whose futility would thereby be exposed.

8. *yet will I leave a remnant.* Not all will
perish by the sword; a remnant will
survive in foreign lands.

9. *I have been anguished.* lit. 'I have
been broken.' In exile they will recall
how God was grieved because of their
hearts which strayed from Him.

*they shall loathe themselves in their own
sight.* This translation (also found in

A.V. and R.V.) assumes that the verb is
kut, a variant of *kuts*. Kimchi gives the
root as *katat*, and he is supported by
Eitan who connects it with the Ethiopic
root which has the meaning 'to be thin'
and renders 'they shall be belittled
against their faces' (i.e. at themselves).
The root occurs again in xx. 43, xxxvi.
31 ; see also on xvi. 47.

10. *they shall know that I am the LORD.*
See on verse 7.

I have not said in vain. It will surely
come to pass.

11-14 RECAPITULATION OF
PRECEDING THREATS

Such a repetition is frequently found in
this Book. 'It must be remembered that

11. Thus saith the Lord GOD:
Smite with thy hand, and stamp
with thy foot, and say: Alas! because
of all the evil abominations of the
house of Israel; for they shall fall by
the sword, by the famine, and by the
pestilence. 12. He that is far off
shall die of the pestilence; and he
that is near shall fall by the sword;
and he that remaineth and is
besieged shall die by the famine;
thus will I spend My fury upon
them. 13. And ye shall know that
I am the LORD, when their slain men
shall be among their idols round
about their altars, upon every high
hill, in all the tops of the mountains,
and under every leafy tree, and
under every thick terebinth, the

11 כֹּה־אָמַר אֲדֹנָי יְהֹוִה הַכֵּה
בְכַפְּךָ וּרְקַע בְּרַגְלְךָ
וֶאֱמָר־אָח אֶל כָּל־
תּוֹעֲבוֹת רָעוֹת בֵּית יִשְׂרָאֵל
אֲשֶׁר בַּחֶרֶב בָּרָעָב וּבַדֶּבֶר
12 יִפֹּלוּ: הָרָחוֹק בַּדֶּבֶר יָמוּת
וְהַקָּרוֹב בַּחֶרֶב יִפּוֹל וְהַנִּשְׁאָר
וְהַנָּצוּר בָּרָעָב יָמוּת וְכִלֵּיתִי
13 חֲמָתִי בָּם: וִידַעְתֶּם כִּי־אֲנִי
יְהֹוָה בִּהְיוֹת חַלְלֵיהֶם בְּתוֹךְ
גִּלּוּלֵיהֶם סְבִיבוֹת
מִזְבְּחוֹתֵיהֶם אֶל כָּל־גִּבְעָה
רָמָה בְּכֹל | רָאשֵׁי הֶהָרִים
וְתַחַת כָּל־עֵץ רַעֲנָן וְתַחַת
כָּל־אֵלָה עֲבֻתָּה מְקוֹם אֲשֶׁר

these passages were not necessarily
delivered at one time; and the repetition
has an epic impressiveness of its own'
(Lofthouse).

11. *smite with thy hand, and stamp with
thy foot.* Gestures expressive of grief
and mourning. Some commentators
understand them as signifying malicious
satisfaction on the part of the prophet
over the pending calamity of his people,
and in support quote xxv. 6 where these
actions unmistakably express exultation
over a fallen enemy. This interpretation is unacceptable. Such an attitude
towards Israel's disaster would be contrary to the prophet's mission and his
belief in Divine mercy. In fact, Ezekiel
explicitly states his deep sympathy with
his people in their misfortune (xi. 13).
The truth is that clapping the hands and
stamping the feet are a display of intense

emotion and excitement whether caused
by joy or sorrow, and are therefore used
in both circumstances.

for they shall fall. As punishment for
their abominations.

12. *far off . . . near.* Far from and
near to the scene of battle. Those who
escape to other countries will die of
pestilence, and those who are near the
battlefield will fall by the sword of the
enemy.

13. *ye shall know that I am the LORD.*
The execution of God's decree will
establish recognition of His Sovereignty
and omnipotence (see on verse 7).

under every leafy tree. 'Trees, generally
solitary and conspicuous, are still revered
as sacred by the fellahin in Palestine'
(Lofthouse).

c

place where they did offer sweet savour to all their idols. 14. And I will stretch out My hand upon them, and make the land desolate and waste, more than the wilderness of Diblah, throughout all their habitations; and they shall know that I am the LORD.'

נָתְנוּ־שָׁם רֵיחַ נִיחֹחַ לְכֹל
14 גִּלּוּלֵיהֶם: וְנָטִיתִי אֶת־יָדִי
עֲלֵיהֶם וְנָתַתִּי אֶת־הָאָרֶץ
שְׁמָמָה וּמְשַׁמָּה מִמִּדְבַּר
דִּבְלָתָה בְּכֹל מוֹשְׁבוֹתֵיהֶם
וְיָדְעוּ כִּי־אֲנִי יְהֹוָה:

7   CHAPTER VII   ז

1. Moreover the word of the LORD came unto me, saying: 2. 'And thou, son of man, thus saith the Lord GOD concerning the land of Israel: An end! the end is come upon the four corners of the land. 3. Now is the

1 וַיְהִי דְבַר־יְהֹוָה אֵלַי לֵאמֹר:
2 וְאַתָּה בֶן־אָדָם כֹּה־אָמַר
אֲדֹנָי יְהֹוִה לְאַדְמַת יִשְׂרָאֵל
קֵץ בָּא הַקֵּץ עַל־אַרְבַּעַת
3 כַּנְפוֹת הָאָרֶץ: עַתָּה הַקֵּץ

v. 2. ארבע ק׳

sweet savour. This phrase is used of the smoke of the sacrificial fat or incense burnt on the altar for the worship of God or an idol.

14. *more than the wilderness of Diblah.* Diblah is identical with Riblah situated on the northern frontier of the country (Num. xxxiv. 11). The letters *d* and *r* interchange as in Deuel and Reuel (Num. i. 14, ii. 14). Mention is made here of this place because it served as the head-quarters of Nebuchadnezzar when he besieged Jerusalem, and it was there that Zedekiah was blinded and his sons slain (2 Kings xxv. 6f.).

they shall know that I am the LORD. The fact that the populated places will suffer the greatest devastation will prove that the judgment was an act of God (Malbim).

CHAPTER VII

THE chapter deals with the imminent destruction of the Judean State, and stresses that the end is come upon the four corners of the land. It repeatedly makes the point that the approaching judgment comes upon the nation as punishment for their evil practices. The latter part gives a detailed and vivid description of the catastrophe, and to add to their distressed feeling, the people are told that their beautiful houses from which they are to be banished will be occupied by their ruthless enemy.

1-4 APPROACHING DESTRUCTION OF THE WHOLE LAND

2. *concerning the land of Israel: An end!* The text may be rendered: 'unto the land of Israel an end (is coming)!' (Metsudath David).

upon the four corners of the land. No town in the land will escape desolation.

3. *now is the end.* The fate of the nation is coming shortly.

33

end upon thee, and I will send Mine anger upon thee, and will judge thee according to thy ways; and I will bring upon thee all thine abominations. 4. And Mine eye shall not spare thee, neither will I have pity; but I will bring thy ways upon thee, and thine abominations shall be in the midst of thee; and ye shall know that I am the LORD.

5. Thus saith the Lord GOD: An evil, a singular evil, behold, it cometh. 6. An end is come, the end is come, it awaketh against thee; behold, it cometh. 7. The turn is come unto thee, O inhabitant of the

עָלַיִךְ וְשִׁלַּחְתִּי אַפִּי בָּךְ
וּשְׁפַטְתִּיךְ כִּדְרָכָיִךְ וְנָתַתִּי
עָלַיִךְ אֵת כָּל־תּוֹעֲבוֹתָיִךְ:
4 וְלֹא־תָחוֹס עֵינִי עָלַיִךְ וְלֹא
אֶחְמוֹל כִּי דְרָכַיִךְ עָלַיִךְ אֶתֵּן
וְתוֹעֲבוֹתַיִךְ בְּתוֹכֵךְ תִּהְיֶיןָ
5 וִידַעְתֶּם כִּי־אֲנִי יְהֹוָה: כֹּה
אָמַר אֲדֹנָי יֱהֹוִה רָעָה אַחַת
6 רָעָה הִנֵּה בָאָה: קֵץ בָּא בָּא
הַקֵּץ הֵקִיץ אֵלָיִךְ הִנֵּה בָּאָה:
7 בָּאָה הַצְּפִירָה אֵלַיִךְ יוֹשֵׁב

---

upon thee. viz. the land of Israel spoken of in the preceding verse.

send Mine anger. The catastrophe will not be accidental but an act of God. The verb is vocalized as the Piel conjugation and may mean, 'let loose, free from restraint.'

I will bring upon thee all thine abominations. i.e. I will punish you for your abominable deeds.

4. *Mine eye shall not spare thee.* Besides being a Father of mercy, He is also a God of justice; or rather, the exercise of justice is in itself an act of mercy, since its purpose is purification from sin and the restoration of harmony between God and man. But they who are inveterately evil fail to use the opportunity which even Divine mercy offers. Cf. *Let favour be shown to the wicked, yet will he not learn righteousness; in the land of uprightness will he deal wrongfully, and will not behold the majesty of the LORD* (Isa. xxvi. 10).

and thine abominations . . . thee. Better, 'while thine abominations shall (still) be in the midst of thee.' God's verdict will be executed upon them while they yet worship idols. It will then be evident

that their images are helpless to save them, and consequently they will learn to recognize that He alone is the Lord (Ehrlich).

5-9   THE POPULATION IS DOOMED

5. *a singular evil.* lit. 'evil which is one,' i.e. a most disastrous evil, referring to the destruction of the Temple (Rashi). The Targum renders: 'an evil after an evil,' apparently reading *achar* (after) instead of *achath* (one); but if that were the intention, the preposition to be expected is *al*, 'evil upon evil.' The sense is probably a calamity which suffices in itself to fulfil God's sentence of national destruction.

6. *it awaketh against thee.* The long predicted doom will now awaken, as it were, from its sleep and be carried into effect. In the Hebrew text there is a play on the words *hakkets* (**the end**) and *hekits* (**it awaketh**).

7. *the turn is come.* The meaning of the noun *tsephirah*, which occurs again in verse 10, is doubtful. Kimchi, followed by A.V., identified it with the Aramaic for 'morning,' *tsaphra:* 'the morning is

land; the time is come, the day of tumult is near, and not of joyful shouting upon the mountains. 8. Now will I shortly pour out My fury upon thee, and spend Mine anger upon thee, and will judge thee according to thy ways; and I will bring upon thee all thine abominations. 9. And Mine eye shall not spare, neither will I have pity; I will bring upon thee according to thy ways, and thine abominations shall be in the midst of thee; and ye shall know that I the Lord do smite. 10. Behold the day; behold, it cometh; the turn is come forth; the rod hath blossomed, arrogancy hath budded. 11. Violence is risen up

הָאָ֔רֶץ בָּ֥א הָעֵ֖ת קָר֣וֹב הַיּ֑וֹם

8 מְהוּמָ֥ה וְלֹא־הֵ֖ד הָרִֽים׃ עַתָּ֣ה מִקָּר֗וֹב אֶשְׁפּ֤וֹךְ חֲמָתִי֙ עָלַ֔יִךְ וְכִלֵּיתִ֤י אַפִּי֙ בָּ֔ךְ וּשְׁפַטְתִּ֖יךְ כִּדְרָכָ֑יִךְ וְנָתַתִּ֣י עָלַ֔יִךְ אֵ֖ת

9 כָּל־תּוֹעֲבוֹתָֽיִךְ׃ וְלֹא־תָח֣וֹס עֵינִ֔י וְלֹ֖א אֶחְמ֑וֹל כִּדְרָכַ֜יִךְ עָלַ֣יִךְ אֶתֵּ֗ן וְתוֹעֲבוֹתַ֛יִךְ בְּתוֹכֵ֥ךְ תִּֽהְיֶ֖יןָ וִֽידַעְתֶּ֕ם כִּ֥י אֲנִ֖י

10 יְהוָ֥ה מַכֶּֽה׃ הִנֵּ֥ה הַיּ֖וֹם הִנֵּ֣ה בָ֑אָה יָֽצְאָה֙ הַצְּפִרָ֔ה צָ֖ץ

11 הַמַּטֶּ֔ה פָּרַ֖ח הַזָּד֑וֹן׃ הֶֽחָמָ֣ס ׀

come,' viz. the dawn of the fatal day. The root-signification may be 'to go round, and in Isa. xxviii. 5 it denotes *a diadem*. This accounts for A.J. *the turn* in the sense of 'the turn of events for evil.' R.V. has 'thy doom' which is derived from a cognate Arabic noun and is accepted by most moderns.

the day of tumult. lit. 'the day tumult,' the day characterized by clamour and confusion when the invading army appears. Preference may be given to the translation proposed by Davidson: 'the day is near, even tumult, and not joyful shouting.'

not of joyful shouting upon the mountains. 'The mountains will no longer resound with the joyous cries of harvest, or the shouts of the familiar idolatrous worship' (Lofthouse). This interpretation takes *hed* to be a shortened form of *hedad*, the sound made by the treaders of grapes (cf. Isa. xvi. 10; Jer. xlviii. 33). Kimchi explains 'not like the echo of mountains,' i.e. the tumult of invasion will be real and not imaginary like the echo which resounds between mountains.

8f. A virtual repetition of verses 3f. with some variations, to give the warning more emphasis.

9. *ye shall know that I the LORD do smite.* By meting out punishment to evildoers commensurate with their crimes, God will be acknowledged by them as the Source of their calamity.

10-13 NONE WILL ESCAPE

10. *the turn is come forth.* See on verse 7. *the rod hath blossomed, arrogancy hath budded.* Both the *rod* and *arrogancy* are an allusion to Nebuchadnezzar; cf. *O Asshur, the rod of Mine anger, in whose hand as a staff is Mine indignation!* (Isa. x. 5); and in Jer. l. 31 Babylon is described as *most arrogant*. The arrogance and striking force of the enemy to chastise Israel are ready for action (Rashi, Kimchi). But, as Lofthouse observes, Ezekiel never attacks Babylon, and therefore suggests the interpretation, 'the boastful confidence of Judah, whether under the protection of Babylon or in rebellion against it, has at last borne its fruit.'

into a rod of wickedness; nought
cometh from them, nor from their
tumult, nor from their turmoil,
neither is there eminency among
them. 12. The time is come, the
day draweth near· let not the buyer
rejoice, nor the seller mourn; for
wrath is upon all the multitude
thereof. 13. For the seller shall not
return to that which is sold, although
they be yet alive; for the vision is
touching the whole multitude thereof, which shall not return; neither
shall any stand possessed of the

קָם לְמַטֵּה־רֶשַׁע לֹא־מֵהֶם
וְלֹא מֵהֲמוֹנָם וְלֹא מֶהֱמֵהֶם
וְלֹא־נֹהַּ בָּהֶם: בָּא הָעֵת הִגִּיעַ 12
הַיּוֹם הַקּוֹנֶה אַל־יִשְׂמָח
וְהַמּוֹכֵר אַל־יִתְאַבָּל כִּי חָרוֹן
אֶל־כָּל־הֲמוֹנָהּ: כִּי הַמּוֹכֵר 13
אֶל־הַמִּמְכָּר לֹא יָשׁוּב וְעוֹד
בַּחַיִּים חַיָּתָם כִּי־חָזוֹן אֶל־
כָּל־הֲמוֹנָהּ לֹא יָשׁוּב וְאִישׁ
בַּעֲוֹנוֹ חַיָּתוֹ לֹא־יִתְחַזָּקוּ:

v. 12. קמץ בז״ק

11. *violence is risen up into a rod of
wickedness.* The violence they have
perpetrated has forged the weapon for
their chastisement. For the doctrine of
sin bearing within itself the seeds of
disaster, cf. *Evil pursueth sinners* (Prov.
xiii. 21).

nought cometh from them. Or, 'none of
them (shall remain)'; so Kimchi followed
by A.V. and R.V. They will either
perish or be carried away into captivity.

their tumult. Or, 'their multitude' (A.V.,
R.V.). Kimchi understands it as 'their
wealth'; that, too, will be lost.

nor from their turmoil. A very uncertain
Hebrew word. R.V. has: 'nor of their
wealth.' Kimchi construes as a duplicated form of *mehem*, 'nor of any of theirs'
(so A.V.), i.e. none of their offspring will
be left alive.

neither is there eminency among them.
The noun *noah* does not occur elsewhere,
and the translation *eminency* (so R.V.) is
based upon an Arabic derivation. Older
commentators identified it with *nehi*,
'wailing' (so A.V. and R.V. margin): so
great will the tragedy be, that the
survivors will not mourn for the
numerous dead.

12. *let not the buyer rejoice, nor the seller
mourn.* In the sale of hereditary land it
is usually the buyer who is happy, while
the impoverished seller is unhappy.
This will not be so in Judea, for neither
of them will remain in possession of the
estate; they will all be overwhelmed in
the catastrophe (cf. Isa. xxiv. 2).

13. *the seller shall not return to that which
is sold.* In normal times an estate
reverted to its original owner in the
Jubilee year (Lev. xxv). But the approaching calamity will make an end
both of the rights of ownership and the
Jubilee institution.

although they be yet alive. lit. 'though
their life be yet among the living.' They
would not recover their land in the
Jubilee year, although they have escaped
death, because they will be in exile
(Kimchi).

for the vision . . . which shall not return.
An alternative rendering is: 'for although
the vision was brought to the whole
multitude, none return (from his wickedness)' (Targum and Jewish commentators).

*neither shall any stand possessed of the
iniquity of his life.* An unintelligible

iniquity of his life. 14. They have blown the horn, and have made all ready, but none goeth to the battle; for My wrath is upon all the multitude thereof. 15. The sword is without, and the pestilence and the famine within; he that is in the field shall die with the sword, and he that is in the city, famine and pestilence shall devour him. 16. But they that shall at all escape of them, shall be on the mountains like doves of the valleys, all of them moaning, every one in his iniquity. 17. All hands shall be slack, and all knees shall drip with water.

14 תָּקְעוּ בַתָּקוֹעַ וְהָכִין הַכֹּל
וְאֵין הֹלֵךְ לַמִּלְחָמָה כִּי חֲרוֹנִי
15 אֶל־כָּל־הֲמוֹנָהּ: הַחֶרֶב
בַּחוּץ וְהַדֶּבֶר וְהָרָעָב מִבָּיִת
אֲשֶׁר בַּשָּׂדֶה בַּחֶרֶב יָמוּת
וַאֲשֶׁר בָּעִיר רָעָב וָדֶבֶר
16 יֹאכְלֶנּוּ: וּפָלְטוּ פְּלִיטֵיהֶם
וְהָיוּ אֶל־הֶהָרִים כְּיוֹנֵי
הַגֵּאָיוֹת כֻּלָּם הֹמוֹת אִישׁ
17 בַּעֲוֹנוֹ: כָּל־הַיָּדַיִם תִּרְפֶּינָה
וְכָל־בִּרְכַּיִם תֵּלַכְנָה מָּיִם:

translation which is not borne out by the Hebrew, which is literally 'neither shall they strengthen themselves, a man whose life is in his iniquity.' Rashi and Kimchi interpret: and the life of every one was corrupted by his iniquity, and they did not strengthen themselves to abandon their wicked ways. Davidson suggests: 'Neither shall any one keep hold of his life in his iniquity,' i.e. those driven out shall not return, and those remaining shall die in their sins.

14-27 COLLAPSE OF ORGANIZED RESISTANCE AMID GENERAL DESPAIR

14. *they have blown the horn* To give the alarm of the approaching invader; but although preparations are made to withstand attack, none will have the courage to face battle, because God's wrath has sapped their powers of resistance.

15. *the sword . . . within.* Cf. Lam. i. 20.
he that is in the field, etc. Cf. vi. 12.

16. *but they that shall at all escape of them, shall be.* Better, 'and should their fugitives escape, they shall be.'

on the mountains. Where the fugitives seek refuge.
like doves of the valleys. They select 'the lofty cliffs and the deep ravines for nesting and roosting places, and always avoid trees, or the neighbourhood of man' (Tristram).
every one in his iniquity. In their perilous plight they will be conscience-stricken and realize that they are suffering the consequences of their sins.

17. *all hands shall be slack.* Despair will render them helpless so that they have no heart for the fight.
all knees shall drip with water. Most moderns understand the phrase metaphorically as 'expressive of complete paralysis of strength' (Davidson). The Jewish commentators explain it of sweat caused by fear. The LXX gives it a literal interpretation: 'and all thighs shall be defiled with moisture,' and this is supported by Ehrlich. He quotes the definition by Siphrë of the *faint-hearted* who is exempt from enlistment in the army (Deut. xx. 8), viz. 'water descends upon his knees.' The meaning is, accordingly, they are unable to contain themselves through cowardly terror.

18. They shall also gird themselves with sackcloth, and horror shall cover them; and shame shall be upon all faces, and baldness upon all their heads. 19. They shall cast their silver in the streets, and their gold shall be as an unclean thing; their silver and their gold shall not be able to deliver them in the day of the wrath of the LORD; they shall not satisfy their souls, neither fill their bowels; because it hath been the stumblingblock of their iniquity. 20. And as for the beauty of their ornament, which was set for a pride, they made the images of their abominations and their detestable things thereof; therefore have I made it unto them as an unclean thing. 21. And I will give it into the hands of the strangers for a prey, and to the wicked of the earth for a

18 וְחָגְרוּ שַׂקִּים וְכִסְּתָה אוֹתָם
פַּלָּצוּת וְאֶל כָּל־פָּנִים בּוּשָׁה
וּבְכָל־רָאשֵׁיהֶם קָרְחָה:
19 כַּסְפָּם בַּחוּצוֹת יַשְׁלִיכוּ
וּזְהָבָם לְנִדָּה יִהְיֶה כַּסְפָּם
וּזְהָבָם לֹא־יוּכַל לְהַצִּילָם
בְּיוֹם עֶבְרַת יְהֹוָה נַפְשָׁם לֹא
יְשַׂבֵּעוּ וּמֵעֵיהֶם לֹא יְמַלֵּאוּ
20 כִּי־מִכְשׁוֹל עֲוֺנָם הָיָה: וּצְבִי
עֶדְיוֹ לְגָאוֹן שָׂמָהוּ וְצַלְמֵי
תוֹעֲבוֹתָם שִׁקּוּצֵיהֶם עָשׂוּ בוֹ
עַל־כֵּן נְתַתִּיו לָהֶם לְנִדָּה:
21 וּנְתַתִּיו בְּיַד־הַזָּרִים לָבַז
וּלְרִשְׁעֵי הָאָרֶץ לְשָׁלָל

18. *gird themselves with sackcloth.* As a sign of mourning over the national catastrophe or a mark of repentance. The former is the more probable.

horror shall cover them. Cf. *the prince shall be clothed with appalment* (verse 27). They will be wholly wrapped in it as though it were a garment (cf. *He put on righteousness as a coat of mail . . . and He put on garments of vengeance for clothing, and was clad with zeal as a cloak,* Isa. lix. 17).

baldness upon all their heads. They will shave or pluck out their hair as a sign of mourning. This was a heathen practice forbidden to Israel (Deut. xiv. 1).

19. *as an unclean thing.* The Hebrew term *niddah* denotes menstrual impurity. On the day of reckoning, the desperate inhabitants will cast away their wealth as something of extreme impurity (cf. xxxvi. 17), because they will neither be able to buy food nor ransom their lives with it.

the stumblingblock of their iniquity. Their wealth has been the cause of their sinning (cf. xliv. 12; Hos. ii. 10).

20. *and as for the beauty . . . pride,* etc. Better, 'and as for their beautiful adornments, they had appointed them for (their) pride, but they made of them their abominable images; therefore have I made these unto them as an unclean thing.' The Hebrew has the singular throughout in the collective sense. The repetition of *an unclean thing* shows that this verse explains the preceding. Like the Israelites when they made the Golden Calf, the present generation donated the precious metal of their jewellery for the manufacture of graven images.

21. *I will give it into the hands of the strangers.* The idols of gold and silver will provide loot for the enemy.

spoil; and they shall profane it.
22. I will also turn My face from
them, and they shall profane My
secret place; and robbers shall enter
into it, and profane it.

23. Make the chain; for the land
is full of bloody crimes, and the city
is full of violence. 24. Wherefore
I will bring the worst of the nations,
and they shall possess their houses;
I will also make the pride of the
strong to cease; and their holy places
shall be profaned. 25. Horror
cometh; and they shall seek peace,
and there shall be none. 26. Calamity
shall come upon calamity, and
rumour shall be upon rumour; and
they shall seek a vision of the
prophet, and instruction shall perish
from the priest, and counsel from

22 וְחִלְּלוּהָ: וַהֲסִבֹּתִי פָנַי מֵהֶם
וְחִלְּלוּ אֶת־צְפוּנִי וּבָאוּ־בָהּ
23 פָּרִיצִים וְחִלְּלוּהָ: עֲשֵׂה
הָרַתּוֹק כִּי הָאָרֶץ מָלְאָה
מִשְׁפַּט דָּמִים וְהָעִיר מָלְאָה
24 חָמָס: וְהֵבֵאתִי רָעֵי גוֹיִם
וְיָרְשׁוּ אֶת־בָּתֵּיהֶם וְהִשְׁבַּתִּי
גְּאוֹן עַזִּים וְנִחֲלוּ מְקַדְשֵׁיהֶם:
25 קְפָדָה־בָא וּבִקְשׁוּ שָׁלוֹם
26 וָאָיִן: הֹוָה עַל־הֹוָה תָּבוֹא
וּשְׁמֻעָה אֶל־שְׁמוּעָה תִּהְיֶה
וּבִקְשׁוּ חָזוֹן מִנָּבִיא וְתוֹרָה
תֹּאבַד מִכֹּהֵן וְעֵצָה מִזְּקֵנִים:

v. 25. וחללוהו ק' כצ"ל v. 21.

profane it. The Israelites had
dedicated their gold and silver to a
'religious' purpose; the Chaldeans will
make a 'profane' use of the metal.

22. I will also turn My face from them.
The Divine Presence will depart from the
Israelites so that they will suffer defeat at
the hands of their enemies, with the
dreadful sequel which is described.

they shall profane My secret place. The
Babylonians will enter the Temple and
desecrate it. The phrase My secret place
is traditionally explained as a reference
to the Holy of Holies, but it may indicate
the Temple generally.

robbers. viz. the Babylonian soldiers
who will loot the holy vessels.

23. make the chain. The prophet is
ordered to make a chain as a symbol that
the remnant of the inhabitants will be
carried away in fetters into captivity.

bloody crimes. lit. 'judgment of bloods,'
which may mean crimes the penalty for
which is death.

24. the worst of the nations. i.e. the
Babylonians (cf. xxviii. 7, xxx. 11 where
they are described as the terrible of the
nations).

the pride of the strong. The allusion may
be to Israel's monarchy and priesthood.

25. they shall seek peace. Of which the
false prophets had assured them (Kimchi).

26. calamity shall come upon calamity.
Cf. destruction followeth upon destruction
(Jer. iv. 20).

rumour shall be upon rumour. News of
one blow will be immediately succeeded
by news of another.

they shall seek a vision of the prophet. In
their bewilderment they will look for
guidance from their prophets, but in
vain (cf. Lam. ii. 9). Nor will they
derive instruction from the priest and
counsel from the elders. The crisis will
leave them without direction from their
religious and national leaders (cf. Jer.
xviii. 18).

the elders. 27. The king shall mourn, and the prince shall be clothed with appalment, and the hands of the people of the land shall be enfeebled; I will do unto them after their way, and according to their deserts will I judge them; and they shall know that I am the LORD.'

הַמֶּ֣לֶךְ יִתְאַבָּ֗ל וְנָשִׂיא֙ יִלְבַּ֣שׁ 27
שְׁמָמָ֔ה וִידֵ֥י עַם־הָאָ֖רֶץ
תִּבָּהַ֑לְנָה מִדַּרְכָּם֙ אֶעֱשֶׂ֣ה
אוֹתָ֔ם וּבְמִשְׁפְּטֵיהֶ֖ם אֶשְׁפְּטֵ֑ם
וְיָדְע֖וּ כִּֽי־אֲנִ֥י יְהוָֽה׃

8   CHAPTER VIII   **ח**

1. And it came to pass in the sixth year, in the sixth month, in the fifth day of the month, as I sat in my house, and the elders of Judah sat

וַיְהִ֣י ׀ בַּשָּׁנָ֣ה הַשִּׁשִׁ֗ית בַּשִּׁשִּׁ֣י 1
בַּחֲמִשָּׁ֣ה לַחֹ֔דֶשׁ אֲנִי֙ יוֹשֵׁ֣ב
בְּבֵיתִ֔י וְזִקְנֵ֥י יְהוּדָ֖ה יֽוֹשְׁבִ֣ים

---

27. the king . . . the prince . . . the people of the land. All classes of the population will find themselves helpless on the day of judgment. The term *am haarets*, 'the people of the land,' has undergone several changes in meaning. Originally it denoted the mass of the people. In Talmudic times it was used for an ignorant man who was not versed in the Torah, or a person not scrupulous about the laws of ritual purity. Still another usage of the phrase has been suggested by Sulzberger who defines it in many Biblical passages, including this verse, as 'members of the national council.'

CHAPTER VIII

IN chapters viii-xi a new series of visions is recounted including the final one of the *Merkabah*. While in the company of the elders of Judah in his house, the spirit of God transported him from Babylon to Jerusalem. Set down in the Temple court, he beheld there the *likeness* which he had seen on two previous occasions in association with the *Merkabah*, and he is shown four scenes of idolatry within the precincts of the Sanctuary. A Divine voice calls his attention to the abominable rites practised by all classes in the House of God, and concludes with a reaffirmation of imminent catastrophe.

1-6 VISION OF THE DIVINE GLORY AND THE 'IMAGE OF JEALOUSY'

1. the sixth year. Of Jehoiachin's captivity, i.e. in 592 or 591 B.C.E.

in the sixth month. An interval of one year and two months elapsed between the present vision and the first when Ezekiel was called to his prophetic mission. Since the period—a lunar year and two months (413 days)—falls short of the number of 430 days during which he had to lie on his sides (iv. 5f.), *Seder Olam* suggests that the year had an intercalary month added (the second Adar). Accordingly Ezekiel had this experience twelve days after he ended the time of his immobility.

the elders of Judah. Who were in captivity and apparently retained their former status. This supports the view that the exiles in Babylon were an organized community (see on i. 1).

before me, that the hand of the Lord GOD fell there upon me. 2. Then I beheld, and lo a likeness as the appearance of fire: from the appearance of his loins and downward, fire; and from his loins and upward, as the appearance of brightness, as the colour of electrum. 3. And the form of a hand was put forth, and I was taken by a lock of my head; and a spirit lifted me up between the earth and the heaven, and brought me in the visions of God to Jerusalem, to the door of the gate of the inner court that looketh toward the north; where was the seat of the image of jealousy, which provoketh to jealousy. 4. And, behold, the glory of the God of

לְפָנָי וַתִּפֹּל עָלַי שָׁם יַד אֲדֹנָי 2 יֱהוִֹה: וָאֶרְאֶה וְהִנֵּה דְמוּת כְּמַרְאֵה־אֵשׁ מִמַּרְאֵה מָתְנָיו וּלְמַטָּה אֵשׁ וּמִמָּתְנָיו וּלְמַעְלָה כְּמַרְאֵה־זֹהַר כְּעֵין 3 הַחַשְׁמַלָה: וַיִּשְׁלַח תַּבְנִית יָד וַיִּקָּחֵנִי בְּצִיצִת רֹאשִׁי וַתִּשָּׂא אֹתִי רוּחַ בֵּין־הָאָרֶץ וּבֵין־ הַשָּׁמַיִם וַתָּבֵא אֹתִי יְרוּשָׁלַמָה בְּמַרְאוֹת אֱלֹהִים אֶל־פֶּתַח שַׁעַר הַפְּנִימִית הַפּוֹנֶה צָפוֹנָה אֲשֶׁר־שָׁם מוֹשַׁב סֵמֶל הַקִּנְאָה 4 הַמַּקְנֶה: וְהִנֵּה־שָׁם כְּבוֹד

פתח בס״פ v. 2.

the hand of the Lord. See on i. 3. Kimchi points out that the phrase *hand of the Lord* is used in the three visions of the *Merkabah* which, he suggests, relate to the exile of Jehoiakim, Jehoiachin and Zedekiah. On this theory he explains why Jerusalem was chosen for the scene of the final vision in which the *Merkabah* departs from the Temple and the sentence of destruction is pronounced upon the city for her idolatry.

2. *fire.* Modern commentators follow the LXX and read *ish* (man) for *esh* (*fire*) in conformity with i. 26; but there the noun is *adam* and no explanation is offered why Ezekiel did not use it here. This verse is obviously based on i. 27 which supports M.T.

3. *the form of a hand was put forth.* lit. 'he put forth the form of a hand and he took me'; the subject is God to be understood from the context. The prophet carefully avoids the anthropomorphic suggestion as far as possible; hence *the form of a hand* instead of 'a hand.'

I was taken by a lock of my head. The noun for *lock* is *tsitsith* used of the fringe in the corner of the garment (Num. xv. 38). He was transported to Jerusalem only in spirit. Kimchi observes that on this occasion Ezekiel is taken by his hair as a sign of displeasure, such as would be shown by an angry master to his offending servant; whereas in the vision which heralded Israel's redemption he is carried to Jerusalem gently and set down *on a very high mountain* (xl. 2).

the visions of God. See on i. 1.

to the door of the gate of the inner court. The word *court* has to be supplied. It appears that he was set down in the outer court in front of the northern gate leading to the inner court. It was there that *the image of jealousy* was situated. The inner court was on a higher level than the outer court on the Temple mount.

the image of jealousy, which provoketh to jealousy. The translation of *kin'ah* here by *ealousy* fails to convey its true

Israel was there, according to the vision that I saw in the plain. 5. Then said He unto me: 'Son of man, lift up thine eyes now the way toward the north.' So I lifted up mine eyes the way toward the north, and beheld northward of the gate of the altar this image of jealousy in the entry.

6. And He said unto me: 'Son of man, seest thou what they do? even the great abominations that the house of Israel do commit here, that I should go far off from My sanctuary? but thou shalt again see yet greater abominations.' 7. And He brought me to the door of the court; and when I looked, behold a hole in

אֱלֹהֵי יִשְׂרָאֵל כַּמַּרְאֶה אֲשֶׁר
5 רָאִיתִי בַּבִּקְעָה: וַיֹּאמֶר אֵלַי
בֶּן־אָדָם שָׂא־נָא עֵינֶיךָ דֶּרֶךְ
צָפוֹנָה וָאֶשָּׂא עֵינַי דֶּרֶךְ צָפוֹנָה
וְהִנֵּה מִצָּפוֹן לְשַׁעַר הַמִּזְבֵּחַ
סֵמֶל הַקִּנְאָה הַזֶּה בַּבִּאָה:
6 וַיֹּאמֶר אֵלַי בֶּן־אָדָם הֲרֹאֶה
אַתָּה מָהֵם עֹשִׂים תּוֹעֵבוֹת
גְּדֹלוֹת אֲשֶׁר בֵּית־יִשְׂרָאֵל ׀
עֹשִׂים פֹּה לְרָחֳקָה מֵעַל
מִקְדָּשִׁי וְעוֹד תָּשׁוּב תִּרְאֶה
7 תּוֹעֵבוֹת גְּדֹלוֹת: וַיָּבֵא אֹתִי
אֶל־פֶּתַח הֶחָצֵר וָאֶרְאֶה
וְהִנֵּה חֹר־אֶחָד בַּקִּיר:

v. 6. מה הם ק׳

---

meaning. Cf. Introduction, p. xvi, where the phrase is explained as 'the image of outraged authority which provoked Him to vindicate His exclusive rights.' The allusion must be to an idolatrous object set up in the Temple, possibly *the graven image of Asherah* placed there by king Manasseh (2 Kings xxi. 7).

4. *the vision that I saw in the plain.* Cf. iii. 23, referring to the vision seen by him at the river Chebar (i. 1ff.). The same vision reappears to him as he looks towards the image.

5. *lift up thine eyes.* Ezekiel, who was standing outside the northern gate leading to the inner court, was commanded to look in the direction of the north where the image was situated.

the gate of the altar. This gate is the same as that in verse 3. The northern gate of the inner court was probably opposite the sacrificial altar which was in the outer court. Hence the name given to it.

6. *seest thou what they do?* By the image Ezekiel is shown men paying homage to it.

that I should go far off from My sanctuary. In practising these abominations they, as it were, compel God's withdrawal from the Temple.

7-13 SCENE OF THE ELDERS PRACTISING SECRET IDOLATRY

7. *the door of the court.* This is the door mentioned in verse 3. Hitherto the prophet was standing outside the entrance of the inner court; now he is brought into its interior where he is shown a hole in the wall of the chamber near the entrance. 'The hole is meant to suggest that entrance into the chamber was obtained secretly by those who practised their rites there' (Davidson).

the wall. 8. Then said He unto me: 'Son of man, dig now in the wall'; and when I had digged in the wall, behold a door. 9. And He said unto me: 'Go in, and see the wicked abominations that they do here.' 10. So I went in and saw; and behold every detestable form of creeping things and beasts, and all the idols of the house of Israel, pourtrayed upon the wall round about. 11. And there stood before them seventy men of the elders of the house of Israel, and in the midst of them stood Jaazaniah the son of Shaphan, every man with his censer in his hand; and a thick cloud of incense went up. 12. Then said He unto me: 'Son of man, hast thou seen

8 וַיֹּאמֶר אֵלַי בֶּן־אָדָם חֲתָר־
נָא בַקִּיר וָאֶחְתֹּר בַּקִּיר וְהִנֵּה
9 פֶּתַח אֶחָד: וַיֹּאמֶר אֵלַי בֹּא
וּרְאֵה אֶת־הַתּוֹעֵבוֹת הָרָעוֹת
10 אֲשֶׁר הֵם עֹשִׂים פֹּה: וָאָבוֹא
וָאֶרְאֶה וְהִנֵּה כָל־תַּבְנִית
רֶמֶשׂ וּבְהֵמָה שֶׁקֶץ וְכָל־
גִּלּוּלֵי בֵּית יִשְׂרָאֵל מְחֻקֶּה
עַל־הַקִּיר סָבִיב ׀ סָבִיב:
11 וְשִׁבְעִים אִישׁ מִזִּקְנֵי בֵית־
יִשְׂרָאֵל וְיַאֲזַנְיָהוּ בֶן־שָׁפָן
עֹמֵד בְּתוֹכָם עֹמְדִים לִפְנֵיהֶם
וְאִישׁ מִקְטַרְתּוֹ בְּיָדוֹ וַעֲתַר
12 עֲנַן־הַקְּטֹרֶת עֹלֶה: וַיֹּאמֶר
אֵלַי הֲרָאִיתָ בֶן־אָדָם אֲשֶׁר

8. *dig now in the wall.* i.e. he was to enlarge the hole in the wall through which his body would be able to pass.

behold a door. Either the enlarged hole served him as a door to get through into the secret chamber, or more probably he discovered a door which was used by the men who practised the cult.

10. *pourtrayed upon the wall.* Cf. xxiii. 14 where images of human beings drawn by the Chaldeans are said to have been depicted on the wall. Some authorities see here the adoption by Israelites of the worship of animals as practised in Egypt. 'At this period, Judah was peculiarly susceptible to the political influence of both Babylon and Egypt, and the cults of both countries may have joined with that of the Canaanites in suggesting new modes of worship' (Lofthouse).

11. *seventy men of the elders.* These were the seventy leaders or Sanhedrin whose duty it was to instruct and guide the people, but who instead led them astray into idolatry; cf. Isa. iii. 12, *O My people, they that lead thee cause thee to err, and destroy the way of thy paths* (Kimchi). Although the institution of a Sanhedrin of seventy is later, the Israelite community from early times had a ruling body of that number to represent them (cf. Exod. xxiv. 1; Num. xi. 16).

Jaazaniah the son of Shaphan. Shaphan, if the same as mentioned here, was a 'scribe' during the reign of Josiah who read to the king the text of the newly discovered book of the law (2 Kings xxii. 10f.). There is reference to his sons Gemariah and Ahikam in Jer. xxxvi. 10, xxxix. 14 who were apparently pious Israelites. If Jaazaniah was their brother, he broke from the tradition of his family.

what the elders of the house of Israel do in the dark, every man in his chambers of imagery? for they say: The Lord seeth us not, the Lord hath forsaken the land.' 13. He said also unto me: 'Thou shalt again see yet greater abominations which they do.' 14. Then He brought me to the door of the gate of the Lord's house which was toward the north; and, behold, there sat the women weeping for Tammuz.

זִקְנֵי בֵית־יִשְׂרָאֵל עֹשִׂים
בַּחֹשֶׁךְ אִישׁ בְּחַדְרֵי מַשְׂכִּיתוֹ
כִּי אֹמְרִים אֵין יְהֹוָה רֹאֶה
אֹתָנוּ עָזַב יְהֹוָה אֶת־הָאָרֶץ:
13 וַיֹּאמֶר אֵלַי עוֹד תָּשׁוּב תִּרְאֶה
תּוֹעֵבוֹת גְּדֹלוֹת אֲשֶׁר־הֵמָּה
14 עֹשִׂים: וַיָּבֵא אֹתִי אֶל־פֶּתַח
שַׁעַר בֵּית־יְהֹוָה אֲשֶׁר אֶל־
הַצָּפוֹנָה וְהִנֵּה־שָׁם הַנָּשִׁים
יֹשְׁבוֹת מְבַכּוֹת אֶת־הַתַּמּוּז:

12. *his chambers of imagery.* This suggests that there was more than one secret chamber where these rites were carried out, or that each worshipper was in a separate cell.

the LORD seeth us not, the LORD hath forsaken the land. They hide their abominable practices from the public eye, but have no scruples about violating the law of God, believing that He is not interested in the affairs of man (cf. Ps. x. 11, lxxiii. 11). Moreover, the evils which had befallen the country proved that He had abandoned His people and the land.

13. Cf. verse 6.

14 THE TAMMUZ CULT

the door of the gate of the LORD'S house. He was now brought into the inner court in front of the northern gate of the Temple.

there sat the women weeping for Tammuz. This is the only place in the Bible where the worship of Tammuz is mentioned. 'It came from Babylonia, and can be traced there as far back as 3,000 B.C.E., so that it is one of the oldest forms of religious worship in the world, and has not altogether disappeared even now.

Tammuz (Akkadian Duzu, from the Sumerian Dumuzi meaning "faithful son"), the youthful husband or son or lover of Ishtar, was looked upon as the god of vegetation and beneficent floods. Every year, at the time of greatest heat, when plants withered and rivers ran dry, he was believed to vanish into the Underworld, and in the following spring to return again . . . The time of his departure was celebrated with public dirges. The worship of Tammuz survived well into the Middle Ages. Arab historians of the 10th and 14th centuries relate that the Syrians of Harran in N. Mesopotamia were accustomed to keep in the month Tammuz the feast of the mourning women (el-bukat) in honour of the god Ta'uz. In a disguised form the worship goes on at the present day among the Yezidis of Kurdistan, descendants of the ancient Assyrians, the emblem of whose rite is a bronze peacock which they call Melek Taus, i.e. probably Tammuz' (Cooke). Maimonides (*Guide*, III. 29) quotes an ancient source which records the following: 'A heathen prophet called Tammuz urged a certain king to worship the seven planets and the twelve constellations. For this, the king killed him. In the night of his death the idols of all the

15. Then said He unto me: 'Hast thou seen this, O son of man? thou shalt again see yet greater abominations than these.' 16. And He brought me into the inner court of the LORD's house, and, behold, at the door of the temple of the LORD, between the porch and the altar, were about five and twenty men, with their backs toward the temple of the LORD, and their faces toward the east; and they worshipped the sun toward the east.

15 וַיֹּאמֶר אֵלַי הֲרָאִיתָ בֶן־אָדָם
עוֹד תָּשׁוּב תִּרְאֶה תּוֹעֵבוֹת
16 גְּדֹלוֹת מֵאֵלֶּה: וַיָּבֵא אֹתִי
אֶל־חֲצַר בֵּית־יְהֹוָה
הַפְּנִימִית וְהִנֵּה־פֶתַח הֵיכַל
יְהֹוָה בֵּין הָאוּלָם וּבֵין הַמִּזְבֵּחַ
כְּעֶשְׂרִים וַחֲמִשָּׁה אִישׁ
אֲחֹרֵיהֶם אֶל־הֵיכַל יְהֹוָה
וּפְנֵיהֶם קֵדְמָה וְהֵמָּה
מִשְׁתַּחֲוִיתֶם קֵדְמָה לַשָּׁמֶשׁ:

world assembled in the Babylonian temple where the golden sun-god resided. He was suspended in mid-air, dropped into the temple and was surrounded by all the images. The sun-god then told them what had happened to the heathen prophet Tammuz and all the idols began to weep until daybreak when they returned to their temples. To commemorate the tragic event, they enacted a law for all times that people should weep and mourn for Tammuz every first day of the month Tammuz.'

16-18 SUN-WORSHIP IN THE INNER COURT

16. *the inner court of the LORD'S house.* The prophet had already been in the inner court (see on verse 14), but he was now brought from the northern gate to the eastern side of the Temple between the porch and the sacrificial altar which stood in the inner court opposite the porch (Kimchi).

their faces toward the east. The entrance to the Temple was on the east side and the Holy of Holies on the west in order to eliminate the popular sun-worship which was practised toward the east. These idolaters turned deliberately in that direction to demonstrate their denial

of God and their belief in the sun-god. The Rabbis detect in the seemingly superfluous phrase *with their backs toward the Temple* a wanton affront of the Divine Presence Whose abode is in the west (Yoma 77a). The Mishnah records that the offending words were recalled in the celebration of the drawing of water during the Festival of Tabernacles. 'When the celebrants reached the gate which leads out to the east, they turned their faces from east to west (thus facing the Temple) and said, "Our fathers who were in this place stood with their back toward the Temple of the Lord and their faces towards the east, and they worshipped the sun towards the east; but as for us, our eyes are turned to the Lord. Rabbi Judah stated: They used to repeat the phrase and say, "We are the LORD'S and our eyes are turned to the LORD" ' (Suk. V. 4).

and they worshipped. The unusual Hebrew form *mishtachawithem* is traditionally explained as a compound of two verbs, *mashchithim* (they destroy) and *mishtachawim* (they worship), signifying the dual nature of their offence: the degradation of the Temple and the worshipping of the sun-god (Talmud Yerushalmi and Targum).

17. Then He said unto me: 'Hast thou seen this, O son of man? Is it a light thing to the house of Judah that they commit the abominations which they commit here in that they fill the land with violence, and provoke Me still more, and, lo, they put the branch to their nose? 18. Therefore will I also deal in fury; Mine eye shall not spare, neither will I have pity; and though they cry in Mine ears with a loud voice, yet will I not hear them.'

17 וַיֹּאמֶר אֵלַי הֲרָאִיתָ בֶן־אָדָם
הֲנָקֵל לְבֵית יְהוּדָה מֵעֲשׂוֹת
אֶת־הַתּוֹעֵבוֹת אֲשֶׁר עָשׂוּ־
פֹה כִּי־מָלְאוּ אֶת־הָאָרֶץ
חָמָס וַיָּשֻׁבוּ לְהַכְעִיסֵנִי וְהִנָּם
שֹׁלְחִים אֶת־הַזְּמוֹרָה אֶל־
18 אַפָּם: וְגַם־אֲנִי אֶעֱשֶׂה בְחֵמָה
לֹא־תָחוֹס עֵינִי וְלֹא אֶחְמֹל
וְקָרְאוּ בְאָזְנַי קוֹל גָּדוֹל וְלֹא
אֶשְׁמַע אוֹתָם:

9 **CHAPTER IX** ס

1. Then He called in mine ears with

1 וַיִּקְרָא בְאָזְנַי קוֹל גָּדוֹל לֵאמֹר

17. is it a light thing to the house of Judah. All the acts of idolatry committed by the house of Judah in the precincts of the Temple are bad enough, but what follows surpasses them in outrageous blasphemy.

they put the branch to their nose. The phrase is very obscure. Some interpret literally. 'The religious custom alluded to in Ezekiel undoubtedly refers to the religion of the Magi. The prophet complains that some of the Jews worship the sun, holding towards their face certain twigs. Exactly the same custom of holding a bundle of twigs in the hands is reported by Strabo (xv. 3, 14), as being observed by the Magi when engaged in prayer. It is the so-called Barsom, still used by the Parsi priests when engaged in worship' (M. Haug, *Essays on the Sacred Language, Writings and Religion of the Parsis*, p. 4). The objection to this explanation is that it fails to account for the exceptional horror in which it is here mentioned. The traditional Jewish interpretation sees in the words an obscene rite, and we have here one of the eighteen 'emendations of the Scribes' (*tikkunë sopherim*) in Scripture made from reverence of God, viz. *appam* (their nose) for *appi* (My nose). Rashi and others explain *zemorah* (branch) as 'the breaking of wind' (*ventris crepitus*). Whatever the act was, Lofthouse thinks 'that the Jewish commentators are right in understanding the words to conceal some shocking or obscene rite . . . If this is so, we can see why this ritual is regarded as worst of all.'

18. will I also deal in fury. Justice demands that Divine chastisement shall be commensurate with the abominable character of their sin.

CHAPTER IX

THE preceding chapter ended with a warning of condign punishment for the people's outrageous sins. Now Ezekiel is shown in a vision the execution of the

a loud voice, saying: 'Cause ye them that have charge over the city to draw near, every man with his destroying weapon in his hand.' 2. And, behold, six men came from the way of the upper gate, which lieth toward the north, every man with his weapon of destruction in his hand; and one man in the midst of them clothed in linen, with a writer's ink-horn on his side. And they went in, and stood beside the brazen altar. 3. And the glory of the God of Israel was gone up from the

קִרְבוּ פְּקֻדּוֹת הָעִיר וְאִישׁ
2 כְּלִי מַשְׁחֵתוֹ בְּיָדוֹ: וְהִנֵּה שִׁשָּׁה
אֲנָשִׁים בָּאִים | מִדֶּרֶךְ שַׁעַר
הָעֶלְיוֹן אֲשֶׁר | מָפְנֶה צָפוֹנָה
וְאִישׁ כְּלִי מַפָּצוֹ בְּיָדוֹ וְאִישׁ־
אֶחָד בְּתוֹכָם לָבֻשׁ בַּדִּים
וְקֶסֶת הַסֹּפֵר בְּמָתְנָיו וַיָּבֹאוּ
וַיַּעַמְדוּ אֵצֶל מִזְבַּח הַנְּחֹשֶׁת:
3 וּכְבוֹד | אֱלֹהֵי יִשְׂרָאֵל נַעֲלָה

stern warning. Deeply moved by the scene of destruction, he intercedes on behalf of the remnant of Israel. But his intercession is in vain; the sentence stands unrepealed.

1-3 THE DESTROYERS ARE SUMMONED TO EXECUTE GOD'S JUDGMENT

1. *He called in mine ears.* It was a Divine voice that spoke to him.

cause . . . to draw near. The Hebrew verb may be parsed as the Piel imperative as A.J. and the English versions, or the Kal perfect or imperative (cf. Ps. lxix. 19), 'have drawn near' (so the LXX and Targum) or 'draw near.' Modern commentators are divided on the point.

that have charge over the city. The Hebrew noun is abstract and may mean 'punishments or appointments,' i.e. 'punishers or appointed men.' Accordingly a variety of translations is possible: 'come near (or, bring near) the officials (or, the punishers) of the city'. Ehrlich treats the noun as vocative, 'approach ye that are to punish,' while Lofthouse prefers, 'the punishments of the city have come.'

2. *six men.* They appeared as human beings to the eyes of the prophet, but the Rabbis declared them to have been powers of destruction in the form of angels charged with the carrying out of God's sentence (Shab. 55a). The seventh, clothed in linen garments with writing implements at his side, had the duty to set a mark upon the righteous who were to be spared. In the Talmud (Yoma 77a) he is identified with the angel Gabriel.

the upper gate. This may be identical with the gate built by king Jotham (2 Kings xv. 35). It was situated in the north-east and received its name because it stood higher than the rest of the Temple court.

which lieth toward the north. In the direction of Babylonia (see on i. 4).

clothed in linen. i.e. a robe indicative of high rank; similarly in Daniel's visions of an angelic being (x. 5, xii. 6).

the brazen altar. Erected by Solomon. According to tradition (Zeb. 59a), the brazen altar of Moses was hidden by Solomon who substituted one made of earth for it which retained the name of the original. The seven men took up their position *beside the brazen altar* in the place where sun-worship was practised (viii. 16).

3. *the glory of the God of Israel was gone up from the cherub.* The seat of the Divine Presence was in the Holy of

cherub, whereupon it was, to the threshold of the house; and He called to the man clothed in linen, who had the writer's inkhorn on his side. 4. And the LORD said unto him: 'Go through the midst of the city, through the midst of Jerusalem, and set a mark upon the foreheads of the men that sigh and that cry for all the abominations that are done in the midst thereof.' 5. And to the others He said in my hearing: 'Go ye through the city after him, and smite; let not your eye spare, neither have ye pity; 6. slay utterly the old man, the young man and the maiden, and little children and

מֵעַל הַכְּרוּב אֲשֶׁר הָיָה עָלָיו
אֶל מִפְתַּן הַבָּיִת וַיִּקְרָא אֶל־
הָאִישׁ הַלָּבֻשׁ הַבַּדִּים אֲשֶׁר
4 קֶסֶת הַסֹּפֵר בְּמָתְנָיו: וַיֹּאמֶר
יְהֹוָה אֵלָו עֲבֹר בְּתוֹךְ הָעִיר
בְּתוֹךְ יְרוּשָׁלָםִ וְהִתְוִיתָ תָּו
עַל־־מִצְחוֹת הָאֲנָשִׁים
הַנֶּאֱנָחִים וְהַנֶּאֱנָקִים עַל כָּל־
הַתּוֹעֵבוֹת הַנַּעֲשׂוֹת בְּתוֹכָהּ:
5 וּלְאֵלֶּה אָמַר בְּאָזְנַי עִבְרוּ
בָעִיר אַחֲרָיו וְהַכּוּ עַל־תָּחֹס
6 עֵינְיכֶם וְאַל־תַּחְמֹלוּ: זָקֵן
בָּחוּר וּבְתוּלָה וְטַף וְנָשִׁים

v. 4. אליו ק'   v. 5. אל ק'   v. 5. עינכם ק'

Holies above the ark-cover between the two cherubim (cf. Num. vii. 89). The use of the singular, *cherub*, is explained by the Talmudic tradition (R.H. 31a) that the departure of the Divine Presence before the invasion of Jerusalem occurred in ten stages, the first two being from the ark-cover to one cherub and from it to the other cherub.

of the house. i.e. the threshold of the Holy of Holies.

4-7 THE RIGHTEOUS TO BE SPARED AND THE REST SLAIN

4. *through the midst of the city, through the midst of Jerusalem.* The repetition implies a reproach, viz. the city of Jerusalem, the dwelling-place of God's glory, will now, through the misdeeds of the inhabitants, be forsaken by Him (Kimchi).

set a mark. The mark on the foreheads

of the righteous was intended to distinguish them from the condemned and give them Divine protection. Similarly, on the night when the Egyptian first-born were slain the houses of the Israelites were marked with blood for protection (Exod. xii. 22f.). Cain was also provided with a sign of Divine protection (Gen. iv. 15), probably on his forehead. The word for *mark* (*taw*) is the Hebrew letter *t*, the last in the Hebrew alphabet. According to one Rabbi (Shab. 55a), God ordered the angel Gabriel to mark on the foreheads of the righteous a *taw* (in ink), the initial of the word *tichyeh*, 'thou shalt live,' and on the foreheads of the wicked a *taw* (in blood), the initial of the word *tamuth*, 'thou shalt die.'

5. *the others.* The six executioners mentioned in verse 2. These were ordered to follow the seventh man and slay all who bore no protective mark.

in my hearing. lit. 'in my ears.'

48

women; but come not near any man upon whom is the mark; and begin at My sanctuary.' Then they began at the elders that were before the house. 7. And He said unto them: 'Defile the house, and fill the courts with the slain; go ye forth.' And they went forth, and smote in the city. 8. And it came to pass, while they were smiting, and I was left, that I fell upon my face, and cried, and said: 'Ah Lord God! wilt Thou destroy all the residue of Israel in Thy pouring out of Thy fury upon Jerusalem?' 9. Then said He unto me: "The iniquity of the house of Israel and Judah is exceeding great,

תַּהֲרֹגוּ לְמַשְׁחִית וְעַל־
כָּל־אִישׁ אֲשֶׁר־עָלָיו הַתָּו
אַל־תִּגָּשׁוּ וּמִמִּקְדָּשִׁי תָּחֵלּוּ
וַיָּחֵלּוּ בָּאֲנָשִׁים הַזְּקֵנִים אֲשֶׁר
7 לִפְנֵי הַבָּיִת: וַיֹּאמֶר אֲלֵיהֶם
טַמְּאוּ אֶת־הַבַּיִת וּמַלְאוּ אֶת־
הַחֲצֵרוֹת חֲלָלִים צֵאוּ וְיָצְאוּ
8 וְהִכּוּ בָעִיר: וַיְהִי כְּהַכּוֹתָם
וְנֵאשְׁאַר אָנִי וָאֶפְּלָה עַל־פָּנַי
וָאֶזְעַק וָאֹמַר אֲהָהּ אֲדֹנָי יֱהֹוִה
הֲמַשְׁחִית אַתָּה אֵת כָּל־
שְׁאֵרִית יִשְׂרָאֵל בְּשָׁפְכְּךָ אֶת־
9 חֲמָתְךָ עַל־יְרוּשָׁלָ͏ִם: וַיֹּאמֶר
אֵלַי עֲוֹן בֵּית־יִשְׂרָאֵל וִיהוּדָה
גָּדוֹל בִּמְאֹד מְאֹד וַתִּמָּלֵא

v. 8. נצ״ל

6. *begin at My sanctuary.* Those who practised idolatry in the house of God were to be the first to experience God's judgment.

the elders that were before the house. The seventy elders who were engaged in heathenish worship within the precincts of the Temple (viii. 11).

7. *defile the house, and fill the courts with the slain.* The presence of a corpse communicates defilement; but that consideration must not weigh with the executioners because the Sanctuary had already been desecrated by idolatry.

go ye forth. And they went forth, and smote in the city. After slaying those in the Sanctuary, they were to turn to the population in the city; and they did so.

8-10 EZEKIEL'S CONSTERNATION AND INTERCESSION

8. *and I was left.* The prophet was the only one left alive in the Temple after the departure of the executioners since, with his exception, none of those present was worthy of being marked with the protective sign. Or the phrase may mean, 'I was left alone with the dead.' The form of the verb is irregular and some MSS. read *wenishar*, the Niphal participle.

wilt Thou destroy all the residue of Israel. After the overthrow of the Northern Kingdom in 722 B.C.E. and the Judean captivity in 597, the population in the Holy City was considered to be the *residue of Israel.*

9. *the iniquity of the house of Israel and Judah.* The remnant of Israel after the

and the land is full of blood, and the city full of wresting of judgment; for they say: The LORD hath forsaken the land, and the LORD seeth not. 10. And as for Me also, Mine eye shall not spare, neither will I have pity, but I will bring their way upon their head.' 11. And, behold, the man clothed in linen, who had the inkhorn on his side, reported, saying: 'I have done according to all that Thou hast commanded me.'

הָאָרֶץ דָּמִים וְהָעִיר מָלְאָה
מֻטֶּה כִּי אָמְרוּ עָזַב יְהֹוָה אֶת־
הָאָרֶץ וְאֵין יְהֹוָה רֹאֶה: וְגַם 10
אֲנִי לֹא־תָחוֹס עֵינִי וְלֹא
אֶחְמֹל דַּרְכָּם בְּרֹאשָׁם נָתָתִּי:
וְהִנֵּה הָאִישׁ | לְבֻשׁ הַבַּדִּים 11
אֲשֶׁר הַקֶּסֶת בְּמָתְנָיו מֵשִׁיב
דָּבָר לֵאמֹר עָשִׂיתִי כַּאֲשֶׁר
צִוִּיתָנִי:

10   CHAPTER X   י

1. Then I looked, and, behold, upon the firmament that was over the head of the cherubim, there appeared above them as it were a sapphire stone, as the appearance of

וָאֶרְאֶה וְהִנֵּה אֶל־הָרָקִיעַ 1
אֲשֶׁר עַל־רֹאשׁ הַכְּרֻבִים
כְּאֶבֶן סַפִּיר כְּמַרְאֵה דְּמוּת

ב״א חמס v. 11. ‏ככל אשר ק׳ v. 9.

fall of the Northern Kingdom had joined Judah, and it is to them the prophet now refers.

full of blood. i.e. deeds of bloodshed were rife.

full of wresting of judgment. Jerusalem was once *full of justice* (Isa. i. 21) but has now lost that distinction.

the LORD hath forsaken the land, and the LORD seeth not. Instead of attributing their calamities to punishment for their sins, they maintained that God had forsaken them and was no longer interested in their fate. This false belief led to a breaking down of moral restraint (see on viii. 12).

10. *as for Me also*, etc. Measure for measure. As they have no pity on the needy and weak, so will I have no pity on them (cf. viii. 18).

11 GOD'S COMMANDS OBEYED
the man clothed in linen. His rank was higher than that of the other six (see on verse 2), and so he reports that the orders have been executed.

CHAPTER X
THE main feature of this chapter is the Divine command to *the man clothed in linen* to take coals of fire from between the cherubim and set the city of Jerusalem ablaze. All else is a repeated description of the *Merkabah* which now departs from the Temple.

1-8 THE VISION OF JERUSALEM CONDEMNED TO DESTRUCTION BY FIRE
1. The verse is in the main a repetition of i. 26.

firmament. See on i. 22.

cherubim. These are identical with the *living creatures* in chapter i.

the likeness of a throne.   2. And He
spoke unto the man clothed in linen,
and said: 'Go in between the wheelwork, even under the cherub, and
fill both thy hands with coals of fire
from between the cherubim, and
dash them against the city.'   And
he went in in my sight.   3. Now the
cherubim stood on the right side of
the house, when the man went in;
and the cloud filled the inner court.
4. And the glory of the LORD
mounted up from the cherub to the
threshold of the house; and the
house was filled with the cloud, and
the court was full of the brightness

2 בְּסֵא נִרְאָה עֲלֵיהֶם: וַיֹּאמֶר
אֶל־הָאִישׁ ׀ לְבֻשׁ הַבַּדִּים
וַיֹּאמֶר בֹּא אֶל־בֵּינוֹת לַגַּלְגַּל
אֶל־תַּחַת לַכְּרוּב וּמַלֵּא
חָפְנֶיךָ גַחֲלֵי־אֵשׁ מִבֵּינוֹת
לַכְּרֻבִים וּזְרֹק עַל־הָעִיר
3 וַיָּבֹא לְעֵינָי: וְהַכְּרֻבִים
עֹמְדִים מִימִין לַבַּיִת בְּבֹאוֹ
הָאִישׁ וְהֶעָנָן מָלֵא אֶת־
4 הֶחָצֵר הַפְּנִימִית: וַיָּרָם
כְּבוֹד־יְהֹוָה מֵעַל הַכְּרוּב עַל
מִפְתַּן הַבָּיִת וַיִּמָּלֵא הַבַּיִת
אֶת־הֶעָנָן וְהֶחָצֵר מָלְאָה

2. *and He spoke.*   It appears that the
Divine Presence, which had previously
departed from the *Merkabah* (ix. 3), now
returns to the Sanctuary (verse 4) before
it leaves again.

the wheelwork . . . cherub.   The singular nouns are used in the collective
sense.   The prophet speaks of *wheelwork*
(*galgal*) instead of the usual *wheels*
(*ophannim*) because *galgal* was the term
applied to them by the angel (verse 13).
In the view of Maimonides (*Guide*, III. 4),
the variant term *galgal* is intended to
explain the nature of the *ophannim:* they
were not celestial bodies but existing
terrestrial objects.

fill both thy hands.   The Talmud (Yoma
77a) remarks that the man clothed in
linen did not take the *coals of fire* direct
from between the cherubim to hand them to him
(as is stated in verse 7).   In this way the
coals lost some of their heat.   Had he
taken the coals himself direct, Israel

would have been utterly destroyed and
no remnant left.

coals of fire.   For coals of fire as a
symbol of purgation, cf. Isa. vi. 6f.,
where one of the seraphim is said to have
touched Isaiah's lips with a coal of fire
to cleanse him from sin.   The general
similarity of that chapter to Ezekiel's
vision should be noted.

he went in.   The man clothed in linen
approached the wheelwork of the *Merkabah*, as he was commanded.

in my sight.   Ezekiel, in his vision, saw
the heavenly agent do this.

3. *the right side of the house.*   Since the
abominations were practised on the north
side of the Temple (viii. 14), the
cherubim took up their position on the
opposite side to mark the contrast.

4. *the house was filled with the cloud.*   The
departure of the Divine glory from the
house left a cloud behind.   The same

of the LORD's glory. 5. And the
sound of the wings of the cherubim
was heard even to the outer court,
as the voice of God Almighty when
He speaketh. 6. And it came to
pass, when He commanded the
man clothed in linen, saying: 'Take
fire from between the wheelwork,
from between the cherubim,' that
he went in, and stood beside a
wheel. 7. And the cherub stretched
forth his hand from between the
cherubim unto the fire that was
between the cherubim, and took
thereof, and put it into the hands of
him that was clothed in linen, who
took it and went out. 8. And there
appeared in the cherubim the form
of a man's hand under their wings.

5 אֶת־נֹגַהּ כְּבוֹד יְהוָה: וְקוֹל
כַּנְפֵי הַכְּרוּבִים נִשְׁמַע עַד
הֶחָצֵר הַחִיצֹנָה כְּקוֹל אֵל־
6 שַׁדַּי בְּדַבְּרוֹ: וַיְהִי בְּצַוֹּתוֹ
אֶת־הָאִישׁ לְבֻשׁ־הַבַּדִּים
לֵאמֹר קַח אֵשׁ מִבֵּינוֹת לַגַּלְגַּל
מִבֵּינוֹת לַכְּרוּבִים וַיָּבֹא
7 וַיַּעֲמֹד אֵצֶל הָאוֹפָן: וַיִּשְׁלַח
הַכְּרוּב אֶת־יָדוֹ מִבֵּינוֹת
לַכְּרוּבִים אֶל־הָאֵשׁ אֲשֶׁר
בֵּינוֹת הַכְּרֻבִים וַיִּשָּׂא וַיִּתֵּן
אֶל־חָפְנֵי לְבֻשׁ הַבַּדִּים וַיִּקַּח
8 וַיֵּצֵא: וַיֵּרָא לַכְּרֻבִים תַּבְנִית
יַד־אָדָם תַּחַת כַּנְפֵיהֶם:

happened when the Presence returned
from the inner court to the house, a
cloud filled the inner court (verse 3).

5. *as the voice of God Almighty.* See on
i. 24.

when He speaketh. Ehrlich prefers to
translate: 'when He (on this occasion)
spoke,' and connects it with *and the
sound of the wings . . . court*, not with
as the voice of God Almighty. The point
is that normally the wings were *let down*
and made no sound while the cherubim
were motionless (i. 24); but in the
present vision, they too made a loud
noise when God spoke which, however,
did not drown the Divine voice, since it
was heard both by the man in linen and
Ezekiel.

6. *it came to pass.* This is the continuation of verse 2, verses 3-5 being in
parenthesis.
he went in, and stood beside a wheel.
Whereas the commentators, Jewish as

well as others, understand the subject to
be the man in linen, Kimchi seems to
identify it with Ezekiel who stood in awe
to see what would happen.

7. *the cherub stretched forth his hand.* See
on verse 2. *The cherub* implies the one
nearest in sight to Ezekiel. 'One would
always be more prominent to the on-
looker than the rest' (Lofthouse).

went out. From the Temple to execute
the command to set fire to the city; but
the fulfilment of the symbolic act took
place six years later.

8. *there appeared . . . the form.* These
expressions imply that the form of the
cherubim as described here existed only
in the prophetic vision but not in reality
(Kimchi).

a man's hand. Each of the cherubim had
under its wings the form of a man's
hand (i. 8).

9. And I looked, and behold four wheels beside the cherubim, one wheel beside one cherub, and another wheel beside another cherub; and the appearance of the wheels was as the colour of a beryl stone. 10. And as for their appearance, they four had one likeness, as if a wheel had been within a wheel. 11. When they went, they went toward their four sides; they turned not as they went, but to the place whither the head looked they followed it; they turned not as they went. 12. And their whole body, and their backs, and their hands, and their wings, and the wheels were full of eyes round about, even the wheels that they four had. 13. As

9 וָאֵרֶא וְהִנֵּה אַרְבָּעָה אוֹפַנִּים
אֵצֶל הַכְּרוּבִים אוֹפַן אֶחָד
אֵצֶל הַכְּרוּב אֶחָד וְאוֹפַן אֶחָד
אֵצֶל הַכְּרוּב אֶחָד וּמַרְאֵה
הָאוֹפַנִּים כְּעֵין אֶבֶן תַּרְשִׁישׁ:
10 וּמַרְאֵיהֶם דְּמוּת אֶחָד
לְאַרְבַּעְתָּם כַּאֲשֶׁר יִהְיֶה
11 הָאוֹפָן בְּתוֹךְ הָאוֹפָן: בְּלֶכְתָּם
אֶל־אַרְבַּעַת רִבְעֵיהֶם יֵלֵכוּ
לֹא יִסַּבּוּ בְּלֶכְתָּם כִּי הַמָּקוֹם
אֲשֶׁר־יִפְנֶה הָרֹאשׁ אַחֲרָיו
יֵלֵכוּ לֹא יִסַּבּוּ בְלֶכְתָּם:
12 וְכָל־בְּשָׂרָם וְגַבֵּהֶם וִידֵיהֶם
וְכַנְפֵיהֶם וְהָאוֹפַנִּים מְלֵאִים
עֵינַיִם סָבִיב לְאַרְבַּעְתָּם
13 אוֹפַנֵּיהֶם: לָאוֹפַנִּים לָהֶם

כצ״ל v. 13.

9-17 REPEATED DESCRIPTION OF THE *MERKABAH*

'Instead of depicting the conflagration of the city, which would have been impossible [since it did not occur for some time afterwards], the prophet's attention is anew drawn to the cherubim, and a fresh description of the living creatures and of the Divine chariot follows' (Davidson). This description heightens the solemnity of the scene in which the *Merkabah* departs.

9. *four wheels beside the cherubim.* The account of the *Merkabah* given in this section differs slightly from that of chapter i. The main object of the repetition, according to Rashi, is to illustrate that, though one of the faces of the four creatures was now changed from

that of an ox to a cherub (verse 14), it was the same *Merkabah* as the prophet had seen in the earlier vision.

10. Cf. i. 16.

11. *the head.* i.e. the cherub which is the principal driving force. Wherever the cherub turned, the wheel followed (Kimchi).

12. *their whole body*, etc. *Body* is literally 'flesh.' The usual interpretation (so Metsudath David) applies the words to the living creatures; but Rashi and Kimchi explain that they do not refer to the cherubim but to the various parts of the wheels; that is to say, the whole of the wheels was full of eyes. Accordingly *backs* means *rings* or *felloes* (as in i. 18) and *hands* are the axles.

for the wheels, they were called in my hearing The wheelwork. 14. And every one had four faces: the first face was the face of the cherub, and the second face was the face of a man, and the third the face of a lion, and the fourth the face of an eagle. 15. And the cherubim mounted up —this is the living creature that I saw by the river Chebar. 16. And when the cherubim went, the wheels went beside them; and when the cherubim lifted up their wings to mount up from the earth, the same wheels also turned not from beside them. 17. When they stood, these stood, and when they mounted up, these mounted up with them; for the spirit of the living creature was in them. 18. And the glory of the LORD went forth from off the threshold of the house, and stood

14 קֹ֣ורָא הַגַּלְגַּ֖ל בְּאָזְנָֽי׃ וְאַרְבָּעָ֣ה
פָנִים֙ לְאֶחָ֔ד פְּנֵ֨י הָאֶחָ֜ד פְּנֵ֣י
הַכְּר֗וּב וּפְנֵ֤י הַשֵּׁנִי֙ פְּנֵ֣י אָדָ֔ם
וְהַשְּׁלִישִׁי֙ פְּנֵ֣י אַרְיֵ֔ה וְהָרְבִיעִ֖י
15 פְּנֵי־נָֽשֶׁר׃ וַיֵּרֹ֖מּוּ הַכְּרוּבִ֑ים
הִ֣יא הַחַיָּ֔ה אֲשֶׁ֥ר רָאִ֖יתִי
16 בִּֽנְהַר־כְּבָֽר׃ וּבְלֶ֨כֶת֙
הַכְּרוּבִ֔ים יֵלְכ֥וּ הָאֹופַנִּ֖ים
אֶצְלָ֑ם וּבִשְׂאֵ֨ת הַכְּרוּבִ֜ים
אֶת־כַּנְפֵיהֶ֗ם לָר֨וּם֙ מֵעַ֣ל
הָאָ֔רֶץ לֹא־יִסַּ֧בּוּ הָאֹופַנִּ֛ים
17 גַּם־הֵ֖ם מֵאֶצְלָֽם׃ בְּעָמְדָ֣ם
יַעֲמֹ֔דוּ וּבְרֹומָ֖ם יֵרֹ֣ומּוּ אֹותָ֑ם
18 כִּ֛י ר֥וּחַ הַחַיָּ֖ה בָּהֶֽם׃ וַיֵּצֵא֙
כְּבֹ֣וד יְהוָ֔ה מֵעַ֖ל מִפְתַּ֥ן הַבָּֽיִת

The wheelwork. See on verse 2.

14. *the face of the cherub.* This description of the four faces varies from that in i. 10. Instead of the face of an ox we have here described that of a cherub. In solving this difficulty, a Rabbi (Chag. 13b) remarked that Ezekiel entreated God to remove the face of the ox, reminiscent of the Golden Calf, since 'an accuser cannot be an advocate.' His prayer was answered and the ox was changed into a cherub. For this reason, in the present vision the creatures are called *cherubim* and not *living creatures* (*chayyoth*) as in chapter i. They were interceders on behalf of Israel. As a modern explanation there is Lofthouse's comment: 'The mention of the cherub must imply that the prophet here identifies with the chariot as a whole (the *cherub* collectively) the animal whose face he noticed most clearly as the chariot moved. The chariot stands at the south side of the Temple (to the south of Ezekiel), and moves eastward (verse 19). Hence, if the face of the man is that which looks in front, the face of the leading cherub which Ezekiel sees most clearly will be that on the left of the human face, i.e. the ox-face; taking the rest in order, he will naturally mention the faces of the man, lion and eagle. This explanation is only redeemed from artificiality by recognizing the naive accuracy of Ezekiel's account.' See also on verse 20.

15. This verse is to be connected with verse 20, what intervenes being inserted to explain the method by which the cherubim *mounted up.*

16. Cf. i. 19, 21.

18-22 THE DIVINE PRESENCE LEAVES THE TEMPLE

18. *from off the threshold of the house.*

over the cherubim. 19. And the cherubim lifted up their wings, and mounted up from the earth in my sight when they went forth, and the wheels beside them; and they stood at the door of the east gate of the LORD'S house; and the glory of the God of Israel was over them above. 20. This is the living creature that I saw under the God of Israel by the river Chebar; and I knew that they were cherubim. 21. Every one had four faces apiece, and every one four

וַיַּעֲמֹד עַל־הַכְּרוּבִים׃

19 וַיִּשְׂאוּ הַכְּרוּבִים אֶת־
כַּנְפֵיהֶם וַיֵּרוֹמּוּ מִן־הָאָרֶץ
לְעֵינַי בְּצֵאתָם וְהָאוֹפַנִּים
לְעֻמָּתָם וַיַּעֲמֹד פֶּתַח שַׁעַר
בֵּית־יְהוָה הַקַּדְמוֹנִי וּכְבוֹד
אֱלֹהֵי יִשְׂרָאֵל עֲלֵיהֶם

20 מִלְמָעְלָה׃ הִיא הַחַיָּה אֲשֶׁר
רָאִיתִי תַּחַת אֱלֹהֵי־יִשְׂרָאֵל
בִּנְהַר כְּבָר וָאֵדַע כִּי כְרוּבִים

21 הֵמָּה׃ אַרְבָּעָה אַרְבָּעָה פָנִים
לְאֶחָד וְאַרְבַּע כְּנָפַיִם לְאֶחָד

The Divine glory, after leaving the Holy of Holies, remained on the threshold, as stated in ix. 3. Now mention is m:de of the third stage of the departure (see on ix. 3).

19. *they stood.* The Hebrew text has the singular form, signifying the uniform position of the cherubim (Kimchi). More probably the phenomenon of the *Merkabah* as a whole is the subject of the verb.

at the door of the east gate. i.e. the eastern gate of the Temple court. Through the same gate *the glory of the LORD* later returns (xliii. 4).

20. *this is the living creature,* etc. On the Jewish interpretation, though the face of the ox was in this vision changed into that of a cherub (see on verse 14), the prophet realized that the *Merkabah* was the same which he had seen in his first vision by the river Chebar. But Lofthouse remarks: 'This verse can only be explained if Ezekiel is understood to be transcribing his own experience exactly. "This is what I saw previously

by the Chebar" has already entered his mind (verse 15). It recurs here, and he naturally uses the word for the animals which he had previously used, instead of "cherub," the word characteristic of this chapter. This recognition of the identity between the two visions he further presses by the last clause of the verse. But why did this second vision suggest to him at first "cherubim" and not simply "living creatures"? The question cannot be answered with certainty. May not the explanation be that the thought of the cherub in ix. 3, and of the general connection between cherubs, God and the ark [of the covenant] suggests to the prophet that the winged supporters of the chariot would naturally be cherubim; hence only after an interval does he recognize explicitly that these winged beings are the living creatures of his former vision? This he still further emphasizes in verse 22.'

21. *every one had four faces apiece.* Each of the four living creatures had four faces, a face in each direction, and each

wings; and the likeness of the hands of a man was under their wings. 22. And as for the likeness of their faces, they were the faces which I saw by the river Chebar, their appearances and themselves; they went every one straight forward.

וּדְמוּת יְדֵי אָדָם תַּחַת כַּנְפֵיהֶם: וּדְמוּת פְּנֵיהֶם הֵמָּה 22 הַפָּנִים אֲשֶׁר רָאִיתִי עַל־נְהַר כְּבָר מַרְאֵיהֶם וְאוֹתָם אִישׁ אֶל־עֵבֶר פָּנָיו יֵלֵכוּ:

11   CHAPTER XI   יא

1. Then a spirit lifted me up, and brought me unto the east gate of the LORD'S house, which looketh eastward; and behold at the door of the gate five and twenty men; and I saw in the midst of them Jaazaniah

וַתִּשָּׂא אֹתִי רוּחַ וַתָּבֵא אֹתִי 1 אֶל־שַׁעַר בֵּית־יְהֹוָה הַקַּדְמוֹנִי הַפּוֹנֶה קָדִימָה וְהִנֵּה בְּפֶתַח הַשַּׁעַר עֶשְׂרִים וַחֲמִשָּׁה אִישׁ וָאֶרְאֶה בְתוֹכָם אֶת־

face had four wings and hands like those of a man.

22. their appearances and themselves. From their appearance and form Ezekiel concluded that these were identical with the faces he had seen before.

they went every one straight forward. This feature which was present in both visions is an additional proof of the identity of the *Merkabah.*

CHAPTER XI

EZEKIEL's attention is directed to the scheming and vain confidence of the leading statesmen in the impregnability of Jerusalem. In a Divine communication, couched in the grimmest terms, he is ordered to disillusion them. In the course of the vision he sees that one of the twenty-five men collapsed and died. Ezekiel interprets this incident as so ominous that he is overcome by it and in dismay asks whether God has decreed the total annihilation of Israel. He then receives a command to convey to the exiles, whose connection with the Holy Land was challenged by the inhabitants of Jerusalem, a message of hope. They are to be assured that they would yet be restored to their homeland, cleansed of its abominations, unified in spirit. Then, with a final admonition, the *Merkabah* leaves the city and rests on the mount of Olives. Finding himself back in Babylon and awakened from his vision, Ezekiel relates his experience to his fellow-exiles.

1-13   THE LEADERS IN JERUSALEM DENOUNCED

1. *a spirit lifted me up.* In a vision the prophet sees himself swept off his feet and carried to another part of the Temple.

unto the east gate. As is evident from viii. 16, the last reference to his position, Ezekiel was standing in the inner court. He is now brought to the outer eastern gate of the court which faced the city.

five and twenty men. They are doubtless the same men who worshipped the sun

the son of Azzur, and Pelatiah the
son of Benaiah, princes of the people.
2. And He said unto me: 'Son of
man, these are the men that devise
iniquity, and that give wicked
counsel in this city; 3. that say:
The time is not near to build houses!
this city is the caldron, and we are
the flesh. 4. Therefore prophesy
against them, prophesy, O son of
man.' 5. And the spirit of the
LORD fell upon me, and He said unto
me: 'Speak: Thus saith the LORD:

יַאֲזַנְיָה בֶן־עַזֻּר וְאֶת־
פְּלַטְיָהוּ בֶן־בְּנָיָהוּ שָׂרֵי הָעָם׃
2 וַיֹּאמֶר אֵלַי בֶּן־אָדָם אֵלֶּה
הָאֲנָשִׁים הַחֹשְׁבִים אָוֶן
וְהַיֹּעֲצִים עֲצַת־רָע בָּעִיר
3 הַזֹּאת׃ הָאֹמְרִים לֹא בְקָרוֹב
בְּנוֹת בָּתִּים הִיא הַסִּיר וַאֲנַחְנוּ
4 הַבָּשָׂר׃ לָכֵן הִנָּבֵא עֲלֵיהֶם
5 הִנָּבֵא בֶן־אָדָם׃ וַתִּפֹּל עָלַי
רוּחַ יְהֹוָה וַיֹּאמֶר אֵלַי אֱמֹר

in the inner court (viii. 16). The contents of chapters viii. belong to the same vision.

Jaazaniah . . . and Pelatiah . . . princes of the people. They were prominent statesmen and known to the colony in exile. For the name Jaazaniah, see on viii. 11, but the person there mentioned is not the same.

2. *devise iniquity.* viz. defiance of the prophet's warnings and planning a revolt against Babylonian authority which, in fact, ended in disaster. Like Jeremiah (xxvii. 12ff.), Ezekiel condemned rebellion against the king of Babylon as a revolt against God's will (see also below, chapter xvii).

3. *the time is not near to build houses.* lit. 'not in the near (future) the building of houses.' In their evil counsel, the rebel leaders urge preparation for war with Babylon; consequently normal occupations, such as house-building, must be deferred for a later period. Rashi, Kimchi and others render: 'It is not near, let us build houses' (so A.V.), that is to say, the prediction of the destruction of the State is not imminent, so we can conduct our lives without taking it into consideration.

this city is the caldron, and we are the flesh. lit. 'it is the caldron,' etc. In assuring themselves of the adequate protection which the walls of Jerusalem would afford them in the event of an attack by the army of Babylon, the planners of the rebellion used a simile familiar at the time. The pot protects the flesh within it from the fire, and the meat is only removed after it has been sufficiently cooked. Similarly, the walls of the city would give protection to its inhabitants, and only a natural death, not the sword of the enemy, would end their lives. Ehrlich offers a different interpretation of the verse. He construes the first clause as interrogative and gives the phrase *to build houses* the meaning which it has in 1 Chron. xvii. 10, viz. 'to establish a dynasty.' Now that Nebuchadnezzar has carried off the king, Jehoiachin, and his household, have we not the opportunity of seizing power for ourselves? As a caldron only serves for cooking meat in it, so the State only exists for us to secure advantage from it! On this view, the rebels are represented as being self-seekers and not patriots.

4. *prophesy . . . prophesy.* The repetition expresses the importance of the call to the prophet and the urgency of the message he is to deliver.

Thus have ye said, O house of Israel; for I know the things that come into your mind. 6. Ye have multiplied your slain in this city, and ye have filled the streets thereof with the slain. 7. Therefore thus saith the Lord GOD: Your slain whom ye have laid in the midst of it, they are the flesh, and this city is the caldron; but ye shall be brought forth out of the midst of it. 8. Ye have feared the sword; and the sword will I bring upon you, saith the Lord GOD. 9. And I will bring you forth out of the midst thereof, and deliver you into the hands of strangers, and will execute judgments among you.

כֹּה־אָמַ֤ר יְהוָה֙ כֵּ֣ן אֲמַרְתֶּ֔ם בֵּ֖ית יִשְׂרָאֵ֑ל וּמַעֲל֥וֹת רֽוּחֲכֶ֖ם 6 אֲנִ֖י יְדַעְתִּֽיהָ׃ הִרְבֵּיתֶ֣ם חַלְלֵיכֶ֔ם בָּעִ֖יר הַזֹּ֑את וּמִלֵּאתֶ֥ם חוּצֹתֶ֖יהָ חָלָֽל׃ 7 לָכֵ֗ן כֹּֽה־אָמַר֮ אֲדֹנָ֣י יְהוִה֒ חַלְלֵיכֶם֙ אֲשֶׁ֣ר שַׂמְתֶּ֣ם בְּתוֹכָ֔הּ הֵ֥מָּה הַבָּשָׂ֖ר וְהִ֣יא הַסִּ֑יר 8 וְאֶתְכֶ֖ם הוֹצִ֥יא מִתּוֹכָֽהּ׃ חֶ֣רֶב יְרֵאתֶ֔ם וְחֶ֕רֶב אָבִ֖יא עֲלֵיכֶ֑ם 9 נְאֻ֖ם אֲדֹנָ֥י יְהוִֽה׃ וְהוֹצֵאתִ֤י אֶתְכֶם֙ מִתּוֹכָ֔הּ וְנָתַתִּ֥י אֶתְכֶ֖ם

v.6. למדנחאי ומלאתים   v.7. סבירין אוציא

5. *thus have ye said.* On this translation, the verse contrasts what these leaders put forward publicly as the motives for their plot, viz. restoring the independence of Judea, and the true, selfish reasons which were in their mind. Kimchi prefers the rendering: 'correctly have ye spoken' (cf. Num. xxvii. 7 for this use of *ken*). The simile you have quoted is apt but in a different sense, is God's retort. The alternative meaning of the simile is given in verse 7.

I know the things that come into your mind. The Hebrew has a singular pronominal suffix attached to the verb *know*, which is literally 'I know it,' i.e. each of the things. The application which these men give to the simile of the caldron and flesh is known to God, says the prophet, but future events will set a different interpretation upon it.

6. *ye have multiplied your slain.* Possibly an allusion to the murder of political opponents who belonged to the pro-Babylonian party (cf. ix. 9).

7. *your slain . . . the caldron.* The figure of the pot and flesh is given a new meaning. The corpses of innocent people slain in the streets of Jerusalem will be the flesh which will *remain* in the pot, but they who engineered the rebellion and shed innocent blood will be dragged out of the city to suffer the punishment they deserve.

ye shall be brought forth. M.T. has the infinitive, 'there will be a bringing forth of you.' Many Hebrew MSS. and printed editions read *otsi*, 'I will bring forth.'

8. *ye have feared the sword.* With all their talk about security (verse 3), the leaders really feared an attack from Babylon and turned to Egypt for help (xvii. 15). Their fears will be justified by events.

9. *and deliver you into the hands of strangers.* Their expulsion from the city, spoken of in verse 7, is not to end in escape to a safe refuge; they will even-

10. Ye shall fall by the sword; I will judge you upon the border of Israel; and ye shall know that I am the LORD. 11. Though this city shall not be your caldron, ye shall be the flesh in the midst thereof; I will judge you upon the border of Israel; 12. and ye shall know that I am the LORD; for ye have not walked in My statutes, neither have ye executed Mine ordinances, but have done after the ordinances of the nations that are round about you.' 13. And it came to pass, when I prophesied, that Pelatiah the son of Benaiah died. Then fell I down upon my face, and cried with a loud voice, and said: 'Ah Lord GOD! wilt Thou make a full end of the remnant of Israel?'

בְּיַד־זָרִים וְעָשִׂיתִי בָכֶם
10 שְׁפָטִים: בַּחֶרֶב תִּפֹּלוּ עַל־
גְּבוּל יִשְׂרָאֵל אֶשְׁפּוֹט אֶתְכֶם
11 וִידַעְתֶּם כִּי־אֲנִי יְהֹוָה: הִיא
לֹא־תִהְיֶה לָכֶם לְסִיר וְאַתֶּם
תִּהְיוּ בְתוֹכָהּ לְבָשָׂר אֶל־
גְּבוּל יִשְׂרָאֵל אֶשְׁפֹּט אֶתְכֶם:
12 וִידַעְתֶּם כִּי־אֲנִי יְהֹוָה אֲשֶׁר
בְּחֻקַּי לֹא הֲלַכְתֶּם וּמִשְׁפָּטַי
לֹא עֲשִׂיתֶם וּכְמִשְׁפְּטֵי הַגּוֹיִם
אֲשֶׁר סְבִיבוֹתֵיכֶם עֲשִׂיתֶם:
13 וַיְהִי כְּהִנָּבְאִי וּפְלַטְיָהוּ בֶן־
בְּנָיָה מֵת וָאֶפֹּל עַל־פָּנַי
וָאֶזְעַק | קוֹל גָּדוֹל וָאֹמַר אֲהָהּ
אֲדֹנָי יֱהֹוִה כָּלָה אַתָּה עֹשֶׂה
14 אֵת שְׁאֵרִית יִשְׂרָאֵל: וַיְהִי

tually be captured and slain by the enemy. This was literally fulfilled, as recorded in 2 Kings xxv. 4ff.

10. *I will judge you upon the border of Israel.* The allusion is to the massacre at Riblah in the land of Hamath, which was on the frontier of the Northern Kingdom (cf. 2 Kings xxv. 18ff.; Jer. lii. 24ff.).

11. This verse reverts to the previous warning (verse 7) that the walls of Jerusalem afford them no protection, and adds that after their flight from the city they would be the *flesh* which fell into the hands of the invaders.

12. *ye shall know that I am the LORD.* When the predicted judgment is executed, they will realize that God is not indifferent to man's conduct and that retribution falls upon the wicked.

13. *Pelatiah . . . died.* Some commentators understand the death of this man as 'symbolical' and that it took place soon after the prophecy, as happened with Hananiah, the opponent of Jeremiah (cf. Jer. xxviii. 17). Lofthouse remarks: 'Far more natural is it to suppose that Ezekiel, by clairvoyance, saw a council which was taking place about this time, felt his spirit roused against it in indignant "prophecy," and there saw one of its members fall dead, and trembled at the thought of the judgment which he had been pronouncing.'

the remnant of Israel. Those who were left in Jerusalem after the first invasion in 597 B.C.E. The prophet understood from the incident that the entire population of Israel was to share the fate of Pelatiah and perish.

14. And the word of the LORD came unto me, saying: 15. 'Son of man, as for thy brethren, even thy brethren, the men of thy kindred, and all the house of Israel, all of them, concerning whom the inhabitants of Jerusalem have said: Get you far from the LORD! unto us is this land given for a possession; 16. therefore say: Thus saith the Lord GOD: Although I have removed them far off among the nations, and although I have scattered them among the countries, yet have I been to them as a little sanctuary in the countries where

15 דְּבַר־יְהֹוָה אֵלַי לֵאמֹר: בֶּן־
אָדָם אַחֶיךָ אַחֶיךָ אַנְשֵׁי
גְאֻלָּתֶךָ וְכָל־בֵּית יִשְׂרָאֵל
כֻּלֹּה אֲשֶׁר אָמְרוּ לָהֶם יֹשְׁבֵי
יְרוּשָׁלַםִ רַחֲקוּ מֵעַל יְהֹוָה
לָנוּ הִיא נִתְּנָה הָאָרֶץ
16 לְמוֹרָשָׁה: לָכֵן אֱמֹר כֹּה־אָמַר
אֲדֹנָי יְהֹוִה כִּי הִרְחַקְתִּים
בַּגּוֹיִם וְכִי הֲפִיצוֹתִים
בָּאֲרָצוֹת וָאֱהִי לָהֶם לְמִקְדָּשׁ
מְעַט בָּאֲרָצוֹת אֲשֶׁר־בָּאוּ

14-21 MESSAGE OF COMFORT BEFORE THE *MERKABAH'S* DEPARTURE

15. *even thy brethren, the men of thy kindred.* This section is probably to be closely connected with what precedes. Ezekiel had expressed concern about the fate of the remnant in the capital. He receives in reply a communication from God which relates not only to them, but also to the groups of Israelites scattered in other lands. They, too, are the prophet's *brethren*, and this term is defined by *the men of thy kindred* which is literally 'the men of thy redemption (*geullah*).' In this phrase is to be detected the law of the *goël*, 'the redeemer,' i.e. the next-of-kin who has the duty of avenging a relative's violent death, marrying his widow, or acquiring the estate in danger of being lost to the family (cf. Num. xxxv. 19; Ruth ii. 20; Lev. xxv. 25). God has a thought for all these exiled Israelites.

all the house of Israel. Including the survivors of the Northern Kingdom.

get you far from the LORD. 'Those left were in possession of the Temple, the abode of God, and had the assurance of His presence, in which those gone forth had no part; for to go into a foreign land was to come under the dominion of other gods according to the words of David, *They have driven me out this day that I should not cleave unto the inheritance of the LORD, saying: Go, serve other gods* (1 Sam. xxvi. 19; cf. Deut. iv. 28, xxviii. 36, 64; Jer. xvi. 13; Hos. ix. 3)' (Davidson).

16. *yet have I been to them as a little sanctuary.* To the humiliating allegation of the inhabitants of Jerusalem that the exiles, being far removed from the Temple, forfeited the Fatherhood and protection of God, comes the Divine retort that they still preserve their relationship to Him by means of their Houses of Worship and Houses of Learning, each of them serving the purpose of a miniature Temple in which the spirit of God was present (Meg. 29a). The Synagogue is even now called *a little sanctuary* in allusion to this verse. The rendering of R.V., 'a sanctuary for a little while,' is less probable, as Ezekiel nowhere expresses the thought that the captivity is soon to be ended.

they are come; 17. therefore say:
Thus saith the Lord GOD: I will
even gather you from the peoples,
and assemble you out of the
countries where ye have been
scattered, and I will give you the
land of Israel. 18. And they shall
come thither, and they shall take
away all the detestable things thereof
and all the abominations thereof
from thence. 19. And I will give
them one heart, and I will put a
new spirit within you; and I will
remove the stony heart out of their
flesh, and will give them a heart of
flesh; 20. that they may walk in My
statutes, and keep Mine ordinances,
and do them; and they shall be My
people, and I will be their God.
21. But as for them whose heart
walketh after the heart of their
detestable things and their abomina-

17 שָׁם: לָכֵן אֱמֹר כֹּה־אָמַר
אֲדֹנָי יֱהֹוִה וְקִבַּצְתִּי אֶתְכֶם
מִן־הָעַמִּים וְאָסַפְתִּי אֶתְכֶם
מִן־הָאֲרָצוֹת אֲשֶׁר נְפֹצוֹתֶם
בָּהֶם וְנָתַתִּי לָכֶם אֶת־
18 אַדְמַת יִשְׂרָאֵל: וּבָאוּ־שָׁמָּה
וְהֵסִירוּ אֶת־כָּל־שִׁקּוּצֶיהָ
וְאֶת־כָּל־תּוֹעֲבוֹתֶיהָ מִמֶּנָּה:
19 וְנָתַתִּי לָהֶם לֵב אֶחָד וְרוּחַ
חֲדָשָׁה אֶתֵּן בְּקִרְבְּכֶם
וַהֲסִרֹתִי לֵב הָאֶבֶן מִבְּשָׂרָם
20 וְנָתַתִּי לָהֶם לֵב בָּשָׂר: לְמַעַן
בְּחֻקֹּתַי יֵלֵכוּ וְאֶת־מִשְׁפָּטַי
יִשְׁמְרוּ וְעָשׂוּ אֹתָם וְהָיוּ־לִי
לְעָם וַאֲנִי אֶהְיֶה לָהֶם
21 לֵאלֹהִים: וְאֶל־לֵב
שִׁקּוּצֵיהֶם וְתוֹעֲבוֹתֵיהֶם לִבָּם

כצ"ל v. 18.

17. *I will give you the land of Israel.* The
inhabitants of Jerusalem had also said,
Unto us is this land given for a possession
(verse 15). This will prove vain boasting. They will be banished from the
land, while the exiles will re-enter it.

18. *they shall take away all the detestable
things.* Their first act will be to purify
the land from the defilement of idolatry.

19. *one heart.* Their heart will no
longer be divided between worship of
God and images, but will be wholly loyal
to Him (cf. Jer. xxxii. 39).

a new spirit. 'The heart is the seat of
the emotions; the spirit is the breath
which animates the actions' (Lofthouse).

stony heart . . . a heart of flesh. Their
former hard and obstinate heart will be
transformed into a sensitive and responsive organ.

20. *they shall be My people, and I will be
their God.* Submission to the will of
God will restore harmonious relationship
between Him and His people. The
ancient covenant will be renewed.

21. *but as for them.* This refers back to
verse 12, the inhabitants of Jerusalem.

after the heart of their detestable things.
Their heart is divided. On the one
hand, they believe in the true God, and
on the other, they follow readily the
desire of their heart to practise idolatry.

tions, I will bring their way upon their own heads, saith the Lord God.'

22. Then did the cherubim lift up their wings, and the wheels were beside them; and the glory of the God of Israel was over them above. 23. And the glory of the LORD went up from the midst of the city, and stood upon the mountain which is on the east side of the city. 24. And a spirit lifted me up, and brought me in the vision by the spirit of God into Chaldea, to them of the captivity. So the vision that I had seen went up from me. 25. Then I spoke unto them of the captivity all the things that the LORD had shown me.

הֵלֵךְ דַּרְכָּם בְּרֹאשָׁם נָתָתִּי
22 נְאֻם אֲדֹנָי יֱהֹוִה: וַיִּשְׂאוּ
הַכְּרוּבִים אֶת־כַּנְפֵיהֶם
וְהָאוֹפַנִּים לְעֻמָּתָם וּכְבוֹד
אֱלֹהֵי יִשְׂרָאֵל עֲלֵיהֶם
23 מִלְמָעְלָה: וַיַּעַל כְּבוֹד יֱהֹוָה
מֵעַל תּוֹךְ הָעִיר וַיַּעֲמֹד עַל־
הָהָר אֲשֶׁר מִקֶּדֶם לָעִיר:
24 וְרוּחַ נְשָׂאַתְנִי וַתְּבִיאֵנִי
כַשְׂדִּימָה אֶל־הַגּוֹלָה בַּמַּרְאֶה
בְּרוּחַ אֱלֹהִים וַיַּעַל מֵעָלַי
הַמַּרְאֶה אֲשֶׁר רָאִיתִי:
25 וָאֲדַבֵּר אֶל־הַגּוֹלָה אֵת כָּל־
דִּבְרֵי יֱהֹוָה אֲשֶׁר הֶרְאָנִי:

12   CHAPTER XII   יב

1. The word of the LORD also came unto me, saying: 2. 'Son of man, thou dwellest in the midst of the

1 וַיְהִי דְבַר־יֱהֹוָה אֵלַי לֵאמֹר:
2 בֶּן־אָדָם בְּתוֹךְ בֵּית־הַמֶּרִי

I will bring their way upon their own heads. They will suffer the consequence of their deeds.

22-23 THE *MERKABAH* LEAVES FOR THE MOUNT OF OLIVES

22. *over them above.* See on x. 18.

23. *upon the mountain.* Having left the city, the *Merkabah* halted on the Mount of Olives on the east side of the city. Commenting on this text, the Rabbis in Midrash Rabbah to Lamentations (Proem xxv) remark, 'For three years and a half the Divine Presence stayed upon the Mount of Olives, hoping that Israel would repent, but they did not.'

24-25 END OF THE VISION

24. *in the vision by the spirit of God.* The transportation of / the prophet from Babylon to Jerusalem and back had not been actual, but took place in a vision (cf. viii. 3).

the vision . . . went up from me. When Ezekiel awoke from his vision, he was permitted to reveal to his fellow-exiles all that he had seen and experienced.

CHAPTER XII

A NEW section begins at this point and extends to the end of chapter xix, containing a fresh series of denunciations of the people's sinfulness which must

rebellious house, that have eyes to see, and see not, that have ears to hear, and hear not; for they are a rebellious house. 3. Therefore, thou son of man, prepare thee stuff for exile, and remove as though for exile by day in their sight; and thou shalt remove from thy place to another place in their sight; it may be they will perceive, for they are a rebellious house. 4. And thou shalt bring forth thy stuff by day in their sight, as stuff for exile; and thou

אַתָּה יֹשֵׁב אֲשֶׁר עֵינַ֫יִם לָהֶם
לִרְאוֹת וְלֹא רָאוּ אָזְנַ֫יִם לָהֶם
לִשְׁמֹ֫עַ וְלֹא שָׁמֵ֫עוּ כִּי בֵּית
3 מְרִי הֵם: וְאַתָּה בֶן־אָדָם
עֲשֵׂה לְךָ֫ כְּלֵי גוֹלָה וּגְלֵה יוֹמָם
לְעֵינֵיהֶם וְגָלִ֫יתָ מִמְּקוֹמְךָ֫
אֶל־מָקוֹם אַחֵר֮ לְעֵינֵיהֶם
אוּלַי יִרְאוּ כִּי בֵּית מְרִי הֵֽמָּה:
4 וְהוֹצֵאתָ֫ כֵלֶ֫יךָ כִּכְלֵי גוֹלָה

eventuate in national downfall. In the present chapter, the prophet receives the command to demonstrate to the captives in Babylon through the medium of symbolical actions the certainty of the nation's approaching doom. They were still possessed of a false confidence in the security of Israel, the indestructibility of the Temple and the permanence of the Davidic dynasty. Ezekiel assumes the rôle of a refugee who tries to escape from a beleaguered city. By so doing he personifies what is about to happen to the population of Judea. The remnant of the people will be banished from their land, and the king who will attempt to flee from the condemned city will be captured and brought to Babylon where he will die. In another symbolical act, Ezekiel portrays the hardships in the besieged Jerusalem. As for the current argument that prophecies which foretell evil need not be taken seriously, he emphatically warns the people that the impending disaster is near at hand and they would be soon convinced of the authenticity of his prediction.

1-16 SYMBOLS OF THE IMMINENT FALL OF JERUSALEM AND BANISHMENT OF THE NATION

2. *that have eyes to see*, etc. The exiles who witnessed the tragedy in 597 B.C.E. learnt no lesson from the event. They even refused to listen to the moral when brought home to them by the prophet in sign and word.

3. *prepare thee stuff for exile.* i.e. articles for use on the journey into exile, such as staff, knapsack, drinking-cup, water-bottle.

by day. i.e. by day-light. He was to make his preparations for flight at a time of the day when his action could be seen, because the purpose was to bring home to the people what was in store for them.

thou shalt remove from thy place to another place. This is explanatory of the preceding phrase, *Remove as though for exile*, which is literally 'go into exile.'

it may be, etc. The meaning is, perhaps they will take notice; the reason for the doubt is *they are a rebellious house*, obdurate despite warnings.

4. *thou shalt bring forth thy stuff.* He is to take the articles out of his house and deposit them in a convenient place where he can lay hands on them when required.

as stuff for exile. In the manner of exiles carrying their scanty baggage.

shalt go forth thyself at even in their sight, as when men go forth into exile. 5. Dig thou through the wall in their sight, and carry out thereby. 6. In their sight shalt thou bear it upon thy shoulder, and carry it forth in the darkness; thou shalt cover thy face, that thou see not the ground; for I have set thee for a sign unto the house of Israel.' 7. And I did so as I was commanded: I brought forth my stuff by day, as stuff for exile, and in the even I digged through the wall with my

יוֹמָם לְעֵינֵיהֶם וְאַתָּה תֵּצֵא
בָעֶרֶב לְעֵינֵיהֶם כְּמוֹצָאֵי
5 גוֹלָה׃ לְעֵינֵיהֶם חֲתָר־לְךָ
6 בַקִּיר וְהוֹצֵאתָ בּוֹ׃ לְעֵינֵיהֶם
עַל־כָּתֵף תִּשָּׂא בָּעֲלָטָה
תוֹצִיא פָּנֶיךָ תְכַסֶּה וְלֹא
תִרְאֶה אֶת־הָאָרֶץ כִּי־מוֹפֵת
7 נְתַתִּיךָ לְבֵית יִשְׂרָאֵל׃ וָאַעַשׂ
כֵּן כַּאֲשֶׁר צֻוֵּיתִי כֵּלַי הוֹצֵאתִי
כִּכְלֵי גוֹלָה יוֹמָם וּבָעֶרֶב
חָתַרְתִּי־לִי בַקִּיר בְּיָד

and thou shalt go forth thyself at even. After leaving the house by day with the articles he is taking with him, he is to make his escape in the evening when the chance of evading the enemy is better.

as when men go forth into exile. Ezekiel should assume a dejected demeanour like persons driven into exile (Kimchi). The phrase may indicate that he is to follow in his symbolical act the same procedure which is adopted by men faced with the grim reality.

5. *dig . . . through the wall.* The noun *kir* which is in the text generally means the wall of a house, while *chomah* usually denotes the wall of a city. Nevertheless some commentators hold that the city-wall is here indicated. This is improbable because of the thickness of such a wall as well as the false assumption that, on the alternative interpretation, Ezekiel had to carry the articles back into the house after having taken them out, and then pass through the hole in the wall with them. His departure from the house in this manner, and not through the door, merely indicates the idea of stealth. It furthermore has allusion to the attempted escape of Zedekiah (cf. 2 Kings xxv. 4).

carry out thereby. The Targum renders: 'go forth by it,' taking the causative form of the verb to mean, 'thou shalt bring thyself out' through the hole.

6. *shalt thou bear it.* Having left his house, he is to proceed to the spot where he secreted his baggage and carry it upon his shoulder.

the darkness. The Hebrew noun is not the usual *choshech* but *alatah* which, apart from verse 12, occurs again only in Gen. xv. 17. It signifies the darkness which follows a sunset.

cover thy face. This direction is variously explained. It may be a mark of humiliation. Others regard it as symbolical of Zedekiah's attempt to avoid recognition by throwing a cloak over his head. When connected with *that thou see not the ground*, 'the more probable meaning is that Zedekiah in his last journey was not even to see the land he was deserting' (Lofthouse).

a sign unto the house of Israel. All this was to be done to serve as a warning of what was to befall the nation.

7. *with my hand.* Digging with the hand, without using tools, indicates great

hand; I carried out in the darkness, and bore it upon my shoulder in their sight.

8. And in the morning came the word of the LORD unto me, saying: 9. 'Son of man, hath not the house of Israel, the rebellious house, said unto thee: What doest thou? 10. Say thou unto them: Thus saith the Lord GOD: Concerning the prince, even this burden, in Jerusalem, and all the house of Israel among whom they are, 11. say: I am your sign: like as I have done, so shall it be done unto them—they shall go into exile, into captivity. 12. And the prince that is among them shall bear upon his shoulder, and go forth in the darkness; they shall dig through the wall to carry out thereby; he shall cover his face, that he see not the ground with his eyes. 13. My net

בְּעֲלָטָה הוֹצֵאתִי עַל־כָּתֵף
8 נָשָׂאתִי לְעֵינֵיהֶם: וַיְהִי דְבַר־
יְהֹוָה אֵלַי בַּבֹּקֶר לֵאמֹר:
9 בֶּן־אָדָם הֲלֹא אָמְרוּ אֵלֶיךָ
בֵּית יִשְׂרָאֵל בֵּית הַמֶּרִי מָה
10 אַתָּה עֹשֶׂה: אֱמֹר אֲלֵיהֶם
כֹּה אָמַר אֲדֹנָי יֱהֹוִה הַנָּשִׂיא
הַמַּשָּׂא הַזֶּה בִּירוּשָׁלַם וְכָל־
בֵּית יִשְׂרָאֵל אֲשֶׁר־הֵמָּה
11 בְתוֹכָם: אֱמֹר אֲנִי מוֹפֶתְכֶם
כַּאֲשֶׁר עָשִׂיתִי כֵּן יֵעָשֶׂה לָהֶם
12 בַּגּוֹלָה בַשְּׁבִי יֵלֵכוּ: וְהַנָּשִׂיא
אֲשֶׁר־בְּתוֹכָם אֶל־כָּתֵף יִשָּׂא
בְּעֲלָטָה וְיֵצֵא בַּקִּיר יַחְתְּרוּ
לְהוֹצִיא בוֹ פָּנָיו יְכַסֶּה יַעַן
אֲשֶׁר לֹא־יִרְאֶה לָעַיִן הוּא
13 אֶת־הָאָרֶץ: וּפָרַשְׂתִּי אֶת־

v. 12. הל' קמוצה

haste, as though there was no time to look for a pick. It also symbolizes fear lest the sound of tools were heard (Kimchi). Davidson compares Isa. xxviii. 2, *with violence*, and gives it here the meaning 'by force.'

8. *in the morning.* Following on the night in which Ezekiel made his escape. We have to deduce that the symbolical act was carried out in detail.

9. *hath not . . . said unto thee.* In Hebrew the interrogative often expresses an affirmation. The meaning is, the people have surely asked thee.

10. *concerning the prince, even this burden, in Jerusalem.* The construction of the verse is obscure. *Prince* is a term for the

Judean king, and the Hebrew word for *burden* often denotes a prophetic message. It may have the double meaning here: the load which you carried is a prophecy relating to the king in Jerusalem. It forebodes what is to happen to him and the people of the house of Israel.

11. *into exile, into captivity.* Not only will they be driven from their homeland (*into exile*), but they will be forced to settle in a district chosen for them by their conquerors (*into captivity*).

12. *the prince.* An allusion to Zedekiah's flight and capture.

he shall cover his face, etc. See on verse 6.

65

also will I spread upon him, and he shall be taken in My snare; and I will bring him to Babylon to the land of the Chaldeans; yet shall he not see it, though he shall die there. 14. And I will disperse toward every wind all that are round about him to help him, and all his troops; and I will draw out the sword after them. 15. And they shall know that I am the LORD, when I shall scatter them among the nations, and disperse them in the countries. 16. But I will leave a few men of them from the sword, from the famine, and from the pestilence; that they may declare all their abominations among the nations whither they come; and they shall know that I am the LORD.'

17. Moreover the word of the LORD came to me, saying: 18. 'Son of man, eat thy bread with quaking,

רִשְׁתִּי עָלָיו וְנִתְפַּשׂ בִּמְצוּדָתִי
וְהֵבֵאתִי אֹתוֹ בָבֶלָה אֶרֶץ
כַּשְׂדִּים וְאוֹתָהּ לֹא־יִרְאֶה
14 וְשָׁם יָמוּת: וְכֹל אֲשֶׁר
סְבִיבֹתָיו עֶזְרֹה וְכָל־אֲגַפָּיו
אֱזָרֶה לְכָל־רוּחַ וְחֶרֶב
15 אָרִיק אַחֲרֵיהֶם: וְיָדְעוּ כִּי־
אֲנִי יְהֹוָה בַּהֲפִיצִי אוֹתָם בַּגּוֹיִם
וְזֵרִיתִי אוֹתָם בָּאֲרָצוֹת:
16 וְהוֹתַרְתִּי מֵהֶם אַנְשֵׁי מִסְפָּר
מֵחֶרֶב מֵרָעָב וּמִדָּבֶר לְמַעַן
יְסַפְּרוּ אֶת־כָּל־תּוֹעֲבוֹתֵיהֶם
בַּגּוֹיִם אֲשֶׁר־בָּאוּ שָׁם וְיָדְעוּ
17 כִּי־אֲנִי יְהֹוָה: וַיְהִי דְבַר־
18 יְהֹוָה אֵלַי לֵאמֹר: בֶּן־אָדָם
לַחְמְךָ בְּרַעַשׁ תֹּאכֵל וּמֵימֶיךָ

v. 14. עזרו ק'

---

13. *My net also will I spread upon him.* The king's intended flight from the doomed city will be frustrated by God. Rashi and Kimchi quote a legend that there was a subterranean passage from Zedekiah's palace to the plains of Jericho through which he attempted to escape. To thwart his plan, God caused a gazelle to run along the top of that passage pursued by Babylonian soldiers. When they reached the exit of the passage, they saw Zedekiah coming from it and so captured him.

yet shall he not see it. Zedekiah was blinded by Nebuchadnezzar at Riblah (cf. 2 Kings xxv. 7; Jer. xxxix. 7).

14. *all that are round about him.* His bodyguard as distinct from the general army.

15f. *they shall know that I am the LORD.* When the prophecies of doom are fulfilled, the remnant of Israel which is scattered among the nations will realize that God is not only the Creator, but also the Ruler of the universe, and that punishment of the wicked is an essential feature of His Sovereignty over mankind. This they will transmit to their conquerors, so that these will also learn the true nature of God (Kimchi).

17-20 THE SUFFERINGS OF JERUSALEM'S INHABITANTS

18. *eat thy bread with quaking.* Another command with symbolical meaning. Ezekiel is to partake of meagre rations of bread and water, to typify the conditions of a siege, and eat and drink in a state of fear and anxiety.

and drink thy water with trembling and with anxiety; 19. and say unto the people of the land: Thus saith the Lord God concerning the inhabitants of Jerusalem in the land of Israel: They shall eat their bread with anxiety, and drink their water with appalment, that her land may be desolate from all that is therein, because of the violence of all them that dwell therein. 20. And the cities that are inhabited shall be laid waste, and the land shall be desolate; and ye shall know that I am the LORD.'

21. And the word of the LORD came unto me, saying: 22. 'Son of man, what is that proverb that ye have in the land of Israel, saying: The days are prolonged, and every vision faileth? 23. Tell them therefore: Thus saith the Lord GOD: I will make this proverb to cease, and they shall no more use it as a proverb in Israel; but say unto

בְּרָגְזָה וּבִדְאָגָה תִּשְׁתֶּה׃
19 וְאָמַרְתָּ אֶל־־עַם־־הָאָרֶץ כֹּה־אָמַר אֲדֹנָי יֱהוִֹה לְיוֹשְׁבֵי יְרוּשָׁלִַם אֶל־־אַדְמַת יִשְׂרָאֵל לַחְמָם בִּדְאָגָה יֹאכֵלוּ וּמֵימֵיהֶם בְּשִׁמָּמוֹן יִשְׁתּוּ לְמַעַן תֵּשַׁם אַרְצָהּ מִמְּלֹאָהּ מֵחֲמַס
20 כָּל־הַיֹּשְׁבִים בָּהּ׃ וְהֶעָרִים הַנּוֹשָׁבוֹת תֶּחֱרַבְנָה וְהָאָרֶץ שְׁמָמָה תִהְיֶה וִידַעְתֶּם כִּי־
21 אֲנִי יְהוָה׃ וַיְהִי דְבַר־יְהוָה
22 אֵלַי לֵאמֹר׃ בֶּן־אָדָם מָה־ הַמָּשָׁל הַזֶּה לָכֶם עַל־אַדְמַת יִשְׂרָאֵל לֵאמֹר יַאַרְכוּ הַיָּמִים
23 וְאָבַד כָּל־חָזוֹן׃ לָכֵן אֱמֹר אֲלֵיהֶם כֹּה־אָמַר אֲדֹנָי יֱהוִֹה הִשְׁבַּתִּי אֶת־הַמָּשָׁל הַזֶּה וְלֹא־יִמְשְׁלוּ אֹתוֹ עוֹד בְּיִשְׂרָאֵל כִּי אִם־דַּבֵּר

19. *the people of the land.* viz. Ezekiel's fellow-exiles.

in the land of Israel. lit. 'to the soil of Israel.' The preposition *el* (to) has here the force of *al* (upon).

her land. i.e. Jerusalem's land, the country of which Jerusalem is the capital.

from all that is therein. lit. 'from its fulness'; it will be stripped of its possessions. The desolation of the land will be the cause of the people's anxiety and appalment.

21-28 A WARNING TO DOUBTERS OF THE PROPHECY

22. *proverb.* A saying current among the people which reflected their attitude of mind. For other instances in the Book, cf. xvi. 44, xviii. 2.

in the land of Israel. Although Ezekiel is in Babylon, he is to address himself to his kinsfolk in Judea.

the days are prolonged, and every vision faileth. A prophet comes with a communication from God predicting a

them: The days are at hand, and the word of every vision. 24. For there shall be no more any vain vision nor smooth divination within the house of Israel. 25. For I am the LORD; I will speak, what word soever it be that I shall speak, and it shall be performed; it shall be no more delayed; for in your days, O rebellious house, will I speak the word, and will perform it, saith the Lord GOD.'

26. Again the word of the LORD came to me, saying: 27. 'Son of man, behold, they of the house of Israel say: The vision that he seeth is for many days to come, and he prophesieth of times that are far off. 28. Therefore say unto them: Thus saith the Lord GOD: There shall none of My words be delayed any more, but the word which I shall speak shall be performed, saith the Lord GOD.'

אֲלֵיהֶם קָרְבוּ הַיָּמִים וּדְבַר
24 כָּל־חָזוֹן: כִּי לֹא יִהְיֶה עוֹד
כָּל־חֲזוֹן שָׁוְא וּמִקְסַם חָלָק
25 בְּתוֹךְ בֵּית יִשְׂרָאֵל: כִּי | אֲנִי
יְהוָה אֲדַבֵּר אֵת אֲשֶׁר אֲדַבֵּר
דָּבָר וְיֵעָשֶׂה לֹא תִמָּשֵׁךְ עוֹד
כִּי בִימֵיכֶם בֵּית הַמֶּרִי אֲדַבֵּר
דָּבָר וַעֲשִׂיתִיו נְאֻם אֲדֹנָי
26 יְהוִה: וַיְהִי דְבַר־יְהוָה אֵלַי
27 לֵאמֹר: בֶּן־אָדָם הִנֵּה בֵית־
יִשְׂרָאֵל אֹמְרִים הֶחָזוֹן אֲשֶׁר־
הוּא חֹזֶה לְיָמִים רַבִּים
וּלְעִתִּים רְחוֹקוֹת הוּא נִבָּא:
28 לָכֵן אֱמֹר אֲלֵיהֶם כֹּה אָמַר
אֲדֹנָי יְהוִה לֹא־תִמָּשֵׁךְ עוֹד
כָּל־דְּבָרַי אֲשֶׁר אֲדַבֵּר דָּבָר
וְיֵעָשֶׂה נְאֻם אֲדֹנָי יְהוִה:

---

national calamity. Time passes, but it does not happen. The proverb, accordingly, expresses carelessness among the people with regard to such forebodings.

23. *the days are at hand, and the word of every vision.* To prove the popular saying invalid, Ezekiel is to emphasize that the prophecy which he delivers, announcing the fall of the State with all its implications, will not be fulfilled in the distant future, but is very near at hand.

24. *vain vision . . . smooth divination.* Opposed to the prophets of God were false prophets who assured the people that all would be well with them and they need pay no attention to predictions of woe. Jeremiah, in particular, had to contend with such opponents (cf. Jer. viii. 11, xiv. 14, xxviii. 1ff.).

25. *I am the LORD; I will speak.* Or, 'for I the Lord will speak.' The subject is emphatic in the Hebrew. That which He speaks will assuredly come to pass by His will. In the past He deferred the execution of His threats to enable the people to avert them by their repentance. On the present occasion the judgment He decrees will be performed *in your days:* there will be no deferment.

26-28. This section repeats the thought of verses 21-25. The repetition is intended to emphasize that the predicted judgment is both absolute and imminent; it does not belong to the class of prophecies which are conditional upon the future conduct of the people.

13 CHAPTER XIII יג

1. And the word of the LORD came
unto me, saying: 2. 'Son of man,
prophesy against the prophets of
Israel that prophesy, and say thou
unto them that prophesy out of
their own heart: Hear ye the word
of the LORD: 3. Thus saith the Lord
GOD: Woe unto the vile prophets,
that follow their own spirit, and
things which they have not seen!
4. O Israel, thy prophets have been
like foxes in ruins. 5. Ye have not

1 וַיְהִי דְבַר־יְהֹוָה אֵלַי לֵאמֹר:
2 בֶּן־אָדָם הִנָּבֵא אֶל־נְבִיאֵי
יִשְׂרָאֵל הַנִּבָּאִים וְאָמַרְתָּ
לִנְבִיאֵי מִלִּבָּם שִׁמְעוּ דְּבַר־
3 יְהֹוָה: כֹּה אָמַר אֲדֹנָי יֱהֹוִה
הוֹי עַל־הַנְּבִיאִים הַנְּבָלִים
אֲשֶׁר הֹלְכִים אַחַר רוּחָם
4 וּלְבִלְתִּי רָאוּ: כְּשֻׁעָלִים
בָּחֳרָבוֹת נְבִיאֶיךָ יִשְׂרָאֵל הָיוּ:

CHAPTER XIII

CONDEMNATION OF FALSE PROPHETS AND PROPHETESSES

AFTER inveighing against the popular
illusions as to the safety and peace of the
country, Ezekiel denounces the persons
who are the originators of such un-
founded and misleading confidence.

1-7 HARMFULNESS OF THE FALSE PROPHETS

2. *prophets of Israel that prophesy.*
'There seems a kind of sarcasm in
prophets of Israel—those whom Israel
accepts and delights to regard as prophets
(Mic. ii. 11); and a similar sarcasm in
that prophesy. They prophesied and
that without limit: their mouths were
always full of *the LORD saith* (verse 6)'
(Davidson).

out of their own heart. Their messages
are not inspired by God but devised by
their own minds. Consequently, their
forecast of the future is nothing but
wishful thinking.

3. *vile prophets.* The Hebrew for *vile*
(*nabal*) denotes a person without percep-
tion of ethical and religious claims. He

says in his heart *there is no God* (Ps.
xiv. 1) Who judges the deeds of man.

things which they have not seen. They
are victims of self-deception.

4. *thy prophets.* They are not God's
messengers but the people's prophets
who attune their words to the desire of
their hearers.

foxes in ruins. The point of the comparison is not certain and is variously
explained. If a man enters through a
breach in a ruined building, the fox
lurking there flees through another
breach and does not make a stand against
him (Rashi). As foxes enter a vineyard
through ruined walls and destroy its
fruits, so the false prophets communicate
their falsehoods to the morally weak to
the detriment of the whole nation
(Kimchi). Possibly the meaning is that
foxes find a natural habitat among ruins,
and similarly among a people in process
of dissolution false prophets discover a
sphere of activity, because in an atmo-
sphere of insecurity there is eagerness to
listen to an optimistic speech. In this
way they intensify national danger and
make the approaching doom still more
certain.

69

gone up into the breaches, neither made up the hedge for the house of Israel, to stand in the battle in the day of the LORD. 6. They have seen vanity and lying divination, that say: The LORD saith; and the LORD hath not sent them, yet they hope that the word would be confirmed! 7. Have ye not seen a vain vision, and have ye not spoken a lying divination, whereas ye say: The LORD saith; albeit I have not spoken?

8. Therefore thus saith the Lord GOD: Because ye have spoken vanity, and seen lies, therefore, behold, I am against you, saith the Lord GOD. 9. And My hand shall be against the

5 לֹא עֲלִיתֶם בַּפְּרָצוֹת וַתִּגְדְּרוּ
גָדֵר עַל־בֵּית יִשְׂרָאֵל לַעֲמֹד
6 בַּמִּלְחָמָה בְּיוֹם יְהוָה: חָזוּ
שָׁוְא וְקֶסֶם כָּזָב הָאֹמְרִים
נְאֻם־יְהוָה וַיהוָה לֹא שְׁלָחָם
7 וְיִחֲלוּ לְקַיֵּם דָּבָר: הֲלוֹא
מַחֲזֵה־שָׁוְא חֲזִיתֶם וּמִקְסַם
כָּזָב אֲמַרְתֶּם וְאֹמְרִים נְאֻם־
8 יְהוָה וַאֲנִי לֹא דִבַּרְתִּי: לָכֵן
כֹּה אָמַר אֲדֹנָי יְהוִה יַעַן
דַּבֶּרְכֶם שָׁוְא וַחֲזִיתֶם כָּזָב
לָכֵן הִנְנִי אֲלֵיכֶם נְאֻם אֲדֹנָי
9 יְהוִה: וְהָיְתָה יָדִי אֶל־־

---

5. *ye have not gone up*, etc. If they had been true prophets, they would have understood that the need of the hour was to warn the people of the peril in which they stood and advise them what measures to adopt in order to avert it. This they had failed to do.

to stand in the battle in the day of the LORD. A day decreed by God is coming when the nation will have to defend the land against invasion. What have the false prophets done to prepare for this ordeal?

6. *they have seen vanity and lying divination.* Their visions, which they profess to have received from God, are the fancy of their deluded minds and their predictions about the future will prove to be lies.

yet they hope, etc. In fact they know nothing of what the future holds for the nation since they receive no enlightenment from God; all they do is to hope that their forecast will be confirmed by events.

7. *have ye not seen a vain vision.* Abrupt changes in person, the second to the third and vice versa, are common in the Biblical style. Their prognostications must prove false, since they are given in the name of God without His authority.

8-16 PUNISHMENT OF THE PEOPLE'S MISLEADERS

9. *My hand shall be against.* The punishment is described in three steps which form a climax. At present these prophets possess influence, they are counsellors and leaders; when Israel is again a nation upon his own land, they shall have no place in the council of the people. Now they occupy a high place in the roll of citizens and bear distinguished names; then their names shall not be written in the writing (i.e. the book or register-roll) of the house of Israel (cf. Isa. iv. 3; Ezra ii. 62). And finally, they shall not have a place in the land at all; Israel will return while they will perish. Jeremiah had already used

prophets that see vanity, and that
divine lies; they shall not be in the
council of My people, neither shall
they be written in the register of the
house of Israel, neither shall they
enter into the land of Israel; and ye
shall know that I am the Lord GOD.
10. Because, even because they have
led My people astray, saying: Peace,
and there is no peace; and when it
buildeth up a slight wall, behold,
they daub it with whited plaster;
11. say unto them that daub it with
whited plaster, that it shall fall;
there shall be an overflowing shower,
and ye, O great hailstones, shall fall,

הַנְּבִיאִים הַחֹזִים שָׁוְא
וְהַקֹּסְמִים כָּזָב בְּסוֹד עַמִּי
לֹא־יִהְיוּ וּבִכְתָב בֵּית־
יִשְׂרָאֵל לֹא יִכָּתֵבוּ וְאֶל־
אַדְמַת יִשְׂרָאֵל לֹא יָבֹאוּ
וִידַעְתֶּם כִּי־אֲנִי אֲדֹנָי יְהֹוִה:
10 יַעַן וּבְיַעַן הִטְעוּ אֶת־עַמִּי
לֵאמֹר שָׁלוֹם וְאֵין שָׁלוֹם וְהוּא
בֹּנֶה חַיִץ וְהִנָּם טָחִים אֹתוֹ
11 תָּפֵל: אֱמֹר אֶל־טָחֵי תָפֵל
וְיִפֹּל הָיָה | גֶּשֶׁם שׁוֹטֵף וְאַתֵּנָה
אַבְנֵי אֶלְגָּבִישׁ תִּפֹּלְנָה וְרוּחַ

v. 9. קמץ בסמוך

similar language in regard to Shemaiah,
a prophet who misled the exiles (cf.
Jer. xxix. 32)' (Davidson).

10. *because, even because.* The repetition
of the conjunction solemnly emphasizes
the offence and the impending judgment
of the false prophets (cf. xxxvi. 3; Lev.
xxvi. 43).

peace, and there is no peace. A reminiscence of Jer. vi. 14, viii. 11 (cf.
also Mic. iii. 5). The Hebrew noun
shalom denotes in such passages national
prosperity and security.

it buildeth up a slight wall. The word
chayits is chosen by Ezekiel because it
signifies a wall consisting of stones
heaped one upon another which are not
cemented together (it has this meaning in
the Mishnah, cf. Shebi. iii. 8), and
conjures up a very forceful metaphor.
Instead of giving the people sound
advice in a time of crisis, the false
prophets have created in them a spirit of
complacency and unwarranted security.
They have not built for them a wall
which will withstand the storm, but
something which will collapse at a touch
and leave them exposed.

whited plaster. Hebrew *taphel*, which
may in this context be a play on *tippol*
(it will fall). A covering of whitewash
conceals the unstable character of the
wall, and when the test comes, that will
be made evident. Of huts inhabited
by Arabs in Palestine, Thomson remarks:
"The mortar used is without lime,
and, when thoroughly saturated by
the rain, becomes as slippery as soap,
and thus the whole fabric tumbles into
a dismal ruin. Indeed, such frail houses
often fall suddenly during great storms,
and crush the inhabitants to death. It
was such facts as these, perhaps, that
suggested to Ezekiel the terms of that
terrible rebuke to the prophets of Israel.'

11. *and ye.* Hebrew *weattenah*, instead
of the usual *weatten*. The hailstones are
addressed as God's agent for the destruction of what the false prophets had
erected. Metsudath David and Malbim
construe the word as another form of
we-etnah, 'I will ordain (lit. give) that
great hailstones fall'; but the same form
occurs in verse 20 where it can only
mean 'ye.'

great hailstones. In the Hebrew, 'stones

and a stormy wind shall break forth,
12. and, lo, when the wall is fallen,
shall it not be said unto you: Where
is the daubing wherewith ye have
daubed it? 13. Therefore thus
saith the Lord GOD: I will even
cause a stormy wind to break forth
in My fury; and there shall be an
overflowing shower in Mine anger,
and great hailstones in fury to
consume it. 14. So will I break
down the wall that ye have daubed
with whited plaster, and bring it
down to the ground, so that the
foundation thereof shall be uncovered; and it shall fall, and ye shall
be consumed in the midst thereof;
and ye shall know that I am the
LORD. 15. Thus will I spend My
fury upon the wall, and upon them
that have daubed it with whited
plaster; and I will say unto you:
The wall is no more, neither they
that daubed it; 16. to wit, the
prophets of Israel that prophesy
concerning Jerusalem, and that see
visions of peace for her, and there is
no peace, saith the Lord GOD.

17. And thou, son of man, set thy
face against the daughters of thy

12 סְעָרוֹת תְּבַקֵּעַ: וְהִנֵּה נָפַל
הַקִּיר הֲלוֹא יֵאָמֵר אֲלֵיכֶם
13 אַיֵּה הַטִּיחַ אֲשֶׁר טַחְתֶּם: לָכֵן
כֹּה אָמַר אֲדֹנָי יְהֹוִה וּבִקַּעְתִּי
רוּחַ־סְעָרוֹת בַּחֲמָתִי וְגֶשֶׁם
שֹׁטֵף בְּאַפִּי יִהְיֶה וְאַבְנֵי
אֶלְגָּבִישׁ בְּחֵמָה לְכָלָה:
14 וְהָרַסְתִּי אֶת־הַקִּיר אֲשֶׁר־
טַחְתֶּם תָּפֵל וְהִגַּעְתִּיהוּ אֶל־
הָאָרֶץ וְנִגְלָה יְסֹדוֹ וְנָפְלָה
וּכְלִיתֶם בְּתוֹכָהּ וִידַעְתֶּם כִּי־
15 אֲנִי יְהֹוָה: וְכִלֵּיתִי אֶת־חֲמָתִי
בַּקִּיר וּבַטָּחִים אֹתוֹ תָּפֵל
וְאֹמַר לָכֶם אֵין הַקִּיר וְאֵין
16 הַטָּחִים אֹתוֹ: נְבִיאֵי יִשְׂרָאֵל
הַנִּבְּאִים אֶל־יְרוּשָׁלַ͏ִם
וְהַחֹזִים לָהּ חֲזוֹן שָׁלֹם וְאֵין
17 שָׁלֹם נְאֻם אֲדֹנָי יְהֹוִה: וְאַתָּה
בֶן־אָדָם שִׂים פָּנֶיךָ אֶל־בְּנוֹת

of *elgabish*'; again only in verse 13 and
xxxviii. 22. In Job xxviii. 18 *gabish*
occurs in the sense of *crystal*.

12. *where is the daubing*, etc. Where is
the assurance of safety from invasion
which you gave to us?

14. *ye shall be consumed in the midst
thereof*. The metaphor is dropped and
the false prophets are told what their
fate will be. They will be overwhelmed
in the disaster which befalls the people
they deluded.

16. *to wit.* There is nothing corresponding to this in the Hebrew. The verse,
of course, defines *they that daubed it*.
An alternative translation is: 'O prophets
of Israel that prophesy,' etc.

17-23 DENUNCIATION OF FALSE
PROPHETESSES

Just as true and false prophets were to be
found in Judea, so were also true and
false prophetesses. Ezekiel now con-
demns the women who, like their male
counterparts, were misleading the people.

people, that prophesy out of their own heart; and prophesy thou against them, 18. and say: Thus saith the Lord GOD: Woe to the women that sew cushions upon all elbows, and make pads for the head of persons of every stature to hunt souls! Will ye hunt the souls of My people, and save souls alive for yourselves? 19. And ye have profaned Me among My people for handfuls of barley and for crumbs of bread, to slay the souls that should not die, and to save the souls alive

עַמֵּךְ הַמִּתְנַבְּאוֹת מִלִּבְּהֶן
18 וְהִנָּבֵא עֲלֵיהֶן: וְאָמַרְתָּ כֹּה־
אָמַר | אֲדֹנָי יֱהֹוִה הוֹי
לִמְתַפְּרוֹת כְּסָתוֹת עַל | כָּל־
אַצִּילֵי יָדַי וְעֹשׂוֹת הַמִּסְפָּחוֹת
עַל־רֹאשׁ כָּל־קוֹמָה לְצוֹדֵד
נְפָשׁוֹת הַנְּפָשׁוֹת תְּצוֹדֵדְנָה
לְעַמִּי וּנְפָשׁוֹת לָכֶנָה תְחַיֶּינָה:
19 וַתְּחַלֶּלְנָה אֹתִי אֶל־עַמִּי
בְּשַׁעֲלֵי שְׂעֹרִים וּבִפְתוֹתֵי
לֶחֶם לְהָמִית נְפָשׁוֹת אֲשֶׁר
לֹא־תְמוּתֶנָה וּלְחַיּוֹת נְפָשׁוֹת

By their magical arts they pretended to be able to foretell the future; and what was worse, their oracles brought dismay to the righteous and assurance to the wicked.

18. *cushions upon all elbows . . . pads for the head of persons.* The details of their practices are obscure, although they must have been familiar to Ezekiel's contemporaries. *Kesathoth* means *cushions* in the Hebrew of the Mishnah, but here it probably signifies 'fillets, bands,' a form of charm. *Mispachoth*, translated *pads*, almost certainly denotes a kind of veil which, as stated here, corresponded to the height of the person and covered the whole body.

to hunt souls. 'The professed object of these superstitious practices is the capture and control of souls—more plainly to slay and to spare, i.e. to determine their fate by a solemn prediction of death or good fortune, as the case may be' (M'Fadyen).

will ye hunt the souls of My people. These practices demoralized the Judeans

and weakened their character, so contributing to their destruction.

and save souls alive for yourselves. The Hebrew may mean, 'and save your own souls (lives)'; i.e. they are actuated by the profit motive; all they are concerned about is receiving their fees.

19. *ye have profaned Me.* By inducing the people to give up their trust in God and put faith in lying divinations, the women caused His name to be profaned.

for handfuls of barley and for crumbs of bread. They accepted such trifling payment for their services. Others think that the barley and bread were employed by these women as materials in their magical art, and the translation should be: 'with handfuls of barley' etc. (so Kimchi). 'W. R. Smith quotes a reference made by Bar Bahlul (middle of the tenth century C.E.) to divination of this kind: "men who give oracles with barley bread or the stones of fruit"' (Cooke).

to slay the souls that should not die, etc. They foretold death for the righteous and promised life to the wicked.

that should not live, by your lying to My people that hearken unto lies. 20. Wherefore thus saith the Lord GOD: Behold, I am against your cushions, wherewith ye hunt the souls as birds, and I will tear them from your arms; and I will let the souls go, even the souls that ye hunt as birds. 21. Your pads also will I tear, and deliver My people out of your hand, and they shall be no more in your hand to be hunted; and ye shall know that I am the LORD. 22. Because with lies ye have cowed the heart of the righteous, when I have not grieved him; and strengthened the hands of the wicked, that he should not

אֲשֶׁר לֹא־תְחַיֶּינָה בְּכַזֶּבְכֶם
20 לְעַמִּי שֹׁמְעֵי כָזָב׃ לָכֵן כֹּה־
אָמַר ׀ אֲדֹנָי יְהוִה הִנְנִי אֶל־
כִּסְּתוֹתֵיכֶנָה אֲשֶׁר אַתֵּנָה
מְצֹדְדוֹת שָׁם אֶת־הַנְּפָשׁוֹת
לְפֹרְחוֹת וְקָרַעְתִּי אֹתָם מֵעַל
זְרוֹעֹתֵיכֶם וְשִׁלַּחְתִּי אֶת־
הַנְּפָשׁוֹת אֲשֶׁר אַתֶּם מְצֹדְדוֹת
אֶת־נְפָשִׁים לְפֹרְחוֹת׃
21 וְקָרַעְתִּי אֶת־מִסְפְּחֹתֵיכֶם
וְהִצַּלְתִּי אֶת־עַמִּי מִיֶּדְכֶן
וְלֹא־יִהְיוּ עוֹד בְּיֶדְכֶן
לִמְצֻדָה וִידַעְתֶּן כִּי־אֲנִי
22 יְהוָה׃ יַעַן הַכְאוֹת לֵב־צַדִּיק
שֶׁקֶר וַאֲנִי לֹא הִכְאַבְתִּיו
וּלְחַזֵּק יְדֵי רָשָׁע לְבִלְתִּי־שׁוּב

20. *as birds.* To be trapped. A.V., 'to make them fly,' follows the Jewish commentators: they frightened innocent people with the threat that their souls would leave their bodies. A.J. is preferable.

from your arms. The suffix *your* is masculine and similarly with *your pads* in the next verse, although these were attached to the clients of the false prophetesses (verse 18) who are addressed. The reference can hardly be to the clients, and possibly the women also used these objects in their incantations. The use of the masculine form when speaking of women is not uncommon in the Bible, and the feminine is resumed in *your hand* in verse 21.

I will let the souls go. God will demonstrate that His might prevails over magical spells.

even the souls. The plural of *nephesh* is everywhere else *nephashoth*, but here *nephashim* with the masculine termination. Rashi comments that it indicates the *men* intended to be the victims of magic. This is not plausible, and the Hebrew construction of the last clause of the verse presents difficulty.

22. *cowed the heart of the righteous, etc.* Their crime was twofold: they disheartened the righteous and seduced them from the right path, and they reassured the sinners and confirmed them in their wickedness.

return from his wicked way, that he be saved alive; 23. therefore ye shall no more see vanity, nor divine divinations; and I will deliver My people out of your hand; and ye shall know that I am the LORD.'

23 מִדַּרְכּוֹ הָרָע לְהַחֲיֹתוֹ: לָכֵן
שָׁוְא לֹא תֶחֱזֶינָה וְקֶסֶם לֹא־
תִקְסַמְנָה עוֹד וְהִצַּלְתִּי אֶת־
עַמִּי מִיֶּדְכֶן וִידַעְתֶּן כִּי־אֲנִי
יְהֹוָה:

14   CHAPTER XIV   יד

1. Then came certain of the elders of Israel unto me, and sat before me. 2. And the word of the LORD came unto me, saying: 3. 'Son of man, these men have set up their idols in their mind, and put the stumblingblock of their iniquity before their face; should I be

1 וַיָּבוֹא אֵלַי אֲנָשִׁים מִזִּקְנֵי
2 יִשְׂרָאֵל וַיֵּשְׁבוּ לְפָנָי: וַיְהִי
3 דְבַר־יְהֹוָה אֵלַי לֵאמֹר: בֶּן־
אָדָם הָאֲנָשִׁים הָאֵלֶּה הֶעֱלוּ
גִלּוּלֵיהֶם עַל־לִבָּם וּמִכְשׁוֹל
עֲוֺנָם נָתְנוּ נֹכַח פְּנֵיהֶם הַאִדָּרֹשׁ

v. 1. סבירין ויבואו

---

he be saved alive. lit. 'to save his life.' The sense is 'by promising him life' (A.V.).

23. *ye shall no more see vanity.* God will abolish their profession in so forceful a manner that even these women will have to acknowledge that He has done it.

CHAPTER XIV

AFTER dealing with the false prophets in the preceding chapter, Ezekiel now turns to the people whose encouragement and patronage are responsible for their activity. They respond to a popular demand and announce what the men who inquire of them want to hear. No genuine revelation from God is possible in such circumstances. All that a true prophet can bring to the people is an exhortation to abandon their evil ways.

1-11 PATRONS OF FALSE PROPHETS
                CONDEMNED

1. *then came.* The purpose of the visit is not explicitly stated and can only be inferred. If this section is connected with what precedes, the elders came to Ezekiel for an explanation of his fierce attack. But it would appear from verse 3 that they too were implicated. More probably, then, they wished to consult him on political questions which were giving them concern; and he is commanded by God to administer a rebuke to them.

3. *have set up their idols in their mind.* More lit. 'have brought up their idols to their hearts,' an idiom for 'have set their mind upon their idols.' The phrase does not imply that they were worshipping idols, but that their thoughts were influenced by pagan ideas, such as believing in magical spells and divination.

75

inquired of at all by them? 4. Therefore speak unto them, and say unto
them: Thus saith the Lord GOD:
Every man of the house of Israel
that setteth up his idols in his mind,
and putteth the stumblingblock of
his iniquity before his face, and
cometh to the prophet—I the LORD
will answer him that cometh according to the multitude of his
idols; 5. that I may take the house of
Israel in their own heart, because
they are all turned away from Me
through their idols.

6. Therefore say unto the house of
Israel: Thus saith the Lord GOD:
Return ye, and turn yourselves from
your idols; and turn away your faces

4 אִדָּרֵשׁ לָהֶם: לָכֵן דַּבֶּר־
אוֹתָם וְאָמַרְתָּ אֲלֵיהֶם כֹּה־
אָמַר ׀ אֲדֹנָי יֱהוִֹה אִישׁ אִישׁ
מִבֵּית יִשְׂרָאֵל אֲשֶׁר יַעֲלֶה
אֶת־גִּלּוּלָיו אֶל־לִבּוֹ
וּמִכְשׁוֹל עֲוֹנוֹ יָשִׂים נֹכַח פָּנָיו
וּבָא אֶל־הַנָּבִיא אֲנִי יְהֹוָה
נַעֲנֵיתִי לוֹ בָהּ בְּרֹב גִּלּוּלָיו:
5 לְמַעַן תְּפֹשׂ אֶת־בֵּית־
יִשְׂרָאֵל בְּלִבָּם אֲשֶׁר נָזֹרוּ
6 מֵעָלַי בְּגִלּוּלֵיהֶם כֻּלָּם: לָכֵן
אֱמֹר ׀ אֶל־בֵּית יִשְׂרָאֵל כֹּה
אָמַר אֲדֹנָי יֱהוִֹה שׁוּבוּ וְהָשִׁיבוּ
מֵעַל גִּלּוּלֵיכֶם וּמֵעַל כָּל־

v. 4. בא ק

This has been a *stumblingblock* to them
wilfully placed by themselves in their
way and leading them into *iniquity*.

should I be inquired. Better, 'shall I
allow Myself to be inquired of,' the
question expressing an emphatic negative. They have come to Ezekiel to seek
guidance in their perplexity, but I shall
certainly not give it to them.

4. *I the LORD will answer him.* The
Hebrew verb is in the Niphal form which
usually has a passive or reflexive force.
If it means 'answer' actively, this usage
occurs only here and in verse 7. Ehrlich
connects the verb with another root
anah, 'to be afflicted,' which is found in
the Niphal with the meaning 'humble
oneself' (cf. Exod. x. 3) and commonly in
Rabbinic Hebrew in the idiom 'I beg
pardon, I excuse myself.' He thinks that
it is so used here with ironical force:
God's reply to a person who inquires of

Him through the prophet is, 'I beg to
be excused in the case of one who comes
with a multitude of idols.'

5. *take . . . in their own heart.* Caught
in the evil inclinations of their heart,
they will experience the retribution which
overwhelms them. But this interpretation is doubtful. Kimchi renders: 'that
I may expose the house of Israel, even
what is in their heart.' Here, too,
Ehrlich has a suggestive explanation to
offer. He gives the verb *taphas* the
meaning 'to hold responsible' which he
also finds in Prov. xxx. 9 (cf. the note in
the Soncino ed.) as well as in Rabbinic
Hebrew. His translation would be: 'in
order to hold the house of Israel responsible for what is in their mind.'

6. *return ye.* The only message which
Ezekiel is able to convey to his inquirers
is a call to repentance by complete
abandonment of their pagan ideas.

from all your abominations. 7. For every one of the house of Israel, or of the strangers that sojourn in Israel, that separateth himself from Me, and taketh his idols into his heart, and putteth the stumbling-block of his iniquity before his face, and cometh to the prophet, that he inquire for him of Me—I the LORD will answer him by Myself, 8. and I will set My face against that man, and will make him a sign and a proverb, and I will cut him off from the midst of My people; and ye shall know that I am the LORD. 9. And when the prophet is enticed and speaketh a word, I the LORD have enticed that prophet, and I will stretch out My hand upon him, and will destroy him from the midst of My people Israel. 10. And they shall bear their iniquity; the iniquity

תוֹעֲבֹתֵיכֶם הָשִׁיבוּ פְנֵיכֶם:
7 כִּי אִישׁ אִישׁ מִבֵּית יִשְׂרָאֵל
וּמֵהַגֵּר אֲשֶׁר־יָגוּר בְּיִשְׂרָאֵל
וְיִנָּזֵר מֵאַחֲרַי וְיַעַל גִּלּוּלָיו
אֶל־לִבּוֹ וּמִכְשׁוֹל עֲוֹנוֹ יָשִׂים
נֹכַח פָּנָיו וּבָא אֶל־הַנָּבִיא
לִדְרָשׁ־לוֹ בִי אֲנִי יְהֹוָה
8 נַעֲנֶה־לוֹ בִי: וְנָתַתִּי פָנַי בָּאִישׁ
הַהוּא וַהֲשִׁמֹתִיהוּ לְאוֹת
וְלִמְשָׁלִים וְהִכְרַתִּיו מִתּוֹךְ
עַמִּי וִידַעְתֶּם כִּי־אֲנִי יְהֹוָה:
9 וְהַנָּבִיא כִי־יְפֻתֶּה וְדִבֶּר דָּבָר
אֲנִי יְהֹוָה פִּתֵּיתִי אֵת הַנָּבִיא
הַהוּא וְנָטִיתִי אֶת־יָדִי עָלָיו
וְהִשְׁמַדְתִּיו מִתּוֹךְ עַמִּי
10 יִשְׂרָאֵל: וְנָשְׂאוּ עֲוֹנָם כַּעֲוֹן

---

7. the strangers. Kimchi defines these as Babylonians who embraced the Jewish faith and joined the community of exiles. More probably when Nebuchadnezzar *carried away all Jerusalem* (2 Kings xxiv. 14), the population included residents who were *strangers*.

8. will make him a sign. A.J. adopts the reading *wahasimothihu* (so Targum, Rashi, Kimchi); R.V. 'will make him an astonishment for a sign' reads *wahashimothihu* (so Metsudath David). The former seems to be the better attested. The exemplary punishment of the sinful among the Israelites will become proverbial and act as a deterrent.

9. I the LORD have enticed that prophet. The meaning appears to be: if the prophet, entering into the "heart" of the

idolaters, the circle and direction of their thoughts, and the general spirit which animates them, gives them a prophetic oracle which coincides with the line of their thoughts, and thus helps to foster their delusions, that prophet himself has been seduced or enticed; and it is the Lord Who has enticed him. The passage has a resemblance to 1 Kings xxii. 23. There a lying spirit came forth from the Lord and entered into the prophets of Ahab and deceived them, so that they entered into the designs of the wicked king and gave an answer favourable to him. Here it is the Lord Himself Who entices the prophet. In both cases this enticement or deception was in punishment for previous sin' (Davidson).

10. they shall bear their iniquity. Both the inquirer and the false prophet are

of the prophet shall be even as the iniquity of him that inquireth; 11. that the house of Israel may go no more astray from Me, neither defile themselves any more with all their transgressions; but that they may be My people, and I may be their God, saith the Lord GOD.'

12. And the word of the LORD came unto me, saying: 13. 'Son of man, when a land sinneth against Me by trespassing grievously, and I stretch out My hand upon it, and break the staff of the bread thereof, and send famine upon it, and cut off from it man and beast; 14. though these three men, Noah, Daniel, and Job, were in it, they should deliver

הַדֹּרֵשׁ כַּעֲוֹן הַנָּבִיא יִהְיֶה׃

11 לְמַעַן לֹא־יִתְעוּ עוֹד בֵּית־ יִשְׂרָאֵל מֵאַחֲרַי וְלֹא־יִטַּמְּאוּ עוֹד בְּכָל־פִּשְׁעֵיהֶם וְהָיוּ־לִי לְעָם וַאֲנִי אֶהְיֶה לָהֶם לֵאלֹהִים נְאֻם אֲדֹנָי יְהוִֹה׃

12 וַיְהִי דְבַר־יְהוָֹה אֵלַי לֵאמֹר׃

13 בֶּן־אָדָם אֶרֶץ כִּי תֶחֱטָא־לִי לִמְעָל־מַעַל וְנָטִיתִי יָדִי עָלֶיהָ וְשָׁבַרְתִּי לָהּ מַטֵּה־ לָחֶם וְהִשְׁלַחְתִּי־בָהּ רָעָב וְהִכְרַתִּי מִמֶּנָּה אָדָם וּבְהֵמָה׃

14 וְהָיוּ שְׁלֹשֶׁת הָאֲנָשִׁים הָאֵלֶּה בְּתוֹכָהּ נֹחַ דֳּנִאֵל וְאִיּוֹב הֵמָּה

v. 14. דניאל ק׳

equally culpable and will suffer the same punishment (cf. Jer. xiv. 15f., xxvii. 15).

11. *that the house of Israel may go no more astray from Me.* The purpose of Divine judgment is not revenge but correction. It is intended to be a deterrent from evil and a medium of reformation.

12-23 THE RIGHTEOUS IN JERUSALEM CANNOT SAVE IT

The question suggests itself to Ezekiel, or may have been put to him, whether the presence of righteous men in Jerusalem may not spare it from destruction. The precedent of Sodom and Gomorrah, in which Abraham's plea on this ground was accepted by God (Gen. xviii. 23ff.), may have been in his mind. The doctrine preached both by Jeremiah and Ezekiel is that each person must suffer for his sins and none can make expiation for him.

13. *a land.* The hypothesis is stated in general terms with special application to the Land of Israel.

break the staff of the bread. See on iv. 16.

man and beast. Since animals are of service to man, they also will be affected by the punishment (Kimchi).

14. *these three men.* Noah, Daniel and Job are mentioned as men renowned for their piety who were saved by their righteousness while others perished in their wickedness. Noah and his family survived the universal destruction in the Flood. Daniel, who lived at the time when Temple and State fell, was elevated to high office in the Babylonian court because he was steadfast in his loyalty to God, whereas his Jewish contemporaries suffered death or humiliation. (Ezekiel refers to his wisdom in xxviii. 3.) Job was spared while his children met with fatal accidents. In none of these instances did their righteous

but their own souls by their righteousness, saith the Lord GOD.

15. If I cause evil beasts to pass through the land, and they bereave it, and it be desolate, so that no man may pass through because of the beasts; 16. though these three men were in it, as I live, saith the Lord GOD, they shall deliver neither sons nor daughters; they only shall be delivered, but the land shall be desolate. 17. Or if I bring a sword upon that land, and say: Let the sword go through the land, so that I cut off from it man and beast; 18. though these three men were in it, as I live, saith the Lord GOD, they shall deliver neither sons nor daughters, but they only shall be delivered themselves. 19. Or if I send a pestilence into that land, and pour out My fury upon it in blood, to cut off from it man and

בְּצִדְקָתָם יַצִּילוּ נַפְשָׁם נְאֻם
15 אֲדֹנָי יֱהֹוִה: לוּ־חַיָּה רָעָה
אַעֲבִיר בָּאָרֶץ וְשִׁכְּלָתָּה
וְהָיְתָה שְׁמָמָה מִבְּלִי עוֹבֵר
16 מִפְּנֵי הַחַיָּה: שְׁלֹשֶׁת הָאֲנָשִׁים
הָאֵלֶּה בְּתוֹכָהּ חַי־אָנִי נְאֻם
אֲדֹנָי יֱהֹוִה אִם־בָּנִים וְאִם־
בָּנוֹת יַצִּילוּ הֵמָּה לְבַדָּם יִנָּצֵלוּ
17 וְהָאָרֶץ תִּהְיֶה שְׁמָמָה: אוֹ
חֶרֶב אָבִיא עַל־הָאָרֶץ הַהִיא
וְאָמַרְתִּי חֶרֶב תַּעֲבֹר בָּאָרֶץ
וְהִכְרַתִּי מִמֶּנָּה אָדָם וּבְהֵמָה:
18 וּשְׁלֹשֶׁת הָאֲנָשִׁים הָאֵלֶּה
בְּתוֹכָהּ חַי־אָנִי נְאֻם אֲדֹנָי
יֱהֹוִה לֹא יַצִּילוּ בָּנִים וּבָנוֹת
19 כִּי הֵם לְבַדָּם יִנָּצֵלוּ: אוֹ דֶבֶר
אֲשַׁלַּח אֶל־הָאָרֶץ הַהִיא
וְשָׁפַכְתִּי חֲמָתִי עָלֶיהָ בְּדָם

v. 15. פתח באתנח v. 19. למדנחאי על

---

character protect the wicked from their fate, and even if all these three pious men lived at one time in a sinful land, they would only be able to save themselves. A similar argument is employed in Jer. xv. 1, *Though Moses and Samuel stood before Me, yet My mind could not be toward this people.* No deduction can be drawn from this verse about the date of the composition of the Books of Daniel and Job. Their fame was apparently traditional before the Books were written.

15. *if I cause evil beasts to pass through the land.* It is to be noted that the four forms of punishment which are enu-

merated correspond to those threatened in Lev. xxvi.

no man may pass through because of the beasts. No mention of such utter desolation is made in regard to the other three afflictions, because they are of such a character that they would not deter men of other countries from passing through the stricken land; but men would not venture into a district which was overrun by wild beasts.

16. *neither sons nor daughters.* Some explain as their own sons and daughters, others as children generally.

19. *in blood.* i.e. causing a high death

79

beast; 20. though Noah, Daniel, and Job, were in it, as I live, saith the Lord GOD, they shall deliver neither son nor daughter; they shall but deliver their own souls by their righteousness. 21. For thus saith the Lord GOD: How much more when I send My four sore judgments against Jerusalem, the sword, and the famine, and the evil beasts, and the pestilence, to cut off from it man and beast. 22. And, behold, though there be left a remnant therein that shall be brought forth, both sons and daughters; behold, when they come forth unto you, and ye see their way and their doings, then ye shall be comforted concerning the evil that I have brought upon Jerusalem, even concerning all that

לְהַכְרִית מִמֶּנָּה אָדָם וּבְהֵמָה:
20 וְנֹחַ דָּנִאֵל וְאִיּוֹב בְּתוֹכָהּ חַי־
אָנִי נְאֻם אֲדֹנָי יֱהֹוִה אִם־בֵּן
אִם־בַּת יַצִּילוּ הֵמָּה
21 בְּצִדְקָתָם יַצִּילוּ נַפְשָׁם: כִּי
כֹה אָמַר אֲדֹנָי יֱהֹוִה אַף כִּי־
אַרְבַּעַת שְׁפָטַי | הָרָעִים חֶרֶב
וְרָעָב וְחַיָּה רָעָה וָדֶבֶר
שִׁלַּחְתִּי אֶל־־יְרוּשָׁלִָם
לְהַכְרִית מִמֶּנָּה אָדָם וּבְהֵמָה:
22 וְהִנֵּה נוֹתְרָה־־בָּהּ פְּלֵטָה
הַמּוּצָאִים בָּנִים וּבָנוֹת הִנָּם
יוֹצְאִים אֲלֵיכֶם וּרְאִיתֶם אֶת־
דַּרְכָּם וְאֶת־עֲלִילוֹתָם
וְנִחַמְתֶּם עַל־הָרָעָה אֲשֶׁר
הֵבֵאתִי עַל־יְרוּשָׁלִָם אֵת

rate. For *blood* in the sense of 'death,' cf. Ps. xxx. 10.

20. *neither son nor daughter.* The singular occurs here as against the plural in verses 16 and 18. Malbim interprets as not one child out of several in a family, thus strengthening the point that is being made.

21. *how much more when I send My four sore judgments.* If when only one of the four punishments is inflicted upon a land the righteous are unable to save the wicked, how much truer will this be in the case of Jerusalem which is to suffer all four (cf. v. 17)!

22. *a remnant therein.* In apparent contradiction to what has been said, a part of the inhabitants of Jerusalem will

survive the catastrophe; but they will be allowed to live to serve a Divine purpose. 'If some of the wicked in Jerusalem escape it is with a special design, viz. that those spared should reveal their great wickedness to the earlier exiles among whom they shall come, and thus show how inevitable the destruction of the city was ' (Davidson).

that shall be brought forth. i.e. carried away as captives to Babylon.

unto you. The Jewish settlement in Babylon consisting of the captives brought there in 597 B.C.E.

then ye shall be comforted. The more recent arrivals will bring with them evidence of their wickedness which had been the cause of Jerusalem's downfall. From this it will be evident that what had

I have brought upon it; 23. and they
shall comfort you, when ye see their
way and their doings, and ye shall
know that I have not done without
cause all that I have done in it, saith
the Lord GOD.'

כָּל־אֲשֶׁר הֵבֵאתִי עָלֶיהָ׃

23 וְנִחֲמוּ אֶתְכֶם כִּי־תִרְאוּ אֶת־
דַּרְכָּם וְאֶת־עֲלִילוֹתָם
וִידַעְתֶּם כִּי לֹא חִנָּם עָשִׂיתִי
אֵת כָּל־אֲשֶׁר־עָשִׂיתִי בָהּ
נְאֻם אֲדֹנָי יְהֹוָה׃

| 15 | CHAPTER XV | טו |

1. And the word of the LORD came
unto me, saying: 2. 'Son of man,
what is the vine-tree more than any
tree, the vine-branch which grew up
among the trees of the forest?
3. Shall wood be taken thereof to
make any work? or will men take a

1 וַיְהִי דְבַר־יְהֹוָה אֵלַי לֵאמֹר׃
2 בֶּן־אָדָם מַה־יִּהְיֶה עֵץ־
הַגֶּפֶן מִכָּל־עֵץ הַזְּמוֹרָה אֲשֶׁר
3 הָיָה בַּעֲצֵי הַיָּעַר׃ הֲיֻקַּח מִמֶּנּוּ
עֵץ לַעֲשׂוֹת לִמְלָאכָה אִם־

נ״א לה   v. 23.

happened was the judgment of God, and
the older captives will take comfort in
that fact since it will teach them that by
loyalty to Him they would escape a
similar fate.

23. *they shall comfort you.* Not directly,
but as explained in the previous note.

CHAPTER XV

PARABLE OF THE VINE

IN this brief chapter, Ezekiel seeks to
justify the pending national catastrophe.
True, Israel is God's vine which He
hoped would bear precious fruit, but it
has degenerated into a wild vine and
become valueless. It does not bear fruit
nor has its thin wood any material value.
Like a log both ends of which are
consumed by fire and the middle section
charred, Israel is weakened by the loss
of the Ten Tribes and by the threat of
his hostile neighbours. The remaining
singed wood is only fit for fuel, and

similarly destruction is the people's fate.
The parable gives the answer to the
complacent thought that Israel, God's
elect, must *ipso facto* be imperishable.
The covenant relationship between Him
and the nation only remains valid if
Israel is loyal to Divine Sovereignty.
Treachery dissolves it.

2. *what is the vine-tree more than any tree.*
The interpretation of the Jewish commentators is: how inferior is the vine-
tree to any other tree! The tree spoken
of is not the fruit-bearing species, but a
wild vine which grows in the forest. It
is inferior to ordinary trees because it is
fruitless and its wood useless as timber.
Modern exegetes prefer to ignore the
ethnachta which divides the verse after
any tree and translate: 'What shall
become of the wood of the vine more
than the wood of the branch (i.e. any
branch) which is among the woods (of
trees) in the forest!'

3. *to make any work.* lit. 'to make for

pin of it to hang any vessel thereon?
4. Behold, it is cast into the fire for
fuel; the fire hath devoured both the
ends of it, and the midst of it is
singed; is it profitable for any work?
5. Behold, when it was whole, it was
meet for no work; how much less,
when the fire hath devoured it, and
it is singed, shall it yet be meet for
any work? 6. Therefore thus saith
the Lord GOD: As the vine-tree
among the trees of the forest, which
I have given to the fire for fuel, so
do I give the inhabitants of Jerusalem. 7. And I will set My face

יֻקְּחוּ מִמֶּנּוּ יָתֵד לִתְלוֹת עָלָיו

4 כָּל־כֶּלִי׃ הִנֵּה לָאֵשׁ נִתַּן
לְאָכְלָה אֵת שְׁנֵי קְצוֹתָיו
אָכְלָה הָאֵשׁ וְתוֹכוֹ נָחָר

5 הֲיִצְלַח לִמְלָאכָה׃ הִנֵּה
בִּהְיוֹתוֹ תָמִים לֹא יֵעָשֶׂה
לִמְלָאכָה אַף כִּי־אֵשׁ
אֲכָלַתְהוּ וַיֵּחָר וְנַעֲשָׂה עוֹד

6 לִמְלָאכָה׃ לָכֵן כֹּה אָמַר
אֲדֹנָי יֱהוִֹה כַּאֲשֶׁר עֵץ־הַגֶּפֶן
בְּעֵץ הַיַּעַר אֲשֶׁר־נְתַתִּיו לָאֵשׁ
לְאָכְלָה כֵּן נָתַתִּי אֶת־יֹשְׁבֵי

7 יְרוּשָׁלִָם׃ וְנָתַתִּי אֶת־פָּנַי

v. 5. קמץ בז"ק

work.' Nobody would think of using
the branch as material for making an
article of furniture.

or will men take a pin of it. The wood is
too thin and pliable even to fashion into
a peg.

4. it is cast into the fire for fuel. The wild
vine is only fit for fuel, and should a
part of the branch (which is probably
bent on account of its length) be thrown
into a fire and taken out after the ends
had been consumed, what is rescued
from the flames is quite useless. The
meaning of the parable is: Israel,
numerically smaller than other peoples,
is compared to a vine (Isa. v. 1ff.) which
has thinner branches than other trees.
By failing to produce the spiritual fruits
for which he is destined, Israel becomes
comparable to the wild vine and is
therefore only fit for the fire of Divine
punishment. This process of judgment
has already begun. Its ends are already
consumed in the destruction of the

Northern Kingdom and the Judean
captivity in 597 B.C.E. What remains,
Jerusalem, is like the singed wood from
which nothing can be made.

5. when it was whole, it was meet for no
work. When a whole branch is valueless,
how can a fragment of it be of use! So,
if the whole nation, consisting of the
twelve tribes, failed in its purpose, what
hope is there of the remnant in
Jerusalem?

6. as the vine-tree among the trees of the
forest. i.e. the wild vine which grows in
a forest and not in a vineyard. That is
now Jerusalem's position; it is no longer
surrounded by the tribes of Israel, but
by heathen peoples.

given. Better, 'appointed, destined'; and
so do I give should be 'so have I appointed,' or 'so will I destine,' the
prophetic perfect which vividly describes
an action as performed although its
fulfilment has yet to take place.

against them; out of the fire are they come forth, and the fire shall devour them; and ye shall know that I am the LORD, when I set My face against them. 8. And I will make the land desolate, because they have acted treacherously, saith the Lord GOD.'

בָּהֶם מֵהָאֵשׁ יָצָ֫אוּ וְהָאֵשׁ
תֹּֽאכְלֵם וִֽידַעְתֶּם כִּֽי־אֲנִי
יְהוָ֔ה בְּשׂוּמִי אֶת־פָּנַי בָּהֶם׃
8 וְנָתַתִּי אֶת־הָאָרֶץ שְׁמָמָה יַ֫עַן
מָ֫עֲלוּ מַ֫עַל נְאֻם אֲדֹנָי יְהוִֽה׃

16   CHAPTER XVI   **טז**

1. Again the word of the LORD came unto me, saying: 2. 'Son of man, cause Jerusalem to know her abominations, 3. and say: Thus saith

1 וַיְהִי דְבַר־יְהוָ֖ה אֵלַי לֵאמֹֽר׃
2 בֶּן־אָדָם הוֹדַע אֶת־יְרֽוּשָׁלַ֫͏ִם
3 אֶת־תּוֹעֲבֹתֶ֑יהָ וְאָמַרְתָּ כֹּֽה־

v. 7. קמץ בז"ק

7. *out of the fire are they come forth,* etc. Jerusalem passed through the fire of the earlier Babylonian invasion and came through it *singed* but not consumed. That is no proof that the city is inviolable; in the next fire it will be devoured by the flames.

ye shall know, etc. When this doom overtakes the city, the inhabitants will know that it has not happened by chance, but that it is the decree of God.

8. *they have acted treacherously.* The Hebrew is the same as that rendered *trespassing grievously* in xiv. 13. It denotes rebellion against God by the practice of idolatry.

CHAPTER XVI

MEDITATING upon the coming end of the kingdom, Ezekiel reviews the people's past history under the form of an allegory and shows how it inevitably leads up to the coming doom. The nation is represented as a female infant born in the open field and abandoned there immediately after birth. A benefactor (God), passing by, saves her life and cares for her until she grows to fair womanhood. He then marries her and

lavishes upon her many tokens of love; but she proves unfaithful to him. So has it been with Israel. His national birth took place in Egypt in the midst of oppression and servitude. God had compassion on the suffering community, sustained them in their affliction, delivered them from their persecutors and took them to be His people. But they abandoned Him for foreign gods and must suffer the fate of the adulteress. Nevertheless, the nation will not be destroyed. God's ancient covenant with Israel, broken by them, will be replaced by a new covenant of everlasting duration.

1-7 THE FOUNDLING SAVED AND
NURTURED TO WOMANHOOD

2. *cause Jerusalem to know her abominations.* By *Jerusalem* the population of Judea is intended. The Targum renders: 'reprove the inhabitants of Jerusalem and tell them their abominations.' According to an opinion expressed in the Mishnah (Meg. iv. 10), this chapter is not to be included among the prophetical readings in the service of the Synagogue. The reason, says Rabbinowitz, is 'because it contains a vehement denunciation of the apostasy and disloyalty of Israel.

the Lord God unto Jerusalem: Thine origin and thy nativity is of the land of the Canaanite; the Amorite was thy father, and thy mother was a Hittite. 4. And as for thy nativity, in the day thou wast born thy navel was not cut, neither wast thou washed in water for cleansing; thou wast not salted at all, nor swaddled at all. 5. No eye pitied thee, to do any of these unto thee, to have compassion upon thee; but thou wast cast out in the open

אָמַר אֲדֹנָי יֱהֹוִה לִירוּשָׁלַם
מְכֹרֹתַיִךְ וּמֹלְדֹתַיִךְ מֵאֶרֶץ
הַכְּנַעֲנִי אָבִיךְ הָאֱמֹרִי וְאִמֵּךְ
חִתִּית: וּמוֹלְדוֹתַיִךְ בְּיוֹם 4
הוּלֶּדֶת אוֹתָךְ לֹא־כָרַּת שָׁרֵּךְ
וּבְמַיִם לֹא־רֻחַצְתְּ לְמִשְׁעִי
וְהָמְלֵחַ לֹא הֻמְלַחַתְּ וְהָחְתֵּל
לֹא חֻתָּלְתְּ: לֹא־חָסָה עָלַיִךְ 5
עַיִן לַעֲשׂוֹת לָךְ אַחַת מֵאֵלֶּה
לְחֻמְלָה עָלָיִךְ וַתֻּשְׁלְכִי אֶל־

v. 4. דגש אחר שורק v. 4. ב' רשין דגושין

The Tosephta (iv. 34) tells of one who read this chapter in public before R. Eliezer, and the Rabbi angrily rebuked him with the words, "Go and make known the abomination of thy mother".'

3. *say.* Kimchi remarks that the command really means, 'put into writing,' because Ezekiel was in Babylon and the message was to be addressed to the inhabitants of Jerusalem.

thine origin . . . Canaanite. 'When Jerusalem's origin is said to be from the land of the Canaanite several references seem combined, e.g. the fact that Jerusalem was a Canaanite city; that Israel first became a family in Canaan (verse 4); and that having originated there its moral character corresponded to its Canaanite origin and had cleaved to it all through its history' (Davidson).

Amorite . . . Hittite. So again in verse 45. These were two of the principal nations which inhabited Canaan. Hence the whole country is described as *the land of the Amorite* (Amos ii. 10) or *the land of the Hittites* (Josh. i. 4).

4. *as for thy nativity.* The reference is to the land of Egypt which is regarded as

the birthplace of Israel as a people. Like a newborn infant who is neglected and deprived of all the attentions which are essential to survival, Israel began his national existence in a state of helpless slavery. Had it not been for God's compassion, Israel would have perished in Egypt.

for cleansing. The otherwise unknown Hebrew noun, *mish'i,* has been connected with the Assyrian root *misu,* 'to wash.'

thou wast not salted at all. It was an ancient custom to rub a child at birth with salt to harden and strengthen its body. In connection with childbirth Dr. Masterman describes present-day customs in Palestine: As soon as the navel is cut, the midwife rubs the child all over with salt, water and oil, and tightly swathes it in clothes for seven days; at the end of that time she removes the dirty clothes, washes the child and anoints it, and then wraps it up again for seven days—and so on till the fortieth day (*Palestine Exploration Fund Quarterly Statement,* 1918, pp. 118f., quoted by Cooke).

5. *to do any of these unto thee.* Not even one of the treatments applied to a child at birth was performed. In the Hebrew

field in the loathsomeness of thy
person, in the day that thou wast
born. 6. And when I passed by
thee, and saw thee wallowing in thy
blood, I said unto thee: In thy
blood, live; yea, I said unto thee:
in thy blood, live; 7. I cause thee to
increase, even as the growth of the
field. And thou didst increase and
grow up, and thou camest to
excellent beauty: thy breasts were
fashioned, and thy hair was grown;
yet thou wast naked and bare.
8. Now when I passed by thee, and

פְּנֵי הַשָּׂדֶה בְּגֹעַל נַפְשֵׁךְ בְּיוֹם
6 הֻלֶּדֶת אֹתָךְ: וָאֶעֱבֹר עָלַיִךְ
וָאֶרְאֵךְ מִתְבּוֹסֶסֶת בְּדָמָיִךְ
וָאֹמַר לָךְ בְּדָמַיִךְ חֲיִי וָאֹמַר
7 לָךְ בְּדָמַיִךְ חֲיִי: רְבָבָה
כְּצֶמַח הַשָּׂדֶה נְתַתִּיךְ וַתִּרְבִּי
וַתִּגְדְּלִי וַתָּבֹאִי בַּעֲדִי עֲדָיִים
שָׁדַיִם נָכֹנוּ וּשְׂעָרֵךְ צִמֵּחַ וְאַתְּ
8 עֵרֹם וְעֶרְיָה: וָאֶעֱבֹר עָלַיִךְ

the new-born child is described as
feminine, and in the ancient world and
much later female babies were commonly
exposed to death by neglect. That was
Israel's condition in Egypt. *No eye
pitied* them to bring the sufferers help,
and were it not for God's intervention
they would have perished.

in the loathsomeness of thy person. lit.
'in the loathing of thy soul,' i.e. in the
loathing of thee, which was evident in
the act of exposure.

6. *when I passed by thee.* As against all
others who looked with pitiless eyes upon
the babe left to die, God had compassion
on it and resolved that it should live.

wallowing in thy blood. The verb *bus*
means 'to trample,' and the form
employed here seems to signify 'kicking
about.' *In thy blood* describes the
unwashed state of the body and emphasizes the abhorrent appearance of the
infant, which adds to the mercy of God
in taking notice of it.

in thy blood, live. The literal interpretation is, although the child was so
repellent a sight, God decreed that it
should live. Homiletically, the phrase
has been understood as 'by (at the cost
of) thy blood, live.' The Midrash
(Pirkë d'R. Eliezer, xxix) explains the

repetition as an allusion to the blood of
circumcision and the blood of the paschal
lamb which the Israelites shed in Egypt
before their exodus and ensured their
redemption. The moral is that self-
sacrifice ensures life, a paradox which is
exemplified by Jewish history.

7. *I cause thee to increase.* Under God's
care the nation increased numerically
(cf. Exod. i. 7, 12).

thou camest to excellent beauty. The
growth of the nation is described
figuratively under the imagery of a girl
developing to maturity. *Excellent beauty*
is literally 'ornament of ornaments' and is
defined in what follows as the physical
attributes of a beautifully formed woman,
viz. a full bust and long hair.

yet thou wast naked and bare. The word
for *naked* (*erom*) need only mean in-
sufficiently clad (cf. Isa. xx. 2ff.), and the
same probably applies to *bare*. 'She
was only a poor Bedouin girl still; a
reference to the poverty of the desert
shepherds who found their way into
Egypt from time to time, and left it as
poor as they entered it' (Lofthouse).
The Jewish commentators interpret:
although Israel in Egypt was physically
developed, he was still spiritually and
morally immature.

looked upon thee, and, behold, thy
time was the time of love, I spread
My skirt over thee, and covered thy
nakedness; yea, I swore unto thee,
and entered into a covenant with
thee, saith the Lord GOD, and thou
becamest Mine. 9. Then washed I
thee with water; yea, I cleansed away
thy blood from thee, and I anointed
thee with oil. 10. I clothed thee
also with richly woven work, and
shod thee with sealskin, and I
wound fine linen about thy head,
and covered thee with silk. 11. I
decked thee also with ornaments,
and I put bracelets upon thy hands,

וָאֶרְאֵךְ וְהִנֵּה עִתֵּךְ עֵת דֹּדִים
וָאֶפְרֹשׂ כְּנָפִי עָלַיִךְ וָאֲכַסֶּה
עֶרְוָתֵךְ וָאֶשָּׁבַע לָךְ וָאָבוֹא
בִבְרִית אֹתָךְ נְאֻם אֲדֹנָי יֱהֹוִה
9 וַתִּהְיִי־לִי׃ וָאֶרְחָצֵךְ בַּמַּיִם
וָאֶשְׁטֹף דָּמַיִךְ מֵעָלָיִךְ וָאֲסֻכֵךְ
10 בַּשָּׁמֶן׃ וָאַלְבִּשֵׁךְ רִקְמָה
וָאֶנְעֲלֵךְ תָּחַשׁ וָאֶחְבְּשֵׁךְ בַּשֵּׁשׁ
11 וָאֲכַסֵּךְ מֶשִׁי׃ וָאֶעְדֵּךְ עֶדִי
וָאֶתְּנָה צְמִידִים עַל־יָדַיִךְ

8-14 GOD'S COVENANT WITH ISRAEL

The foundling, now grown to beautiful
womanhood, is espoused by her Rescuer.
The relationship between God and
Israel is frequently depicted by the
prophets under the metaphor of marriage.

8. *thy time was the time of love.* She
reached marriageable age. Kimchi interprets, this is an allusion to the vision
of the burning bush in which God
announced to Moses that the time was
come for Israel's redemption.

I spread My skirt over thee. A Biblical
idiom for marriage (cf. Ruth iii. 9).
God declared to Israel, *Ye shall be unto
me a kingdom of priests, and a holy nation*
(Exod. xix. 6).

covered thy nakedness. God provided
for Israel's needs.

I swore unto thee. The words, *Wherefore
say unto the children of Israel: I am the
LORD, and I will bring you out from
under the burdens of the Egyptians* (Exod.
vi. 6), are interpreted by the Rabbis
(Tanchuma, Waëra, 2) to imply an oath.

entered into a covenant with thee. Cf.
Exod. xxiv. 8.

9. *then washed I thee with water*, etc.
Descriptive of the purification of a bride
as a preparation for her marriage (cf.
Ruth iii. 3). This may be a symbolical
reference to the purification of the
Israelites before the revelation of the
Torah on mount Sinai (Exod. xix. 10).

10. *I clothed thee also with richly woven
work.* The Bridegroom gave lavish
presents of garments, etc. to His bride.
The language is, of course, figurative, but
Jewish tradition read historical facts into
some of the details. According to the
Targum, the allusion is to the costly
garments which the Israelites obtained
from the Egyptians at the time of the
exodus.

sealskin. One of the coverings of the
ark was made of this material (Exod.
xxv. 5).

silk. The Targum renders 'coloured
garments' and takes both this word and
fine linen (cf. Exod. xxxix. 27) as representing the garments which distinguished
Israel's priests.

11. *I put bracelets upon thy hands.* The
Targum understands it as emblematical
of the two tablets of stone on which the
Ten Commandments were engraven.

and a chain on thy neck. 12. And I put a ring upon thy nose, and earrings in thine ears, and a beautiful crown upon thy head. 13. Thus wast thou decked with gold and silver; and thy raiment was of fine linen, and silk, and richly woven work; thou didst eat fine flour, and honey, and oil; and thou didst wax exceeding beautiful, and thou wast meet for royal estate. 14. And thy renown went forth among the nations for thy beauty; for it was perfect, through My splendour which I had put upon thee, saith the Lord GOD.

15. But thou didst trust in thy beauty and play the harlot because of thy renown, and didst pour out thy

וְרָבִיד עַל־גְּרוֹנֵךְ : וָאֶתֵּן נֶזֶם 12
עַל־אַפֵּךְ וַעֲגִילִים עַל־–
אָזְנָיִךְ וַעֲטֶרֶת תִּפְאֶרֶת
בְּרֹאשֵׁךְ : וַתַּעְדִּי זָהָב וָכֶסֶף 13
וּמַלְבּוּשֵׁךְ שֵׁשׁ וָמֶשִׁי וְרִקְמָה
סֹלֶת וּדְבַשׁ וָשֶׁמֶן אָכָלְתְּי
וַתִּיפִי בִּמְאֹד מְאֹד וַתִּצְלְחִי
לִמְלוּכָה : וַיֵּצֵא לָךְ שֵׁם בַּגּוֹיִם 14
בְּיָפְיֵךְ כִּי | כָּלִיל הוּא בַּהֲדָרִי
אֲשֶׁר־שַׂמְתִּי עָלַיִךְ נְאֻם
אֲדֹנָי יֱהֹוִה : וַתִּבְטְחִי בְיָפְיֵךְ 15
וַתִּזְנִי עַל־שְׁמֵךְ וַתִּשְׁפְּכִי

v. 13. ' יתיר י' v. 13. יתיר י'

12. I put a ring upon thy nose. A jewel attached to the nostril. According to the Targum, this is an allusion to the ark in the Sanctuary; *earrings* represent the protecting cloud of Divine Glory in the wilderness, and *a beautiful crown upon thy head* is a reference to the presence of the guiding angel at the head of the Israelites during their journey through the wilderness.

13. fine flour, and honey, and oil. Her food was of the richest kind. 'Ezekiel does not mention wine, nor does he include wine among articles of sacrifice. Hebrews, like other oriental peoples, were vegetarians, except on rare occasions' (Lofthouse).

thou wast meet for royal estate. Understood by Kimchi as referring to the kingdom of David. Davidson translates 'thou didst attain to royal estate,' which he explains: 'It was Israel herself, personified as a woman, that attained to royalty, that is, to be an independent State among the States around, a queen among other queens.'

14. thy renown went forth among the nations for thy beauty. The growing power and prosperity of the nation is described in these terms. Perhaps there is special allusion to David of whom it was said, *The fame of David went out into all lands; and the LORD brought the fear of him upon all nations* (1 Chron. xiv. 17).

through My splendour which I had put upon thee. Whatever greatness was attained by the Israelite nation was not self-earned, but bestowed by its Protector.

15-34 ISRAEL'S INFIDELITY

Despite the many favours and boundless mercy shown to the foundling, culminating in the honour of 'marriage,' she proved grossly unfaithful to her covenant.

15. thou didst trust . . . renown. Aware of her loveliness and her renown as a beautiful woman, she felt that she need not be dependent upon her 'Husband,' since she would have many admirers who would lavish gifts upon her. Similarly Israel lost his sense of reliance upon God, and forsook His worship for the idolatry

harlotries on every one that passed by; his it was. 16. And thou didst take of thy garments, and didst make for thee high places decked with divers colours, and didst play the harlot upon them; the like things shall not come, neither shall it be so. 17. Thou didst also take thy fair jewels of My gold and of My silver, which I had given thee, and madest for thee images of men, and didst play the harlot with them; 18. and thou didst take thy richly woven garments and cover them, and didst set Mine oil and Mine incense before

אֶת־תַּזְנוּתַיִךְ עַל־כָּל־
16 עוֹבֵר לוֹ־יֶהִי: וַתִּקְחִי
מִבְּגָדַיִךְ וַתַּעֲשִׂי־לָךְ בָּמוֹת
טְלֻאוֹת וַתִּזְנִי עֲלֵיהֶם לֹא
17 בָאוֹת וְלֹא יִהְיֶה: וַתִּקְחִי כְּלֵי
תִפְאַרְתֵּךְ מִזְּהָבִי וּמִכַּסְפִּי
אֲשֶׁר נָתַתִּי לָךְ וַתַּעֲשִׂי־לָךְ
18 צַלְמֵי זָכָר וַתִּזְנִי־בָם: וַתִּקְחִי
אֶת־בִּגְדֵי רִקְמָתֵךְ וַתְּכַסִּים
וְשַׁמְנִי וּקְטָרְתִּי נָתַתִּ לִפְנֵיהֶם:

v. 18. יתיר

of his neighbours' gods in the belief that these would assure him success. Ehrlich, ignoring the Hebrew accentuation, construes: 'but thou didst trust in thy beauty and play the harlot, (and thou didst trust) in thy renown and didst pour out,' etc.

on every one that passed by. Her lapses were not casual but persistent. She behaved like a harlot who solicited the passers-by (cf. Gen. xxxviii. 14f.).

his it was. Referring to her harlotry, i.e. she readily responded to any man who wanted her (Rashi). Kimchi explains the phrase to mean, her longing was for any man who came her way. The Hebrew is literally 'to him let it be'; the phrase gives the woman's actual words when she sees a man who arouses her desire. The verse graphically describes how prone Israel was to be attracted by any form of idolatry which he chanced to encounter.

16. *didst make for thee high places decked with divers colours.* The garments given to her by her 'Husband' were used by the adulteress to lure her lovers. The reference is to garments of various colours which she piled up for her harlotries, and so suggestive of the *bamah* used for idolatrous worship (see on vi. 3). In this allegory the prophet

alludes to the numerous *high places* which Israel had built for idol-worship from materials bestowed upon him by God (Kimchi). Davidson thinks that the garments were converted into tents which were associated with idolatry (cf. 1 Kings xiii. 32; 2 Kings xvii. 29, xxiii. 7).

the like things shall not come, neither shall it be so. The Hebrew is difficult, being literally 'they (feminine) are not coming and it (masculine) will not be.' The words are evidently an expression of disgust: such lewdness is without parallel.

17. *of My gold and of My silver, which I had given thee.* Cf. (I) *multiplied unto her silver and gold, which they used for Baal* (Hos. ii. 10).

images of men. Following the metaphor of the adulterous wife, the prophet speaks of the images she worships as *men.* It may be that they had human form.

18. *cover them.* viz. the images. The heathens used to dress up their idols (cf. Jer. x. 9).

didst set Mine oil and Mine incense before them. The rich gifts which God bestowed on Israel were used as offerings to idols.

them. 19. My bread also which I gave thee, fine flour, and oil, and honey, wherewith I fed thee, thou didst even set it before them for a sweet savour, and thus it was; saith the Lord GOD. 20. Moreover thou hast taken thy sons and thy daughters, whom thou hast borne unto Me, and these hast thou sacrificed unto them to be devoured. Were thy harlotries a small matter, 21. that thou hast slain My children, and delivered them up, in setting them apart unto them? 22. And in all thine abominations and thy harlotries thou hast not remembered the days of thy youth, when thou

19 וְלַחְמִי אֲשֶׁר־נָתַתִּי לָךְ סֹלֶת
וְשֶׁמֶן וּדְבַשׁ הֶאֱכַלְתִּיךְ
וּנְתַתִּיהוּ לִפְנֵיהֶם לְרֵיחַ נִיחֹחַ
20 וַיְהִי נְאֻם אֲדֹנָי יֱהֹוִה: וַתִּקְחִי
אֶת־בָּנַיִךְ וְאֶת־בְּנוֹתַיִךְ אֲשֶׁר
יָלַדְתְּ לִי וַתִּזְבָּחִים לָהֶם
לֶאֱכוֹל הַמְעַט מִתַּזְנֻתֵךְ:
21 וַתִּשְׁחֲטִי אֶת־בָּנַי וַתִּתְּנִים
22 בְּהַעֲבִיר אוֹתָם לָהֶם: וְאֵת
כָּל־תּוֹעֲבֹתַיִךְ וְתַזְנֻתַיִךְ לֹא
זָכַרְתִּ אֶת־יְמֵי נְעוּרַיִךְ

v. 20. מתזנותיך ק׳   v. 22. יתירי׳

19. *honey.* Disallowed as part of an offering to God (Lev. ii. 11). 'It was one of the most familiar products of Palestine, and was probably used in idolatrous rites; it was also offered to the gods of Babylonia, and occurred in Athenian ritual' (Lofthouse).

thus it was; saith the Lord GOD. All this really happened and cannot be denied, since God testifies to its truth.

20. *whom thou hast borne unto Me.* By entering into a covenant with God, Israel had been elevated to the rank of 'the children of God' (cf. *Ye are the children of the LORD your God,* Deut. xiv. 1). These children, who were to be reared as His loyal servants, were slaughtered and afterwards burnt by their parents as sacrifices to Molech (Kimchi). The barbarous rite of child sacrifice seems to have been rife among the Canaanites and other eastern peoples, as is evident from Lev. xviii. 21, 24 and Deut. xviii. 9f. In spite of repeated warnings against this practice, it was occasionally resorted to by Israelites. Ahaz, king of Judah, is stated to have passed his son through the fire (2 Kings xvi. 3). He

was probably the first to introduce the hideous practice in Israel. Later, Manasseh also sacrificed his son to Molech (2 Kings xxi. 6). That the rite was observed is evident from the denunciations of the prophets (cf. Isa. lvii. 5; Jer. vii. 31, xix. 5).

unto them. viz. the *images of men* spoken of in verse 17.

to be devoured. In the fire of Molech worship.

21. *that thou hast slain My children.* This is to be connected with the concluding clause of the preceding verse *were thy harlotries a small matter.* Not satisfied with the evil of worshipping pagan gods, Israel went to the extreme of child sacrifice. From this verse it may be deduced that the victim of the Molech cult was, like animal sacrifices, first slaughtered and then burnt.

in setting them apart. Or, as A.V. and R.V., 'in causing them to pass (through the fire).'

22. *thou hast not remembered,* etc. This was the cause of the behaviour which is so strongly censured. Were Israel mind-

wast naked and bare, and wast wallowing in thy blood.

23. And it came to pass after all thy wickedness—woe, woe unto thee! saith the Lord GOD—24. that thou hast built unto thee an eminent place, and hast made thee a lofty place in every street. 25. Thou hast built thy lofty place at every head of the way, and hast made thy beauty an abomination, and hast opened thy feet to every one that passed by, and multiplied thy harlotries. 26. Thou hast also played the harlot with the Egyptians, thy neighbours, great of flesh; and hast multiplied thy

בְּהְיוֹתֵךְ עֵירֹם וְעֶרְיָה

23 מִתְבּוֹסֶסֶת בְּדָמֵךְ הָיִית: וַיְהִי
אַחֲרֵי כָּל־רָעָתֵךְ אוֹי אוֹי
24 לָךְ נְאֻם אֲדֹנָי יֱהֹוִה: וַתִּבְנִי־
לָךְ גֶּב וַתַּעֲשִׂי־לָךְ רָמָה
25 בְּכָל־רְחוֹב: אֶל־כָּל־רֹאשׁ
דֶּרֶךְ בָּנִית רָמָתֵךְ וַתְּתַעֲבִי
אֶת־יָפְיֵךְ וַתְּפַשְּׂקִי אֶת־
רַגְלַיִךְ לְכָל־עוֹבֵר וַתַּרְבִּי
26 אֶת־תַּזְנוּתֵךְ: וַתִּזְנִי אֶל־בְּנֵי־
מִצְרַיִם שְׁכֵנַיִךְ גִּדְלֵי בָשָׂר

v. 25. תזנותיך ק'

---

ful of his origins and the part God played therein, he could not be guilty of his infidelities. 'The insertion of such an appeal at this point is surely a touch of genius' (Lofthouse).

23. *and it came to pass after all thy wickedness,* etc. According to this rendering of A.J. (so A.V. and R.V.), the opening clause of the verse is to be connected with verse 24, the concluding clause being in parenthesis. Some modern commentators rightly point out that a parenthesis of this kind is unusual in Hebrew. Kimchi and other Jewish exegetes interpret: 'and so it was also after all thy wickedness,' i.e. thou wert naked and bare in the days of thy youth (verse 22) and thou art again in the same state now as a result of thy wickedness. This disconnects the first clause of verse 23 from verse 24. The prophet then proceeds to bewail Israel's tragedy: *Woe, woe unto thee,* thy disaster is grievous, since thou hast lost so much through thy misdeeds. The Targum explains the repeated *woe* as: woe unto thee because of thy sinfulness and woe unto thee because thou hast not repented of thy sin.

24. *an eminent place.* Perhaps an elevated platform on which an idolatrous image was set.

25. *at every head of the way.* i.e. at every cross-road where the idol would be conspicuous.

hast made thy beauty an abomination. Thou hast put thy beauty to an abominable use. Instead of its being for the delectation of thy 'Husband,' thou hast prostituted it.

26. *played the harlot with the Egyptians.* The idolatries of Israel were not confined to aping the religious rites of their Canaanite neighbours. By making alliances with foreign powers, they came also under the influence of their ideas and customs. Here Ezekiel refers to alliances with Egypt, Assyria (verse 28) and Chaldea (verse 29). These were also condemned under the allegory of a harlot by Hosea (ii. 4), Isaiah (lvii. 7ff.) and Jeremiah (ii. 18f.). The alliance with Egypt which the prophet has in mind may be that made by Solomon (1 Kings iii. 1).

great of flesh. An expression denoting excessive sensuality. Such was a charac-

harlotry, to provoke Me. 27. Behold, therefore I have stretched out My hand over thee, and have diminished thine allowance, and delivered thee unto the will of them that hate thee, the daughters of the Philistines, that are ashamed of thy lewd way. 28. Thou hast played the harlot also with the Assyrians, without having enough; yea, thou hast played the harlot with them, and yet thou wast not satisfied. 29. Thou hast moreover multiplied thy harlotry with the land of traffic, even with Chaldea; and yet thou didst not have enough herewith. 30. How

וָאֵט אֶת־חֻקֵּךְ
27 לְהַכְעִיסֵנִי: וְהִנֵּה נָטִיתִי יָדִי
עָלַיִךְ וָאֶגְרַע חֻקֵּךְ וָאֶתְּנֵךְ
בְּנֶפֶשׁ שֹׂנְאֹתַיִךְ בְּנוֹת פְּלִשְׁתִּים
הַנִּכְלָמוֹת מִדַּרְכֵּךְ זִמָּה:
28 וַתִּזְנִי אֶל־בְּנֵי אַשּׁוּר מִבִּלְתִּי
שָׂבְעָתֵךְ וַתִּזְנִים וְגַם לֹא
29 שָׂבָעַתְּ: וַתַּרְבִּי אֶת־תַּזְנוּתֵךְ
אֶל־אֶרֶץ כְּנַעַן כַּשְׂדִּימָה
30 וְגַם־בְּזֹאת לֹא שָׂבָעַתְּ: מָה

teristic feature of Egypt (cf. xxiii. 20). Israel's alliance with Egypt and adoption of its obscene idolatries mark the climax of his degeneration.

to provoke Me. This emphasizes the seriousness of the offence. The tendency to worship so many foreign gods was not so much prompted by a desire to satisfy their base instincts as to provoke and defy the true God.

27. *I have stretched out My hand over thee.* To inflict punishment for the acts of infidelity.

have diminished thine allowance. A betrayed husband punishes his wife by withdrawing or reducing her maintenance (cf. Hos. ii. 11). The language here is figurative of the loss of territory to the Philistines in the time of king Ahaz; cf. 2 Chron. xxviii. 18 (Malbim). Cooke suggests that the reference may be 'to what happened in 701 B.C.E., at the time of the Assyrian invasion, as Sennacherib records it: "his (Hezekiah's) cities which I have plundered I separated from his land, and gave them to Mitinti, king of Ashdod, Padi, king of Ekron, and Silbel, king of Gaza, and diminished his land".'

delivered thee unto the will of them that hate thee. The Philistines were the

arch-enemies of the people of Israel and now satisfied their desire for revenge.

daughters. The Targum translates 'cities' and it is so generally understood.

that are ashamed of thy lewd way. Israel's conduct was so disgraceful that even their enemies, the Philistines, were ashamed of them. The language is ironical.

28. *without having enough.* Not satisfied with a political flirtation with Egypt, Israel also ingratiated himself with Assyria to secure the safety of his kingdom. Even this was not enough for him. He also turned to Chaldea—anywhere in fact, but not to God.

29. *the land of traffic.* lit. 'the land of Canaan.' The word *Canaan* came to mean 'merchant' because the Canaanites, and in particular the Phoenicians, were renowned as traders (cf. Zech. xiv. 21 where *trafficker* is literally Canaanite).

even with Chaldea. This country was at the time an important commercial centre (cf. xvii. 4).

30. *how weak is thy heart.* i.e. how degenerate, morally weak. The feminine form of the noun for *heart*, which occurs nowhere else, is used here to emphasize the woman's debased character (Kimchi).

weak is thy heart, saith the Lord
God, seeing thou doest all these
things, the work of a wanton harlot;
31. in that thou buildest thine
eminent place in the head of every
way, and makest thy lofty place in
every street; and hast not been as a
harlot that enhanceth her hire.
32. Thou wife that committest
adultery, that takest strangers instead of thy husband—33. to all
harlots gifts are given; but thou hast
given thy gifts to all thy lovers, and
hast bribed them to come unto thee
from every side in thy harlotries.
34. And the contrary is in thee from
other women, in that thou didst
solicit to harlotry, and wast not
solicited; and in that thou givest
hire, and no hire is given unto thee,
thus thou art contrary.

35. Wherefore, O harlot, hear the
word of the Lord! 36. Thus saith

אֲמֻלָה לִבָּתֵךְ נְאֻם אֲדֹנָי יְהוִֹה
בַּעֲשׂוֹתֵךְ אֶת־כָּל־אֵלֶּה
מַעֲשֵׂה אִשָּׁה זוֹנָה שַׁלָּטֶת:
31 בִּבְנוֹתַיִךְ גַּבֵּךְ בְּרֹאשׁ כָּל־
דֶּרֶךְ וְרָמָתֵךְ עָשִׂיתִי בְּכָל־
רְחֹוב וְלֹא־הָיִיתִי כַּזּוֹנָה
32 לְקַלֵּס אֶתְנָן: הָאִשָּׁה הַמְּנָאָפֶת
תַּחַת אִישָׁהּ תִּקַּח אֶת־זָרִים:
33 לְכָל־זֹנוֹת יִתְּנוּ־נֵדֶה וְאַתְּ
נָתַתְּ אֶת־נְדָנַיִךְ לְכָל־
מְאַהֲבַיִךְ וַתִּשְׁחֳדִי אוֹתָם
לָבוֹא אֵלַיִךְ מִסָּבִיב
34 בְּתַזְנוּתָיִךְ: וַיְהִי־בָךְ הֵפֶךְ
מִן־הַנָּשִׁים בְּתַזְנוּתַיִךְ וְאַחֲרַיִךְ
לֹא זוּנָּה וּבְתִתֵּךְ אֶתְנָן וְאֶתְנַן
לֹא־נִתַּן־לָךְ וַתְּהִי לְהֶפֶךְ:
35 לָכֵן זוֹנָה שִׁמְעִי דְבַר־יְהוִֹה:

v. 31. יתיר י׳.   v. 31. יתיר י׳   v. 34. הב׳ בדגש   v. 34. הב׳ בפתח

a wanton harlot. lit. 'domineering,'
unrestrained by any moral principle.
31. *that enhanceth her hire.* Kimchi renders: 'that scoffeth at her hire,' i.e. the ordinary harlot scorns the payment offered to
her and asks for more. The Israelite nation,
on the other hand, prostitutes herself not
for gain but to indulge in unbridled lust.
32. *instead of thy husband.* Better,
'under thy husband,' i.e. while married
(cf. for this idiom, Num. v. 19).

33. *thou hast given thy gifts to all thy
lovers.* From the wealth which God has
bestowed on the nation, tribute was paid
to neighbouring nations to obtain their
goodwill.

34. *in that thou didst solicit to harlotry,
and wast not solicited.* Israel eagerly
sought alliances with his neighbours,
even bribing them, but they did not seek
an alliance with him. The same point
is made by other prophets. Hosea says
bitingly, *Ephraim hath hired lovers*
(viii. 9), and Jeremiah makes Israel
declare, *I have loved strangers, and after
them will I go* (ii. 25).

35-43 PUNISHMENT OF THE UNFAITHFUL PEOPLE

35. *O harlot.* 'All the scorn of the
previous section is gathered up into the
insulting appellative' (Lofthouse).

the Lord God: Because thy filthiness was poured out, and thy nakedness uncovered through thy harlotries with thy lovers; and because of all the idols of thy abominations, and for the blood of thy children, that thou didst give unto them; 37. therefore, behold, I will gather all thy lovers, unto whom thou hast been pleasant, and all them that thou hast loved, with all them that thou hast hated; I will even gather them against thee from every side, and will uncover thy nakedness unto them, that they may see all thy nakedness. 38. And I will judge thee, as women that break wedlock and shed blood are judged; and I will bring upon thee the blood of fury and jealousy. 39. I will also give thee into their hand, and they shall throw down thine eminent

36 כֹּה־אָמַ֞ר אֲדֹנָ֣י יֱהֹוִ֗ה יַ֚עַן הִשָּׁפֵ֣ךְ נְחֻשְׁתֵּ֗ךְ וַתִּגָּלֶ֤ה עֶרְוָתֵךְ֙ בְּתַזְנוּתַ֖יִךְ עַל־מְאַהֲבָ֑יִךְ וְעַ֤ל כָּל־גִּלּוּלֵי֙ תוֹעֲבוֹתַ֔יִךְ וְכִדְמֵ֣י 37 בָנַ֔יִךְ אֲשֶׁ֥ר נָתַ֖תְּ לָהֶֽם: לָכֵ֗ן הִנְנִ֤י מְקַבֵּץ֙ אֶת־כָּל־מְאַהֲבַ֙יִךְ֙ אֲשֶׁ֣ר עָרַ֣בְתְּ עֲלֵיהֶ֔ם וְאֵת֙ כָּל־אֲשֶׁ֣ר אָהַ֔בְתְּ עַ֖ל כָּל־אֲשֶׁ֣ר שָׂנֵ֑את וְקִבַּצְתִּ֙י אֹתָ֤ם עָלַ֙יִךְ֙ מִסָּבִ֔יב וְגִלֵּיתִ֤י עֶרְוָתֵךְ֙ אֲלֵהֶ֔ם וְרָא֖וּ אֶת־ 38 כָּל־עֶרְוָתֵֽךְ: וּשְׁפַטְתִּ֔יךְ מִשְׁפְּטֵ֖י נֹֽאֲפ֣וֹת וְשֹׁפְכֹ֣ת דָּ֑ם וּנְתַתִּ֕יךְ דַּ֖ם חֵמָ֥ה וְקִנְאָֽה: 39 וְנָתַתִּ֨י אֹתָ֜ךְ בְּיָדָ֗ם וְהָרְס֤וּ גַבֵּךְ֙

---

36. *thy filthiness was poured out.* This rendering follows the Targum and other Jewish authorities. The verb is used in a similar context in verse 15 and xxiii. 8, but the meaning of the noun, *nechosheth,* is uncertain. It usually denotes 'copper'; and Geiger suggested that here it signifies much the same as the parallel *nakedness,* comparing its meaning in the Mishnah, 'the copper rim of a stove.'

that thou didst give unto them. As sacrifices to the pagan gods.

37. *all thy lovers.* Figurative of the nations with whom alliances had been made (cf. Hos. ii. 9).

that thou hast hated. 'Either Philistines and Edomites, with whom no alliances had been made, or, as the expression implies, the lovers of whom Judah had

become weary and had grown to loathe; the word has this meaning in Prov. v. 12' (Lofthouse).

will uncover thy nakedness unto them. They will be used by God to bring national humiliation upon His sinful people.

38. *I will judge thee, as women . . . are judged.* lit. 'I will judge thee with judgments of,' etc., referring to the punishment for adultery and child murder. For the latter, see verses 20f., 36.

I will bring upon thee the blood of fury and jealousy. lit. 'I will give (or, make) thee the blood of,' etc. The sense is, I will make thee the object of My bloody fury and jealousy, i.e. of My fury and jealousy which can only be assuaged by thy blood.

39. *into their hand.* viz. of her lovers mentioned in verse 37.

place, and break down thy lofty places; and they shall strip thee of thy clothes, and take thy fair jewels; and they shall leave thee naked and bare. 40. They shall also bring up an assembly against thee, and they shall stone thee with stones, and thrust thee through with their swords. 41. And they shall burn thy houses with fire, and execute judgments upon thee in the sight of many women; and I will cause thee to cease from playing the harlot, and thou shalt also give no hire any more. 42. So will I satisfy My fury upon thee, and My jealousy shall depart from thee, and I will be quiet,

וְהֶעֱלוּ ׃ וְעָרְיָה עֵירֹם וְהִנִּיחוּךְ 40 וְנִתְצוּ רָמֹתַיִךְ וְהִפְשִׁיטוּ אוֹתָךְ בְּגָדָיִךְ וְלָקְחוּ כְּלֵי תִפְאַרְתֵּךְ

בָּאֶבֶן אוֹתָךְ וְרָגְמוּ קָהָל עָלַיִךְ

וְשָׂרְפוּ בְּחַרְבוֹתָם וּבִתְּקוּךְ 41 שְׁפָטִים בָךְ וְעָשׂוּ בָאֵשׁ בָּתַּיִךְ וְהִשְׁבַּתִּיךְ רַבּוֹת נָשִׁים לְעֵינֵי תִתְּנִי־ לֹא אֶתְנָן וְגַם־ מִזּוֹנָה

וְסָרָה בָּךְ חֲמָתִי וַהֲנִחֹתִי עוֹד ׃ 42 וְלֹא וְשָׁקַטְתִּי מִמֵּךְ קִנְאָתִי

v. 41. הב׳ בפתח

---

eminent place. See on verse 24.

naked and bare. In the same state as at the time when she was a foundling in the field. The meaning of the allegory is that the invaders of Judea will destroy her buildings and carry away her wealth.

40. *they shall also bring up an assembly against thee.* The punishment of the nation is described in terms of the sentence passed upon an adulteress. When a person was stoned to death, it was done publicly. The accusers began the execution and the people then joined in (cf. Deut. xiii. 10). Judea's 'lovers' will summon other nations to combine in the attack upon her.

they shall stone thee with stones. The penalty, *both the adulterer and the adulteress shall surely be put to death* (Lev. xx. 10), is defined by the Rabbis as death by strangulation, and only when the crime of incest was included and Scripture adds the phrase *their blood shall be upon them* (e.g. Lev. xx. 11f.) was stoning used. Accordingly Kimchi remarks that to disgrace an adulteress, people used to throw stones at her in public, stab her and burn her house. Applied to Judea, the words predict that her fortresses and walls will be destroyed by her enemies.

thrust thee through. The Hebrew verb *bittek* occurs nowhere else. The cognate word in Assyrian means 'to cut in pieces.'

41. *they shall burn thy houses with fire.* A prediction of the burning of the Temple, the king's palace and the houses in Jerusalem by Nebuchadnezzar (cf. 2 Kings xxv. 9).

in the sight of many women. There seems to have been a practice of making other women witness the execution of the adulteress as a warning. Judea's overthrow will be witnessed by neighbouring nations.

I will cause thee to cease, etc. With the destruction of the State, the political manoeuvrings with other nations, hitherto indulged in, will come to an end.

thou shalt also give no hire any more. No longer will Judea be in a position to bribe her neighbours for their friendship.

42. *so will I satisfy My fury.* 'Any judgment as to the seeming harshness of this "anthropopathism," whereby God is represented as "raging Himself out," should be modified by recollecting that we are not yet free of the allegory. The expression itself implies restoration and returning favour (cf. verse 60)' (Lofthouse).

and will be no more angry. 43. Because thou hast not remembered the days of thy youth, but hast fretted Me in all these things; lo, therefore I also will bring thy way upon thy head, saith the Lord GOD; or hast thou not committed this lewdness above all thine abominations?

44. Behold, every one that useth proverbs shall use this proverb against thee, saying: As the mother, so her daughter. 45. Thou art thy mother's daughter, that loatheth her husband and her children; and thou art the sister of thy sisters, who loathed their husbands and their children; your mother was a Hittite, and your father an Amorite. 46. And thine elder sister is Samaria, that

43 יַעַן אֲשֶׁר לֹא־ אֶכְעַס עוֹד :
זָכַרְתִּ אֶת־יְמֵי נְעוּרַיִךְ
וַתִּרְגְּזִי־לִי בְּכָל־אֵלֶּה וְגַם־
אֲנִי הֵא דַרְכֵּךְ ׀ בְּרֹאשׁ נָתַתִּי
נְאֻם אֲדֹנָי יְהוִֹה וְלֹא עָשִׂיתִי
אֶת־הַזִּמָּה עַל כָּל־־

44 תּוֹעֲבֹתָיִךְ : הִנֵּה כָּל־הַמֹּשֵׁל
עָלַיִךְ יִמְשֹׁל לֵאמֹר כְּאִמָּה

45 בִתָּהּ : בַּת־אִמֵּךְ אַתְּ גֹּעֶלֶת
אִישָׁהּ וּבָנֶיהָ וַאֲחוֹת אֲחוֹתֵךְ
אַתְּ אֲשֶׁר גָּעֲלוּ אַנְשֵׁיהֶן וּבְנֵיהֶן
אִמְּכֶן חִתִּית וַאֲבִיכֶן אֱמֹרִי :

46 וַאֲחוֹתֵךְ הַגְּדוֹלָה שֹׁמְרוֹן הִיא

v. 43. יתיר י׳　　v. 43. יתיר י׳

will be no more angry. Better, 'will be no more provoked to anger.'

43. *because thou hast not remembered the days of thy youth.* All these calamities will befall them because they had been forgetful of, and ungrateful for, the kindnesses God had done for them in their national infancy.

I also will bring. lit. 'I have given,' the prophetic perfect.

or hast thou not committed . . . abominations? So Metsudath David, but the Targum and other Jewish authorities render: 'It never occurred to thee to repent thine abominations,' understanding the noun *zimmah* as 'thought.'

44-58 JUDEA'S GUILT EXCEEDS
THAT OF SODOM AND SAMARIA

44. *the mother.* i.e. the Hittite (verse 3). The people of Judah are as sinful as the original inhabitants of Canaan. Another interpretation is suggested by Davidson: 'as the mother (the Israelite nation as a

whole) so is her daughter (Jerusalem),' and he understands this section as addressed to the capital.

45. *that loatheth her husband and her children.* This verse explains the proverb just cited. The low state of morality which obtained among the Canaanites is found in Judea and Jerusalem.

the sister of thy sisters. The *sisters* are Samaria and Sodom whom Jerusalem resembles in the pursuit of wickedness.

your mother was a Hittite, etc. See on verse 3. Here the suffix is plural and seems to apply to the three *sisters.*

46. *thine elder sister is Samaria.* Ehrlich takes *sister* to indicate only a neighbouring city or State, without any reference to relationship. Samaria, as the capital, stands for the Northern Kingdom and is described as *elder* because it was larger in size and more numerous in population than Judah.

dwelleth at thy left hand, she and her daughters; and thy younger sister, that dwelleth at thy right hand, is Sodom and her daughters. 47. Yet hast thou not walked in their ways, nor done after their abominations; but in a very little while thou didst deal more corruptly than they in all thy ways. 48. As I live, saith the Lord GOD, Sodom thy sister hath not done, she nor her daughters, as thou hast done, thou and thy daughters. 49. Behold, this was the iniquity of thy sister Sodom: pride, fulness of bread, and careless ease was in her and in her daughters; neither did she strengthen the hand of the poor and needy. 50. And they were haughty, and committed abomination before Me; therefore I removed them when I saw it. 51. Neither hath Samaria committed even half of thy sins; but thou hast multiplied thine abominations more

וּבְנוֹתֶיהָ הַיּוֹשֶׁבֶת עַל־־
שְׂמֹאולֵךְ וַאֲחוֹתֵךְ הַקְּטַנָּה
מִמֵּךְ הַיּוֹשֶׁבֶת מִימִינֵךְ סְדֹם
47 וּבְנוֹתֶיהָ: וְלֹא בְדַרְכֵיהֶן
הָלַכְתְּ וּכְתוֹעֲבוֹתֵיהֶן עָשִׂיתִ
כִּמְעַט קָט וַתַּשְׁחִתִי מֵהֵן
48 בְּכָל־דְּרָכָיִךְ: חַי־אָנִי נְאֻם
אֲדֹנָי יֱהֹוִה אִם־עָשְׂתָה סְדֹם
אֲחוֹתֵךְ הִיא וּבְנוֹתֶיהָ כַּאֲשֶׁר
49 עָשִׂית אַתְּ וּבְנוֹתָיִךְ: הִנֵּה־זֶה
הָיָה עֲוֹן סְדֹם אֲחוֹתֵךְ גָּאוֹן
שִׂבְעַת־לֶחֶם וְשַׁלְוַת הַשְׁקֵט
הָיָה לָהּ וְלִבְנוֹתֶיהָ וְיַד־עָנִי
וְאֶבְיוֹן לֹא הֶחֱזִיקָה:
50 וַתִּגְבְּהֶינָה וַתַּעֲשֶׂינָה תוֹעֵבָה
לְפָנָי וָאָסִיר אֶתְהֶן כַּאֲשֶׁר
51 רָאִיתִי: וְשֹׁמְרוֹן כַּחֲצִי
חַטֹּאתַיִךְ לֹא חָטָאָה וַתַּרְבִּי
אֶת־־תּוֹעֲבוֹתַיִךְ מֵהֵנָּה

v. 46. יתיר׳.   v. 47. יתיר ר׳

---

at thy left hand. i.e. the north.

her daughters. The subordinate townships, as in verse 27.

47. nor done after their abominations. But even surpassed them in sinfulness.

in a very little while, etc. For only twenty-three years after Samaria's fall did Israel remain faithful to God; soon after Hezekiah's death and the accession of Manasseh the corruption of Judah set in (Kimchi). The word *kat* in the phrase *very little* has puzzled modern commentators, but Eitan corroborates it

by reference to a similar root in Ethiopic.

49. this was the iniquity of thy sister Sodom. Her security and prosperity produced in her a sense of pride and egoism. These vices induced in the inhabitants heartlessness towards the poor and other acts which God abominated.

50. I removed them. God destroyed the whole locality (Gen. xix. 25).

when I saw it. Cf. *I will go down now, and see whether they have done altogether according to the cry of it* (Gen. xviii. 21).

E

than they, and hast justified thy sisters by all thine abominations which thou hast done. 52. Thou also, bear thine own shame, in that thou hast given judgment for thy sisters; through thy sins that thou hast committed more abominable than they, they are more righteous than thou; yea, be thou also confounded, and bear thy shame, in that thou hast justified thy sisters.

53. And I will turn their captivity, the captivity of Sodom and her daughters, and the captivity of Samaria and her daughters, and the captivity of thy captives in the midst of them; 54. that thou mayest bear thine own shame, and mayest be ashamed because of all that thou hast done, in that thou art a comfort unto them. 55. And thy sisters, Sodom and her daughters, shall return to their former estate, and Samaria and her daughters shall

וַתְּצַדְּקִי אֶת־אֲחוֹתֵ֖ךְ בְּכָל־

52 תּוֹעֲבֹתַ֫יִךְ אֲשֶׁר עָשִׂ֑יתִי׃ גַּם־ אַ֣תְּ ׀ שְׂאִי כְלִמָּתֵךְ אֲשֶׁר פִּלַּלְתְּ לַאֲחוֹתֵךְ בְּחַטֹּאתַ֫יִךְ אֲשֶׁר־הִתְעַבְתְּ מֵהֵן תִּצְדַּ֫קְנָה מִמֵּךְ וְגַם־אַתְּ בּ֫וֹשִׁי וּשְׂאִי כְלִמָּתֵךְ בְּצַדֶּקְתֵּךְ אַחְיוֹתֵךְ׃

53 וְשַׁבְתִּי אֶת־שְׁבִיתְהֶן אֶת־ שְׁבִ֫ית סְדֹם֙ וּבְנוֹתֶ֫יהָ וְאֶת־ שְׁבִ֫ית שֹׁמְרוֹן וּבְנוֹתֶ֫יהָ וּשְׁבִ֫ית

54 שְׁבִיתַ֫יִךְ בְּתוֹכָהְנָה׃ לְמַ֫עַן תִּשְׂאִי כְלִמָּתֵךְ וְנִכְלַ֫מְתְּ מִכֹּל אֲשֶׁר עָשִׂית בְּנַחֲמֵךְ אֹתָֽן׃

55 וַאֲחוֹתַ֫יִךְ סְדֹם וּבְנוֹתֶ֫יהָ תָּשֹׁ֫בְןָ לְקַדְמָתָ֫ן וְשֹׁמְרוֹן וּבְנוֹתֶ֫יהָ

---

v. 51. אחותיך ק׳ v. 51. יתיר י׳ v. 53. שבות ק׳ v. 53. שבות ק׳ v. 53. ושבות ק׳

51. more than they. Than Samaria and the other cities of the Northern Kingdom.

hast justified thy sisters. In comparison with Judea's guilt, Sodom and Samaria would appear almost righteous. Cf. *Backsliding Israel hath proved herself more righteous than treacherous Judah* (Jer. iii. 11).

52. thou . . . sisters. This translation follows the order of the Hebrew, but the meaning becomes clearer in Davidson's rendering: 'thou also, which hast (in that thou hast) given judgment for (in behalf of) thy sisters, bear thy shame'; and he continues: 'through thy sins which thou hast committed more abominable than they, they are more righteous than thou.' The more grievous guilt of Judah has the effect of mitigating

the severity of the punishment upon her erring *sisters;* what a disgrace!

53. I will turn their captivity. Besides the literal application, the phrase is also used in the more general sense of 'restore the fortunes of.'

in the midst of them. Judah is to be restored together with Sodom and Samaria.

54. in that thou art a comfort unto them. Judah was a *comfort* to them in her greater guilt. If God restores her, He must assuredly restore them who had sinned less!

55. Jeremiah similarly prophesied the restoration of Israel's neighbours (cf. Jer. xii. 14ff., xlviii. 47, xlix. 6, 39).

return to their former estate, and thou and thy daughters shall return to your former estate. 56. For thy sister Sodom was not mentioned by thy mouth in the day of thy pride; 57. before thy wickedness was uncovered, as at the time of the taunt of the daughters of Aram, and of all that are round about her, the daughters of the Philistines, that have thee in disdain round about. 58. Thou hast borne thy lewdness and thine abominations, saith the LORD.

59. For thus saith the Lord GOD: I will even deal with thee as thou hast done, who hast despised the oath in breaking the covenant.

תָּשֹׁבְןָ לְקַדְמָתֶן וְאַתְּ וּבְנוֹתַיִךְ
56 תְּשֻׁבֶינָה לְקַדְמַתְכֶן׃ וְלוֹא
הָיְתָה סְדֹם אֲחוֹתֵךְ לִשְׁמוּעָה
57 בְּפִיךְ בְּיוֹם גְּאוֹנָיִךְ׃ בְּטֶרֶם
תִּגָּלֶה רָעָתֵךְ כְּמוֹ עֵת חֶרְפַּת
בְּנוֹת־אֲרָם וְכָל־סְבִיבוֹתֶיהָ
בְּנוֹת פְּלִשְׁתִּים הַשָּׁאטוֹת
58 אוֹתָךְ מִסָּבִיב׃ אֶת־זִמָּתֵךְ
וְאֶת־תּוֹעֲבוֹתַיִךְ אַתְּ נְשָׂאתִים
59 נְאֻם יְהֹוָה׃ כִּי כֹה אָמַר אֲדֹנָי
יְהֹוִה וְעָשִׂית אוֹתָךְ כַּאֲשֶׁר
עָשִׂית אֲשֶׁר־בָּזִית אָלָה

v. 59. וְעָשִׂיתִי ק'

56. *for thy sister Sodom was not mentioned,* etc. The name of Sodom was not mentioned from contempt of its evil reputation; but this was an act of hypocrisy on the part of one who was of still worse character. Rashi and others render as a question: 'was not thy sister Sodom mentioned . . .?' That is to say, since Judah in her heyday had realized that Sodom's fall was due to selfish pride (verse 49), her own failings of similar nature and greater intensity were thus even more serious.

57. *before thy wickedness was uncovered.* Disaster was, in ancient times, interpreted as God's punishment of sin, a doctrine contested in the Book of Job. Before calamity overwhelmed Judah, she could profess a righteousness which she did not possess; but when the day of reckoning came, her true character was exposed.

the taunt of the daughters of Aram, etc. Ezekiel is alluding to an occasion when the peoples mentioned had humiliated the kingdom of Judah, and the Jewish

commentators quote what happened in the reign of Ahaz as recorded in 2 Chron. xxviii. 5, 18.

58. *thou hast borne thy lewdness.* Either thou hast suffered, or thou wilt suffer (prophetic perfect), punishment for thine abominable sins; or, thou canst no longer disclaim guilt.

59-63 RESTORATION AFTER THE EXPIATION OF SIN

The Hebrew prophets never left their people in despair. The most vehement denunciation and the direst threats are followed by words of hope. Judah has been unmindful of, and faithless to, the covenant with God and must suffer the consequences; but He will remember and renew it for ever. Whatever may be in store for the nation in the near future, He will not completely repudiate them.

59. *I will even deal with thee as thou hast done.* In Hebrew law a husband could not condone his wife's adultery and he had to take action against her. In like

60. Nevertheless I will remember My covenant with thee in the days of thy youth, and I will establish unto thee an everlasting covenant. 61. Then shalt thou remember thy ways, and be ashamed, when thou shalt receive thy sisters, thine elder sister and thy younger; and I will give them unto thee for daughters, but not because of thy covenant. 62. And I will establish My covenant with thee, and thou shalt know that I am the LORD; 63. that thou mayest remember, and be confounded, and never open thy mouth any more, because of thy shame; when I have

לְהָפֵר בְּרִית: וְזָכַרְתִּי אֲנִי 60
אֶת־בְּרִיתִי אוֹתָךְ בִּימֵי
נְעוּרָיִךְ וַהֲקִימוֹתִי לָךְ בְּרִית
עוֹלָם: וְזָכַרְתְּ אֶת־דְּרָכַיִךְ 61
וְנִכְלַמְתְּ בְּקַחְתֵּךְ אֶת־
אֲחוֹתַיִךְ הַגְּדֹלוֹת מִמֵּךְ אֶל־
הַקְּטַנּוֹת מִמֵּךְ וְנָתַתִּי אֶתְהֶן
לָךְ לְבָנוֹת וְלֹא מִבְּרִיתֵךְ:
וַהֲקִימֹתִי אֲנִי אֶת־בְּרִיתִי 62
אִתָּךְ וְיָדַעַתְּ כִּי־אֲנִי יְהוָה:
לְמַעַן תִּזְכְּרִי וָבֹשְׁתְּ וְלֹא 63
יִהְיֶה־לָּךְ עוֹד פִּתְחוֹן פֶּה
מִפְּנֵי כְּלִמָּתֵךְ בְּכַפְּרִי־לָךְ

manner, God must punish His people's infidelity.

60. *nevertheless I will remember My covenant.* The pronoun *I* is emphatic in the Hebrew. God can do what man is unable to do. With the human being adultery renders the marriage covenant null; God, however, will *remember* it and permit the nation's sufferings to wipe out the guilty past.

in the days of thy youth. The period of the exodus and the wanderings. Cf. the parallel passage in Jer. ii. 2, *I remember for thee the affection of thy youth . . . how thou wentest after Me in the wilderness.* *I will establish unto thee an everlasting covenant.* God will enter into a new covenant with His people which will be eternal (cf. xxxvii. 26; Jer. xxxi. 30ff.).

61. *be ashamed.* The magnanimity of God in overlooking past sins, making a new covenant with the nation and even presenting them with Sodom and Samaria, will arouse in them a deep feeling of remorse.

but not because of thy covenant. Judea will not be restored to her ancient glory and include Samaria and Sodom in her territory in fulfilment of the former covenant since that has been broken. This will happen in consequence of the new covenant. An alternative Midrashic explanation is: the incorporation of these provinces into Judea was not provided for in the covenant made with Abraham as described in Gen. xv. 18ff. Therefore this new promise is a sign of Judea's restoration to God's love.

62. *I will establish.* The subject *I* is again emphatic and may be intended to act as a contrast to *but not because of thy covenant* which precedes. What He now promises is a voluntary act on His part. *thou shalt know that I am the LORD.* Both in the impending punishment and the subsequent restoration they may learn the nature of God.

63. *when I have forgiven thee all that thou hast done.* lit. 'when I have covered over for thee,' concealed it from My sight.

99

forgiven thee all that thou hast done,
saith the Lord God.'

לְכָל־אֲשֶׁר עָשִׂית נְאֻם אֲדֹנָי
יֱהוִֹה:

---

17   CHAPTER XVII   יז

1. And the word of the LORD came
unto me, saying: 2. 'Son of man,
put forth a riddle, and speak a
parable unto the house of Israel,
3. and say: Thus saith the Lord
GOD:

A great eagle with great wings
And long pinions,

1 וַיְהִי דְבַר־יְהוָֹה אֵלַי לֵאמֹר:
2 בֶּן־אָדָם חוּד חִידָה וּמְשֹׁל
מָשָׁל אֶל־־בֵּית יִשְׂרָאֵל:
3 וְאָמַרְתָּ כֹּה־אָמַר | אֲדֹנָי יֱהוִֹה
הַנֶּשֶׁר הַגָּדוֹל גְּדוֹל הַכְּנָפַיִם
אֶרֶךְ הָאֵבֶר

The manifestation of God's grace after
national apostasy will overwhelm them
with shame of their disloyalty in the past.
They will have no 'opening of the mouth'
(so lit., again only in xxix. 21 but in a
different sense), no plea for self-justifica-
tion and complaint of His hard treatment
of His people.

CHAPTER XVII

AFTER his condemnation of the people,
Ezekiel censures king Zedekiah's act of
treachery towards Nebuchadnezzar in
breaking his solemn oath of loyalty and
in seeking military aid from Egypt.
The prophet predicts the extinction of
Zedekiah's dynasty and the fall of
Jerusalem. This oracle was delivered
shortly before the disaster in 586 B.C.E.
In an easily understood allegory Ezekiel
likens Babylon and Egypt to two great
eagles. One, Babylon, broke off the top
of the cedar, i.e. carried off king Jehoiachin to Babylon and replaced him
by the inferior Zedekiah. But this
vine of low stature, who owed his kingship
to Nebuchadnezzar, revolted and turned
to Egypt, the other great eagle, for help.

In conclusion, the prophet speaks of the
Messianic Age when the Davidic dynasty
will be re-established and exercise
world-wide rule.

1-10 RIDDLE OF THE GREAT EAGLE

2. *riddle . . . parable.* Ezekiel is commanded to convey his message in the
form of a riddle which requires some
intelligence to solve, but at the same
time to develop the application so as to
bring it nearer to the form of a *mashal*,
an allegory whose meaning is less
disguised and more readily grasped.

3. *a great eagle.* i.e. Nebuchadnezzar,
the mighty king of Babylon, comparable
to the eagle which is the king of birds.
Another point of comparison is the
tendency of each to swoop down on his
prey. The plunderer of a nation is often
described as an eagle (cf. Deut. xxviii.
49; Isa. xlvi. 11; Jer. xlviii. 40; Hos.
viii. 1).

with great wings, etc. Like the eagle
whose wings enable it to fly long dis-
tances, so Nebuchadnezzar's power extends over a wide area.

Full of feathers, which had
divers colours,
Came unto Lebanon,
And took the top of the cedar;

4 He cropped off the topmost of
the young twigs thereof,
And carried it into a land of
traffic;
He set it in a city of merchants.

5 He took also of the seed of the
land,
And planted it in a fruitful soil;
He placed it beside many waters,
He set it as a slip.

6 And it grew, and became a
spreading vine
Of low stature,

מָלֵא הַנּוֹצָה
אֲשֶׁר־לוֹ הָרִקְמָה
בָּא אֶל־הַלְּבָנוֹן
וַיִּקַּח אֶת־צַמֶּרֶת הָאָרֶז׃

4 אֵת רֹאשׁ יְנִיקוֹתָיו קָטָף
וַיְבִיאֵהוּ אֶל־אֶרֶץ כְּנַעַן
בְּעִיר רֹכְלִים שָׂמוֹ׃

5 וַיִּקַּח מִזֶּרַע הָאָרֶץ
וַיִּתְּנֵהוּ בִּשְׂדֵה־זָרַע
קַח עַל־מַיִם רַבִּים
צַפְצָפָה שָׂמוֹ׃

6 וַיִּצְמַח וַיְהִי לְגֶפֶן סֹרַחַת
שִׁפְלַת קוֹמָה

---

divers colours. Alluding perhaps to the many different nations subject to Nebuchadnezzar and contributing to his military power.

Lebanon. Represents the Land of Israel and more particularly the kingdom of Judah.

the top of the cedar. If *the cedar* alludes to Jerusalem, *the top* is the nobility of the city, especially the princes of the house of David.

4. *the topmost of the young twigs.* The allusion is to the young king, Jehoiachin, carried off by Nebuchadnezzar to Babylon in the year 597 B.C.E. (cf. 2 Kings xxiv. 15).

a land of traffic . . . a city of merchants. The land of Chaldea and the city of Babylon (see on xvi. 29).

5. *the seed of the land.* i.e. a member of the royal family. After deposing Jehoiachin, Nebuchadnezzar appointed Zedekiah, his uncle, as king (2 Kings xxiv. 17).

planted it in a fruitful soil. Nebuchadnezzar permitted Zedekiah to exercise his kingship in the homeland of Judea.

he placed it. Hebrew *kach*, which the English versions construe as an unusual form of *lakach*. In Rabbinic Hebrew it signifies 'stalk, shoot' which gives the required parallel to the noun in the next clause. It is then to be understood as also governed by *he set it.*

beside many waters. Here is doubtless a reference to Babylon; cf. *O thou that dwellest upon many waters* (Jer. li. 13). The meaning is that although Nebuchadnezzar set Zedekiah upon the throne, the Judean king was to feel himself dependent upon Babylon like a stalk which draws its sustenance from near-by water.

a slip. *Tsaphtsaphah* in Rabbinic Hebrew denotes a species of willow.

6. *a spreading vine of low stature.* Though Judea still continued as a kingdom, Nebuchadnezzar's policy was to keep it in the condition of vassal State dependent upon Babylon (cf. verse 14).

Whose tendrils might turn toward him,
And the roots thereof be under
him;
So it became a vine, and brought
forth branches,
And shot forth sprigs.

7 There was also another great
eagle with great wings
And many feathers;
And, behold, this vine did bend
Its roots toward him,
And shot forth its branches
toward him, from the beds of
its plantation,
That he might water it.

8 It was planted in a good soil
By many waters,
That it might bring forth
branches, and that it might
bear fruit,

לִפְנוֹת דָּלִיּוֹתָיו אֵלָיו
וְשָׁרָשָׁיו תַּחְתָּיו יִהְיוּ
וַתְּהִי לְגֶפֶן וַתַּעַשׂ בַּדִּים
וַתְּשַׁלַּח פֹּארֹת:
7 וַיְהִי נֶשֶׁר־אֶחָד גָּדוֹל
גָּדוֹל כְּנָפַיִם
וְרַב נוֹצָה
וְהִנֵּה הַגֶּפֶן הַזֹּאת
כָּפְנָה שָׁרֲשֶׁיהָ עָלָיו
וְדָלִיּוֹתָיו שִׁלְחָה־לּוֹ
לְהַשְׁקוֹת אוֹתָהּ
מֵעֲרֻגוֹת מַטָּעָהּ:
8 אֶל־שָׂדֶה טּוֹב
אֶל־מַיִם רַבִּים הִיא שְׁתוּלָה
לַעֲשׂוֹת עָנָף וְלָשֵׂאת פֶּרִי

v. 7. הל׳ רפה

---

whose tendrils might turn toward him.
Toward the eagle, i.e. Nebuchadnezzar.
Zedekiah occupied the throne, but he
was to serve the Babylonian king.

the roots thereof be under him. Under
Nebuchadnezzar. Kimchi renders:
'under it': the roots were intended to
remain under the trunk and not spread
abroad. This means, Zedekiah was only
granted a local authority; his foreign
policy had to be subservient to Babylon.

branches . . . sprigs. No mention is
made of fruit being produced by the
vine, because Zedekiah's children were
all put to death by Nebuchadnezzar
(2 Kings xxv. 7).

7. *another great eagle.* The Hebrew for
another is literally 'one.' This eagle, described as less powerful than the other,
is Pharaoh Hophra, the king of Egypt to
whom Zedekiah appealed for help in
contravention of his covenant with
Babylon. Pharaoh himself later fell
victim to Nebuchadnezzar (cf. Jer.
xliv. 30).

this vine . . . toward him. Zedekiah
turned to Egypt to aid him in his
attempt to free himself from the Babylonian yoke.

from the beds of its plantation. i.e. from
Judea where the nation ruled by Zedekiah
was dwelling.

8. *it was planted in a good soil,* etc.
Zedekiah, whose throne was safe and
protected by Babylon, would have
succeeded in strengthening his kingdom
and securing the throne for his children.
He had, therefore, no need to look to
Egypt for support.

That it might be a stately vine.

9 Say thou: Thus saith the Lord
GOD: Shall it prosper?

Shall he not pull up the roots
thereof,

And cut off the fruit thereof, that
it wither,

Yea, wither in all its sprouting
leaves?

Neither shall great power or
much people be at hand

When it is plucked up by the
roots thereof.

10 Yea, behold, being planted, shall
it prosper?

Shall it not utterly wither, when
the east wind toucheth it?

In the beds where it grew it shall
wither.'

11. Moreover the word of the
LORD came unto me, saying: 12.
'Say now to the rebellious house:

לִהְיוֹת לְגֶפֶן אַדָּרֶת:

9 אֱמֹר כֹּה אָמַר

אֲדֹנָי יֱהֹוִה תִּצְלָח

הֲלוֹא אֶת־שָׁרָשֶׁיהָ יְנַתֵּק

וְאֶת־פִּרְיָהּ | יְקוֹסֵס וְיָבֵשׁ

כָּל־טַרְפֵּי צִמְחָהּ תִּיבָשׁ

וְלֹא־בִזְרֹעַ גְּדוֹלָה וּבְעַם־רָב

לְמַשְׂאוֹת אוֹתָהּ מִשָּׁרָשֶׁיהָ:

10 וְהִנֵּה שְׁתוּלָה הֲתִצְלָח

הֲלוֹא כְגַעַת בָּהּ רוּחַ הַקָּדִים

תִּיבַשׁ יָבֹשׁ

עַל־עֲרֻגֹת צִמְחָהּ תִּיבָשׁ:

11 וַיְהִי דְבַר־יְהֹוָה אֵלַי לֵאמֹר:

12 אֱמָר־נָא לְבֵית הַמֶּרִי הֲלֹא

v. 9. v. 10. קָמֵץ בְּז"ק כ' דְּגוּשָׁה

9. say thou. Addressed to Ezekiel.

shall he not pull up. The subject of the
verb is the first eagle, Nebuchadnezzar.
The vine will be uprooted, its fruit cut
off and its leaves wither. Zedekiah's
monarchy will be destroyed, all the heirs
to the throne killed, and all the nobles of
Judea will perish.

neither shall great power . . . be at hand.
Pharaoh, who made a military alliance
with Zedekiah, will not come to his
rescue at the critical moment. As so
often with Ezekiel, here too he drops the
metaphor and speaks in plain terms,
referring to *great power* and *much people*.
The rendering of A.V. and R.V., 'even
without great or much people to pluck it
up by the roots thereof,' is closer to
the Hebrew and means that Nebuchadnezzar will not require a display of great
force and a numerous army to destroy
the Judean kingdom.

10. *when the east wind toucheth it.* The
allusion is to the Babylonian empire
which was situated north-east of the
Holy Land. Zedekiah's confidence in
his military preparations, which led to
his rebellion against Babylon, is held by
the prophet to be an empty dream.

in the beds where it grew it shall wither.
Cf. verse 7. Though the vine was
planted in fertile soil where it could have
grown luxuriantly, it would not withstand the force of *the east wind*.

11-21 INTERPRETATION OF THE
PARABLE

12. *say now.* The prophet is now
commanded to explain the meaning of
the parable.

the rebellious house. i.e. the people of
Israel (cf. ii. 5), more exactly, the
kingdom of Judah.

Know ye not what these things mean? tell them: Behold, the king of Babylon came to Jerusalem, and took the king thereof, and the princes thereof, and brought them to him to Babylon; 13. and he took of the seed royal, and made a covenant with him, and brought him under an oath, and the mighty of the land he took away; 14. that his might be a lowly kingdom, that it might not lift itself up, but that by keeping his covenant it might stand. 15. But he rebelled against him in sending his ambassadors into Egypt, that they might give him horses and much people. Shall he prosper? shall he escape that doeth such things? shall he break the covenant, and yet escape? 16. As I live, saith the Lord GOD, surely in the place where

יְדַעְתֶּם מָה־אֵלֶּה אֱמֹר הִנֵּה־
בָא מֶלֶךְ־בָּבֶל יְרוּשָׁלַ֙͏ִם וַיִּקַּח
אֶת־מַלְכָּהּ וְאֶת־שָׂרֶיהָ וַיָּבֵא
13 אוֹתָם אֵלָיו בָּבֶלָה: וַיִּקַּח
מִזֶּרַע הַמְּלוּכָה וַיִּכְרֹת אִתּוֹ
בְּרִית וַיָּבֵא אֹתוֹ בְּאָלָה וְאֶת־
14 אֵילֵי הָאָרֶץ לָקָח: לִהְיוֹת
מַמְלָכָה שְׁפָלָה לְבִלְתִּי
הִתְנַשֵּׂא לִשְׁמֹר אֶת־בְּרִיתוֹ
15 לְעָמְדָהּ: וַיִּמְרָד־בּוֹ לִשְׁלֹחַ
מַלְאָכָיו מִצְרַיִם לָתֶת־לוֹ
סוּסִים וְעַם־רָב הֲיִצְלָח
הֲיִמָּלֵט הָעֹשֵׂה אֵלֶּה וְהֵפֵר
16 בְּרִית וְנִמְלָט: חַי־אָנִי נְאֻם
אֲדֹנָי יֱהֹוִה אִם־לֹא בִּמְקוֹם

v. 15. קמץ בלא א״סף

---

the king thereof, and the princes thereof. King Jehoiachin and his princes, represented in the parable by the top of the cedar and the topmost of the young twigs respectively (verses 3f.), were carried away as captives to Babylon.

13. *the seed royal.* The reference is to Zedekiah whom Nebuchadnezzar placed on the throne after deposing Jehoiachin. This is the interpretation of *the seed of the land* being planted in *a fruitful soil* (verse 5).

a covenant . . . an oath. Made in the name of God to secure Zedekiah's loyalty to Babylonian suzerainty (cf. 2 Chron. xxxvi 13).

the mighty of the land he took away. Influential leaders of Judea were also taken to Babylon as hostages to guarantee

the observance of the terms of the treaty (cf. 2 Kings xxiv. 15).

14. *a lowly kingdom.* Nebuchadnezzar's purpose was that Judea should remain a vassal State of Babylon. This is the meaning of the *vine of low stature* (verse 6).

15. *Egypt.* This is the interpretation of the other great eagle towards which the vine bent its branches (verse 7).

horses and much people. War horses and troops.

shall he prosper? Can he succeed in his plan?

shall he break the covenant, and yet escape? One who breaks a sacred covenant taken in the name of God cannot hope for Divine support in his undertaking.

the king dwelleth that made him king, whose oath he despised, and whose covenant he broke, even with him in the midst of Babylon he shall die. 17. Neither shall Pharaoh with his mighty army and great company succour him in the war, when they cast up mounds and build forts, to cut off many souls; 18. seeing he hath despised the oath by breaking the covenant, when, lo, he had given his hand, and hath done all these things, he shall not escape. 19. Therefore thus saith the Lord GOD: As I live, surely Mine oath that he hath despised, and My covenant that he hath broken, I will even bring it upon his own head. 20. And I will spread My net upon him, and he shall be taken in My snare, and I will bring him to Babylon, and will plead with him

הַמֶּלֶךְ הַמַּמְלִיךְ אֹתוֹ אֲשֶׁר
בָּזָה אֶת־אָלָתוֹ וַאֲשֶׁר הֵפֵר
אֶת־בְּרִיתוֹ אִתּוֹ בְתוֹךְ־בָּבֶל
17 יָמוּת: וְלֹא בְחַיִל גָּדוֹל
וּבְקָהָל רָב בַּיַעֲשֶׂה אוֹתוֹ פַרְעֹה
בַּמִּלְחָמָה בִּשְׁפֹּךְ סֹלְלָה
וּבִבְנוֹת דָּיֵק לְהַכְרִית נְפָשׁוֹת
18 רַבּוֹת: וּבָזָה אָלָה לְהָפֵר
בְּרִית וְהִנֵּה נָתַן יָדוֹ וְכָל־אֵלֶּה
19 עָשָׂה לֹא יִמָּלֵט: לָכֵן כֹּה־
אָמַר אֲדֹנָי יֱהוִֹה חַי־אָנִי אִם־
לֹא אָלָתִי אֲשֶׁר בָּזָה וּבְרִיתִי
אֲשֶׁר הֵפִיר וּנְתַתִּיו בְּרֹאשׁוֹ:
20 וּפָרַשְׂתִּי עָלָיו רִשְׁתִּי וְנִתְפַּשׂ
בִּמְצוּדָתִי וַהֲבִיאוֹתִיהוּ בָבֶלָה

16. *in the midst of Babylon he shall die.* Nebuchadnezzar who, after slaughtering Zedekiah's sons, carried him to Babylon where he died, had thereby virtually destroyed the kingdom. This is the interpretation of *shall he not pull up the roots thereof,* etc. (verse 9).

17. *neither shall Pharaoh . . . succour him in the war.* lit. 'shall Pharaoh do it in the war.' Kimchi renders: 'neither shall Pharaoh . . . wage war against him,' against Nebuchadnezzar when he besieges Jerusalem. Pharaoh did not fulfil the terms of his treaty with Judea. This is the intention of *neither shall great power or much people be at hand,* etc. (verse 9).

they cast up. The subject is the Babylonians.

mounds . . . forts. Military constructions to invest a city.

18. *he had given his hand.* As a pledge of faithfully carrying out the terms of the covenant.

19. *Mine oath . . . My covenant.* See on verse 13. The violation of an undertaking given in the name of God, even with a heathen like the king of Babylon, is equal to breaking a covenant with God Himself. The sanctity of an oath could not be more emphatically stressed.

bring it upon his own head. The guilt of his treachery will recoil on his head.

20. *I will spread My net upon him.* See on xii. 13.

will plead with him there. Humiliated and imprisoned in Babylon on account

there for his treachery that he hath
committed against Me. 21. And
all his mighty men in all his bands
shall fall by the sword, and they
that remain shall be scattered toward
every wind; and ye shall know that
I the LORD have spoken it.

22. Thus saith the Lord GOD:
Moreover I will take, even I, of the
lofty top of the cedar, and will set it;
I will crop off from the topmost of
its young twigs a tender one, and I
will plant it upon a high mountain
and eminent; 23. in the mountain of
the height of Israel will I plant it;
and it shall bring forth boughs, and
bear fruit, and be a stately cedar;
and under it shall dwell all fowl of

וְנִשְׁפַּטְתִּי אִתּוֹ שָׁם מַעֲלוֹ אֲשֶׁר
21 מָעַל־בִּי: וְאֵת כָּל־מִבְרָחָו
בְּכָל־אֲנַפָּיו בַּחֶרֶב יִפֹּלוּ
וְהַנִּשְׁאָרִים לְכָל־רוּחַ יִפָּרֵשׂוּ
וִידַעְתֶּם כִּי אֲנִי יְהֹוָה דִּבַּרְתִּי׃
22 * כֹּה אָמַר אֲדֹנָי יֱהֹוִה וְלָקַחְתִּי
אָנִי מִצַּמֶּרֶת הָאֶרֶז הָרָמָה
וְנָתָתִּי מֵרֹאשׁ יְנִקוֹתָיו רַךְ
אֶקְטֹף וְשָׁתַלְתִּי אָנִי עַל הַר־
23 גָּבֹהַ וְתָלוּל: בְּהַר מְרוֹם
יִשְׂרָאֵל אֶשְׁתֳּלֶנּוּ וְנָשָׂא עָנָף
וְעָשָׂה פֶרִי וְהָיָה לְאֶרֶז אַדִּיר
וְשָׁכְנוּ תַחְתָּיו כֹּל צִפּוֹר כָּל־

v. 21. מברחיו ק׳   v. 22. הפטרת האזינו

of his violation of the covenant, Zedekiah
will be conscious of his guilt.

21. *all his mighty men.* M.T. reads
mibrachaw which is derived from the
root *barach*, 'to flee,' and can only be
translated 'his fugitives.' Many Hebrew
MSS., however, have the reading
mibcharaw (presupposed also by the
Targum) which means 'his chosen men,
choice troops,' as in Dan. xi. 15 (*chosen
people*).

ye shall know. When the predicted
retribution has been accomplished, they
will realize that the prophet was speaking
in the name of God when he opposed
the plan against Babylon.

22-24 PROMISE OF RESTORATION

As is the common practice of the
prophets, a message of doom is tempered
by hope of a brighter future which would
follow.

22. *even I.* The repetition of the
personal pronoun is to emphasize that

this time it will be God, not Nebuchadnezzar, Who will cut off a twig from the
cedar. Whereas Nebuchadnezzar removed it to Babylon for destruction
(verses 3f.), God will bring it back to the
holy city and replant it in the sacred soil
where it will grow into a great cedar.

will set it. Restore it to its former
splendour. Some interpret this as referring to the restoration under Zerub-
babel, a descendant of Jehoiachin. The
Targum and Rashi understand it as an
allusion to the Messianic kingdom.

a high mountain. The mount of Zion.

23. *the mountain of the height of Israel.*
A designation of Jerusalem.

and bear fruit. Unlike Zedekiah who
perished together with his sons, the re-
established dynasty will endure and the
kingship pass from father to son.

be a stately cedar. Jerusalem will again
become the centre of a great kingdom.

under it shall dwell all fowl of every wing.
As birds build their nest in the branches

every wing, in the shadow of the branches thereof shall they dwell. 24. And all the trees of the field shall know that I the LORD have brought down the high tree, have exalted the low tree, have dried up the green tree, and have made the dry tree to flourish; I the LORD have spoken and have done it.'

כָּנָף בְּצֵל דָּלִיּוֹתָיו תִּשְׁכֹּנָּה׃

24 וְיָדְעוּ כָּל־עֲצֵי הַשָּׂדֶה כִּי אֲנִי יְהוָה הִשְׁפַּלְתִּי | עֵץ גָּבֹהַּ הִגְבַּהְתִּי עֵץ שָׁפָל הוֹבַשְׁתִּי עֵץ לָח וְהִפְרַחְתִּי עֵץ יָבֵשׁ אֲנִי יְהוָה דִּבַּרְתִּי וְעָשִׂיתִי׃

18   CHAPTER XVIII   יח

1. And the word of the LORD came unto me, saying: 2. 'What mean ye, that ye use this proverb in the land of Israel, saying:

1 וַיְהִי דְבַר־יְהוָה אֵלַי לֵאמֹר׃ 2 מַה־לָכֶם אַתֶּם מֹשְׁלִים אֶת־ הַמָּשָׁל הַזֶּה עַל־אַדְמַת

of the tree, so will many nations place themselves under the protection of the restored Davidic monarchy.

24. all the trees of the field. The allegory is continued. The revived Davidic dynasty is compared to a lofty cedar (verse 23), the heathen nations to ordinary trees. When, in contrast to its present helplessness, Israel is elevated to the position of a universal kingdom, the peoples of the world will acknowledge the Sovereignty and intervention of God in the affairs of man.

brought down the high tree, have exalted the low tree. All peoples will then know that it is by the will of God that the haughty are humbled and the lowly elevated.

CHAPTER XVIII
RESPONSIBILITY OF THE INDIVIDUAL

IT seems that Ezekiel's fellow-exiles uttered charges against Divine justice in regard to their fate. Considering themselves better men than their fathers, they attributed their suffering to the sins of their ancestors, voicing their bewilderment and chagrin in the proverb once

current in Jerusalem, *The fathers have eaten sour grapes, and the children's teeth are set on edge* (Jer. xxxi. 28). To this allegation the prophet devotes the whole of this chapter, which may be divided into two principal parts: (i) Every individual is held responsible for his own conduct whether he be good or bad; neither the wrongdoings nor the righteous deeds of others—not even those of the next-of-kin—determine the fate of a man. The righteous will enjoy God's favour, and the wicked will be doomed. (ii) Man is not the slave of a predestined fate; his conduct is not dictated by instinct and inherent inclination. He is free to choose between good and evil; he has the power to repent and amend his former way of life. As a fitting summary, Ezekiel concludes with an urgent call to the house of Israel to cast away all their sins and make for themselves *a new heart and a new spirit*, for God is not only a just Judge but also a merciful Father Who delights in the well-being of His children.

1-20 THE DOCTRINE OF INDIVIDUAL
RESPONSIBILITY

1. *saying.* i.e. that he might transmit it to Israel.

The fathers have eaten sour grapes,
And the children's teeth are set on edge?

3. As I live, saith the Lord GOD, ye shall not have occasion any more to use this proverb in Israel. 4. Behold, all souls are Mine; as the soul of the father, so also the soul of the son is Mine; the soul that sinneth, it shall die.

5. But if a man be just, and do that which is lawful and right, 6. and hath

יִשְׂרָאֵל לֵאמֹר
אָבוֹת יֹאכְלוּ בֹסֶר
וְשִׁנֵּי הַבָּנִים תִּקְהֶינָה׃
3 חַי־אָנִי נְאֻם אֲדֹנָי יְהוִה אִם־
יִהְיֶה לָכֶם עוֹד מְשֹׁל הַמָּשָׁל
4 הַזֶּה בְּיִשְׂרָאֵל׃ הֵן כָּל־
הַנְּפָשׁוֹת לִי הֵנָּה כְּנֶפֶשׁ הָאָב
וּכְנֶפֶשׁ הַבֵּן לִי־הֵנָּה הַנֶּפֶשׁ
5 הַחֹטֵאת הִיא תָמוּת׃ וְאִישׁ
כִּי־יִהְיֶה צַדִּיק וְעָשָׂה מִשְׁפָּט

---

2. *in the land of Israel.* Kimchi renders: 'concerning the Land of Israel' (so A.V., R.V.), that is to say, concerning the tragedy which befell that land.

the fathers have eaten sour grapes, etc. In Jer. xxxi. 28 the verb is in the perfect, but here in the imperfect mood: 'the fathers eat.' The proverb means, 'Is it just that one generation should be punished for the sins of its predecessors?' What may have given rise to this belief was the statement made in the name of God that the sins of Manasseh were the cause of Israel's downfall (cf. 2 Kings xxi. 10-12), although the disaster happened about half-a-century later. But the people misunderstood the words. What they implied was that Manasseh was the originator of evils which were continued by later generations who suffered the consequences of *their own sins.* Similarly in the Decalogue, *visiting the iniquity of the fathers upon the children unto the third and fourth generation of them that hate Me* (Exod. xx. 5) is interpreted in the Talmud (Ber. 7a) as signifying that only if the children are, like their fathers, sinners against God, will they suffer also for the sins of their fathers as well as their own. In another passage (Makk. 24a), a different view is propounded, viz. that Moses promulgated the doctrine that God is *visiting the iniquity of the fathers upon the children* (Exod. xxxiv. 7). Then came Ezekiel with the declaration which annulled it: *The soul that sinneth, it shall die.*

3. *ye shall not have occasion.* The current proverb will no more be used because experience will prove it to be untrue.

4. *all souls are Mine.* Since God is the Creator and Owner of all individuals, they must each stand in the same relationship to Him. Even father and son, who are physically related to one another, are separate entities in the sight of God; therefore the failings of the father cannot determine the destiny of the son.

it shall die. The repetition of the pronoun *it* is to stress that only the individual sinner will suffer the consequences and no one else. The verbs *die* and *live* (verse 9, etc.) in this connection denote the loss of God's favour and consequent suffering and its reverse.

5. *be just, and do that which is lawful and right.* This general statement is defined by the particulars which follow.

not eaten upon the mountains,
neither hath lifted up his eyes to the
idols of the house of Israel, neither
hath defiled his neighbour's wife,
neither hath come near to a woman
in her impurity; 7. and hath not
wronged any, but hath restored his
pledge for a debt, hath taken nought
by robbery, hath given his bread to
the hungry, and hath covered the
naked with a garment; 8. he that
hath not given forth upon interest,
neither hath taken any increase, that
hath withdrawn his hand from
iniquity, hath executed true justice
between man and man, 9. hath

6 וּצְדָקָ֑ה אֶל־הֶהָרִים֙ לֹ֣א
אָכָ֔ל וְעֵינָיו֙ לֹ֣א נָשָׂ֔א אֶל־
גִּלּוּלֵ֖י בֵּ֣ית יִשְׂרָאֵ֑ל וְאֶת־אֵ֤שֶׁת
רֵעֵ֙הוּ֙ לֹ֣א טִמֵּ֔א וְאֶל־אִשָּׁ֥ה
7 נִדָּ֖ה לֹ֥א יִקְרָֽב׃ וְאִישׁ֙ לֹ֣א
יוֹנֶ֔ה חֲבֹלָת֥וֹ חוֹב֙ יָשִׁ֔יב גְּזֵלָ֖ה
לֹ֣א יִגְזֹ֑ל לַחְמוֹ֙ לְרָעֵ֣ב יִתֵּ֔ן
8 וְעֵירֹ֖ם יְכַסֶּה־בָּֽגֶד׃ בַּנֶּ֣שֶׁךְ
לֹא־יִתֵּ֗ן וְתַרְבִּית֙ לֹ֣א יִקָּ֔ח
מֵעָ֙וֶל֙ יָשִׁ֣יב יָד֔וֹ מִשְׁפַּ֤ט אֱמֶת֙
יַעֲשֶׂ֔ה בֵּ֥ין אִ֖ישׁ לְאִֽישׁ׃

v. 8. ק קמץ בז"ק   v. 6. קמץ בז"ק

---

6. hath not eaten upon the mountains. He
has not worshipped the idols which were
installed on mountains and high places,
and has not partaken of the sacrificial
meal which was part of the ritual.

neither hath lifted up his eyes to the idols.
In prayer and expectation of aid. Cf.
I will lift up mine eyes unto the mountains:
from whence shall my help come? (Ps.
cxxi. 1).

of the house of Israel. viz. Baal in
Samaria and the golden calves set up by
Jeroboam in Bethel and Dan.

his neighbour's wife. He is innocent of
the sin of adultery.

come near . . . impurity. Cf. Lev. xviii.
19, xx. 18.

hath not wronged any. Cf. Lev. xxv.
14 (the same verb) where the Torah
forbids fraudulent dealing in any trans-
action. Here and in the following two
verses the prophet enumerates duties,
both negative and positive, towards one's
fellow-man.

hath restored his pledge for a debt. This
alludes to the law in Exod. xxii. 25f.
which declares it the duty of the creditor
to return to the borrower any article
pledged for a debt which is necessary for
his subsistence or comfort.

hath taken nought by robbery. For the
prohibition of robbery with violence, cf.
Lev. xix. 13.

hath given his bread to the hungry . . .
covered the naked with a garment. Cf.
Deut. xv. 7-11; the language is reminiscent of Isa. lviii. 7.

8. interest . . . increase. For the law
on the subject, cf. Exod. xxii. 24;
Lev. xxv. 35ff.; Deut. xxiii. 20. The
repetition here implies that he did not
lend money on the express condition of
receiving interest, nor did he accept
interest offered to him voluntarily by
the debtor on paying his debt (Kimchi).

withdrawn his hand from iniquity. The
iniquity here intended is giving false
weight or measure (cf. Lev. xix. 35).

true justice between man and man. When
acting as judge between disputants.

walked in My statutes, and hath
kept Mine ordinances, to deal truly;
he is just, he shall surely live, saith
the Lord GOD.

10. If he beget a son that is a
robber, a shedder of blood, and that
doeth to a brother any of these things,
11. whereas he himself had not done
any of these things, for he hath even
eaten upon the mountains, and
defiled his neighbour's wife, 12. hath
wronged the poor and needy, hath
taken by robbery, hath not restored
the pledge, and hath lifted up his
eyes to the idols, hath committed
abomination, 13. hath given forth
upon interest, and hath taken
increase; shall he then live? he shall
not live—he hath done all these
abominations; he shall surely be put
to death, his blood shall be upon
him.

9 בְּחֻקּוֹתַי יְהַלֵּךְ וּמִשְׁפָּטַי שָׁמַר
לַעֲשׂוֹת אֱמֶת צַדִּיק הוּא חָיֹה
10 יִֽחְיֶה֙ נְאֻ֣ם אֲדֹנָ֣י יֱהֹוִ֔ה׃ וְהוֹלִ֣יד
בֵּן־פָּרִיץ שֹׁפֵךְ דָּם וְעָשָׂה
11 אָח מֵאַחַד מֵאֵלֶּה׃ וְה֣וּא אֶת־
כָּל־אֵלֶּה לֹא עָשָׂה כִּי גַם
אֶל־הֶהָרִים֙ אָכַל וְאֶת־אֵשֶׁת
12 רֵעֵהוּ טִמֵּא׃ עָנִי וְאֶבְיוֹן הוֹנָה
גְּזֵלוֹת גָּזָל חֲבֹל לֹא יָשִׁיב
וְאֶל־הַגִּלּוּלִים֙ נָשָׂא עֵינָיו
13 תּוֹעֵבָה עָשָׂה׃ בַּנֶּשֶׁךְ נָתַן
וְתַרְבִּית לָקַח וָחָי לֹא יִֽחְיֶ֔ה
אֵת כָּל־הַתּוֹעֵבוֹת הָאֵלֶּה
עָשָׂה מוֹת יוּמָת דָּמָיו בּוֹ יִהְיֶה׃

v. 10.   v. 12. קמץ בז״ק   v. 13. קמץ בז״ק צירי בסמוך

---

9. *My statutes . . . Mine ordinances.*
He has been generally observant of the
Divine laws.

to deal truly. When obeying God's
demands, he is prompted not by personal
motive, but solely by the truth as
revealed in the Torah.

he is just. It is such obedience to the
demands of the Divine law 'expressed in
terms of practical conduct' that ennobles
and sanctifies man's mind and elevates
him to the rank of a just and righteous
man.

he shall surely live. However erring his
forefathers may have been. Contrast
verse 13.

10. *robber.* The meaning of the Hebrew
noun *parits* is 'one who breaks through'
the lawful bounds, a man of violence.

any of these things. Any of the sins, such
as robbery, etc., from which the father
refrained. If the son committed one of

these crimes, he would not be forgiven
because of the righteousness of his father,
but would perish in his own sin.

11. *had not done any of these things*, etc.
The reference is to the laws mentioned
in verses 7-9 as having been observed by
his father. The son's life was in every
respect the reverse of his father's.

12. *hath wronged the poor and needy.* In
their poverty they could not buy the
protection of judges and rulers and so
became easy victims of exploitation.

abomination. i.e. an immoral offence.

13. *shall he then live?* Should such a
wicked man escape retribution because
of the righteousness of his father?

he shall surely be put to death. For such
crimes as murder, idolatry and adultery
in accordance with the laws stated in
Num. xxxv. 16; Deut. xvii. 5; Lev.
xx. 10.

his blood shall be upon him. He brough

14. Now, lo, if he beget a son, that seeth all his father's sins, which he hath done, and considereth, and doeth not such like, 15. that hath not eaten upon the mountains, neither hath lifted up his eyes to the idols of the house of Israel, hath not defiled his neighbour's wife, 16. neither hath wronged any, hath not taken aught to pledge, neither hath taken by robbery, but hath given his bread to the hungry, and hath covered the naked with a garment, 17. that hath withdrawn his hand from the poor, that hath not received interest nor increase, hath executed Mine ordinances, hath walked in My statutes; he shall not die for the iniquity of his father, he shall surely live. 18. As for his father, because he cruelly oppressed, committed robbery on his brother, and did that which is not good among his people, behold, he dieth for his iniquity. 19. Yet say ye: Why doth not the son bear the iniquity of the father with him? When the son hath done that which is lawful and right, and hath kept

וְהִנֵּה הוֹלִיד בֵּן וַיַּרְא אֶת־ 14
כָּל־חַטֹּאת אָבִיו אֲשֶׁר עָשָׂה
וַיִּרְאֶ֯ וְלֹא יַעֲשֶׂה כָּהֵן: עַל־ 15
הֶהָרִים לֹא אָכָל וְעֵינָיו לֹא
נָשָׂא אֶל־גִּלּוּלֵי בֵּית יִשְׂרָאֵל
אֶת־אֵשֶׁת רֵעֵהוּ לֹא טִמֵּא:
וְאִישׁ לֹא הוֹנָה חֲבֹל לֹא חָבָל 16
וּגְזֵלָה לֹא גָזָל לַחְמוֹ לָרָעֵב
נָתָן וְעֵרוֹם כִּסָּה־בָּגֶד: מֵעָנִי 17
הֵשִׁיב יָדוֹ נֶשֶׁךְ וְתַרְבִּית לֹא
לָקָח מִשְׁפָּטַי עָשָׂה בְּחֻקּוֹתַי
הָלָךְ הוּא לֹא יָמוּת בַּעֲוֺן אָבִיו
חָיֹה יִחְיֶה: אָבִיו כִּי־עָשַׁק 18
עֹשֶׁק גָּזַל גֵּזֶל אָח וַאֲשֶׁר לֹא־
טוֹב עָשָׂה בְּתוֹךְ עַמָּיו וְהִנֵּה־
מֵת בַּעֲוֺנוֹ: וַאֲמַרְתֶּם מַדֻּעַ 19
לֹא־נָשָׂא הַבֵּן בַּעֲוֺן הָאָב וְהַבֵּן
מִשְׁפָּט וּצְדָקָה עָשָׂה אֵת כָּל־

---

v. 14. וירְאה ק׳   v. 15. קמץ בז״ק   v. 16. קמץ בז״ק   v. 17. קמץ בז״ק

death upon himself by his deeds; but only upon himself, not upon his children.

14. *considereth.* Reflecting upon his father's conduct, he appreciates that it is evil and decides to shun that way of life. This translation follows the *kerë;* R.V. and feareth' is according to the *kethib.*

doeth not such like. As the pious kings Hezekiah and Josiah did not follow in the sinful ways of their predecessors.

16. *hath not taken aught to pledge.* He did not withhold the pledge from the debtor when he should have restored it.

17. *hath withdrawn his hand from the poor.*

He refrained from oppressing the helpless poor (see on verse 12).

18. *brother.* i.e. fellow-Israelite, as in Lev. xxv. 35.

among his people. This phrase may be a parallel to *brother.* Kimchi understands it as 'publicly'; he committed his crime openly without consideration for public opinion.

he dieth for his iniquity. He, and not his righteous son, suffers the penalty.

19. *yet say ye.* The current belief that even the innocent son is punished for the sin of his father is stated and refuted by the prophet. The son, he stresses, is

all My statutes, and hath done them, he shall surely live. 20. The soul that sinneth, it shall die; the son shall not bear the iniquity of the father with him, neither shall the father bear the iniquity of the son with him; the righteousness of the righteous shall be upon him, and the wickedness of the wicked shall be upon him.

21. But if the wicked turn from all his sins that he hath committed, and keep all My statutes, and do that which is lawful and right, he shall surely live, he shall not die. 22. None of his transgressions that he hath committed shall be remembered against him; for his righteousness that he hath done he shall live. 23. Have I any pleasure at all that the wicked should die? saith the Lord GOD; and not rather that he should return from his ways, and live?

חֻקּוֹתַי שָׁמַר וַיַּעֲשֶׂה אֹתָם חָיֹה
20 יִחְיֶה: הַנֶּפֶשׁ הַחֹטֵאת הִיא
תָמוּת בֵּן לֹא־יִשָּׂא ׀ בַּעֲוֺן
הָאָב וְאָב לֹא יִשָּׂא בַּעֲוֺן הַבֵּן
צִדְקַת הַצַּדִּיק עָלָיו תִּהְיֶה
וְרִשְׁעַת רָשָׁע עָלָיו תִּהְיֶה:
21 וְהָרָשָׁע כִּי יָשׁוּב מִכָּל־
חַטֹּאתָו אֲשֶׁר עָשָׂה וְשָׁמַר אֶת־
כָּל־חֻקּוֹתַי וְעָשָׂה מִשְׁפָּט
וּצְדָקָה חָיֹה יִחְיֶה לֹא יָמוּת:
22 כָּל־פְּשָׁעָיו אֲשֶׁר עָשָׂה לֹא
יִזָּכְרוּ לוֹ בְּצִדְקָתוֹ אֲשֶׁר־
23 עָשָׂה יִחְיֶה: הֶחָפֹץ אֶחְפֹּץ
מוֹת רָשָׁע נְאֻם אֲדֹנָי יְהוִֹה
הֲלוֹא בְּשׁוּבוֹ מִדְּרָכָיו וְחָיָה:

not affected by the evil deeds of his father.

20. *the soul that sinneth, it shall die.* This verse gives the clearest expression of the prophet's doctrine with regard to the responsibility of the individual.

21-29 THE POWER OF PENITENCE

The doctrine of personal accountability is supported by the efficacy of repentance. No individual is punished for his sins after he has repented them; how much less should he be penalized for the sins of another

21. *turn . . . and keep.* The two stages of genuine repentance are defined: turning away from a sin committed and loyal obedience to the will of God. The essential elements of penitence, as taught in the Torah and by the Rabbis, are

regret for past sins and a determination to avoid them in the future: remorse and amendment.

22. *remembered against him.* As the effect of repentance, the sins are, so to speak, expunged by God from the man's record and he suffers no penalty for their commission.

23. *have I any pleasure,* etc. God is the Judge of man and in that capacity cannot overlook misdeeds. But He is also a merciful and loving Father Who hopes for the amendment of His children so that it is not necessary for Him to punish them.

not rather that he should return from his ways, and live? The repentance of the wicked causes no change in the will of God, since His will has always been that man should live. The change in the

24. But when the righteous turneth away from his righteousness, and committeth iniquity, and doeth according to all the abominations that the wicked man doeth, shall he live? None of his righteous deeds that he hath done shall be remembered; for his trespass that he trespassed, and for his sin that he hath sinned, for them shall he die. 25. Yet ye say: The way of the LORD is not equal. Hear now, O house of Israel: Is it My way that is not equal? is it not your ways that are unequal? 26. When the righteous man turneth away from his righteousness, and committeth iniquity, he shall die therefor; for his iniquity that he hath done shall

24 וּבְשׁוּב צַדִּיק מִצִּדְקָתוֹ וְעָשָׂה
עָוֶל כְּכֹל הַתּוֹעֵבוֹת אֲשֶׁר־
עָשָׂה הָרָשָׁע יַעֲשֶׂה וָחָי כָּל־
צִדְקֹתָו אֲשֶׁר־עָשָׂה לֹא
תִזָּכַרְנָה בְּמַעֲלוֹ אֲשֶׁר־מָעַל
וּבְחַטָּאתוֹ אֲשֶׁר־חָטָא בָּם
25 יָמוּת: וַאֲמַרְתֶּם לֹא יִתָּכֵן
דֶּרֶךְ אֲדֹנָי שִׁמְעוּ־נָא בֵּית
יִשְׂרָאֵל הֲדַרְכִּי לֹא יִתָּכֵן הֲלֹא
26 דַרְכֵיכֶם לֹא יִתָּכֵנוּ: בְּשׁוּב־
צַדִּיק מִצִּדְקָתוֹ וְעָשָׂה עָוֶל
וּמֵת עֲלֵיהֶם בְּעַוְלוֹ אֲשֶׁר־

v. 24. צדקתיו ק

fate of the individual is effected by his own change of heart which is subject to his will (Malbim).

24. *none of his righteous deeds . . . shall be remembered.* Just as the misdeeds of the repentant sinner are forgiven, so the former righteous acts of the wicked will not stand to his credit. According to a Talmudic interpretation (Kidd. 40b), this refers only to an apostate who is so vicious that he regrets his good deeds in the past.

for his trespass . . . and for his sin. The Hebrew *ma'al* (trespass) means in the first instance 'treachery.' The evil-doer's sin is twofold: he becomes a rebel against God, regretting his former righteous way of life; and he wilfully adopts a sinful life. For both these offences he suffers the penalty (Malbim).

25. *the way of the LORD . . . equal.* i.e. His manner of ruling the universe is inconsistent.

is it not your ways that are unequal? It seems that the doctrine taught by the prophet gave rise to the criticism: if man

is free to change his way of life from wickedness to righteousness and *vice versa*, this implies a change in the attitude of God towards man and so points to a defect in His nature. To this reasoning the prophet replies that it is not God Who makes the change but man himself. God always bestows His blessing upon man, but it is for him to be worthy of receiving it. As rain cannot fertilize the soil unless it has been cultivated, so man can only benefit from God's benevolence when he has retained his moral capacity for its reception (Malbim). Biblical phrases which apparently ascribe inconstancy to God, such as *it repented the LORD that He had made man* (Gen. vi. 6), are only an anthropomorphic form of expression.

26. *shall die therefor.* The last word is literally 'because of them.' The apostate will die for two sins: he abandons the righteousness of the past and commits iniquity in the present.

for his iniquity that he hath done shall he die. The change in his fate is the sequel

he die.   27. Again, when the wicked
man turneth away from his wickedness that he hath committed, and
doeth that which is lawful and right,
he shall save his soul alive.   28. Because he considereth, and turneth
away from all his transgressions
that he hath committed, he shall
surely live, he shall not die.   29. Yet
saith the house of Israel: The way of
the Lord is not equal.   O house of
Israel, is it My ways that are not
equal? is it not your ways that are
unequal?   30. Therefore I will judge
you, O house of Israel, every one
according to his ways, saith the
Lord God. Return ye, and turn
yourselves from all your transgressions; so shall they not be a
stumblingblock of iniquity unto you.
31. Cast away from you all your
transgressions, wherein ye have
transgressed; and make you a new
heart and a new spirit; for why will

27 עָשָׂה יָמוּת׃ וּבְשׁוּב רָשָׁע
מֵרִשְׁעָתוֹ אֲשֶׁר עָשָׂה וַיַּעַשׂ
מִשְׁפָּט וּצְדָקָה הוּא אֶת־נַפְשׁוֹ
28 יְחַיֶּה׃ וַיִּרְאֶה וַיָּשׁוֹב מִכָּל־
פְּשָׁעָיו אֲשֶׁר עָשָׂה חָיוֹ יִחְיֶה
29 לֹא יָמוּת׃ וְאָמְרוּ בֵּית יִשְׂרָאֵל
לֹא יִתָּכֵן דֶּרֶךְ אֲדֹנָי הַדְּרָכַי
לֹא יִתָּכֵנוּ בֵּית יִשְׂרָאֵל הֲלֹא
30 דַרְכֵיכֶם לֹא יִתָּכֵן׃ לָכֵן אִישׁ
כִּדְרָכָיו אֶשְׁפֹּט אֶתְכֶם בֵּית
יִשְׂרָאֵל נְאֻם אֲדֹנָי יְהוִה שׁוּבוּ
וְהָשִׁיבוּ מִכָּל־פִּשְׁעֵיכֶם
וְלֹא־יִהְיֶה לָכֶם לְמִכְשׁוֹל
31 עָוֺן׃ הַשְׁלִיכוּ מֵעֲלֵיכֶם אֶת־
כָּל־פִּשְׁעֵיכֶם אֲשֶׁר פְּשַׁעְתֶּם
בָּם וַעֲשׂוּ לָכֶם לֵב חָדָשׁ וְרוּחַ

v. 28. יתיר ו׳

of a change in his conduct and not
brought about by a change in Divine
dispensation.

27. *turneth away from his wickedness*, etc.
Likewise, should the wicked man regret
his former iniquities and lead a righteous
life, his escape from the fate which would
have been his, if he had not repented, is
the natural effect of his own cause.

lawful and right. 'Things *lawful* are
things which may be judged by the law-
courts; things *right* are acts of righteousness, deeds of religious courage and of
mercy of which God alone is judge'
(Barnes).

28. *considereth.* His amendment is due
to his realization of the punishment
involved in sin.

30-32 A CALL TO REPENTANCE

30. *every one*, etc. Each individual i
judged separately.

turn yourselves. lit. 'cause to return.
Rashi and Kimchi render: 'make other
to return.'

*so shall they not be a stumblingblock o
iniquity.* Perhaps a more correct trans
lation would be: 'so that iniquity be no
a stumblingblock to you,' or 'so tha
(your transgression) be not a stumbling
block of iniquity to you.'

31. *cast away.* i.e. repent your sins.

a new heart and a new spirit. Cf. xi. 1
A firm resolve to lead a life of faithfulnes
and obedience to the law of God.

ye die, O house of Israel? 32. For
I have no pleasure in the death of
him that dieth, saith the Lord GOD;
wherefore turn yourselves, and live.

חָדָשָׁה וְלָמָּה תָמֻתוּ בֵּית
32 יִשְׂרָאֵל: כִּי לֹא אֶחְפֹּץ בְּמוֹת
הַמֵּת נְאֻם אֲדֹנָי יֱהֹוִה וְהָשִׁיבוּ
וִחְיוּ: *

19   CHAPTER XIX   יט

1. Moreover, take thou up a lamentation for the princes of Israel, 2. and
say:

How was thy mother a lioness;

1 וְאַתָּה שָׂא קִינָה אֶל־נְשִׂיאֵי
2 יִשְׂרָאֵל: וְאָמַרְתָּ
מָה אִמְּךָ לָבִיא

v. 32. עד כאן

why will ye die?   Not by My wish but as
the inevitable consequence of your
actions.

32. *I have no pleasure.*   See on verse 23.
Lofthouse remarks: 'It is obvious that
Ezekiel here passes by several considera-
tions which would rise to our minds.
He neglects the influences of heredity
and environment, and of character.
Children do suffer from their parents; a
man's past does condition his present.
The problem is not for us so simple as
for Ezekiel.   But it must be remembered,
first, that Ezekiel is opposing a definite
error, and second, that he does not
actually deny such influences; his argument is simply, "Where good is done, it
cannot receive the punishment of evil";
and this is true.'

CHAPTER XIX

DIRGE OVER THE KINGS AND
PEOPLE OF JUDAH

AFTER stressing the forthcoming calamity
and justifying the Divine dispensation,
Ezekiel becomes a sympathetic mourner.
Speaking in God's behalf, he gives
expression to his grief over the tragic fate
of the last kings of Judah and over the
fall of the State.   Comparing the young
Judean rulers to whelps, he bemoans
their disastrous end.   Jehoahaz, who

reigned only three months, was banished
by Pharaoh and led in chains to Egypt
where he died in 608 B.C.E.   Jehoiakim,
the brother and successor of Jehoahaz,
was taken captive by Nebuchadnezzar
and transported to Babylon, dying on
the way in 597 B.C.E. (According to some
authorities he died in Babylon.)   Jehoiachin, who succeeded his father, was
exiled by Nebuchadnezzar to Babylon
after reigning for three months.
Zedekiah, the son of Josiah, was placed
on the throne by Nebuchadnezzar,
revolted against his overlord, was captured and blinded by him and brought
to Babylon in 586 B.C.E.   With that
event Judah's national life collapsed and
the dynasty came to an end.
   The elegy falls into two sections.
Verses 1-9 relate to the fate of the last
Judean kings; and verses 10-14 refer to
the fall of Judah.

1-9 ELEGY OVER JUDAH'S KINGS

1. *the princes of Israel.*   viz. Jehoahaz,
Jehoiakim and Zedekiah.   Ezekiel always
employs the term *prince* instead of 'king.'

2. *thy mother a lioness.*   The designation
mother is applied to the house of David,
compared to a *lioness* because Judah
(cf. Gen. xlix. 9), and particularly the
kingdom of David, are symbolized as a
lion.

Among lions she couched,
In the midst of the young lions
She reared her whelps!

3 And she brought up one of her
whelps,
He became a young lion;
And he learned to catch the prey,
He devoured men.

4 Then the nations assembled
against him,
He was taken in their pit;
And they brought him with
hooks
Unto the land of Egypt.

5 Now when she saw that she was
disappointed,
And her hope was lost,
Then she took another of her
whelps,

בֵּין אֲרָיֹות רָבָצָה
בְּתֹוךְ כְּפִרִים
רִבְּתָה גוּרֶיהָ׃

3 וַתַּעַל אֶחָד מִגֻּרֶיהָ
כְּפִיר הָיָה
וַיִּלְמַד לִטְרָף־טֶרֶף
אָדָם אָכָל׃

4 וַיִּשְׁמְעוּ אֵלָיו גֹּויִם
בְּשַׁחְתָּם נִתְפָּשׂ
וַיְבִאֻהוּ בַחַחִים
אֶל־אֶרֶץ מִצְרָיִם׃

5 וַתֵּרֶא כִּי נֹוחֲלָה
אָבְדָה תִּקְוָתָהּ
וַתִּקַּח אֶחָד מִגֻּרֶיהָ

v. 4. פתח באתנח

among lions she couched. Judah dwelt securely and fearlessly among the nations as long as he remained faithful to the will of God.

3. *one of her whelps.* The allusion is to Jehoahaz who succeeded his father, Josiah, after his death in the battle of Megiddo. For his reign, cf. 2 Kings xxiii. 31-33, and note also the mention of his fate in Jer. xxii. 10-12.

he became a young lion. He came to the throne at the age of twenty-three.

he devoured men. He ventured to wage war against Egypt.

4. *the nations assembled against him.* lit. 'listened unto him.' Egypt and her vassal States took up the challenge of Jehoahaz.

in their pit; and they brought him with hooks. The allegory is continued. The lion was captured by falling into a pit prepared for him and then bound in fetters: an allusion to the capture of Jehoahaz by the Egyptians. 'Pits and nets used in hunting are mentioned in the Gilgamesh Epic, Tablet i, col. 3, 9f.' (Cooke). For *hooks*, çf. xxix. 4, xxxviii. 4.

5. *she saw.* The subject is the mother lioness.

she was disappointed. The Hebrew verb *yachal* in the Niphal means 'to wait' (expectantly), and from it is derived the noun *tocheleth*, 'hope.' Its use here is difficult, and Kimchi (so the Targum) explains it as an instance where a verb has opposite meanings, 'she gave up hope.'

she took another of her whelps. Modern commentators hold that Jehoiachin is intended, and Jehoiakim is omitted from the last kings of Judah in the elegy because he died a peaceful end. But the Jewish commentators identify the second *whelp* with Jehoiakim, the half-brother and successor of Jehoahaz. From the

And made him a young lion.

6 And he went up and down among
the lions,

He became a young lion;

And he learned to catch the prey,

He devoured men.

7 And he knew their castles,

And laid waste their cities;

And the land was desolate, and
the fulness thereof,

Because of the noise of his
roaring.

8 Then the nations cried out
against him

כְּפִיר שָׂמָתְהוּ׃

6 וַיִּתְהַלֵּךְ בְּתוֹךְ־אֲרָיוֹת

כְּפִיר הָיָה

וַיִּלְמַד לִטְרָף־טֶרֶף

אָדָם אָכֵל׃

7 וַיֵּדַע אַלְמְנוֹתָיו

וְעָרֵיהֶם הֶחֱרִיב

וַתֵּשַׁם אֶרֶץ וּמְלֹאָהּ

מִקּוֹל שַׁאֲגָתוֹ׃

8 וַיִּתְּנוּ עָלָיו גּוֹיִם

various accounts of Jehoiakim's fate (cf. 2 Kings xxiv. 1ff.; Jer. xxii. 18f.; Dan. i. 1f.; 2 Chron. xxxvi. 6f.) it appears that he was twice taken prisoner by Nebuchadnezzar. The first time he was carried to Babylon, as stated in Daniel, and subsequently reinstated. After three years' subservience to Nebuchadnezzar, he again rebelled against him, as recorded in 2 Kings xxiv. 1 where *he turned, and rebelled* is idiomatic for 'he again rebelled.' As the consequence of this rebellion he was finally dethroned and taken to Babylon. It is this final phase of his career which the prophet predicted in the words, *He shall be buried with the burial of an ass, drawn and cast forth beyond the gates of Jerusalem* (Jer. xxii. 19).

made him a young lion. Though Pharaoh-necoh placed Jehoiakim on the throne (2 Kings xxiii. 34), the appointment is attributed to the Judean nation because it was made with their approval. He was twenty-five years old when he began to reign.

6. *he went up and down among the lions.* He vacillated between an alliance with Pharaoh-necoh and with Nebuchadnezzar.

he devoured men. He defied Nebuchad-nezzar which resulted in much bloodshed.

7. *he knew their castles.* The Hebrew phrase is difficult. The noun *almenothaw* normally means 'his widows,' but is taken as an unusual form of *armenothaw*, 'his castles, citadels,' as in Isa. xiii. 22. The verb is translated 'devastated' by the Targum, a sense which cannot be established in Hebrew. It is, however, commonly used of carnal knowledge; and so Rashi and Kimchi interpret as 'he knew their widows,' i.e. his policy brought about the death of a large number of men and rape of their women.

laid waste their cities. Through his evil deeds he caused the destruction of the cities of the Holy Land. So Kimchi, but Rashi understands it to mean that he impoverished the cities by levying heavy taxes (cf. 2 Kings xxiii. 35).

the land was desolate . . . his roaring. Judea in general deteriorated because of his misrule. The expression *noise of his roaring* is used to fit in with the allegory of the Judean king as a lion.

8. *the nations cried out against him.* The Hebrew verb is literally 'gave' with no object. Either 'voice' or 'snare' is to be un-

On every side from the provinces;
And they spread their net over
him,
He was taken in their pit.

9 And they put him in a cage with
hooks,
And brought him to the king of
Babylon;
That they might bring him into
strongholds,
So that his voice should no more
be heard
Upon the mountains of Israel.

10 Thy mother was like a vine, in
thy likeness,
Planted by the waters;
She was fruitful and full of
branches
By reason of many waters.

11 And she had strong rods
To be sceptres for them that
bore rule;

סָבִיב מִמְּדִינוֹת
וַיִּפְרְשׂוּ עָלָיו רִשְׁתָּם
בְּשַׁחְתָּם נִתְפָּשׂ׃
9 וַיִּתְּנֻהוּ בַסּוּגַר בַּחַחִים
וַיְבִאֻהוּ אֶל־מֶלֶךְ בָּבֶל
יְבִאֻהוּ בַּמְּצֹדוֹת
לְמַעַן לֹא־יִשָּׁמַע קוֹלוֹ
עוֹד אֶל־הָרֵי יִשְׂרָאֵל׃
10 אִמְּךָ כַגֶּפֶן בְּדָמְךָ
עַל־מַיִם שְׁתוּלָה
פֹּרִיָּה וַעֲנֵפָה
הָיְתָה מִמַּיִם רַבִּים׃
11 וַיִּהְיוּ־לָהּ מַטּוֹת עֹז
אֶל־שִׁבְטֵי מֹשְׁלִים

derstood. With the latter object it would mean, 'the nations laid a snare for him.'
on every side from the provinces. Several nations joined Nebuchadnezzar in the war against Jehoiakim, as stated in 2 Kings xxiv. 2.

9. *cage.* The Hebrew noun *sugar* is either derived from the verb *sagar*, 'shut up,' or is a loan-word from the Assyrian *sigaru*, 'cage.' 'Assurbanipal refers to a cage placed at the east gate of Nineveh in which he kept an Arabian monarch imprisoned' (Lofthouse).

brought him to the king of Babylon. Jehoiakim was twice taken captive by Nebuchadnezzar (see on verse 5). The reference here is to his first dethronement when he was imprisoned in Babylon for some time. Jehoiachin is not included in the elegy because his reign of only three months was considered negligible. Zedekiah is not treated separately since his fate was the same as that of Jehoiakim.

his voice should no more be heard. This is mentioned as a contrast to *the noise of his roaring* (verse 7). His rule over Judea (*the mountains of Israel*) came to an end.

10-14 ELEGY OVER THE FALL OF JUDAH

10. *thy mother.* The State of Judah.

a vine. For the allegory, cf. chapters xv and xvii.

in thy likeness. So most Jewish commentators. A.V. and R.V. have 'in thy blood,' i.e. in thy natural vigour.

planted by the waters; she was fruitful. Figurative of government by righteous kings in former days when the nation prospered and was powerful.

by reason of many waters. Cf. xvii. 5.

11. *strong rods to be sceptres.* Strong and resolute kings ruled over the nation.

And her stature was exalted
Among the thick branches,
And she was seen in her height
With the multitude of her tendrils.

12 But she was plucked up in fury,
She was cast down to the ground,
And the east wind dried up her fruit;
Her strong rods were broken off and withered,
The fire consumed her.

13 And now she is planted in the wilderness,
In a dry and thirsty ground.

14 And fire is gone out of the rod of her branches,
It hath devoured her fruit,
So that there is in her no strong rod
To be a sceptre to rule.'
This is a lamentation, and it was for a lamentation.

נַתִּגְבַּהּ קוֹמָתוֹ
עַל־בֵּין עֲבֹתִים
וַיֵּרָא בְגָבְהוֹ
בְּרֹב דָּלִיֹּתָיו׃

12 וַתֻּתַּשׁ בְּחֵמָה
לָאָרֶץ הֻשְׁלָכָה
וְרוּחַ הַקָּדִים הוֹבִישׁ פִּרְיָהּ
הִתְפָּרְקוּ וְיָבֵשׁוּ מַטֵּה עֻזָּהּ
אֵשׁ אֲכָלָתְהוּ׃

13 וְעַתָּה שְׁתוּלָה בַמִּדְבָּר
בְּאֶרֶץ צִיָּה וְצָמָא׃

14 וַתֵּצֵא אֵשׁ מִמַּטֵּה בַדֶּיהָ
פִּרְיָהּ אָכָלָה
וְלֹא־הָיָה בָהּ מַטֵּה עֹז
שֵׁבֶט לִמְשׁוֹל
קִינָה הִיא וַתְּהִי לְקִינָה׃

מ בז״ק   v. 14.

her stature was exalted among the thick branches. Judea then held a position of honour and influence among the surrounding peoples.

12. *she was cast down to the ground.* Her fall from high position to her present lowly state is so spectacular that it could only be due to God's will.

the east wind dried up her fruit. The allusion is to the invading army of Nebuchadnezzar whose seat of government was situated north-east of the Holy Land (cf. xvii. 10). Not only did he destroy the kingdom of Judah, but he also put to death all the heirs of Zedekiah and so made an end of the Davidic dynasty.

the fire consumed her. Kimchi renders: 'consumed it,' referring to *her strong rods* which in the Hebrew is singular with a collective force. The 'strong rod' is figurative of the last king, Zedekiah.

13. *now she is planted in the wilderness.* Descriptive of the existing condition of the people in Babylonian captivity.

14. *fire is gone out of the rod.* The fire which consumed the nation originated in its rulers. The cause of ruin is to be traced to Zedekiah's rebellion against Babylon.

to be a sceptre to rule. The royal house had perished so that no heir to the throne was left.

this is a lamentation, and it was for a lamentation. The elegy was spoken by the prophet before the disaster occurred, and it became the theme of general lamentation over the fall of the State.

20   CHAPTER XX   ב

1. And it came to pass in the seventh year, in the fifth month, the tenth day of the month, that certain of the elders of Israel came to inquire of the LORD, and sat before me. 2. And the word of the LORD came unto me, saying: 3. 'Son of man, speak unto the elders of Israel, and say unto them: Thus saith the Lord GOD: Are ye come to inquire of Me? As I live, saith the Lord GOD, I will not be inquired of by you. 4. Wilt thou judge them, son of

1 וַיְהִי | בַּשָּׁנָה הַשְּׁבִיעִית בַּחֲמִשִׁי
בֶּעָשׂוֹר לַחֹדֶשׁ בָּאוּ אֲנָשִׁים
מִזִּקְנֵי יִשְׂרָאֵל לִדְרֹשׁ אֶת־
יְהֹוָה וַיֵּשְׁבוּ לְפָנָי: * וַיְהִי 2
דְבַר־יְהֹוָה אֵלַי לֵאמֹר: בֶּן־ 3
אָדָם דַּבֵּר אֶת־זִקְנֵי יִשְׂרָאֵל
וְאָמַרְתָּ אֲלֵהֶם כֹּה אָמַר אֲדֹנָי
יֱהֹוִה הֲלִדְרֹשׁ אֹתִי אַתֶּם בָּאִים
חַי־אָנִי אִם־אִדָּרֵשׁ לָכֶם נְאֻם
אֲדֹנָי יֱהֹוִה: הֲתִשְׁפֹּט אֹתָם 4

v. 2. הפטרת קדושים

CHAPTER XX

AN INQUIRY ABOUT JERUSALEM'S FATE

THE discourse in this chapter is a reply to some of the elders who came to the prophet to inquire about the ultimate fate of Jerusalem, and perhaps also to request that he might invoke God's mercy to annul His decree regarding the impending destruction of the State. On Divine authority Ezekiel replies that the tragic fate of Jerusalem is irrevocable, because the same stubbornness and disobedience to the law of God which characterized their ancestors in Egypt, the wilderness and the Holy Land are still prevalent among their contemporaries. Yet the destruction of the Temple and the fall of the State will not mean the end of the covenant which God had made with Israel. Any attempt on their part to terminate that covenant and to assimilate themselves to other nations will be frustrated by His intervention. The wicked who persisted in eliminating God from their lives will perish, and only the righteous remnant will return to a reborn and purified Zion, and there dedicate themselves to the service of God.

1-4 THE ELDERS' INQUIRY

1. *in the seventh year.* Of Jehoiachin's captivity, i.e. 590 B.C.E., four years before the destruction of the Temple. For previous visits of this kind, cf. viii. 1, xiv. 1.

in the fifth month, the tenth day of the month. i.e. the tenth of Ab, the fatal day on which Jerusalem was eventually sacked. An ominous coincidence!

to inquire of the LORD. To seek enlightenment from the prophet about the future of Jerusalem and Judea. The nature of the inquiry is not specified and must be gathered from the context.

3. *I will not be inquired of by you.* In xxxvi. 37 the opposite is stated: *I will yet for this be inquired of by the house of Israel.* Commenting on this contradiction, the Midrash observes that this is one of the passages which teach that God does, as it were, change His mind so as to annul His decrees (Cant. Rabba vii. 8).

4. *wilt thou judge them?* The purport of the question is: wilt thou act as champion, or advocate, on their behalf? The

man, wilt thou judge them? cause them to know the abominations of their fathers; 5. and say unto them: Thus saith the Lord GOD: In the day when I chose Israel, and lifted up My hand unto the seed of the house of Jacob, and made Myself known unto them in the land of Egypt, when I lifted up My hand unto them, saying: I am the LORD your God; 6. in that day I lifted up My hand unto them, to bring them forth out of the land of Egypt into a land that I had sought out for them, flowing with milk and honey, which is the beauty of all lands; 7. and I said unto them: Cast ye

הֲתִשְׁפּוֹט בֶּן־אָדָם אֶת־
תּוֹעֲבֹת אֲבוֹתָם הוֹדִיעֵם:
5 וְאָמַרְתָּ אֲלֵיהֶם כֹּה־אָמַר
אֲדֹנָי יֱהֹוִה בְּיוֹם בָּחֳרִי
בְיִשְׂרָאֵל וָאֶשָּׂא יָדִי לְזֶרַע
בֵּית יַעֲקֹב וָאִוָּדַע לָהֶם בְּאֶרֶץ
מִצְרָיִם וָאֶשָּׂא יָדִי לָהֶם לֵאמֹר
6 אֲנִי יְהֹוָה אֱלֹהֵיכֶם: בַּיּוֹם
הַהוּא נָשָׂאתִי יָדִי לָהֶם
לְהוֹצִיאָם מֵאֶרֶץ מִצְרָיִם
אֶל־אֶרֶץ אֲשֶׁר־תַּרְתִּי לָהֶם
זָבַת חָלָב וּדְבַשׁ צְבִי הִיא
7 לְכָל־הָאֲרָצוֹת: וָאֹמַר
אֲלֵהֶם אִישׁ שִׁקּוּצֵי עֵינָיו

answer is: the present is not the time for thee to assume that rôle. Thy task is to *cause them to know* the reason of their dangerous plight which will be evident to them when they survey the national past.

5-9 ISRAEL'S SINFULNESS IN EGYPT

5. *the day when I chose Israel.* The choice of Israel began in Egypt on the day when God sent Moses and Aaron to them.

lifted up My hand. Lifting up the hand is the gesture in taking an oath. The nature of the oath is stated in verse 6.

unto the seed of the house of Jacob. In Exod. vi. 8 the promise is said to have been made to Abraham, Isaac and Jacob. Since the first two had other sons, Ishmael and Esau respectively, it is explained that the fulfilment was to be restricted to the seed of Jacob.

made Myself known. Through Moses (cf. Exod. iii. 6ff.).

I am the LORD your God. Cf. Exod. vi. 2, 7. The expression denotes release and protection for Israel.

6. *in that day.* The Divine choice of Israel under oath was followed by another promising redemption for them from Egyptian slavery and acquisition of the Land of Promise (cf. Exod. vi. 6f.).

the beauty of all lands. Its geographical features and climate make it the most beautiful of all lands. Cf. *Fair in situation, the joy of the whole earth, even mount Zion . . . the city of the great King* (Ps. xlviii. 3). 'Palestine, therefore, not merely by its situation, but by its comparative fertility, might well be considered the prize of the Eastern world, the possession of which was the mark of God's peculiar favour . . . and a land of which the blessings were so evidently the gift of God' (Stanley).

away every man the detestable things of his eyes, and defile not yourselves with the idols of Egypt; I am the LORD your God. 8. But they rebelled against Me, and would not hearken unto Me; they did not every man cast away the detestable things of their eyes, neither did they forsake the idols of Egypt; then I said I would pour out My fury upon them, to spend My anger upon them in the midst of the land of Egypt. 9. But I wrought for My name's sake, that it should not be profaned in the sight of the nations, among whom they were, in whose sight I made Myself known unto them, so as to bring them forth out of the land of Egypt. 10. So I caused them to go forth out of the land of Egypt, and brought them into the wilderness. 11. And I gave them My statutes, and taught them

הַשְׁלִיכוּ וּבְגִלּוּלֵי מִצְרַיִם
אַל־תִּטַּמָּאוּ אֲנִי יְהֹוָה
אֱלֹהֵיכֶם: וַיַּמְרוּ־בִי וְלֹא 8
אָבוּ לִשְׁמֹעַ אֵלַי אִישׁ אֶת־
שִׁקּוּצֵי עֵינֵיהֶם לֹא הִשְׁלִיכוּ
וְאֶת־גִּלּוּלֵי מִצְרַיִם לֹא עָזָבוּ
וָאֹמַר לִשְׁפֹּךְ חֲמָתִי עֲלֵיהֶם
לְכַלּוֹת אַפִּי בָּהֶם בְּתוֹךְ אֶרֶץ
מִצְרָיִם: וָאַעַשׂ לְמַעַן שְׁמִי 9
לְבִלְתִּי הֵחֵל לְעֵינֵי הַגּוֹיִם
אֲשֶׁר־הֵמָּה בְתוֹכָם אֲשֶׁר
נוֹדַעְתִּי אֲלֵיהֶם לְעֵינֵיהֶם
לְהוֹצִיאָם מֵאֶרֶץ מִצְרָיִם:
וָאוֹצִיאֵם מֵאֶרֶץ מִצְרַיִם 10
וָאֲבִאֵם אֶל־הַמִּדְבָּר: וָאֶתֵּן 11

7. *cast ye away . . . the detestable things.* The implication is that the Israelites followed some of the religious practices of their Egyptian neighbours, a fact attested by Josh. xxiv. 14. Nevertheless 'it is noteworthy that the characteristic beliefs of Egypt have left no trace on Israelite thought' (Lofthouse).

I am the LORD your God. Who alone is to be worshipped.

8. *they rebelled against Me, and would not hearken.* What is here narrated is not recorded in the Pentateuch. It may well be believed that while the Israelites were in Egypt, the pure faith inherited from the patriarchs was contaminated by local heathenish ideas and practices. According to the Midrash Rabba, Exod. iv. 3, the wicked among the Israelites perished and were buried during the plague of darkness, so that the Egyptians should not say that an epidemic had been inflicted by God on His people.

I said. i.e. I intended. On the strict principle of justice, the Israelites should have perished in Egypt. Only for the sake of the honour of His name God spared and redeemed them from bondage.

9. *it should not be profaned.* Were the Israelites not liberated from Egypt, the nations would not attribute it to Divine retribution but to His lack of power (cf. Num. xiv. 16; Deut. ix. 28).

I made Myself known unto them. God had revealed Himself to Israel and conveyed to them His intention to liberate them. All this was well known to the Egyptians. Failure to carry out the proclaimed redemption would have caused a profanation of the name of God.

10-17 ISRAEL'S CONDUCT IN THE WILDERNESS

10. 'Ezekiel here makes no reference

Mine ordinances, which if a man do, he shall live by them.   12. Moreover also I gave them My sabbaths, to be a sign between Me and them, that they might know that I am the LORD that sanctify them.   13. But the house of Israel rebelled against Me in the wilderness; they walked not in My statutes, and they rejected Mine ordinances, which if a man do, he shall live by them, and My sabbaths they greatly profaned; then I said I would pour out My fury upon them in the wilderness, to consume them.   14. But I wrought for My name's sake, that it should not be profaned in the sight of the

לָהֶם֙ אֶת־חֻקּוֹתַ֔י וְאֶת־
מִשְׁפָּטַ֖י הוֹדַ֣עְתִּי אוֹתָ֑ם אֲשֶׁ֨ר
יַעֲשֶׂ֤ה אוֹתָם֙ הָֽאָדָ֔ם וָחַ֖י בָּהֶֽם׃
12 וְגַ֤ם אֶת־שַׁבְּתוֹתַי֙ נָתַ֣תִּי לָהֶ֔ם
לִהְי֣וֹת לְא֔וֹת בֵּינִ֖י וּבֵֽינֵיהֶ֑ם
לָדַ֕עַת כִּ֛י אֲנִ֥י יְהוָ֖ה מְקַדְּשָֽׁם׃
13 וַיַּמְרוּ־בִ֣י בֵֽית־יִשְׂרָאֵ֣ל
בַּמִּדְבָּ֗ר בְּחֻקּוֹתַ֤י לֹא־הָלָ֨כוּ֙
וְאֶת־מִשְׁפָּטַ֣י מָאָ֔סוּ אֲשֶׁ֨ר
יַעֲשֶׂ֤ה אֹתָם֙ הָֽאָדָ֔ם וָחַ֖י בָּהֶ֑ם
וְאֶת־שַׁבְּתֹתַ֖י חִלְּל֣וּ מְאֹ֑ד
וָאֹמַ֞ר לִשְׁפֹּ֨ךְ חֲמָתִ֧י עֲלֵיהֶ֛ם
14 בַּמִּדְבָּ֖ר לְכַלּוֹתָֽם׃ וָאֶֽעֱשֶׂ֖ה
לְמַ֣עַן שְׁמִ֑י לְבִלְתִּ֤י הֵחֵל֙ לְעֵינֵ֔י

v. 13. הל׳ בקמץ   v. 13. קמץ ברביע

to the Red Sea; his thought of God's wrath and Israel's disobedience obscures what was to the Hebrew God's crowning mercy' (Lofthouse).

11. *I gave them My statutes.* The reference is to the Revelation on mount Sinai.

which if a man do, he shall live by them. A quotation from Lev. xviii. 5. Obedience to the Divine laws, both those relating to the duties of man towards God and those dealing with his duties towards his fellow-men, leads to social and national happiness and stability.

12. *My sabbaths.* The plural includes festivals which are given in the Pentateuch the designation of *sabbath;* cf. Lev. xxiii. 24, 39.

a sign between Me and them. Cf. Exod.

xxxi. 17. 'The Sabbath was more than a day of rest. Its observance by the Israelite was a constantly recurring acknowledgment of God as the Creator of the universe. It would be an open denial of God for an Israelite to desecrate the Sabbath' (Hertz).

13. *they walked not in My statutes.* During their sojourn in the wilderness, they worshipped the Golden Calf, left of the manna until the morning (Exod. xvi. 20), tried God in Rephidim (Exod. xvii) and committed other acts of disobedience.

My sabbaths they greatly profaned. Instances are recorded in Exod. xvi. 27f. and Num. xv. 32f.

14. *it should not be profaned.* See on verse 9, and cf. Exod. xxxii. 12ff.; Num. xiv. 12ff.

nations, in whose sight I brought them out. 15. Yet also I lifted up My hand unto them in the wilderness, that I would not bring them into the land which I had given them, flowing with milk and honey, which is the beauty of all lands; 16. because they rejected Mine ordinances, and walked not in My statutes, and profaned My sabbaths —for their heart went after their idols. 17. Nevertheless Mine eye spared them from destroying them, neither did I make a full end of them in the wilderness. 18. And I said unto their children in the wilderness: Walk ye not in the statutes of your fathers, neither observe their ordinances, nor defile yourselves with their idols; 19. I am the LORD your God; walk in My statutes, and keep Mine ordinances, and do them; 20. and hallow My sabbaths, and they shall be a sign between Me and you, that ye may know that I am the LORD your God.

הַגּוֹיִם אֲשֶׁר הוֹצֵאתִים
15 לְעֵינֵיהֶם: וְגַם־אֲנִי נָשָׂאתִי
יָדִי לָהֶם בַּמִּדְבָּר לְבִלְתִּי
הָבִיא אוֹתָם אֶל־הָאָרֶץ
אֲשֶׁר־נָתַתִּי זָבַת חָלָב וּדְבַשׁ
צְבִי הִיא לְכָל־הָאֲרָצוֹת:
16 יַעַן בְּמִשְׁפָּטַי מָאָסוּ וְאֶת־
חֻקּוֹתַי לֹא־הָלְכוּ בָהֶם וְאֶת־
שַׁבְּתוֹתַי חִלֵּלוּ כִּי אַחֲרֵי
17 גִּלּוּלֵיהֶם לִבָּם הֹלֵךְ: וַתָּחָס
עֵינִי עֲלֵיהֶם מִשַּׁחֲתָם וְלֹא־
עָשִׂיתִי אוֹתָם כָּלָה בַּמִּדְבָּר:
18 וָאֹמַר אֶל־בְּנֵיהֶם בַּמִּדְבָּר
בְּחוּקֵּי אֲבוֹתֵיכֶם אַל־תֵּלֵכוּ
וְאֶת־מִשְׁפְּטֵיהֶם אַל־
תִּשְׁמֹרוּ וּבְגִלּוּלֵיהֶם אַל־
19 תִּטַּמָּאוּ: אֲנִי יְהוָה אֱלֹהֵיכֶם
בְּחֻקּוֹתַי לֵכוּ וְאֶת־מִשְׁפָּטַי
20 שִׁמְרוּ וַעֲשׂוּ אֹתָם: וְאֶת־
שַׁבְּתוֹתַי קַדֵּשׁוּ וְהָיוּ לְאוֹת
בֵּינִי וּבֵינֵיכֶם לָדַעַת כִּי אֲנִי

v. 16. קמץ ברביע   v. 18. דגש אחר שורק

15. *I would not bring them into the land.* On account of the sin of the spies (cf. Num. xiv. 29f.).

the beauty of all lands. See on verse 6.

17. *neither did I make a full end of them.* Though the generation which left Egypt perished in the wilderness, their children entered the Promised Land.

18-26 SINFULNESS OF THE
SUCCEEDING GENERATION

18. *their children.* The offspring of the adults who left Egypt.

the statutes of your fathers. The Egyptian practices which they had acquired while living in their land.

19. *I am the LORD your God; walk in My statutes.* The younger generation were

21. But the children rebelled against Me; they walked not in My statutes, neither kept Mine ordinances to do them, which if a man do, he shall live by them; they profaned My sabbaths; then I said I would pour out My fury upon them, to spend My anger upon them in the wilderness. 22. Nevertheless I withdrew My hand, and wrought for My name's sake, that it should not be profaned in the sight of the nations, in whose sight I brought them forth. 23. I lifted up My hand unto them also in the wilderness, that I would scatter them among the nations, and disperse them through the countries; 24. because they had not executed Mine ordinances, but had rejected My statutes, and had profaned My sabbaths, and their eyes were after their fathers' idols. 25. Wherefore

21 יְהֹוָה אֱלֹהֵיכֶם: ׃ וַיַּמְרוּ־בִי
הַבָּנִים בְּחֻקּוֹתַי לֹא־הָלָכוּ
וְאֶת־־מִשְׁפָּטַי לֹא־שָׁמְרוּ
לַעֲשׂוֹת אוֹתָם אֲשֶׁר יַעֲשֶׂה
אוֹתָם הָאָדָם וָחַי בָּהֶם אֶת־
שַׁבְּתוֹתַי חִלֵּלוּ וָאֹמַר לִשְׁפֹּךְ
חֲמָתִי עֲלֵהֶם לְכַלּוֹת אַפִּי בָּם
22 בַּמִּדְבָּר: וַהֲשִׁבֹתִי אֶת־יָדִי
וָאַעַשׂ לְמַעַן שְׁמִי לְבִלְתִּי הֵחֵל
לְעֵינֵי הַגּוֹיִם אֲשֶׁר־הוֹצֵאתִי
23 אֹתָם לְעֵינֵיהֶם: נַּם־־אֲנִי
נָשָׂאתִי אֶת־יָדִי לָהֶם בַּמִּדְבָּר
לְהָפִיץ אֹתָם בַּגּוֹיִם וּלְזָרוֹת
24 אוֹתָם בָּאֲרָצוֹת: יַעַן מִשְׁפָּטַי
לֹא־עָשׂוּ וְחֻקּוֹתַי מָאָסוּ וְאֶת־
שַׁבְּתוֹתַי חִלֵּלוּ וְאַחֲרֵי גִלּוּלֵי
25 אֲבוֹתָם הָיוּ עֵינֵיהֶם: וְגַם־

v. 20.   v. 21. הל׳ בקמץ   v. 24. קמץ בז״ק עד כאן

not only exhorted to avoid the sins of their fathers, but to accept the way of God as that alone in which they should walk, if they were to enjoy a secure national existence.

21. the children rebelled against Me. The Jewish commentators quote as a case of rebellion against God the incident of the Baal of Peor (Num. xxv. 1-9).

22. I withdrew My hand. The Divine hand was outstretched to make an end of the sinful generation, but He withdrew it and spared the people.

23. I would scatter them among the nations. While they were still in the wilderness, God decreed that their descendants, after being settled in the Holy Land, would

be exiled and dispersed among the nations, because they were yet in need of purification in the furnace of national suffering (cf. Deut. iv. 27ff., xxviii. 64ff.; Ps. cvi. 26f.). Commenting on the words, *and the people wept that night* (Num. xiv. 1), the Talmud observes that it was the night of the ninth of Ab, and the Holy One, blessed be He, said, 'Because you wept that night without cause, I will convert it into an anniversary of weeping for the destruction of both Temples' (Taan. 29a). But all such threats were conditional, and the meaning is that the unrighteous spirit which was evinced in the wilderness, if persisted in when the nation was established in its land, would lead to captivity and dispersion.

I gave them also statutes that were not good, and ordinances whereby they should not live; 26. and I polluted them in their own gifts, in that they set apart all that openeth the womb, that I might destroy them, to the end that they might know that I am the LORD.

27. Therefore, son of man, speak unto the house of Israel, and say unto them: Thus saith the Lord GOD: In this moreover have your fathers blasphemed Me, in that they dealt treacherously with Me. 28. For when I had brought them into the land, which I lifted up My hand to

אֲנִי נָתַתִּי לָהֶם חֻקִּים לֹא
טוֹבִים וּמִשְׁפָּטִים לֹא יִחְיוּ
26 בָּהֶם: וָאֲטַמֵּא אוֹתָם
בְּמַתְּנוֹתָם בְּהַעֲבִיר כָּל־
פֶּטֶר רָחַם לְמַעַן אֲשִׁמֵּם לְמַעַן
אֲשֶׁר יֵדְעוּ אֲשֶׁר אֲנִי יְהֹוָה:
27 לָכֵן דַּבֵּר אֶל־בֵּית יִשְׂרָאֵל
בֶּן־אָדָם וְאָמַרְתָּ אֲלֵיהֶם כֹּה
אָמַר אֲדֹנָי יְהֹוִה עוֹד זֹאת
גִּדְּפוּ אוֹתִי אֲבוֹתֵיכֶם בְּמַעֲלָם
28 בִּי מָעַל: וָאֲבִיאֵם אֶל־
הָאָרֶץ אֲשֶׁר נָשָׂאתִי אֶת־יָדִי

25. *statutes that were not good.* The thought that God could actually give the Israelites *statutes that were not good* was repugnant to the Jewish mind. Accordingly, Rashi explains that, since they rejected the discipline of the Torah, God allowed the evil dictates of their heart to have unrestricted sway over them. Kimchi and others interpret that, as a punishment for rejecting the Divine statutes, God delivers them to their enemies who impose upon them exacting and rigorous statutes (*not good*). Because they discarded those laws *which if a man do, he shall live by them,* they would become subject to laws which signify death. The verb *I gave* therefore has the meaning of 'I caused to give.' Rashi's explanation seems to come nearer to Biblical doctrine which ascribes to God the inevitable consequence of man's choice of action. Thus He is said to have hardened Pharaoh's heart where the intention is that He let the king harden his heart. See on the phrase, *I the LORD have enticed that prophet* (xiv. 9).

26. *I polluted them in their own gifts.* 'The penalty of sin is further delusion and worse sin, the end of which is death' (Davidson). God had ordained that the firstborn, *all that openeth the womb,* should be 'sanctified' to Him (Exod. xiii. 2). So far as the children were concerned, this was a law which preserved them alive since nowhere does He command child-sacrifice. They rejected this law, and God allowed them to turn an act of 'sanctification' into an act of 'pollution' when they burnt their children to Molech.

27-29 ISRAEL'S SINFULNESS IN
THE HOLY LAND

27. *moreover have your fathers blasphemed Me.* In addition to their wickedness in Egypt and the wilderness, they continued their sinning when they were in their own land. The verb 'blaspheme' signifies, in a wider sense, committing a cardinal sin. The phrase, *the same blasphemeth the LORD* (Num. xv. 30), is interpreted in the Talmud of idolatry (Kerith. 7b).

give unto them, then they saw every high hill, and every thick tree, and they offered there their sacrifices, and there they presented the provocation of their offering, there also they made their sweet savour, and there they poured out their drink-offerings. 29. Then I said unto them: What meaneth the high place whereunto ye go? So the name thereof is called Bamah unto this day.

30. Wherefore say unto the house of Israel: Thus saith the Lord GOD: When ye pollute yourselves after the manner of your fathers, and go astray after their abominations, 31. and when, in offering your gifts,

לָתֵת אוֹתָהּ לָהֶם וַיִּרְאוּ כָל־
גִּבְעָה רָמָה וְכָל־עֵץ עָבוֹת
וַיִּזְבְּחוּ־שָׁם אֶת־זִבְחֵיהֶם
וַיִּתְּנוּ־שָׁם כַּעַס קָרְבָּנָם
וַיָּשִׂימוּ שָׁם רֵיחַ נִיחוֹחֵיהֶם
וַיַּסִּיכוּ שָׁם אֶת־נִסְכֵּיהֶם:
29 וָאֹמַר אֲלֵהֶם מָה הַבָּמָה
אֲשֶׁר־אַתֶּם הַבָּאִים שָׁם
וַיִּקָּרֵא שְׁמָהּ בָּמָה עַד הַיּוֹם
30 הַזֶּה: לָכֵן אֱמֹר ׀ אֶל־בֵּית
יִשְׂרָאֵל כֹּה אָמַר אֲדֹנָי יֱהֹוִה
הַבְּדֶרֶךְ אֲבוֹתֵיכֶם אַתֶּם
נִטְמְאִים וְאַחֲרֵי שִׁקּוּצֵיהֶם
31 אַתֶּם זֹנִים: וּבִשְׂאֵת מַתְּנֹתֵיכֶם

---

28. *then they saw*, etc. On entering the Promised Land, they adopted the forms of worship practised by the Canaanites. Shrines were set up on hill-tops and under leafy trees (see on vi. 13).

the provocation of their offering. By their idolatrous offerings they provoked God to anger.

sweet savour. This term is used of the odour of flesh, fat, meal-offering or incense burnt upon the altar for the worship of God or an idol.

drink-offerings. Libations of wine.

29. *what meaneth the high place.* i.e. who permitted you the use of a *high place?* Ezekiel apparently gives the Hebrew term *bamah* a contemptuous derivation as a compound of *ba* (go) and *mah* (what).

the name thereof is called Bamah unto this day. The term *bamah*, borrowed from heathendom, was later applied to the

structure even when used for the worship of God.

30-44 AS IN THE PAST SO IN THE FUTURE GOD WILL HAVE REGARD FOR THE HONOUR OF HIS NAME

In reply to the inquiry of the elders of Israel, Ezekiel reviewed the past of the nation; now he applies the teaching to the future.

30. *when ye pollute yourselves.* This verse and the first half of the next verse are antecedents to the clause, *shall I then be inquired of by you?* The meaning is, if you still indulge in the abominable practices of idolatry, how can you expect a Divine revelation?

31. *in offering your gifts.* As an act of homage to the images you worship, the *gifts* taking the form of the sacrifice of their children.

in making your sons to pass through the fire, ye pollute yourselves with all your idols, unto this day; shall I then be inquired of by you, O house of Israel? As I live, saith the Lord GOD, I will not be inquired of by you; 32. and that which cometh into your mind shall not be at all; in that ye say: We will be as the nations, as the families of the countries, to serve wood and stone. 33. As I live, saith the Lord GOD, surely with a mighty hand, and with an outstretched arm, and with fury poured out, will I be king over you; 34. and I will bring you out from the peoples, and will gather you out of the countries wherein ye are scattered, with a mighty hand, and with an outstretched arm, and with fury poured out; 35. and I will bring

בְּהַעֲבִיר בְּנֵיכֶם בָּאֵשׁ אַתֶּם
נִטְמְאִים לְכָל־־גִּלּוּלֵיכֶם
עַד־הַיּוֹם וַאֲנִי אִדָּרֵשׁ לָכֶם
בֵּית יִשְׂרָאֵל חַי־אָנִי נְאֻם אֲדֹנָי
יֱהֹוִה אִם־־אִדָּרֵשׁ לָכֶם:
32 וְהָעֹלָה עַל־רוּחֲכֶם הָיוֹ לֹא
תִהְיֶה אֲשֶׁר ׀ אַתֶּם אֹמְרִים
נִהְיֶה כַגּוֹיִם כְּמִשְׁפְּחוֹת
הָאֲרָצוֹת לְשָׁרֵת עֵץ וָאָבֶן:
33 חַי־אָנִי נְאֻם אֲדֹנָי יֱהֹוִה אִם־
לֹא בְּיָד חֲזָקָה וּבִזְרוֹעַ נְטוּיָה
וּבְחֵמָה שְׁפוּכָה אֶמְלוֹךְ
34 עֲלֵיכֶם: וְהוֹצֵאתִי אֶתְכֶם
מִן־הָעַמִּים וְקִבַּצְתִּי אֶתְכֶם
מִן־הָאֲרָצוֹת אֲשֶׁר נְפוֹצוֹתֶם
בָּם בְּיָד חֲזָקָה וּבִזְרוֹעַ נְטוּיָה
35 וּבְחֵמָה שְׁפוּכָה: וְהֵבֵאתִי

---

ye pollute yourselves. Such 'pollution' creates a barrier between them and God which makes impossible the achievement of their desire, viz. enlightenment from Him on what the immediate future holds in store.

32. *we will be as the nations.* Apparently a wave of assimilation swept over the exiles in Babylon or over the remnant in Jerusalem. Humiliated, subject to foreign domination and driven from their soil, they regarded the covenant between them and God as ended. They were free to discard His service and adopt the form of worship practised by other nations. But that intention, declares God, *shall not be at all.*

33. *will I be king over you.* The delusion which had seized hold of them will be dispelled by the severest measures. God's *mighty hand* and *outstretched arm,* revealed in the past for their protection, will soon become manifest in drastic fashion to remind them of their distinctiveness as His people.

34. *I will bring you out,* etc. As against the hope of the Judeans to lose their identity among their neighbours, God tells them that by mighty acts He will remove them from their present environment and ultimately restore their distinctive character.

you into the wilderness of the peoples, and there will I plead with you face to face. 36. Like as I pleaded with your fathers in the wilderness of the land of Egypt, so will I plead with you, saith the Lord GOD. 37. And I will cause you to pass under the rod, and I will bring you into the bond of the covenant; 38. and I will purge out from among you the rebels, and them that transgress against Me; I will bring them forth out of the land where they sojourn, but they shall not enter into the land of Israel; and ye shall know that I am the LORD. 39. As for you, O house of Israel, thus saith the Lord GOD:

אֶתְכֶם אֶל־־מִדְבַּר הָעַמִּים
וְנִשְׁפַּטְתִּי אִתְּכֶם שָׁם פָּנִים
אֶל־פָּנִים: כַּאֲשֶׁר נִשְׁפַּטְתִּי 36
אֶת־אֲבוֹתֵיכֶם בְּמִדְבַּר אֶרֶץ
מִצְרָיִם כֵּן אִשָּׁפֵט אִתְּכֶם נְאֻם
אֲדֹנָי יֱהוִֹה: וְהַעֲבַרְתִּי אֶתְכֶם 37
תַּחַת הַשָּׁבֶט וְהֵבֵאתִי אֶתְכֶם
בְּמָסֹרֶת הַבְּרִית: וּבָרוֹתִי 38
מִכֶּם הַמֹּרְדִים וְהַפּוֹשְׁעִים
בִּי מֵאֶרֶץ מְגוּרֵיהֶם אוֹצִיא
אוֹתָם וְאֶל־אַדְמַת יִשְׂרָאֵל
לֹא יָבוֹא וִידַעְתֶּם כִּי־אֲנִי
יְהוָֹה: וְאַתֶּם בֵּית־יִשְׂרָאֵל 39
כֹּה־אָמַר | אֲדֹנָי יֱהוִֹה אִישׁ

v. 87. חסר א׳

---

35. *the wilderness of the peoples.* i.e. the desert which bordered on the land where they were dwelling, viz. between Syria and Babylon. As in the wilderness of Egypt they were constituted the people of God, so in the desert, cut off from intercourse with heathen nations, they will be made again into His people. There God will *plead,* i.e. remonstrate and reason with them, *face to face* with none to distract their attention from Him.

36. *the wilderness of the land of Egypt.* The experience of the remote past, in the infancy of the nation, will be repeated in its rebirth.

37. *I will cause you to pass under the rod.* In separating the tithe of herd or flock, it was the practice to make the animals pass one by one under the rod and the tenth was separated and declared holy (cf. Lev. xxvii. 32). Similarly, the Judeans, before their deliverance from

exile, will be scrutinized by their Shepherd; the wicked will perish and the righteous be saved.

I will bring you into the bond of the covenant. As the selected sheep are dedicated to the Sanctuary, so the Judeans who pass under God's rod will be reconsecrated under the covenant whereby Israel is a *holy nation* (Exod. xix. 6).

38. *the land where they sojourn.* The land of captivity.

but they shall not enter into the land of Israel. The rebels will perish in the *wilderness of the peoples* as once the rebellious generation perished in the wilderness of Egypt.

39. *as for you,* etc. The verse has been understood in two ways. First, as addressed to the contemporary generation as distinguished from those who, spoken of in the preceding verses, were

Go ye, serve every one his idols, even because ye will not hearken unto Me; but My holy name shall ye no more profane with your gifts, and with your idols. 40. For in My holy mountain, in the mountain of the height of Israel, saith the Lord GOD, there shall all the house of Israel, all of them, serve Me in the land; there will I accept them, and there will I require your heave-offerings, and the first of your gifts, with all your holy things. 41. With your sweet savour will I accept you, when I bring you out from the peoples, and gather you out of the countries wherein ye have been scattered; and I will be sanctified in

גִּלּוּלָיו֙ לְכ֣וּ עֲבֹ֔דוּ וְאַחַ֖ר אִם־
אֵֽינְכֶ֤ם שֹׁמְעִים֙ אֵלָ֔י וְאֶת־שֵׁ֥ם
קָדְשִׁ֛י לֹ֥א תְחַלְּלוּ־ע֖וֹד
40 בְּמַתְּנֽוֹתֵיכֶ֖ם וּבְגִלּֽוּלֵיכֶֽם: כִּ֣י
בְהַר־קָדְשִׁ֞י בְּהַ֣ר | מְר֣וֹם
יִשְׂרָאֵ֗ל נְאֻם֙ אֲדֹנָ֣י יְהֹוִ֔ה שָׁ֣ם
יַֽעַבְדֻ֜נִי כָּל־בֵּ֧ית יִשְׂרָאֵ֛ל
כֻּלֹּ֖ה בָּאָ֑רֶץ שָׁ֤ם אֶרְצֵם֙ וְשָׁ֣ם
אֶדְר֗וֹשׁ אֶת־תְּרֽוּמֹֽתֵיכֶ֛ם
וְאֶת־רֵאשִׁ֥ית מַשְׂאֽוֹתֵיכֶ֖ם
41 בְּכָל־קָדְשֵׁיכֶֽם: בְּרֵ֣יחַ נִיחֹ֣חַ
אֶרְצֶ֣ה אֶתְכֶ֔ם בְּהוֹצִיאִ֤י
אֶתְכֶם֙ מִן־הָ֣עַמִּ֔ים וְקִבַּצְתִּ֣י
אֶתְכֶ֔ם מִן־הָ֣אֲרָצ֔וֹת אֲשֶׁ֥ר
נְפֹצֹתֶ֖ם בָּ֑ם וְנִקְדַּשְׁתִּ֥י בָכֶ֖ם

to share in the future restoration. Since they refuse to obey God, let them completely abandon themselves to the worship of their idols. Alternatively, it is interpreted as ironical advice: 'Go ye, serve every one his idols; but afterwards (I swear that) ye shall hearken unto Me and no more profane My holy name with your (abominable) gifts (which you are now offering) and with your idols (which you are now worshipping).' The latter is preferable.

40. the mountain of the height of Israel. i.e. mount Zion, the site of the Temple.

there shall all the house of Israel, all of them, serve Me. The present worship, contaminated with idolatry, will be discarded; and the true service, acceptable to God, will come into its own when the scattered house of Israel is regathered.

in the land. The Land of Israel.

there will I require your heave-offerings. When they are restored to the Holy Land, God will not only accept, but even *require*, their offerings. The term *terumah* usually signifies the dues of the priests or gifts for religious purposes. Here it is more generally used of the Temple offerings.

the first of your gifts. These include the first-ripe fruit which had to be carried to Jerusalem and presented to the priest (Deut. xxvi. 2ff.), the firstborn of the cattle and the redemption fee of the firstborn male child paid to the priest (Exod. xiii. 2, 12ff.), and the first portion of the dough (Num. xv. 20f.).

all your holy things. Referring to sacrifices on the altar and other kinds of offerings.

41. sweet savour. See on verse 28.

I will be sanctified in you. In contradistinction to the profanation of God's

you in the sight of the nations. 42. And ye shall know that I am the Lord, when I shall bring you into the land of Israel, into the country which I lifted up My hand to give unto your fathers. 43. And there shall ye remember your ways, and all your doings, wherein ye have polluted yourselves; and ye shall loathe yourselves in your own sight for all your evils that ye have committed. 44. And ye shall know that I am the Lord, when I have wrought with you for My name's sake, not according to your evil ways, nor according to your corrupt doings, O ye house of Israel, saith the Lord God.'

42 לְעֵינֵי הַגּוֹיִם: וִידַעְתֶּם כִּי־
אֲנִי יְהֹוָה בַּהֲבִיאִי אֶתְכֶם אֶל־
אַדְמַת יִשְׂרָאֵל אֶל־הָאָרֶץ
אֲשֶׁר נָשָׂאתִי אֶת־יָדִי לָתֵת
43 אוֹתָהּ לַאֲבוֹתֵיכֶם: וּזְכַרְתֶּם־
שָׁם אֶת־דַּרְכֵיכֶם וְאֵת כָּל־
עֲלִילוֹתֵיכֶם אֲשֶׁר נִטְמֵאתֶם
בָּם וּנְקֹטֹתֶם בִּפְנֵיכֶם בְּכָל־
רָעוֹתֵיכֶם אֲשֶׁר עֲשִׂיתֶם:
44 וִידַעְתֶּם כִּי־אֲנִי יְהֹוָה
בַּעֲשׂוֹתִי אִתְּכֶם לְמַעַן שְׁמִי
לֹא כְדַרְכֵיכֶם הָרָעִים
וְכַעֲלִילוֹתֵיכֶם הַנִּשְׁחָתוֹת
בֵּית יִשְׂרָאֵל נְאֻם אֲדֹנָי יֱהֹוִה:

21 CHAPTER XXI כא

1. And the word of the Lord came 1 וַיְהִי דְבַר־יְהֹוָה אֵלַי לֵאמֹר:

name wrought by the captivity of His people in the eyes of the nations of the world, the restoration of Israel to his land will serve as a means to make the Divine name holy in their sight.

42. *ye shall know that I am the LORD.* It will be evident beyond all doubt that the might of God had restored them to their land, and they will have to acknowledge that He, and none other, is God.

43. *there shall ye remember your ways.* The manifestation of God's mercy will make them ashamed of their evil past and reform their hearts.

ye shall loathe yourselves. See on vi. 9.

44. *for My name's sake, not according to your evil ways.* Their self-loathing will be the deeper when they realize that the transformation of their fortunes is not due to their merits. They really deserved to perish because of their evil ways; if they have escaped that fate it is for the reason that God is jealous for His good name. May they take the lesson to heart and refrain from doing anything which can cause His name to be profaned!

CHAPTER XXI

IN this chapter the prophet repeats with solemn emphasis his solemn warning of the imminent invasion and fall of

unto me, saying: 2. 'Son of man, set thy face toward the South, and preach toward the South, and prophesy against the forest of the field in the South; 3. and say to the forest of the South: Hear the word of the LORD: Thus saith the Lord GOD: Behold, I will kindle a fire in thee, and it shall devour every green tree in thee, and every dry tree, it shall not be quenched, even a flaming flame; and all faces from the south to the north shall be seared thereby. 4. And all flesh shall see

2 בֶּן־אָדָם שִׂים פָּנֶיךָ דֶּרֶךְ תֵּימָנָה וְהַטֵּף אֶל־דָּרוֹם וְהִנָּבֵא אֶל־יַעַר הַשָּׂדֶה נֶגֶב׃ 3 וְאָמַרְתָּ לְיַעַר הַנֶּגֶב שְׁמַע דְּבַר־יְהוָה כֹּה־אָמַר אֲדֹנָי יֱהוִֹה הִנְנִי מַצִּית־בְּךָ ׀ אֵשׁ וְאָכְלָה בְךָ כָל־עֵץ־לַח וְכָל־עֵץ יָבֵשׁ לֹא־תִכְבֶּה לַהֶבֶת שַׁלְהֶבֶת וְנִצְרְבוּ־בָהּ 4 כָּל־פָּנִים מִנֶּגֶב צָפוֹנָה׃ וְרָאוּ

Jerusalem. At first he speaks in metaphors, then he passes on to plain language. The scene of the forest in the South devoured by fire is replaced by that of Jerusalem devastated by the sword. He proceeds to describe in vivid terms the drawn sword in the hand of the Babylonian king who would execute God's judgment unsparingly. After the oracle on the devouring sword comes a description of Nebuchadnezzar standing at the cross-roads and practising divination to decide whether he should first attack Ammon or Jerusalem. The lot fell on the latter; but Ammon, too, would eventually be destroyed by the sword of Nebuchadnezzar.

In A.V. and R.V., verses 1-5 are attached to the preceding chapter, xxi beginning with verse 6 of the Hebrew.

1-5 THE CONFLAGRATION IN THE FOREST

2. set thy face toward. Turn in the direction of the South, i.e. the Land of Israel which lay due south of Babylon where the prophet was living.

preach. The verb means in the first instance 'to drop (words)' and so 'to preach.' In later Hebrew the noun for 'preacher' was derived from this root.

the forest. Jerusalem is compared to a forest. As a forest has good and bad trees, so Jerusalem harboured righteous and wicked inhabitants (Kimchi). An indication that Jerusalem will be devastated, and free for anyone to enter like a forest or field (Rashi). The whole of the land, not only the capital, was threatened (cf. verse 7).

South. The Hebrew is *negeb*, whereas earlier in the verse it is *darom*. The latter means 'the sunny district,' the former 'the hot, arid land' and denotes the district from Beer-sheba to Kadesh-barnea.

3. *green tree . . . and every dry tree.* A figure for the righteous and the wicked.

it shall not be quenched, even a flaming flame. The literal translation of the Hebrew is: 'a flame, an intense flame, (which) shall not be quenched.' Any resistance which the Judeans will oppose to the Babylonian army (the *flame*) will not overcome it.

all faces . . . shall be seared thereby. All the inhabitants of the land will suffer from the cruelty of the invader, even the righteous.

4. *all flesh shall see.* The destruction

that I the Lord have kindled it; it shall not be quenched.' 5. Then said I: 'Ah Lord God! they say of me: Is he not a maker of parables?'

6. Then the word of the Lord came unto me, saying: 7. 'Son of man, set thy face toward Jerusalem, and preach toward the sanctuaries, and prophesy against the land of Israel; 8. and say to the land of Israel: Thus saith the Lord: Behold, I am against thee, and will draw forth My sword out of its sheath, and will cut off from thee the righteous and the wicked. 9. Seeing then that I will cut off from thee the righteous and the wicked, therefore shall My sword go forth out of its

כָּל־בָּשָׂ֖ר כִּ֣י אֲנִ֣י יְהוָ֑ה
5 בְּעַרְתִּ֖יהָ לֹ֥א תִכְבֶּֽה׃ וָאֹמַ֕ר
אֲהָהּ֙ אֲדֹנָ֣י יְהוִ֔ה הֵ֖מָּה אֹמְרִ֣ים
לִ֕י הֲלֹ֛א מְמַשֵּׁ֥ל מְשָׁלִ֖ים הֽוּא׃
6 וַיְהִ֥י דְבַר־יְהוָ֖ה אֵלַ֥י לֵאמֹֽר׃
7 בֶּן־אָדָ֗ם שִׂ֤ים פָּנֶ֙יךָ֙ אֶל־
יְר֣וּשָׁלַ֔͏ִם וְהַטֵּ֖ף אֶל־מִקְדָּשִׁ֑ים
וְהִנָּבֵ֖א אֶל־אַדְמַ֥ת יִשְׂרָאֵֽל׃
8 וְאָמַרְתָּ֙ לְאַדְמַ֣ת יִשְׂרָאֵ֔ל כֹּ֤ה
אָמַ֣ר יְהוָ֔ה הִנְנִ֣י אֵלַ֔יִךְ
וְהוֹצֵאתִ֥י חַרְבִּ֖י מִתַּעְרָ֑הּ
וְהִכְרַתִּ֥י מִמֵּ֖ךְ צַדִּ֥יק וְרָשָֽׁע׃
9 יַ֛עַן אֲשֶׁר־הִכְרַ֥תִּי מִמֵּ֖ךְ צַדִּ֣יק
וְרָשָׁ֑ע לָכֵ֗ן תֵּצֵ֤א חַרְבִּ֖י

will be of such a nature and extent that all the world will recognize it as an act of Divine retribution.

5. *is he not a maker of parables?* Ezekiel's contention is that since his oracles are delivered in the form of metaphors, the people do not take his messages seriously, but regard him merely as a skilful composer of parables. Thereupon he is told to translate his figures of speech into plain language.

6-10 INTERPRETATION OF THE BLAZING FOREST

7. *toward Jerusalem.* This explains the vague expression, *toward the South*, in verse 2.

preach toward the sanctuaries. The interpretation of *preach toward the South* (verse 2). The plural *sanctuaries* denotes the various buildings which together comprised the Temple.

the land of Israel. This defines *the forest of the field* (verse 2).

8. *My sword.* Symbolized by the flame. *the righteous and the wicked.* This is the meaning of *every green tree and every dry tree* (verse 3). The indiscriminate punishment of the righteous and wicked, as proclaimed here, is not only in contradiction to Ezekiel's teaching (cf. xviii. 20), but is also contrary to the doctrine of Gen. xviii. 23, 25. This difficulty did not escape the attention of the Rabbis. Commenting on the verse, they observe that the righteous spoken of here were not righteous in the full sense of the word, but were relatively so in comparison with the extreme wicked (A.Z. 4a). In an alternative explanation, they remark that once permission is given to the destroying angel to carry out his task, he makes no distinction between the good and bad, and even begins with the former (Mechilta to Exod. xii. 22; B.K. 60a).

sheath against all flesh from the
south to the north; 10. and all flesh
shall know that I the LORD have
drawn forth My sword out of its
sheath; it shall not return any more.
11. Sigh therefore, thou son of man;
with the breaking of thy loins and
with bitterness shalt thou sigh
before their eyes. 12. And it shall
be, when they say unto thee:
Wherefore sighest thou? that thou
shalt say: Because of the tidings, for
it cometh; and every heart shall
melt, and all hands shall be slack,
and every spirit shall be faint, and
all knees shall drip with water;
behold, it cometh, and it shall be
done, saith the Lord GOD.'

13. And the word of the LORD
came unto me, saying: 14. 'Son of
man, prophesy, and say: Thus saith

מִתַּעְרָהּ אֶל־כָּל־בָּשָׂר מִנֶּגֶב
10 צָפוֹן: וְיָדְעוּ כָּל־בָּשָׂר כִּי אֲנִי
יְהוָֹה הוֹצֵאתִי חַרְבִּי מִתַּעְרָהּ
11 לֹא תָשׁוּב עוֹד: וְאַתָּה בֶן־
אָדָם הֵאָנַח בְּשִׁבְרוֹן מָתְנַיִם
וּבִמְרִירוּת תֵּאָנַח לְעֵינֵיהֶם:
12 וְהָיָה כִּי־יֹאמְרוּ אֵלֶיךָ עַל־
מָה אַתָּה נֶאֱנָח וְאָמַרְתָּ אֶל־
שְׁמוּעָה כִי־בָאָה וְנָמֵס כָּל־
לֵב וְרָפוּ כָל־יָדַיִם וְכִהֲתָה
כָל־רוּחַ וְכָל־בִּרְכַּיִם
תֵּלַכְנָה מַּיִם הִנֵּה בָאָה וְנִהְיָתָה
13 נְאֻם אֲדֹנָי יְהוִֹה: וַיְהִי דְבַר־
14 יְהוָֹה אֵלַי לֵאמֹר: בֶּן־אָדָם
הִנָּבֵא וְאָמַרְתָּ כֹּה אָמַר יְהוָֹה

v. 11. פתח באתנח   v. 12. קמץ בז"ק

9. *against all flesh.* The judgment upon Israel will be an occasion for judging all other peoples.

10. *it shall not return any more.* Until it has completed its destructive work.

11-12 EZEKIEL TO SIGH OVER WHAT IS TO COME

The prophet must have been deeply affected by God's revelation to him; he should not hide his emotion but openly display it.

11. *with the breaking of thy loins.* i.e. with shattering emotion. The Biur takes the meaning to be 'with distress and despair,' the opposite of the words addressed to Jeremiah, *Gird up thy loins* (Jer. i. 17), be active and confident.

before their eyes. In the presence of the people that they should inquire about the reason of his sighing.

12. *because of the tidings.* The disastrous news of the destruction of the Temple which will reach the Jewish exiles in Babylon. The prophet was to behave as though he had actually received the tidings.

every heart shall melt. So long as the Temple was still in existence, the exiles cherished the hope of returning to their homeland. But with the destruction of the Temple, that hope would be lost.

all knees shall drip with water. See on vii. 17.

it cometh, and it shall be done. The news which, when it comes, will be a true account of what had happened.

the LORD: Say:

> A sword, a sword, it is sharpened,
> And also furbished:
>
> 15 It is sharpened that it may make
>   a sore slaughter,
>   It is furbished that it may
>   glitter—
>   Or shall we make mirth?—
>   Against the rod of My son, con-
>   temning every tree.
>
> 16 And it is given to be furbished,
>   That it may be handled;
>   The sword, it is sharpened,
>   Yea, it is furbished,
>   To give it into the hand of the
>   slayer.

אָמֹר
חֶרֶב חֶרֶב הוּחַדָּה
וְגַם־מְרוּטָה:
15 לְמַעַן טְבֹחַ טֶבַח הוּחַדָּה
לְמַעַן הֱיֵה־לָה בָּרָק מֹרָטָּה
אוֹ נָשִׂישׂ
שֵׁבֶט בְּנִי מֹאֶסֶת כָּל־עֵץ:
16 וַיִּתֵּן אֹתָהּ לְמָרְטָה
לִתְפֹּשׂ בַּכָּף
הִיא הוּחַדָּה חֶרֶב
וְהִיא מֹרָטָה
לָתֵת אוֹתָהּ בְּיַד־הוֹרֵג:

**13-22   GOD'S SWORD IS PREPARED
TO STRIKE**

14. *a sword, a sword, it is sharpened.* The sword to be drawn by God (verse 8) is ready for action. The repetition of *a sword* is intended for emphasis. According to the Targum, two massacres are predicted: by Nebuchadnezzar and by Ishmael the son of Nethaniah at the instigation of Ammon (cf. Jer. xli).

furbished. So that it flashes and strikes terror in the heart of the people.

15. *or shall we make mirth?* The second half of the verse is extremely difficult and most modern commentators resort to speculative emendation of the text. A.J. interprets this clause as parenthetical, expressing the thought of the Judeans that, far from being terrified at the sight of the sword, they should rather rejoice because it will not be used against them but against the other nations. Another explanation is: is there cause for complacency that the sword is drawn only against Israel's enemies?

against the rod of My son, contemning every tree. At once comes the Divine retort destructive of such complacency. There can be no occasion here for self-satisfaction. The sharpened and flashing sword is destined for use only against Judea; it rejects any other people. There is nothing in the Hebrew to correspond with *against,* and the verb *ma'as* means 'to reject' as well as 'to despise.' The translation may accordingly be: '(the sword) is the rod of My son, it rejecteth every (other) tree.' The word *rod* is commonly used for God's chastisement (cf. Isa. x. 24, xxx. 31; Lam. iii. 1), and the instrument of human punishment (cf. Prov. xiii. 24, *He that spareth his rod hateth his son*). Since Jerusalem is compared to a forest (verse 2), the nations are referred to as 'trees.'

16. *it is given.* The Hebrew is literally 'and he gave it,' viz. God, Who had drawn the sword from its sheath (verse 8), has handed it over to be furbished and then delivered into the hand of the executioner. Lofthouse remarks that 'the vagueness of the last clause heightens the weirdness and mystery of the whole.'

17. Cry and wail, son of man; for it is upon My people, it is upon all the princes of Israel; they are thrust down to the sword with My people; smite therefore upon thy thigh. 18. For there is a trial; and what if it contemn even the rod? It shall be no more, saith the Lord GOD. 19. Thou therefore, son of man, prophesy, and smite thy hands together; and let the sword be doubled the third time, the sword of those to be slain; it is the sword of the great one that is to be slain, which compasseth them about. 20. I have set the point of the sword against all their gates, that their heart may melt, and their stumblings be multiplied; ah! it is /made

17 זְעַק וְהֵילֵל בֶּן־אָדָם כִּי־הִיא
הָיְתָה בְעַמִּי הִיא בְּכָל־נְשִׂיאֵי
יִשְׂרָאֵל מְגוּרֵי אֶל־חֶרֶב הָיוּ
אֶת־עַמִּי לָכֵן סְפֹק אֶל־
18 יָרֵךְ: כִּי בֹחַן וּמָה אִם־גַּם־
שֵׁבֶט מֹאֶסֶת לֹא יִהְיֶה נְאֻם
19 אֲדֹנָי יְהוִֹה: וְאַתָּה בֶן־אָדָם
הִנָּבֵא וְהַךְ כַּף אֶל־כָּף
וְתִכָּפֵל חֶרֶב שְׁלִישִׁתָה חֶרֶב
חֲלָלִים הִיא חֶרֶב חָלָל הַגָּדוֹל
20 הַחֹדֶרֶת לָהֶם: לְמַעַן | לָמוּג
לֵב וְהַרְבֵּה הַמִּכְשֹׁלִים עַל
כָּל־ ־שַׁעֲרֵיהֶם נָתַתִּי
אִבְחַת־חֶרֶב אָח עֲשׂוּיָה

v. 17. סבירין למען v. 19. למדנחאי על

17. *the princes of Israel.* The allusion is to the last kings of Judah and Zedekiah's children.

smite therefore upon thy thigh. A gesture of grief and dismay.

18. *there is a trial*, etc. The portrayal of the furbished sword serves as a test to see whether the people will take the warning to heart. Rashi's interpretation of the verse is preferable: '(My son) has been tried,' by other but less drastic punishments of God. 'What, then, (will become of him) if also the sword which rejecteth (the other nations should strike him)? He will cease to exist.'

19. *smite thy hands together.* The Jewish commentators understand the action as indicating sorrow, but verse 22 rather suggests anger. The prophet is to strike his hands together to summon the agent of destruction.

let the sword be doubled the third time. An obscure phrase which the Jewish

commentators take to mean that Ezekiel is urged to announce that the third disaster, that which overtakes Zedekiah, will be twice as formidable as the two previous calamities in the reigns of Jehoiakim and Jehoiachin. Another interpretation reads into the words an instruction to brandish the sword with a double motion, backward and forward, three times.

the great one that is to be slain. The reference is possibly to Zedekiah (cf. verse 30). Alternatively, the singular has collective force. The meaning will then be: the sword will devour many, and among them will be eminent men, kings and princes.

which compasseth them about. The devouring sword will surround them like a besieging army so that few, if any, will escape.

20. *the point.* The Hebrew noun *ibchath* occurs nowhere else. Some Jewish

glittering, it is sharpened for slaughter. 21. Go thee one way to the right, or direct thyself to the left; whither is thy face set? 22. I will also smite My hands together, and I will satisfy My fury; I the LORD have spoken it.'

23. And the word of the LORD came unto me, saying: 24. 'Now, thou son of man, make thee two ways, that the sword of the king of Babylon may come; they twain shall come forth out of one land; and mark a sign-post, mark it clear at

לְבָרָק מֹעֲטָה לְטֶבַח:
21 הִתְאַחֲדִי הֵימִנִי הָשִׂימִי
הַשְׂמִילִי אָנָה פָּנַיִךְ מֻעָדוֹת:
22 וְגַם־אֲנִי אַכֶּה כַפִּי אֶל־כַּפִּי
וַהֲנִחֹתִי חֲמָתִי אֲנִי יְהֹוָה
23 דִּבַּרְתִּי: וַיְהִי דְבַר־יְהֹוָה
24 אֵלַי לֵאמֹר: וְאַתָּה בֶן־אָדָם
שִׂים־לְךָ | שְׁנַיִם דְּרָכִים לָבוֹא
חֶרֶב מֶלֶךְ־בָּבֶל מֵאֶרֶץ אֶחָד
יֵצְאוּ שְׁנֵיהֶם וְיָד בָּרֵא בְרֹאשׁ־

v. 21. חסר א'

---

commentators hold that it is the equivalent of *tibchath*, 'the slaughter of,' and most moderns emend accordingly. Others suggest a connection with the Arabic noun meaning 'consternation.' A.J., following R.V., departs from the order of the Hebrew which is: 'That their heart may melt, and their stumblings be multiplied, against all their gates I have set the point of the sword.'

ah! it is made glittering. As the effect of sharpening and furbishing. R.V., more lit., 'ah! it is made as lightning.' Lofthouse comments: 'The prophet's voice rises to a shriek'

it is sharpened. This translation adopts the emendation *merutah* for *me'uttah*. M.T. must be rendered: 'it is wrapped' (so A.V.), to preserve its sharpness.

21. *go thee . . . to the left.* The verbs have the feminine form indicating that the 'sword' (a feminine noun in Hebrew), representing the king of Babylon, is addressed. He hesitated at the cross-roads and cast lots whether to attack Judea on the right or Ammon on the left (verse 26). So he is urged to reach a decision in which direction he will advance

22. *I will also smite My hands together.* See on verse 19.

I will satisfy My fury. When God has carried out His sentence, His anger will be appeased (cf. v. 13).

23-28   NEBUCHADNEZZAR AT THE CROSS-ROADS

24. *make thee two ways.* Ezekiel receives a command from God to make a drawing of a road which, at a certain point, branches in two directions, one leading to Jerusalem and the other to Ammon.

the sword . . . may come. The imagery of the *sword* in the previous section now receives precise definition.

they twain shall come forth out of one land. The two diverging paths issue from one road which has its beginning in Babylon.

mark . . . mark it clear. The Hebrew verb is *barë*, the Piel of *bara* which means 'to cut,' 'shape,' and when used in connection with God 'to create.' A.J. evidently regards it as a variant of *ba'ar* in the Piel, 'to make plain,' while Kimchi and other Jewish commentators understand it as the equivalent of *barar*, in its late Hebrew sense of 'to choose.' Its normal usage is probable here: 'cut out,' from a log of wood (cf. xxiii. 47 where the verb is translated *despatch them with their swords*, lit. 'cut them down'). The noun for *sign-post* is literally 'hand' and

the head of the way to the city. 25. Thou shalt make a way, that the sword may come to Rabbah of the children of Ammon, and to Judah in Jerusalem the fortified. 26. For the king of Babylon standeth at the parting of the way, at the head of the two ways, to use divination; he shaketh the arrows to and fro, he inquireth of the teraphim, he looketh in the liver. 27. In his right hand

כה דֶּרֶךְ עִיר בָּרֵא: דֶּרֶךְ תָּשִׂים
לָבוֹא חֶרֶב אֵת רַבַּת בְּנֵי־
עַמּוֹן וְאֶת־יְהוּדָה בִירוּשָׁלַ͏ִם
כו בְּצוּרָה: כִּי־עָמַד מֶלֶךְ־
בָּבֶל אֶל־אֵם הַדֶּרֶךְ בְּרֹאשׁ
שְׁנֵי הַדְּרָכִים לִקְסָם־קָסֶם
קִלְקַל בַּחִצִּים שָׁאַל בַּתְּרָפִים
כז רָאָה בַּכָּבֵד: בִּימִינוֹ הָיָה |

may be understood as the figure of a hand with its finger pointing towards a road, or more generally 'a post' (cf. *a monument* in 1 Sam. xv. 12; Isa. lvi. 5).

the head of the way. i.e. the cross-roads.

to the city. viz. to each of the cities of Jerusalem and Rabbah.

25. *thou shalt make a way.* The destination of the road is now indicated: either Jerusalem the capital of Judea or Rabbah the capital of Ammon. The *sword* of Nebuchadnezzar was to make one of them its objective.

to Rabbah . . . to Judah. The text has *eth* for *to*, the sign of the accusative, here of direction (cf. *toward* (eth) *the way of the wilderness*, 2 Sam. xv. 23).

Judah in Jerusalem the fortified. The phrase sounds peculiar if so rendered. The meaning may be 'Judah with (i.e. which includes) Jerusalem the fortified.' A contrast is drawn between Rabbah, a city which could be taken without difficulty, and Jerusalem with its strong walls which would require a long siege to capture. This consideration might induce Nebuchadnezzar to make the former his first objective, but he will decide by using the art of divination.

26. *the parting of the way.* lit. 'the mother of the way,' defined by the clause which follows.

to use divination. For an indication which road he should take. The *divination* assumed three forms to make the outcome more certain.

he shaketh the arrows to and fro. The normal method was for two arrows, inscribed with the names of the two objectives, to be shaken in a quiver and one of them drawn out. This was the method commonly employed by the Arabs; but see on verse 27.

teraphim. On the nature of this instrument of divination, Ibn Ezra on Gen. xxxi. 19 quotes two views: that it was a kind of clock showing the hours, or an image made to speak at certain times. His own opinion is that it was an image of a human being and, in support, cites the incident of Michal placing in the bed the *teraphim* which David's pursuers mistook for him (1 Sam. xix. 13). Exactly how they were used for the purpose is not known.

he looketh in the liver. This is the only place in the Bible where this method of divination is mentioned. 'According to primitive ideas the liver was the seat of life, because it is filled with blood; hence to obtain the omens, from a living organ as it were, a sheep was first sacrificed, and then its liver was examined to find out the colour and marks which appeared on it. The clay model of a sheep's liver, divided by cross lines and inscribed with

is the lot Jerusalem, to set battering rams, to open the mouth for the slaughter, to lift up the voice with shouting, to set battering rams against the gates, to cast up mounds, to build forts. 28. And it shall be unto them as a false divination in their sight, who have weeks upon weeks! but it bringeth iniquity to remembrance, that they may be taken.

29. Therefore thus saith the Lord GOD: Because ye have made your iniquity to be remembered, in that

הַקֶּסֶם יְרוּשָׁלַ͏ִם לָשׂוּם כָּרִים
לִפְתֹּחַ פֶּה בְּרֶצַח לְהָרִים קוֹל
בִּתְרוּעָה לָשׂוּם כָּרִים עַל־
שְׁעָרִים לִשְׁפֹּךְ סֹלְלָה לִבְנוֹת
דָּיֵק: 28 וְהָיָה לָהֶם כִּקְסָום־
שָׁוְא בְּעֵינֵיהֶם שְׁבֻעֵי שְׁבֻעוֹת
לָהֶם וְהוּא־מַזְכִּיר עָוֹן
לְהִתָּפֵשׂ: 29 לָכֵן כֹּה־אָמַר
אֲדֹנָי יֱהוִֹה יַעַן הַזְכַּרְכֶם

v. 28. ר יתיר

omens in each division, may be seen in the British Museum' (Cooke). Lofthouse quotes Plato, *Timaeus*, xxxii: 'The faculty of prognostication belongs to that part of the soul which is situated in the liver, because that part has no share in reason or thought.'

27. *in his right hand.* The inference appears to be that he drew an arrow with each hand, but the one drawn by the right hand provided the required indication.

to set battering rams. The fact that Jerusalem was strongly fortified is to be ignored by Nebuchadnezzar, so the divination informed him. By the use of his military machines he would overcome the city (cf. iv. 2).

to open the mouth for the slaughter. i.e. to proclaim the annihilation of Jerusalem; an assurance of victory for the Babylonian army.

to lift up the voice with shouting. Battlecries to terrify the inhabitants of the city which was being attacked and throw them into panic.

mounds . . . forts. Earthworks erected by the city walls from which to attack the defenders standing upon them.

28. *it shall be unto them as a false divination.* When the inhabitants of Jerusalem hear of Nebuchadnezzar's decision to march against them, they will not treat it seriously, relying upon the false prophets who were assuring them that the city was inviolable.

who have weeks upon weeks! A very obscure phrase. Rashi follows the Targum and explains 'seven times seven,' i.e. were Nebuchadnezzar to divine forty-nine times and all pointed to the capture of Jerusalem, its inhabitants persisted in their confidence that the campaign against them would fail. Kimchi and other authorities translate: 'to them who have sworn oaths' (so A.V.; R.V. has, 'which have sworn oaths unto them'); they feel secure as if the Babylonians had sworn peace with them. Perhaps the meaning is: so sure were the inhabitants of Jerusalem of the futility of the divination practised by the Babylonians that they even swore again and again that the omens would never come true

it bringeth iniquity to remembrance. This complacent attitude of the Judeans adds to their guilt and hastens their downfall. A.V. and R.V. agree with Rashi in translating: 'he (Nebuchadnezzar) bringeth iniquity to remembrance'; the meaning is then, 'Nebuchadnezzar's presence is an accusation before God of the king and the people because of their breaking their allegiance to Him (cf. xvii). The consequence of this accusa-

your transgressions are uncovered,
so that your sins do appear in all
your doings; because that ye are
come to remembrance, ye shall be
taken with the hand. 30. And thou,
O wicked one, that art to be slain,
the prince of Israel, whose day is
come, in the time of the iniquity of
the end; 31. thus saith the Lord
GOD: The mitre shall be removed,
and the crown taken off; this shall be
no more the same: that which is
low shall be exalted, and that which
is high abased. 32. A ruin, a ruin,
a ruin, will I make it; this also shall

עֲוֺנְכֶם בְּהִגָּלוֹת פִּשְׁעֵיכֶם
לְהֵרָאוֹת חַטֹּאותֵיכֶם בְּכֹל
עֲלִילוֹתֵיכֶם יַעַן הִזָּכֶרְכֶם
30 בַּכַּף תִּתָּפֵשׂוּ: וְאַתָּה חָלָל
רָשָׁע נְשִׂיא יִשְׂרָאֵל אֲשֶׁר־בָּא
31 יוֹמוֹ בְּעֵת עֲוֺן קֵץ: כֹּה אָמַר
אֲדֹנָי יֱהֹוִה הָסִיר הַמִּצְנֶפֶת
וְהָרִים הָעֲטָרָה זֹאת לֹא־זֹאת
הַשָּׁפָלָה הַגְבֵּהַּ וְהַגָּבֹהַּ
32 הַשְׁפִּיל: עַוָּה עַוָּה עַוָּה
אֲשִׂימֶנָּה גַּם־זֹאת לֹא הָיָה

מלא ו' v. 29.

---

tion, or bringing guilt to remembrance,
is that they shall be taken, i.e. captured,
the city and the people, by the foe'
(Davidson).

29-32 DEPOSITION OF JUDEA'S KING

29. *in that your transgressions are uncovered.* Let the people of Judea not
delude themselves with false hopes.
Overwhelming disaster is coming upon
them, because their more recent misdeeds
are so glaring and challenging that they
call their former iniquities to remembrance before God. He cannot overlook
the record of their wilful disobedience
which demands the most severe punishment.

30. *O wicked one, that art to be slain.*
Kimchi mentions an alternative rendering: 'profane wicked prince of Israel,'
which appears in A.V.

prince of Israel. The allusion is to king
Zedekiah.

whose day is come. The time of his
deposition has been determined by God.

in the time of the iniquity of the end. He
will be deposed when the guilt of Judah
has its sequel in the end of the dynasty

and the time of the captivity. The
phrase occurs again in verse 34 and
xxxv. 5.

31. *the mitre shall be removed, and the
crown taken off.* He will be removed
from his throne and will never again rule
over Judea. Although *mitre* is elsewhere
used of the headgear of the High Priest,
it signifies a 'turban'; and the king, as
well as the High Priest, may each have
worn one of a distinguishing type.

this shall be no more the same. lit. 'this
not this'; 'everything will be flung into
confusion' (Lofthouse). There will be
an upheaval in which Zedekiah's throne
will be upset.

that which is low shall be exalted. Jehoiachin, now in disgrace in Babylon,
will be restored to honour (cf. 2 Kings
xxv. 27ff.).

that which is high abased. Zedekiah,
who now occupies an exalted office, will
be degraded.

32. *a ruin, a ruin, a ruin.* The repetition
of the noun points to the completeness of
the impending disaster.

this also shall be no more, etc. Even the
restoration of the crown to Jehoiachin,

be no more, until he come whose
right it is, and I will give it him.

33. And thou, son of man, prophesy, and say: Thus saith the
Lord GOD concerning the children
of Ammon, and concerning their
taunt; and say thou:

> O sword, O sword keen-edged,
> Furbished for the slaughter,
> To the uttermost, because of the
> glitterings;

34 While they see falsehood unto
thee,
While they divine lies unto thee,
To lay thee upon the necks of
the wicked that are to be slain,
Whose day is come, in the time
of the iniquity of the end!—

עַד־בֹּא אֲשֶׁר־לוֹ הַמִּשְׁפָּט
33 וּנְתַתִּיו: וְאַתָּה בֶן־אָדָם
הִנָּבֵא וְאָמַרְתָּ כֹּה אָמַר אֲדֹנָי
יֱהֹוִה אֶל־בְּנֵי עַמּוֹן וְאֶל־
חֶרְפָּתָם וְאָמַרְתָּ
חֶרֶב חֶרֶב פְּתוּחָה
לְטֶבַח מְרוּטָה
לְהָכִיל לְמַעַן בָּרָק:
34 בַּחֲזוֹת לָךְ שָׁוְא
בִּקְסָם־לָךְ כָּזָב
לָתֵת אוֹתָךְ
אֶל־צַוְּארֵי חַלְלֵי רְשָׁעִים
אֲשֶׁר־בָּא יוֹמָם בְּעֵת עֲוֹן קֵץ:

referred to in the preceding verse, will
only be temporary. The ultimate restoration will happen at an unspecified
time in the future with the advent of the
Messiah. The phrase *until he come
whose right it is* recalls the Messianic
prophecy in Gen. xlix. 10.

33-37 THREAT AGAINST AMMON

'The prophet's excitement, growing in
verse 32, now rises higher; he seizes the
sword again, but this time he turns
against the Ammonites who might have
thought that they would escape when
Judah was invaded. The full force,
however, of the prophet's mood is spent,
and as the sword is sheathed (verse 35)
the prophecy ends with a prediction of
ruin at once general and vague' (Lofthouse).

33. *concerning their taunt.* The Ammonites were hostile to Judea at the time
of crisis when Nebuchadnezzar attacked
Jehoiakim (cf. 2 Kings xxiv. 2). They

were not to imagine that they would
escape a like fate at his hands.

furbished for the slaughter. Cf. verses
14ff.

to the uttermost, etc. Davidson's translation is preferable: 'it is furbished to the
uttermost (lit. as far as it can hold or
receive) in order that it may glitter.'
The destructive sword is prepared to its
extreme sharpness to be an effective
instrument of punishment.

34. *they see falsehood unto thee.* The
hopes of victory which the Ammonite
soothsayers were holding out were
nought but misleading falsehoods.

to lay thee upon the necks of the wicked.
The latter part of the clause refers to the
princes and people of Judea. Contrary
to the assurance of the diviners, Ammon
will share the fate of Jerusalem, and its
slain, as it were, fall upon the dead bodies
of the Judeans and form one heap.

in the time of the iniquity of the end. See
on verse 30.

35 Cause it to return into its
    sheath!—
    In the place where thou wast
      created, in the land of thine
      origin,
    Will I judge thee.

36 And I will pour out Mine
    indignation upon thee,
    I will blow upon thee with the
      fire of My wrath;
    And I will deliver thee into the
      hand of brutish men,
    Skilful to destroy.

37 Thou shalt be for fuel to the fire;
    Thy blood shall be in the midst
      of the land,
    Thou shalt be no more re-
      membered;
    For I the LORD have spoken it.'

35 הָשֵׁב אֶל־תַּעְרָהּ
בִּמְקוֹם אֲשֶׁר־נִבְרֵאת
בְּאֶרֶץ מְכֻרוֹתַיִךְ
אֶשְׁפֹּט אֹתָךְ׃

36 וְשָׁפַכְתִּי עָלַיִךְ זַעְמִי
בְּאֵשׁ עֶבְרָתִי אָפִיחַ עָלָיִךְ
וּנְתַתִּיךְ בְּיַד אֲנָשִׁים בֹּעֲרִים
חָרָשֵׁי מַשְׁחִית׃

37 לָאֵשׁ תִּהְיֶה לְאָכְלָה
דָּמֵךְ יִהְיֶה בְּתוֹךְ הָאָרֶץ
לֹא תִזָּכֵרִי
כִּי אֲנִי יְהֹוָה דִּבַּרְתִּי׃

22   CHAPTER XXII   כב

1. Moreover the word of the LORD
came unto me, saying: 2. 'Now,

1 וַיְהִי דְבַר־יְהֹוָה אֵלַי לֵאמֹר׃

v. 1. הפטרת אחרי מות

---

35. *cause it to return into its sheath!*
The symbolic action by Ezekiel who
flourishes the sword is to end; it will be
followed in due course by God's judgment and retribution. Kimchi construes as a question: 'shall I cause it to
return into its sheath?'

in the place, etc. A prediction of the
invasion of Ammon by the Babylonians.

36. *I will blow upon thee with the fire of
My wrath.* As fire grows more intense
through the blowing of the bellows, so
will God's indignation against Ammon
grow fiercer.

brutish men. The Babylonians are described as ruthless so that the Ammonites
could expect no mercy at their hands.
Kimchi mentions an alternative rendering: 'men who will devour them like
fire,' a parallel to the next phrase,
skilful to destroy.

37. *thy blood shall be in the midst of the
land.* Unlike Judea and Egypt (cf.
xxii. 15, xxix. 12), the Ammonites will
not survive in dispersion, but be destroyed
in their own land.

thou shalt be no more remembered. 'In
striking contrast to Israel's destiny. The
neighbouring nations and their religion
led to nothing; whereas Israel, in spite of
many failures, both survived and grew,
a clear proof of the distinctive character
of Israel's faith' (Cooke).

CHAPTER XXII

GRAVE INDICTMENT OF JERUSALEM

THE chapter falls into three sections.
The first (1-16) deals with the cardinal
sins of bloodshed, idolatry, adultery and
oppression—crimes which have defiled
the Holy City. Exile and dispersion are

thou, son of man, wilt thou judge, wilt thou judge the bloody city? then cause her to know all her abominations. 3. And thou shalt say: Thus saith the Lord GOD: O city that sheddest blood in the midst of thee, that thy time may come, and that makest idols unto thyself to defile thee; 4. thou art become guilty in thy blood that thou hast shed, and art defiled in thine idols which thou hast made; and thou hast caused thy days to draw near, and art come even unto thy years; therefore have I made thee a reproach unto the nations, and a

2 וְאַתָּה בֶן־אָדָם הֲתִשְׁפֹּט הֲתִשְׁפֹּט אֶת־עִיר הַדָּמִים וְהוֹדַעְתָּהּ אֵת כָּל־

3 תּוֹעֲבוֹתֶיהָ: וְאָמַרְתָּ כֹּה אָמַר אֲדֹנָי יֱהוִֹה עִיר שֹׁפֶכֶת דָּם בְּתוֹכָהּ לָבוֹא עִתָּהּ וְעָשְׂתָה גִלּוּלִים עָלֶיהָ לְטָמְאָה:

4 בְּדָמֵךְ אֲשֶׁר־שָׁפַכְתְּ אָשַׁמְתְּ וּבְגִלּוּלַיִךְ אֲשֶׁר־עָשִׂית טָמֵאת וַתַּקְרִיבִי יָמַיִךְ וַתָּבוֹא עַד־שְׁנוֹתַיִךְ עַל־כֵּן נְתַתִּיךְ חֶרְפָּה לַגּוֹיִם וְקַלָּסָה לְכָל־

v. 4. למדנחאי עת כתיב עד ק׳ נ״א בגוים v. 4.

therefore inevitable. The second (17-22) compares God's judgment to the refiner's furnace. As the fire burns the dross from the ore, so does God's punishment consume the wicked. The third section (23-31) accuses the whole population, from the highest to the lowest, of corruption and evil-doing. There is no one left to *stand in the breach.* The doom of Jerusalem is sealed.

1-16 THE SINS OF JERUSALEM
2. *wilt thou judge,* etc. See on xx. 4.
the bloody city. Though guilty of other sins, stress is laid on the heinous crime of bloodshed.
cause her to know all her abominations. In pronouncing judgment upon the corrupt city, the prophet is told to inform its inhabitants of the details of the indictment.
3. *O city that sheddest blood in the midst of thee.* The inhabitants were guilty of bloodshed openly in the midst of the city, an indication of moral debasement more serious than when murder is committed in secret.
that thy time may come. Their doom is

sealed on account of their acts of violence which resulted in the loss of innocent lives.
makest idols unto thyself to defile thee. The highest degree of ritual and moral impurity is contracted from idolatry. Hence the mention here of the defilement caused by the worship of idols. Instead of *unto thyself,* R.V. renders more lit.: 'against herself' (the Hebrew has the third person feminine throughout); i.e. the idols which are worshipped are Jerusalem's enemies, the cause of the coming downfall.
4. *guilty in thy blood . . . defiled in thine idols.* While bloodshed determines guilt and punishment, idolatry corrupts the soul and contributes to the state of mind which leads to crime.
thou hast caused thy days to draw near. By their misdeeds they have hastened the time of retribution.
art come even unto thy years. They have also brought upon themselves the years of dispersion and exile which are to follow the overthrow of the State (Malbim).
I made thee a reproach. The verb is in the prophetic perfect which views what

mocking to all the countries! 5. Those that are near, and those that are far from thee, shall mock thee, thou defiled of name and full of tumult.

6. Behold, the princes of Israel, every one according to his might, have been in thee to shed blood. 7. In thee have they made light of father and mother; in the midst of thee have they dealt by oppression with the stranger; in thee have they wronged the fatherless and the widow. 8. Thou hast despised My holy things, and hast profaned My sabbaths. 9. In thee have been talebearers to shed blood; and in thee they have eaten upon the mountains; in the midst of thee they have committed lewdness. 10. In thee have they uncovered their fathers' nakedness; in thee

5 הָאֲרָצוֹת׃ הַקְּרֹבוֹת
וְהָרְחֹקוֹת מִמֵּךְ יִתְקַלְּסוּ־בָךְ
טְמֵאַת הַשֵּׁם רַבַּת הַמְּהוּמָה׃
6 הִנֵּה נְשִׂיאֵי יִשְׂרָאֵל אִישׁ לִזְרֹעוֹ
7 הָיוּ בָךְ לְמַעַן שְׁפָךְ־דָּם׃ אָב
וָאֵם הֵקַלּוּ בָךְ לַגֵּר עָשׂוּ
בַעֹשֶׁק בְּתוֹכֵךְ יָתוֹם וְאַלְמָנָה
8 הוֹנוּ בָךְ׃ קָדָשַׁי בָּזִית וְאֶת־
9 שַׁבְּתֹתַי חִלָּלְתְּ׃ אַנְשֵׁי רָכִיל
הָיוּ בָךְ לְמַעַן שְׁפָךְ־דָּם וְאֶל־
הֶהָרִים אָכְלוּ בָךְ זִמָּה עָשׂוּ
10 בְתוֹכֵךְ׃ עֶרְוַת־אָב גִּלָּה־

is to be as though it has happened. God will make Jerusalem an object of mockery among the nations.

5. *thou defiled of name and full of tumult.* The distant peoples will despise them because of their evil reputation, and their near neighbours taunt them because of the confusion and turmoil created in Jerusalem by famine, pestilence and massacre.

6. *the princes of Israel.* The members of the royal household and leading officials of the State.

according to his might. lit. 'a man to his arm'; each according to the opportunities afforded by his exalted rank. Davidson renders: 'have been high-handed in thee, to shed blood'; they were arbitrary so that their power was law.

7. *they made light of father and mother.* The subject *they* does not refer to *the princes of Israel*, but the people of Judea generally. They were faithless to the Torah which repeatedly enjoined the honouring of parents and fair treatment of the stranger, orphan and widow.

8. *thou hast despised My holy things.* They had shown contempt for the Temple by bringing blemished animals for sacrifice.

My sabbaths. See on xx. 12.

9. *talebearers to shed blood.* Talebearing in itself is forbidden by the Torah (Lev. xix. 16); but their slanders which aimed at the death penalty upon innocent persons were doubly hideous.

they have eaten upon the mountains. See on xviii. 6.

they have committed lewdness. A general charge which the prophet goes on to explain in detail. In this verse three cardinal sins are enumerated: bloodshed, idolatry and unchastity.

10. *they uncovered their fathers' nakedness.* The reference is to incestuous marriage with a stepmother, prohibited in Lev. xviii. 7f. The text has the verb in the singular, and Kimchi explains that the allusion is to king Amon who, according to Rabbinic tradition, had intercourse with his mother. The ancient versions, including the Targum, presuppose a

have they humbled her that was unclean in her impurity. 11. And each hath committed abomination with his neighbour's wife; and each hath lewdly defiled his daughter-in-law; and each in thee hath humbled his sister, his father's daughter. 12. In thee have they taken gifts to shed blood; thou hast taken interest and increase, and thou hast greedily gained of thy neighbours by oppression, and hast forgotten Me, saith the Lord GOD.

13. Behold, therefore, I have smitten My hand at thy dishonest gain which thou hast made, and at thy blood which hath been in the midst of thee. 14. Can thy heart endure, or can thy hands be strong, in the days that I shall deal with

בָּךְ טֻמְאַת הַנִּדָּה עִנּוּ־בָךְ׃

11 וְאִישׁ ׀ אֶת־אֵשֶׁת רֵעֵהוּ עָשָׂה תּוֹעֵבָה וְאִישׁ אֶת־כַּלָּתוֹ טִמֵּא בְזִמָּה וְאִישׁ אֶת־אֲחֹתוֹ בַת־

12 אָבִיו עִנָּה־בָךְ׃ שֹׁחַד לָקְחוּ־בָךְ לְמַעַן שְׁפָּךְ־דָּם נֶשֶׁךְ וְתַרְבִּית לָקַחַתְּ וַתְּבַצְּעִי רֵעַיִךְ בַּעֹשֶׁק וְאֹתִי שָׁכַחַתְּ נְאֻם

13 אֲדֹנָי יֱהוִֹה׃ וְהִנֵּה הִכֵּיתִי כַפִּי אֶל־בִּצְעֵךְ אֲשֶׁר עָשִׂית וְעַל־דָּמֵךְ אֲשֶׁר הָיוּ בְּתוֹכֵךְ׃

14 הֲיַעֲמֹד לִבֵּךְ אִם־תֶּחֱזַקְנָה יָדַיִךְ לַיָּמִים אֲשֶׁר אֲנִי עֹשֶׂה

plural verb. Perhaps the singular was used because *fathers'* is also singular in the Hebrew.

they humbled her . . . in her impurity. They not only committed rape, but at a time when the woman's condition rendered intercourse forbidden (cf. Lev. xviii. 19, xx. 18).

11. *abomination.* Adultery is abhorrent to God.

daughter-in-law . . . sister. Cf. Lev. xviii. 15, 9.

12. *taken gifts to shed blood.* Judges accepted bribes to condemn the innocent to death. The acceptance of bribes by judges even in less serious cases is condemned in Deut. xvi. 19.

interest and increase. Cf. Lev. xxv. 36f.

of thy neighbours. Their deeds of extortion were not restricted to strangers, but also included their friends. The prophet began his indictment with bloodshed (verse 2); and after referring to

other grave sins, he reverts to bloodshed and violence, because these major crimes sealed their fate (see on verse 3).

hast forgotten Me. Who ordained laws against the acts committed by the Judeans. The shocking picture of national depravity drawn by Ezekiel is confirmed by other prophets (cf. Jer. v. 7ff., vi. 13, vii. 5f., xxii. 3).

13. *smitten My hand at thy dishonest gain.* See on xxi. 19. The Rabbis, commenting on this verse, make the observation: Ezekiel enumerated twenty-four sins of which Israel was guilty; but the one with which he concluded his indictment is robbery, signifying that violence outweighs them all.

14. *can thy heart endure, or can thy hands be strong . . .?* Will your fortitude stand the strain, and will you have the strength to defend yourselves against the imminent attack of your enemies? The intended answer is, of course, negative.

thee? I the LORD have spoken it, and will do it. 15. And I will scatter thee among the nations, and disperse thee through the countries; and I will consume thy filthiness out of thee. 16. And thou shalt be profaned in thyself, in the sight of the nations; and thou shalt know that I am the LORD.'

17. And the word of the LORD came unto me, saying: 18. 'Son of man, the house of Israel is become dross unto Me; all of them are brass and tin and iron and lead, in the midst of the furnace; they are the dross of silver. 19. Therefore thus saith the Lord GOD: Because ye are all become dross, therefore, behold, I will gather you into the midst of Jerusalem. 20. As they gather silver and brass and iron and lead

אוֹתָךְ אֲנִי יְהֹוָה דִּבַּרְתִּי

15 וְעָשִׂיתִי: וַהֲפִיצוֹתִי אֹתָךְ בַּגּוֹיִם וְזֵרִיתִיךְ בָּאֲרָצוֹת וַהֲתִמֹּתִי טֻמְאָתֵךְ מִמֵּךְ:

16 וְנִחַלְתְּ בָּךְ לְעֵינֵי גוֹיִם וְיָדַעַתְּ

17 כִּי־אֲנִי יְהֹוָה:· וַיְהִי דְבַר־

18 יְהֹוָה אֵלַי לֵאמֹר: בֶּן־אָדָם הָיוּ־לִי בֵית־יִשְׂרָאֵל לְסִג כֻּלָּם נְחֹשֶׁת וּבְדִיל וּבַרְזֶל וְעוֹפֶרֶת בְּתוֹךְ כּוּר סִיגִים

19 כֶּסֶף הָיוּ: לָכֵן כֹּה אָמַר אֲדֹנָי יְהֹוָה יַעַן הֱיוֹת כֻּלְּכֶם לְסִגִים לָכֵן הִנְנִי קֹבֵץ אֶתְכֶם אֶל־

20 תּוֹךְ יְרוּשָׁלָ͏ִם: קְבֻצַת כֶּסֶף וּנְחֹשֶׁת וּבַרְזֶל וְעוֹפֶרֶת וּבְדִיל

v. 16. ע״כ   v. 18. לסיג ק׳

---

15. *I will consume thy filthiness out of thee.* The forthcoming exile in Babylon will have a purifying effect upon the nation.

16. *thou shalt be profaned in thyself, in the sight of the nations.* The humiliation of Judea's captivity, witnessed by her neighbours, will create feelings of shame and remorse. A.V., 'thou shalt take thine inheritance in thyself,' is based on Kimchi and apparently means that formerly Israel was God's inheritance, but now he belongs only to himself, and must rely on his own resources.

thou shalt know that I am the LORD. When the prediction is verified by events, the nation will realize that it is God's doing.

17-22 THE SMELTING FURNACE

18. *is become dross.* Israel is no longer comparable to pure metal, but to base metal containing a large proportion of dross.

all of them are brass, etc. The people are like crude ore, a mixture of various minerals, which has to undergo the process of smelting.

the dross of silver. The Hebrew construction is difficult and is literally 'dross silver they were.' The two nouns may be construed as in apposition and interpreted as 'dross of silver.' Alternatively, *sigë*, the noun in the construct state, is to be understood, 'dross, dross of silver'; or the meaning is: they who are now dross were once pure silver.

19. *into the midst of Jerusalem.* Jerusalem is to be the furnace. The allusion may be to the gathering of most of the inhabitants of the land into this city for the final stand against the enemy, and

and tin into the midst of the furnace, to blow the fire upon it, to melt it; so will I gather you in Mine anger and in My fury, and I will cast you in, and melt you. 21. Yea, I will gather you, and blow upon you with the fire of My wrath, and ye shall be melted in the midst thereof. 22. As silver is melted in the midst of the furnace, so shall ye be melted in the midst thereof; and ye shall know that I the LORD have poured out My fury upon you.'

23. And the word of the LORD came unto me, saying: 24. 'Son of man, say unto her: Thou art a land that is not cleansed, nor rained upon in the day of indignation. 25. There is a conspiracy of her prophets in the midst thereof, like a roaring lion ravening the prey; they have devoured souls, they take treasure and precious things, they have made her widows many in the midst thereof.

אֶל־תּוֹךְ כּוּר לָפַחַת־עָלָיו
אֵשׁ לְהַנְתִּיךְ כֵּן אֶקְבֹּץ בְּאַפִּי
וּבַחֲמָתִי וְהִנַּחְתִּי וְהִתַּכְתִּי
אֶתְכֶם: וְכִנַּסְתִּי אֶתְכֶם 21
וְנָפַחְתִּי עֲלֵיכֶם בְּאֵשׁ עֶבְרָתִי
וְנִתַּכְתֶּם בְּתוֹכָהּ: כְּהִתּוּךְ 22
כֶּסֶף בְּתוֹךְ כּוּר כֵּן תֻּתְּכוּ
בְתוֹכָהּ וִידַעְתֶּם כִּי־אֲנִי יְהוָה
שָׁפַכְתִּי חֲמָתִי עֲלֵיכֶם: וַיְהִי 23
דְבַר־יְהוָה אֵלַי לֵאמֹר: בֶּן־ 24
אָדָם אֱמָר־לָהּ אַתְּ אֶרֶץ לֹא
מְטֹהָרָה הִיא לֹא גֻשְׁמָהּ בְּיוֹם
זָעַם: קֶשֶׁר נְבִיאֶיהָ בְּתוֹכָהּ 25
כַּאֲרִי שׁוֹאֵג טֹרֵף טָרֶף נֶפֶשׁ
אָכָלוּ חֹסֶן וִיקָר יִקָּחוּ
אַלְמְנוֹתֶיהָ הִרְבּוּ בְתוֹכָהּ:

v. 24. הש׳ רפה והה׳ במפיק v. 25. כצ״ל v. 25. קמץ ברביע v. 25. קמץ בז״ק

the horrors of the siege will be part of the refining process.

20. Mine anger . . . My fury. This will be the fire which will heat the furnace in which the nation is to be smelted. The next verse speaks of the fire of My wrath.

23-31 CORRUPTION OF THE ENTIRE NATION

24. a land that is not cleansed. The Bible often speaks of the land being defiled by the iniquities of its inhabitants (cf. xxxvi. 17f.; Num. xxxv. 34; Deut. xxi. 23). The Judeans made no effort to purify their land.

nor rained upon in the day of indignation. 'In the East, rain is the great giver of plenty and fertility. Judah is both

defiled and parched up as her punishment falls upon her' (Lofthouse).

25. a conspiracy of her prophets. The false prophets made a pact among themselves that they should all predict peace and security for the nation.

like a roaring lion . . . they have devoured souls. As the lion roars to frighten his prey and then rends it, so do the false prophets employ loud oratory to confuse the people and gain their confidence, thereby causing disaster to them and their families (Kimchi).

they have devoured souls, etc. They allied themselves with the autocratic princes and venal judges who for personal gain condemned the innocent to death and confiscated their property.

147

26. Her priests have done violence to My law, and have profaned My holy things; they have put no difference between the holy and the common, neither have they taught difference between the unclean and the clean, and have hid their eyes from My sabbaths, and I am profaned among them. 27. Her princes in the midst thereof are like wolves ravening the prey: to shed blood, and to destroy souls, so as to get dishonest gain. 28. And her prophets have daubed for them with whited plaster, seeing falsehood, and divining lies unto them, saying: Thus saith the Lord GOD, when the LORD hath not spoken. 29. The people of the land have used oppression, and exercised robbery,

26 כֹּהֲנֶ֜יהָ חָמְס֣וּ תֽוֹרָתִי֮ וַיְחַלְּל֣וּ קָדָשַׁ֒י֒ בֵּֽין־קֹ֣דֶשׁ לְחֹל֙ לֹ֣א הִבְדִּ֔ילוּ וּבֵ֧ין־הַטָּמֵ֛א לְטָה֖וֹר לֹ֣א הוֹדִ֑יעוּ וּמִשַׁבְּתוֹתַי֙ הֶעְלִ֣ימוּ עֵֽינֵיהֶ֔ם וָאֵחַ֖ל בְּתוֹכָֽם׃

27 שָׂרֶ֣יהָ בְקִרְבָּ֗הּ כִּזְאֵבִ֛ים טֹ֥רְפֵי טָ֖רֶף לִשְׁפָּךְ־דָּ֑ם לְאַבֵּ֣ד נְפָשׁ֔וֹת לְמַ֖עַן בְּצֹ֥עַ בָּֽצַע׃

28 וּנְבִיאֶ֗יהָ טָח֤וּ לָהֶם֙ תָּפֵ֔ל חֹזִ֣ים שָׁ֔וְא וְקֹסְמִ֥ים לָהֶ֖ם כָּזָ֑ב אֹֽמְרִים֙ כֹּ֣ה אָמַ֣ר אֲדֹנָ֣י יְהֹוִ֔ה וַֽיהֹוָ֖ה לֹ֥א דִבֵּֽר׃

29 עַ֤ם הָאָ֙רֶץ֙ עָ֣שְׁקוּ עֹ֔שֶׁק וְגָזְל֖וּ גָּזֵ֑ל

26. *her priests have done violence to My law.* Either by failing in their duty to instruct the people in the Torah (cf. Mal. ii. 7), or by violating its teachings. The latter seems more probable in the light of the next clause.

have profaned My holy things. They ignored the regulations which had as their purpose safeguarding the sanctity of the Temple and its services.

difference between the holy and the common, etc. This was a duty specifically imposed upon the priests (cf. Lev. x. 10f.). Various limitations were placed on the use of what came within the category of *holy*, and it was necessary for the people to know them and so avoid the sin of 'trespass.'

between the unclean and the clean. Laws concerning animals fit or unfit for consumption, and the ritual purity of the individual and the family.

hid their eyes from My sabbaths. The priests looked on indifferently at the desecration of the sacred days by the people (cf. Jer. xvii. 21ff.).

27. *her princes.* See on verse 6.

so as to get dishonest gain. The men of authority abused their power to enrich themselves. Even the crime of judicial murder was perpetrated to achieve this end.

28. *her prophets have daubed for them with whited plaster.* After referring to the misdeeds of the priests and the princes, Ezekiel reverts to the false prophets whom he holds responsible for their base conduct. Not only did they not check them, they even abetted the evil deeds by putting a 'worthless white-wash' over their tottering structure (see on xiii. 10).

29. *the people of the land.* See on vii. 27.

have used oppression. They enacted oppressive regulations which embittered the lot of the masses.

and have wronged the poor and
needy, and have oppressed the
stranger unlawfully. 30. And I
sought for a man among them, that
should make up the hedge, and
stand in the breach before Me for
the land, that I should not destroy it;
but I found none. 31. Therefore
have I poured out Mine indignation
upon them; I have consumed them
with the fire of My wrath; their own
way have I brought upon their
heads, saith the Lord GOD.'

וְעָנִי וְאֶבְיוֹן הוֹנוּ וְאֶת־הַגֵּר
30 עָשְׁקוּ בְּלֹא מִשְׁפָּט: וָאֲבַקֵּשׁ
מֵהֶם אִישׁ גֹּדֵר־גָּדֵר וְעֹמֵד
בַּפֶּרֶץ לְפָנַי בְּעַד הָאָרֶץ
לְבִלְתִּי שַׁחֲתָהּ וְלֹא מָצָאתִי:
31 וָאֶשְׁפֹּךְ עֲלֵיהֶם זַעְמִי בְּאֵשׁ
עֶבְרָתִי כִּלִּיתִים דַּרְכָּם
בְּרֹאשָׁם נָתַתִּי נְאֻם אֲדֹנָי
יֱהֹוִה:

23   CHAPTER XXIII   כג

1. And the word of the LORD came
unto me, saying: 2. 'Son of man,
there   were   two   women,   the

1 וַיְהִי דְבַר־יְהֹוָה אֵלַי לֵאמֹר:
2 בֶּן־אָדָם שְׁתַּיִם נָשִׁים בְּנוֹת

---

have wronged the poor and needy. By
making extortionate demands upon them.
oppressed the stranger. Transgressing
the law to love the stranger (Lev. xix. 34).
unlawfully. This term qualifies all the
offences enumerated. Their actions had
been 'without justice' (so lit.).

30. make up the hedge, and stand in the
breach. The corruption has affected all
classes of the population and left not even
one capable of averting the disaster which
approaches. 'There is no real conflict
between this passage and xiv. 14. There
the goodness of the individual is thought
of as counterbalancing the wickedness
of the many; here, the individual who
"makes up the fence" inspires the many
with his own goodness' (Lofthouse).

31. therefore have I poured out Mine
indignation upon them. The moral collapse of the people must have its sequel
in their destruction. Here, again, the
prophet uses the past tense instead of the
future, because in his mind the direful
event which he predicts is as though
already accomplished.

CHAPTER XXIII
THE TWO ADULTEROUS SISTERS

THE prophet portrays in vivid allegory
the history of the two kingdoms centred
respectively in Samaria and Jerusalem.
They are compared to two sisters,
Oholah and Oholibah, who were unfaithful to their husbands and sought association with strange men. Similarly, the
nation of Israel from its inception in
Egypt abandoned the service of God and
worshipped the idols of its neighbours.
Samaria contracted political alliances
with foreign Powers against the counsel
of God's prophets, and the result was
moral degradation and national downfall.
The younger sister, Oholibah, the
kingdom of Judah, learned no lesson from
that fate and followed the same path.
Jerusalem will therefore share the doom
of Samaria and drink to the full the cup
from which she had drunk.

1-4 OHOLAH AND OHOLIBAH
2. the daughters of one mother. Samaria
and Jerusalem both had their origin in
the nation of Israel (cf. xvi. 46; Jer. iii. 7).

daughters of one mother; 3. and they committed harlotries in Egypt; they committed harlotries in their youth; there were their bosoms pressed, and there their virgin breasts were bruised. 4. And the names of them were Oholah the elder, and Oholibah her sister; and they became Mine, and they bore sons and daughters. And as for their names, Samaria is Oholah, and Jerusalem Oholibah.

5. And Oholah played the harlot when she was Mine; and she doted on her lovers, on the Assyrians, warriors, 6. clothed with blue,

3 אִם־אַחַת הָיוּ: וַתִּזְנֶינָה
בְּמִצְרַיִם בִּנְעוּרֵיהֶן זָנוּ שָׁמָּה
מֹעֲכוּ שְׁדֵיהֶן וְשָׁם עִשּׂוּ דַּדֵּי
4 בְּתוּלֵיהֶן: וּשְׁמוֹתָן אָהֳלָה
הַגְּדוֹלָה וְאָהֳלִיבָה אֲחוֹתָהּ
וַתִּהְיֶינָה לִי וַתֵּלַדְנָה בָּנִים
וּבָנוֹת וּשְׁמוֹתָן שֹׁמְרוֹן אָהֳלָה
5 וִירוּשָׁלַם אָהֳלִיבָה: וַתִּזֶן
אָהֳלָה תַּחְתָּי וַתַּעְגַּב עַל־
מְאַהֲבֶיהָ אֶל־אַשּׁוּר
6 קְרוֹבִים: לְבֻשֵׁי תְכֵלֶת פַּחוֹת

3. *they committed harlotries in Egypt.* 'The two kingdoms are represented ideally as already existing in Egypt. This is not so far from the truth. The great tribes of Judah and Ephraim from the first stood apart, and in their attitude there lay already the germs of the two kingdoms as appears in the song of Deborah' (Davidson). For Israelite idolatry in Egypt, cf. xx. 8.

there were their bosoms pressed, etc. The prophets commonly refer to idolatry under the image of sexual licence. The 'sisters' lost their chastity during their maidenhood in Egypt, i.e. corrupted themselves with the cults of the Egyptians.

4. *they became Mine.* The covenant relationship between God and Israel is often symbolized as marriage (cf. Hos. ii. 21f.).

Samaria is Oholah, and Jerusalem Oholibah. The Jewish commentators explain the name given to Samaria as 'her tent,' i.e. her 'tent' for worship (see on xvi. 16) is her own and not God's, since in Samaria they worshipped the calves introduced by Jeroboam; and the name

given to Jerusalem denotes 'My tent is in her,' i.e. in her midst is God's sanctuary. Modern exegetes do not accept this sharp distinction and question whether the 'i' in Oholibah denotes 'my,' comparing the name Oholibamah, the wife of Esau (Gen. xxxvi. 2). They prefer the meanings 'she who has a tent' and 'a tent is in her.' The two sisters are alike in possessing a shrine (tent).

5-10 THE ASSOCIATION OF SAMARIA WITH ASSYRIA

5. *when she was Mine.* lit. 'under Me,' under My control as her 'Husband.'

the Assyrians, warriors. The Hebrew word *kerobim* is variously explained. A.J. connects it with *kerab*, 'war' (cf. 2 Sam. xvii. 11; Ps. cxliv. 1). Ehrlich cites Esth. i 14, *and the next* (karob) *unto him,* referring to one who had ready access to the king, and understands the word here as indicating that the court of Samaria entered into close relations with the Assyrians. Rashi, Kimchi and others render: 'the Assyrians, her neighbours' (so A.V., R.V.), i.e. they became on friendly terms with the Assyrians and made them their 'neighbours,' or re-

governors and rulers, handsome young men all of them, horsemen riding upon horses. 7. And she bestowed her harlotries upon them, the choicest men of Assyria all of of them; and on whomsoever she doted, with all their idols she defiled herself. 8. Neither hath she left her harlotries brought from Egypt; for in her youth they lay with her, and they bruised her virgin breasts; and they poured out their lust upon her. 9. Wherefore I delivered her into the hand of her lovers, into the hand of the Assyrians, upon whom she doted. 10. These uncovered her nakedness; they took her sons and her daughters, and her they slew with the sword; and she became a byword among women, for judgments were executed upon her.

11. And her sister Oholibah saw

וּסְגָנִים בַּחוּרֵי חֶמֶד כֻּלָּם
7 פָּרָשִׁים רֹכְבֵי סוּסִים: וַתִּתֵּן
תַּזְנוּתֶיהָ עֲלֵיהֶם מִבְחַר בְּנֵי־
אַשּׁוּר כֻּלָּם וּבְכָל־אֲשֶׁר־
עָגְבָה בְּכָל־גִּלּוּלֵיהֶם
8 נִטְמָאָה: וְאֶת־תַּזְנוּתֶיהָ
מִמִּצְרַיִם לֹא עָזָבָה כִּי אוֹתָהּ
שָׁכְבוּ בִנְעוּרֶיהָ וְהֵמָּה עִשּׂוּ
דַּדֵּי בְתוּלֶיהָ וַיִּשְׁפְּכוּ תַזְנוּתָם
9 עָלֶיהָ: לָכֵן נְתַתִּיהָ בְּיַד־
מְאַהֲבֶיהָ בְּיַד בְּנֵי אַשּׁוּר אֲשֶׁר
10 עָגְבָה עֲלֵיהֶם: הֵמָּה גִּלּוּ
עֶרְוָתָהּ בָּנֶיהָ וּבְנוֹתֶיהָ לָקָחוּ
וְאוֹתָהּ בַּחֶרֶב הָרָגוּ וַתְּהִי־שֵׁם
לַנָּשִׁים וּשְׁפוּטִים עָשׂוּ בָהּ:
11 וַתֵּרֶא אֲחוֹתָהּ אָהֳלִיבָה

v. 8. קמץ בז״ק   v. 10. קמץ בז״ק

garded them as 'relatives.' The first approach of Israel to Assyria was by king Menahem (2 Kings xv. 19f.; cf. Hos. v. 13, xii. 2).

6. *clothed with blue . . . riding upon horses.* The inhabitants of Samaria were attracted by the beautiful uniforms of the Assyrian warriors, by their high-ranking officers and elegant appearance, and by their martial bearing.

7. *with all their idols she defiled herself.* Their eagerness for an alliance with Assyria was carried into effect, and the consequence was the introduction of Assyrian forms of idolatry.

8. *neither hath she left her harlotries brought from Egypt.* They superimposed Assyrian idolatry upon the cults which they learnt in Egypt.

9. *wherefore I delivered her into the hand of her lovers.* Because they abandoned their devotion to God in their infatuation with Assyria, God made the Assyrians the force which destroyed their kingdom.

10. *these.* The Assyrians whom Samaria had courted.

uncovered her nakedness. Symbolic of the ravishing of the kingdom and the captivity of its inhabitants.

they took. Into captivity.

she became a byword among women. lit. 'a name to women'; the fate of this harlot at the hand of her lover should serve as a warning example to other women. In plain language, what happened to Samaria should have been a deterrent to Jerusalem.

this, yet was she more corrupt in her
doting than she, and in her harlotries
more than her sister in her harlotries.
12. She doted upon the Assyrians,
governors and rulers, warriors,
clothed most gorgeously, horsemen
riding upon horses, all of them
handsome young men. 13. And
I saw that she was defiled; they
both took one way. 14. And she
increased her harlotries; for she saw
men pourtrayed upon the wall, the
images of the Chaldeans pourtrayed
with vermilion, 15. girded with
girdles upon their loins, with pendant turbans upon their heads, all
of them captains to look upon, the
likeness of the sons of Babylon, even

וַתַּשְׁחֵת עֲגָבָתָהּ מִמֶּנָּה וְאֶת־
תַּזְנוּתֶיהָ מִזְּנוּנֵי אֲחוֹתָהּ:
12 אֶל־בְּנֵי אַשּׁוּר עָגָבָה פַּחוֹת
וּסְגָנִים קְרֹבִים לְבֻשֵׁי מִכְלוֹל
פָּרָשִׁים רֹכְבֵי סוּסִים בַּחוּרֵי
13 חֶמֶד כֻּלָּם: וָאֵרֶא כִּי נִטְמָאָה
14 דֶּרֶךְ אֶחָד לִשְׁתֵּיהֶן: וַתּוֹסֶף
אֶל־תַּזְנוּתֶיהָ וַתֵּרֶא אַנְשֵׁי
מְחֻקֶּה עַל־הַקִּיר צַלְמֵי
כַשְׂדִּיִּים חֲקֻקִים בַּשָּׁשַׁר:
15 חֲגוֹרֵי אֵזוֹר בְּמָתְנֵיהֶם סְרוּחֵי
טְבוּלִים בְּרָאשֵׁיהֶם מַרְאֵה
שָׁלִשִׁים כֻּלָּם דְּמוּת בְּנֵי־

v. 12. הג׳ בקמץ   v. 14. כשדים ק׳

11-21 THE RELATIONS OF OHOLIBAH
WITH ASSYRIA AND BABYLON

11. *yet was she more corrupt.* Though
Judea saw what happened to Samaria on
account of her reliance on foreign
Powers and disloyalty to God, she
adopted the same policy and even
intensified it (cf. Jer. iii. 8, 11).

12. *rulers.* Hebrew *seganim*; only the
plural occurs in the Bible. The singular
is common in Rabbinic literature as the
title of the deputy High Priest.

warriors. Hebrew *kerobim* (see on verse
5). This verse may allude to king
Ahaz's appeal to Tiglath-pileser for help
(cf. 2 Kings xvi. 7).

13. *I saw that she was defiled.* God
looked on the corrupting effect which
followed on the alliance, but bided His
time.

they both took one way. Both kingdoms
followed the same road of national corruption and decay.

14. *for she saw men pourtrayed upon the
wall.* 'At present, an Oriental woman
of good position would never see strange
men save in pictures; and though Hebrew
women had more freedom, Ezekiel
compares Judah's desire for closer ac-
quaintance with Babylon to a wanton
girl's desire for a world from which she
would naturally be secluded' (Lofthouse).
Not satisfied with Assyrians as a 'lover,'
Judea also lusted after Babylon.

15. *girded with girdles upon their loins.*
Waist-belts were a feature of the
Babylonian attire unknown in the Land
of Israel, as stated in Shab. 9b. The
Judeans preferred Babylonian garb to
their own, a mark of the tendency to
assimilation.

pendant turbans. i.e. turbans wound
around the head with fillets hanging
down behind.

captains. Hebrew *shalishim*, the noun
used in Exod. xiv. 7. It is now explained
as 'third man' who occupied the chariot

of Chaldea, the land of their nativity. 16. And as soon as she saw them she doted upon them, and sent messengers unto them into Chaldea. 17. And the Babylonians came to her into the bed of love, and they defiled her with their lust; and she was polluted with them, and her soul was alienated from them. 18. So she uncovered her harlotries, and uncovered her nakedness; then My soul was alienated from her, like as My soul was alienated from her sister. 19. Yet she multiplied her harlotries, remembering the days of her youth, wherein she had played the harlot in the land of Egypt. 20. And she doted upon concubinage

בְּבֶל כַּשְׂדִּים אֶרֶץ מוֹלַדְתָּם:

16 וַתַּעְגַּב עֲלֵיהֶם לְמַרְאֵה עֵינֶיהָ וַתִּשְׁלַח מַלְאָכִים אֲלֵיהֶם

17 כַּשְׂדִּימָה: וַיָּבֹאוּ אֵלֶיהָ בְנֵי־ בָבֶל לְמִשְׁכַּב דֹּדִים וַיְטַמְּאוּ אוֹתָהּ בְּתַזְנוּתָם וַתִּטְמָא־בָם:

18 וַתְּגַל תַּזְנוּתֶיהָ וַתְּגַל אֶת־עֶרְוָתָהּ וַתֵּקַע נַפְשִׁי מֵעָלֶיהָ כַּאֲשֶׁר נָקְעָה נַפְשִׁי מֵעַל אֲחוֹתָהּ:

19 וַתַּרְבֶּה אֶת־תַּזְנוּתֶיהָ לִזְכֹּר אֶת־יְמֵי נְעוּרֶיהָ אֲשֶׁר זָנְתָה

20 בְּאֶרֶץ מִצְרָיִם: וַתַּעְגְּבָה עַל

v. 16. ותעגבה ק'

with the king and driver, an officer of high rank.

the land of their nativity. Unlike Israel who was attracted by foreign customs, the Babylonians strictly conformed to their own national dress.

16. *as soon as she saw them.* The sight of the martial Chaldeans at once aroused an ardent desire to be allied with them. Another rendering is: 'and she doted upon them after the sight of her eyes.'

17. *the Babylonians came to her*, etc. The Babylonians took full advantage of Judea's infatuation, with the result that the land was defiled by them.

her soul was alienated from them. lit. 'was dislocated.' Sated passion had its reaction in a revulsion of feeling. The allusion is to the rebellions of Jehoiakim and Zedekiah against Babylon's domination.

18. *she uncovered her harlotries.* Tired of

Babylon and lost to all shame, Judea looked for other 'lovers.'

My soul was alienated from her. Such degrading national behaviour had the same consequence as with Samaria. God decided to withdraw His protection and leave her to her fate, as a husband does with a faithless wife. Jeremiah uses the same phrase in vi. 8. 'God is interwoven with Israel, as it were, but sin will wrench Him away from the people— a striking metaphor expressing God's love on the one hand, and the powerful effect of sin on the other' (Soncino Bible, *Jeremiah*, p. 45).

19. *the land of Egypt.* Judea even renewed her old association with Egypt. Zedekiah made overtures to Egypt for help against Babylon (cf. xvii. 15).

20. *upon concubinage with them.* Rashi and Kimchi render: 'upon (becoming one of) their concubines.' Judea was ready to become one of the many vassal States

with them, whose flesh is as the flesh of asses, and whose issue is like the issue of horses. 21. Thus thou didst call to remembrance the lewdness of thy youth, when they from Egypt bruised thy breasts for the bosom of thy youth.

22. Therefore, O Oholibah, thus saith the Lord GOD: Behold, I will raise up thy lovers against thee, from whom thy soul is alienated, and I will bring them against thee on every side: 23. the Babylonians and all the Chaldeans, Pekod and Shoa and Koa, and all the Assyrians with them, handsome young men, governors and rulers all of them, captains and councillors, all of them riding upon horses. 24. And they shall come against thee with hosts, chariots, and wheels, and with an assembly of peoples; they shall set themselves in array against thee with buckler and shield and helmet

פְּלַגְשֵׁיהֶם אֲשֶׁר בְּשַׂר חֲמוֹרִים
בְּשָׂרָם וְזִרְמַת סוּסִים זִרְמָתָם:
21 וַתִּפְקְדִי אֵת זִמַּת נְעוּרָיִךְ
בַּעְשׂוֹת מִמִּצְרַיִם דַּדַּיִךְ לְמַעַן
22 שְׁדֵי נְעוּרָיִךְ: לָכֵן אָהֳלִיבָה
כֹּה־אָמַר אֲדֹנָי יְהֹוִה הִנְנִי
מֵעִיר אֶת־מְאַהֲבַיִךְ עָלַיִךְ
אֵת אֲשֶׁר־נָקְעָה נַפְשֵׁךְ מֵהֶם
23 וַהֲבֵאתִים עָלַיִךְ מִסָּבִיב: בְּנֵי
בָבֶל וְכָל־כַּשְׂדִּים פְּקוֹד
וְשׁוֹעַ וְקוֹעַ כָּל־בְּנֵי אַשּׁוּר
אוֹתָם בַּחוּרֵי חֶמֶד פַּחוֹת
וּסְגָנִים כֻּלָּם שָׁלִשִׁים וּקְרוּאִים
24 רֹכְבֵי סוּסִים כֻּלָּם: וּבָאוּ
עָלַיִךְ הֹצֶן רֶכֶב וְגַלְגַּל וּבִקְהַל
עַמִּים צִנָּה וּמָגֵן וְקוֹבַע יָשִׂימוּ

of Egypt to be under that country's protection.

whose flesh, etc. 'Ezekiel here uses proverbial phrases to express his contemptuous loathing' (Lofthouse). As a harlot is attracted by sexual potency, so Judea was allured by the military power of Egypt.

21. *the lewdness of thy youth.* Forgetful of the lessons taught by their national history, they renewed the errors of their past in Egypt (cf. verse 3).

22-35 PUNISHMENT OF THE UNFAITHFUL OHOLIBAH

22. *therefore.* Because of their monstrous infidelities.

thy lovers. Enumerated in the next verse. These peoples to whom the Judeans had surrendered themselves will be the agents of God's punishment.

23. *and all the Chaldeans.* Who, together with the Babylonians, comprised the empire.

Pekod and Shoa and Koa. These are now identified with Pukudu, Sutu and Kutu, races inhabiting the land east of the Tigris and bordering on Elam or Persia.

councillors. lit. 'called' to give counsel; distinguished (cf. Num. i. 16, xvi. 2).

24. *with hosts.* Kimchi follows the Targum and renders 'armed'; R.V. has 'with weapons.' The word does not occur elsewhere and its meaning is uncertain.

round about; and I will commit the judgment unto them, and they shall judge thee according to their judgments. 25. And I will set My jealousy against thee, and they shall deal with thee in fury; they shall take away thy nose and thine ears, and thy residue shall fall by the sword; they shall take thy sons and thy daughters, and thy residue shall be devoured by the fire. 26. They shall also strip thee of thy clothes, and take away thy fair jewels. 27. Thus will I make thy lewdness to cease from thee, and thy harlotry brought from the land of Egypt, so that thou shalt not lift up thine eyes unto them, nor remember Egypt any more.

28. For thus saith the Lord GOD: Behold, I will deliver thee into the hand of them whom thou hatest,

עָלַיִךְ סָבִיב וְנָתַתִּי לִפְנֵיהֶם
מִשְׁפָּט וּשְׁפָטוּךְ בְּמִשְׁפְּטֵיהֶם:
25 וְנָתַתִּי קִנְאָתִי בָּךְ וְעָשׂוּ אוֹתָךְ
בְּחֵמָה אַפֵּךְ וְאָזְנַיִךְ יָסִירוּ
וְאַחֲרִיתֵךְ בַּחֶרֶב תִּפּוֹל הֵמָּה
בָּנַיִךְ וּבְנוֹתַיִךְ יִקָּחוּ וְאַחֲרִיתֵךְ
26 תֵּאָכֵל בָּאֵשׁ: וְהִפְשִׁיטוּךְ
אֶת־בְּגָדָיִךְ וְלָקְחוּ כְּלֵי
27 תִפְאַרְתֵּךְ: וְהִשְׁבַּתִּי זִמָּתֵךְ
מִמֵּךְ וְאֶת־זְנוּתֵךְ מֵאֶרֶץ
מִצְרָיִם וְלֹא־תִשְׂאִי עֵינַיִךְ
אֲלֵיהֶם וּמִצְרַיִם לֹא תִזְכְּרִי־
28 עוֹד: כִּי כֹה אָמַר אֲדֹנָי יֱהֹוִה
הִנְנִי נֹתְנָךְ בְּיַד אֲשֶׁר שָׂנֵאת

v. 25. קמץ בז"ק

I will commit the judgment unto them. God will inform them of the sentence which He has pronounced upon guilty Judea and they are to execute.

according to their judgments. Which were notoriously ruthless, as the next verse describes.

25. *I will set My jealousy against thee.* The description of God as 'jealous' in such a connection means that He metes out retribution for the offences against Him (cf. the *Soncino Chumash* on Num. xxv. 11). Ehrlich interprets that God will set upon the face of the nation the mark of His jealousy as does a wronged husband upon his wife's face.

they shall take away thy nose and thine ears. In ancient times this disfigurement was perpetrated upon an adulteress. Here the words are figurative of the nation's deprivation of its leading men who will be led away as captives.

thy residue shall fall by the sword. The mass of the people will also suffer in addition to the leaders, many of them being slain.

they shall take. As slaves into captivity.

thy residue shall be devoured. The houses and property will be destroyed or plundered.

26. *they shall also strip thee.* Cf. xvi. 39.

27. *will I make thy lewdness to cease.* With the fall of the State and in the Babylonian exile the lust after idolatry among the Judeans vanished entirely (see on xxii. 15).

brought from the land of Egypt. Practised since the time they sojourned in that land.

28. *whom thou hatest.* i.e. the Babylonians (see on verse 17).

into the hand of them from whom thy soul is alienated; 29. and they shall deal with thee in hatred, and shall take away all thy labour, and shall leave thee naked and bare; and the nakedness of thy harlotries shall be uncovered, both thy lewdness and thy harlotries. 30. These things shall be done unto thee, for that thou hast gone astray after the nations, and because thou art polluted with their idols. 31. In the way of thy sister hast thou walked; therefore will I give her cup into thy hand. 32. Thus saith the Lord GOD:

> Thou shalt drink of thy sister's cup,
> Which is deep and large;
> Thou shalt be for a scorn and a derision;
> It is full to the uttermost.

33 Thou shalt be filled with drunkenness and sorrow,
> With the cup of astonishment and appalment,
> With the cup of thy sister Samaria.

בְּיַד אֲשֶׁר־נָקְעָה נַפְשֵׁךְ מֵהֶם:

29 וְעָשׂוּ אוֹתָךְ בְּשִׂנְאָה וְלָקְחוּ כָּל־יְגִיעֵךְ וַעֲזָבוּךְ עֵרֹם וְעֶרְיָה וְנִגְלָה עֶרְוַת זְנוּנָיִךְ

30 וְזִמָּתֵךְ וְתַזְנוּתָיִךְ: עָשֹׂה אֵלֶּה לָךְ בִּזְנוֹתֵךְ אַחֲרֵי גוֹיִם עַל אֲשֶׁר־נִטְמֵאת בְּגִלּוּלֵיהֶם:

31 בְּדֶרֶךְ אֲחוֹתֵךְ הָלָכְתְּ וְנָתַתִּי

32 כוֹסָהּ בְּיָדֵךְ: כֹּה אָמַר אֲדֹנָי יְהֹוִה
כּוֹס אֲחוֹתֵךְ תִּשְׁתִּי הָעֲמֻקָה וְהָרְחָבָה תִּהְיֶה לִצְחֹק וּלְלַעַג מִרְבָּה לְהָכִיל:

33 שִׁכָּרוֹן וְיָגוֹן תִּמָּלֵאִי כּוֹס שַׁמָּה וּשְׁמָמָה כּוֹס אֲחוֹתֵךְ שֹׁמְרוֹן:

---

29. all thy labour. The fruits of their toil (cf. the use of the noun in Ps. cxxviii. 2).

shall be uncovered. The magnitude of the national guilt will become evident from the drastic nature of the punishment.

30. thou hast gone astray after the nations. By seeking alliances with them instead of relying upon the protection of God.

thou art polluted with their idols. These alliances with foreign Powers resulted in the debasement of the religion.

31. thy sister. Oholah—Samaria.

therefore will I give her cup into thy hand. The cup of bitterness from which the Northern Kingdom had drunk in the time of the Assyrian invasion will pass into the hands of the Southern Kingdom when attacked by the Babylonians.

32. thou shalt be for a scorn and a derision. Kimchi construes: 'it (the cup) shall be for scorn,' etc. The cup of God's fury will bring scorn upon Judea from the surrounding nations. This interpretation is more correct grammatically, since *thou shalt be* requires tiheyi for tiheyah.

it is full to the uttermost. The cup is filled to the brim, indicating the large draught of bitterness which the people will have to drink. A.V. and R.V. render: 'it containeth much,' making the phrase a description of the size of the cup.

34 Thou shalt even drink it and
 drain it,
And thou shalt craunch the
 sherds thereof,
And shalt tear thy breasts;
For I have spoken it,
Saith the Lord GOD.

35. Therefore thus saith the Lord
GOD: Because thou hast forgotten
Me, and cast Me behind thy back,
therefore bear thou also thy lewdness and thy harlotries.'

36. The LORD said moreover unto
me: 'Son of man, wilt thou judge
Oholah and Oholibah? then declare
unto them their abominations. 37.
For they have committed adultery,
and blood is in their hands, and with
their idols have they committed
adultery; and their sons, whom they
bore unto Me, they have also set
apart unto them to be devoured.
38. Moreover this they have done
unto Me: they have defiled My
sanctuary in the same day, and have

34 וְשָׁתִית אוֹתָהּ וּמָצִית
וְאֶת־חֲרָשֶׂיהָ תְּגָרֵמִי
וְשָׁדַיִךְ תְּנַתֵּקִי
כִּי אֲנִי דִבַּרְתִּי
נְאֻם אֲדֹנָי יֱהֹוִה׃

35 לָכֵן כֹּה אָמַר אֲדֹנָי יֱהֹוִה יַעַן
שָׁכַחַתְּ אוֹתִי וַתַּשְׁלִיכִי אוֹתִי
אַחֲרֵי גַוֵּךְ וְגַם־אַתְּ שְׂאִי

36 זִמָּתֵךְ וְאֶת־תַּזְנוּתָיִךְ׃ וַיֹּאמֶר
יְהֹוָה אֵלַי בֶּן־אָדָם הֲתִשְׁפּוֹט
אֶת־אׇהֳלָה וְאֶת־אׇהֳלִיבָה
וְהַגֵּד לָהֶן אֵת תּוֹעֲבוֹתֵיהֶן׃

37 כִּי נִאֵפוּ וְדָם בִּידֵיהֶן וְאֶת־
גִּלּוּלֵיהֶן נִאֵפוּ וְגַם אֶת־בְּנֵיהֶן
אֲשֶׁר יָלְדוּ־לִי הֶעֱבִירוּ לָהֶם

38 לְאׇכְלָה׃ עוֹד זֹאת עָשׂוּ לִי
טִמְּאוּ אֶת־מִקְדָּשִׁי בַּיּוֹם

---

34. *craunch the sherds thereof.* In order
to suck the liquid which is soaked in the
material of the vessel. *Craunch* is a
form of the verb 'crunch.'

shall tear thy breasts. In a fit of madness
through drinking the cup of bitterness.

35. *cast Me behind thy back.* You have
completely forgotten Me like an object
which is deliberately flung behind one's
back as something worthless.

bear thou also thy lewdness. Suffer the
consequences of it.

36-49 FURTHER INDICTMENT OF
 OHOLAH AND OHOLIBAH

Some commentators regard this section
as a recapitulation of the preceding; it is
better understood as an additional charge.

36. *Oholah and Oholibah.* 'The coupling
of the still standing Jerusalem with the
fallen Samaria has great dramatic and
rhetorical force' (Lofthouse)

37. *adultery . . . blood . . . idols.* These
are the heinous crimes of which they are
accused. They are specified in detail in
what follows.

whom they bore unto Me. Who should
have been reared to serve Me. At birth
they were entered into the covenant of
God by circumcision; later they were
sacrificed by their parents to the hideous
cult of Molech (Kimchi).

38. *in the same day.* Explained in the
next verse.

profaned My sabbaths. 39. For when they had slain their children to their idols, then they came the same day into My sanctuary to profane it; and, lo, thus have they done in the midst of My house. 40. And furthermore ye have sent for men that come from far; unto whom a messenger was sent, and, lo, they came; for whom thou didst wash thyself, paint thine eyes, and deck thyself with ornaments; 41. and sattest upon a stately bed, with a table prepared before it, whereupon thou didst set Mine incense and Mine oil. 42. And the voice of a multitude being at ease was therein; and for the sake of men, they were so many, brought drunken from the wilderness, they put bracelets upon

הַהוּא וְאֶת־שַׁבְּתוֹתַי חִלֵּלוּ׃
39 וּבְשַׁחֲטָם אֶת־בְּנֵיהֶם
לְגִלּוּלֵיהֶם וַיָּבֹאוּ אֶל־מִקְדָּשִׁי
בַּיּוֹם הַהוּא לְחַלְּלוֹ וְהִנֵּה־כֹה
40 עָשׂוּ בְּתוֹךְ בֵּיתִי׃ וְאַף כִּי
תִשְׁלַחְנָה לַאֲנָשִׁים בָּאִים
מִמֶּרְחָק אֲשֶׁר מַלְאָךְ שָׁלוּחַ
אֲלֵיהֶם וְהִנֵּה־בָאוּ לַאֲשֶׁר
רָחַצְתְּ כָּחַלְתְּ עֵינַיִךְ וְעָדִית
41 עֶדִי׃ וְיָשַׁבְתְּ עַל־מִטָּה
כְבוּדָּה וְשֻׁלְחָן עָרוּךְ לְפָנֶיהָ
וּקְטָרְתִּי וְשַׁמְנִי שַׂמְתְּ עָלֶיהָ׃
42 וְקוֹל הָמוֹן שָׁלֵו בָהּ וְאֶל־
אֲנָשִׁים מֵרֹב אָדָם מוּבָאִים
סוֹבָאִים מִמִּדְבָּר וַיִּתְּנוּ

their hands, and beautiful crowns upon their heads. 43. Then said I of her that was worn out by adulteries: Still they commit harlotries with her, even her. 44. For every one went in unto her, as men go in unto a harlot; so went they in unto Oholah and unto Oholibah, the lewd women. 45. But righteous men, they shall judge them as adulteresses are judged, and as women that shed blood are judged; because they are adulteresses, and blood is in their hands.

46. For thus saith the Lord GOD: An assembly shall be brought up against them, and they shall be made

צְמִידִים֙ אֶל־יְדֵיהֶ֔ן וַעֲטֶ֥רֶת
43 תִּפְאֶ֖רֶת עַל־רָאשֵׁיהֶֽן׃ וָאֹמַ֕ר
לַבָּלָ֖ה נִֽאוּפִ֑ים עַ֛תָּ יִזְנֶ֥ה
44 תַזְנוּתֶ֖יהָ וָהִֽיא׃ וַיָּב֣וֹא אֵלֶ֔יהָ
כְּב֖וֹא אֶל־אִשָּׁ֣ה זוֹנָ֑ה כֵּ֣ן בָּ֗אוּ
אֶל־אָֽהֳלָ֔ה וְאֶל־אָהֳלִיבָ֖ה
45 אִשֹּׁ֥ת הַזִּמָּֽה׃ וַאֲנָשִׁ֣ים צַדִּיקִ֗ם
הֵ֚מָּה יִשְׁפְּט֣וּ אוֹתְהֶ֔ם מִשְׁפַּ֖ט
נֹֽאֲפ֑וֹת וּמִשְׁפַּ֖ט שֹׁפְכֹ֣ת דָּ֑ם
כִּ֣י נֹֽאֲפֹ֣ת הֵ֔נָּה וְדָ֖ם בִּֽידֵיהֶֽן׃
46 כִּ֣י כֹּ֤ה אָמַר֙ אֲדֹנָ֣י יֱהֹוִ֔ה הַעֲלֵ֥ה
עֲלֵיהֶ֖ם קָהָ֑ל וְנָתֹ֥ן אֶתְהֶֽן

difficulties. A.V. has 'and with men of the common sort were brought Sabeans from the wilderness,' which is influenced by Kimchi whose interpretation is: 'among the men who came in multitudes were also Sabeans brought from the wilderness,' the Sabeans being a nomadic people. On this explanation, the Israelites, both in the north and south, are charged with making indiscriminate alliances, even with Bedouins who roam the wilderness. R.V. reads: 'and with men of the common sort were brought drunkards from the wilderness,' which approximates to A.J. The meaning, then, is that Judea has sunk so low that she enters into alliances with the most degraded types. Even to attract such as these they try to make themselves enticing.

43. *still they commit harlotries with her, even her.* Rashi interprets: I thought that now that she is worn out by her harlotry, her immoralities would come to an end, but she has remained the same. The general sense is that the people were

not sated with their imported idolatries but persisted with them.

44. *women.* The plural form *ishshoth* does not occur again. Kimchi suggests that it is used here to express a sense of abhorrence; they are unlike normal women.

45. *righteous men, they shall judge them.* The Targum and Jewish commentators understand the reference to be to the Babylonian and Assyrian 'judges' who, compared with Oholah and Oholibah, are *righteous.*

as adulteresses are judged. Inflicting upon them penalties reserved for women guilty of adultery and murder. By the latter the sacrifice of children is meant.

46. *shall be brought up . . . and they shall be made.* The text has both verbs in the infinitive. The prophet is commanded to impress upon the people that God will bring against them a group of peoples who will make them the object of horror and spoliation.

159

a horror and a spoil. 47. And the assembly shall stone them with stones, and despatch them with their swords; they shall slay their sons and their daughters, and burn up their houses with fire. 48. Thus will I cause lewdness to cease out of the land, that all women may be taught not to do after your lewdness. 49. And your lewdness shall be recompensed upon you, and ye shall bear the sins of your idols; and ye shall know that I am the Lord God.'

47 לְזַעֲוָה וְלָבַז: וְרָגְמוּ עֲלֵיהֶן
אֶבֶן קָהָל וּבָרֵא אוֹתְהֶן
בְּחַרְבוֹתָם בְּנֵיהֶם וּבְנֹתֵיהֶם
יַהֲרֹגוּ וּבָתֵּיהֶן בָּאֵשׁ יִשְׂרֹפוּ:
48 וְהִשְׁבַּתִּי זִמָּה מִן־הָאָרֶץ
וְנִוַּסְּרוּ כָּל־הַנָּשִׁים וְלֹא
49 תַעֲשֶׂינָה כְּזִמַּתְכֶנָה: וְנָתְנוּ
זִמַּתְכֶנָה עֲלֵיכֶן וַחֲטָאֵי
גִלּוּלֵיכֶן תִּשֶּׂאינָה וִידַעְתֶּם כִּי
אֲנִי אֲדֹנָי יְהוִה:

24   CHAPTER XXIV   כד

1. And the word of the Lord came   1 וַיְהִי דְבַר־יְהוָה אֵלַי בַּשָּׁנָה

v. 46. פתח בס״פ v. 49. יתיר י׳

---

47. *shall stone them with stones.* See on xvi. 40. Ehrlich construes: 'and they shall stone her with stones (the singular used collectively) thrown by the assembly,' the subject of the verb being indefinite.

48. *will I cause lewdness to cease.* See on verse 27.

all women may be taught. i.e. the surrounding nations will take warning.

49. *shall be recompensed.* lit. 'they (the assembly of nations) shall award (the punishment of) your lewdness upon you.'

ye shall bear the sins of your idols. i.e. you shall suffer the penalty for the sins incurred in connection with your idols.

CHAPTER XXIV

BEGINNING OF THE SIEGE OF JERUSALEM

THE chapter is prefaced by a memorable date, the tenth of the tenth month (Tebeth). This day, on which Nebu-

chadnezzar began the siege of Jerusalem, was appointed as a fast (Zech. viii. 19) and still remains in the Jewish calendar. After Ezekiel had written down the day of the week and the exact date on which the prophecy came to him that the city was being invested, he forthwith illustrated the siege by a parable. He returns to the figure of the caldron which the remnant in Jerusalem once used for their illusory hopes. A rusted pot with flesh is set on the fire. All the contents are consumed. The empty pot is set on the fire again so that rust and metal alike may be melted. The parable represents the siege: the pot is Jerusalem, the flesh is the inhabitants, and the rust is the wickedness of the people. The latter part of the chapter deals with the death of Ezekiel's wife which took place on the evening of that day. The prophet was not to observe the customary rites of mourning. The import of the attitude he was to adopt towards them was that in the national catastrophe the people

160

G

unto me in the ninth year, in the
tenth month, in the tenth day of the
month, saying: 2. 'Son of man, write
thee the name of the day, even of
this selfsame day; this selfsame day
the king of Babylon hath invested
Jerusalem. 3. And utter a parable
concerning the rebellious house, and
say unto them: Thus saith the Lord
GOD:

Set on the pot, set it on,
And also pour water into it;
4 Gather into it the pieces belonging
to it,
Even every good piece, the thigh,
and the shoulder;
Fill it with the choice bones.

הַתְּשִׁיעִית בַּחֹדֶשׁ הָעֲשִׂירִי
בֶּעָשׂוֹר לַחֹדֶשׁ לֵאמֹר: בֶּן־ 2
אָדָם כְּתָוב־לְךָ אֶת־שֵׁם
הַיּוֹם אֶת־עֶצֶם הַיּוֹם הַזֶּה
סָמַךְ מֶלֶךְ־בָּבֶל אֶל־
יְרוּשָׁלִַם בְּעֶצֶם הַיּוֹם הַזֶּה:
וּמְשֹׁל אֶל־בֵּית־הַמֶּרִי מָשָׁל 3
וְאָמַרְתָּ אֲלֵיהֶם כֹּה אָמַר אֲדֹנָי
יְהֹוִה
שְׁפֹת הַסִּיר שְׁפֹת
וְגַם־יְצֹק בּוֹ מָיִם:
אֱסֹף נְתָחֶיהָ אֵלֶיהָ 4
כָּל־נֵתַח טוֹב יָרֵךְ וְכָתֵף
מִבְחַר עֲצָמִים מַלֵּא:

v. 2. כתב ק'

---

would be too bewildered and overwhelmed to feel personal bereavement.

1-14 TRUE MEANING OF THE
PARABLE OF THE CALDRON

1. *in the ninth year.* Of the reign of
Zedekiah, early in 587 B.C.E. The same
date is given in 2 Kings xxv. 1; Jer. lii. 4.

2. *the name of the day.* i.e. the day of
the week.

this selfsame day. The day of the month.
The prophet was to place on record the
beginning of the siege on the day the
information was communicated to him.
The purpose was to demonstrate the
authenticity of the oracle. There was no
other way of communication open to
him because of the great distance between
Babylon and Jerusalem.

hath invested. lit. 'hath leaned (his
weight) towards.'

3. *utter a parable . . . set on the pot.*
The imagery of the caldron, previously
used by the inhabitants of Jerusalem for
their deceptive hopes (xi. 3), is now to be
given its true interpretation by the
prophet in the light of current events.
Setting the caldron on the stove and
pouring water into it, the first stage in
the process of cooking, represent the
siege of Jerusalem which is the preliminary to conquest.

4. *gather into it the pieces.* The pieces of
flesh gathered in the pot symbolize the
inhabitants of the city and the fugitives
from other towns who sought refuge
there.

every good piece. The leaders of the
people.

the choice bones. Perhaps the commanders of the forces and the fighting
men.

161

5 Take the choice of the flock,

And pile also the bones under it;

Make it boil well,

That the bones thereof may also

be seethed in the midst of it.

6. Wherefore thus saith the Lord
GOD: Woe to the bloody city, to the
pot whose filth is therein, and whose
filth is not gone out of it! bring it out
piece by piece; no lot is fallen upon
it. 7. For her blood is in the midst
of her; she set it upon the bare rock;
she poured it not upon the ground,
to cover it with dust; 8. that it might
cause fury to come up, that venge-

5 מִבְחַר הַצֹּאן לָקוֹחַ
וְגַם דּוּר הָעֲצָמִים תַּחְתֶּיהָ
רַתַּח רְתָחֶיהָ
גַּם־בָּשְׁלוּ עֲצָמֶיהָ בְּתוֹכָהּ׃
6 לָכֵן כֹּה־אָמַר ׀ אֲדֹנָי יֱהֹוִה
אוֹי עִיר הַדָּמִים סִיר אֲשֶׁר
חֶלְאָתָהּ בָהּ וְחֶלְאָתָהּ לֹא
יָצְאָה מִמֶּנָּה לִנְתָחֶיהָ לִנְתָחֶיהָ
הוֹצִיאָהּ לֹא־נָפַל עָלֶיהָ
7 גּוֹרָל׃ כִּי דָמָהּ בְּתוֹכָהּ הָיָה
עַל־צְחִיחַ סֶלַע שָׂמָתְהוּ לֹא
שְׁפָכַתְהוּ עַל־הָאָרֶץ לְכַסּוֹת
8 עָלָיו עָפָר׃ לְהַעֲלוֹת חֵמָה

v. 6. ההו״א רפה

5. the choice of the flock. The pieces of
flesh are to be from the best sheep, an
allusion to the presence of the aristocracy
in the besieged city.

under it. Under the flesh, i.e. the bones
are also to be put into the caldron.

make it boil well. lit. 'cause its boilings
to boil,' bring the water to boiling point.

that the bones thereof, etc. A graphic
allusion to the extreme ferocity of the
Babylonian attack.

6. *wherefore.* That the people should
thoroughly understand the import of the
parable its message is stated in plain
language.

filth. This is a more exact rendering of
the Hebrew *chel'ah* than R.V. 'rust.'
Here it denotes the bloodstains of the
innocent who were murdered in Jerusalem.

bring it out piece by piece. The population within the city will perish or be

exiled not in one mass, but in sections at
different times.

no lot is fallen upon it. The contents are
to be taken out at random, indicating that
the deportation from Jerusalem will be
indiscriminate.

7. *for her blood,* etc. Her crimes are
unpardoned because she committed them
openly and unshamedly, making no
attempt to conceal the blood which was
shed. It is still uncovered and cries for
God's judgment (cf. Gen. iv. 10;
Job xvi. 18). The Rabbis interpreted
the verse as referring to the blood of the
prophet Zechariah who was murdered
within the precincts of the sanctuary.
The blood seethed at the appearance of
the Babylonian general, and he
slaughtered the members of the Sanhedrin and schoolchildren over it to
stop it from seething (Midrash to Lam.,
Proem xxiii).

to cover it with dust. They treated
human blood with even less concern

ance might be taken, I have set her blood upon the bare rock, that it should not be covered. 9. Therefore thus saith the Lord GOD: Woe to the bloody city! I also will make the pile great, 10. heaping on the wood, kindling the fire, that the flesh may be consumed; and preparing the mixture, that the bones also may be burned; 11. then will I set it empty upon the coals thereof, that it may be hot, and the bottom thereof may burn, and that the impurity of it may be molten in it, that the filth of it may be consumed. 12. It hath wearied itself with toil;

לְנָקָם נָקָם נָתַתִּי אֶת־דָּמָהּ
עַל־צְחִיחַ סָלַע לְבִלְתִּי
9 הִכָּסוֹת: לָכֵן כֹּה אָמַר אֲדֹנָי
יֱהוִֹה אוֹי עִיר הַדָּמִים גַּם־אֲנִי
10 אַגְדִּיל הַמְּדוּרָה: הַרְבֵּה
הָעֵצִים הַדְלֵק הָאֵשׁ הָתֵם
הַבָּשָׂר וְהַרְקַח הַמֶּרְקָחָה
11 וְהָעֲצָמוֹת יֵחָרוּ: וְהַעֲמִידֶהָ
עַל־גֶּחָלֶיהָ רֵקָה לְמַעַן תֵּחַם
וְחָרָה נְחֻשְׁתָּהּ וְנִתְּכָה בְתוֹכָהּ
טֻמְאָתָהּ תִּתֻּם חֶלְאָתָהּ:
12 תְּאֻנִים הֶלְאָת וְלֹא־תֵצֵא

---

than animal blood which had to be covered with dust (cf. Lev. xvii. 13).

8. *I have set her blood upon the bare rock.* In view of Jerusalem's callousness, God will preserve the bloodstains to exact a severe penalty from those responsible.

9. *therefore.* God, as the supreme Judge, pronounces sentence.

I also will make the pile great. They heaped sin on sin; God will also heap fuel for their punishment.

10. *heaping on the wood . . . that the flesh may be consumed.* Divine judgment will be executed to the full upon the guilty.

preparing the mixture. Of spices, usually added when the flesh has been sufficiently cooked (Kimchi). Rashi explains: 'and made it into a thin mixture'; i.e. on account of the intense heat the flesh is disintegrated and reduced to a thin substance resembling powdered spices. Both interpretations are based on the common use of the root *rakach* in connection with the compounding of ointments or perfumes.

the bones also may be burned. So thorough will the punishment be that it will include men upon whom the nation depends: the rulers, commanders and army, who are to the people what the bones are in the human frame.

11. *set it empty upon the coals.* After all the contents of the pot had been consumed by prolonged boiling, the empty pot will be melted by the heat of the fire together with the filth that clung to it. This is a symbol of the city's purification after being emptied of its inhabitants.

bottom thereof. lit. 'the copper thereof.' This meaning of *nechosheth* is found in Rabbinic Hebrew (cf. Kelim viii. 3, ix. 1, 3).

12. *it hath wearied itself with toil.* This translation seems to imply that the men of Jerusalem made a strong effort to get rid of its 'filth'; but the thought does not suit the context which emphasized their indifference to the evidence of their guilt. Preference may therefore be given to R.V. margin: 'she hath wearied (Me) with toil.' Justice demands of God that He should remove the 'filth,' and this He has to do by the drastic

yet its great filth goeth not forth out
of it, yea, its noisome filth. 13. Because of thy filthy lewdness, because
I have purged thee and thou wast
not purged, thou shalt not be
purged from thy filthiness any more,
till I have satisfied My fury upon
thee. 14. I the LORD have spoken
it; it shall come to pass, and I will
do it; I will not go back, neither will
I spare, neither will I repent;
according to thy ways, and according
to thy doings, shall they judge thee,
saith the Lord GOD.'

15. Also the word of the LORD
came unto me, saying: 16. 'Son of
man, behold, I take away from thee
the desire of thine eyes with a stroke;

מִמֶּנָּה רַבַּת חֶלְאָתָהּ בָּאֵשׁ
חֶלְאָתָהּ: בְּטֻמְאָתֵךְ זִמָּה יַעַן 13
טִהַרְתִּיךְ וְלֹא טָהַרְתְּ
מִטֻּמְאָתֵךְ לֹא תִטְהֲרִי־עוֹד
עַד־הֲנִיחִי אֶת־חֲמָתִי בָּךְ׃
אֲנִי יְהֹוָה דִּבַּרְתִּי בָּאָה וְעָשִׂיתִי 14
לֹא־אֶפְרַע וְלֹא־אָחוּס וְלֹא
אֶנָּחֵם כִּדְרָכַיִךְ וְכַעֲלִילוֹתַיִךְ
שְׁפָטוּךְ נְאֻם אֲדֹנָי יְהֹוִה׃ וַיְהִי 15
דְבַר־יְהֹוָה אֵלַי לֵאמֹר׃ בֶּן־ 16
אָדָם הִנְנִי לֹקֵחַ מִמְּךָ אֶת־
מַחְמַד עֵינֶיךָ בְּמַגֵּפָה וְלֹא

process of melting down the 'caldron,'
i.e. by destroying Jerusalem. The word
for *toil* (teunim) does not occur elsewhere
but is connected with *awen* which is
frequently used with *amal*, the common
noun for 'labour' (cf. Ps. x. 7, lv. 11).
its great filth goeth not forth out of it. In
any other way than by burning.
its noisome filth. This rendering understands the Hebrew *beësh* as 'ill-smelling,
repulsive.' A.V. has 'her scum shall be
in the fire', and R.V. 'her rust (goeth not
forth) by fire.' Davidson translates: 'let
her rust be in the fire!' and comments:
'Previous efforts to purify Jerusalem have
been in vain, her uncleanness will go out
only by fire.' This agrees with the
interpretation of Jewish commentators.

13. *because of thy filthy lewdness.* A.V.
and R.V. render: 'in thy filthiness is
lewdness,' and Kimchi explains: 'thou art
still in thy filthy lewdness.' A.J. is
probable.
*because I have purged thee and thou wast
not purged.* All efforts to bring the
people to moral reformation through

prophetic admonition have failed. Only
the purging effect of God's wrath will
achieve that end.

14. *I the LORD have spoken it.* Such is
the Divine judgment upon the nation.
The Hebrew uses the prophetic perfect.
In fact, the process had begun with the
siege of Jerusalem.

I will not go back. The verb *para'*
usually means 'let loose, let alone.' It
is not found elsewhere in the sense used
here, 'refrain.'

shall they judge thee. The Chaldeans
who are the executors of God's judgment
will inflict upon them the punishment
which is commensurate with their
heinous crimes.

15-27 THE SYMBOL OF EZEKIEL'S
BEREAVEMENT

16. *the desire of thine eyes.* i.e. Ezekiel's
wife.

with a stroke. Suddenly without her
having been previously sick; perhaps a
sign of the sudden fall of the Temple.

yet neither shalt thou make lamentation nor weep, neither shall thy tears run down. 17. Sigh in silence; make no mourning for the dead, bind thy headtire upon thee, and put thy shoes upon thy feet, and cover not thine upper lip, and eat not the bread of men.' 18. So I spoke unto the people in the morning, and at even my wife died; and I did in the morning as I was commanded. 19. And the people said unto me: 'Wilt thou not tell us what these things are to us, that thou doest so?' 20. Then I said unto them: 'The word of the LORD

תֵּסְפֹּד וְלֹא תִבְכֶּה וְלוֹא תָבוֹא
17 דִּמְעָתֶךָ: הֵאָנֵק | דֹּם מֵתִים
אֵבֶל לֹא־תַעֲשֶׂה פְּאֵרְךָ
חֲבוֹשׁ עָלֶיךָ וּנְעָלֶיךָ תָּשִׂים
בְּרַגְלֶיךָ וְלֹא תַעְטֶה עַל־
שָׂפָם וְלֶחֶם אֲנָשִׁים לֹא תֹאכֵל:
18 וָאֲדַבֵּר אֶל־הָעָם בַּבֹּקֶר
וַתָּמָת אִשְׁתִּי בָּעָרֶב וָאַעַשׂ
19 בַּבֹּקֶר כַּאֲשֶׁר צֻוֵּיתִי: וַיֹּאמְרוּ
אֵלַי הָעָם הֲלֹא־תַגִּיד לָנוּ
מָה־אֵלֶּה לָּנוּ כִּי אַתָּה עֹשֶׂה:
20 וָאֹמַר אֲלֵיהֶם דְּבַר־יְהֹוָה

neither shalt thou make lamentation nor weep. He is to suppress his natural feelings; he is not to lament nor perform any other rites of mourning over his wife's sudden death. This unusual behaviour enjoined on the prophet was to serve as an augury that the blow which was soon to befall the nation would be too stunning for normal expressions of grief.

17. *sigh in silence.* And not with loud cries of lament as was customary in such circumstances (cf. 'Make bitter weeping, and make passionate wailing (over the dead),' Ecclus. xxxviii. 17).

put thy shoes upon thy feet. Cf. 2 Sam. xv. 30. To remove the shoes remains a sign of mourning among Jews.

cover not thine upper lip. The usual practice was for mourners to loosen their headgear and enshroud the head down to the upper lip (cf. Mic. iii. 7).

eat not the bread of men. It is still Jewish law that the first meal of mourners after the burial should be supplied to them by others.

18. *in the morning.* The phrase occurs twice, and the interpretation of the verse depends upon whether the words indicate the same point of time or not. One view is, 'On one morning he tells the people what he had learnt; in the evening his wife dies; next morning no customary signs of grief are shown by the bereaved husband' (Lofthouse). Ehrlich, on the other hand, understands both to refer to the same morning, and he interprets: I spoke to the people in the morning, my wife having died the previous evening, and on the same morning carried out the instructions given to me by God. Rashi and Kimchi do not discuss the point, but Metsudath David offers the first explanation.

19. *what these things are to us.* Noticing his extraordinary behaviour in not observing the traditional rites, the people suspected that it had a reason which affected them.

20. *the word of the LORD came unto me.* He prefaces his message with the assurance that he was obeying God's

came unto me, saying: 21. Speak unto the house of Israel: Thus saith the Lord GOD: Behold, I will profane My sanctuary, the pride of your power, the desire of your eyes, and the longing of your soul; and your sons and your daughters whom ye have left behind shall fall by the sword. 22. And ye shall do as I have done: ye shall not cover your upper lips, nor eat the bread of men; 23. and your tires shall be upon your heads, and your shoes upon your feet; ye shall not make lamentation nor weep; but ye shall pine away in your iniquities, and moan one toward another. 24. Thus shall Ezekiel be unto you a sign; according to all that he hath done

21 הָיָה אֵלַי לֵאמֹר: אֱמֹר |
לְבֵית יִשְׂרָאֵל כֹּה־אָמַר אֲדֹנָי
יְהֹוִה הִנְנִי מְחַלֵּל אֶת־מִקְדָּשִׁי
גְּאוֹן עֻזְּכֶם מַחְמַד עֵינֵיכֶם
וּמַחְמַל נַפְשְׁכֶם וּבְנֵיכֶם
וּבְנוֹתֵיכֶם אֲשֶׁר עֲזַבְתֶּם
22 בַּחֶרֶב יִפֹּלוּ: וַעֲשִׂיתֶם כַּאֲשֶׁר
עָשִׂיתִי עַל־שָׂפָם לֹא תַעְטוּ
וְלֶחֶם אֲנָשִׁים לֹא תֹאכֵלוּ:
23 וּפְאֵרֵכֶם עַל־רָאשֵׁיכֶם
וְנַעֲלֵיכֶם בְּרַגְלֵיכֶם לֹא
תִסְפְּדוּ וְלֹא תִבְכּוּ וּנְמַקֹּתֶם
בַּעֲוֹנֹתֵיכֶם וּנְהַמְתֶּם אִישׁ אֶל־
24 אָחִיו: וְהָיָה יְחֶזְקֵאל לָכֶם
לְמוֹפֵת כְּכֹל אֲשֶׁר־עָשָׂה

command in what he did, and they rightly thought that his sudden loss and consequent behaviour had a symbolic significance for the nation.

21. *I will profane My sanctuary.* By delivering it into the hands of heathens. You will suffer bereavement of *the desire of your eyes* as did Ezekiel by the death of his wife (*the desire of thine eyes*, verse 16).

your sons and your daughters whom ye have left behind. Apparently the Judeans who were deported to Babylon with Jehoiachin left members of their families behind in Jerusalem. The news of their death there will reach the exiles in Babylon.

22. *ye shall do as I have done.* Having heard of the death of their children in Jerusalem, the exiles will be too overcome to observe the laws of mourning, as indicated in the action of the prophet.

Rashi gives an alternative explanation: the exiles will refrain from mourning from fear of the Babylonians who will be responsible for their bereavement.

23. *ye shall pine away in your iniquities.* Cf. xxxiii. 10; Lev. xxvi. 39. 'At this point the analogy between Ezekiel's grief and the nation's ceases. The latter will include the bitterness of a guilty conscience—an actual consciousness of sin' (Lofthouse).

moan one toward another. The exiles will not make loud lamentation, but *moan*, giving almost inaudible expression of their remorse (cf. the use of the verb in Prov. v. 11f.).

24. *then shall Ezekiel be unto you a sign.* The prophet repeats the exact words which God had communicated to him; hence the mention of himself in the third person.

shall ye do; when this cometh, then
shall ye know that I am the Lord
GOD.

25. And thou, son of man, shall it
not be in the day when I take from
them their stronghold, the joy of
their glory, the desire of their eyes,
and the yearning of their soul, their
sons and their daughters, 26. that in
that day he that escapeth shall come
unto thee, to cause thee to hear it
with thine ears? 27. In that day
shall thy mouth be opened together
with him that is escaped, and thou
shalt speak, and be no more dumb;
so shalt thou be a sign unto them;
and they shall know that I am the
LORD.'

תַּעֲשׂוּ בְּבֹאָהּ וִידַעְתֶּם כִּי אֲנִי
25 אֲדֹנָי יְהֹוִה: וְאַתָּה בֶן־אָדָם
הֲלוֹא בְּיוֹם קַחְתִּי מֵהֶם אֶת־
מָעֻזָּם מְשׂוֹשׂ תִּפְאַרְתָּם אֶת־
מַחְמַד עֵינֵיהֶם וְאֶת־מַשָּׂא
26 נַפְשָׁם בְּנֵיהֶם וּבְנוֹתֵיהֶם: בַּיּוֹם
הַהוּא יָבוֹא הַפָּלִיט אֵלֶיךָ
27 לְהַשְׁמָעוּת אָזְנָיִם : בַּיּוֹם
הַהוּא יִפָּתַח פִּיךָ אֶת־הַפָּלִיט
וּתְדַבֵּר וְלֹא תֵאָלֵם עוֹד וְהָיִיתָ
לָהֶם לְמוֹפֵת וְיָדְעוּ כִּי־אֲנִי
יְהֹוָה:

shall ye do. Abstaining from signs of
mourning as the prophet had done in his
bereavement.

when this cometh. On their hearing the
news of the fall of Jerusalem and the
destruction of the Temple.

then shall ye know, etc. That the
calamitous event was the decree of God.

25. their stronghold, etc. These terms
describe the Temple. It had been their
stronghold, upon which they had relied
for immunity, and the joy of their glory,
the magnificent edifice which had been
their pride. Whether the desire of their
eyes is an epithet for the Temple is
uncertain. Though the Hebrew accentuation is against it, Kimchi regards
the whole verse up to their sons, etc.
as descriptive of the Temple, and their
sons and their daughters as a separate
clause governed by when I take. Metsudath David understands the desire . . .
their soul as qualifying the words that
follow.

26. in that day he that escapeth shall come.
The phrase in that day cannot refer to
the day of Jerusalem's fall spoken of in
the preceding verse, since there was a
considerable interval between that event
and the arrival of the fugitive (cf. xxxiii.
21). Kimchi therefore understands the
phrase to mean more generally 'in that
period.'

to cause thee to hear it. lit. 'for the
causing of ears to hear.'

27. shall thy mouth be opened together with
him that is escaped. With the tidings of
the destruction of Jerusalem brought by
the fugitive, the authenticity of the
prophet's message will be established.

and be no more dumb. As he was at the
beginning of his career (cf. iii. 26f.;
xxxiii. 22).

so shalt thou be a sign unto them. His
mission as a messenger of God will be
accepted by the community in Babylon.

they shall know, etc. See on verse 24.

25   CHAPTER XXV   כה

1. And the word of the LORD came unto me, saying: 2. 'Son of man, set thy face toward the children of Ammon, and prophesy against them; 3. and say unto the children of Ammon: Hear the word of the Lord GOD: Thus saith the Lord GOD: Because thou saidst: Aha! against My sanctuary, when it was profaned, and against the land of Israel, when it was made desolate, and against the house of Judah, when they went into captivity; 4. therefore, behold, I will

1 וַיְהִי דְבַר־יְהֹוָה אֵלַי לֵאמֹר׃
2 בֶּן־אָדָם שִׂים פָּנֶיךָ אֶל־בְּנֵי
3 עַמּוֹן וְהִנָּבֵא עֲלֵיהֶם׃ וְאָמַרְתָּ
לִבְנֵי עַמּוֹן שִׁמְעוּ דְּבַר־אֲדֹנָי
יְהֹוִה כֹּה־אָמַר אֲדֹנָי יְהֹוִה
יַעַן אָמְרֵךְ הֶאָח אֶל־מִקְדָּשִׁי
כִי־נִחָל וְאֶל־אַדְמַת יִשְׂרָאֵל
כִּי נָשַׁמָּה וְאֶל־בֵּית יְהוּדָה
4 כִּי הָלְכוּ בַגּוֹלָה׃ לָכֵן הִנְנִי

v. 3. קמץ בלא אס״ף

CHAPTERS XXV-XXXII
ORACLES AGAINST THE NATIONS

WITH the preceding chapter Ezekiel's denunciation of Israel's sins and prophecy of Jerusalem's doom come to an end. Before he reverts to the theme of Judea's future, her restoration and spiritual regeneration, he proclaims the downfall of the heathen nations in the next eight chapters. The nations singled out for condemnation are Israel's neighbours, seven in number. The nearest are Ammon, Moab, Edom and the Philistines; those farther away are Tyre, Zidon and Egypt (for similar denunciations, cf. Isa. xiii-xxvii and Jer. xlvi-li). The sins of these nations, on account of which they are doomed, are twofold: not only did they take no warning from Israel's chastisement and made no effort to amend their evil ways, but they indulged in malicious joy over Israel's calamity. Also, their presence was a constant physical and spiritual danger to Israel's restoration and thereby a frustration of the Divine plan for humanity in the moral sphere.

CHAPTER XXV
ORACLES AGAINST FOUR NEIGHBOURING PEOPLES

1-7 AGAINST AMMON

2. *Ammon.* This people, dwelling on the other side of the Jordan north-east of Jerusalem, were racially connected with Israel (cf. Gen. xix. 38). Though the Israelites had respected their territory when journeying to Canaan (Deut. ii. 19, 37), they bore animosity and waged several wars against them. After the Israelite tribes on the east of the Jordan had been carried away by the Assyrians, the Ammonites seized their land (Jer. xlix. 1). On the fall of Jerusalem they instigated the treacherous murder of Gedaliah, appointed governor by the Babylonian king (Jer. xl. 14), and obstructed Judea's restoration in the time of Nehemiah (Neh. iv. 1). Still later they are found aiding the Syrians in the Maccabean war (cf. 1 Macc. v. 6).

3. *unto the children of Ammon.* Ehrlich understands the preposition as 'concerning' and *hear* as addressed to Ezekiel's compatriots in Babylon. It is to be noted that the verb is plural, whereas Ammon is spoken of in the singular.

My sanctuary . . . the land of Israel . . the house of Judah. The Ammonite maliciously rejoiced over the destruction of the Temple, the ravaging of Judea and the deportation of the population.

deliver thee to the children of the
east for a possession, and they shall
set their encampments in thee, and
make their dwellings in thee; they
shall eat thy fruit, and they shall
drink thy milk. 5. And I will make
Rabbah a pasture for camels, and
the children of Ammon a couching-
place for flocks; and ye shall know
that I am the LORD. 6. For thus
saith the Lord GOD: Because thou
hast clapped thy hands, and stamped
with the feet, and rejoiced with all
the disdain of thy soul against the
land of Israel; 7. therefore, behold,
I stretch out My hand upon thee,
and will deliver thee for a spoil to
the nations; and I will cut thee off
from the peoples, and I will cause
thee to perish out of the countries;
I will destroy thee, and thou shalt
know that I am the LORD.

נְתַתִּ֤יךְ לִבְנֵי־קֶ֙דֶם֙ לְמֽוֹרָשָׁ֔ה
וְיִשְּׁב֤וּ טִירֽוֹתֵיהֶם֙ בָּ֔ךְ וְנָ֥תְנוּ
בָ֖ךְ מִשְׁכְּנֵיהֶ֑ם הֵ֚מָּה יֹאכְל֣וּ
פִרְיֵ֔ךְ וְהֵ֖מָּה יִשְׁתּ֥וּ חֲלָבֵֽךְ׃
5 וְנָתַתִּ֤י אֶת־רַבָּה֙ לִנְוֵ֣ה גְמַלִּ֔ים
וְאֶת־בְּנֵ֥י עַמּ֖וֹן לְמִרְבַּץ־צֹ֑אן
6 וִֽידַעְתֶּ֖ם כִּֽי־אֲנִ֥י יְהוָֽה׃ כִּ֣י
כֹ֤ה אָמַר֙ אֲדֹנָ֣י יְהוִ֔ה יַ֚עַן
מַחְאֲךָ֣ יָ֔ד וְרַקְעֲךָ֖ בְּרָ֑גֶל
וַתִּשְׂמַ֤ח בְּכָל־שָֽׁאטְךָ֙ בְּנֶ֔פֶשׁ
7 אֶל־אַדְמַ֖ת יִשְׂרָאֵֽל׃ לָכֵ֡ן
הִנְנִ֨י נָטִ֤יתִי אֶת־יָדִי֙ עָלֶ֔יךָ
וּנְתַתִּ֥יךָ לבז לַגּוֹיִ֖ם וְהִכְרַתִּ֣יךָ
מִן־הָֽעַמִּ֔ים וְהַאֲבַדְתִּ֖יךָ מִן־
הָאֲרָצ֑וֹת אַשְׁמִ֣ידְךָ֔ וְיָדַעְתָּ֖
v. 7. לבן ק׳

4. the children of the east. The nomad
tribes of the Arabian desert. Josephus
(*Antiquities* X, ix. 7) records that five
years after his campaign against Judea,
Nebuchadnezzar successfully warred
against the Ammonites and Moabites.
In their weakened state they could not
resist the plundering Bedouins. But
since the prophet speaks of the attackers
settling in the towns of Ammon, a later
and more serious invasion is intended.
Kimchi explains the phrase as referring
to the peoples of Persia and Media whose
territory was situated north-east of
Ammon.

5. Rabbah. The capital of Ammon (cf.
xxi. 25). From being a great city, the
site will be overgrown and camels
pasture in what were once its streets.

ye shall know. The words may be
regarded as addressed to the Ammonites
or the Judean captives (see on verse 3 and
contrast the end of verse 7). In either
case, it will be evident that the fate of
Ammon is an act of Divine punishment.

**6. clapped thy hands, and stamped with
the feet.** Expressing gloating over
Judea's disaster (see on vi. 11).

with all the disdain of thy soul. Their
exultation over the calamity was
prompted by hatred and contempt.

7. stretch out My hand upon thee. To
execute judgment.

I will destroy thee. Ammon will never
rise again as a nation. It is noteworthy
that Jeremiah xlix. 6 predicts the return
of Ammonite captives to their country.
Perhaps two invasions of Ammon were
predicted, that by Ezekiel being the later.

8. Thus saith the Lord GOD: Because that Moab and Seir do say: Behold, the house of Judah is like unto all the nations, 9. therefore, behold, I will open the flank of Moab on the side of the cities, on the side of his cities which are on his frontiers, the beauteous country of Beth-jeshimoth, Baal-meon, and Kiriathaim, 10. together with the children of Ammon, unto the children of the east, and I will give them for a possession, that the children of Ammon may not be remembered among the nations; 11. and I will execute judgments upon Moab; and they shall know that I am the LORD.

12. Thus saith the Lord GOD: Because that Edom hath dealt against the house of Judah by taking

8 כִּי־אָנִי יְהֹוָה: כֹּה אָמַר אֲדֹנָי יְהֹוָה יַעַן אָמַר מוֹאָב וְשֵׂעִיר הִנֵּה כְּכָל־הַגּוֹיִם בֵּית

9 יְהוּדָה: לָכֵן הִנְנִי פֹתֵחַ אֶת־ כֶּתֶף מוֹאָב מֵהֶעָרִים מֵעָרָיו מִקָּצֵהוּ צְבִי אֶרֶץ בֵּית הַיְשִׁימֹת בַּעַל מְעוֹן

10 וְקִרְיָתְמָה: לִבְנֵי־קֶדֶם עַל־ בְּנֵי עַמּוֹן וּנְתַתִּיהָ לְמוֹרָשָׁה לְמַעַן לֹא־תִזָּכֵר בְּנֵי־עַמּוֹן

11 בַּגּוֹיִם: וּבְמוֹאָב אֶעֱשֶׂה שְׁפָטִים וְיָדְעוּ כִּי־אָנִי יְהֹוָה:

12 כֹּה אָמַר אֲדֹנָי יְהֹוָה יַעַן עֲשׂוֹת אֱדוֹם בִּנְקֹם נָקָם לְבֵית יְהוּדָה

v. 9. וקריתימה ק'

8-11 AGAINST MOAB

8. *Moab.* Like Ammon a kindred people to Israel; their country was situated east of the Dead Sea. There was constant strife between the two nations, and Moab joined in the attack upon Judah by the Babylonians (2 Kings xxiv. 2).

and Seir. Seir stands for 'Edom.' They are mentioned together probably because they were allies in support of Babylon. A specific denunciation of Edom follows in verse 12.

the house of Judah is like unto all the nations. They taunted the afflicted Judeans with being no different from other nations and mocked their claim to be a people chosen by God.

9. *open the flank of Moab.* God will expose Moab to attack by invaders who will penetrate the fortified cities on the frontiers and overrun the whole country. The three towns named were the fortresses upon which Moab relied for security. Beth-jeshimoth was situated

in the south of the Plains of Moab, to the north-east of the Dead Sea. It is mentioned in Num. xxxiii. 49; Josh. xii. 3, xiii. 20. Baal-meon is more fully named Beth-baal-meon in Josh. xiii. 17. It is located by the Dead Sea a few miles inland, with Kirjathaim to its south. Both Baal-meon and Kiriathaim occur in Mesha's inscription on the Moabite Stone.

10. *together with the children of Ammon,* etc. Moab will suffer the same fate as Ammon. Rashi connects this verse with the opening words of the preceding verse: *I will open.* God will open the fortified cities of Moab through which the armies of the children of the east will march on to Ammon.

11. *upon Moab.* The children of the east will destroy the Ammonites and then do likewise to the Moabites.

12-14 AGAINST EDOM

12. *Edom hath dealt against the house o*

vengeance, and hath greatly of-
fended, and revenged himself upon
them; 13. therefore thus saith the
Lord GOD: I will stretch out My
hand upon Edom, and will cut off
man and beast from it; and I will
make it desolate from Teman, even
unto Dedan shall they fall by the
sword. 14. And I will lay My
vengeance upon Edom by the hand
of My people Israel; and they shall
do in Edom according to Mine
anger and according to My fury;
and they shall know My vengeance,
saith the Lord GOD.

15. Thus saith the Lord GOD:
Because the Philistines have dealt by
revenge, and have taken vengeance
with disdain of soul to destroy, for
the old hatred; 16. therefore thus
saith the Lord GOD: Behold, I will
stretch out My hand upon the
Philistines, and I will cut off the

וְיַֽאַשְׁמ֥וּ אָשֹׁ֖ום וְנִקְמ֥וּ בָהֶֽם׃
13 לָכֵ֗ן כֹּ֤ה אָמַר֙ אֲדֹנָ֣י יֱהֹוִ֔ה
וְנָטִ֤תִי יָדִי֙ עַל־אֱד֔וֹם וְהִכְרַתִּ֥י
מִמֶּ֖נָּה אָדָ֣ם וּבְהֵמָ֑ה וּנְתַתִּ֤יהָ
חָרְבָּה֙ מִתֵּימָ֔ן וּדְדָ֖נֶה בַּחֶ֥רֶב
14 יִפֹּֽלוּ׃ וְנָתַתִּ֤י אֶת־נִקְמָתִי֙
בֶֽאֱד֔וֹם בְּיַ֖ד עַמִּ֣י יִשְׂרָאֵ֑ל וְעָשׂ֣וּ
בֶֽאֱד֗וֹם כְּאַפִּי֙ וְכַֽחֲמָתִ֔י וְיָֽדְע֖וּ
אֶת־נִקְמָתִ֑י נְאֻ֖ם אֲדֹנָ֥י יֱהֹוִֽה׃
15 כֹּ֤ה אָמַר֙ אֲדֹנָ֣י יֱהֹוִ֔ה יַ֛עַן עֲשׂ֥וֹת
פְּלִשְׁתִּ֖ים בִּנְקָמָ֑ה וַיִּנָּֽקְמ֤וּ נָקָם֙
בִּשְׁאָ֣ט בְּנֶ֔פֶשׁ לְמַשְׁחִ֖ית אֵיבַ֥ת
16 עוֹלָֽם׃ לָכֵ֗ן כֹּ֤ה אָמַר֙ אֲדֹנָ֣י
יֱהֹוִ֔ה הִנְנִ֨י נוֹטֶ֤ה יָדִי֙ עַל־
פְּלִשְׁתִּ֔ים וְהִכְרַתִּ֖י אֶת־

Judah. Edom was nearer in kinship to
Israel than Ammon and Moab, being
descendants of Esau (Gen. xxxvi. 43).
Their hostility to Judea in the time of
crisis is frequently condemned in strong
language (cf. Obad. 1off.; Ps. cxxxvii. 7).
from Teman, even unto Dedan. The
former was a district in the extreme
north of Edom called after Esau's
grandson (Gen. xxxvi. 11); while the
latter was in the extreme south. The
meaning is, therefore, that the entire
country will be ravaged (cf. Obad. 18).
14. by the hand of My people Israel. The
Edomites were finally defeated and
incorporated in the Jewish State by the
Maccabees.

15-17 AGAINST THE PHILISTINES
15. *the Philistines have dealt by revenge.*
The Philistines, who inhabited the

southern coast of the Holy Land, are
believed to have come from the island of
Crete and also known under the name of
Cerethim. The designation, *the Cherethites and the Pelethites* (cf. 2 Sam. viii.
18) is assumed to have been that of a
bodyguard of king David consisting of
Philistines. Hence the dual name
Kerethi Pelethi. The hostile acts of the
Philistines against Israel at various
periods were of such ferocity as to be
capable of being committed only by an
outraged people seeking vengeance. For
Philistine cruelties towards Judea at the
time of the fall of Jerusalem, cf. Joel
iv. 4ff.

to destroy, for the old hatred. Another
translation is: 'to (be) a destroyer with
everlasting hatred.' Kimchi explains:
they inflicted upon them such destruction
as would create perpetual hatred.

Cherethites, and destroy the remnant of the sea-coast. 17. And I will execute great vengeance upon them with furious rebukes; and they shall know that I am the LORD, when I shall lay My vengeance upon them.'

כְּרֵתִים וְהַאֲבַדְתִּי אֶת־
שְׁאֵרִית חוֹף הַיָּם: וְעָשִׂיתִי בָם 17
נְקָמוֹת גְּדֹלוֹת בְּתוֹכְחוֹת חֵמָה
וְיָדְעוּ כִּי־אֲנִי יְהוָה בְּתִתִּי
אֶת־נִקְמָתִי בָּם:

26   CHAPTER XXVI   כו

1. And it came to pass in the eleventh year, in the first day of the month, that the word of the LORD came unto me, saying: 2. 'Son of

וַיְהִי בְּעַשְׁתֵּי־עֶשְׂרֵה שָׁנָה 1
בְּאֶחָד לַחֹדֶשׁ הָיָה דְבַר־
יְהוָה אֵלַי לֵאמֹר: בֶּן־אָדָם 2

v. 1. חצי הספר בפסוקים

---

16. Cherethites. See on verse 15 and cf. Zeph. ii. 5.

the remnant of the sea-coast. The part of the coast, so far spared in the overthrow of Judea, will be utterly destroyed.

17. *great vengeance upon them.* Measure for measure (cf. the occurence of *vengeance* in verse 15).

furious rebukes. The direst forms of punishment.

CHAPTER XXVI

AGAINST TYRE

THIS and the following two chapters deal with the fate of Tyre. The Divine communication was made to the prophet in the year, and probably in the very month, of the fall of Jerusalem. Tyre represents Phoenicia which bordered on the Land of Israel, and at one time her territory extended as far as Kadesh in Galilee and Carmel. It is worthy of note that, though friendly relations always existed between Phoenicia and Israel, the prophet portrays her destruction in more threatening colours and in greater detail than with any other nation. In proclaiming Tyre's downfall, he could not have been motivated by his personal or the national feeling of revenge. Tyre had, in fact, forfeited her right of existence by her excessive commercialism. Her lust for material gain knew no bounds, and their wealth produced in the population a sense of pride and arrogance which resulted in a complete disregard for human suffering. The demoralization of Tyre was strikingly evidenced by her malicious joy over the destruction of Jerusalem, and particularly by her exultant boasting: *Aha, she is broken . . . I shall be filled with her that is laid waste* (verse 2). After a siege of thirteen years (as recorded in Josephus, *Antiquities* X, xi. 1), Nebuchadnezzar subdued Tyre and so made way for its disappearance from the scene of history.

1-6 THE SIN AND OVERTHROW OF TYRE

1. *in the eleventh year.* Of the reign of Zedekiah, the year in which Jerusalem was captured.

first day of the month. Since the month is not stated, it is probable that the reference is to the fifth month in which the fate of Jerusalem was sealed.

יַּעַן אֲשֶׁר־אָמְרָה צֹּר עַל־
יְרוּשָׁלַ͏ִם
הֶאָח נִשְׁבְּרָה דַּלְתוֹת הָעַמִּים
נָסֵבָּה אֵלָי
אִמָּלְאָה הׇחֳרָבָה׃
3 לָכֵן כֹּה אָמַר אֲדֹנָי יֱהֹוִה
הִנְנִי עָלַיִךְ צֹר
וְהַעֲלֵיתִי עָלַיִךְ גּוֹיִם רַבִּים
כְּהַעֲלוֹת הַיָּם לְגַלָּיו׃
4 וְשִׁחֲתוּ חֹמוֹת צֹר
וְהָרְסוּ מִגְדָּלֶיהָ
וְסִחֵיתִי עֲפָרָהּ מִמֶּנָּה
וְנָתַתִּי אוֹתָהּ לִצְחִיחַ סָלַע׃
5 מִשְׁטַח חֲרָמִים תִּהְיֶה
בְּתוֹךְ הַיָּם

man, because that Tyre hath said
against Jerusalem:
> Aha, she is broken that was the
> gate of the peoples;
> She is turned unto me;
> I shall be filled with her that is
> laid waste;
3 Therefore thus saith the Lord
  GOD:
> Behold, I am against thee, O
> Tyre,
> And will cause many nations to
> come up against thee,
> As the sea causeth its waves to
> come up.
4 And they shall destroy the walls
  of Tyre,
> And break down her towers;
> I will also scrape her dust from
> her,
> And make her a bare rock.
5 She shall be a place for the
  spreading of nets
> In the midst of the sea;

---

2. *she is broken that was the gate of the peoples*. Jerusalem, which had attracted merchants from many countries, was no more. Therefore, thought the men of Tyre, her trade will henceforth be diverted to them. Their selfish satisfaction over Jerusalem's calamity and desire to benefit from it brought about their own ruin. Though the actual fall of Jerusalem might not yet have been known to Tyre, it was already spoken of there as an accomplished fact because of its imminent certainty. In the Hebrew, *gate* is plural, perhaps thought of as consisting of two leaves.

she is turned unto me. Better, 'it is turned'; the subject may be 'gate' or 'merchandise' to be understood.

shall be filled with her that is laid waste. Jerusalem's loss will be Tyre's gain.

3. *many nations*. Nebuchadnezzar and his satellites (cf. 2 Kings xxv. 2).

as the sea. 'All through these chapters the prophet seems to hear the waves beating upon the doomed city' (Lofthouse).

4. *I will also scrape*, etc. After the destruction of Tyre by her invaders, all traces of her former glory will be swept away as by a tidal wave. What was once a magnificent city will then have the appearance of a bare rock.

5. *a place for the spreading of nets*. The fishermen will find the dry, rocky island a suitable place for drying their nets.

in the midst of the sea. Tyre was built upon an island of rock, hence her name *Tsor*, meaning 'rock.'

For I have spoken it, saith the
Lord GOD;
And she shall become a spoil to
the nations.

6 And her daughters that are in the
field
Shall be slain with the sword;
And they shall know that I am
the LORD.

7. For thus saith the Lord GOD:
Behold, I will bring upon Tyre
Nebuchadrezzar king of Babylon,
king of kings, from the north, with
horses, and with chariots, and with
horsemen, and a company, and much
people.

8 He shall slay with the sword
Thy daughters in the field;
And he shall make forts against
thee,
And cast up a mound against
thee,
And set up bucklers against thee.

9 And he shall set his battering
engines
Against thy walls,

כִּי אֲנִי דִבַּרְתִּי נְאֻם אֲדֹנָי יְהוִֹה
וְהָיְתָה לְבַז לַגּוֹיִם:
6 וּבְנוֹתֶיהָ אֲשֶׁר בַּשָּׂדֶה
בַּחֶרֶב תֵּהָרַגְנָה
וְיָדְעוּ כִּי־אֲנִי יְהוָה:
7 כִּי כֹה אָמַר אֲדֹנָי יְהוִֹה הִנְנִי
מֵבִיא אֶל־צֹר נְבוּכַדְרֶאצַּר
מֶלֶךְ־בָּבֶל מִצָּפוֹן מֶלֶךְ
מְלָכִים בְּסוּס וּבְרֶכֶב
וּבְפָרָשִׁים וְקָהָל וְעַם־רָב:
8 בְּנוֹתַיִךְ בַּשָּׂדֶה
בַּחֶרֶב יַהֲרֹג
וְנָתַן עָלַיִךְ דָּיֵק
וְשָׁפַךְ עָלַיִךְ סֹלְלָה
וְהֵקִים עָלַיִךְ צִנָּה:
9 וּמְחִי קָבָלּוֹ
יִתֵּן בְּחֹמֹתָיִךְ

---

6. *her daughters that are in the field.* The
towns and villages on the mainland of
which Tyre was the capital. Not she
alone, but the population of all the
Phoenician cities will perish.

7-14 NEBUCHADNEZZAR THE
EXECUTOR OF GOD'S JUDGMENT

7. *Nebuchadrezzar.* This spelling of the
name by Ezekiel, which is also found in
the Book of Jeremiah, is nearer the
Babylonian *Nabu-kudurri-usur*, meaning
'Nebo protect (my) labour.'

king of kings. Who had dominion over
many vassal kings (cf. Dan. ii. 37;
Ezra vii. 12).

from the north. i.e. Babylon (see on i. 4)
much people. Drawn from the nation
he had subjected.

8. *thy daughters in the field.* See on
verse 6. The Babylonian military operation against Tyre is described in chrono-
logical order. The first to suffer were
the cities on the mainland. Then came
the attack on the island-city by means of
forts or movable towers, mounds and
bucklers, the last being probably large
shields which gave cover to the besiegers.
Finally the battering rams came into
operation (verse 9).

9. *battering engines.* lit. 'the smiting of
his attacking engine'; a different noun for
battering rams is used in xxi. 27.

And with his axes
He shall break down thy towers.

10 By reason of the abundance of
his horses
Their dust shall cover thee;
At the noise of the horsemen,
And of the wheels, and of the
chariots,
Thy walls shall shake,
When he shall enter into thy
gates,
As men enter into a city
Wherein is made a breach.

11 With the hoofs of his horses
Shall he tread down all thy
streets;
He shall slay thy people with the
sword,
And the pillars of thy strength
Shall go down to the ground.

12 And they shall make a spoil of
thy riches,
And make a prey of thy merchandise;
And they shall break down thy
walls,
And destroy the houses of thy
delight;
And thy stones and thy timber
and thy dust
Shall they lay in the midst of the
waters.

וּמִגְדְּלֹתַ֫יִךְ
יִתֹּץ בְּחַרְבוֹתָיו׃

10 מִשִּׁפְעַת סוּסָיו
יְכַסֵּךְ אֲבָקָם
מִקּוֹל פָּרַשׁ
וְגַלְגַּל וָרֶ֫כֶב
תִּרְעַ֫שְׁנָה חוֹמוֹתַ֫יִךְ
בְּבוֹאוֹ בִּשְׁעָרַ֫יִךְ
כִּמְבוֹאֵי עִיר מְבֻקָּעָה׃

11 בְּפַרְסוֹת סוּסָיו
יִרְמֹס אֶת־כָּל־חוּצוֹתָ֫יִךְ
עַמֵּךְ בַּחֶ֫רֶב יַהֲרֹג
וּמַצְּבוֹת עֻזֵּךְ
לָאָ֫רֶץ תֵּרֵד׃

12 וְשָׁלְלוּ חֵילֵךְ
וּבָזְזוּ רְכֻלָּתֵךְ
וְהָרְסוּ חוֹמוֹתַ֫יִךְ
וּבָתֵּי חֶמְדָּתֵךְ יִתֹּ֫צוּ
וַאֲבָנַ֫יִךְ וְעֵצַ֫יִךְ וַעֲפָרֵךְ
בְּתוֹךְ מַ֫יִם יָשִׂ֫ימוּ׃

הר׳ בפתח v. 10.

is axes. lit. 'his swords.'

*0. their dust shall cover thee . . . thy
alls shall shake.* The description of
ne effect of the conqueror's army is
yperbolical.

herein is made a breach. The hostile
rmy will enter the breached city without
neeting resistance.

1. the pillars of thy strength. The
ewish commentators define them as the

towers and strongholds of the proud city.
Modern authorities rather think of
ornamental pillars, of which Herodotus
tells that Tyre possessed two in honour
of the national deity, Melkarth.

12. *stones . . . timber.* The rubble of
the destroyed buildings, etc.

shall they lay in the midst of the waters.
What remains of the city will be swept
into the sea by the conquerors.

13 And I will cause the noise of thy
    songs to cease,
    And the sound of thy harps
    shall be no more heard.
14 And I will make thee a bare rock;
    Thou shalt be a place for the
    spreading of nets,
    Thou shalt be built no more;
    For I the Lord have spoken,
    Saith the Lord God.

15. Thus saith the Lord God to
Tyre: Shall not the isles shake at
the sound of thy fall, when the
wounded groan, when the slaughter
is made in the midst of thee?
16. Then all the princes of the sea
shall come down from their thrones,
and lay away their robes, and strip
off their richly woven garments;
they shall clothe themselves with
trembling; they shall sit upon the
ground, and shall tremble every
moment, and be appalled at thee.
17. And they shall take up a lamentation for thee, and say to thee:

    How art thou destroyed, that
    wast peopled from the seas,

13 וְהִשְׁבַּתִּי הֲמוֹן שִׁירָיִךְ
וְקוֹל כִּנּוֹרַיִךְ לֹא יִשָּׁמַע עוֹד׃
14 וּנְתַתִּיךְ לִצְחִיחַ סֶלַע
מִשְׁטַח חֲרָמִים תִּהְיֶה
לֹא תִבָּנֶה עוֹד
כִּי אֲנִי יְהֹוָה דִּבַּרְתִּי
נְאֻם אֲדֹנָי יְהֹוִה׃
15 כֹּה אָמַר אֲדֹנָי יְהֹוִה לְצוֹר
הֲלֹא ׀ מִקּוֹל מַפַּלְתֵּךְ בֶּאֱנֹק
חָלָל בֵּהָרֵג הֶרֶג בְּתוֹכֵךְ
16 יִרְעֲשׁוּ הָאִיִּים׃ וְיָרְדוּ מֵעַל
כִּסְאוֹתָם כֹּל נְשִׂיאֵי הַיָּם
וְהֵסִירוּ אֶת־מְעִילֵיהֶם וְאֶת־
בִּגְדֵי רִקְמָתָם יִפְשֹׁטוּ חֲרָדוֹת ׀
יִלְבָּשׁוּ עַל־הָאָרֶץ יֵשֵׁבוּ
וְחָרְדוּ לִרְגָעִים וְשָׁמְמוּ עָלָיִךְ׃
17 וְנָשְׂאוּ עָלַיִךְ קִינָה וְאָמְרוּ לָךְ
אֵיךְ אָבַדְתְּ נוֹשֶׁבֶת מִיַּמִּים

v. 16. קמץ בפשטא   v. 15. כצ״ל

14. *bare rock; thou shalt be a place for the
spreading of nets.* See on verses 4f.
Kimchi renders: 'she shall be a place . . .
she shall be built,' etc., construing the
verbs as third person feminine, since the
second person feminine would require a
different form.

thou shalt be built no more. Tyre was
completely destroyed by Nebuchadnezzar and, as foretold by Ezekiel, was
never rebuilt. The city now called Tyre,
which was captured by Alexander the
Great in 332 B.C.E., is another city with
the same name, built on the mainland
opposite the old Tyre (Kimchi).

15-18   TYRE'S FATE DISMAYS THE NATION.
15. *the isles.* The coastal States along the
Mediterranean with which Tyre was
commercially associated.

at the sound of thy fall. The prophet
depicts the crash of the city's collapse
and the agonized moaning of the injured
as audible to the neighbouring States.

16. *shall come down from their thrones.*
To express their sympathy with Tyre
the rulers of the adjacent States will go
into mourning.

17. *how.* Hebrew *ech* (elsewhere *echah*)
introduces a dirge.

The renowned city,
That wast strong in the sea,
Thou and thy inhabitants,
That caused your terror to be
On all that inhabit the earth!

18 Now shall the isles tremble
In the day of thy fall;
Yea, the isles that are in the sea
Shall be affrighted at thy going
out.

19. For thus saith the Lord GOD:
When I shall make thee a desolate
city, like the cities that are not
inhabited; when I shall bring up the
deep upon thee, and the great waters
shall cover thee; 20. then will I bring
thee down with them that descend
into the pit, to the people of old
time, and will make thee to dwell in
the nether parts of the earth, like
the places that are desolate of old,

הָעִיר הַהֻלָּלָה
אֲשֶׁר הָיְתָה חֲזָקָה בַיָּם
הִיא וְיֹשְׁבֶיהָ
אֲשֶׁר־נָתְנוּ חִתִּיתָם
לְכָל־יוֹשְׁבֶיהָ:
18 עַתָּה יֶחְרְדוּ הָאִיֵּן
יוֹם מַפַּלְתֵּךְ
וְנִבְהֲלוּ הָאִיִּים
אֲשֶׁר־בַּיָּם מִצֵּאתֵךְ:
19 כִּי כֹה אָמַר אֲדֹנָי יֱהֹוִה בְּתִתִּי
אֹתָךְ עִיר נֶחֱרֶבֶת כֶּעָרִים
אֲשֶׁר לֹא־נוֹשָׁבוּ בְּהַעֲלוֹת
עָלַיִךְ אֶת־תְּהוֹם וְכִסּוּךְ
20 הַמַּיִם הָרַבִּים: וְהוֹרַדְתִּיךְ
אֶת־יוֹרְדֵי בוֹר אֶל־עַם
עוֹלָם וְהוֹשַׁבְתִּיךְ בְּאֶרֶץ
תַּחְתִּיּוֹת כָּחֳרָבוֹת מֵעוֹלָם

כצ״ל v. 20.

---

at wast peopled from the seas. Kimchi
xplains the phrase as: 'that wast
nriched from the merchandise brought
) thee over the seas.'

rong in the sea. Tyre was the most
owerful of the coastal States.

t all that inhabit the earth. The
Iebrew is literally 'to all its inhabitants'
hich seems most probably to signify
10se who inhabited the coast of the
Iediterranean, although we should have
xpected to read 'their (the waters')
habitants.'

3. shall the isles tremble. The Targum
d Kimchi distinguish between the first
un (spelt ha-iyyin) and the second
oelt ha-iyyim), defining them respec-

tively as 'the coastal regions' and 'the
isles,' the latter being specifically
qualified by that are in the sea.

at thy going out. When the Tyrian
population is driven into captivity,
consternation will overcome their neighbours.

19-21 TYRE'S DESCENT INTO THE UNDERWORLD

19. when I shall make thee, etc. The
whole verse is antecedent to the following
verse.

20. will I bring thee down . . . the pit.
Ezekiel envisages Tyre descending into
the underworld which is inhabited by the
dead of former ages.

with them that go down to the pit,
that thou be not inhabited; and I
will set glory in the land of the
living; 21. I will make thee a terror,
and thou shalt be no more; though
thou be sought for, yet shalt thou
never be found again, saith the Lord
GOD.'

אֶת־יוֹרְדֵי בוֹר לְמַעַן לֹא
תֵשְׁבִי וְנָתַתִּי צְבִי בְּאֶרֶץ
חַיִּים: בַּלָּהוֹת אֶתְּנֵךְ וְאֵינֵךְ 21
וּתְבֻקְשִׁי וְלֹא־תִמָּצְאִי עוֹד
לְעוֹלָם נְאֻם אֲדֹנָי יֱהֹוִה:

27   CHAPTER XXVII   כז

1. Moreover the word of the LORD
came unto me, saying: 2. 'And thou,
son of man, take up a lamentation for
Tyre, 3. and say unto Tyre, that
dwelleth at the entry of the sea, that

וַיְהִי דְבַר־יְהֹוָה אֵלַי לֵאמֹר: 1
וְאַתָּה בֶן־אָדָם שָׂא עַל־צֹר 2
קִינָה: וְאָמַרְתָּ לְצוֹר הַיֹּשֶׁבְתִּי 3
עַל־מְבוֹאֹת יָם רֹכֶלֶת

v. 3. הישבת ק'

---

that thou be not inhabited. The destruction will be complete and irreparable.

I will set glory in the land of the living.
A difficult clause which interrupts the
sequence. Modern exegetes emend the
text to make it apply to Tyre: 'so that
thou shalt not remain in the land of the
living.' According to the Jewish commentators Ezekiel draws a contrast
between the fate of Tyre and Judea.
The land of the living is taken to be a
designation of the Holy Land (as the
Midrash explains Ps. cxvi. 9), in contradistinction to *the nether parts of the
earth* to which Tyre is assigned. As
against the latter's hope to profit by
Jerusalem's fall (verse 2), God decrees
Tyre's disappearance and Israel's restoration.

21. *a terror.* A cause of dismay to other
peoples (cf. verses 15ff.).

CHAPTER XXVII

LAMENTATION OVER TYRE'S DOWNFALL

IN this chapter Ezekiel pictures Tyre as
a magnificent ship constructed from the
best material, furnished with the choicest
equipment and manned by the most
skilful sailors. He then describes in
graphic imagery and in a remarkably
detailed style the various types of
merchandise which made up the ship's
cargo. Sailing proudly on the high
seas, it was overtaken by a tempest and
suffered shipwreck. Everything on board
was lost. The disaster caused intense
consternation among the neighbouring
cities; and seamen, merchants and kings
uttered lamentation over the catastrophe.

1-11 THE SHIP: ITS BEAUTY AND
                  CREW

2. *and thou.* This may be contrasted
with xxvi. 16f. where it is stated that *all
the princes of the sea* will *take up a lamentation for thee.* Ezekiel, too, is called
upon to utter a dirge.

take up. lit. 'raise.' This verb is always
used in connection with a lamentation
because it was uttered in a loud voice.

3. *entry of the sea.* The Hebrew has the
plural 'entries,' signifying the two sections of the harbour which were known
respectively as 'the Sidonian' and 'the

is the merchant of the peoples unto
many isles: Thus saith the Lord
God:

  Thou, O Tyre, hast said:
  I am of perfect beauty.

4 Thy borders are in the heart of
   the seas,
  Thy builders have perfected thy
   beauty.

5 Of cypress-trees from Senir have
   they fashioned
  All thy planks;
  They have taken cedars from
   Lebanon
  To make masts for thee.

6 Of the oaks of Bashan
  Have they made thine oars;
  Thy deck have they made of
   ivory inlaid in larch,

הָעַמִּים אֶל־אִיִּים רַבִּים כֹּה
אָמַר אֲדֹנָי יֱהֹוִה
צוֹר אַתְּ אָמַרְתְּ
אֲנִי כְּלִילַת יֹפִי׃

4 בְּלֵב יַמִּים גְּבוּלָיִךְ
בֹּנַיִךְ כָּלְלוּ יָפְיֵךְ׃

5 בְּרוֹשִׁים מִשְּׂנִיר בָּנוּ לָךְ
אֵת כָּל־לֻחֹתָיִם
אֶרֶז מִלְּבָנוֹן לָקָחוּ
לַעֲשׂוֹת תֹּרֶן עָלָיִךְ׃

6 אַלּוֹנִים מִבָּשָׁן
עָשׂוּ מִשּׁוֹטָיִךְ
קַרְשֵׁךְ עָשׂוּ־שֵׁן בַּת־אֲשֻׁרִים

v. 5. קמץ בז״ק

Egyptian,' the former facing the town of Sidon to the north-east of the island.

the merchant of the peoples unto many isles. Tyre traded with the numerous settlements in that part of the world.

I am of perfect beauty. Tyre coveted the praise which was once bestowed upon Jerusalem (cf. Lam. ii. 15 where the same phrase occurs).

4. *thy borders are in the heart of the seas.* Built on a rocky island, Tyre was the Venice of antiquity. Consequently the simile of a ship was most appropriately applied to her. Unlike a small boat which has to hug the shore, the ship, to which Tyre is likened, sails over the high seas.

5. *cypress-trees.* This timber was also used for building the Temple (1 Kings v. 24).

Senir. A mountainous district in Transjordan known by several names. It was called 'Hermon'; the Sidonians, who were the original inhabitants, named it 'Sirion,' and the Amorites 'Senir,' meaning 'snow' in their language. It was known as 'Sion'; cf. *The Soncino Chumash* on Deut. iii. 9.

cedars from Lebanon. Lebanon was famous for its cedars.

6. *the oaks of Bashan.* This territory was east of the Jordan; its *oaks* are mentioned again in Isa. ii. 13 and Zech. xi. 2.

thy deck. lit. 'thy boards' in the collective singular.

ivory inlaid in larch. This rendering follows the Targum and Rashi who read *bath ashurim* as one word meaning 'in the larch,' the wood of a coniferous tree, defined as box-wood or a species called by the Arabs 'sherbin.' It would then be identical with *teashshur* which occurs in Isa. xli. 19, lx. 13. Kimchi and Metsudath David understand the text as: 'the Ashurites made thy deck out of ivory brought from the isles of the Kittites' (so A.V.); but this interpreta-

179

From the isles of the Kittites.

7 Of fine linen with richly woven
    work from Egypt
    Was thy sail,
    That it might be to thee for an
      ensign;
    Blue and purple from the isles
      of Elishah
    Was thine awning.

8 The inhabitants of Sidon and
    Arvad
    Were thy rowers;
    Thy wise men, O Tyre, were in
      thee,
    They were thy pilots.

9 The elders of Gebal and the wise
    men thereof
    Were in thee thy calkers;

מֵאִיֵּי כִתִּים׃

7 שֵׁשׁ בְּרִקְמָה מִמִּצְרַיִם
הָיָה מִפְרָשֵׂךְ
לִהְיוֹת לָךְ לְנֵס
תְּכֵלֶת וְאַרְגָּמָן מֵאִיֵּי אֱלִישָׁה
הָיָה מְכַסֵּךְ׃

8 יֹשְׁבֵי צִידוֹן וְאַרְוַד
הָיוּ שָׁטִים לָךְ
חֲכָמַיִךְ צוֹר הָיוּ בָךְ
הֵמָּה חֹבְלָיִךְ׃

9 זִקְנֵי גְבַל וַחֲכָמֶיהָ
הָיוּ בָךְ מַחֲזִיקֵי בִּדְקֵךְ

v. 6. כתיים ק'

tion would require the word to be read as *ashshurim* (cf. Gen. xxv. 3).

the isles of the Kittites. i.e. Cyprus, 'called after the town Kition (Larnaka), but probably the name embraced the coasts of Asia Minor and Greece or perhaps even of Italy' (Davidson).

7. *from Egypt.* See on xvi. 10.

for an ensign. A flag of identification. As no distinctive flags were used on ships in ancient times, the colour of the sails served that purpose.

purple. Some authorities define *argaman* as 'red.' Support for this view is given in *Midrash Haggadol* on *Numbers*, ed. Fisch, p. 209.

the isles of Elishah. Elishah was a son of Javan who became the founder of a people (Gen. x. 4). Italy, Sicily and Greece have been suggested for their territory. 'Dido's other name, Elissa, would suggest Carthage, or perhaps more generally the North African coast-land. Racial and commercial ties between Carthage and Tyre were close' (Lofthouse).

awning. lit. 'covering'; usually understood as a deck-awning. Others propose 'cabin,' a part of the ship partitioned off by the material named.

8. *Sidon.* Sidon seems to have been at that time a vassal of Tyre. It 'lay to the north of Tyre, about half-way between it and Beirut, and was probably the oldest Phoenician town, Tyre being a colony. Sidon is the firstborn of Canaan (Gen. x. 15), and is called Great Sidon in Josh. xix. 28 . . . At a later time Tyre eclipsed her mother in power and wealth' (Davidson).

Arvad. Arvad is named as a son of Canaan in Gen. x. 18. 'Arvad is an island town founded by Sidonian fugitives, north of Tripoli, now *Ruwad*' (Lofthouse). Its inhabitants were renowned for their seamanship.

9. *Gebal.* Cf. 1 Kings v. 32 where the Gebalites are stated to have been engaged in building the Temple. It is the modern Jebel, mid-way between Tripoli and Beirut.

thy calkers. lit. 'the strengtheners of thy breach,' i.e. ship-carpenters.

All the ships of the sea with their
    mariners were in thee
To exchange thy merchandise.
10 Persia and Lud and Put were in
    thine army,
Thy men of war;
They hanged the shield and
    helmet in thee,
They set forth thy comeliness.
11. The men of Arvad and Helech
were upon thy walls round about,
and the Gammadim were in thy
towers; they hanged their shields
upon thy walls round about; they
have perfected thy beauty. 12. Tarshish was thy merchant by reason of

כָּל־אֳנִיּוֹת הַיָּם וּמַלָּחֵיהֶם
הָיוּ בָךְ
לַעֲרֹב מַעֲרָבֵךְ׃
10 פָּרַס וְלוּד וּפוּט הָיוּ בְחֵילֵךְ
אַנְשֵׁי מִלְחַמְתֵּךְ
מָגֵן וְכוֹבַע תִּלּוּ־בָךְ
הֵמָּה נָתְנוּ הֲדָרֵךְ׃
11 בְּנֵי אַרְוַד וְחֵילֵךְ עַל־
חוֹמוֹתַיִךְ סָבִיב וְגַמָּדִים
בְּמִגְדְּלוֹתַיִךְ הָיוּ שִׁלְטֵיהֶם
תִּלּוּ עַל־חוֹמוֹתַיִךְ סָבִיב
12 הֵמָּה כָּלְלוּ יָפְיֵךְ׃ תַּרְשִׁישׁ

---

to exchange thy merchandise. From far
and wide the nations brought their wares
to Tyre and exchanged them for Tyrian
goods.

10. *Persia.* Mentioned here for the first
time in the Bible. Attracted by the
might and wealth of Tyre, her mercenaries came from distant lands, such as
Persia, Lud and Put.

Lud and Put. Though Lud and Put
occur together here and in xxx. 5, they
are of different descent. *Lud* is Semitic
and *Put* Hamitic (cf. Gen. x. 6, 22).
Some identify *Lud* with the Lydians of
western Asia Minor; others suggest the
'Lubdi,' a people inhabiting the land
between the Upper Tigris and the
Euphrates. *Put* is the Egyptian 'Punt'
on the western coast of the Red Sea.

hanged the shield and helmet in thee. It
was the practice in ancient times to hang
weapons on towers and fortresses (cf.
Cant. iv. 4).

they set forth thy comeliness. The subject
of the verb is the foreign troops with
their magnificent weapons.

11. *Arvad.* See on verse 8.

and Helech. So translated it is an
unidentified people. Rashi, Kimchi and
others render: 'and thine army' (A.V.
and R.V. 'with thine army'). Ehrlich
explains the conjunction as the equivalent of the Arabic *pha* and translates:
'The men of Arvad constituted thine
army upon thy walls.'

upon thy walls. To protect the city from
hostile attack.

Gammadim. A people not mentioned
elsewhere. The Targum understood it
as 'Cappadocians' and Kimchi as
'pygmies,' who acted as observers on the
towers so as not to be noticed by the
enemy; or, because they were high up on
the towers, they looked small like
pygmies. The LXX translates by a
word meaning 'guards.'

12-25 THE COMMERCE OF TYRE

12. *Tarshish.* Identified with Tartessus,
a Phoenician port and mining district in
southern Spain.

181

the multitude of all kinds of riches; with silver, iron, tin, and lead, they traded for thy wares. 13. Javan, Tubal, and Meshech, they were thy traffickers; they traded the persons of men and vessels of brass for thy merchandise. 14. They of the house of Togarmah traded for thy wares with horses and horsemen and mules. 15. The men of Dedan were thy traffickers; many isles were the mart of thy hand; they brought thee as tribute horns of ivory and

סְחֹרְתֵּךְ מֵרֹב כָּל־הוֹן בְּכֶסֶף
בַּרְזֶל בְּדִיל וְעוֹפֶרֶת נָתְנוּ
עִזְבוֹנָיִךְ: יָוָן תֻּבַל וָמֶשֶׁךְ ‏13
הֵמָּה רֹכְלָיִךְ בְּנֶפֶשׁ אָדָם וּכְלֵי
נְחֹשֶׁת נָתְנוּ מַעֲרָבֵךְ: מִבֵּית ‏14
תּוֹגַרְמָה סוּסִים וּפָרָשִׁים
וּפְרָדִים נָתְנוּ עִזְבוֹנָיִךְ: בְּנֵי ‏15
דְדָן רֹכְלַיִךְ אִיִּים רַבִּים
סְחֹרַת יָדֵךְ קַרְנוֹת שֵׁן וְהָובְנִים

v. 15. והבנים ק׳

by reason of the multitude of all kinds of riches. The wealth of Tyre attracted commerce from as far west as Tarshish.

they traded for thy wares. They exchanged their metals for Tyrian goods. The noun *izzabon* is found only in this chapter. It is derived from the verb *azab*, 'to abandon, leave,' and the noun signifies that which is 'left' with the purchaser.

13. *Javan, Tubal, and Meshech.* Names of three sons of Japheth (Gen. x. 2). *Javan* is the Hebrew term for the Ionians, the Greeks of Asia Minor. *Tubal* and *Meshech* are usually identified with the Tibareni and Maschi who lived south-east and south respectively of the Black Sea. These peoples supplied Tyre with slaves and copper.

the persons of men. lit. 'with the soul of man,' i.e. 'human soul, human being,' used in the collective sense. In Joel iv. 6 Tyre is condemned for having sold Judeans *to* Javan who then traded in them.

brass. The Hebrew *nechosheth* is more strictly translated 'copper.' It was a pure metal; cf. *out of whose hills thou mayest dig nechosheth* (Deut. viii. 9).

14. *Togarmah.* This was the name of one of the sons of Gomer (Gen. x. 3), and is supposed to denote Armenia which

Herodotus mentions as famed for its horses and mules. In xxxviii. 6 Togarmah is described as situated in the extreme north.

horsemen. If this is the sense of *parashim*, they were mercenaries who drove the war-chariots of Tyre. More probably the meaning is 'steeds, war-horses,' as contrasted with *susim*, horses employed for peaceful purposes. The noun may possibly have that signification in Isa. xxviii. 28; Jer. xlvi. 4; Joel ii. 4.

15. *Dedan.* See on xxv. 13. Since, however, Dedan occurs again in verse 20, in its proper place in connection with the Arabian tribes, it has been suggested that this was a different Dedan, situated on the Persian Gulf.

the mart of thy hand. Cf. *the merchants of thy hand* in verse 21. The phrase *of thy hand* probably means 'in thy service.'

as tribute. Not in exchange for goods but the payments by lands under Tyrian domination.

horns of ivory. Tusks of elephants shaped like horns.

ebony. The Hebrew is *hobnim*, a loan word which appears in Egyptian a *heben*, in Greek as *hebenos* and Latin a *hebenum*. The Targum (followed b Rashi) understood the meaning to b

ebony. 16. Aram was thy merchant by reason of the multitude of thy wealth; they traded for thy wares with carbuncles, purple, and richly woven work, and fine linen, and coral, and rubies. 17. Judah, and the land of Israel, they were thy traffickers; they traded for thy merchandise wheat of Minnith, and balsam, and honey, and oil, and balm. 18. Damascus was thy merchant for the multitude of thy wealth, by reason of the multitude of all riches, with the wine of Helbon, and white wool. 19. Vedan and Javan traded with yarn for thy wares; massive iron, cassia, and

16 הֵשִׁיבוּ אֶשְׁכָּרֵךְ׃ אֲרָם
סֹחַרְתֵּךְ מֵרֹב מַעֲשָׂיִךְ בְּנֹפֶךְ
אַרְגָּמָן וְרִקְמָה וּבוּץ וְרָאמֹת
וְכַדְכֹּד נָתְנוּ בְּעִזְבוֹנָיִךְ׃
17 יְהוּדָה וְאֶרֶץ יִשְׂרָאֵל הֵמָּה
רֹכְלָיִךְ בְּחִטֵּי מִנִּית וּפַנַּג וּדְבַשׁ
וָשֶׁמֶן וָצֹרִי נָתְנוּ מַעֲרָבֵךְ׃
18 דַּמֶּשֶׂק סֹחַרְתֵּךְ בְּרֹב מַעֲשָׂיִךְ
מֵרֹב כָּל־הוֹן בְּיֵין חֶלְבּוֹן
19 וְצֶמֶר צָחַר׃ וְדָן וְיָוָן מְאוּזָּל
בְּעִזְבוֹנַיִךְ נָתָנּוּ בַּרְזֶל עָשׁוֹת

v. 19. דגש אחר שורק הב' בדגש

'peacocks,' but Kimchi gives the correct translation.

16. *Aram.* Syria supplied Tyre with precious stones and beautiful fabrics. The Syrian town, Damascus, is mentioned in verse 18. Some Hebrew MSS. and the LXX read 'Edom.'

thy wealth. lit. 'thy works,' i.e. the manufactured articles exported to Tyre by other peoples.

17. *Minnith.* An Ammonite town mentioned in Judg. xi. 33. 2 Chron. xxvii. 5 records the large quantities of wheat and barley which the Ammonites paid to king Jotham as tribute.

balsam. The Hebrew word *pannag* occurs nowhere else and is of doubtful meaning. Kimchi understood it as the name of another place from which wheat was exported.

balm. Gilead was famous for its balm (cf. Jer. viii. 22).

18. *thy wealth.* See on verse 16.

wine of Helbon. 'Now Chalbum, nine miles north of Damascus in Anti-Lebanus; it is mentioned as a wine

district in Assyrian lists. Persian kings drank no other wine, and the district is still famous as a wine centre' (Lofthouse).

white. The Hebrew *tsachar* occurs in another form in Judg. v. 10. On the analogy of the Arabic, some authorities prefer the translation 'reddish-grey, tawny.'

19. *Vedan.* The place cannot be identified with certainty. Aden, or Waddan near the Arab city Medina, has been conjectured.

Javan. Certainly not the same as the land in verse 13. A Greek colony in Arabia has been suggested.

yarn. This rendering of *me'uzzal* is obtained by identifying the root *azal* (with *aleph*) with the Aramaic *azal* (with *ain*), 'to spin.' Several Hebrew MSS. and the LXX read *mē'uzzal*, 'from Uzzal.' The name occurs in Gen. x. 27 and is taken to be the old designation of Sanaa, the capital of Yemen in Southern Arabia. The translation will then be: 'Vedan and Javan exported thy wares from Uzzal.'

massive iron. Kimchi explains as 'bright iron,' which is found in A.V. and R.V.,

calamus, were among thy merchandise. 20. Dedan was thy trafficker in precious cloths for riding. 21. Arabia, and all the princes of Kedar, they were the merchants of thy hand; in lambs, and rams, and goats, in these were they thy merchants. 22. The traffickers of Sheba and Raamah, they were thy traffickers; they traded for thy wares with chief of all spices, and with all precious stones, and gold. 23. Haran and Canneh and Eden, the traffickers of Sheba, Asshur was

קִדָּה וְקָנֶה בְּמַעֲרָבֵךְ הָיָה:
20 דְּדָן רֹכַלְתֵּךְ בְבִגְדֵי־חֹפֶשׁ
21 לְרִכְבָּה: עֲרַב וְכָל־נְשִׂיאֵי
קֵדָר הֵמָּה סֹחֲרֵי יָדֵךְ בְּכָרִים
וְאֵילִם וְעַתּוּדִים בָּם סֹחֲרָיִךְ:
22 רֹכְלֵי שְׁבָא וְרַעְמָה הֵמָּה
רֹכְלָיִךְ בְּרֹאשׁ כָּל־בֹּשֶׂם
וּבְכָל־אֶבֶן יְקָרָה וְזָהָב נָתְנוּ
23 עִזְבוֹנָיִךְ: חָרָן וְכַנֵּה וָעֶדֶן
רֹכְלֵי שְׁבָא אַשּׁוּר כִּלְמַד

connecting *ashoth* with the verb *ashath* found in Jer. v. 28, *they are become sleek*. In Mishnaic Hebrew *esheth* means 'wrought metal, metal bars,' and that is probably its significance here.

cassia, and calamus. These spices were used as ingredients of the oil for anointing the Tabernacle and the priests (Exod. xxx. 23f.).

20. *Dedan.* See on verse 15.

precious cloths. lit. 'clothes of freedom,' which several moderns take to mean 'wide-spread garments,' i.e. saddle-cloths.

21. *Arabia.* A term for the nomadic Bedouins of the eastern deserts.

Kedar. A nomad race in the Syrian-Arabian desert, probably descended from Kedar, the second son of Ishmael (Gen. xxv. 13). They were renowned for their flocks (Isa. lx. 7).

lambs. The Targum renders: 'oxen,' and Kimchi remarks that its reading of the text was *bepharim* for *becharim.* M.T. suits the context better.

22. *Sheba and Raamah.* Raamah was the son of Cush and the father of Sheba (Gen. x. 7). The Sabaeans were a powerful people living in the south-west of Arabia. 'The ruins of their capital Marib still remain, six days' journey east of Sanaa, the capital of Yemen. Their caravans (Job vi. 19) traded to Syria and other countries with gold, precious stones and aromatics (1 Kings x. 2, 10; Isa. lx. 6; Jer. vi. 20; Ps. lxxii. 15)' (Davidson). Raamah is supposed to have inhabited the region of the Persian Gulf.

chief of all spices. i.e. spices of the best quality.

23. *Haran.* An ancient and well-known city in Mesopotamia. On account of its geographical position, being situated on the route from Babylon to Syria, it was an important commercial centre. It was from Haran that Abraham migrated to Canaan (Gen. xii. 4).

Canneh. Some identify it with *Calneh* in Gen. x. 10, otherwise called *Calno* (Isa. x. 9), a city in Babylon.

Eden. Cf. 2 Kings xix. 12; Isa. xxxvii. 12; Amos i. 5. On Assyrian inscriptions it is called Bit-Adini, situated on either side of the Euphrates, due south of Haran.

the traffickers of Sheba. The peoples of Haran, Canneh and Eden, who traded

as thine apprentice in traffic. 24. These were thy traffickers in gorgeous fabrics, in wrappings of blue and richly woven work, and in chests of rich apparel, bound with cords and cedar-lined, among thy merchandise. 25. The ships of Tarshish brought thee tribute for thy merchandise;

So wast thou replenished, and made very heavy

In the heart of the seas.

24 רְכֻלָּתֵךְ׃ הֵמָּה רֹכְלַיִךְ
בְּמַכְלֻלִים בִּגְלוֹמֵי תְּכֵלֶת
וְרִקְמָה וּבְגִנְזֵי בְּרֹמִים
בַּחֲבָלִים חֲבֻשִׁים וַאֲרֻזִים
25 בְּמַרְכֻלְתֵּךְ׃ אֳנִיּוֹת תַּרְשִׁישׁ
שָׁרוֹתַיִךְ מַעֲרָבֵךְ
וַתִּמָּלְאִי וַתִּכְבְּדִי מְאֹד
בְּלֵב יַמִּים׃

also with Sheba, brought their wares to Phoenicia.

Asshur. The name normally indicates Assyria, which is inappropriate in this connection since that people had long been on the decline. Some identify it with Sura on the Euphrates, or with a town situated on the west side of the Tigris, now the ruined site of Kalat Serkat.

as thine apprentice. The Hebrew reads *asshur kilmad*, which A.V. and R.V. translate: 'Asshur (and) Chilmad' on the authority of the LXX. The latter has been identified with Kalwadha near Bagdad. The Targum has 'and the Medes' (*umadai*). A.J. construes as the preposition *k*, 'as,' and *lemad*, a derivative of *lamad*, 'to learn'; but this is most improbable Hebrew for *as thine apprentice*. It seems best to understand *asshur kilmad* as a place-name which is unknown.

24. *gorgeous fabrics.* lit. 'things perfected'; a general term which is detailed by what follows.

wrappings. Or, 'cloaks.' The Hebrew *gelomë* occurs nowhere else except in the verb *and wrapped it* (2 Kings ii. 8). The word is Aramaic and has cognates in other Semitic languages. It occurs frequently in Rabbinic Hebrew.

rich apparel. The Hebrew *beromim* is not found elsewhere. It appears to denote garments made of materials which consisted of different coloured strands.

bound with cords. This refers either to the *chests* or to the clothing in them. Another suggestion is that *chabalim, chabushim* and *aruzim* (*cedar-lined*) denote manufactured articles; the first two being 'cords' and 'belts' respectively, and the last, articles made of cedar-wood.

25. *ships of Tarshish.* See on verse 12.

brought thee tribute for thy merchandise. Kimchi renders: 'were thy caravans for thy merchandise.' The noun *sharotha-yich* is thus connected with the verb *shur*, 'to journey' (cf. Isa. lvii. 9); a cognate noun in Arabic means 'caravan.' Fleets of large ships from remote Tarshish brought a variety of rich cargo to Tyre. With this clause the list of the nations which traded with Tyre is concluded. The latter part of the verse resumes the description of the gallant ship where it broke off in verse 9.

made very heavy. A ship overladen with cargo is in danger of being wrecked during a storm. Similarly, Tyre's overweening pride contributed to her downfall.

in the heart of the seas. An allusion to Tyre's geographical location (see on verse 4).

26 Thy rowers have brought thee
   Into great waters;
   The east wind hath broken thee
   In the heart of the seas.

27 Thy riches, and thy wares, thy
     merchandise,
   Thy mariners, and thy pilots,
   Thy calkers, and the exchangers
     of thy merchandise,
   And all thy men of war, that are
     in thee,
   With all thy company which is
     in the midst of thee,
   Shall fall into the heart of the
     seas
   In the day of thy ruin.

28 At the sound of the cry of thy
     pilots
   The waves shall shake.

29 And all that handle the oar,
   The mariners, and all the pilots
     of the sea,
   Shall come down from their
     ships,
   They shall stand upon the land,

26 בְּמַיִם רַבִּים הֱבִיאוּךְ
הַשָּׁטִים אֹתָךְ
רוּחַ הַקָּדִים שְׁבָרֵךְ
בְּלֵב יַמִּים:
27 הוֹנֵךְ וְעִזְבוֹנַיִךְ מַעֲרָבֵךְ
מַלָּחַיִךְ וְחֹבְלָיִךְ
מַחֲזִיקֵי בִדְקֵךְ
וְעֹרְבֵי מַעֲרָבֵךְ
וְכָל־אַנְשֵׁי מִלְחַמְתֵּךְ
אֲשֶׁר־בָּךְ
וּבְכָל־קְהָלֵךְ אֲשֶׁר בְּתוֹכֵךְ
יִפְּלוּ בְּלֵב יַמִּים
בְּיוֹם מַפַּלְתֵּךְ:
28 לְקוֹל זַעֲקַת חֹבְלָיִךְ
יִרְעֲשׁוּ מִגְרֹשׁוֹת:
29 וְיָרְדוּ מֵאֳנִיּוֹתֵיהֶם
כֹּל תֹּפְשֵׂי מָשׁוֹט
מַלָּחִים כֹּל חֹבְלֵי הַיָּם
אֶל־הָאָרֶץ יַעֲמֹדוּ:

הרי׳ בחולם   v. 28.

26-36   THE SHIPWRECK

26. great waters. i.e. the deep and dangerous open sea.

the east wind hath broken thee. For the danger of the east wind at sea, cf. Exod. xiv. 21; Ps. xlviii. 8. The Talmud (Git. 31b) describes the east wind as making furrows in the sea like a ploughed field.

27. shall fall into the heart of the seas. Both crew and cargo will be completely lost in the shipwreck.

28. *the waves.* This translation of *migroshoth* is based on Isa. lvii. 20, *the troubled* (nigrash) *sea.* Elsewhere in the Bible *migrash* denotes the pasture-land surrounding a city; hence Kimchi's explanation 'suburbs' which is found in A.V. and R.V. Ezekiel probably intends the neighbouring districts along the coast.

29. *shall come down from their ships.* After the disaster which overtook Tyre, sailors will refuse to sail in their ships dreading a like fate.

30 And shall cause their voice to be
    heard over thee,
    And shall cry bitterly,
    And shall cast up dust upon
    their heads,
    They shall roll themselves in the
    ashes;
31 And they shall make themselves
    utterly bald for thee,
    And gird them with sackcloth,
    And they shall weep for thee in
    bitterness of soul
    With bitter lamentation.
32 And in their wailing they shall
    take up a lamentation for thee,
    And lament over thee:
    Who was there like Tyre, forti-
    fied
    In the midst of the sea?
33 When thy wares came forth out
    of the seas,
    Thou didst fill many peoples;
    With the multitude of thy riches
    and of thy merchandise
    Didst thou enrich the kings of
    the earth.
34 Now that thou art broken by the
    seas
    In the depths of the waters,

30 וְהִשְׁמִ֧יעוּ עָלַ֛יִךְ בְּקוֹלָ֖ם
וְיִזְעֲק֖וּ מָרָ֑ה
וְיַעֲל֤וּ עָפָר֙ עַל־רָ֣אשֵׁיהֶ֔ם
בָּאֵ֖פֶר יִתְפַּלָּֽשׁוּ׃
31 וְהִקְרִ֤יחוּ אֵלַ֙יִךְ֙ קָרְחָ֔א
וְחָגְר֖וּ שַׂקִּ֑ים
וּבָכ֥וּ אֵלַ֛יִךְ בְּמַר־נֶ֖פֶשׁ
מִסְפֵּ֥ד מָֽר׃
32 וְנָשְׂא֨וּ אֵלַ֤יִךְ בְּנִיהֶם֙ קִינָ֔ה
וְקוֹנְנ֖וּ עָלָ֑יִךְ
מִ֣י כְצ֔וֹר כְּדֻמָּ֖ה
בְּת֥וֹךְ הַיָּֽם׃
33 בְּצֵ֤את עִזְבוֹנַ֙יִךְ֙ מִיַּמִּ֔ים
הִשְׂבַּ֖עַתְּ עַמִּ֣ים רַבִּ֑ים
בְּרֹ֤ב הוֹנַ֙יִךְ֙ וּמַעֲרָבַ֔יִךְ
הֶעֱשַׁ֖רְתְּ מַלְכֵי־אָֽרֶץ׃
34 עֵ֛ת נִשְׁבֶּ֥רֶת מִיַּמִּ֖ים
בְּמַעֲמַקֵּי־מָ֑יִם

v. 31. א׳   v. 32. במקום ה׳ הב׳ בחיריק

---

30. *shall cause their voice to be heard over thee.* They will raise a lament over Tyre's ruin.

cast up dust upon their heads, etc. Signs of mourning.

31. *make themselves utterly bald.* See on vii. 18.

32. *who was there like Tyre?* In power and wealth.

fortified. The translation of A.J. cannot be supported. The Hebrew *kedummah* can only be derived from the root *damam*, 'to be silent,' and must be rendered 'like her that is brought to silence' (so R.V.). Tyre had been a busy and thriving city, her port resounding with the cries of sailors; now it is dead and reduced to utter silence.

33. *out of the seas.* Tyre's exports had been conveyed to many countries along the sea-routes, satisfying the needs of their inhabitants.

34. *by the seas.* By the agency of the seas. The sea, which was the source of her eminence, has become the cause of her ruin.

And thy merchandise and all thy
company
Are fallen in the midst of thee,

מַעֲרָבֵךְ וְכָל־קְהָלֵךְ
בְּתוֹכֵךְ נָפָלוּ׃

35 All the inhabitants of the isles
Are appalled at thee,
And their kings are horribly
afraid,
They are troubled in their
countenance;

35 כֹּל יֹשְׁבֵי הָאִיִּים
שָׁמְמוּ עָלָיִךְ
וּמַלְכֵיהֶם שָׂעֲרוּ שַׂעַר
רָעֲמוּ פָּנִים׃

36 The merchants among the
peoples hiss at thee;
Thou art become a terror,
And never shalt be any more.'

36 סֹחֲרִים בָּעַמִּים שָׁרְקוּ עָלָיִךְ
בַּלָּהוֹת הָיִית
וְאֵינֵךְ עַד־עוֹלָם׃

28   CHAPTER XXVIII   כח

1. And the word of the LORD came

1 וַיְהִי דְבַר־יְהוָֹה אֵלַי לֵאמֹר׃

---

35. *all the inhabitants of the isles are appalled.* They dreaded that a similar doom would overtake them.

horribly afraid . . . troubled in their countenance. Inwardly broken in spirit and outwardly showing anxiety on their faces.

36. *hiss.* The Hebrew verb denotes amazement and dismay.

never shalt be any more. See on xxvi. 14. 'This figure of the mighty and overladen ship, proudly venturing out into the waters which are to be her ruin, is the most striking example in the Bible of the thought familiar to Hebrews and Greeks alike—that pride prepares the way for its own fall' (Lofthouse).

CHAPTER XXVIII

FATE OF THE PRINCE OF TYRE

THIS is the conclusion of the three chapters directed against Tyre. Here the guilt and punishment of Tyre are laid at the door of *the prince of Tyre* who is regarded as the embodiment of the people. The root cause of Tyre's collapse was her abundance of wealth. In her vast material resources, which she attributed exclusively to her genius, she found her only purpose in life. Spiritual values had no place in the minds of her population; self-glorification and self-sufficiency reigned supreme. Such arrogance and demoralization must lead to destruction. In a lament of striking imaginative power, Ezekiel describes the fall of Tyre and her expulsion from the Garden of Eden, repeating his message that the multitude of her sins produced the fire which would eventually consume her. In conclusion he turns to Zidon, which lay about twenty miles north of Tyre, and pronounces her doom. With the destruction of Israel's immediate neighbours, who were to him *a pricking brier and a piercing thorn*, his national existence will be resumed. By the execution of judgment upon the heathen nations for their iniquities and fulfilment of His promise to restore Israel to his ancient glory, God's holy name will be sanctified throughout the world.

unto me, saying: 2. 'Son of man, say
unto the prince of Tyre: Thus saith
the Lord GOD:

Because thy heart is lifted up,
And thou hast said: I am a god,
I sit in the seat of God,
In the heart of the seas;
Yet thou art man, and not God,
Though thou didst set thy heart
    as the heart of God—
3 Behold, thou art wiser than
    Daniel!
There is no secret that they can
    hide from thee!
4 By thy wisdom and by thy
    discernment
Thou hast gotten thee riches,
And hast gotten gold and silver
Into thy treasures;
5 In thy great wisdom by thy
    traffic
Hast thou increased thy riches,
And thy heart is lifted up because
    of thy riches—

בֶּן־אָדָם אֱמֹר לִנְגִיד צֹר 2
כֹּה־אָמַר | אֲדֹנָי יֱהֹוִה
יַעַן גָּבַהּ לִבְּךָ
וַתֹּאמֶר אֵל אָנִי
מוֹשַׁב אֱלֹהִים יָשַׁבְתִּי
בְּלֵב יַמִּים
וְאַתָּה אָדָם וְלֹא־אֵל
וַתִּתֵּן לִבְּךָ כְּלֵב אֱלֹהִים:
הִנֵּה חָכָם אַתָּה מִדָּנִאֵל 3
כָּל־סָתוּם לֹא עֲמָמוּךָ:
בְּחָכְמָתְךָ וּבִתְבוּנָתְךָ 4
עָשִׂיתָ לְּךָ חָיִל
וַתַּעַשׂ זָהָב וָכֶסֶף
בְּאוֹצְרוֹתֶיךָ:
בְּרֹב חָכְמָתְךָ בִּרְכֻלָּתְךָ 5
הִרְבִּיתָ חֵילֶךָ
וַיִּגְבַּהּ לְבָבְךָ בְּחֵילֶךָ:

v. 8. מדניאל

1-10 GUILT AND PUNISHMENT OF THE PRINCE OF TYRE

2. *the prince of Tyre.* It is conjectured
that Ithobal II was ruler of Tyre at the
time. The attitude of the king also
reflected the feelings of his subjects.

thy heart is lifted up. Haughtiness to the
point of self-deification was his besetting
sin.

*I sit in the seat of God, in the heart of the
seas.* He regarded his realm, cut off
from the land by the sea, as a Divine
abode. 'The beauty and splendour of
the place, its richness and renown,
possibly also its isolation, make it
something not of the earth' (Davidson).

didst set thy heart as the heart of God.
Ehrlich regards *heart* here, as often elsewhere, the seat of intellect; so the meaning is, 'though thou didst hold thine
understanding to be as the understanding
of God.'

3. *thou art wiser than Daniel!* A sarcastic
comparison. In xiv. 14 Daniel was
mentioned as an outstanding example of
piety, here of wisdom. Of him the
Babylonian king said, *No secret causeth
thee trouble* (Dan. iv. 6).

hide. lit. 'make dim,' obscure; again in
xxxi. 8.

4. *by thy wisdom . . . thou hast gotten
thee riches.* The Tyrian ruler did

6 Therefore thus saith the Lord
    GOD:
Because thou hast set thy heart
As the heart of God;
7 Therefore, behold, I will bring
    strangers upon thee,
The terrible of the nations;
And they shall draw their swords
    against the beauty of thy
    wisdom,
And they shall defile thy bright-
    ness.
8 They shall bring thee down to
    the pit;
And thou shalt die the deaths of
    them that are slain,
In the heart of the seas.
9 Wilt thou yet say before him that
    slayeth thee:
I am God?
But thou art man, and not God,
In the hand of them that defile
    thee.
10 Thou shalt die the deaths of the
    uncircumcised

6 לָכֵן כֹּה אָמַר אֲדֹנָי יְהֹוִה
יַעַן תִּתְּךָ אֶת־לְבָבְךָ
כְּלֵב אֱלֹהִים׃
7 לָכֵן הִנְנִי מֵבִיא עָלֶיךָ זָרִים
עָרִיצֵי גּוֹיִם
וְהֵרִיקוּ חַרְבוֹתָם
עַל־יְפִי חָכְמָתֶךָ
וְחִלְּלוּ יִפְעָתֶךָ׃
8 לַשַּׁחַת יוֹרִדֻךָ
וָמַתָּה מְמוֹתֵי חָלָל
בְּלֵב יַמִּים׃
9 הֶאָמֹר תֹּאמַר
אֱלֹהִים אָנִי לִפְנֵי הֹרְגֶךָ
וְאַתָּה אָדָם וְלֹא־אֵל
בְּיַד מְחַלְלֶיךָ׃
10 מוֹתֵי עֲרֵלִים תָּמוּת

possess wisdom of a sort—commercial acumen to amass wealth.

6. *as the heart of God.* See on verse 2.

7. *therefore.* Because his overweening pride resulted in self-deification, he is doomed to annihilation.

strangers . . . the terrible of the nations. viz. the Chaldeans (cf. xxx. 11, xxxii. 12).

against the beauty of thy wisdom. They will destroy the material wealth which he had acquired by his wisdom and in which he gloried inordinately.

shall defile thy brightness. More lit. 'profane.' He thought of his status as Godlike; the Chaldeans will profane it.

8. *shalt die,* etc. God is eternal; he will meet with a violent end in the heart of the seas. Though his kingdom was surrounded by the sea and in a very strong strategical position, it will be no protection to him.

9. *I am God.* Will he persist in claiming to be divine when he faces his executioners?

that defile thee. Kimchi renders: 'that slay thee.' A.V. similarly 'that slayeth thee, and R.V. 'that woundeth thee.'

10. *the deaths of the uncircumcised.* 'The term *uncircumcised* is employed by the prophet not in its usual sense, but in reference to the dead, who suffer death from the sword, and whose bodies either lie unburied and dishonoured or are flung indiscriminately into the earth with no funeral honours' (Davidson).

By the hand of strangers;
For I have spoken, saith the
Lord GOD.'

11. Moreover the word of the
LORD came unto me, saying: 12. 'Son
of man, take up a lamentation for
the king of Tyre, and say unto him:
Thus saith the Lord GOD: Thou seal
most accurate, full of wisdom, and
perfect in beauty, 13. thou wast in
Eden the garden of God; every
precious stone was thy covering,
the carnelian, the topaz, and the
emerald, the beryl, the onyx, and
the jasper, the sapphire, the car-
buncle, and the smaragd, and gold;
the workmanship of thy settings and
of thy sockets was in thee, in the day
that thou wast created they were
prepared. 14. Thou wast the far-

בְּיַד זָרִים

כִּי אֲנִי דִבַּ֫רְתִּי

נְאֻם אֲדֹנָי יְהֹוִה:

11 וַיְהִי דְבַר־יְהֹוָה אֵלַי לֵאמֹר:

12 בֶּן־אָדָם שָׂא קִינָה עַל־מֶ֫לֶךְ
צוֹר וְאָמַרְתָּ לּוֹ כֹּה אָמַר אֲדֹנָי
יְהֹוִה אַתָּה חוֹתֵם תָּכְנִית מָלֵא

13 חָכְמָה וּכְלִיל יֹפִי: בְּעֵ֫דֶן
גַּן־אֱלֹהִים הָיִ֫יתָ כָּל־אֶ֫בֶן
יְקָרָה מְסֻכָתֶךָ אֹ֫דֶם פִּטְדָה
וְיָהֲלֹם תַּרְשִׁישׁ שֹׁ֫הַם וְיָשְׁפֵה
סַפִּיר נֹ֫פֶךְ וּבָרְקַת וְזָהָב
מְלֶ֫אכֶת תֻּפֶּ֫יךָ וּנְקָבֶ֫יךָ בָּךְ

14 בְּיוֹם הִבָּרַאֲךָ כּוֹנָ֫נוּ: אַתְּ־

---

strangers. See on verse 7.

11-19 LAMENT OVER THE PRINCE OF TYRE

12. unto him. Better, 'concerning him.'
It is improbable that Ezekiel had
personal contact with the Tyrian king.

thou seal most accurate. A phrase of
doubtful meaning. The noun tochnith
(most accurate) appears to be akin to
tochen and mathkoneth, 'measurement.'
If translated, 'thou wert one who sealeth
measurement,' the sense is: he was
perfect in physical form.

13. thou wast in Eden the garden of God.
Cf. xxxi. 8f. Tyre, which abounded in
material luxuries, is idealized and likened
to the earthly Paradise created by God,
Eden.

every precious stone was thy covering.
This is usually understood in the sense

that his robe was decorated with a
variety of jewels. Ehrlich suggests that
it was the royal umbrella or canopy under
which he walked. The nine precious
stones enumerated are identical with
those which were set in three of the four
rows of the High Priest's breastplate
(Exod. xxviii. 17-20). The LXX adds
the three which are omitted to complete
the twelve.

and gold. The precious metal also
figured in the covering.

of thy settings and of thy sockets. Referring to the settings of the gems. Kimchi
takes the words to indicate musical
instruments, 'tabrets and pipes' (so A.V.,
R.V.).

they were prepared. It was as though
these magnificent objects had been
specially created and reserved for him
on the day he was born.

covering cherub; and I set thee, so that thou wast upon the holy mountain of God; thou hast walked up and down in the midst of stones of fire. 15. Thou wast perfect in thy ways from the day that thou wast created, till unrighteousness was found in thee. 16. By the multitude of thy traffic they filled the midst of thee with violence, and thou hast sinned; therefore have I cast thee as profane out of the mountain of God; and I have destroyed thee, O covering cherub, from the midst of the stones of fire. 17. Thy heart was lifted up because of thy beauty, thou hast corrupted thy wisdom by reason of thy brightness; I have cast thee to the ground, I have laid thee before kings, that

כְּרוּב מִמְשַׁח הַסּוֹכֵךְ וּנְתַתִּיךָ
בְּהַר קֹדֶשׁ אֱלֹהִים הָיִיתָ בְּתוֹךְ
אַבְנֵי־אֵשׁ הִתְהַלָּכְתָּ: תָּמִים 15
אַתָּה בִּדְרָכֶיךָ מִיּוֹם הִבָּרְאָךְ
עַד־נִמְצָא עַוְלָתָה בָּךְ: בְּרֹב 16
רְכֻלָּתְךָ מָלוּ תוֹכְךָ חָמָס
וַתֶּחֱטָא וָאֲחַלֶּלְךָ מֵהַר
אֱלֹהִים וָאַבֶּדְךָ כְּרוּב הַסֹּכֵךְ
מִתּוֹךְ אַבְנֵי־אֵשׁ: גָּבַהּ לִבְּךָ 17
בְּיָפְיֶךָ שִׁחַתָּ חָכְמָתְךָ עַל־
יִפְעָתֶךָ עַל־אֶרֶץ הִשְׁלַכְתִּיךָ
לִפְנֵי מְלָכִים נְתַתִּיךָ לְרַאֲוָה

v. 16. חסר א'

---

14. *thou wast the far-covering cherub.* This rendering, which is based on Rashi, takes the word *mimshach* to mean 'far-extending.' The king of Tyre is compared to a *cherub* because the cherubim in the Tabernacle and in Solomon's Temple spread their wings over the ark, symbolizing protection. Similarly, the king is described as the protector of *the garden of God*, Tyre.

I set thee . . . the holy mountain of God. The phrase *the holy mountain of God* is best interpreted as synonymous with *the garden of God* as descriptive of Tyre. His accession to the throne is ascribed to the Divine will.

thou hast walked . . . stones of fire. The meaning is quite uncertain and all the commentators, ancient and modern, are hard driven to suggest an interpretation. If, as appears probable, *stones of fire* are jewels, an additional reference is made to the splendour of the king's appearance. As he walked about, he appeared to be surrounded by flashing rays of light.

15. *thou wast perfect.* Before his vast wealth filled him with conceit and

ambition, there was no fault to be found with his conduct.

16. *thou hast sinned.* The prince is identified here with the city of Tyre for whose conduct of affairs he is held responsible. With the growth of commerce there was an increase of corruption, for which he must pay the penalty.

cast thee. Addressed to the prince. Being *profane* he can no longer inhabit *the mountain of God* for which holiness and purity are essential qualifications. The verbs in this and the following verses are in the prophetic perfect. The punishment was still to be inflicted.

destroyed . . . stones of fire. He would be stripped of his power and magnificence, and cease to be a *covering cherub*, a protection, to Tyre and her population.

17. *thou hast corrupted thy wisdom by reason of thy brightness.* True wisdom cannot be exercised where there is a spirit of arrogance. The qualities which made Tyre pre-eminent were neutralized by pride, so that instead of making still

they may gaze upon thee. 18. By the multitude of thine iniquities, in the unrighteousness of thy traffic, thou hast profaned thy sanctuaries; therefore have I brought forth a fire from the midst of thee, it hath devoured thee, and I have turned thee to ashes upon the earth in the sight of all them that behold thee. 19. All they that know thee among the peoples shall be appalled at thee; thou art become a terror, and thou shalt never be any more.'

20. And the word of the LORD came unto me, saying: 21. 'Son of man, set thy face toward Zidon, and prophesy against it, 22. and say: Thus saith the Lord GOD:

> Behold, I am against thee, O Zidon,
> And I will be glorified in the midst of thee;
> And they shall know that I am the LORD, when I shall have executed

18 בָּךְ׃ מֵרֹב עֲוֹנֶיךָ בְּעֶוֶל
רְכֻלָּתְךָ חִלַּלְתָּ מִקְדָּשֶׁיךָ
וָאוֹצִא־אֵשׁ מִתּוֹכְךָ הִיא
אֲכָלַתְךָ וָאֶתֶּנְךָ לְאֵפֶר עַל־
הָאָרֶץ לְעֵינֵי כָּל־רֹאֶיךָ׃
19 כָּל־יוֹדְעֶיךָ בָּעַמִּים שָׁמְמוּ
עָלֶיךָ בַּלָּהוֹת הָיִיתָ וְאֵינְךָ
20 עַד־עוֹלָם׃ וַיְהִי דְבַר־יְהֹוָה
21 אֵלַי לֵאמֹר׃ בֶּן־אָדָם שִׂים
פָּנֶיךָ אֶל־צִידוֹן וְהִנָּבֵא
22 עָלֶיהָ׃ וְאָמַרְתָּ כֹּה אָמַר אֲדֹנָי
יְהֹוִה
הִנְנִי עָלַיִךְ צִידוֹן
וְנִכְבַּדְתִּי בְּתוֹכֵךְ
וְיָדְעוּ כִּי־אֲנִי יְהֹוָה בַּעֲשׂוֹתִי

greater progress she will suffer eclipse and ruin.

that they may gaze upon thee. Gloat over the city's collapse.

18. *thou hast profaned thy sanctuaries.* The allusion is obscure. Rashi explains the Hebrew *mikdashĕcha* (*thy sanctuaries*) as 'thy holiness'; while Kimchi, quoting Amos vii. 13, *the king's sanctuary*, gives it in both passages the meaning of 'palaces.' This, however, is doubtful. The term has possibly to be connected with *the garden of God* and *the holy mountain of God* which had been used in the description of Tyre. She once deserved to be called 'thy holy places' over which the prince bore sway; but through moral debasement that title can no longer be applied and the city will be destroyed.

a fire from the midst of thee. The evil in the midst of Tyre will be the flame which reduces her to a heap of burnt ruins.

19. *shall be appalled at thee.* See on xxvii. 35.

a terror. See on xxvi. 21.

thou shalt never be any more. See on xxvi. 14.

20-26 DOWNFALL OF ZIDON

21. *toward Zidon.* Or, 'against Zidon' (A.V.). See on xxvii. 8. Zidon and Tyre are coupled in a prophecy of doom in Isa. xxiii.

22. *when I shall have executed judgments in her.* By meting out punishment to the guilty, God's universal Sovereignty is vindicated as well as His attribute of justice.

judgments in her, and shall be sanctified in her.

23 For I will send into her pestilence
And blood in her streets;
And the wounded shall fall in the midst of her
By the sword upon her on every side;

and they shall know that I am the LORD. 24. And there shall be no more a pricking brier unto the house of Israel, nor a piercing thorn of any that are round about them, that did have them in disdain; and they shall know that I am the Lord GOD.

25. Thus saith the Lord GOD: When I shall have gathered the house of Israel from the peoples among whom they are scattered, and shall be sanctified in them in the sight of the nations, then shall they dwell in their own land which I gave to My servant Jacob. 26. And they shall dwell safely therein, and shall build houses, and plant vine-

בָּהּ שְׁפָטִים וְנִקְדַּשְׁתִּי בָהּ׃

23 וְשִׁלַּחְתִּי־בָהּ
דֶּבֶר וָדָם בְּחוּצוֹתֶיהָ
וְנִפְלַל חָלָל בְּתוֹכָהּ
בְּחֶרֶב עָלֶיהָ מִסָּבִיב

24 וְיָדְעוּ כִּי־אֲנִי יְהֹוָה׃ וְלֹא־
יִהְיֶה עוֹד לְבֵית יִשְׂרָאֵל סִלּוֹן
מַמְאִיר וְקוֹץ מַכְאִב מִכֹּל
סְבִיבֹתָם הַשָּׁאטִים אוֹתָם
וְיָדְעוּ כִּי אֲנִי אֲדֹנָי יְהֹוָה׃

25 כֹּה־אָמַר אֲדֹנָי יֱהֹוִה בְּקַבְּצִי
אֶת־בֵּית יִשְׂרָאֵל מִן־
הָעַמִּים אֲשֶׁר נָפֹצוּ בָם
וְנִקְדַּשְׁתִּי בָם לְעֵינֵי הַגּוֹיִם
וְיָשְׁבוּ עַל־אַדְמָתָם אֲשֶׁר

26 נָתַתִּי לְעַבְדִּי לְיַעֲקֹב׃ וְיָשְׁבוּ
עָלֶיהָ לָבֶטַח וּבָנוּ בָתִּים וְנָטְעוּ

v. 25. הפטרת וארא

in her. The abrupt change from the second to the third person is not uncommon in the language of the prophets.

23. *fall.* The text has the unusual *niphlal* instead of *naphal* which is read in a few Hebrew MSS. Probability is in favour of the rare form, since it is impossible to explain how the common verb came to be altered. It perhaps denotes intensity: 'the wounded shall fall in heaps.'

by the sword upon her. i.e. the sword which will come upon her.

they shall know, etc. It will be acknowledged that the doom of Zidon was not by chance but the decree of God.

24. *there shall be no more,* etc. The verse is to be interpreted generally, and not only of Tyre and Zidon. The judgment of God upon the nations, who were the hostile neighbours of Israel, will remove a source of danger and oppression from him so that he will enjoy both restoration and security.

25. *shall be sanctified in them.* God's holiness will be recognized by all as the effect of the fulfilment of His promise to restore Israel to his land.

My servant Jacob. An appellation of the people of Israel (cf. xxxvii. 25; Jer. xxx. 10). It occurs many times in the latter section of the Book of Isaiah.

26. *build houses, and plant vineyards.*

yards; yea, they shall dwell safely; when I have executed judgments upon all those that have them in disdain round about them; and they shall know that I am the LORD their God.'

כְּרָמִים וְיָשְׁבוּ לָבֶטַח בַּעֲשׂוֹתִי שְׁפָטִים בְּכֹל הַשָּׁאטִים אֹתָם מִסְּבִיבֹתָם וְיָדְעוּ כִּי אֲנִי יְהֹוָה אֱלֹהֵיהֶם׃

29   CHAPTER XXIX   כט

1. In the tenth year, in the tenth month, in the twelfth day of the month, the word of the LORD came

1 בַּשָּׁנָה הָעֲשִׂרִית בָּעֲשִׂרִי בִּשְׁנֵים עָשָׂר לַחֹדֶשׁ הָיָה

These operations are only undertaken by a people when it feels security of tenure.

they shall know that I am the LORD their God. 'This oft-repeated phrase is not a mere formula. The prophet's idea is that God does all, brings all calamities, causes all catastrophes and revolutions in States, and guides the fortunes of Israel in the sight of the nations, with one great design in view—to make Himself, the true and only God, known to all mankind' (Davidson).

CHAPTER XXIX

AGAINST EGYPT

AFTER Tyre comes the prophecy against Egypt extending over four chapters, xxix-xxxii. Though this first prophecy against Egypt, in the tenth year and tenth month, is dated about seven months earlier than that against Tyre, the latter is placed first in the Book because its fulfilment preceded the Egyptian defeat. The second prophecy against Egypt is dated twenty-seven years from the accession to the throne by Nebuchadnezzar. The following two prophecies are dated the eleventh year, the year of the destruction of Jerusalem, and two in the twelfth year. The oracle against Egypt is exceedingly fierce and elaborate because of her importance as a world

Power and her influence upon Israel which was particularly evil. Egypt's sin was twofold. Her arrogance was notorious and her rôle in the history of Israel was that of a deceiver. As a great Power, she succeeded in subjugating Israel politically and imposing upon him an alliance which proved to be, in the prophet's words, *a broken reed*, and a calamity in his foreign relations. The alliance was constantly denounced by the prophets not only as a political delusion, but also as a factor in weakening Israel's reliance upon God. This *reed* must therefore be destroyed for ever. In conclusion the prophet raises a dirge over the doomed Pharaoh, and in graphic language pictures his descent to the nether-world where he joins the company of other fallen tyrants.

1-16 ALLEGORY OF EGYPT'S DOOM AND ITS INTERPRETATION

1. *in the tenth year.* Of the reign of Zedekiah, about seven months before the fall of Jerusalem, 586 B.C.E. There were several prophecies by Ezekiel against Egypt delivered at various times later than the tenth year of the reign of Zedekiah. They are grouped together in one series, though the first of them is dated before that concerning Tyre in chapter xxvi.

unto me, saying: 2. 'Son of man,
set thy face against Pharaoh king of
Egypt, and prophesy against him
and against all Egypt; 3. speak, and
say: Thus saith the Lord GOD:

Behold, I am against thee,
Pharaoh

King of Egypt,

The great dragon that lieth

In the midst of his rivers,

That hath said: My river is mine
own,

And I have made it for myself.

4. And I will put hooks in thy jaws,
and I will cause the fish of thy rivers
to stick unto thy scales; and I will
bring thee up out of the midst of thy
rivers, and all the fish of thy rivers
shall stick unto thy scales. 5. And
I will cast thee into the wilderness,

2 דְּבַר־יְהֹוָה אֵלַי לֵאמֹר: בֶּן־
אָדָם שִׂים פָּנֶיךָ עַל־פַּרְעֹה
מֶלֶךְ מִצְרָיִם וְהִנָּבֵא עָלָיו
3 וְעַל־מִצְרַיִם כֻּלָּהּ: דַּבֵּר
וְאָמַרְתָּ כֹּה־אָמַר ׀ אֲדֹנָי יֱהֹוִה
הִנְנִי עָלֶיךָ
פַּרְעֹה מֶלֶךְ־מִצְרַיִם
הַתַּנִּים הַגָּדוֹל הָרֹבֵץ
בְּתוֹךְ יְאֹרָיו
אֲשֶׁר אָמַר לִי יְאֹרִי
וַאֲנִי עֲשִׂיתִנִי:
4 וְנָתַתִּי חַחִיִּים בִּלְחָיֶיךָ
וְהִדְבַּקְתִּי דְגַת־יְאֹרֶיךָ
בְּקַשְׂקְשֹׂתֶיךָ וְהַעֲלִיתִיךָ
מִתּוֹךְ יְאֹרֶיךָ וְאֵת כָּל־דְּגַת
יְאֹרֶיךָ בְּקַשְׂקְשֹׂתֶיךָ תִּדְבָּק:
5 וּנְטַשְׁתִּיךָ הַמִּדְבָּרָה

v. 4. חחים ק׳

2. *Pharaoh.* viz. Hophra, named in
Jer. xliv. 30. He was the fourth king of
the twenty-sixth dynasty who reigned
from 589 to 570 B.C.E.

3. *the great dragon.* i.e. the crocodile.
The river Nile, which overflowed its
banks periodically and brought fertility
to the land, was the source of Egypt's
prosperity and pride. The arrogant
Pharaoh personified his country as did
the prince of Tyre.

his rivers. The tributaries and canals
of the main river.

my river is mine own, etc. Like the prince
of Tyre, Pharaoh thought of himself as
more than human, the creator of the
strength and productivity of Egypt.

The exalted position which his country
occupied in the world at that time was
due to his exceptional powers.

4. *hooks in thy jaws.* As the crocodile is
captured and drawn by hooks from the
river, so will Egypt be defeated by her
enemies and lose the wealth yielded by
her river.

I will cause the fish, etc. The fishes
which adhere to the scales of the crocodile
typify the whole nation. Both king and
people will perish.

shall stick unto thy scales. Ehrlich agrees
with Metsudath David in construing as
a relative clause: '(which) stick unto thy
scales.'

5. *into the wilderness.* Dry land spells

Thee and all the fish of thy
rivers;
Thou shalt fall upon the open
field;
Thou shalt not be brought together, nor gathered;
To the beasts of the earth and to
the fowls of the heaven
Have I given thee for food.
6 And all the inhabitants of Egypt
shall know
That I am the LORD,
Because they have been a staff of
reed
To the house of Israel.
7 When they take hold of thee with
the hand, thou dost break,
And rend all their shoulders;
And when they lean upon thee,
thou breakest,
And makest all their loins to be
at a stand.
8. Therefore thus saith the Lord
GOD: Behold, I will bring a sword
upon thee, and will cut off from thee

אוֹתְךָ֙ וְאֵ֣ת כָּל־דְּגַ֣ת יְאֹרֶ֔יךָ
עַל־פְּנֵ֥י הַשָּׂדֶ֖ה תִּפּ֑וֹל
לֹ֤א תֵֽאָסֵף֙ וְלֹ֣א תִקָּבֵ֔ץ
לְחַיַּ֥ת הָאָ֛רֶץ וּלְע֥וֹף הַשָּׁמַ֖יִם
נְתַתִּ֥יךָ לְאָכְלָֽה׃
6 וְיָֽדְעוּ֙ כָּל־יֹשְׁבֵ֣י מִצְרַ֔יִם
כִּ֖י אֲנִ֣י יְהֹוָ֑ה
יַ֧עַן הֱיוֹתָ֛ם מִשְׁעֶ֥נֶת קָנֶ֖ה
לְבֵ֥ית יִשְׂרָאֵֽל׃
7 בְּתָפְשָׂ֨ם בְּךָ֤ בַכַּף֙ תֵּר֔וֹץ
וּבָקַעְתָּ֥ לָהֶ֖ם כָּל־כָּתֵ֑ף
וּבְהִֽשָּׁעֲנָ֤ם עָלֶ֙יךָ֙ תִּשָּׁבֵ֔ר
וְהַעֲמַדְתָּ֥ לָהֶ֖ם כָּל־מָתְנָֽיִם׃
8 לָכֵ֗ן כֹּ֤ה אָמַר֙ אֲדֹנָ֣י יֱהֹוִ֔ה הִנְנִ֛י
מֵבִ֥יא עָלַ֖יִךְ חָ֑רֶב וְהִכְרַתִּ֥י

v. 7. בכף ק׳

certain death for the crocodile and fishes cast upon it out of the water. Driven away from the Nile, the Egyptian people will be destroyed.

not be brought together, nor gathered. The fallen will not be given burial as human dignity requires, but will lie about abandoned and neglected to become a prey to the beasts and birds of prey (cf. xxxix. 17ff.).

6. *a staff of reed.* Which provides no support and breaks when one leans upon it. Egypt was described by the officer of Sennacherib, king of Assyria, as a *bruised reed . . . whereon if a man lean, it will go into his hand, and pierce it* (Isa. xxxvi. 6). She proved untrustworthy as an ally of Israel.

7. *rend all their shoulders.* Anyone who depends upon Egypt finds the support giving way so that he falls and dislocates his shoulder.

makest all their loins to be at a stand. lit. 'causest all their loins to stand'; i.e. a person who leans upon another adopts a bent posture. In the case of Egypt, anybody leaning upon her soon feels the necessity to stand erect. The root of the verb is *amad;* and Kimchi mentions that some explain the verb as though it were from the root *ma'ad* (cf. *make their loins continually to totter,* ham'ad, Ps. lxix. 24), while Rashi remarks that some emend the verb accordingly. They both reject the suggested rendering.

8. *therefore.* As the effect of Egypt's arrogance. The imagery is now translated into plain language.

man and beast. 9. And the land of Egypt shall be desolate and waste, and they shall know that I am the LORD; because he hath said: The river is mine, and I have made it. 10. Therefore, behold, I am against thee, and against thy rivers, and I will make the land of Egypt utterly waste and desolate, from Migdol to Syene even unto the border of Ethiopia. 11. No foot of man shall pass through it, nor foot of beast shall pass through it, neither shall it be inhabited forty years. 12. And I will make the land of Egypt desolate in the midst of the countries that are desolate, and her cities among the cities that are laid waste shall be desolate forty years; and I will scatter the Egyptians among the nations, and will disperse them through the countries.

13. For thus saith the Lord GOD: At the end of forty years will I

9 מִמֶּךָ אָדָם וּבְהֵמָה: וְהָיְתָה
אֶרֶץ־מִצְרַיִם לִשְׁמָמָה
וְחָרְבָּה וְיָדְעוּ כִּי־אֲנִי יְהֹוָה
יַעַן אָמַר יְאֹר לִי וַאֲנִי עָשִׂיתִי:
10 לָכֵן הִנְנִי אֵלֶיךָ וְאֶל־יְאֹרֶיךָ
וְנָתַתִּי אֶת־אֶרֶץ מִצְרַיִם
לְחָרְבוֹת חֹרֶב שְׁמָמָה מִמִּגְדֹּל
11 סְוֵנֵה וְעַד־גְּבוּל כּוּשׁ: לֹא
תַעֲבָר־בָּהּ רֶגֶל אָדָם וְרֶגֶל
בְּהֵמָה לֹא תַעֲבָר־בָּהּ וְלֹא
12 תֵשֵׁב אַרְבָּעִים שָׁנָה: וְנָתַתִּי
אֶת־אֶרֶץ מִצְרַיִם שְׁמָמָה
בְּתוֹךְ ׀ אֲרָצוֹת נְשַׁמּוֹת וְעָרֶיהָ
בְּתוֹךְ עָרִים מָחֳרָבוֹת תִּהְיֶיןָ
שְׁמָמָה אַרְבָּעִים שָׁנָה וַהֲפִצֹתִי
אֶת־מִצְרַיִם בַּגּוֹיִם וְזֵרִיתִים
13 בָּאֲרָצוֹת: כִּי כֹּה אָמַר אֲדֹנָי

9. *the river is mine*, etc. Cf. verse 3. Pride is an offence to God and punished by Him with humiliation.

10. *from Migdol to Syene.* The whole country will be involved in the punishment. *Migdol*, meaning 'a tower,' was a frontier fortress at the north-east corner of Lower Egypt (cf. Exod. xiv. 2; Jer. xliv. 1), about twelve miles south of Pelusium, on the northern border. *Syene*, or *Seweneh*, now known as Assoun, is opposite Migdol at the extreme south, on the frontier of Ethiopia.

11. *nor foot of beast shall pass through it.* Even animals will desert the land owing to the lack of pasture.

forty years. Cf. iv. 6 where the desolation of Judea is predicted for a similar period. The recovery of Egypt was foretold by other prophets (cf. Isa. xix. 24; Jer. xlvi. 26). The Midrash states that famine was decreed for Egypt in the time of Joseph to last forty-two years; but with the coming of Jacob to the country, after two years, it ended prematurely. Now the Egyptians would have to suffer the balance of forty years.

12. *in the midst of the countries that are desolate.* The state of desolation in Egypt will be so extreme that it will appear patently so even in comparison with other lands which have been ravaged by an invading army.

13. *at the end of forty years.* After forty

gather the Egyptians from the peoples whither they were scattered; 14. and I will turn the captivity of Egypt, and will cause them to return into the land of Pathros, into the land of their origin; and they shall be there a lowly kingdom. 15. It shall be the lowliest of the kingdoms, neither shall it any more lift itself up above the nations; and I will diminish them, that they shall no more rule over the nations. 16. And it shall be no more the confidence of the house of Israel, bringing iniquity to remembrance, when they turn after them; and they shall know that I am the Lord GOD.'

17. And it came to pass in the seven and twentieth year, in the first month, in the first day of the

יְהוָה מִקֵּץ אַרְבָּעִים שָׁנָה
אֲקַבֵּץ אֶת־מִצְרַיִם מִן־
הָעַמִּים אֲשֶׁר־נָפֹצוּ שָׁמָּה:
14 וְשַׁבְתִּי אֶת־שְׁבוּת מִצְרַיִם
וַהֲשִׁבֹתִי אֹתָם אֶרֶץ פַּתְרוֹס
עַל־אֶרֶץ מְכוּרָתָם וְהָיוּ שָׁם
15 מַמְלָכָה שְׁפָלָה: מִן־
הַמַּמְלָכוֹת תִּהְיֶה שְׁפָלָה
וְלֹא־תִתְנַשֵּׂא עוֹד עַל־הַגּוֹיִם
וְהִמְעַטְתִּים לְבִלְתִּי רְדוֹת
16 בַּגּוֹיִם: וְלֹא־יִהְיֶה־עוֹד לְבֵית
יִשְׂרָאֵל לְמִבְטָח מַזְכִּיר עָוֹן
בִּפְנוֹתָם אַחֲרֵיהֶם וְיָדְעוּ כִּי
17 אֲנִי אֲדֹנָי יְהוִה: וַיְהִי בְּעֶשְׂרִים
וָשֶׁבַע שָׁנָה בָּרִאשׁוֹן בְּאֶחָד

years Egypt will be restored, though only to rank as a weak kingdom with its former pride shattered. The restoration at the end of the period named probably coincides with the decline of the Babylonian empire.

14. *I will turn the captivity.* See on xvi. 53.

the land of Pathros . . . the land of their origin. Pathros, meaning 'south land,' was the name of Upper Egypt. Herodotus considered it to be the source from which Egyptian rule developed.

a lowly kingdom. Small in size and humble in status.

15. *the lowliest of the kingdoms.* Egypt will become not merely *a lowly kingdom* (verse 14), but inferior to all other nations.

16. *no more the confidence.* In her weakened and lowly condition she will no more be able to seduce Israel to turn to her for help.

bringing iniquity to remembrance. Israel's reliance upon Egypt instead of trusting in God was an offence in His sight. For the phrase, cf. xxi. 28; Num. v. 15.

when they turn after them. Seeking an alliance.

they shall know. The subject is Israel. Metsudath David takes it to be 'the nations' in general.

17-21 EGYPT A REWARD TO NEBUCHADNEZZAR FOR HIS CAMPAIGN AGAINST TYRE

17. *the seven and twentieth year.* The Jewish commentators, relying upon *Seder Olam,* explain this of the reign of

month, the word of the Lord came
unto me, saying: 18. 'Son of man,
Nebuchadrezzar king of Babylon
caused his army to serve a great
service against Tyre; every head
was made bald, and every shoulder
was peeled; yet had he no wages, nor
his army, from Tyre, for the service
that he had served against it; 19.
therefore thus saith the Lord GOD:
Behold, I will give the land of Egypt
unto Nebuchadrezzar king of Babylon; and he shall carry off her
abundance, and take her spoil, and
take her prey; and it shall be the
wages for his army. 20. I have
given him the land of Egypt as his
hire for which he served, because
they wrought for Me, saith the
Lord GOD.

לַחֹדֶשׁ הָיָה דְבַר־יְהֹוָה
אֵלַי לֵאמֹר: בֶּן־אָדָם ‏18
נְבוּכַדְרֶאצַּר מֶלֶךְ־בָּבֶל
הֶעֱבִיד אֶת־חֵילוֹ עֲבֹדָה
גְדוֹלָה אֶל־צֹר כָּל־רֹאשׁ
מֻקְרָח וְכָל־כָּתֵף מְרוּטָה
וְשָׂכָר לֹא־הָיָה לוֹ וּלְחֵילוֹ
מִצֹּר עַל־הָעֲבֹדָה אֲשֶׁר־
עָבַד עָלֶיהָ: לָכֵן כֹּה אָמַר ‏19
אֲדֹנָי יְהֹוִה הִנְנִי נֹתֵן
לִנְבוּכַדְרֶאצַּר מֶלֶךְ־בָּבֶל
אֶת־אֶרֶץ מִצְרָיִם וְנָשָׂא הֲמֹנָהּ
וְשָׁלַל שְׁלָלָהּ וּבָזַז בִּזָּהּ וְהָיְתָה
שָׂכָר לְחֵילוֹ: פְּעֻלָּתוֹ אֲשֶׁר־ ‏20
עָבַד בָּהּ נָתַתִּי לוֹ אֶת־אֶרֶץ
מִצְרָיִם אֲשֶׁר עָשׂוּ לִי נְאֻם

Nebuchadnezzar. He came to the
throne in 605 B.C.E. which yields the
date 578. Modern authorities, on the
other hand, relate the number to that
given in verse 1, *the tenth year* (586), and
accordingly date this section 570. It
was 'written after Nebuchadnezzar's
thirteen years' siege of Tyre had come to
an end, and inserted among the prophecies relating to Egypt already collected. Nebuchadnezzar had served a
great service for God against Tyre, for
which neither he nor his army had
received wages. God will recompense
him for his service against Tyre by
giving him the land of Egypt' (Davidson).

18. *Nebuchadrezzar.* For this spelling
of the name, see on xxvi. 7.

*every head was made bald, and every
shoulder was peeled.* The Babylonian
besiegers of Tyre had their heads made
bald and the skin of their shoulders
chafed by carrying loads of stone and
timber in the campaign against the town.
A vivid description of the laborious work
involved in the long siege of Tyre. 'As
Nebuchadnezzar had no fleet, the arm of
the sea between Tyre and the mainland
had to be filled up; hence the bearing of
burdens' (Lofthouse).

yet had he no wages. So far the Babylonians had received no award from God for
carrying out His task.

19. *therefore.* Because Nebuchadnezzar
and his soldiers had no pay for their
Tyrian campaign, they will be com-
pensated by the spoil taken from Egypt.

20. *they wrought for Me.* A.J. apparently understands the Babylonians

21. In that day will I cause a horn to shoot up unto the house of Israel, and I will give thee the opening of the mouth in the midst of them; and they shall know that I am the LORD.'

21 אֲדֹנָי יֱהֹוִה: בַּיּוֹם הַהוּא אַצְמִיחַ קֶרֶן לְבֵית יִשְׂרָאֵל וּלְךָ אֶתֵּן פִּתְחוֹן־פֶּה בְּתוֹכָם וְיָדְעוּ כִּי־אֲנִי יְהֹוָה׃

30 CHAPTER XXX ל

1. And the word of the LORD came unto me, saying: **2.** 'Son of man, prophesy, and say: Thus saith the Lord GOD:

Wail ye: Woe worth the day!

3 For the day is near,

Even the day of the LORD is near,

1 וַיְהִי דְבַר־יְהֹוָה אֵלַי לֵאמֹר׃
2 בֶּן־אָדָם הִנָּבֵא וְאָמַרְתָּ כֹּה אָמַר אֲדֹנָי יֱהֹוִה הֵילִילוּ הָהּ לַיּוֹם׃
3 כִּי־קָרוֹב יוֹם וְקָרוֹב יוֹם לַיהֹוָה

v. 21. עד כאן

as the subject of the clause. The Targum, followed by Rashi and Kimchi, take as its subject the preceding phrase, *the land of Egypt.* The translation is then: 'they did to Me,' in seducing Israel from God.

21. *in that day,* etc. The reference is to Cyrus and the return from the Babylonian exile, and the phrase *that day* denotes 'at that time' (Kimchi). Rashi understands it as alluding to the prediction of Egypt's restoration at the end of forty years (verse 13). That restoration will coincide with the dawn of Israel's release from captivity. Probably *horn* is to be interpreted as the symbol of power and prosperity, and Ezekiel predicts in general terms that in the future Israel will be restored to his former glory.

I will give thee the opening of the mouth. The fulfilment of Ezekiel's prediction will establish the authenticity of his message. No longer will he feel his speech restrained by the scepticism of his people.

CHAPTER XXX
THE IMMINENT FALL OF EGYPT

EGYPT, a world Power and centre of pagan worship, is to lose both attributes. Her collapse will be a blow to heathendom in general and a demonstration of the Sovereignty of the true God. All her allies and dependent States will share her fate. Nebuchadnezzar is to be used as the agent for the execution of the Divine decree against her, and the destruction of population and land will be extensive and thorough.

1-19 THE FATE IN STORE FOR EGYPT

1. No date is assigned to this prophecy. It was possibly the same as in xxix. 1.

2. *wail ye.* Addressed to the Egyptians.

woe worth the day. The day of reckoning which looms ahead for Egypt. '*Worth* is derived from an Anglo-Saxon root meaning "be," and is cognate with the German "werden" ' (Lofthouse).

3. *the day is near.* More accurately 'a day is near,' defined by the following

A day of clouds, it shall be the
    time of the nations.

4 And a sword shall come upon
    Egypt,
    And convulsion shall be in
    Ethiopia,
    When the slain shall fall in
    Egypt;
    And they shall take away her
    abundance,
    And her foundations shall be
    broken down.

5. Ethiopia, and Put, and Lud, and
all the mingled people, and Cub, and
the children of the land that is in
league, shall fall with them by the
sword.

6 Thus saith the LORD:
    They also that uphold Egypt
    shall fall,
    And the pride of her power shall
    come down;
    From Migdol to Syene shall they
    fall in it by the sword,
    Saith the Lord GOD.

יוֹם עָנָן עֵת גּוֹיִם יִהְיֶה׃

4 וּבָאָה חֶרֶב בְּמִצְרַיִם
וְהָיְתָה חַלְחָלָה בְּכוּשׁ
בִּנְפֹל חָלָל בְּמִצְרַיִם
וְלָקְחוּ הֲמוֹנָהּ
וְנֶהֶרְסוּ יְסֹדוֹתֶיהָ׃

5 כּוּשׁ וּפוּט וְלוּד וְכָל־הָעֶרֶב
וְכוּב וּבְנֵי אֶרֶץ הַבְּרִית אִתָּם
בַּחֶרֶב יִפֹּלוּ׃

6 כֹּה אָמַר יְהוָֹה
וְנָפְלוּ סֹמְכֵי מִצְרַיִם
וְיָרַד גְּאוֹן עֻזָּהּ
מִמִּגְדֹּל סְוֵנֶה
בַּחֶרֶב יִפְּלוּ־בָהּ
נְאֻם אֲדֹנָי יֱהוִֹה׃

v. 4. מלרע

---

the day of the LORD. It will be the
occasion when God's judgment will be
passed upon the world.

a day of clouds. As the clouds herald a
storm, so will the day of the LORD bring
drastic punishment upon those who
deserve it.

the time of the nations. All the heathen
peoples will be involved, Egypt among
them.

4. a sword. An attack by Babylon is
meant.

convulsion shall be in Ethiopia. Ethiopia,
being under the domination of Egypt,
will be alarmed for her safety and
terrified lest she share Egypt's doom.

her foundations shall be broken down.
The reference is to the allies and
mercenaries upon whom Egypt relied
for military strength. They are specified
in the next verse.

5. Ethiopia. Or Cush, like Egypt a son
of Ham (Gen. x. 6); there was not only a
blood-relationship between them but
also a close political connection.

Put, and Lud. See on xxvii. 10.

all the mingled people. Cf. all the kings
of the mingled people (Jer. xxv. 24). It
probably denotes Egypt's mercenaries
who were drawn from various races.

Cub. The name of a people which has
not been identified.

that is in league. lit. 'the land of the
covenant,' i.e. in alliance with Egypt.

6. from Migdol to Syene. See on xxix. 10.

7 And they shall be desolate in the midst of the countries that are desolate,

And her cities shall be in the midst of the cities that are wasted.

8 And they shall know that I am the LORD,

When I have set a fire in Egypt,

And all her helpers are destroyed.

9 In that day shall messengers go forth from before Me in ships

To make the confident Ethiopians afraid;

And there shall come confusion upon them in the day of Egypt;

For, lo, it cometh.

10 Thus saith the Lord GOD:

I will also make the multitude of Egypt to cease,

By the hand of Nebuchadrezzar king of Babylon.

7 וְנָשַׁמּוּ בְתֹוךְ אֲרָצֹות נְשַׁמֹּות
וְעָרָיו בְּתֹוךְ־עָרִים נֶחֱרָבֹות
תִּהְיֶינָה׃
8 וְיָדְעוּ כִּי־אֲנִי יְהֹוָה
בְּתִתִּי־אֵשׁ בְּמִצְרַיִם
וְנִשְׁבְּרוּ כָּל־עֹזְרֶיהָ׃
9 בַּיֹּום הַהוּא יֵצְאוּ
מַלְאָכִים מִלְּפָנַי בַּצִּים
לְהַחֲרִיד אֶת־כּוּשׁ בֶּטַח
וְהָיְתָה חַלְחָלָה בָהֶם
בְּיֹום מִצְרַיִם
כִּי הִנֵּה בָּאָה׃
10 כֹּה אָמַר אֲדֹנָי יֱהֹוִה
וְהִשְׁבַּתִּי אֶת־הֲמֹון מִצְרַיִם
בְּיַד נְבוּכַדְרֶאצַּר
מֶלֶךְ־בָּבֶל׃

---

7. in the midst of the countries, etc. See on xxix. 12.

8. a fire. A common figure in the Bible for the devastation caused by war.

9. in that day. Defined at the end of the verse as *the day of Egypt*, the time of her downfall.

shall messengers go forth from before Me. Lofthouse comments: 'God speaks as if He had come in person into Egypt, like another and more terrible Nebuchadnezzar'; but this is an incorrect interpretation of the phrase *from before Me*. The Jewish commentators rightly explain it as 'on My mission,' more exactly 'at My will, on My orders.'

in ships. The Hebrew *tsim* (again in Num. xxiv. 24, and the singular *tsi* in Isa. xxxiii. 21) is a loan-word from the Egyptian *t'ai.* The rivers of Ethiopia are mentioned in Isa. xviii. 1 and they were used by messengers to reach different parts of the country.

to make . . . afraid. More lit. 'to make Ethiopia (which had been) in a state of confidence afraid.'

in the day of Egypt. Another reading is *keyom* '(as) in the day of Egypt.' The rendering of A.J. is probable. Kimchi's interpretation is: the tidings of the approaching army will cause the Ethiopians as much alarm and consternation as they felt at the time of Egypt's collapse (cf. verse 4).

10. the multitude of Egypt. The native population as distinct from the mercenaries.

by the hand of Nebuchadrezzar. Cf. xxix. 19.

11 He and his people with him, the
   terrible of the nations,
   Shall be brought in to destroy
   the land;
   And they shall draw their swords
   against Egypt,
   And fill the land with the slain.

12 And I will make the rivers dry,
   And will give the land over into
   the hand of evil men;
   And I will make the land
   desolate,
   And all that is therein, by the
   hand of strangers;
   I the LORD have spoken it.

13 Thus saith the Lord GOD:
   I will also destroy the idols,
   And I will cause the things of
   nought to cease from Noph;
   And there shall be no more a
   prince out of the land of
   Egypt;
   And I will put a fear in the land
   of Egypt.

14 And I will make Pathros desolate,
   And I will set a fire in Zoan,

11 הוּא וְעַמּוֹ אִתּוֹ עָרִיצֵי גוֹיִם
מוּבָאִים לְשַׁחֵת הָאָרֶץ
וְהֵרִיקוּ חַרְבוֹתָם
עַל־מִצְרַיִם
וּמָלְאוּ אֶת־הָאָרֶץ חָלָל:
12 וְנָתַתִּי יְאֹרִים חָרָבָה
וּמָכַרְתִּי אֶת־הָאָרֶץ
בְּיַד־רָעִים
וַהֲשִׁמֹּתִי אֶרֶץ
וּמְלֹאָהּ בְּיַד־זָרִים
אֲנִי יְהֹוָה דִּבַּרְתִּי:
13 כֹּה־אָמַר אֲדֹנָי יְהֹוִה
וְהַאֲבַדְתִּי גִלּוּלִים
וְהִשְׁבַּתִּי אֱלִילִים מִנֹּף
וְנָשִׂיא מֵאֶרֶץ־מִצְרַיִם
לֹא יִהְיֶה־עוֹד
וְנָתַתִּי יִרְאָה בְּאֶרֶץ מִצְרָיִם:
14 וַהֲשִׁמֹּתִי אֶת־פַּתְרוֹס
וְנָתַתִּי אֵשׁ בְּצֹעַן

---

11. *he.* viz. Nebuchadnezzar.

the terrible of the nations. Cf. xxviii. 7; again in xxxi. 12, xxxii. 12.

12. *I will make the rivers dry.* The drying up of the Egyptian canals and the destruction of its system of irrigation would inevitably bring desolation upon the country (cf. Isa. xix. 5ff.).

evil men. Men who will prove themselves lawless and without pity.

13. *Noph.* Memphis, the capital of Lower Egypt, was the site for the temples of the Egyptian gods, Ptah and Apis. In the destruction of Egypt's population, her religious institutions will also be involved.

a fear. Cf. Isa. xix. 16.

14. *Pathros.* See on xxix. 14.

Zoan. Tanis or San, on the eastern bank of the second arm of the Nile (cf. Num. xiii. 22; Ps. lxxviii. 12, 43).

And will execute judgments in No.

15 And I will pour My fury upon Sin, the stronghold of Egypt; And I will cut off the multitude of No.

16 And I will set a fire in Egypt; Sin shall be in great convulsion, And No shall be rent asunder; And in Noph shall come adversaries in the day-time.

17 The young men of Aven and of Pi-beseth shall fall by the sword; And these cities shall go into captivity.

18 At Tehaphnehes also the day shall withdraw itself, When I shall break there the yokes of Egypt,

וְעָשִׂיתִי שְׁפָטִים בְּנֹא:

15 וְשָׁפַכְתִּי חֲמָתִי
עַל־סִין מָעוֹז מִצְרָיִם
וְהִכְרַתִּי אֶת־הֲמוֹן נֹא:

16 וְנָתַתִּי אֵשׁ בְּמִצְרַיִם
חוּל תָּחִיל סִין
וְנֹא תִּהְיֶה לְהִבָּקֵעַ
וְנֹף צָרֵי יוֹמָם:

17 בַּחוּרֵי אָוֶן
וּפִי־בֶסֶת בַּחֶרֶב יִפֹּלוּ
וְהֵנָּה בַּשְּׁבִי תֵלַכְנָה:

18 וּבִתְחַפְנְחֵס חָשַׂךְ הַיּוֹם
בְּשִׁבְרִי־שָׁם
אֶת־מֹטוֹת מִצְרָיִם

v. 16.   ב״א חשך   v. 18. תחול ק׳

No. Identified with Thebes, the capital of Upper Egypt. It is named *No-amon* in Nahum iii. 8 (cf. *Amon of No*, Jer. xlvi. 25), the town being associated with the worship of the god Amon.

15. *Sin.* Probably Pelusium on the eastern frontier of Egypt.

16. *No shall be rent asunder.* Though a fortress, it will be breached and penetrated by the invading army.

shall come adversaries in the day-time. The text is difficult, the literal translation being: 'Noph the adversaries of by day.' The sense is: confident in their overwhelming strength and despising Egyptian resistance, the invaders will attack not at night but in the day-time.

17. *Aven.* Or, 'On,' i.e. Heliopolis in Lower Egypt, the centre of sun-worship. Hence it is also called *Beth-shemesh*, 'house of the sun' (Jer. xliii. 13).

Pi-beseth. Bubastis, now Tel Basta, about forty miles north-east of Cairo, meaning 'the city of the cat-shaped idol.' All the places enumerated in verses 13-18 seem to have been the centres of different forms of idolatry.

these cities. lit. 'and these.' Kimchi quotes his father who explained the pronoun as referring to the women of the two cities, viz. the wives of the young men who are said at the beginning of the verse to fall by the sword.

18. *Tehaphnehes.* In Jer. ii. 16, xliii. 7ff. the name of the city is *Tahpanhes*. It is probably the modern Tel el-Defenne, Daphnae, one of the chief fortresses of ancient Egypt.

the day shall withdraw itself. A figure for utter despair and helplessness. Another reading for *chasach* is *chashach*, 'the day will grow dark.'

the yokes of Egypt. The tyranny which Egypt inflicted upon other nations.

And the pride of her power shall
cease in her;
As for her, a cloud shall cover
her,
And her daughters shall go into
captivity.

19 Thus will I execute judgments in
Egypt;
And they shall know that I am
the LORD.'

20. And it came to pass in the
eleventh year, in the first month, in
the seventh day of the month, that
the word of the LORD came unto me,
saying: 21. 'Son of man, I have
broken the arm of Pharaoh king of
Egypt; and, lo, it hath not been
bound up to be healed, to put a
roller, that it be bound up and wax
strong, that it hold the sword.
22. Therefore thus saith the Lord
GOD: Behold, I am against Pharaoh
king of Egypt, and will break his
arms, the strong, and that which
was broken; and I will cause
the sword to fall out of his hand.

וְנִשְׁבַּת־בָּהּ גְּאוֹן עֻזָּהּ
הִיא עָנָן יְכַסֶּנָּה
וּבְנוֹתֶיהָ בַּשְּׁבִי תֵלַכְנָה׃
19 וְעָשִׂיתִי שְׁפָטִים בְּמִצְרָיִם
וְיָדְעוּ כִּי־אֲנִי יְהֹוָה׃
20 וַיְהִי בְּאַחַת עֶשְׂרֵה שָׁנָה
בָּרִאשׁוֹן בְּשִׁבְעָה לַחֹדֶשׁ הָיָה
21 דְבַר־יְהֹוָה אֵלַי לֵאמֹר׃ בֶּן־
אָדָם אֶת־זְרוֹעַ פַּרְעֹה מֶלֶךְ־
מִצְרַיִם שָׁבָרְתִּי וְהִנֵּה לֹא־
חֻבְּשָׁה לָתֵת רְפֻאוֹת לָשׂוּם
חִתּוּל לְחָבְשָׁהּ לְחָזְקָהּ לִתְפֹּשׂ
22 בֶּחָרֶב׃ לָכֵן כֹּה־אָמַר אֲדֹנָי
יֱהֹוִה הִנְנִי אֶל־פַּרְעֹה מֶלֶךְ־
מִצְרַיִם וְשָׁבַרְתִּי אֶת־זְרֹעֹתָיו
אֶת־הַחֲזָקָה וְאֶת־הַנִּשְׁבָּרֶת
וְהִפַּלְתִּי אֶת־הַחֶרֶב מִיָּדוֹ׃

---

her daughters. The Targum renders:
'the inhabitants of her towns.' The
Hebrew for *daughters* often occurs in the
sense of smaller towns adjacent to a large
city.

19. *they shall know that I am the* LORD.
The ultimate purpose of these chastise-
ments is to vindicate the Sovereignty of
God.

20-26   DEFEAT OF EGYPT BY NEBUCHADNEZZAR

20. *the eleventh year.* Of the reign of
Zedekiah, about four months before the
fall of Jerusalem.

21. *broken the arm of Pharaoh.* The
allusion is to the advance of Pharaoh

Hophra to relieve Jerusalem while it was
besieged by the Babylonians. It brought
only a temporary respite. The Egyptian
army withdrew and the Babylonians
renewed the attack (Jer. xxxvii. 5ff.).
Egypt's decisive defeat at the hands of
Nebuchadnezzar is recorded in 2 Kings
xxiv. 7.

roller. The Hebrew *chittul* denotes 'a
bandage'; the verb from the same root
occurred in xvi. 4, *swaddled* (*chuttalt*).
The damage done to Egypt was irreparable.

22. *will break his arms.* Defeat will
follow defeat until Egypt is rendered
completely powerless.

23. And I will scatter the Egyptians among the nations, and will disperse them through the countries. 24. And I will strengthen the arms of the king of Babylon, and put My sword in his hand; but I will break the arms of Pharaoh, and he shall groan before him with the groanings of a deadly wounded man. 25. And I will hold up the arms of the king of Babylon, and the arms of Pharaoh shall fall down; and they shall know that I am the Lord, when I shall put My sword into the hand of the king of Babylon, and he shall stretch it out upon the land of Egypt. 26. And I will scatter the Egyptians among the nations, and disperse them through the countries; and they shall know that I am the Lord.'

23 וַהֲפִצוֹתִי אֶת־מִצְרַיִם בַּגּוֹיִם
24 וְזֵרִיתִם בָּאֲרָצוֹת: וְחִזַּקְתִּי
אֶת־זְרֹעוֹת מֶלֶךְ בָּבֶל
וְנָתַתִּי אֶת־חַרְבִּי בְּיָדוֹ
וְשָׁבַרְתִּי אֶת־זְרֹעוֹת פַּרְעֹה
וְנָאַק נַאֲקוֹת חָלָל לְפָנָיו:
25 וְהַחֲזַקְתִּי אֶת־זְרֹעוֹת מֶלֶךְ
בָּבֶל וּזְרֹעוֹת פַּרְעֹה תִּפֹּלְנָה
וְיָדְעוּ כִּי־אֲנִי יְהֹוָה בְּתִתִּי
חַרְבִּי בְּיַד מֶלֶךְ־בָּבֶל וְנָטָה
אוֹתָהּ אֶל־אֶרֶץ מִצְרַיִם:
26 וַהֲפִצוֹתִי אֶת־מִצְרַיִם בַּגּוֹיִם
וְזֵרִיתִי אוֹתָם בָּאֲרָצוֹת וְיָדְעוּ
כִּי־אֲנִי יְהֹוָה:

31   CHAPTER XXXI   לא

1. And it came to pass in the eleventh year, in the third month, in the first day of the month, that the

1 וַיְהִי בְּאַחַת עֶשְׂרֵה שָׁנָה
בַּשְּׁלִישִׁי בְּאֶחָד לַחֹדֶשׁ הָיָה

---

23. Cf. xxix. 12, xxx. 26.

24. *put My sword in his hand.* Nebuchadnezzar being God's instrument for punishing Egypt.

25f. The two preceding verses are repeated in substance for final emphasis.

CHAPTER XXXI

ASSYRIA'S FATE A WARNING TO EGYPT

THE eclipse of Assyria is held up to Egypt as an example of Divine punishment for self-exaltation and arrogance. Mighty Assyria, the powerful conqueror of many nations, had vanished in ruins from the stage of history. A similar fate will befall Egypt, the mistress of many peoples. Only at the beginning and the end of the chapter is Pharaoh, the representative of Egypt, explicitly mentioned; the middle section deals with the eminence and subsequent decline of Assyria as the prototype of Egypt's doom.

1-9 EGYPT LIKENED TO A CEDAR

1. *the eleventh year.* Of Zedekiah's reign.

the third month. About two months before the capture of Jerusalem.

word of the LORD came unto me,
saying: 2. 'Son of man, say unto
Pharaoh king of Egypt, and to his
multitude:

> Whom art thou like in thy great-
> ness?

3 Behold, the Assyrian was a cedar
in Lebanon,

> With fair branches, and with a
> shadowing shroud,
> And of a high stature;
> And its top was among the thick
> boughs.

4 The waters nourished it,

> The deep made it to grow;
> Her rivers ran round
> About her plantation,
> And she sent out her conduits
> Unto all the trees of the field.

2 דְּבַר־יְהֹוָה אֵלַי לֵאמֹר: בֶּן־
אָדָם אֱמֹר אֶל־פַּרְעֹה מֶלֶךְ־
מִצְרַיִם וְאֶל־הֲמוֹנוֹ
אֶל־מִי דָּמִיתָ בְגָדְלֶךָ:
3 הִנֵּה אַשּׁוּר אֶרֶז בַּלְּבָנוֹן
יְפֵה עָנָף וְחֹרֶשׁ מֵצַל
וּגְבַהּ קוֹמָה
וּבֵין עֲבֹתִים הָיְתָה צַמַּרְתּוֹ:
4 מַיִם גִּדְּלוּהוּ
תְּהוֹם רֹמְמָתְהוּ
אֶת־נַהֲרֹתֶיהָ הֹלֵךְ
סְבִיבוֹת מַטָּעָהּ
וְאֶת־תְּעָלֹתֶיהָ שִׁלְּחָה
אֶל כָּל־עֲצֵי הַשָּׂדֶה:

v. 4. הל׳ רפה

---

2. his multitude. The Egyptian people.

whom art thou like in thy greatness?
Incomparably great and powerful though
he might think himself to be, he cannot
escape the judgment which God had
passed upon him.

3. the Assyrian was a cedar in Lebanon.
As the cedar is taller than any other tree
in Lebanon, so was Assyria the mightiest
people in his time. Most moderns
emend *ashshur* (Assyria) into *te'ashshur*,
the tree mentioned in Isa. xli. 19,
translated *larch* (see on xxvii. 6). Thereby they eliminate all reference to Assyria
and explain the whole chapter as
addressed directly to Pharaoh. Ehrlich,
on the other hand, defends the integrity
of M.T. and accepts the Jewish interpretation which is here followed.

with a shadowing shroud. The Hebrew
is literally 'a thicket providing shade,'
alluding to its many interlocked branches.

its top was among the thick boughs. The
topmost branch was not isolated but
encircled by leafy and thick boughs, a
feature which lends beauty and grandeur
to a tree. For the application, see on
xix. 11.

4. her rivers ran round about her plantation.
This rendering ignores the sign of the
accusative before *her rivers* and makes a
noun in the feminine plural the subject of
a verb in the masculine singular.
Kimchi translates: 'it (viz. the deep) led
her rivers round about her plantation,'
understanding *holech* as the equivalent of
holich (more strictly *holichah*). The
LXX construes similarly. The pronoun
in *her plantation* refers to *the deep*, the
subterranean reservoir of waters; i.e. the
plantation drew its nourishment from
there.

she sent out her conduits, etc. Following
the explanation just given, the text
means that the deep not only supplied the

5 Therefore its stature was exalted
Above all the trees of the field;
And its boughs were multiplied,
And its branches became long,
Because of the multitude of
  waters, when it shot them
  forth.

6 All the fowls of heaven made
Their nests in its boughs,
And all the beasts of the field did
  bring forth their young
Under its branches,
And under its shadow dwelt
All great nations.

7 Thus was it fair in its greatness,
In the length of its branches;
For its root was
By many waters.

8 The cedars in the garden of God
Could not hide it;
The cypress-trees were not
Like its boughs,

5 עַל־כֵּן֙ גָּבְהָ֣א קֹֽמָת֔וֹ
מִכֹּ֖ל עֲצֵ֣י הַשָּׂדֶ֑ה
וַתִּרְבֶּ֤ינָה סַרְעַפֹּתָיו֙
וַתֶּאֱרַ֣כְנָה פֹארֹתָ֔יו
מִמַּ֥יִם רַבִּ֖ים בְּשַׁלְּח֥וֹ׃
6 בִּסְעַפֹּתָ֣יו קִֽנְנ֗וּ
כָּל־ע֣וֹף הַשָּׁמַ֔יִם
וְתַ֤חַת פֹּֽארֹתָיו֙ יָֽלְד֔וּ
כֹּ֖ל חַיַּ֣ת הַשָּׂדֶ֑ה
וּבְצִלּוֹ֙ יֵֽשְׁב֔וּ
כֹּ֖ל גּוֹיִ֥ם רַבִּֽים׃
7 וַיְּ֣יף בְּגָדְל֔וֹ
בְּאֹ֖רֶךְ דָּלִיּוֹתָ֑יו
כִּֽי־הָיָ֥ה שָׁרְשׁ֖וֹ
אֶל־מַ֥יִם רַבִּֽים׃
8 אֲרָזִ֣ים לֹֽא־עֲמָמֻ֘הוּ֙
בְּגַן־אֱלֹהִ֔ים
בְּרוֹשִׁ֗ים
לֹ֤א דָמוּ֙ אֶל־סְעַפֹּתָ֔יו

v. 5. פארתיו ק v. 5. א׳ במקום ה׳

great rivers for the cedar, but also filled the smaller canals which nourished the other trees. In other words, Assyria received an exceptionally large supply from the deep as compared with the other nations and so its might was increased above theirs. This thought is elaborated in the next verse.

5. *when it shot them forth.* When the deep sent *the multitude of waters* forth to nourish the cedar.

6. *all the fowls . . . all the beasts.* These

are figures for the peoples which passed under Assyrian domination (cf. verse 12).

7. *in the length of its branches.* An allusion to Assyria's widespread conquests.

8. *in the garden of God.* The phrase here signifies the world (Rashi).

hide. Better, 'obscure' (see on xxviii. 3). There were other great nations in the world, compared with the cypress, etc., contemporaneous with Assyria, but she stood out pre-eminent among them.

And the plane-trees were not
As its branches;
Nor was any tree in the garden
of God
Like unto it in its beauty.

9 I made it fair
By the multitude of its branches;
So that all the trees of Eden,
That were in the garden of God,
envied it.

10. Therefore thus saith the
Lord GOD: Because thou art exalted
in stature, and he hath set his top
among the thick boughs, and his
heart is lifted up in his height;
11. I do even deliver him into the
hand of the mighty one of the
nations; he shall surely deal with
him; I do drive him out according
to his wickedness. 12. And
strangers, the terrible of the nations,
do cut him off, and cast him down;
upon the mountains and in all the
valleys his branches are fallen, and
his boughs lie broken in all the

וְעַרְמֹנִים לֹא־הָיוּ כִּפְאֹרֹתָיו
כָּל־עֵץ בְּגַן־אֱלֹהִים
לֹא־דָמָה אֵלָיו בְּיָפְיוֹ׃
9 יָפֶה עֲשִׂיתִיו
בְּרֹב דָּלִיּוֹתָיו
וַיְקַנְאֻהוּ כָּל־עֲצֵי־עֵדֶן
אֲשֶׁר בְּגַן הָאֱלֹהִים׃
10 לָכֵן כֹּה אָמַר אֲדֹנָי יְהֹוִה יַעַן
אֲשֶׁר גָּבַהְתָּ בְּקוֹמָה וַיִּתֵּן
צַמַּרְתּוֹ אֶל־בֵּין עֲבוֹתִים וְרָם
11 לְבָבוֹ בְּגָבְהוֹ׃ וְאֶתְּנֵהוּ בְּיַד
אֵל גּוֹיִם עָשׂוֹ יַעֲשֶׂה לוֹ בְּרִשְׁעוֹ
12 גֵּרַשְׁתִּיהוּ׃ וַיִּכְרְתֻהוּ זָרִים
עָרִיצֵי גוֹיִם וַיִּטְּשֻׁהוּ אֶל־
הֶהָרִים וּבְכָל־גֵּאָיוֹת נָפְלוּ
דָלִיּוֹתָיו וַתִּשָּׁבַרְנָה פֹארֹתָיו

9. *I made it fair.* The supreme position
held by Assyria was the work of God.

Eden . . . the garden of God. As in
xxviii. 13, but here descriptive of the
world which He had created.

10-14 DESTRUCTION OF ASSYRIAN
SUPREMACY

10. *thou.* Addressed to Assyria. The
sudden change from the second person
to the third in what follows is common in
Biblical style.

11. *the mighty one of the nations.* viz.
Nebuchadnezzar.

according to his wickedness. An alternative reading is: 'in his wickedness.'
The clause should probably be rendered:
'he (Nebuchadnezzar) shall deal with

him (Assyria) according to (or, in) his
wickedness; I (God) have driven him
out.' God has decreed Assyria's expulsion from His garden; as a mighty Power
it will vanish from the scene.

12. *strangers, the terrible of the nations.*
See on xxviii. 7.

do cut him off. The imagery of the cedar
is continued.

and cast him down. In the Hebrew the
verb is the same as *do leave him* at the
end of the verse and may be similarly
translated. The fallen cedar is left
abandoned as something useless.

his branches are fallen. Explained by the
Jewish commentators as the Assyrian
forces. Others consider them to be the
dependent States.

channels of the land; and all the peoples of the earth do go down from his shadow, and do leave him. 13. Upon his carcass all the fowls of the heaven do dwell, and upon his branches are all the beasts of the field; 14. to the end that none of all the trees by the waters exalt themselves in their stature, neither set their top among the thick boughs, nor that their mighty ones stand up in their height, even all that drink water; for they are all delivered unto death, to the nether parts of the earth, in the midst of the children of men, with them that go down to the pit.

15. Thus saith the Lord GOD: In the day when he went down to the nether-world I caused the deep to mourn and cover itself for him, and

בְּכָל־אֲפִיקֵי הָאָרֶץ וַיֵּרְדוּ
מִצִּלּוֹ כָּל־עַמֵּי הָאָרֶץ
13 וַיִּטְּשֻׁהוּ: עַל־מַפַּלְתּוֹ יִשְׁכְּנוּ
כָּל־עוֹף הַשָּׁמָיִם וְאֶל־
פֹּרֹאתָיו הָיוּ כֹּל חַיַּת הַשָּׂדֶה:
14 לְמַעַן אֲשֶׁר לֹא־יִגְבְּהוּ
בְקוֹמָתָם כָּל־עֲצֵי־מַיִם
וְלֹא־יִתְּנוּ אֶת־צַמַּרְתָּם
אֶל־בֵּין עֲבֹתִים וְלֹא־יַעַמְדוּ
אֵלֵיהֶם בְּגָבְהָם כָּל־שֹׁתֵי מָיִם
כִּי־כֻלָּם נִתְּנוּ לַמָּוֶת אֶל־אֶרֶץ
תַּחְתִּית בְּתוֹךְ בְּנֵי אָדָם אֶל־
15 יוֹרְדֵי בוֹר: כֹּה־אָמַר אֲדֹנָי
יֱהֹוִה בְּיוֹם רִדְתּוֹ שְׁאוֹלָה
הֶאֱבַלְתִּי כִּסֵּתִי עָלָיו אֶת־

v. 14. הא׳ בצרי

do leave him. Assyria's protection having ceased, her vassals desert her.

13. *fowls of the heaven . . . beasts of the field.* Not to be understood as in verse 6, but in a literal sense. The dead of Assyria will become food for birds and beasts of prey.

14. *to the end that*, etc. The fall of proud Assyria should act as a warning to the other nations who may be tempted to follow her example.

the trees by the waters. lit. 'the trees of water,' i.e. nourished by the waters of the deep.

all that drink water. Depend upon the deep as the source of sustenance, like Assyria. They, too, can be cut down and abandoned; so let them not be proud and over-confident.

they are all delivered unto death. Nations, like human beings, are mortal.

the nether parts of the earth. Sheol, the abode of the dead.

the pit. Another term for Sheol (cf. Ps. xvi. 10).

15-18 ASSYRIA'S FALL A WARNING TO EGYPT

15. *he went down.* The subject is Assyria. *The nether-world* is Sheol in the Hebrew. Cf. the scene described in Isa. xiv where the fallen king of Babylon descends to the nether-world.

I caused the deep to mourn, etc. The collapse of Assyria will cause a great upheaval in the world and fill it with consternation. In figurative language, even the deep is plunged into mourning by God and 'covered' (cf. *I will cover the sun with a cloud*, xxxii. 7).

I restrained the rivers thereof, and the great waters were stayed; and I caused Lebanon to mourn for him, and all the trees of the field fainted for him. 16. I made the nations to shake at the sound of his fall, when I cast him down to the nether-world with them that descend into the pit; and all the trees of Eden, the choice and best of Lebanon, all that drink water, were comforted in the nether parts of the earth. 17. They also went down into the nether-world with him unto them that are slain by the sword; yea, they that were his arm, that dwelt under his shadow in the midst of the nations.

18. To whom art thou thus like in glory and in greatness among the trees of Eden? yet shalt thou be brought down with the trees of Eden unto the nether parts of the earth; thou shalt lie in the midst of the uncircumcised, with them that

תְּהוֹם וָאֶמְנַע נַהֲרוֹתֶיהָ
וַיִּכָּלְאוּ מַיִם רַבִּים וָאַקְדִּר
עָלָיו לְבָנוֹן וְכָל־עֲצֵי הַשָּׂדֶה

16 עָלָיו עֻלְפֶּה: מִקּוֹל מַפַּלְתּוֹ
הִרְעַשְׁתִּי גוֹיִם בְּהוֹרִדִי אֹתוֹ
שְׁאֹלָה אֶת־יוֹרְדֵי בוֹר וַיִּנָּחֲמוּ
בְּאֶרֶץ תַּחְתִּית כָּל־עֲצֵי־
עֵדֶן מִבְחַר וְטוֹב־לְבָנוֹן כָּל־

17 שֹׁתֵי מָיִם: גַּם־הֵם אִתּוֹ יָרְדוּ
שְׁאֹלָה אֶל־חַלְלֵי־חָרֶב
וּזְרֹעוֹ יָשְׁבוּ בְצִלּוֹ בְּתוֹךְ גּוֹיִם:

18 אֶל־מִי דָמִיתָ כָּכָה בְּכָבוֹד
וּבְגֹדֶל בַּעֲצֵי־עֵדֶן וְהוֹרַדְתָּ
אֶת־עֲצֵי־עֵדֶן אֶל־אֶרֶץ
תַּחְתִּית בְּתוֹךְ עֲרֵלִים תִּשְׁכַּב

I restrained the rivers thereof. The rivers which *run round about her plantation* (verse 4) are now dried up. 'This deep which had nourished the great cedar is covered with mourning and paralysed by his fall; she is motionless, her waters congeal' (Davidson).

fainted. The Hebrew has the singular, indicating that each of them fainted. *Lebanon*, i.e. its cedars, etc., and *all the trees of the field*, represent other important nations of that time; they are overcome by fear for their own safety.

16. *I made the nations to shake*, etc. This explains the metaphor of the previous verse.

them that descend into the pit. As in verse 14.

trees of Eden. Cf. verse 9.

that drink water. That depend upon water for their life and growth.

were comforted in the nether parts of the earth. The nations whose glory and power lay in the past are comforted by the sight of Assyria joining their company (cf. Isa. xiv. 10 of Babylon).

17. *they also went down.* Referring to the *trees of Eden* (verse 16).

his arm. Assyria's allies.

that dwelt under his shadow. Cf. verses 6 and 12. With their protector gone, they suffer destruction.

18. *to whom art thou thus like*, etc. After describing the eminence and decline of Assyria, the prophet reverts to his theme of verse 2. If the giant cedar, Assyria, was cut down, can Egypt hope to escape?

in the midst of the uncircumcised. See on xxviii. 10.

are slain by the sword. This is Pharaoh and all his multitude, saith the Lord GOD.'

אֶת־חַלְלֵי־חֶרֶב הוּא פַּרְעֹה
וְכָל־הֲמוֹנֹה נְאֻם אֲדֹנָי יְהֹוִה:

| 32 | CHAPTER XXXII | לב |

1. And it came to pass in the twelfth year, in the twelfth month, in the first day of the month, that the word of the LORD came unto me, saying: 2. 'Son of man, take up a lamentation for Pharaoh king of Egypt, and say unto him:

> Thou didst liken thyself unto a young lion of the nations;
> Whereas thou art as a dragon in the seas;
> And thou didst gush forth with thy rivers,

1 וַיְהִי בִּשְׁתֵּי עֶשְׂרֵה שָׁנָה בִּשְׁנֵי־
עָשָׂר חֹדֶשׁ בְּאֶחָד לַחֹדֶשׁ הָיָה
2 דְבַר־יְהֹוָה אֵלַי לֵאמֹר: בֶּן־
אָדָם שָׂא קִינָה עַל־פַּרְעֹה
מֶלֶךְ־מִצְרַיִם וְאָמַרְתָּ אֵלָיו
כְּפִיר גּוֹיִם נִדְמֵיתָ
וְאַתָּה כַּתַּנִּים בַּיַּמִּים
וַתָּגַח בְּנַהֲרוֹתֶיךָ
וַתִּדְלַח־מַיִם בְּרַגְלֶיךָ

this is Pharaoh. The concluding words indicate that the oracle of the chapter is ultimately directed at Egypt.

CHAPTER XXXII
FINAL PROPHECY AGAINST EGYPT

THIS chapter, which concludes the section dealing with the judgment upon the nations, is dated about one year and a half after the fall of Jerusalem. Israel could now see how vain had been his trust in Egypt, and the prophetic warnings against an alliance with that country had received complete vindication. This realization lends colour and force to Ezekiel's prediction of Egypt's destruction. Babylon is to be used as the Divine instrument for the execution of judgment upon her. Her calamity will strike terror into the hearts of many peoples who will raise lamentations over her doom. The prophet himself utters a dirge over her ignominious end in Sheol where she finds other nations which suffered a similar fate. This chapter is described by Davidson as 'one of the most weird passages in literature.'

1-16 DIRGE OVER PHARAOH

1. *the twelfth year.* Reckoned from the beginning of Zedekiah's reign, the year 584 B.C.E.

2. *lamentation.* No feeling of pity is implied; it is a 'doom-song.'

whereas thou art as a dragon in the seas. Egyptian ambition made her think of herself as a lion roaming proudly among the nations and inspiring them with terror, whereas she was in fact like a crocodile (see on xxix. 3) whose domain is limited to the waters. Egypt dreamt of far-flung conquests; but she should have restricted herself to her own land.

thou didst gush forth with thy rivers. Or, 'in thy rivers.' The root-meaning of the verb is 'burst forth.' It may imply that Egypt's army used to break out beyond the national frontiers to subjugate neighbouring peoples. Lofthouse, on the other hand, explains it as 'blowing water from thy nostrils; a further suggestion of the careless pride of the crocodile, as the following words suggest his brutal destructiveness.'

And didst trouble the waters with
thy feet,
And foul their rivers.

3 Thus saith the Lord GOD:
I will therefore spread out My
net over thee
With a company of many
peoples;
And they shall bring thee up in
My net.

4 And I will cast thee upon the
land,
I will hurl thee upon the open
field,
And will cause all the fowls of
the heaven to settle upon thee,
And I will fill the beasts of the
whole earth with thee.

5 And I will lay thy flesh upon the
mountains,
And fill the valleys with thy
foulness.

6 I will also water with thy blood
the land wherein thou swimmest, even to the mountains;

וַתִּרְפֹּס נַהֲרֹתָם׃

3 כֹּה אָמַר אֲדֹנָי יֱהֹוִה
וּפָרַשְׂתִּי עָלֶיךָ אֶת־רִשְׁתִּי
בִּקְהַל עַמִּים רַבִּים
וְהֶעֱלוּךָ בְּחֶרְמִי׃

4 וּנְטַשְׁתִּיךָ בָאָרֶץ
עַל־פְּנֵי הַשָּׂדֶה אֲטִילֶךָ
וְהִשְׁכַּנְתִּי עָלֶיךָ
כָּל־עוֹף הַשָּׁמַיִם
וְהִשְׂבַּעְתִּי מִמְּךָ
חַיַּת כָּל־הָאָרֶץ׃

5 וְנָתַתִּי אֶת־בְּשָׂרְךָ
עַל־הֶהָרִים
וּמִלֵּאתִי הַגֵּאָיוֹת רָמוּתֶךָ׃

6 וְהִשְׁקֵיתִי אֶרֶץ צָפָתְךָ
מִדָּמְךָ אֶל־הֶהָרִים

---

didst trouble the waters. The crocodile
moved into rivers beyond the Nile,
churning up the waters and befouling
them.

3. *spread out My net.* Cf. xii. 13, xvii. 20.
God has decreed to put an end to the
crocodile's harmful activities by catching
it in His net.

with a company of many peoples. Babylon
and her allies (cf. verses 11f.).

4. *I will cast thee upon the land.* See on
xxix. 5.

all the fowls, etc. Cf. xxxi. 13.

5. *mountains . . . valleys.* Cf. xxxi. 12.
The meaning is probably that the
population will be dispersed and perish

in foreign lands, or the Egyptian warriors
will fall in battle there.

with thy foulness. This translation is
based on an alternative given by Rashi.
A.V. and R.V. render: 'with thy height,'
filled with the long carcase of the
crocodile. The second half of the verse
amplifies the thought of the first half.

6. *the land wherein thou swimmest.* A
designation for Egypt in which the Nile
overflowed and spread all over the
country. But the more probable translation is: 'I will give (the land) to drink
of thine out-flowing, (that is) from thy
blood, to the mountains.' The blood of
the slain will be poured out upon the
land.

And the channels shall be full of
   thee.

7 And when I shall extinguish thee,
    I will cover the heaven,
   And make the stars thereof black;
   I will cover the sun with a cloud,
   And the moon shall not give her
    light.

8 All the bright lights of heaven
   Will I make black over thee,
   And set darkness upon thy land,
   Saith the Lord GOD.

9. I will also vex the hearts of many peoples, when I shall bring thy destruction among the nations, into the countries which thou hast not known. 10. Yea, I will make many peoples appalled at thee, and their kings shall be horribly afraid for thee, when I shall brandish My sword before them; and they shall tremble at every moment, every man for his own life, in the day of thy fall.

11. For thus saith the Lord GOD:

וַאֲפִקִים יִמָּלְאוּן מִמֶּךָּ׃

7 וְכִסֵּיתִי בְכַבּֽוֹתְךָ שָׁמַיִם
וְהִקְדַּרְתִּי אֶת־כֹּכְבֵיהֶם
שֶׁמֶשׁ בֶּעָנָן אֲכַסֶּנּוּ
וְיָרֵחַ לֹא־יָאִיר אוֹרֽוֹ׃

8 כָּל־מְאוֹרֵי אוֹר בַּשָּׁמַיִם
אַקְדִּירֵם עָלֶיךָ
וְנָתַתִּי חֹשֶׁךְ עַל־אַרְצְךָ
נְאֻם אֲדֹנָי יְהוִֹה׃

9 וְהִכְעַסְתִּי לֵב עַמִּים רַבִּים
בַּהֲבִיאִי שִׁבְרְךָ בַּגּוֹיִם עַל־
אֲרָצוֹת אֲשֶׁר לֹא־יְדַעְתָּם׃

10 וַהֲשִׁמּוֹתִי עָלֶיךָ עַמִּים רַבִּים
וּמַלְכֵיהֶם יִשְׂעֲרוּ עָלֶיךָ שַׂעַר
בְּעוֹפְפִי חַרְבִּי עַל־פְּנֵיהֶם
וְחָרְדוּ לִרְגָעִים אִישׁ לְנַפְשׁוֹ

11 בְּיוֹם מַפַּלְתֶּךָ׃ כִּי כֹּה אָמַר

---

of thee. i.e. of thy blood.

7. *I shall extinguish thee.* According to the Jewish commentators, Egypt is compared to a great fire which, when extinguished, sends up a cloud of smoke obscuring the sky. Modern interpreters think rather of a star which is withdrawn from the heavens (cf. Isa. xiv. 12).

I will cover the heaven, etc. The day of Divine judgment is often described by the prophets as an occasion of darkness (cf. Isa. xiii. 10; Joel ii. 10; Amos viii. 9).

8. *bright lights.* lit. 'luminaries of light'; the heavenly bodies.

9. *vex the hearts.* i.e. terrify.

when I shall bring, etc. The sense is: 'when I cause the news of thy destruction to come among the nations.' The verb is employed similarly in Lev. xiv. 2, where *he shall be brought unto the priest* should be: 'it (the information about the condition of the leper) is communicated to the priest,' since the text continues, *And the priest shall go forth out of the camp* to make an examination.

into the countries which thou hast not known. The dismay aroused by Egypt's fall will be felt even in countries unknown to her.

10. *My sword.* viz. Babylon, the instrument of God's judgment, as explained in the next verse.

The sword of the king of Babylon shall come upon thee. 12. By the swords of the mighty will I cause thy multitude to fall;

The terrible of the nations are
they all;
And they shall spoil the pride of
Egypt,
And all the multitude thereof
shall be destroyed.

13 I will destroy also all the beasts
thereof
From beside many waters;
Neither shall the foot of man
trouble them any more,
Nor the hoofs of beasts trouble
them.

14 Then will I make their waters to
settle,
And cause their rivers to run like
oil,
Saith the Lord GOD.

15 When I shall make the land of
Egypt desolate and waste,
A land destitute of that whereof
it was full,
When I shall smite all them that
dwell therein,
Then shall they know that I am
the LORD.

16 This is the lamentation wherewith they shall lament;

אֲדֹנָי יֱהֹוִה חֶרֶב מֶלֶךְ־בָּבֶל

12 תְּבוֹאֶךָ: בְּחַרְבוֹת גִּבּוֹרִים
אַפִּיל הֲמוֹנֶךָ
עָרִיצֵי גוֹיִם כֻּלָּם
וְשָׁדְדוּ אֶת־גְּאוֹן מִצְרַיִם
וְנִשְׁמַד כָּל־הֲמוֹנָהּ:

13 וְהַאֲבַדְתִּי אֶת־כָּל־בְּהֶמְתָּהּ
מֵעַל מַיִם רַבִּים
וְלֹא תִדְלָחֶם רֶגֶל־אָדָם עוֹד
וּפַרְסוֹת בְּהֵמָה לֹא תִדְלָחֵם:

14 אָז אַשְׁקִיעַ מֵימֵיהֶם
וְנַהֲרוֹתָם כַּשֶּׁמֶן אוֹלִיךְ
נְאֻם אֲדֹנָי יֱהֹוִה:

15 בְּתִתִּי אֶת־אֶרֶץ מִצְרַיִם
שְׁמָמָה וּנְשַׁמָּה
אֶרֶץ מִמְּלֹאָהּ
בְּהַכּוֹתִי אֶת־כָּל־יוֹשְׁבֵי בָהּ
וְיָדְעוּ כִּי־אֲנִי יֱהֹוָה:

16 קִינָה הִיא וְקוֹנְנוּהָ

---

12. *the terrible of the nations.* A designation for the Babylonians (see on xxviii. 7).

13. *from beside many waters.* The cattle which used to feed along the banks of the Nile and beside the numerous canals in Egypt will no longer be there, because the desolation of the land will be complete.
foot of man trouble them, etc. The waters will not be stirred up by the foot of man or beast, because none will be left in the land.
any more. The Hebrew word *od* signifies here, as well as in other passages of Scripture, 'for a long time' (Kimchi).

14. *to settle . . . to run like oil.* As a result of the desolation, Egypt's waters will remain undisturbed and flow smoothly like a river of oil.

15. *and waste.* Against the accentuation Kimchi connects this with the clause that follows: 'and the country shall be desolated (destitute) of all that whereof it was full' (so A.V.). The next clause is literally '(the) land from its fulness' and is without a verb.

16. *this is the lamentation.* As in the beginning (verse 2), so at the conclusion

The daughters of the nations
shall lament therewith;
For Egypt, and for all her multitude, shall they lament therewith,
Saith the Lord GOD.'

17. It came to pass also in the
twelfth year, in the fifteenth day of
the month, that the word of the
LORD came unto me, saying: 18. 'Son
of man, wail for the multitude of
Egypt, and cast them down, even
her, with the daughters of the
mighty nations, unto the nether
parts of the earth, with them that
go down into the pit.

19. Whom dost thou pass in
beauty?
Go down, and be thou laid with
the uncircumcised.

בְּנוֹת הַגּוֹיִם תְּקוֹנֶנָּה אוֹתָהּ
עַל־מִצְרַיִם וְעַל־כָּל־
הֲמוֹנָהּ תְּקוֹנֶנָּה אוֹתָהּ
נְאֻם אֲדֹנָי יְהוִֹה׃

17 וַיְהִי בִּשְׁתֵּי עֶשְׂרֵה שָׁנָה
בַּחֲמִשָּׁה עָשָׂר לַחֹדֶשׁ הָיָה
18 דְבַר־יְהוָה אֵלַי לֵאמֹר׃ בֶּן־
אָדָם נְהֵה עַל־הֲמוֹן מִצְרַיִם
וְהוֹרִדֵהוּ אוֹתָהּ וּבְנוֹת גּוֹיִם
אַדִּרִם אֶל־אֶרֶץ תַּחְתִּיּוֹת
אֶת־יוֹרְדֵי בוֹר׃

19 מִמִּי נָעָמְתָּ
רְדָה וְהָשְׁכְּבָה אֶת־עֲרֵלִים׃

of the section, emphasis is laid upon the
nature of the oracle against Egypt.

the daughters. Women used to be
engaged professionally to wail (cf. Jer.
ix. 16).

17-32 DIRGE OVER THE NATION'S DESCENT TO SHEOL

'As a dirge over the nations of antiquity
nothing could be more striking than this
passage. In the last 150 years all the
great Powers in Ezekiel's world, except
one, had been successively flung down.
No such disasters had ever been crowded
into a similar period. Babylon herself,
though Ezekiel seems not to have
expected this, is shortly to fall with a
like crash. These sixteen verses are the
death-song of the world in which Israel
had grown up; in the new world, which
was to take its place, the nation of Israel
was to be replaced by the church of
Judaism' (Lofthouse).

17. *the twelfth year.* See on verse 1.

the fifteenth day of the month. Presumably the twelfth month as in verse 1,

so that there is an interval of a fortnight
between the two communications.

18. *cast them down.* The dirge is to be
uttered before the actual event had
occurred, and will have the effect of
bringing it about.

the daughters of the mighty nations. A
designation for other States and peoples
which experience a similar doom.

the nether parts of the earth. In the
shadowy existence which continues after
death in subterranean regions, the nations
are represented as preserving their
collective identity.

19. *whom dost thou pass in beauty?* The
text has the feminine since Egypt as a
nation is addressed. It changes to the
masculine when the king is intended.
The question implies: even if you were
superior to other great Powers, you will
not escape their fate.

go down. To Sheol, despite your having
surpassed them.

the uncircumcised. See on xxviii. 10.

20. They shall fall in the midst of them that are slain by the sword; she is delivered to the sword; draw her down and all her multitudes. 21. The strong among the mighty shall speak of him out of the midst of the nether-world with them that helped him; they are gone down, they lie still, even the uncircumcised, slain by the sword. 22. Asshur is there and all her company; their graves are round about them; all of them slain, fallen by the sword; 23. whose graves are set in the uttermost parts of the pit, and her company is round about her grave; all of them slain, fallen by the sword, who caused terror in the land of the living. 24. There is Elam and all her multitude round about her grave; all of them slain, fallen by the sword, who are gone down uncircumcised into the nether parts

20 בְּתוֹךְ חֲלָלֵי־חֶרֶב יִפֹּלוּ חֶרֶב
נִתָּנָה מָשְׁכוּ אוֹתָהּ וְכָל־
21 הֲמוֹנֶיהָ: יְדַבְּרוּ־לוֹ אֵלֵי
גִבּוֹרִים מִתּוֹךְ שְׁאוֹל אֶת־
עֹזְרָיו יָרְדוּ שָׁכְבוּ הָעֲרֵלִים
22 חַלְלֵי־חָרֶב: שָׁם אַשּׁוּר וְכָל־
קְהָלָהּ סְבִיבוֹתָיו קִבְרֹתָיו
כֻּלָּם חֲלָלִים הַנֹּפְלִים בֶּחָרֶב:
23 אֲשֶׁר נִתְּנוּ קִבְרֹתֶיהָ בְּיַרְכְּתֵי־
בוֹר וַיְהִי קְהָלָהּ סְבִיבוֹת
קְבֻרָתָהּ כֻּלָּם חֲלָלִים נֹפְלִים
בַּחֶרֶב אֲשֶׁר־נָתְנוּ חִתִּית
24 בְּאֶרֶץ חַיִּים: שָׁם עֵילָם וְכָל־
הֲמוֹנָהּ סְבִיבוֹת קְבֻרָתָהּ כֻּלָּם
חֲלָלִים הַנֹּפְלִים בַּחֶרֶב
אֲשֶׁר־יָרְדוּ עֲרֵלִים | אֶל־

v. 20. קמץ בז״ק

20. they shall fall. Referring to the Egyptians.

she is delivered to the sword. Or, 'the sword is extended,' lit. 'given.'

draw her down. The prophet is probably addressing the nations already in Sheol, exhorting them to drag Egypt down into their midst.

21. *shall speak of him.* Better, 'speak of him.' The leaders of the nations already in Sheol are represented as speaking about Pharaoh and his allies on their appearance in their midst, referring to them in the third person in the words that follow.

with them that helped him. The words are to be connected with *of him*, both being governed by *speak*.

they are gone down, etc. The Egyptians

have been reduced to the same condition as the rest of them.

22. *all her company.* The nations allied with Assyria.

their graves are round about them. lit. 'his graves are round about him,' which is variously explained as: the Egyptian dead around Assyria's or vice versa, the king surrounded by his dead warriors.

23. *in the uttermost parts of the pit.* i.e. very deep down in the pit where they are inaccessible. This describes their complete disappearance from the land of the living which they had terrorized (Kimchi).

24. *Elam.* Once a mighty Power, she became subordinated to Assyria. The prophet refers to the time when she was great and powerful.

of the earth, who caused their
terror in the land of the living; yet
have they borne their shame with
them that go down to the pit.
25. They have set her a bed in the
midst of the slain with all her
multitude; her graves are round
about them; all of them uncircumcised, slain by the sword; because
their terror was caused in the land
of the living, yet have they borne
their shame with them that go down
to the pit; they are put in the midst
of them that are slain. 26. There
is Meshech, Tubal, and all her
multitude; her graves are round
about them; all of them uncircumcised, slain by the sword; because
they caused their terror in the land
of the living. 27. And they that are
inferior to the uncircumcised shall
not lie with the mighty that are gone
down to the nether-world with their
weapons of war, whose swords are
laid under their heads, and whose
iniquities are upon their bones;
because the terror of the mighty was
in the land of the living. 28. But

אֶרֶץ תַּחְתִּיּוֹת אֲשֶׁר נָתְנוּ
חִתִּיתָם בְּאֶרֶץ חַיִּים וַיִּשְׂאוּ
כְלִמָּתָם אֶת־יוֹרְדֵי בוֹר׃
25 בְּתוֹךְ חֲלָלִים נָתְנוּ מִשְׁכָּב
לָהּ בְּכָל־הֲמוֹנָהּ סְבִיבוֹתָיו
קִבְרֹתֶהָ כֻּלָּם עֲרֵלִים חַלְלֵי־
חֶרֶב כִּי־נִתַּן חִתִּיתָם בְּאֶרֶץ
חַיִּים וַיִּשְׂאוּ כְלִמָּתָם אֶת־
יוֹרְדֵי בוֹר בְּתוֹךְ חֲלָלִים נִתָּן׃
26 שָׁם מֶשֶׁךְ תֻּבַל וְכָל־הֲמוֹנָהּ
סְבִיבוֹתָיו קִבְרוֹתֶיהָ כֻּלָּם
עֲרֵלִים מְחֻלְלֵי חֶרֶב כִּי־נָתְנוּ
27 חִתִּיתָם בְּאֶרֶץ חַיִּים׃ וְלֹא
יִשְׁכְּבוּ אֶת־גִּבּוֹרִים נֹפְלִים
מֵעֲרֵלִים אֲשֶׁר יָרְדוּ־שְׁאוֹל
בִּכְלֵי־מִלְחַמְתָּם וַיִּתְּנוּ אֶת־
חַרְבוֹתָם תַּחַת רָאשֵׁיהֶם וַתְּהִי
עֲוֺנֹתָם עַל־עַצְמוֹתָם כִּי־
חִתִּית גִּבּוֹרִים בְּאֶרֶץ חַיִּים׃

who caused their terror, etc. Cf. Isa.
xxii. 6 for Elam's military prowess. An
oracle against her is found in Jer. xlix.
35ff.

25. Much of this verse reproduces the
preceding. Lofthouse remarks: 'These
repetitions have a special and surprising
literary effectiveness.'

set her a bed in the midst of the slain.
Elam, because of her ruthless tyranny,
rests in shame with the other nations
which played a similar rôle.

26. Meshech, Tubal. See on xxvii. 13,
and cf. xxxviii. 2.

all her multitude. Referring to each of
the two peoples.

27. they that are inferior, etc. Meshech
and Tubal meet with a more humiliating
end than the other nations. The latter,
once warlike Powers, descend to Sheol
with their military equipment; but
Meshech and Tubal rest among those
stripped of their arms. It is not stated
what were their exceptional iniquities
which earned for them this special fate.

thou, in the midst of the uncircumcised shalt thou be broken and lie,
even with them that are slain by the
sword. 29. There is Edom, her
kings and all her princes, who for
all their might are laid with them
that are slain by the sword; they
shall lie with the uncircumcised, and
with them that go down to the pit.
30. There are the princes of the
north, all of them, and all the
Zidonians, who are gone down with
the slain, ashamed for all the terror
which they caused by their might,
and they lie uncircumcised with
them that are slain by the sword,
and bear their shame with them that
go down to the pit. 31. These shall
Pharaoh see, and shall be comforted
over all his multitude; even Pharaoh
and all his army, slain by the sword,
saith the Lord GOD. 32. For I have
put My terror in the land of the
living; and he shall be laid in the
midst of the uncircumcised, with
them that are slain by the sword,
even Pharaoh and all his multitude,
saith the Lord GOD.'

28 וְאַתָּה בְּתוֹךְ עֲרֵלִים תִּשָּׁבַר
וְתִשְׁכַּב אֶת־חַלְלֵי־חָרֶב:
29 שָׁמָּה אֱדוֹם מְלָכֶיהָ וְכָל־
נְשִׂיאֶיהָ אֲשֶׁר־נִתְּנוּ בִגְבוּרָתָם
אֶת־חַלְלֵי־חָרֶב הֵמָּה אֶת־
עֲרֵלִים יִשְׁכָּבוּ וְאֶת־יֹרְדֵי
30 בוֹר: שָׁמָּה נְסִיכֵי צָפוֹן כֻּלָּם
וְכָל־צִדֹנִי אֲשֶׁר־יָרְדוּ אֶת־
חֲלָלִים בְּחִתִּיתָם מִגְּבוּרָתָם
בּוֹשִׁים וַיִּשְׁכְּבוּ עֲרֵלִים אֶת־
חַלְלֵי־חֶרֶב וַיִּשְׂאוּ כְלִמָּתָם
31 אֶת־יוֹרְדֵי בוֹר: אוֹתָם יִרְאֶה
פַרְעֹה וְנִחַם עַל־כָּל־הֲמוֹנֹה
חַלְלֵי־חֶרֶב פַּרְעֹה וְכָל־
32 חֵילוֹ נְאֻם אֲדֹנָי יְהוִה: כִּי־
נָתַתִּי אֶת־חִתִּיתִי בְּאֶרֶץ חַיִּים
וְהֻשְׁכַּב בְּתוֹךְ עֲרֵלִים אֶת־
חַלְלֵי־חֶרֶב פַּרְעֹה וְכָל־
הֲמוֹנֹה נְאֻם אֲדֹנָי יְהוִה:

v. 28.   v. 30. הג׳ רפה   v. 32. חתיתי ק הב׳ בפתח

28. *thou.* i.e. Pharaoh.

even with them that are slain by the sword.
And apparently not *with the mighty,* etc.
described in the preceding verse.

29. *Edom.* See on xxv. 12.

kings . . . princes. Cf. Gen. xxxvi. 31ff.

30. *the princes of the north.* Ehrlich
agrees with Kimchi in interpreting the
phrase of the Babylonian satellite kings.
The prophet is then deliberately vague
because he was living in Babylon.

Many moderns understand it as the
rulers of Syria.

Zidonians. A general term for the
Phoenicians.

31. *shall be comforted.* In xxxi. 16 the
fallen nations derive comfort from
Egypt's eclipse; here Egypt finds con-
solation in the sight of others having
shared her doom.

32. *I have put My terror in the land of the
living.* Ultimately it is God's might
that prevails in the world. The *kethib*
reads 'his (Pharaoh's) terror.'

33 CHAPTER XXXIII לג

1. And the word of the LORD came unto me, saying: 2. 'Son of man, speak to the children of thy people, and say unto them: When I bring the sword upon a land, if the people of the land take a man from among them, and set him for their watchman; 3. if, when he seeth the sword come upon the land, he blow the horn, and warn the people; 4. then whosoever heareth the sound of the horn, and taketh not warning, if the sword come, and take him away, his blood shall be upon his own head;

1 וַיְהִי דְבַר־יְהוָֹה אֵלַי לֵאמֹר׃
2 בֶּן־אָדָם דַּבֵּר אֶל־בְּנֵי־
עַמְּךָ וְאָמַרְתָּ אֲלֵיהֶם אֶרֶץ
כִּי־אָבִיא עָלֶיהָ חָרֶב וְלָקְחוּ
עַם־הָאָרֶץ אִישׁ אֶחָד
מִקְצֵיהֶם וְנָתְנוּ אֹתוֹ לָהֶם
3 לְצֹפֶה׃ וְרָאָה אֶת־הַחֶרֶב
בָּאָה עַל־הָאָרֶץ וְתָקַע
בַּשּׁוֹפָר וְהִזְהִיר אֶת־הָעָם׃
4 וְשָׁמַע הַשֹּׁמֵעַ אֶת־קוֹל
הַשּׁוֹפָר וְלֹא נִזְהָר וַתָּבוֹא חֶרֶב
וַתִּקָּחֵהוּ דָּמוֹ בְרֹאשׁוֹ יִהְיֶה׃

CHAPTERS XXXIII-XXXIX

ISRAEL'S RESTORATION PREDICTED

CHAPTER XXXIII

WITH this chapter a new phase opens in Ezekiel's career. After announcing the doom of the heathen peoples, he reverts to the destiny of his own nation. But he no longer warns and threatens, because his predictions have become a tragic reality. He is now charged with the task of preparing the remnant of Israel for the coming restoration. As the root cause of Israel's calamity was sin, the prophet dwells again at length on its consequences, the responsibility which accompanies free will and the power of repentance. He opens the chapter by defining his rôle as that of a watchman in wartime whose duty is to warn his people of the approaching enemy, and concludes it with the assurance that, since his earlier prophecies had been fulfilled, his words will not now be disregarded.

1-9 THE PROPHET A WATCHMAN

2. *speak to the children of thy people.* Having delivered several prophecies against heathen nations, Ezekiel is now charged with the task of speaking again to his people.

when I bring the sword upon a land. God determines the fate of a land, whether it should have peace or war.

from among them. lit. 'from the end of them.' Ehrlich explains the word as meaning 'from the most worthy of them' and compares its use in Gen. xlvii. 2.

3. *he blow the horn.* The horn was sounded as a signal of alarm (cf. Amos iii. 6).

4. *his blood shall be upon his own head.* He is responsible for his death and no blame attaches to the watchman whose warning was ignored.

5. he heard the sound of the horn, and took not warning, his blood shall be upon him; whereas if he had taken warning, he would have delivered his soul. 6. But if the watchman see the sword come, and blow not the horn, and the people be not warned, and the sword do come, and take any person from among them, he is taken away in his iniquity, but his blood will I require at the watchman's hand.

7. So thou, son of man, I have set thee a watchman unto the house of Israel; therefore, when thou shalt hear the word at My mouth, warn them from Me. 8. When I say unto the wicked: O wicked man, thou shalt surely die, and thou dost not speak to warn the wicked from his way; that wicked man shall die in his iniquity, but his blood will I require at thy hand. 9. Nevertheless, if thou warn the wicked of his way to turn from it, and he turn not from his way; he shall die in his iniquity, but thou hast delivered thy soul.

10. Therefore, O thou son of man, say unto the house of Israel:

5 אֵת קוֹל הַשּׁוֹפָר שָׁמַע וְלֹא
נִזְהָר דָּמוֹ בּוֹ יִהְיֶה וְהוּא נִזְהָר
6 נַפְשׁוֹ מִלֵּט: וְהַצֹּפֶה כִּי־
יִרְאֶה אֶת־הַחֶרֶב בָּאָה
וְלֹא־תָקַע בַּשּׁוֹפָר וְהָעָם
לֹא־נִזְהָר וַתָּבוֹא חֶרֶב וַתִּקַּח
מֵהֶם נָפֶשׁ הוּא בַּעֲוֹנוֹ נִלְקָח
וְדָמוֹ מִיַּד־הַצֹּפֶה אֶדְרֹשׁ:
7 וְאַתָּה בֶן־אָדָם צֹפֶה נְתַתִּיךָ
לְבֵית יִשְׂרָאֵל וְשָׁמַעְתָּ מִפִּי
דָּבָר וְהִזְהַרְתָּ אֹתָם מִמֶּנִּי:
8 בְּאָמְרִי לָרָשָׁע רָשָׁע מוֹת
תָּמוּת וְלֹא דִבַּרְתָּ לְהַזְהִיר
רָשָׁע מִדַּרְכּוֹ הוּא רָשָׁע בַּעֲוֹנוֹ
יָמוּת וְדָמוֹ מִיָּדְךָ אֲבַקֵּשׁ:
9 וְאַתָּה כִּי־הִזְהַרְתָּ רָשָׁע
מִדַּרְכּוֹ לָשׁוּב מִמֶּנָּה וְלֹא־שָׁב
מִדַּרְכּוֹ הוּא בַּעֲוֹנוֹ יָמוּת וְאַתָּה
10 נַפְשְׁךָ הִצַּלְתָּ: וְאַתָּה בֶן־
אָדָם אֱמֹר אֶל־בֵּית יִשְׂרָאֵל

v. 6. קמץ בז״ק

---

5. *delivered his soul.* Saved his life.

6. *he is taken away in his iniquity.* Though he was worthy of death on account of his sins, nevertheless the watchman who had failed in his duty is held guilty by God of that man's violent end.

7. *so thou.* 'There is great dramatic force in this sudden application of the rule to the prophet' (Lofthouse).

when thou shalt hear the word at My mouth. The prophet's duty is comparable to that of a watchman. He must warn Israel of the danger which results from unrepented sin.

9. *thou hast delivered thy soul.* Ezekiel is then not held responsible, and being free from guilt will not be punished by God.

Thus ye speak, saying: Our transgressions and our sins are upon us, and we pine away in them; how then can we live? 11. Say unto them: As I live, saith the Lord GOD, I have no pleasure in the death of the wicked, but that the wicked turn from his way and live; turn ye, turn ye from your evil ways; for why will ye die, O house of Israel?

12. And thou, son of man, say unto the children of thy people: The righteousness of the righteous shall not deliver him in the day of his transgression; and as for the wickedness of the wicked, he shall not stumble thereby in the day that he turneth from his wickedness; neither shall he that is righteous be

כֵּן אֲמַרְתֶּם לֵאמֹר כִּי־
פְּשָׁעֵינוּ וְחַטֹּאתֵינוּ עָלֵינוּ וּבָם
אֲנַחְנוּ נְמַקִּים וְאֵיךְ נִחְיֶה:
11 אֱמֹר אֲלֵיהֶם חַי־אָנִי | נְאֻם |
אֲדֹנָי יֱהֹוִה אִם־אֶחְפֹּץ בְּמוֹת
הָרָשָׁע כִּי אִם־בְּשׁוּב רָשָׁע
מִדַּרְכּוֹ וְחָיָה שׁוּבוּ שׁוּבוּ
מִדַּרְכֵיכֶם הָרָעִים וְלָמָּה
12 תָמוּתוּ בֵּית יִשְׂרָאֵל: וְאַתָּה
בֶן־אָדָם אֱמֹר אֶל־בְּנֵי־
עַמְּךָ צִדְקַת הַצַּדִּיק לֹא
תַצִּילֶנּוּ בְּיוֹם פִּשְׁעוֹ וְרִשְׁעַת
הָרָשָׁע לֹא־יִכָּשֶׁל בָּהּ בְּיוֹם
שׁוּבוֹ מֵרִשְׁעוֹ וְצַדִּיק לֹא יוּכַל

10-20 ANSWER TO THE PEOPLE'S DESPAIR

10. thus ye speak. Kimchi renders: 'rightly do ye say,' giving *ken* the meaning it has in Num. xxvii. 7 and elsewhere. Your despondency is justified only as long as you cleave to your sins.

how then can we live? They now realized that their evil ways were the cause of their calamities, but they had not yet grasped the sublime doctrine that sincere repentance can expunge the punishment of sin.

11. I have no pleasure in the death of the wicked. Cf. xviii. 23. Unlike man who punishes his enemy for the sake of revenge, God's purpose in chastening the wicked is to move them to penitence and so escape the full consequences of their guilt.

for why will ye die, O house of Israel? That is not inevitable; the Divine decree can be averted by repentance.

12. the righteousness . . . day of his transgression. At first sight the verse seems to assert that a man's past is not taken into account by God Who judges him by his moral state at a particular moment. Davidson correctly interprets the passage as follows: 'His (Ezekiel's) purpose is to teach the general truth that the past of one's life does not of necessity determine the future either in itself or in the judgment of God. This, next to the assurance of God's gracious will regarding men (verse 11), was the truth most needed to comfort the people and awaken them out of the stupor which lay on them into a moral life and activity again.'

not stumble thereby. The penitent sinner will not suffer for his past wickedness.

able to live thereby in the day that he sinneth. 13. When I say to the righteous, that he shall surely live; if he trust to his righteousness, and commit iniquity, none of his righteous deeds shall be remembered; but for his iniquity that he hath committed, for it shall he die. 14. Again, when I say unto the wicked: Thou shalt surely die; if he turn from his sin, and do that which is lawful and right; 15. if the wicked restore the pledge, give back that which he had taken by robbery, walk in the statutes of life, committing no iniquity; he shall surely live, he shall not die. 16. None of his sins that he hath committed shall be remembered against him; he hath done that which is lawful and right; he shall surely live. 17. Yet the children of thy people say: The way of the Lord is not equal; but as for them, their way is not equal. 18. When the righteous turneth from his righteousness, and committeth iniquity, he shall even die thereby. 19. And when the wicked turneth from his wickedness, and doeth that which is lawful and right, he shall live thereby. 20. Yet ye say: The way of the Lord is not

לִֽחְי֣וֹת בָּ֔הּ בְּי֖וֹם חַטָּאתֽוֹ׃

13 בְּאָמְרִ֤י לַצַּדִּיק֙ חָיֹ֣ה יִֽחְיֶ֔ה וְהֽוּא־בָטַ֥ח עַל־צִדְקָת֖וֹ וְעָ֣שָׂה עָ֑וֶל כָּל־צִדְקֹתָיו֙ לֹ֣א תִזָּכַ֔רְנָה וּבְעַוְל֥וֹ אֲשֶׁר־עָשָׂ֖ה

14 בּ֥וֹ יָמֽוּת׃ וּבְאָמְרִ֣י לָֽרָשָׁ֔ע מ֥וֹת תָּמ֑וּת וְשָׁ֣ב מֵֽחַטָּאת֔וֹ

15 וְעָשָׂ֥ה מִשְׁפָּ֖ט וּצְדָקָֽה׃ חֲבֹ֨ל יָשִׁ֤יב רָשָׁע֙ גְּזֵלָ֣ה יְשַׁלֵּ֔ם בְּחֻקּ֤וֹת הַֽחַיִּים֙ הָלַ֔ךְ לְבִלְתִּ֖י עֲשׂ֣וֹת

16 עָ֑וֶל חָי֥וֹ יִֽחְיֶ֖ה לֹ֥א יָמֽוּת׃ כָּל־חַטֹּאתָו֙ אֲשֶׁ֣ר חָטָ֔א לֹ֥א תִזָּכַ֖רְנָה ל֑וֹ מִשְׁפָּ֧ט וּצְדָקָ֛ה

17 עָשָׂ֖ה חָי֥וֹ יִֽחְיֶֽה׃ וְאָמְרוּ֙ בְּנֵ֣י עַמְּךָ֔ לֹ֥א יִתָּכֵ֖ן דֶּ֣רֶךְ אֲדֹנָ֑י וְהֵ֖מָּה דַּרְכָּ֥ם לֹֽא־יִתָּכֵֽן׃

18 בְּשֽׁוּב־צַדִּ֥יק מִצִּדְקָת֖וֹ

19 וְעָ֣שָׂה עָ֑וֶל וּמֵ֖ת בָּהֶֽם׃ וּבְשׁ֣וּב רָשָׁ֗ע מֵֽרִשְׁעָתוֹ֙ וְעָשָׂ֣ה מִשְׁפָּ֣ט וּצְדָקָ֑ה עֲלֵיהֶ֖ם ה֥וּא יִֽחְיֶֽה׃

20 וַאֲמַרְתֶּ֕ם לֹ֥א יִתָּכֵ֖ן דֶּ֣רֶךְ אֲדֹנָ֑י

v. 13. צדקתיו ק׳   v. 16. חטאתיו ק׳

---

live thereby. Escape punishment for his sin by reason of his former righteousness.

13. *to the righteous.* Better, 'concerning the righteous'; similarly 'concerning the wicked' in the next verse.

none of his righteous deeds shall be remembered. See on xviii. 24.

14. *if he turn . . . lawful and right.* See on xviii. 27.

15. *if the wicked restore the pledge.* See on xviii. 7.

the statutes of life. The laws of God in general which prolong life.

he shall not die. As was previously determined by Divine judgment.

17. *the way of the Lord is not equal, etc.* See on xviii. 25.

18f. Cf. xviii. 26f.

equal. O house of Israel, I will judge you every one after his ways.'

21. And it came to pass in the twelfth year of our captivity, in the tenth month, in the fifth day of the month, that one that had escaped out of Jerusalem came unto me, saying: 'The city is smitten.' 22. Now the hand of the LORD had been upon me in the evening, before he that was escaped came; and He had opened my mouth against his coming to me in the morning; and my mouth was opened, and I was no more dumb. 23. Then the word of the LORD came unto me, saying: 24. 'Son of man, they that inhabit those waste places in the land of

אִישׁ כִּדְרָכָיו אֶשְׁפּוֹט אֶתְכֶם
בֵּית יִשְׂרָאֵל: וַיְהִי בִּשְׁתֵּי 21
עֶשְׂרֵה שָׁנָה בָּעֲשִׂרִי בַּחֲמִשָּׁה
לַחֹדֶשׁ לְגָלוּתֵנוּ בָּא־אֵלַי
הַפָּלִיט מִירוּשָׁלַםִ לֵאמֹר
הֻכְּתָה הָעִיר: וְיַד־יְהֹוָה 22
הָיְתָה אֵלַי בָּעֶרֶב לִפְנֵי בּוֹא
הַפָּלִיט וַיִּפְתַּח אֶת־פִּי עַד־
בּוֹא אֵלַי בַּבֹּקֶר וַיִּפָּתַח פִּי
וְלֹא נֶאֱלַמְתִּי עוֹד: וַיְהִי 23
דְּבַר־יְהֹוָה אֵלַי לֵאמֹר: בֶּן־ 24
אָדָם יֹשְׁבֵי הֶחֳרָבוֹת הָאֵלֶּה

---

20. *after his ways.* i.e. after his ways in the present.

21-29 NEWS OF JERUSALEM'S FALL REACHES EZEKIEL: HIS PROPHECY CONCERNING THE REMNANT IN JUDEA

21. *in the twelfth year of our captivity.* i.e. the captivity of Jehoiachin (i. 2) which began in 597 B.C.E. Apparently there was an interval of eighteen months before the news of the disaster reached Ezekiel in Babylon. Modern commentators consider this far too long and alter *twelfth* to 'eleventh,' which is the reading of some Hebrew MSS. and ancient versions. Metsudath David offers an explanation which overcomes the difficulty without altering M.T. The city fell in the fourth month of the eleventh year of Zedekiah (cf. Jer. xxxix. 2), i.e. Tammuz 586 B.C.E. But the Hebrew new year begins in Tishri, which is not the first but the seventh of the months. There is thus a dual system of reckoning: one which regards the year as a series of months beginning with Nisan in the spring, the other

regarding the year as a period beginning in the autumn on the first day of the seventh month. Accordingly, the interval between the fourth month in the eleventh year (586) and the tenth month in the twelfth year (585) is only six months.

22. *the hand of the LORD had been upon me.* See on i. 3.

He had opened my mouth. The silence imposed upon Ezekiel (cf. iii. 26f.) was removed by the arrival of the fugitive, as predicted in xxiv. 26f. The corroboration of the prophet's predictions established his authority as a messenger of God among the exiles, and he was now given permission to 'open his mouth' in a new series of exhortations to prepare them for the coming restoration.

against his coming. Rashi explains the text as 'before his coming,' i.e. on the evening before the fugitive's arrival Ezekiel was released from the bond of silence.

24. *they that inhabit those waste places.* viz. they who were left in the ruined

Israel speak, saying: Abraham was
one, and he inherited the land; but
we are many; the land is given us for
inheritance. 25. Wherefore say unto
them: Thus saith the Lord GOD:
Ye eat with the blood, and lift up
your eyes unto your idols, and shed
blood; and shall ye possess the
land? 26. Ye stand upon your
sword, ye work abomination, and ye
defile every one his neighbour's wife;
and shall ye possess the land?
27. Thus shalt thou say unto them:
Thus saith the Lord GOD: As I live,
surely they that are in the waste
places shall fall by the sword, and

עַל־אַדְמַת יִשְׂרָאֵל אֹמְרִים
לֵאמֹר אֶחָד הָיָה אַבְרָהָם
וַיִּירַשׁ אֶת־הָאָרֶץ וַאֲנַחְנוּ
רַבִּים לָנוּ נִתְּנָה הָאָרֶץ
25 לְמוֹרָשָׁה: לָכֵן אֱמֹר אֲלֵהֶם
כֹּה־אָמַר | אֲדֹנָי יְהֹוִה עַל־
הַדָּם | תֹּאכֵלוּ וְעֵינֵכֶם תִּשְׂאוּ
אֶל־גִּלּוּלֵיכֶם וְדָם תִּשְׁפֹּכוּ
26 וְהָאָרֶץ תִּירָשׁוּ: עֲמַדְתֶּם
עַל־חַרְבְּכֶם עֲשִׂיתֶן תּוֹעֵבָה
וְאִישׁ אֶת־אֵשֶׁת רֵעֵהוּ
טִמֵּאתֶם וְהָאָרֶץ תִּירָשׁוּ:
27 כֹּה־תֹאמַר אֲלֵהֶם כֹּה־אָמַר
אֲדֹנָי יְהֹוִה חַי־אָנִי אִם־לֹא
אֲשֶׁר בֶּחֳרָבוֹת בַּחֶרֶב יִפֹּלוּ

cities with Gedaliah as governor (2 Kings
xxv. 22).

Abraham was one. The survivors in the
land confidently hoped that they would
stay there permanently and form the
nucleus of the future Israel. Was not
the land given to one individual, the
patriarch Abraham? They were more
than one and dwelt on its soil; so how
greater was their claim to the land as his
heirs!

25. *wherefore say unto them.* Ezekiel
is commanded to utter a warning against
such confidence. Their hope would not
be fulfilled while they persisted in the
sins which had been the cause of the
national catastrophe.

ye eat with the blood. Kimchi and
Metsudath David understand the phrase
as a heathen practice of consuming the
flesh of a sacrificial animal while the
worshippers sat round its collected

blood (cf. Lev. xix. 26). Rashi interprets
the language figuratively: you murder
the rich and live on what you take from
them. Another possible explanation is
that they violated the law of Lev. iii. 17,
xvii. 10 by not removing the blood before
the flesh is eaten.

lift up your eyes unto your idols. See on
xviii. 6.

and shed blood. See on xxii. 9.

shall ye possess the land? The Holy Land
does not tolerate idolatry and bloodshed
within its borders. It was because of
such crimes that the original inhabitants,
the Canaanites, were cast out (cf. Lev.
xviii. 24ff.).

26. *ye stand upon your sword.* The sense
appears to be: you are constantly engaged
in acts of violence.

27. *in the waste places.* The inhabitants
of the towns devastated by the enemy

him that is in the open field will I give to the beasts to be devoured, and they that are in the strongholds and in the caves shall die of the pestilence. 28. And I will make the land most desolate, and the pride of her power shall cease; and the mountains of Israel shall be desolate, so that none shall pass through. 29. Then shall they know that I am the Lord, when I have made the land most desolate, because of all their abominations which they have committed.

30. And as for thee, son of man, the children of thy people that talk of thee by the walls and in the doors of the houses, and speak one to another, every one to his brother, saying: Come, I pray you, and hear what is the word that cometh forth from the Lord; 31. and come unto thee as the people cometh, and sit before thee as My people, and hear

וַאֲשֶׁר֙ עַל־פְּנֵ֣י הַשָּׂדֶ֔ה לַחַיָּ֥ה
נְתַתִּ֖יו לְאָכְל֑וֹ וַאֲשֶׁ֥ר בַּמְּצָד֛וֹת
וּבַמְּעָר֖וֹת בַּדֶּ֥בֶר יָמֽוּתוּ׃

28 וְנָתַתִּ֤י אֶת־הָאָ֨רֶץ֙ שְׁמָמָ֣ה
וּמְשַׁמָּ֔ה וְנִשְׁבַּ֖ת גְּא֣וֹן עֻזָּ֑הּ
וְשָֽׁמְמ֛וּ הָרֵ֥י יִשְׂרָאֵ֖ל מֵאֵ֥ין

29 עוֹבֵֽר׃ וְיָדְע֖וּ כִּֽי־אֲנִ֣י יְהֹוָ֑ה
בְּתִתִּ֤י אֶת־הָאָ֨רֶץ֙ שְׁמָמָ֣ה
וּמְשַׁמָּ֔ה עַ֥ל כָּל־תּוֹעֲבֹתָ֖ם

30 אֲשֶׁ֥ר עָשֽׂוּ׃ וְאַתָּ֣ה בֶן־אָדָ֗ם
בְּנֵ֤י עַמְּךָ֙ הַנִּדְבָּרִ֣ים בְּךָ֔ אֵ֣צֶל
הַקִּיר֖וֹת וּבְפִתְחֵ֣י הַבָּתִּ֑ים
וְדִבֶּר־חַ֣ד אֶת־אַחַ֗ד אִ֤ישׁ
אֶת־אָחִיו֙ לֵאמֹ֔ר בֹּֽאוּ־נָ֣א
וְשִׁמְע֔וּ מָ֣ה הַדָּבָ֔ר הַיּוֹצֵ֖א מֵאֵ֥ת

31 יְהֹוָֽה׃ וְיָב֣וֹאוּ אֵלֶ֗יךָ כִּמְבוֹא־
עָ֜ם וְיֵשְׁב֤וּ לְפָנֶ֨יךָ֙ עַמִּ֔י וְשָֽׁמְע֣וּ

will be included in the work of destruction.

in the open field. They who fled from the cities before the arrival of the troops will not escape, but be devoured by beasts of prey.

shall die of the pestilence. Which is the effect of overcrowding and underfeeding.

30-33 THE EXILES' ATTITUDE TO EZEKIEL

30. *that talk of thee.* The Jewish commentators understand this to mean that the Judean exiles spoke about Ezekiel in hostile and malicious tones. It is more probable that by the event, he became the topic of conversation among them and they discussed his sayings.

by the walls. Where shade was to be found from the sun's heat.

in the doors of the houses. A natural place for small groups to gather and converse.

what is the word that cometh forth from the LORD. They displayed curiosity to know what his message was, but not a desire to act upon it.

31. *as the people cometh.* They come to the prophet to hear his words, ostensibly to receive instruction in the will of God.

as My people. There is nothing to correspond to *as* in the text, but it has to be supplied: as though they were in fact God's people eager to learn and obey His laws.

thy words, but do them not—for with their mouth they show much love, but their heart goeth after their covetousness; 32. and, lo, thou art unto them as a love song of one that hath a pleasant voice, and can play well on an instrument; so they hear thy words, but they do them not— 33. when this cometh to pass— behold, it cometh—then shall they know that a prophet hath been among them.'

אֶת־דְּבָרֶיךָ וְאוֹתָם לֹא יַעֲשׂוּ כִּי־עֲגָבִים בְּפִיהֶם הֵמָּה עֹשִׂים אַחֲרֵי בִצְעָם לִבָּם הֹלֵךְ: 32 וְהִנְּךָ לָהֶם כְּשִׁיר עֲגָבִים יְפֵה קוֹל וּמֵטִב נַגֵּן וְשָׁמְעוּ אֶת־דְּבָרֶיךָ וְעֹשִׂים 33 אֵינָם אוֹתָם: וּבְבֹאָהּ הִנֵּה בָאָה וְיָדְעוּ כִּי נָבִיא הָיָה בְתוֹכָם:

34   CHAPTER XXXIV   לד

1. And the word of the LORD came unto me, saying: 2. 'Son of man, prophesy against the shepherds of Israel, prophesy, and say unto them,

1 וַיְהִי דְבַר־יְהֹוָה אֵלַי לֵאמֹר: 2 בֶּן־אָדָם הִנָּבֵא עַל־רוֹעֵי יִשְׂרָאֵל הִנָּבֵא וְאָמַרְתָּ אֲלֵיהֶם

with their mouth they show much love. They speak with admiration of the prophet's discourse, but in their hearts are thoughts of self-interest which conflict with the principles he expressed.

32. *thou art unto them as a love song.* The hearers were attracted by the beauty of his language, and listened to him only as one does to an entertainer. His exhortation made no impression upon them.

33. *when this cometh to pass.* When *all* the predictions have been fulfilled, they will realize that his words were not just fine oratory, but true prophecy.

CHAPTER XXXIV
PAST SELFISH SHEPHERDS AND FUTURE IDEAL SHEPHERDS

As a prerequisite to Israel's recovery and regeneration, the former corrupt and selfish leaders must be replaced by conscientious and noble rulers. Hence the prophet's first message in his programme of reconstruction is devoted to Israel's past and future governors. God Himself will intervene on behalf of His flock. He will gather them from among the nations and bring them back to their homeland. A scion of the house of David, a just and ideal ruler, will reign over them; then they will enjoy prosperity, security and peace. With this chapter, Jer. xxiii. 1-8 may be compared.

1-10 THE EVIL SHEPHERDS

2. *the shepherds of Israel.* The allusion is to the kings, princes and leaders. The earliest occurrence of this metaphor of shepherd and flock to signify leader and people is in the plea of Moses: *that the congregation of the LORD be not as sheep which have no shepherd* (Num. xxvii. 17). *that have fed themselves.* Instead of

even to the shepherds: Thus saith
the Lord GOD: Woe unto the
shepherds of Israel that have fed
themselves! should not the shepherds
feed the sheep? 3. Ye did eat the
fat, and ye clothed you with the
wool, ye killed the fatlings; but ye
fed not the sheep. 4. The weak
have ye not strengthened, neither
have ye healed that which was sick,
neither have ye bound up that which
was broken, neither have ye brought
back that which was driven away,
neither have ye sought that which
was lost; but with force have ye
ruled over them and with rigour.
5. So were they scattered, because
there was no shepherd; and they
became food to all the beasts of the
field, and were scattered. 6. My
sheep wandered through all the
mountains, and upon every high
hill; yea, upon all the face of the

לָרֹעִים כֹּה־אָמַר ׀ אֲדֹנָי יֱהֹוִֹה
הוֹי רֹעֵי יִשְׂרָאֵל אֲשֶׁר הָיוּ
רֹעִים אוֹתָם הֲלוֹא הַצֹּאן יִרְעוּ
הָרֹעִים׃ אֶת־הַחֵלֶב 3
תֹּאכֵלוּ וְאֶת־הַצֶּמֶר
תִּלְבָּשׁוּ הַבְּרִיאָה תִּזְבָּחוּ
הַצֹּאן לֹא תִרְעוּ׃ אֶת־ 4
הַנַּחְלוֹת לֹא חִזַּקְתֶּם וְאֶת־
הַחוֹלָה לֹא־רִפֵּאתֶם
וְלַנִּשְׁבֶּרֶת לֹא חֲבַשְׁתֶּם וְאֶת־
הַנִּדַּחַת לֹא הֲשֵׁבֹתֶם וְאֶת־
הָאֹבֶדֶת לֹא בִקַּשְׁתֶּם וּבְחָזְקָה
רְדִיתֶם אֹתָם וּבְפָרֶךְ׃
וַתְּפוּצֶינָה מִבְּלִי רֹעֶה 5
וַתִּהְיֶינָה לְאָכְלָה לְכָל־
חַיַּת הַשָּׂדֶה וַתְּפוּצֶינָה׃ יִשְׁגּוּ 6
צֹאנִי בְּכָל־הֶהָרִים וְעַל כָּל־
גִּבְעָה רָמָה וְעַל כָּל־פְּנֵי

v. 3. קמץ בז״ק

---

promoting the welfare of the people and
safeguarding their interests, their aim was
to enrich themselves at the expense of the
masses.

3. *but ye fed not the sheep.* The only
concern of the rulers was to increase their
possessions by extortionate demands and
acts of injustice. Even after having
pandered to their greed, they gave no
thought to the needs of the masses.

4. *weak . . . sick . . . driven away . . .
lost.* The last word is better translated
'strayed.' All these terms have the
feminine form, since they apply to classes

of sheep which need extra care from a
shepherd. They correspond to the poor,
oppressed, widows, orphans, etc. among
the population.

with force have ye ruled over them. Not
with consideration and justice.

5. *they became food to all the beasts of the
field.* Unprotected by their rulers, the
people became the prey of neighbouring
peoples.

and were scattered. As sheep flee in all
directions when attacked by a beast of
prey, so was the population dispersed
through the inroads upon them.

229

earth were My sheep scattered, and there was none that did search or seek. 7. Therefore, ye shepherds, hear the word of the LORD: 8. As I live, saith the Lord GOD, surely forasmuch as My sheep became a prey, and My sheep became food to all the beasts of the field, because there was no shepherd, neither did My shepherds search for My sheep, but the shepherds fed themselves, and fed not My sheep; 9. therefore, ye shepherds, hear the word of the LORD: 10. Thus saith the Lord GOD: Behold, I am against the shepherds; and I will require My sheep at their hand, and cause them to cease from feeding the sheep; neither shall the shepherds feed themselves any more; and I will deliver My sheep from their mouth, that they may not be food for them.

11. For thus saith the Lord GOD: Behold, here am I, and I will search for My sheep, and seek them out. 12. As a shepherd seeketh out his

הָאָרֶץ נָפֹצוּ צֹאנִי וְאֵין דּוֹרֵשׁ
7 וְאֵין מְבַקֵּשׁ: לָכֵן רֹעִים שִׁמְעוּ
8 אֶת־דְּבַר יְהֹוָה: חַי־אָנִי
נְאֻם | אֲדֹנָי יֱהֹוִה אִם־לֹא יַעַן
הֱיוֹת־צֹאנִי | לָבַז וַתִּהְיֶינָה
צֹאנִי לְאָכְלָה לְכָל־חַיַּת
הַשָּׂדֶה מֵאֵין רֹעֶה וְלֹא־דָרְשׁוּ
רֹעַי אֶת־צֹאנִי וַיִּרְעוּ הָרֹעִים
אוֹתָם וְאֶת־צֹאנִי לֹא רָעוּ:
9 לָכֵן הָרֹעִים שִׁמְעוּ דְבַר־־
10 יְהֹוָה: כֹּה־־אָמַר אֲדֹנָי יֱהֹוִה
הִנְנִי אֶל־־הָרֹעִים וְדָרַשְׁתִּי
אֶת־צֹאנִי מִיָּדָם וְהִשְׁבַּתִּים
מֵרְעוֹת צֹאן וְלֹא־יִרְעוּ עוֹד
הָרֹעִים אוֹתָם וְהִצַּלְתִּי צֹאנִי
מִפִּיהֶם וְלֹא־תִהְיֶיןָ לָהֶם
11 לְאָכְלָה: כִּי כֹּה אָמַר אֲדֹנָי
יֱהֹוִה הִנְנִי־אָנִי וְדָרַשְׁתִּי אֶת־
12 צֹאנִי וּבִקַּרְתִּים: כְּבַקָּרַת

6. *there was none that did search or seek.* The leaders proved useless in the national crisis. They could not rally their people who fled in panic to hide in the mountains and hills from the invader.

8. *My shepherds.* Since the people of Israel is *My sheep*, the rulers are described as *My shepherds*, perhaps with the implication 'they are answerable to Me' (cf. verse 10).

9. *therefore, ye shepherds.* A repetition of verse 7 for solemn emphasis.

10. *I will require My sheep at their hand.*

God will hold the shepherds to account for the loss of the flock.

cause them to cease from feeding the sheep. Their status as rulers will be brought to an end.

I will deliver . . . mouth. The extortionate governors are scathingly described as beasts of prey.

11-22 GOD WILL BE THEIR SHEPHERD

11. *here am I.* Having dismissed the unfaithful herdsmen, God Himself will assume the rôle of shepherd.

flock in the day that he is among his
sheep that are separated, so will
I seek out My sheep; and I will
deliver them out of all places whither
they have been scattered in the day
of clouds and thick darkness.
13. And I will bring them out from
the peoples, and gather them from
the countries, and will bring them
into their own land; and I will feed
them upon the mountains of Israel,
by the streams, and in all the
habitable places of the country.
14. I will feed them in a good
pasture, and upon the high mountains of Israel shall their fold be;
there shall they lie down in a good
fold, and in a fat pasture shall they
feed upon the mountains of Israel.
15. I will feed My sheep, and I will
cause them to lie down, saith the
Lord GOD. 16. I will seek that
which was lost, and will bring back
that which was driven away, and
will bind up that which was broken,

רֹעֶה עֶדְרוֹ בְּיוֹם הֱיוֹתוֹ
בְתוֹךְ־צֹאנוֹ נִפְרָשׁוֹת כֵּן
אֲבַקֵּר אֶת־צֹאנִי וְהִצַּלְתִּי
אֶתְהֶם מִכָּל־הַמְּקוֹמֹת
אֲשֶׁר־נָפֹצוּ שָׁם בְּיוֹם עָנָן
13 וַעֲרָפֶל׃ וְהוֹצֵאתִים מִן־
הָעַמִּים וְקִבַּצְתִּים מִן־
הָאֲרָצוֹת וַהֲבִיאוֹתִים אֶל־
אַדְמָתָם וּרְעִיתִים אֶל־הָרֵי
יִשְׂרָאֵל בָּאֲפִיקִים וּבְכֹל
14 מוֹשְׁבֵי הָאָרֶץ׃ בְּמִרְעֶה־
טוֹב אֶרְעֶה אֹתָם וּבְהָרֵי
מְרוֹם־יִשְׂרָאֵל יִהְיֶה נְוֵהֶם שָׁם
תִּרְבַּצְנָה בְּנָוֶה טּוֹב וּמִרְעֶה
שָׁמֵן תִּרְעֶינָה אֶל־הָרֵי
15 יִשְׂרָאֵל׃ אֲנִי אֶרְעֶה צֹאנִי
וַאֲנִי אַרְבִּיצֵם נְאֻם אֲדֹנָי יֱהֹוִה׃
16 אֶת־הָאֹבֶדֶת אֲבַקֵּשׁ וְאֶת־
הַנִּדַּחַת אָשִׁיב וְלַנִּשְׁבֶּרֶת

12. *among his sheep that are separated.*
As the shepherd goes in search of
strayed sheep, so will God seek out His
dispersed flock. Ehrlich connects
niphrashoth with a similar root in Arabic
meaning 'torn (by wild beasts)'; the
interpretation will then be: as a shepherd
makes an examination of his flock after
an attack to discover which have been
injured.

clouds and thick darkness. Symbolic of
calamity.

13. *I will feed them,* etc. Under God's

care, Israel will, on his return to his
homeland, be well fed.

14. *upon the high mountains.* The hills
of Palestine are now mostly barren as
the effect of centuries of neglect in which
the top soil has been washed away, but
in ancient times they were fertile areas.

15. *I will feed . . . cause them to lie down.*
A dutiful shepherd watches over his
flock both when the sheep are feeding
and when they lie down to rest.

16. *I will seek,* etc. In contrast to what
is described in verse 4.

and will strengthen that which was sick; and the fat and the strong I will destroy, I will feed them in justice. 17. And as for you, O My flock, thus saith the Lord GOD: Behold, I judge between cattle and cattle, even the rams and the he-goats. 18. Seemeth it a small thing unto you to have fed upon the good pasture, but ye must tread down with your feet the residue of your pasture? and to have drunk of the settled waters, but ye must foul the residue with your feet? 19. And as for My sheep, they eat that which ye have trodden with your feet, and they drink that which ye have fouled with your feet.

20. Therefore thus saith the Lord GOD unto them: Behold, I, even I, will judge between the fat cattle and the lean cattle. 21. Because ye thrust with side and with shoulder,

אֶחֱבֹשׁ וְאֶת־הַחוֹלָה אֲחַזֵּק
וְאֶת־הַשְּׁמֵנָה וְאֶת־הַחֲזָקָה
אַשְׁמִיד אֶרְעֶנָּה בְמִשְׁפָּט׃
17 וְאַתֵּנָה צֹאנִי כֹּה אָמַר אֲדֹנָי
יֱהֹוִה הִנְנִי שֹׁפֵט בֵּין־שֶׂה לָשֶׂה
18 לָאֵילִים וְלָעַתּוּדִים׃ הַמְעַט
מִכֶּם הַמִּרְעֶה הַטּוֹב תִּרְעוּ
וְיֶתֶר מִרְעֵיכֶם תִּרְמְסוּ
בְּרַגְלֵיכֶם וּמִשְׁקַע־מַיִם
תִּשְׁתּוּ וְאֵת הַנּוֹתָרִים
19 בְּרַגְלֵיכֶם תִּרְפֹּשׂוּן׃ וְצֹאנִי
מִרְמַס רַגְלֵיכֶם תִּרְעֶינָה
וּמִרְפַּשׂ רַגְלֵיכֶם תִּשְׁתֶּינָה׃
20 לָכֵן כֹּה אָמַר אֲדֹנָי יֱהֹוִה
אֲלֵיהֶם הִנְנִי־אָנִי וְשָׁפַטְתִּי
בֵּין־שֶׂה בִרְיָה וּבֵין שֶׂה רָזָה׃
21 יַעַן בְּצַד וּבְכָתֵף תֶּהְדֹּפוּ

I will destroy. The ancient versions read *eshmor* (I will guard) for *ashmid*, and most moderns emend accordingly. But, as Lofthouse remarks, 'The thought is now passing from the shepherds to the sheep; of tle latter, those who have misused their strength are to be punished like the former. God does not act like other shepherds nor like the kings who favour the strong and rich.'

I will feed them in justice. God will also take care of them; they will receive their deserts at His hand.

17. *between cattle and cattle.* God will judge between the oppressed poor and their rich oppressors.

the rams and the he-goats. These are the **strong** among the flock which push the others aside at the time of grazing: a figure for the unscrupulous powerful members of the nation.

18. *seemeth it a small thing unto you.* The *rams and the he-goats,* i.e. the ruling classes, are addressed. The charge against them is twofold: not only did they appropriate the best for themselves but they spoiled what was left over which could have been of benefit to the rest.

19. *as for My sheep.* i.e. the weak and helpless whose rights had been violated by the powerful.

20. *the fat cattle and the lean cattle.* See on verse 17.

21. *side . . . shoulder . . . horns.* These denote the exercise of brute force.

and push all the weak with your horns, till ye have scattered them abroad; 22. therefore will I save My flock, and they shall no more be a prey; and I will judge between cattle and cattle. 23. And I will set up one shepherd over them, and he shall feed them, even My servant David; he shall feed them, and he shall be their shepherd. 24. And I the LORD will be their God, and My servant David prince among them; I the LORD have spoken. 25. And I will make with them a covenant of peace, and will cause evil beasts to cease out of the land; and they shall dwell safely in the wilderness, and sleep in the woods. 26. And I will make them and the places round about My hill a blessing; and I will

וּבְקַרְנֵיכֶם תְּנַגְּחוּ כָּל־
הַנַּחְלוֹת עַד אֲשֶׁר הֲפִיצוֹתֶם
אוֹתָנָה אֶל־הַחוּצָה:
22 וְהוֹשַׁעְתִּי לְצֹאנִי וְלֹא־
תִהְיֶינָה עוֹד לָבַז וְשָׁפַטְתִּי בֵּין
23 שֶׂה לָשֶׂה: וַהֲקִמֹתִי עֲלֵיהֶם
רֹעֶה אֶחָד וְרָעָה אֶתְהֶן אֵת
עַבְדִּי דָוִיד הוּא יִרְעֶה אֹתָם
24 וְהוּא יִהְיֶה לָהֶן לְרֹעֶה: וַאֲנִי
יְהֹוָה אֶהְיֶה לָהֶם לֵאלֹהִים
וְעַבְדִּי דָוִד נָשִׂיא בְתוֹכָם אֲנִי
25 יְהֹוָה דִּבַּרְתִּי: וְכָרַתִּי לָהֶם
בְּרִית שָׁלוֹם וְהִשְׁבַּתִּי חַיָּה־
רָעָה מִן־הָאָרֶץ וְיָשְׁבוּ
בַמִּדְבָּר לָבֶטַח וְיָשְׁנוּ
26 בַיְּעָרִים: וְנָתַתִּי אוֹתָם
וּסְבִיבוֹת גִּבְעָתִי בְּרָכָה

ביערים ק' v. 25.

22. *My flock.* The same Hebrew word as *My sheep* in verse 19 with the same definition.

23-31 APPOINTMENT OF AN IDEAL
SHEPHERD OVER THE NATION

23. *one shepherd . . . My servant David.* The allusion is to the Messianic age. The sufferings caused by unjust rulers having ended by the intervention of God, Israel will enjoy peace and prosperity under the sway of an ideal shepherd, of whom David is the prototype.

24. *I the LORD will be their God,* etc. The acceptance of the Sovereignty of God will precede the rule of the Messianic prince.

25. *a covenant of peace.* The new covenant will ensure peace and security from all hostile forces. The *evil beasts* may be interpreted figuratively of bad rulers and aggressive neighbours or literally (cf. xiv. 15).

wilderness . . . woods. Normally these are the places where wild beasts roam and are dangerous to human beings. Under the new covenant they will become safe (cf. Hos. ii. 20).

26. *I will make them . . . a blessing.* Israel, now regathered in the Holy Land round about God's *hill* (Zion), will be blessed with what He provides for the people.

233

cause the shower to come down in its season; there shall be showers of blessing. 27. And the tree of the field shall yield its fruit, and the earth shall yield her produce, and they shall be safe in their land; and they shall know that I am the LORD, when I have broken the bars of their yoke, and have delivered them out of the hand of those that made bondmen of them. 28. And they shall no more be a prey to the nations, neither shall the beast of the earth devour them; but they shall dwell safely, and none shall make them afraid. 29. And I will raise up unto them a plantation for renown, and they shall be no more consumed with hunger in the land, neither bear the shame of the nations any more. 30. And they shall know that I the LORD their God am with them, and that they, the house of Israel, are My people, saith the Lord GOD. 31. And ye My sheep, the sheep of My pasture, are men, and I am your God, saith the Lord GOD.'

וְהוֹרַדְתִּי הַגֶּשֶׁם בְּעִתּוֹ גִּשְׁמֵי
27 בְרָכָה יִהְיוּ: וְנָתַן עֵץ הַשָּׂדֶה
אֶת־פִּרְיוֹ וְהָאָרֶץ תִּתֵּן יְבוּלָהּ
וְהָיוּ עַל־אַדְמָתָם לָבֶטַח
וְיָדְעוּ כִּי־אֲנִי יְהֹוָה בְּשִׁבְרִי
אֶת־מֹטוֹת עֻלָּם וְהִצַּלְתִּים
28 מִיַּד הָעֹבְדִים בָּהֶם: וְלֹא־
יִהְיוּ עוֹד בַּז לַגּוֹיִם וְחַיַּת
הָאָרֶץ לֹא תֹאכְלֵם וְיָשְׁבוּ
29 לָבֶטַח וְאֵין מַחֲרִיד: וַהֲקִמֹתִי
לָהֶם מַטָּע לְשֵׁם וְלֹא־יִהְיוּ
עוֹד אֲסֻפֵי רָעָב בָּאָרֶץ וְלֹא־
יִשְׂאוּ עוֹד כְּלִמַּת הַגּוֹיִם:
30 וְיָדְעוּ כִּי־אֲנִי יְהֹוָה אֱלֹהֵיהֶם
אִתָּם וְהֵמָּה עַמִּי בֵּית יִשְׂרָאֵל
31 נְאֻם אֲדֹנָי יֱהֹוִה: וְאַתֵּן צֹאנִי
צֹאן מַרְעִיתִי אָדָם אַתֶּם אֲנִי
אֱלֹהֵיכֶם נְאֻם אֲדֹנָי יֱהֹוִה:

showers of blessing. i.e. showers which bring blessing in the form of abundant harvests.

27. *the bars of their yoke.* Their servitude in captivity.

28. *neither shall the beast of the earth devour them.* The figure of the flock is continued.

29. *a plantation for renown.* The Land of Israel will be famed far and wide for its extraordinary fertility.

neither bear the shame of the nations any more. The inhabitants of the Holy Land will no more suffer the humiliation of having to look to other nations for material assistance.

31. *are men.* When Israel acknowledges God, then He treats him as a human being and not as an animal, although he is designated *sheep.* So the verse is explained by some Jewish commentators. Kimchi's interpretation is: only if one follows the teachings of the Torah does he deserve the description of *man.* This way of explaining the words hardly suits the context. An alternative is: 'Ye are My flock, nay, ye are more, ye are *Adam* (so the Hebrew), My special creation of old' (Barnes).

35   CHAPTER XXXV   לה

1. Moreover the word of the LORD came unto me, saying: 2. 'Son of man, set thy face against mount Seir, and prophesy against it, 3. and say unto it: Thus saith the Lord GOD: Behold, I am against thee, O mount Seir, and I will stretch out My hand against thee, and I will make thee most desolate. 4. I will lay thy cities waste, and thou shalt be desolate; and thou shalt know that I am the LORD. 5. Because thou hast had a hatred of old, and hast hurled the children of Israel unto the power of the sword in the time of their calamity, in the time of the iniquity of the end; 6. therefore, as I live,

1 וַיְהִי דְבַר־יְהֹוָה אֵלַי לֵאמֹר׃

2 בֶּן־אָדָם שִׂים פָּנֶיךָ עַל־הַר

3 שֵׂעִיר וְהִנָּבֵא עָלָיו׃ וְאָמַרְתָּ
לוֹ כֹּה אָמַר אֲדֹנָי יֱהֹוִה הִנְנִי
אֵלֶיךָ הַר־שֵׂעִיר וְנָטִיתִי יָדִי
עָלֶיךָ וּנְתַתִּיךָ שְׁמָמָה וּמְשַׁמָּה׃

4 עָרֶיךָ חָרְבָּה אָשִׂים וְאַתָּה
שְׁמָמָה תִהְיֶה וְיָדַעְתָּ כִּי־אֲנִי

5 יְהֹוָה׃ יַעַן הֱיוֹת לְךָ אֵיבַת
עוֹלָם וַתַּגֵּר אֶת־בְּנֵי־יִשְׂרָאֵל
עַל־יְדֵי־חָרֶב בְּעֵת אֵידָם

6 בְּעֵת עֲוֹן קֵץ׃ לָכֵן חַי־אָנִי

CHAPTER XXXV

THREAT AGAINST EDOM

AFTER denouncing the evil shepherds of the past and promising ideal rulership as the first step along the path of restoration, Ezekiel proceeds to the next obstruction which must be removed if a restored Israel is to prosper. All the nations which oppressed Israel and retarded his progress must vanish from the stage of history. Edom, in particular, the archenemy of Israel, had forfeited his right to national existence, and his fall is an essential preliminary to Israel's final redemption and the universal recognition of God's Sovereignty. The prophet Obadiah proclaimed the same message with striking emphasis: *And saviours shall come up on mount Zion to judge the mount of Esau; and the kingdom shall be the LORD'S* (Obad. 21).

2. *mount Seir.* The original home of Edom was the mountainous country of Seir east of the Arabah. The term *mount Seir* is also used for the entire territory inhabited by the Edomites which extended westward to the south of Judea.

4. *thou shalt know.* So grievous will the desolation be that the Edomites will detect in it the work of God.

5. *a hatred of old.* Towards Israel. Edom's enmity goes back to the relationship between his ancestor Esau and Jacob. A.V. translates 'a perpetual hatred,' R.V. 'a perpetual enmity'; and for this interpretation, cf. Amos. i. 11.

hast hurled . . . power of the sword. R.V. is closer to the text: 'hast given over the children of Israel to the power of the sword.' The translation of A.V., 'hast shed (the blood of) the children of Israel by the force of the sword,' is based on Kimchi.

in the time of their calamity. The Edomites aided the Babylonians in their campaign which destroyed the Judean State (Obad. 10ff.).

in the time of the iniquity of the end. The

saith the Lord GOD, I will prepare
thee unto blood, and blood shall
pursue thee; surely thou hast hated
thine own blood, therefore blood
shall pursue thee. 7. Thus will I
make mount Seir most desolate, and
cut off from it him that passeth
through and him that returneth.
8. And I will fill his mountains with
his slain; in thy hills and in thy
valleys and in all thy streams shall
they fall that are slain with the
sword. 9. I will make thee perpetual desolations, and thy cities
shall not return; and ye shall know
that I am the LORD. 10. Because
thou hast said: These two nations
and these two countries shall be
mine, and we will possess it;
whereas the LORD was there;
11. therefore, as I live, saith the

נְאֻם אֲדֹנָי יְהוִֹה כִּי־לְדָם
אֶעֶשְׂךָ וְדָם יִרְדֲּפֶךָ אִם־לֹא
דָם שָׂנֵאתָ וָדָם יִרְדֲּפֶךָ: וְנָתַתִּי 7
אֶת־הַר שֵׂעִיר לְשִׁמְמָה
וּשְׁמָמָה וְהִכְרַתִּי מִמֶּנּוּ עֹבֵר
וָשָׁב: וּמִלֵּאתִי אֶת־הָרָיו 8
חֲלָלָיו גִּבְעוֹתֶיךָ וְגֵיאוֹתֶיךָ
וְכָל־אֲפִיקֶיךָ חַלְלֵי־חֶרֶב
יִפְּלוּ בָהֶם: שִׁמְמוֹת עוֹלָם 9
אֶתֶּנְךָ וְעָרֶיךָ לֹא תָשֹׁבְנָה
וִידַעְתֶּם כִּי־אֲנִי יְהוָֹה: יַעַן 10
אֲמָרְךָ אֶת־שְׁנֵי הַגּוֹיִם
וְאֶת־שְׁתֵּי הָאֲרָצוֹת לִי
תִהְיֶינָה וִירַשְׁנוּהָ וַיהוָֹה שָׁם
הָיָה: לָכֵן חַי־אָנִי נְאֻם אֲדֹנָי 11

v. 9. תשובנה ק'

iniquity which completed their full
measure of guilt and brought about their
punishment. The phrase occurred in
xxi. 30.

6. *will prepare thee unto blood.* Because
Edom had shed the blood of Israelites,
his blood would be shed.

surely thou hast hated thine own blood.
i.e. Edom hated Israel to whom he was
related by blood-ties.

7. *him that passeth . . . returneth.* A
Hebrew idiom whereby two opposites
denote totality. The slaughter of the
Edomites will be complete.

8. *I will fill his mountains with his slain.*
Wherever they flee for safety they will
be overtaken and slain by their enemies.

9. *thy cities shall not return.* In contrast
to Egypt whose refugees will return to
their land (xxix. 14), Edom is to remain

desolate for ever. The *kethib* represent
a reading which signifies 'shall not be
re-inhabited.'

ye shall know. The subject is th
Edomites; less probably, as Lofthous
explains, the *mountains* and *hills* o
verse 8.

10. *these two nations . . . shall be mine*
Not only did Edom have a hand in th
overthrow of Israel, but also claimed th
right to take possession of his territory
The *two nations* are the Kingdoms c
Israel and Judah.

we will possess it. The object is th
territory of the *two nations.*

whereas the LORD was there. Thoug
God had ejected His people from the lan
and His Divine Presence departed fro
it (xi. 23), yet He was still there in th
sense that the land was His and He alor
had the right to dispose of it.

236

Lord GOD, I will do according to thine anger and according to thine envy, which thou hast used out of thy hatred against them; and I will make Myself known among them, when I shall judge thee. 12. And thou shalt know that I the LORD have heard all thy blasphemies which thou hast spoken against the mountains of Israel, saying: They are laid desolate, they are given us to devour. 13. And ye have magnified yourselves against Me with your mouth, and have multiplied your words against Me; I have heard it. 14. Thus saith the Lord GOD: When the whole earth rejoiceth, I will make thee desolate. 15. As thou didst rejoice over the inheritance of the house of Israel, because it was desolate, so will I do unto thee; thou shalt be desolate, O mount Seir, and all Edom, even all of it; and they shall know that I am the LORD.

יְהֹוָה וְעָשִׂיתִי כְּאַפְּךָ
וּבְקִנְאָתְךָ אֲשֶׁר עָשִׂיתָה
מִשִּׂנְאָתֶיךָ בָּם וְנוֹדַעְתִּי בָם
12 כַּאֲשֶׁר אֶשְׁפְּטֶךָ: וְיָדַעְתָּ כִּי
אֲנִי יְהֹוָה שָׁמַעְתִּי | אֶת־כָּל־
נָאֲצוֹתֶיךָ אֲשֶׁר אָמַרְתָּ עַל־
הָרֵי יִשְׂרָאֵל לֵאמֹר | שָׁמֵמָה
13 לָנוּ נִתְּנוּ לְאָכְלָה: וַתַּגְדִּילוּ
עָלַי בְּפִיכֶם וְהַעְתַּרְתֶּם עָלַי
14 דִּבְרֵיכֶם אֲנִי שָׁמָעְתִּי: כֹּה
אָמַר אֲדֹנָי יְהֹוִה כִּשְׂמֹחַ כָּל־
הָאָרֶץ שְׁמָמָה אֶעֱשֶׂה־לָּךְ:
15 כְּשִׂמְחָתְךָ לְנַחֲלַת בֵּית־
יִשְׂרָאֵל עַל אֲשֶׁר־שָׁמֵמָה כֵּן
אֶעֱשֶׂה־לָּךְ שְׁמָמָה תִהְיֶה
הַר־שֵׂעִיר וְכָל־אֱדוֹם כֻּלָּה
וְיָדְעוּ כִּי־אֲנִי יְהֹוָה:

v. 12. שממו ק'

11. *do according to thine anger*, etc. Edom will be fully requited for the malicious feelings he displayed to Israel.

among them. viz. Israel. By punishing the Edomites for their misdeeds towards Israel, God will be recognized as the protector of His people.

12. *all thy blasphemies.* The *mountains of Israel* belonged to God; therefore the words used by Edom about them were blasphemous.

13. *ye have magnified yourselves against Me.* The attitude of Edom towards Israel constituted defiance of God.

14. *when the whole earth rejoiceth, I will make thee desolate.* According to Kimchi, this verse is the antecedent to the following. That is to say, all the world will rejoice over Edom's desolation as Edom rejoiced over Jerusalem's desolation. This interpretation agrees with that given by Davidson who translates: 'to the rejoicing of the whole earth, I will make thee desolate.'

15. *the inheritance of the house of Israel.* Edom's guilt consisted in his gloating over the destruction of what was a Divine gift, intended to be an everlasting inheritance of Israel. Therefore he incurred the penalty of having his own land desolated.

237

36   CHAPTER XXXVI   לו

1. And thou, son of man, prophesy unto the mountains of Israel, and say: Ye mountains of Israel, hear the word of the LORD. 2. Thus saith the Lord GOD: Because the enemy hath said against you: Aha! even the ancient high places are ours in possession; 3. therefore prophesy, and say: Thus saith the Lord GOD: Because, even because they have made you desolate, and swallowed you up on every side, that ye might be a possession unto the rest of the

1 וְאַתָּה בֶן־אָדָם הִנָּבֵא אֶל־
הָרֵי יִשְׂרָאֵל וְאָמַרְתָּ הָרֵי
יִשְׂרָאֵל שִׁמְעוּ דְּבַר־יְהֹוָה: 2 כֹּה אָמַר אֲדֹנָי יֱהֹוִה יַעַן אָמַר
הָאוֹיֵב עֲלֵיכֶם הֶאָח וּבָמוֹת
עוֹלָם לְמוֹרָשָׁה הָיְתָה לָּנוּ:
3 לָכֵן הִנָּבֵא וְאָמַרְתָּ כֹּה אָמַר
אֲדֹנָי יֱהֹוִה יַעַן בְּיַעַן שַׁמּוֹת
וְשָׁאֹף אֶתְכֶם מִסָּבִיב
לִהְיוֹתְכֶם מוֹרָשָׁה לִשְׁאֵרִית

CHAPTER XXXVI

RESTORATION AND REGENERATION OF ISRAEL

THIS chapter is the sequel to the preceding; and as Ezekiel had been commanded to prophesy *against mount Seir* (xxxv. 2), he is now commanded to prophesy *unto the mountains of Israel*. His theme is Israel's future, which he began in chapter xxxiii. Israel's restoration will be twofold, material and spiritual. Delivered from foreign domination, the Land of Israel will undergo a transformation. The desolate hills and valleys will once more be fertile, yielding abundant fruit to their rightful owner, and the forsaken cities will again be inhabited by Israelites as numerous as the sheep formerly brought to Jerusalem on the pilgrim festivals. In addition to material prosperity, Israel, after his purification in the furnace of exile, will be attentive to the law of God, and a new spirit will prevail in his midst. God's holy name, profaned among the heathens, will be reasserted and His Kingship re-established. 'The chapter is the brightest in the whole Book' (Lofthouse).

1-7 REDEMPTION OF THE LAND OF ISRAEL

1. *prophesy unto the mountains of Israel.* The prophecy of Israel's salvation follows immediately that of the fall of Edom, because the latter was necessary for the former to take place (Kimchi).

2. *the ancient high places.* The term *bamoth* (*high places*) in the mouth of a Hebrew prophet normally denotes idolatrous altars; but as used by the *enemy* it is a designation for the Holy Land in general on account of its hilly character. It occurs in the sense of 'heights' in Deut. xxxii. 13; Mic. iii. 12.

ours in possession. Cf. xxxv. 10.

3. *they have made you desolate, and swallowed you.* The verbs have the infinitive form, and Kimchi interprets that the peoples were planning to make the mountains of Israel desolate; but the context describes what had happened.

the rest of the nations. Surrounding Judea, especially Edom, who coveted the land after the Babylonian army had withdrawn.

nations, and ye are taken up in the lips of talkers, and the evil report of the people; 4. therefore, ye mountains of Israel, hear the word of the Lord GOD: Thus saith the Lord GOD to the mountains and to the hills, to the streams and to the valleys, to the desolate wastes and to the cities that are forsaken, which are become a prey and derision to the residue of the nations that are round about; 5. therefore thus saith the Lord GOD: Surely in the fire of My jealousy have I spoken against the residue of the nations, and against all Edom, that have appointed My land unto themselves for a possession with the joy of all their heart, with disdain of soul, to cast it out for a prey; 6. therefore prophesy concerning the land of Israel, and say unto the mountains and to the hills, to the streams and to the valleys: Thus saith the Lord

הַגּוֹיִם וַתֵּעֲלוּ עַל־־שְׂפַת

4 לָשׁוֹן וְדִבַּת־עָם: לָכֵן הָרֵי

יִשְׂרָאֵל שִׁמְעוּ דְּבַר־אֲדֹנָי

יְהֹוִה כֹּה־אָמַר אֲדֹנָי יְהֹוִה

לֶהָרִים וְלַגְּבָעוֹת לָאֲפִיקִים

וְלַגֵּאָיוֹת וְלֶחֳרָבוֹת הַשֹּׁמֵמוֹת

וְלֶעָרִים הַנֶּעֱזָבוֹת אֲשֶׁר הָיוּ

לָבַז וּלְלַעַג לִשְׁאֵרִית הַגּוֹיִם

5 אֲשֶׁר מִסָּבִיב: לָכֵן כֹּה־אָמַר

אֲדֹנָי יְהֹוִה אִם־לֹא בְּאֵשׁ

קִנְאָתִי דִבַּרְתִּי עַל־שְׁאֵרִית

הַגּוֹיִם וְעַל־אֱדוֹם כֻּלָּא אֲשֶׁר

נָתְנוּ־אֶת־אַרְצִי | לָהֶם

לְמוֹרָשָׁה בְּשִׂמְחַת כָּל־לֵבָב

בִּשְׁאָט נֶפֶשׁ לְמַעַן מִגְרָשָׁהּ

6 לָבַז: לָכֵן הִנָּבֵא עַל־אַדְמַת

יִשְׂרָאֵל וְאָמַרְתָּ לֶהָרִים

וְלַגְּבָעוֹת לָאֲפִיקִים וְלַגֵּאָיוֹת

כֹּה־אָמַר | אֲדֹנָי יְהֹוִה הִנְנִי

כצ״ל v. 5.

e are taken up in the lips of talkers. They speak of the defeated Judeans with ontempt. In the Hebrew *talkers* is literally 'tongue' which Ehrlich explains as a word for 'nation' as speaking a distinctive anguage. It is used in this sense in sa. lxvi. 18; Zech. viii. 23 and the rayer Book (cf. ed. Singer, p. 40).

. to the mountains and to the hills. zekiel proclaims the reversal of the oom to which he had given utterance in i. 3.

My jealousy. Davidson defines the ord as 'injured self-consciousness; it is

the reaction of God's sense of Himself against the injurious conduct of Edom and the nations in relation to Him or that which is His (cf. *My* land).'

to cast it out for a prey. Their whole purpose was to deprive Israel of his homeland and to render him defenceless against his enemies. This is the interpretation given by most Jewish commentators, but the Hebrew does not naturally bear it. Malbim takes *migrash* in its usual sense (see on xxvii. 28), and the meaning may be: 'that its open country should be for spoil.'

GOD: Behold, I have spoken in My jealousy and in My fury, because ye have borne the shame of the nations; 7. therefore thus saith the Lord GOD: I have lifted up My hand: Surely the nations that are round about you, they shall bear their shame. 8. But ye, O mountains of Israel, ye shall shoot forth your branches, and yield your fruit to My people Israel; for they are at hand to come. 9. For, behold, I am for you, and I will turn unto you, and ye shall be tilled and sown; 10. and I will multiply men upon you, all the house of Israel, even all of it; and the cities shall be inhabited, and the waste places shall be builded; 11. and I will multiply upon you man and beast, and they shall increase and be fruitful; and I will cause you to be inhabited after your former estate, and will do better unto you than at your beginnings; and ye shall know that I am the

בְּקִנְאָתִי וּבַחֲמָתִי דִּבַּרְתִּי יַעַן
7 כְּלִמַּת גּוֹיִם נְשָׂאתֶם: לָכֵן
כֹּה אָמַר אֲדֹנָי יֱהוִֹה אֲנִי
נָשָׂאתִי אֶת־יָדִי אִם־לֹא
הַגּוֹיִם אֲשֶׁר־לָכֶם מִסָּבִיב
8 הֵמָּה כְּלִמָּתָם יִשָּׂאוּ: וְאַתֶּם
הָרֵי יִשְׂרָאֵל עַנְפְּכֶם תִּתֵּנוּ
וּפֶרְיְכֶם תִּשְׂאוּ לְעַמִּי יִשְׂרָאֵל
9 כִּי קֵרְבוּ לָבוֹא: כִּי הִנְנִי
אֲלֵיכֶם וּפָנִיתִי אֲלֵיכֶם
וְנֶעֱבַדְתֶּם וְנִזְרַעְתֶּם:
10 וְהִרְבֵּיתִי עֲלֵיכֶם אָדָם כָּל־
בֵּית יִשְׂרָאֵל כֻּלֹּה וְנֹשְׁבוּ
הֶעָרִים וְהֶחֳרָבוֹת תִּבָּנֶינָה:
11 וְהִרְבֵּיתִי עֲלֵיכֶם אָדָם
וּבְהֵמָה וְרָבוּ וּפָרוּ וְהוֹשַׁבְתִּי
אֶתְכֶם כְּקַדְמוֹתֵיכֶם וְהֵיטִבֹתִי
מֵרִאשֹׁתֵיכֶם וִידַעְתֶּם כִּי־אֲנִי

6. *ye have borne the shame of the nations.* The shame inflicted upon Judea by the nations in their derision and intrusion.

7. *I have lifted up My hand.* See on xx. 5. *they shall bear their shame.* They will experience the humiliation which they had inflicted upon the Judeans.

8-15 REPOPULATION AND PROSPERITY OF THE LAND

8. *they are at hand to come.* In prophetic perspective the end of the exile is not far off.

9. *I am for you.* The opposite of *I am against thee* (xxxv. 3, said of mount Seir). God's favour will again be bestowed upon the Land of Israel and its desolate soil will become exceedingly fruitful.

10. *all the house of Israel, even all of it.* The two Kingdoms will be restored to the land. Their reunion is the theme of the latter part of the next chapter.

11. *increase and be fruitful.* A reminiscence of Gen. i. 22.

after your former estate. In pre-exilic times.

will do better unto you than at your beginnings. While their numbers will be restored to their former strength, their

Lord 12. Yea, I will cause men to walk upon you, even My people Israel, and they shall possess thee, and thou shalt be their inheritance; and thou shalt no more henceforth bereave them of children. 13. Thus saith the Lord GOD: Because they say unto you: Thou land art a devourer of men, and hast been a bereaver of thy nations; 14. therefore thou shalt devour men no more, neither bereave thy nations any more, saith the Lord GOD; 15. neither will I suffer the shame of the nations any more to be heard against thee, neither shalt thou bear the reproach of the peoples any more, neither shalt thou cause thy nations to stumble any more, saith the Lord GOD.'

16. Moreover the word of the LORD came unto me, saying: 17. 'Son of man, when the house of Israel dwelt in their own land, they defiled it by their way and by their doings; their way before Me was as the uncleanness of a woman in her

יְהוָֹה׃ וְהוֹלַכְתִּי עֲלֵיכֶם אָדָם 12
אֶת־עַמִּי יִשְׂרָאֵל וִירֵשׁוּךָ
וְהָיִיתָ לָהֶם לְנַחֲלָה וְלֹא־
תוֹסִף עוֹד לְשַׁכְּלָם׃ כֹּה אָמַר 13
אֲדֹנָי יְהוִֹה יַעַן אֹמְרִים לָכֶם
אֹכֶלֶת אָדָם אָתִּי וּמְשַׁכֶּלֶת
גּוֹיַךְ הָיִית׃ לָכֵן אָדָם לֹא־ 14
תֹאכְלִי עוֹד וְגוֹיַךְ לֹא
תְכַשְּׁלִי־עוֹד נְאֻם אֲדֹנָי יֱהוִֹה׃
וְלֹא־אַשְׁמִיעַ אֵלַיִךְ עוֹד 15
כְּלִמַּת הַגּוֹיִם וְחֶרְפַּת עַמִּים
לֹא תִשְׂאִי־עוֹד וְגוֹיַךְ לֹא־
תַכְשִׁלִי עוֹד נְאֻם אֲדֹנָי יֱהוִֹה׃
וַיְהִי דְבַר־יְהוָֹה אֵלַי 16
לֵאמֹר׃ בֶּן־אָדָם בֵּית 17
יִשְׂרָאֵל יֹשְׁבִים עַל־אַדְמָתָם
וַיְטַמְּאוּ אוֹתָהּ בְּדַרְכָּם
וּבַעֲלִילוֹתָם כְּטֻמְאַת הַנִּדָּה

v. 13. את ק׳. v. 13. גוייך ק׳ v. 14. וגוייך ק׳ v. 14. תשכלי ק׳ v. 15. וגוייך ק׳ v. 16. הפטרת פרשת פרה

prosperity will exceed that of bygone days.

12. I will cause men to walk upon you. The prophet is still addressing the mountains. The desolate and forsaken mountains will once again be traversed by their rightful owners.

possess thee. viz. the land. The Hebrew unusually has the masculine form in the remainder of the sentence; contrast the next verse.

bereave them of children. The havoc caused by war, pestilence and famine will not recur.

13. thou land art a devourer of men, etc.

The hostile neighbours alleged that the Land of Israel destroyed its inhabitants. The Canaanites, the original population, had perished, and now the Israelites were undergoing a similar fate. Cf. Num. xiii. 32 where the spies reported of Canaan it is a land that eateth up the inhabitants thereof.

14. neither bereave thy nations any more. Israel's experience on his return will disprove the allegation.

15. shame of the nations. See on verse 6.

16-38 MORAL PURIFICATION OF ISRAEL

17. as the uncleanness of a woman in her impurity. Metaphorically Israel is com-

impurity. 18. Wherefore I poured out My fury upon them for the blood which they had shed upon the land, and because they had defiled it with their idols; 19. and I scattered them among the nations, and they were dispersed through the countries; according to their way and according to their doings I judged them. 20. And when they came unto the nations, whither they came, they profaned My holy name; in that men said of them: These are the people of the LORD, and are gone forth out of His land. 21. But I had pity for My holy name, which the house of Israel had profaned among the nations, whither they came. 22. Therefore say unto the house of Israel: Thus saith the Lord GOD: I do not this for your sake,

18 הָיְתָה דַרְכָּם לְפָנָי: וָאֶשְׁפֹּךְ
חֲמָתִי עֲלֵיהֶם עַל־הַדָּם
אֲשֶׁר־שָׁפְכוּ עַל־הָאָרֶץ
19 וּבְגִלּוּלֵיהֶם טִמְּאוּהָ: וָאָפִיץ
אֹתָם בַּגּוֹיִם וַיִּזָּרוּ בָּאֲרָצוֹת
כְּדַרְכָּם וְכַעֲלִילוֹתָם
20 שְׁפַטְתִּים: וַיָּבוֹא אֶל־הַגּוֹיִם
אֲשֶׁר־בָּאוּ שָׁם וַיְחַלְּלוּ אֶת־
שֵׁם קָדְשִׁי בֶּאֱמֹר לָהֶם עַם־
יְהוָה אֵלֶּה וּמֵאַרְצוֹ יָצָאוּ:
21 וָאֶחְמֹל עַל־שֵׁם קָדְשִׁי אֲשֶׁר
חִלְּלֻהוּ בֵּית יִשְׂרָאֵל בַּגּוֹיִם
22 אֲשֶׁר־בָּאוּ שָׁמָּה: לָכֵן אֱמֹר
לְבֵית־יִשְׂרָאֵל כֹּה אָמַר אֲדֹנָי
יְהוִה לֹא לְמַעַנְכֶם אֲנִי עֹשֶׂה

---

v. 20. סבירין ויבואו

pared with a wife and God to a husband. Therefore in the times of unfaithfulness to Him, Israel is spoken of as having the state of *a woman in her impurity*. She is temporarily avoided by her husband, becoming reunited with him after purification. Similarly, Israel's banishment from the soil was due to moral impurity, but restoration to his homeland will follow upon purification (Kimchi).

18. *for the blood . . . their idols*. That the sins of homicide and idolatry were among the chief causes of Israel's banishment was stressed in xvi. 36, xxiii. 37.

20. *when they came*. lit. 'when he came,' the subject being *the house of Israel* in verse 17. The Rabbis homiletically interpreted the singular verb as referring to God. He, so to speak, went into exile with His people; cf. *in all their affliction He was afflicted* (Isa. lxiii. 9).

they profaned My holy name. By their misdeeds and consequent dispersion they caused the desecration of God's name; because the nations understood Israel's exile to foreign lands as an indication that God was unable to protect him.

and are gone forth out of His land. Though they bore the title of *the people of the LORD*, He could not save them and they were driven from His land.

21. *I had pity for My holy name*. Not for Israel who had incurred punishment; but the Divine name, as it were, had suffered indignity without cause.

22. *I do not this for your sake*. Israel's coming salvation is not determined by his merits, but by the necessity to reassert the name of God which, through its association with His people, had been profaned among the nations.

O **house** of Israel, but for My holy name, which ye have profaned among the nations, whither ye came. 23. And I will sanctify My great name, which hath been profaned among the nations, which ye have profaned in the midst of them; and the nations shall know that I am the LORD, saith the Lord GOD, when I shall be sanctified in you before their eyes.

24. For I will take you from among the nations, and gather you out of all the countries, and will bring you into your own land.

25. And I will sprinkle clean water upon you, and ye shall be clean; from all your uncleannesses, and from all your idols, will I cleanse you. 26. A new heart also will I give you, and a new spirit will I put within you; and I will take away the stony heart out of your flesh, and I will give you a heart of flesh.

27. And I will put My spirit within

בֵּית יִשְׂרָאֵל כִּי אִם־לְשֵׁם־
קָדְשִׁי אֲשֶׁר חִלַּלְתֶּם בַּגּוֹיִם
23 אֲשֶׁר־בָּאתֶם שָׁם: וְקִדַּשְׁתִּי
אֶת־שְׁמִי הַגָּדוֹל הַמְחֻלָּל
בַּגּוֹיִם אֲשֶׁר חִלַּלְתֶּם בְּתוֹכָם
וְיָדְעוּ הַגּוֹיִם כִּי־אֲנִי יְהֹוָה
נְאֻם אֲדֹנָי יֱהֹוִה בְּהִקָּדְשִׁי בָכֶם
24 לְעֵינֵיהֶם: וְלָקַחְתִּי אֶתְכֶם
מִן־הַגּוֹיִם וְקִבַּצְתִּי אֶתְכֶם
מִכָּל־הָאֲרָצוֹת וְהֵבֵאתִי
אֶתְכֶם אֶל־אַדְמַתְכֶם:
25 וְזָרַקְתִּי עֲלֵיכֶם מַיִם טְהוֹרִים
וּטְהַרְתֶּם מִכֹּל טֻמְאוֹתֵיכֶם
וּמִכָּל־גִּלּוּלֵיכֶם אֲטַהֵר
26 אֶתְכֶם: וְנָתַתִּי לָכֶם לֵב חָדָשׁ
וְרוּחַ חֲדָשָׁה אֶתֵּן בְּקִרְבְּכֶם
וַהֲסִרֹתִי אֶת־לֵב הָאֶבֶן
מִבְּשַׂרְכֶם וְנָתַתִּי לָכֶם לֵב
27 בָּשָׂר: וְאֶת־רוּחִי אֶתֵּן

v. 25. כצ״ל   v. 23. כצ״ל

23. *I will sanctify My great name.* By restoring the exiled Israelites to their homeland. That will be a demonstration that the captivity was not the effect of God's weakness.

when I shall be sanctified in you. Or, 'when I show Myself holy through you.' God will vindicate the holiness of His name through Israel by the act of redemption.

before their eyes. There is an alternative reading 'before your eyes'; but M.T. is supported by xxxviii. 16.

25. *I will sprinkle clean water upon you.* Since Israel's evil ways were compared to *the uncleanness of a woman in her impurity* (verse 17), the forgiveness of his sins is characterized as purification by cleansing water.

all your uncleannesses. Sin defiles both body and soul.

26. *a new heart also will I give you,* etc. This verse is virtually a repetition of xi. 19.

27. *My spirit.* i.e. the holy spirit of God.

you, and cause you to walk in My statutes, and ye shall keep Mine ordinances, and do them.

28. And ye shall dwell in the land that I gave to your fathers; and ye shall be My people, and I will be your God. 29. And I will save you from all your uncleannesses; and I will call for the corn, and will increase it, and lay no famine upon you. 30. And I will multiply the fruit of the tree, and the increase of the field, that ye may receive no more the reproach of famine among the nations. 31. Then shall ye remember your evil ways, and your doings that were not good; and ye shall loathe yourselves in your own sight for your iniquities and for your abominations. 32. Not for your sake do I this, saith the Lord GOD, be it known unto you; be ashamed

בְּקִרְבְּכֶם וְעָשִׂיתִי אֵת אֲשֶׁר־
בְּחֻקַּי תֵּלֵכוּ וּמִשְׁפָּטַי תִּשְׁמְרוּ
28 וַעֲשִׂיתֶם: וִישַׁבְתֶּם בָּאָרֶץ
אֲשֶׁר נָתַתִּי לַאֲבֹתֵיכֶם וִהְיִיתֶם
לִי לְעָם וְאָנֹכִי אֶהְיֶה לָכֶם
29 לֵאלֹהִים: וְהוֹשַׁעְתִּי אֶתְכֶם
מִכֹּל טֻמְאוֹתֵיכֶם וְקָרָאתִי
אֶל־הַדָּגָן וְהִרְבֵּיתִי אֹתוֹ
וְלֹא־אֶתֵּן עֲלֵיכֶם רָעָב:
30 וְהִרְבֵּיתִי אֶת־פְּרִי הָעֵץ
וּתְנוּבַת הַשָּׂדֶה לְמַעַן אֲשֶׁר
לֹא־תִקְחוּ עוֹד חֶרְפַּת רָעָב
31 בַּגּוֹיִם: וּזְכַרְתֶּם אֶת־
דַּרְכֵיכֶם הָרָעִים וּמַעַלְלֵיכֶם
אֲשֶׁר לֹא־טוֹבִים וּנְקֹטֹתֶם
בִּפְנֵיכֶם עַל עֲוֺנֹתֵיכֶם וְעַל
32 תּוֹעֲבֹתֵיכֶם: לֹא לְמַעַנְכֶם
אֲנִי־עֹשֶׂה נְאֻם אֲדֹנָי יֱהֹוִה
יִוָּדַע לָכֶם בּוֹשׁוּ וְהִכָּלְמוּ

and cause you to walk in My statutes. Animated with this spirit, they will willingly observe the laws of God.

28. *ye shall dwell in the land.* As the consequence of spiritual regeneration, Israel will remain in possession of the land (cf. xxviii. 25, xxxvii. 25).

29. *I will save you from all your uncleannesses.* The nation's tendency to lapse into sin will be overcome by the power of the new spirit.

I will call for the corn. Summon it to appear; God will restore the fertility of the land (cf. xxxiv. 26f.).

30. *the reproach of famine among the nations.* See on xxxiv. 29.

31. *ye shall loathe yourselves.* See on vi. 9.

32. *not for your sake do I this.* Israel must not be complacent about his former misdeeds and imagine that God had pardoned them by His act of redemption. They should be remembered with deeper shame because He has restored the people to the land.

and confounded for your ways, O house of Israel.

33. Thus saith the Lord GOD: In the day that I cleanse you from all your iniquities, I will cause the cities to be inhabited, and the waste places shall be builded. **34.** And the land that was desolate shall be tilled, whereas it was a desolation in the sight of all that passed by. **35.** And they shall say: This land that was desolate is become like the garden of Eden; and the waste and desolate and ruined cities are fortified and inhabited. **36.** Then the nations that are left round about you shall know that I the LORD have builded the ruined places, and planted that which was desolate; I the LORD have spoken it, and I will do it.

37. Thus saith the Lord GOD: I will yet for this be inquired of by the house of Israel, to do it for them; I will increase them with men like a

33 מִדַּרְכֵיכֶם בֵּית יִשְׂרָאֵל ׃ כֹּה
אָמַר אֲדֹנָי יֱהֹוִה בְּיוֹם טַהֲרִי
אֶתְכֶם מִכֹּל עֲוֺנוֹתֵיכֶם
וְהוֹשַׁבְתִּי אֶת־הֶעָרִים וְנִבְנוּ
34 הֶחֳרָבוֹת ׃ וְהָאָרֶץ הַנְּשַׁמָּה
תֵּעָבֵד תַּחַת אֲשֶׁר הָיְתָה
שְׁמָמָה לְעֵינֵי כָּל־עוֹבֵר ׃
35 וְאָמְרוּ הָאָרֶץ הַלֵּזוּ הַנְּשַׁמָּה
הָיְתָה כְּגַן־עֵדֶן וְהֶעָרִים
הֶחֳרֵבוֹת וְהַנְשַׁמּוֹת וְהַנֶּהֱרָסוֹת
36 בְּצוּרוֹת יָשָׁבוּ ׃ וְיָדְעוּ הַגּוֹיִם
אֲשֶׁר יִשָּׁאֲרוּ סְבִיבוֹתֵיכֶם כִּי ׀
אֲנִי יְהֹוָה בָּנִיתִי הַנֶּהֱרָסוֹת
נָטַעְתִּי הַנְּשַׁמָּה אֲנִי יְהֹוָה
37 דִּבַּרְתִּי וְעָשִׂיתִי ׃ * כֹּה
אָמַר אֲדֹנָי יֱהֹוִה עוֹד זֹאת
אִדָּרֵשׁ לְבֵית־יִשְׂרָאֵל לַעֲשׂוֹת
לָהֶם אַרְבֶּה אֹתָם כַּצֹּאן

v. 35. הר׳ בצירי   v. 36. ע״כ לספרדים   v. 37. הפטרה לשבת וחול המועד של פסח והספרדים מתחילין היתה עלי

33. *in the day that I cleanse you.* This verse and the next are antecedents to verse 35. Render: 'and cause the cities to be inhabited . . . then shall they say.'

34. *whereas it was a desolation in the sight of all that passed by.* Even the completely devastated places, which were thought by passers-by to be beyond reclamation, will be restored to their former state. Ehrlich construes the verse: 'shall be tilled—whereas it was a desolation—in the sight of all that pass by.'

35. *they shall say.* The transformation which had taken place in the Holy Land will create amazement.

36. *the nations that are left round about you shall know.* What has occurred will be recognized as the work of God, not of man.

I the LORD have spoken it. It was predicted by His prophets.

37. *I will yet for this be inquired of by the house of Israel.* Their prayer will be for an increase of population after the severe losses caused by war and exile. That will be one of the principal concerns in the restored nation.

245

flock. 38. As the flock for sacrifice, as the flock of Jerusalem in her appointed seasons, so shall the waste cities be filled with flocks of men; and they shall know that I am the LORD.'

אָדָם: 38 כְּצֹאן קָדָשִׁים כְּצֹאן
יְרוּשָׁלַ‍ם בְּמוֹעֲדֶיהָ כֵּן תִּהְיֶינָה
הֶעָרִים הֶחֳרֵבוֹת מְלֵאוֹת צֹאן
אָדָם וְיָדְעוּ כִּי־אֲנִי יְהוָה:

37   CHAPTER XXXVII   לז

1. The hand of the LORD was upon me, and the LORD carried me out in a spirit, and set me down in the midst of the valley, and it was full of bones; 2. and He caused me to pass by them round about, and,

1 הָיְתָה עָלַי יַד־יְהוָֹה וַיּוֹצִיאֵנִי
בְרוּחַ יְהוָֹה וַיְנִיחֵנִי בְּתוֹךְ
הַבִּקְעָה וְהִיא מְלֵאָה עֲצָמוֹת:
2 וְהֶעֱבִירַנִי עֲלֵיהֶם סָבִיב |

v. 38. הר' בצירי v. 38. עד כאן לאשכנזים

38. *as the flock for sacrifice,* etc. The desolate cities of the Holy Land will teem with inhabitants as Jerusalem was once filled with cattle for sacrifices on the three pilgrim festivals.

they shall know that I am the LORD. The fulfilment of God's word will lead to the strengthening of the people's faith in Him.

CHAPTER XXXVII

VISION OF THE DRY BONES AND THE SYMBOL OF UNITY

THE prophecy of Israel's regeneration is illustrated in the most graphic manner by a vision concerning the rebirth of the nation. The prophet finds himself in a valley full of scattered dry bones. Under the vivifying effect of the spirit of God the bones knit together and are covered with sinews, flesh and skin. Ultimately the breath of life is infused into them and they stand up a great host. No more inspiriting message could have been communicated to the despairing exiles to revive their national will to live. In the second half of the chapter (verses 15-28) Ezekiel by a symbolic act predicts the reunion of the two Kingdoms which will be ruled by one king of the house of David. The purified and restored Israel

will never again be uprooted from their soil, but *they shall dwell therein, they, and their children, and their children's children, for ever; and David My servant shall be their prince for ever* (verse 25).

1-14 THE VISION OF ISRAEL'S RESURRECTION

1. *the hand of the LORD was upon me.* See on i. 3.

the valley. Probably the same valley where he saw a vision in the earlier days of his career (iii. 22) (Kimchi). A.J there has *plain,* but the Hebrew is the same in both passages.

it was full of bones. There is a discussion in the Talmud (Sanh. 92b) whether the prophet's account of the dry bones in the valley was an allegory or something which he saw. With regard to the latter view several suggestions are made as to the identity of the persons who were resurrected. One opinion is that they were the Ephraimites who miscalculated the duration of the Egyptian bondage, left the country thirty years before the appointed time of the release, and were slain in the wilderness.

2. *round about.* Rashi comments that because Ezekiel was debarred from

behold, there were very many in the
open valley; and, lo, they were very
dry. 3. And He said unto me: 'Son
of man, can these bones live?' And
I answered: 'O Lord GOD, Thou
knowest.' 4. Then He said unto
me: 'Prophesy over these bones, and
say unto them: O ye dry bones, hear
the word of the LORD: 5. Thus saith
the Lord GOD unto these bones:
Behold, I will cause breath to enter
into you, and ye shall live. 6. And
I will lay sinews upon you, and will
bring up flesh upon you, and cover
you with skin, and put breath in you,
and ye shall live; and ye shall know
that I am the LORD.' 7. So I
prophesied as I was commanded;

סָבִיב וְהִנֵּה רַבּוֹת מְאֹד עַל־
פְּנֵי הַבִּקְעָה וְהִנֵּה יְבֵשׁוֹת
3 מְאֹד: וַיֹּאמֶר אֵלַי בֶּן־אָדָם
הֲתִחְיֶינָה הָעֲצָמוֹת הָאֵלֶּה
וָאֹמַר אֲדֹנָי יֱהֹוִה אַתָּה יָדָעְתָּ:
4 וַיֹּאמֶר אֵלַי הִנָּבֵא עַל־
הָעֲצָמוֹת הָאֵלֶּה וְאָמַרְתָּ
אֲלֵיהֶם הָעֲצָמוֹת הַיְבֵשׁוֹת
5 שִׁמְעוּ דְּבַר־יְהֹוָה: כֹּה אָמַר
אֲדֹנָי יֱהֹוִה לָעֲצָמוֹת הָאֵלֶּה
הִנֵּה אֲנִי מֵבִיא בָכֶם רוּחַ
6 וִחְיִיתֶם: וְנָתַתִּי עֲלֵיכֶם גִּדִים
וְהַעֲלֵתִי עֲלֵיכֶם בָּשָׂר
וְקָרַמְתִּי עֲלֵיכֶם עוֹר וְנָתַתִּי
בָכֶם רוּחַ וִחְיִיתֶם וִידַעְתֶּם
7 כִּי־אֲנִי יְהֹוָה: וְנִבֵּאתִי כַּאֲשֶׁר

contact with the dead, being a *kohen*
(descendant in the male line from Aaron),
he was not set down inside the valley
among the bones but on the outer edge
of the valley. Kimchi disputes this
interpretation on the ground that on
another occasion (cf. v. 1) Ezekiel,
though a *kohen*, was ordered to shave his
head and beard, an act forbidden to a
priest; and it is expressly stated in the
preceding verse *and set me down in the
midst of the valley*. His view is that the
matter of contracting ritual defilement
did not arise with Ezekiel, since the
experience was not actual and only a
vision.

in the open valley. lit. 'upon the face of
the valley.'

they were very dry. i.e. the flesh had

gone completely, depicting how forlorn
was the hope of the nation's revival.

3. *Thou knowest.* It is beyond human
power to make the bones live. Only
God, if He so will, can do it.

5. *I will cause breath to enter into you.*
After the bones had been covered with
sinews, flesh and skin, God will put
breath into them, as stated in the next
verse. Apparently, the final stage in
the process of giving life to the bones is
mentioned first to bring out the purpose
of the scene.

6. *sinews . . . flesh . . . skin . . . put
breath.* Perhaps the intention is that
the physical and political rehabilitation
of the people will be completed by their
spiritual revitalization.

and as I prophesied, there was a
noise, and behold a commotion, and
the bones came together, bone to its
bone. 8. And I beheld, and, lo,
there were sinews upon them, and
flesh came up, and skin covered them
above; but there was no breath in
them. 9. Then said He unto me:
'Prophesy unto the breath, prophesy,
son of man, and say to the breath:
Thus saith the Lord GOD: Come
from the four winds, O breath, and
breathe upon these slain, that they
may live.' 10. So I prophesied as
He commanded me, and the breath
came into them, and they lived, and
stood up upon their feet, an exceeding great host. 11. Then He said
unto me: 'Son of man, these bones
are the whole house of Israel;
behold, they say: Our bones are
dried up, and our hope is lost; we

צִוֵּיתִי וַיְהִי־קוֹל כְּהִנָּבְאִי
וְהִנֵּה־רַעַשׁ וַתִּקְרְבוּ עֲצָמוֹת
8 עֶצֶם אֶל־עַצְמוֹ: וְרָאִיתִי
וְהִנֵּה־עֲלֵיהֶם גִּדִים וּבָשָׂר
עָלָה וַיִּקְרַם עֲלֵיהֶם עוֹר
מִלְמָעְלָה וְרוּחַ אֵין בָּהֶם:
9 וַיֹּאמֶר אֵלַי הִנָּבֵא אֶל־הָרוּחַ
הִנָּבֵא בֶן־אָדָם וְאָמַרְתָּ אֶל־
הָרוּחַ כֹּה־אָמַר | אֲדֹנָי יְהֹוִה
מֵאַרְבַּע רוּחוֹת בֹּאִי הָרוּחַ
וּפְחִי בַּהֲרוּגִים הָאֵלֶּה וְיִחְיוּ:
10 וְהִנַּבֵּאתִי כַּאֲשֶׁר צִוָּנִי וַתָּבוֹא
בָהֶם הָרוּחַ וַיִּחְיוּ וַיַּעַמְדוּ עַל־
רַגְלֵיהֶם חַיִל גָּדוֹל מְאֹד
11 מְאֹד: וַיֹּאמֶר אֵלַי בֶּן־אָדָם
הָעֲצָמוֹת הָאֵלֶּה כָּל־בֵּית
יִשְׂרָאֵל הֵמָּה הִנֵּה אֹמְרִים
יָבְשׁוּ עַצְמוֹתֵינוּ וְאָבְדָה

---

7. *a noise . . . a commotion.* The *noise*
(lit. 'sound') grew into a *commotion* by the
coming together of the bones to form
human frames.

8. *flesh came up.* Upon the sinews.
'Ezekiel prepares the way for the
description of the actual coming of the
breath with distinct literary art' (Lofthouse).

9. *come from the four winds, O breath.*
The breath of life which had departed
from the bodies is thought of as having
been dispersed in all directions, and is
summoned to return from wherever it
may be. Or, as Davidson comments:
'The wind from the four corners of the

heavens is but a symbol of the universal
life-giving spirit of God.'

11. *these bones are the whole house of Israel.*
The interpretation of the vision. These
dried bones are a representation of the
entire people of Israel, both the Northern
and Southern Kingdoms, destroyed and
desolate, bereft of vitality.

behold, they say. The subject is the
survivors of the two Kingdoms, scattered
and in exile. They have lost the
semblance of nationhood as fleshless
bones can no longer be regarded as
human beings.

our hope is lost. Of ever again being a
living nation. The words, with the

are clean cut off. 12. Therefore prophesy, and say unto them: Thus saith the Lord GOD: Behold, I will open your graves, and cause you to come up out of your graves, O My people; and I will bring you into the land of Israel. 13. And ye shall know that I am the LORD, when I have opened your graves, and caused you to come up out of your graves, O My people. 14. And I will put My spirit in you, and ye shall live, and I will place you in your own land; and ye shall know that I the LORD have spoken, and performed it, saith the LORD.'

15. And the word of the LORD came unto me, saying: 16. 'And thou, son of man, take thee one stick, and write upon it: For Judah, and for the children of Israel his companions; then take another stick,

יב תִּקְוָתֵנוּ נִגְזַרְנוּ לָנוּ: לָכֵן הִנָּבֵא
וְאָמַרְתָּ אֲלֵיהֶם כֹּה־אָמַר
אֲדֹנָי יֱהֹוִה הִנֵּה אֲנִי פֹתֵחַ אֶת־
קִבְרוֹתֵיכֶם וְהַעֲלֵיתִי אֶתְכֶם
מִקִּבְרוֹתֵיכֶם עַמִּי וְהֵבֵאתִי
אֶתְכֶם אֶל־אַדְמַת יִשְׂרָאֵל:
יג וִידַעְתֶּם כִּי־אֲנִי יְהֹוָה בְּפִתְחִי
אֶת־קִבְרוֹתֵיכֶם וּבְהַעֲלוֹתִי
אֶתְכֶם מִקִּבְרוֹתֵיכֶם עַמִּי:
יד וְנָתַתִּי רוּחִי בָכֶם וִחְיִיתֶם
וְהִנַּחְתִּי אֶתְכֶם עַל־אַדְמַתְכֶם
וִידַעְתֶּם כִּי אֲנִי יְהֹוָה דִּבַּרְתִּי
טו וְעָשִׂיתִי נְאֻם־יְהֹוָה: * וַיְהִי
דְבַר־יְהֹוָה אֵלַי לֵאמֹר:
טז וְאַתָּה בֶן־אָדָם קַח־לְךָ עֵץ
אֶחָד וּכְתֹב עָלָיו לִיהוּדָה
וְלִבְנֵי יִשְׂרָאֵל חֲבֵרָו וּלְקַח

v. 14. עד כאן v. 15. הפטרת ויגש v. 16. חבריו ק׳

addition of the negative, were made the theme of Imber's *Hatikwah*, the Jewish national anthem.

we are clean cut off. They compared themselves to limbs severed from the body, never again to be united in a living organism.

12. *I will open your graves.* Figuratively the *graves* are the foreign countries where they are languishing in captivity.

13. *ye shall know that I am the LORD*, etc. When the miracle of Israel's national revival is performed, the people's faith in God will be firmly established.

14. *I will put My spirit in you.* This is the explanation of the *breath* entering the bones to revive them. Israel's restoration could not be achieved by human power, but only by the spirit of God.

15-28 THE REUNION OF THE TWO KINGDOMS

16. *take thee one stick.* The prediction of national resurrection, as symbolized in the vision of the dry bones, is followed by the symbolic action of the reunion of the two Kingdoms to indicate that unity is an essential factor in preserving the life of the nation.

write upon it: For Judah . . . his companions. The stick, emblem of the royal sceptre, was to be inscribed with those words. Judah represented the Southern

and write upon it: For Joseph, the stick of Ephraim, and of all the house of Israel his companions; 17. and join them for thee one to another into one stick, that they may become one in thy hand. 18. And when the children of thy people shall speak unto thee, saying: Wilt thou not tell us what thou meanest by these? 19. say unto them: Thus saith the Lord GOD: Behold, I will take the stick of Joseph, which is in the hand of Ephraim, and the tribes of Israel his companions; and I will put them unto him together with the stick of Judah, and make them one stick, and they shall be one in My hand. 20. And the sticks whereon thou writest shall be in thy hand before their eyes. 21. And say unto them: Thus saith the Lord GOD: Behold, I will take the children of Israel from among the nations, whither they are gone, and

עֵץ אֶחָד וּכְתֹב עָלָיו לְיוֹסֵף
עֵץ אֶפְרַיִם וְכָל־בֵּית יִשְׂרָאֵל
17 חֲבֵרָו וְקָרֵב אֹתָם אֶחָד אֶל־
אֶחָד לְךָ לְעֵץ אֶחָד וְהָיוּ
18 לַאֲחָדִים בְּיָדֶךָ: וְכַאֲשֶׁר
יֹאמְרוּ אֵלֶיךָ בְּנֵי עַמְּךָ לֵאמֹר
הֲלוֹא־תַגִּיד לָנוּ מָה־אֵלֶּה
19 לָךְ: דַּבֵּר אֲלֵהֶם כֹּה־אָמַר
אֲדֹנָי יֱהֹוִה הִנֵּה אֲנִי לֹקֵחַ אֶת־
עֵץ יוֹסֵף אֲשֶׁר בְּיַד־אֶפְרַיִם
וְשִׁבְטֵי יִשְׂרָאֵל חֲבֵרָו וְנָתַתִּי
אוֹתָם עָלָיו אֶת־עֵץ יְהוּדָה
וַעֲשִׂיתִם לְעֵץ אֶחָד וְהָיוּ אֶחָד
20 בְּיָדִי: וְהָיוּ הָעֵצִים אֲשֶׁר
תִּכְתֹּב עֲלֵיהֶם בְּיָדְךָ
21 לְעֵינֵיהֶם: וְדַבֵּר אֲלֵהֶם
כֹּה־אָמַר אֲדֹנָי יֱהֹוִה הִנֵּה
אֲנִי לֹקֵחַ אֶת־בְּנֵי יִשְׂרָאֵל
מִבֵּין הַגּוֹיִם אֲשֶׁר הָלְכוּ־שָׁם

v. 16. חבריו ק׳   v. 19. חבריו ק׳

Kingdom ruled by a dynasty descended from that tribe; *his companions* refers to the tribe of Benjamin which joined the tribe of Judah.

for Joseph, the stick of Ephraim. The Northern Kingdom was named after Ephraim because its first king was Jeroboam, a descendant of that tribe.

all the house of Israel his companions. The reference is to the other nine tribes which, together with Ephraim, constituted the Northern Kingdom.

17. *into one stick.* He was to hold both sticks together end to end to make them appear as one stick.

19. *I will put them,* etc. God explains the meaning of the symbolic act. All the tribes which united with Ephraim to form a separate Kingdom will be joined with Judah to constitute a single realm.

21. *say unto them.* The prophet was to explain to the people the meaning of the symbol while holding the two sticks in his hand.

will gather them on every side, and
bring them into their own land;
22. and I will make them one nation
in the land, upon the mountains of
Israel, and one king shall be king to
them all; and they shall be no more
two nations, neither shall they be
divided into two kingdoms any more
at all; 23. neither shall they defile
themselves any more with their
idols, nor with their detestable
things, nor with any of their transgressions; but I will save them out
of all their dwelling-places, wherein
they have sinned, and will cleanse
them; so shall they be My people,
and I will be their God. 24. And
My servant David shall be king over
them, and they all shall have one
shepherd; they shall also walk in
Mine ordinances, and observe My
statutes, and do them. 25. And
they shall dwell in the land that I
have given unto Jacob My servant,
wherein your fathers dwelt; and
they shall dwell therein, they, and

וְקִבַּצְתִּי אֹתָם מִסָּבִיב
וְהֵבֵאתִי אוֹתָם אֶל־אַדְמָתָם:
22 וְעָשִׂיתִי אֹתָם לְגוֹי אֶחָד בָּאָרֶץ
בְּהָרֵי יִשְׂרָאֵל וּמֶלֶךְ אֶחָד
יִהְיֶה לְכֻלָּם לְמֶלֶךְ וְלֹא
יִהְיֶה־עוֹד לִשְׁנֵי גוֹיִם וְלֹא
יֵחָצוּ עוֹד לִשְׁתֵּי מַמְלָכוֹת
23 עוֹד: וְלֹא יִטַּמְּאוּ עוֹד
בְּגִלּוּלֵיהֶם וּבְשִׁקּוּצֵיהֶם וּבְכֹל
פִּשְׁעֵיהֶם וְהוֹשַׁעְתִּי אֹתָם
מִכֹּל מוֹשְׁבֹתֵיהֶם אֲשֶׁר חָטְאוּ
בָהֶם וְטִהַרְתִּי אוֹתָם וְהָיוּ־
לִי לְעָם וַאֲנִי אֶהְיֶה לָהֶם
24 לֵאלֹהִים: וְעַבְדִּי דָוִד מֶלֶךְ
עֲלֵיהֶם וְרוֹעֶה אֶחָד יִהְיֶה
לְכֻלָּם וּבְמִשְׁפָּטַי יֵלֵכוּ
וְחֻקּוֹתַי יִשְׁמְרוּ וְעָשׂוּ אוֹתָם:
25 וְיָשְׁבוּ עַל־הָאָרֶץ אֲשֶׁר נָתַתִּי
לְעַבְדִּי לְיַעֲקֹב אֲשֶׁר יָשְׁבוּ־
בָהּ אֲבוֹתֵיכֶם וְיָשְׁבוּ עָלֶיהָ

v. 22. יהיו ק׳

---

*will gather them . . . bring them into
their own land.* The reunion of the two
Kingdoms is to be preceded by the
gathering together of the dispersed in
foreign countries and their return to
Zion.

23. *I will save them out of all their
dwelling-places.* Although those who
were living among pagan nations had
adopted their idolatry, God will restore
them to their land, but will also purge
them of their heathenism.

24. *My servant David shall be king over
them.* See on xxxiv. 23.

shall have one shepherd. While *king*
signifies a political ruler, *shepherd* denotes
a spiritual leader. The Messiah will
combine both offices (Malbim).

25. *unto Jacob.* Though Abraham and
Isaac were also promised the land, only
Jacob is mentioned in this connection
because he was the ancestor of Israel
alone, whereas the other two patriarchs
were also the ancestors of Ishmael and

their children, and their children's children, for ever; and David My servant shall be their prince for ever. 26. Moreover I will make a covenant of peace with them—it shall be an everlasting covenant with them; and I will establish them, and multiply them, and will set My sanctuary in the midst of them for ever. 27. My dwelling-place also shall be over them; and I will be their God, and they shall be My people. 28. And the nations shall know that I am the LORD that sanctify Israel, when My sanctuary shall be in the midst of them for ever.'

הֵמָּה וּבְנֵיהֶם וּבְנֵי בְנֵיהֶם עַד־
עוֹלָם וְדָוִד עַבְדִּי נָשִׂיא לָהֶם
26 לְעוֹלָם: וְכָרַתִּי לָהֶם בְּרִית
שָׁלוֹם בְּרִית עוֹלָם יִהְיֶה אוֹתָם
וּנְתַתִּים וְהִרְבֵּיתִי אוֹתָם וְנָתַתִּי
אֶת־מִקְדָּשִׁי בְּתוֹכָם לְעוֹלָם:
27 וְהָיָה מִשְׁכָּנִי עֲלֵיהֶם וְהָיִיתִי
לָהֶם לֵאלֹהִים וְהֵמָּה יִהְיוּ־לִי
28 לְעָם: וְיָדְעוּ הַגּוֹיִם כִּי אֲנִי
יְהוָה מְקַדֵּשׁ אֶת־יִשְׂרָאֵל
בִּהְיוֹת מִקְדָּשִׁי בְּתוֹכָם
לְעוֹלָם:

38   CHAPTER XXXVIII   לח

1. And the word of the LORD came   1 וַיְהִי דְבַר־יְהוָה אֵלַי לֵאמֹר:

v. 28. עד כאן

Esau respectively, who were not included in the promise.

shall be their prince for ever. The term *prince* in this context is a designation for the Messiah. Ezekiel frequently uses *prince* for the future ideal ruler in the concluding part of his Book (Malbim).

26. *a covenant of peace.* In the coming age Israel will be blessed with harmony both physically and spiritually.

an everlasting covenant. The covenant of peace to be made with Israel will never again be broken. This assurance indicates that the prophecy of the restoration and reunion of the Kingdoms relates to the Messianic era.

I will establish them. i.e. permanently. The Hebrew is literally 'I will give them'; A.V. and R.V., 'I will place them.'

27. *My dwelling-place also shall be over them.* The Divine Presence will abide in the midst of Israel for ever, and the

reciprocal relationship between God and His people will be firmly established. In the opinion of Kimchi, the preposition *over,* instead of the usual 'among them,' signifies that the presence of God would inspire them with awe. He cites the Hebrew idiom: 'fear shall be *over them,* or *upon them.*' A.V. and R.V. render: 'with them.'

28. *the nations shall know,* etc. The sanctification of Israel will manifest itself to the world in his national prosperity and spiritual achievement. 'The ideas in this verse lead naturally over to the episode of Gog's invasion, the issues of which so remarkably illustrate them' (Davidson).

CHAPTER XXXVIII

THE FINAL DELIVERANCE OF ISRAEL

THIS chapter and the next deal with the abortive attack of Gog upon Israel.

unto me, saying: 2. 'Son of man, set thy face toward Gog, of the land of Magog, the chief prince of Meshech and Tubal, and prophesy against him, 3. and say: Thus saith the Lord GOD: Behold, I am against thee, O Gog, chief prince of Meshech and Tubal; 4. and I will turn thee about, and put hooks into thy jaws, and I will bring thee forth, and all thine army, horses and horsemen, all of them clothed most gorgeously, a great company with buckler and shield, all of them

2 בֶּן־אָדָם שִׂים פָּנֶיךָ אֶל־גּוֹג
אֶרֶץ הַמָּגוֹג נְשִׂיא רֹאשׁ מֶשֶׁךְ
3 וְתֻבָל וְהִנָּבֵא עָלָיו: וְאָמַרְתָּ
כֹּה אָמַר אֲדֹנָי יֱהוִֹה הִנְנִי
אֵלֶיךָ גּוֹג נְשִׂיא רֹאשׁ מֶשֶׁךְ
4 וְתֻבָל: וְשׁוֹבַבְתִּיךָ וְנָתַתִּי
חַחִים בִּלְחָיֶיךָ וְהוֹצֵאתִי
אוֹתְךָ וְאֶת־כָּל־חֵילְךָ סוּסִים
וּפָרָשִׁים לְבֻשֵׁי מִכְלוֹל כֻּלָּם
קָהָל רָב צִנָּה וּמָגֵן תֹּפְשֵׂי

The preceding chapter closed with the assurance that Israel would be restored finally to the land of his fathers which would become the permanent abode of the Divine Presence. This restoration, however, would not pass unchallenged. Formidable armies from the extreme north under the leadership of Gog would invade Israel after his return. But the invasion by Gog and his confederates, which had been predicted by former prophets (cf. verse 17, xxxix. 8), would end in the utter destruction of their forces. No specific date for the coming invasion by Gog is given. The character of the two chapters is apocalyptic and relates to the indefinite future, the advent of the Messiah, indicated by the phrase *the end of days*. After the victory peace and security will be established in Israel for ever, the Sovereignty of God re-asserted and His holy name sanctified throughout the world.

1-13 GOG'S CAMPAIGN A PROVIDENTIAL ACT

2. *Gog, of the land of Magog.* The identity of Gog is obscure, and probably he is to be understood not so much as a particular person but rather as an apocalyptic figure. Magog is the designation of the country of Gog. Magog,

Meshech and Tubal are mentioned in Gen. x. 2 among the sons of Japheth. In Rabbinic literature, Gog and Magog (the latter as an individual) are frequently referred to as the leaders of a hostile army against Israel before the coming of the Messiah. The Midrash Tanchuma (Korach, end) interprets *Gog u-Magog* to mean the assembly of enemy nations, pointing out that the numerical value of the two Hebrew words is seventy, the supposed number of peoples in the ancient world. The Palestinian Talmud (Meg. 71b) identifies Magog with Gothia, the land of the Goths (the reading in the Babylonian Talmud, Yoma 10a is 'Kandia,' perhaps Crete). Josephus (*Antiquities* I, vi. 1) associates the Magogites with the Scythians, the ancestors of the Gothians who inhabited the region of the Caucasus mountains.

Meshech and Tubal. See on xxvii. 13.

4. *I will turn thee about.* i.e. God will cause him to be diverted from the goal at which he is aiming.

put hooks into thy jaws. Cf. xxix. 4. Gog and his hosts will be captured by God and led against their will to their doom.

clothed most gorgeously. As in xxiii. 12.

handling swords: 5. Persia, Cush, and Put with them, all of them with shield and helmet; 6. Gomer, and all his bands; the house of Togarmah in the uttermost parts of the north, and all his bands; even many peoples with thee. 7. Be thou prepared, and prepare for thyself, thou, and all thy company that are assembled unto thee, and be thou guarded of them. 8. After many days thou shalt be mustered for service, in the latter years thou shalt come against the land that is brought back from the sword, that is gathered out of many peoples, against the mountains of Israel, which have been a continual waste; but it is brought forth out of the peoples, and they dwell

⁵ חַרְבוֹת כֻּלָם ׃ פָּרַס כּוּשׁ וּפוּט

⁶ אִתָּם כֻּלָם מָגֵן וְכוֹבָע ׃ גֹּמֶר וְכָל־אֲגַפֶּיהָ בֵּית תּוֹגַרְמָה יַרְכְּתֵי צָפוֹן וְאֶת־כָּל־אֲגַפָּיו עַמִּים רַבִּים אִתָּךְ ׃

⁷ הִכֹּן וְהָכֵן לְךָ אַתָּה וְכָל־קְהָלֶךָ הַנִּקְהָלִים עָלֶיךָ

⁸ וְהָיִיתָ לָהֶם לְמִשְׁמָר ׃ מִיָּמִים רַבִּים תִּפָּקֵד בְּאַחֲרִית הַשָּׁנִים תָּבוֹא | אֶל־אֶרֶץ | מְשׁוֹבֶבֶת מֵחֶרֶב מְקֻבֶּצֶת מֵעַמִּים רַבִּים עַל הָרֵי יִשְׂרָאֵל אֲשֶׁר־הָיוּ לְחָרְבָּה תָּמִיד | וְהִיא מֵעַמִּים הוּצָאָה וְיָשְׁבוּ לָבֶטַח כֻּלָם ׃

---

5. *Persia, Cush and Put.* See on xxvii. 10.

6. *Gomer.* The eldest son of Japheth (Gen. x. 2). Some scholars identify Gomer with the Cimmerians, the Greek name for the Armenians. The Targum renders: 'Garmamia.' In the Talmudic passages cited on verse 2 the reading is 'Germania,' which has been identified with Kerman in south Persia.

bands. Cf. xii.

Togarmah. See on xxvii. 14.

7. *be thou prepared, and prepare for thyself.* Gog is ironically exhorted to make himself prepared and also to spur on his allies to make themselves ready for the campaign against Israel.

be thou guarded of them. A.V. and R.V. more lit., 'be thou a guard unto them'; be the commander of the combined forces.

8. *after many days thou shalt be mustered*

for service. The attack by Gog will take place in the distant future when Israel had been restored and for a time had enjoyed peace and security. Kimchi was apparently aware of the story told in the Koran (Sura xviii) that Alexander the Great built a wall around Gog and Magog to shut them off from the rest of the world; and he understands the clause to mean that, after having been excluded from the outside world, Gog will make a reappearance upon the stage of history.

the land that is brought back from the sword. The gravity of Gog's crime will lie in the fact that his attack was directed against a land which had been desolated and whose people have been redeemed from the countries of their dispersion.

a continual waste. This is the literal translation, but *tamid* here signifies 'for a long time,' meaning the period of the exile.

it is brought forth . . . peoples. The subject, which is feminine in the Hebrew,

safely all of them. 9. And thou shalt ascend, thou shalt come like a storm, thou shalt be like a cloud to cover the land, thou, and all thy bands, and many peoples with thee.

10. Thus saith the Lord GOD: It shall come to pass in that day, that things shall come into thy mind, and thou shalt devise an evil device;

11. and thou shalt say: I will go up against the land of unwalled villages; I will come upon them that are at quiet, that dwell safely, all of them dwelling without walls, and having neither bars nor gates; 12. to take the spoil and to take the prey; to turn thy hand against the waste places that are now inhabited, and against the people that are gathered out of the nations, that have gotten cattle and goods, that dwell in the middle of the earth. 13. Sheba, and Dedan, and the merchants of

9 וְעָלִיתָ כַּשֹּׁאָה תָבוֹא כֶּעָנָן
לְכַסּוֹת הָאָרֶץ תִּהְיֶה אַתָּה
וְכָל־אֲגַפֶּיךָ וְעַמִּים רַבִּים
10 אוֹתָךְ׃ כֹּה אָמַר אֲדֹנָי יְהֹוִה
וְהָיָה ׀ בַּיּוֹם הַהוּא יַעֲלוּ
דְבָרִים עַל־לְבָבֶךָ וְחָשַׁבְתָּ
11 מַחֲשֶׁבֶת רָעָה׃ וְאָמַרְתָּ
אֶעֱלֶה עַל־אֶרֶץ פְּרָזוֹת
אָבוֹא הַשֹּׁקְטִים יֹשְׁבֵי לָבֶטַח
כֻּלָּם יֹשְׁבִים בְּאֵין חוֹמָה
וּבְרִיחַ וּדְלָתַיִם אֵין לָהֶם׃
12 לִשְׁלֹל שָׁלָל וְלָבֹז בַּז לְהָשִׁיב
יָדְךָ עַל־חֳרָבוֹת נוֹשָׁבוֹת
וְאֶל־עַם מְאֻסָּף מִגּוֹיִם עֹשֶׂה
מִקְנֶה וְקִנְיָן יֹשְׁבֵי עַל־טַבּוּר
13 הָאָרֶץ׃ שְׁבָא וּדְדָן וְסֹחֲרֵי

can only refer to *the land.* Ehrlich interprets: 'so that it was excluded from (no longer reckoned among) the nations,' and the continuation would then mean: 'but (the returned exiles), all of them, inhabited (it) in security.'

9. *like a storm . . . like a cloud.* A figure for the strength and terrifying appearance of Gog's approaching armies (cf. Jer. iv. 13).

10. *in that day.* At the time when Israel is again settled in his land.

thou shalt devise an evil device. viz. the invasion of the Land of Israel.

11. *the land of unwalled villages.* In the condition of peace and feeling secure, Israel will have made no preparations against attack by building walls around his cities. The defenceless state of the

land will be an incentive to Gog to make it the object of his campaign.

12. *to turn thy hand against.* An idiom indicating 'to take strong measures against' (cf. Isa. i. 25).

that dwell in the middle of the earth. lit. 'in the navel of the earth'; the phrase occurs again in Judg. ix. 37. The Land of Israel was considered to be geographically the centre of the world as the navel is in the centre of the body (cf. v. 5). This is mentioned to stress the viciousness of Gog's plan. He dwelt in the far north, a great distance from the Land of Israel; so the people of the latter could have had no aggressive designs upon him.

13. *Sheba, and Dedan, and the merchants of Tarshish.* For these nations and the

Tarshish, with all the magnates thereof, shall say unto thee: Comest thou to take the spoil? hast thou assembled thy company to take the prey? to carry away silver and gold, to take away cattle and goods, to take great spoil?

14. Therefore, son of man, prophesy, and say unto Gog: Thus saith the Lord GOD: In that day when My people Israel dwelleth safely, shalt thou not know it? 15. And thou shalt come from thy place out of the uttermost parts of the north, thou, and many peoples with thee, all of them riding upon horses, a great company and a mighty army; 16. and thou shalt come up against My people Israel, as a cloud to cover the land; it shall be in the end of days, and I will bring thee against My land, that the nations may know Me, when I shall be sanctified through thee, O Gog, before their eyes.

תַּרְשִׁישׁ וְכָל־כְּפִירֶיהָ יֹאמְרוּ לְךָ הֲלִשְׁלֹל שָׁלָל אַתָּה בָא הֲלָבֹז בַּז הִקְהַלְתָּ קְהָלֶךָ לָשֵׂאת ׀ כֶּסֶף וְזָהָב לָקַחַת מִקְנֶה וְקִנְיָן לִשְׁלֹל שָׁלָל גָּדוֹל: 14 לָכֵן הִנָּבֵא בֶן־אָדָם וְאָמַרְתָּ לְגוֹג כֹּה אָמַר אֲדֹנָי יְהֹוִה הֲלוֹא ׀ בַּיּוֹם הַהוּא בְּשֶׁבֶת עַמִּי יִשְׂרָאֵל לָבֶטַח תֵּדָע: 15 וּבָאתָ מִמְּקוֹמְךָ מִיַּרְכְּתֵי צָפוֹן אַתָּה וְעַמִּים רַבִּים אִתָּךְ רֹכְבֵי סוּסִים כֻּלָּם קָהָל גָּדוֹל וְחַיִל רָב: 16 וְעָלִיתָ עַל־עַמִּי יִשְׂרָאֵל כֶּעָנָן לְכַסּוֹת הָאָרֶץ בְּאַחֲרִית הַיָּמִים תִּהְיֶה וַהֲבִאוֹתִיךָ עַל־אַרְצִי לְמַעַן דַּעַת הַגּוֹיִם אֹתִי בְּהִקָּדְשִׁי בְךָ לְעֵינֵיהֶם גּוֹג:

special articles of their trading, see on xxvii. 22, 15, 12. They hoped to derive personal gain by purchasing the goods plundered by Gog's armies.

the magnates thereof. lit. 'the lions thereof,' a figure for the leading merchants (cf. *thou didst liken thyself unto a young lion of the nations,* xxxii, 2).

14-23 DESTRUCTION OF GOG'S HORDES

14. *therefore.* Such being the design of Gog, the prophet is commanded to tell him that, far from succeeding, his attack will be an occasion when God's name will be sanctified by his defeat.

shalt thou not know it? viz. the state of Israel's peace and confidence which had led to his unpreparedness, so that thou wilt choose him for thy victim.

16. *as a cloud.* Which covers the earth with gloom; so will Gog invade with a vast army which covers a wide battle area.

I will bring thee against My land. 'How can it be just that God should Himself lead the barbarians to a crime for which He destroys them? To the Hebrews God is the ultimate cause of all things; if the savage comes, God must have brought him; if he is destroyed, God

K

17. Thus saith the Lord GOD:
Art thou he of whom I spoke in old
time by My servants the prophets of
Israel, that prophesied in those days
for many years, that I would bring
thee against them? 18. And it shall
come to pass in that day, when Gog
shall come against the land of Israel,
saith the Lord GOD, that My fury
shall arise up in My nostrils.
19. For in My jealousy and in the
fire of My wrath have I spoken:
Surely in that day there shall be a
great shaking in the land of Israel;
20. so that the fishes of the sea, and
the fowls of the heaven, and the
beasts of the field and all creeping
things that creep upon the ground,

17 כֹּה־אָמַר אֲדֹנָי יֱהוִֹה הַאַתָּה־
הוּא אֲשֶׁר־דִּבַּרְתִּי בְּיָמִים
קַדְמוֹנִים בְּיַד עֲבָדַי נְבִיאֵי
יִשְׂרָאֵל הַנִּבְּאִים בַּיָּמִים הָהֵם
שָׁנִים לְהָבִיא אֹתְךָ עֲלֵיהֶם:
18 *וְהָיָה | בַּיּוֹם הַהוּא בְּיוֹם
בּוֹא גוֹג עַל־אַדְמַת יִשְׂרָאֵל
נְאֻם אֲדֹנָי יֱהוִֹה תַּעֲלֶה חֲמָתִי
19 בְּאַפִּי: וּבְקִנְאָתִי בְאֵשׁ־
עֶבְרָתִי דִבַּרְתִּי אִם־לֹא |
בַּיּוֹם הַהוּא יִהְיֶה רַעַשׁ גָּדוֹל
20 עַל אַדְמַת יִשְׂרָאֵל: וְרָעֲשׁוּ
מִפָּנַי דְּגֵי הַיָּם וְעוֹף הַשָּׁמַיִם
וְחַיַּת הַשָּׂדֶה וְכָל־הָרֶמֶשׂ
הָרֹמֵשׂ עַל־הָאֲדָמָה וְכֹל

v. 18. הפטרת שבת וחול חמועד של סוכות.

must have planned to destroy him'
(Lofthouse). Though the purpose of
Gog's campaign is said to be lust for
destruction and spoil, it is an act designed
in God's wisdom to bring mankind to
the realization that He is King of the
universe.

17. *art thou he of whom I spoke in old time.*
As Gog's invasion had been predicted
long ago although his name had not been
specified, God now identifies him with
the man spoken of in the prophecies.

by My servants the prophets. The
reference cannot be to Zechariah who
was later than Ezekiel, and chapter xiv
of his Book may be dependent upon this
chapter. The allusion may be to
Zephaniah (cf. his chapter i), Jeremiah
(cf. iv. 5ff.) and possibly other predictions which are not recorded.

in many years. Or, 'many years ago,'

before the fulfilment of the prophecy
(Kimchi).

18. *My fury*, etc. Cf. Deut. xxxii. 22;
Ps. xviii. 9. It denotes the Divine
anger manifesting itself as a destructive
force.

19. *in My jealousy.* This translation of
the term *kin'ah* in connection with God
is inadequate and misleading. The
proper meaning of the word is 'vindication.' When man outrages His moral
law, He is roused to action with the
purpose of vindicating it.

shaking. If an earthquake is intended,
such a phenomenon is often part of an
apocalyptic outlook. Rashi explains it
of lightning and thunder.

20. *shall shake at My presence.* Universal
panic will be caused by God's manifestation in behalf of Israel.

257

and all the men that are upon the face of the earth, shall shake at My presence, and the mountains shall be thrown down, and the steep places shall fall, and every wall shall fall to the ground. 21. And I will call for a sword against him throughout all My mountains, saith the Lord GOD; every man's sword shall be against his brother. 22. And I will plead against him with pestilence and with blood; and I will cause to rain upon him, and upon his bands, and upon the many peoples that are with him, an overflowing shower, and great hailstones, fire, and brimstone. 23. Thus will I magnify Myself, and sanctify Myself, and I will make Myself known in the eyes of many nations; and they shall know that I am the LORD.

הָאָדָם אֲשֶׁר עַל־פְּנֵי הָאֲדָמָה וְנֶהֶרְסוּ הֶהָרִים וְנָפְלוּ הַמַּדְרֵגוֹת וְכָל־חוֹמָה לָאָרֶץ תִּפּוֹל: וְקָרָאתִי עָלָיו 21 לְכָל־הָרַי חֶרֶב נְאֻם אֲדֹנָי יְהֹוִה חֶרֶב אִישׁ בְּאָחִיו תִּהְיֶה: וְנִשְׁפַּטְתִּי אִתּוֹ בְּדֶבֶר וּבְדָם 22 וְגֶשֶׁם שׁוֹטֵף וְאַבְנֵי אֶלְגָּבִישׁ אֵשׁ וְגָפְרִית אַמְטִיר עָלָיו וְעַל־אֲגַפָּיו וְעַל־עַמִּים רַבִּים אֲשֶׁר אִתּוֹ: וְהִתְגַּדִּלְתִּי 23 וְהִתְקַדִּשְׁתִּי וְנוֹדַעְתִּי לְעֵינֵי גּוֹיִם רַבִּים וְיָדְעוּ כִּי־אֲנִי יְהֹוָה:

39   CHAPTER XXXIX   לט

1. And thou, son of man, prophesy   וְאַתָּה בֶן־אָדָם הִנָּבֵא עַל־גּוֹג 1

---

steep places. The Targum and Peshitta render 'towers,' perhaps reading *migdaloth* for *madregoth;* but the noun occurs in Cant. ii. 14 where it is parallel to *rock* and so signifies something natural, not manufactured.

21. *against him.* viz. Gog.

throughout all My mountains. The enemy is represented as having overrun the Holy Land.

every man's sword shall be against his brother. In the panic created by God's presence, the heathen hordes will not distinguish between friend and foe but wildly strike with their swords, killing one another. This happened in the past (cf. Judg. vii. 22; 1 Sam. xiv. 20).

22. *I will plead against him.* By exercising His judgment upon Gog, God will demonstrate his guilt.

great hailstones. As in xiii. 11, 13.

23. *they shall know that I am the LORD.* The demonstration of God's omnipotence and His deliverance of Israel will bring about universal recognition of His Sovereignty.

CHAPTER XXXIX

THE FATE OF GOG'S HORDES

THE prophet proceeds to give a more detailed and vivid account of the disaster which is to befall Gog's armies. So vast will be the multitudes of the enemy that

against Gog, and say: Thus saith
the Lord GOD: Behold, I am against
thee, O Gog, chief prince of
Meshech and Tubal; 2. and I will
turn thee about and lead thee on,
and will cause thee to come up from
the uttermost parts of the north;
and I will bring thee upon the
mountains of Israel; 3. and I will
smite thy bow out of thy left hand,
and will cause thine arrows to fall
out of thy right hand. 4. Thou
shalt fall upon the mountains of
Israel, thou, and all thy bands, and
the peoples that are with thee;
I will give thee unto the ravenous
birds of every sort and to the beasts
of the field, to be devoured. 5. Thou
shalt fall upon the open field; for
I have spoken it, saith the Lord
GOD. 6. And I will send a fire on
Magog, and on them that dwell
safely in the isles; and they shall

וְאָמַרְתָּ כֹּה אָמַר אֲדֹנָי יְהוִה
הִנְנִי אֵלֶיךָ גּוֹג נְשִׂיא רֹאשׁ מֶשֶׁךְ
וְתֻבָל: וְשֹׁבַבְתִּיךָ וְשִׁשֵּׁאתִיךָ ²
וְהַעֲלִיתִיךָ מִיַּרְכְּתֵי צָפוֹן
וַהֲבִאוֹתִיךָ עַל־־הָרֵי
יִשְׂרָאֵל: וְהִכֵּיתִי קַשְׁתְּךָ מִיַּד ³
שְׂמֹאולֶךָ וְחִצֶּיךָ מִיַּד יְמִינְךָ
אַפִּיל: עַל־־הָרֵי יִשְׂרָאֵל ⁴
תִּפּוֹל אַתָּה וְכָל־־אֲגַפֶּיךָ
וְעַמִּים אֲשֶׁר אִתָּךְ לְעֵיט צִפּוֹר
כָּל־־כָּנָף , וְחַיַּת הַשָּׂדֶה
נְתַתִּיךָ לְאָכְלָה: עַל־פְּנֵי ⁵
הַשָּׂדֶה תִּפּוֹל כִּי אֲנִי דִבַּרְתִּי
נְאֻם אֲדֹנָי יְהוִה: וְשִׁלַּחְתִּי־ ⁶
אֵשׁ בְּמָגוֹג וּבְיֹשְׁבֵי הָאִיִּים

v. 2. א׳ מלא ואו׳   v. 3. נחה

he wood from his weapons will serve
he Israelites as fuel for seven years, and
: will take them seven months to bury
.is dead.   Birds and beasts are to enjoy
 great feast, devouring the flesh of the
ighty and drinking the blood of the
rinces.   After reiterating the whole-
ome effect which the annihilation of
jog's followers will have upon Israel
nd upon mankind in general, Ezekiel
eclares in a final, triumphant oracle
hat the restoration of Israel, confirmed
y the destruction of his enemies, will be
omplete and his regeneration lasting,
or I have poured out My spirit upon the
ouse of Israel.

1-10 THE ANNIHILATION OF GOG

behold, I am, etc.   As in xxxviii. 3.

, I will turn thee about.   See on xxxviii. 4.

lead thee on.   The Hebrew verb is otherwise unknown.

I will bring thee.   See on xxxviii. 16.

upon the mountains of Israel. Cf. xxxviii.
21.   'Most invaders would be content
with ravaging the plains; this horde
leaves no hilly spot untouched' (Lofthouse).

3. *I will smite thy bow out of thy left hand.*
The skill in archery which distinguished
the foe would be of no avail with God
as Israel's Ally; cf. *then shall the LORD
go forth, and fight against those nations*
(Zech. xiv. 3).

4. *I will give thee.*   lit. 'I have given thee,'
the prophetic perfect.

6. *on Magog,* etc.   Not only will the
invaders be slain in the Land of Israel,
but the countries from which they came
will also suffer at God's hand.

know that I am the LORD.   7. And
My holy name will I make known
in the midst of My people Israel;
neither will I suffer My holy name
to be profaned any more; and the
nations shall know that I am the
LORD, the Holy One in Israel.
8. Behold, it cometh, and it shall
be done, saith the Lord GOD; this
is the day whereof I have spoken.
9. And they that dwell in the cities
of Israel shall go forth, and shall
make fires of the weapons and use
them as fuel, both the shields and
the bucklers, the bows and the
arrows, and the handstaves, and the
spears, and they shall make fires of
them seven years; 10. so that they
shall take no wood out of the field,
neither cut down any out of the
forests, for they shall make fires of
the weapons; and they shall spoil
those that spoiled them, and rob
those that robbed them, saith the
Lord GOD.

11. And it shall come to pass in
that day, that I will give unto Gog

לְבֶ֫טַח וְיָדְע֖וּ כִּי־אֲנִ֥י יְהוָֽה׃
7 וְאֶת־שֵׁ֤ם קָדְשִׁי֙ אוֹדִ֣יעַ בְּתוֹךְ֙
עַמִּ֣י יִשְׂרָאֵ֔ל וְלֹֽא־אַחֵ֥ל אֶת־
שֵֽׁם־קָדְשִׁ֖י ע֑וֹד וְיָדְע֣וּ הַגּוֹיִ֗ם
כִּי־אֲנִ֤י יְהוָה֙ קָד֖וֹשׁ בְּיִשְׂרָאֵֽל׃
8 הִנֵּ֤ה בָאָה֙ וְנִֽהְיָ֔תָה נְאֻ֖ם אֲדֹנָ֣י
יְהוִ֑ה ה֣וּא הַיּ֔וֹם אֲשֶׁ֖ר דִּבַּֽרְתִּי׃
9 וְֽיָצְא֞וּ יֹשְׁבֵ֣י ׀ עָרֵ֣י יִשְׂרָאֵ֗ל
וּבִֽעֲר֡וּ וְ֠הִשִּׂיקוּ בְּנֶ֨שֶׁק וּמָגֵ֤ן
וְצִנָּה֙ בְּקֶ֣שֶׁת וּבְחִצִּ֔ים וּבְמַקֵּ֥ל
יָ֖ד וּבְרֹ֑מַח וּבִעֲר֥וּ בָהֶ֛ם אֵ֖שׁ
10 שֶׁ֣בַע שָׁנִֽים׃ וְלֹֽא־יִשְׂא֨וּ עֵצִ֜ים
מִן־הַשָּׂדֶ֗ה וְלֹ֤א יַחְטְבוּ֙ מִן־
הַיְּעָרִ֔ים כִּ֥י בַנֶּ֖שֶׁק יְבַֽעֲרוּ־
אֵ֑שׁ וְשָׁלְל֣וּ אֶת־שֹׁלְלֵיהֶ֗ם
וּבָֽזְז֛וּ אֶת־בֹּֽזְזֵיהֶ֖ם נְאֻ֖ם אֲדֹנָ֥י
11 יְהוִֽה׃ וְהָיָ֣ה בַיּ֣וֹם הַה֗וּא אֶתֵּ֣ן

v. 8. קמץ בז״ק

7. *neither will I suffer My holy name to
be profaned any more.* The dispersion
of Israel and his subsequent sufferings
led to the profanation of God's holy
name, because they were interpreted by
heathen nations as due to His inability to
protect His people.

the Holy One in Israel. That the Divine
Presence abides in the midst of Israel
will then become evident to those nations
who had placed so false a construction
upon His people's exile.

8. *it cometh, and it shall be done.* i.e. the
catastrophe upon Gog is so certain that
it is as good as accomplished.

9. *shall go forth.* The inhabitants of the
Land of Israel, who hitherto had not left

their homes to meet Gog in battle, will
now come out to gather the wooden parts
of the weapons for fuel. It is to be noted
that in the state of security assured by
God, the weapons themselves serve no
useful purpose and are not gathered and
stored for a future war.

seven years. So great will the quantity
be, that it will suffice for seven years.

10. *they shall take no wood out of the field*
They will have no need to fetch wood
from the field or forest during the seven
years.

11-16 BURIAL OF THE SLAIN AND
CLEANSING OF THE LAND

11. *in that day.* Foretold in the preceding section.

a place fit for burial in Israel, the
valley of them that pass through on
the east of the sea; and it shall stop
them that pass through; and there
shall they bury Gog and all his
multitude; and they shall call it
The valley of Hamon-gog. 12. And
seven months shall the house of
Israel be burying them, that they
may cleanse the land. 13. Yea, all
the people of the land shall bury
them, and it shall be to them a
renown; in the day that I shall be
glorified, saith the Lord GOD.
14. And they shall set apart men of
continual employment, that shall
pass through the land to bury with
them that pass through those that
remain upon the face of the land,

לְגוֹג ׀ מְקוֹם־שָׁם קֶבֶר
בְּיִשְׂרָאֵל גֵּי הָעֹבְרִים קִדְמַת
הַיָּם וְחֹסֶמֶת הִיא אֶת־
הָעֹבְרִים וְקָבְרוּ שָׁם אֶת־גּוֹג
וְאֶת־כָּל־הֲמוֹנֹה וְקָרְאוּ גֵּיא
הֲמוֹן גּוֹג: וּקְבָרוּם בֵּית   12
יִשְׂרָאֵל לְמַעַן טַהֵר אֶת־
הָאָרֶץ שִׁבְעָה חֳדָשִׁים: וְקָבְרוּ   13
כָּל־עַם הָאָרֶץ וְהָיָה לָהֶם
לְשֵׁם יוֹם הִכָּבְדִי נְאֻם אֲדֹנָי
יְהֹוִה: וַאֲנָשֵׁי תָמִיד יַבְדִּילוּ   14
עֹבְרִים בָּאָרֶץ מְקַבְּרִים אֶת־
הָעֹבְרִים אֶת־הַנּוֹתָרִים עַל־

a place fit for burial. lit. 'a place of
there burial,' a place where there will be
burial for him and his host.
the valley of them that pass through. i.e.
the valley through which one passes to
(there is nothing corresponding to on in
the text) the east of the sea, viz. the Dead
Sea. An alternative explanation given
by Davidson is: 'The expression is
probably a proper name; the "valley of
the passers through" may have been so
named as the usual route of communication between the east and west of the sea.'
it shall stop them that pass through. The
valley where the slain are to be buried is
the thoroughfare for traffic between east
and west, but it will be blocked by the
multitude of dead bodies (Rashi). The
rendering of A.V., 'it shall stop the
(noses of the) passengers,' because of the
stench, is based on Kimchi.
Hamon-gog. Meaning 'the multitude of
Gog.'
12. shall the house of Israel be burying them.
An unburied corpse is a reproach to God

and causes defilement of the land (cf.
Deut. xxi. 23). Therefore Israel will
have to bury the slain to cleanse the land.
There will be so many that the task will
last seven months.

13. all the people of the land shall bury
them. The whole population of Israel
will take part in the burial of their
enemies, and their act of honouring these
dead will bring them renown among the
nations (Rashi). The renown will be
due to the vast number of the slain as
proved by the length of time the burial
took (Metsudath David). The latter
explanation fits in better with the continuation: the greatness of Israel's
victory will bring honour to God's name.

14. they shall set apart men of continual
employment. After seven months, during
which the corpses found will have been
buried, men are to be appointed to do
nothing else but search throughout the
land for any body or bones which were
not detected.
to bury with them that pass through. The

to cleanse it; after the end of seven months shall they search. 15. And when they that pass through shall pass through the land, and any seeth a man's bone, then shall he set up a sign by it, till the buriers have buried it in the valley of Hamon-gog. 16. And Hamonah shall also be the name of a city. Thus shall they cleanse the land.

17. And thou, son of man, thus saith the Lord GOD: Speak unto the birds of every sort, and to every beast of the field: Assemble yourselves, and come; gather yourselves on every side to My feast that I do prepare for you, even a great feast, upon the mountains of Israel, that ye may eat flesh and drink blood.

פְּנֵי הָאָרֶץ לְטַהֲרָהּ מִקְצֵה
שִׁבְעָה־חֳדָשִׁים יַחְקֹרוּ׃
15 וְעָבְרוּ הָעֹבְרִים בָּאָרֶץ וְרָאָה
עֶצֶם אָדָם וּבָנָה אֶצְלוֹ צִיּוּן
עַד קָבְרוּ אֹתוֹ הַמְקַבְּרִים
16 אֶל־גֵּיא הֲמוֹן גּוֹג׃ וְגַם שֶׁם־
עִיר הֲמוֹנָה וְטִהֲרוּ הָאָרֶץ׃
17 וְאַתָּה בֶן־אָדָם כֹּה־אָמַר ׀
אֲדֹנָי יֱהֹוִה אֱמֹר לְצִפּוֹר כָּל־
כָּנָף וּלְכֹל ׀ חַיַּת הַשָּׂדֶה
הִקָּבְצוּ וָבֹאוּ הֵאָסְפוּ מִסָּבִיב
עַל־זִבְחִי אֲשֶׁר אֲנִי זֹבֵחַ לָכֶם
זֶבַח גָּדוֹל עַל הָרֵי יִשְׂרָאֵל
וַאֲכַלְתֶּם בָּשָׂר וּשְׁתִיתֶם דָּם׃

v. 16.　v. 17. עד כאן מלעיל

appointed men will bury the remains they find with the assistance of passers-by. What is meant by this phrase is explained in the next verse.

shall they search. i.e. begin the task of searching.

15. *when they that pass through shall pass through the land.* This refers to wayfarers who, if they saw a human bone, would mark the spot by a sign, so that the employed men may notice it and remove it for burial in the valley of Hamon-gog.

16. *Hamonah shall also be the name of a city.* 'A city shall also be built in commemoration of Gog's overthrow; naturally the city must be supposed situated near the valley of Hamon-gog, because its name Hamonah (multitude), if the city were situated elsewhere, would not of itself suggest any connection with Gog' (Davidson).

thus shall they cleanse the land. This concluding clause provides the reason for the great care taken to remove the corpses and name the city after the vast burial-place. The city would help to cleanse the land, because it would serve as a reminder to keep away from the defiled area.

17-24 THE VICTORY FEAST AND VINDICATION OF GOD'S JUDGMENT

17. *My feast.* lit. 'My sacrifice.' The two ideas are interconnected, since one was usually the occasion of the other. 'To an Israelite, the sacrifice here described is a grim parody of the true sacrifice, since the "guests" drink the blood, a rite absolutely forbidden in Israel' (Lofthouse).

that ye may eat flesh and drink blood. The food and drink for the feast will consist of the dead bodies of Gog's warriors. The celebration to which the birds and beasts are invited would, of

18. The flesh of the mighty shall ye
eat, and the blood of the princes of
the earth shall ye drink; rams,
lambs, and goats, bullocks, fatlings
of Bashan are they all of them.
19. And ye shall eat fat till ye be
full, and drink blood till ye be
drunken, of My feast which I have
prepared for you.   20. And ye shall
be filled at My table with horses and
horsemen, with mighty men, and
with all men of war, saith the Lord
GOD.   21. And I will set My glory
among the nations, and all the
nations shall see My judgment that
I have executed, and My hand that
I have laid upon them.   22. So the
house of Israel shall know that I am
the LORD their God, from that day
and forward.   23. And the nations
shall know that the house of Israel
went into captivity for their iniquity,
because they broke faith with Me,
and I hid My face from them; so

18 בְּשַׂר גִּבּוֹרִים תֹּאכֵלוּ וְדַם־
נְשִׂיאֵי הָאָרֶץ תִּשְׁתּוּ אֵילִים
כָּרִים וְעַתּוּדִים פָּרִים מְרִיאֵי
19 בָשָׁן כֻּלָּם: וַאֲכַלְתֶּם־חֵלֶב
לְשָׂבְעָה וּשְׁתִיתֶם דָּם לְשִׁכָּרוֹן
מִזִּבְחִי אֲשֶׁר־זָבַחְתִּי לָכֶם:
20 וּשְׂבַעְתֶּם עַל־שֻׁלְחָנִי סוּס
וָרֶכֶב גִּבּוֹר וְכָל־אִישׁ
מִלְחָמָה נְאֻם אֲדֹנָי יֱהֹוִה:
21 וְנָתַתִּי אֶת־כְּבוֹדִי בַּגּוֹיִם וְרָאוּ
כָל־הַגּוֹיִם אֶת־מִשְׁפָּטִי אֲשֶׁר
עָשִׂיתִי וְאֶת־יָדִי אֲשֶׁר־שַׂמְתִּי
22 בָהֶם: וְיָדְעוּ בֵּית יִשְׂרָאֵל כִּי
אֲנִי יְהֹוָה אֱלֹהֵיהֶם מִן־הַיּוֹם
23 הַהוּא וָהָלְאָה: וְיָדְעוּ הַגּוֹיִם
כִּי בַעֲוֹנָם גָּלוּ בֵית־יִשְׂרָאֵל
עַל אֲשֶׁר מָעֲלוּ־בִי וָאַסְתִּר

v. 19. מלעיל

course, take place before the corpses were
interred, although their ultimate burial
has already been recorded.
18. *rams*, etc.   The animals enumerated
are those which were brought upon the
sacrificial altar, and are used as a figure
for the leading men (cf. Isa. xxxiv. 6ff.;
Jer. li. 40).
Bashan.   In Transjordan, famous for
its breeds of cattle (cf. Deut. xxxii. 14;
Ps. xxii. 13).
20. *ye shall be filled*.   The invited birds
and beasts are still being addressed.
My table.   God being the 'Host' at the
feast.
horsemen.   The Hebrew *recheb* is more
strictly 'chariot' (as in A.V. and R.V.)

and represents 'charioteers'; but there
are passages where the meaning seems
to be 'rider' (cf. Isa. xxi. 7, 9).

21. *I will set My glory among the nations.*
The overthrow of Gog's formidable force
will be acknowledged to be a Divine act.

22. *the house of Israel shall know.*   The
miraculous deliverance will also confirm
Israel's faith and confidence in God.

23. *the nations shall know.*   The manifestation of God's omnipotence in the
defeat of Gog and His intervention on
behalf of His people will prove to the
nations that Israel's suffering in exile
was not due to His inability to save him
but to his sin.

I gave them into the hand of their adversaries, and they fell all of them by the sword. 24. According to their uncleanness and according to their transgressions did I unto them; and I hid My face from them.

25. Therefore thus saith the Lord GOD: Now will I bring back the captivity of Jacob, and have compassion upon the whole house of Israel; and I will be jealous for My holy name. 26. And they shall bear their shame, and all their breach of faith which they have committed against Me, when they shall dwell safely in their land, and none shall make them afraid; 27. when I have brought them back from the peoples, and gathered them out of their enemies' lands, and am sanctified in them in the sight of many nations. 28. And they shall know that I am the LORD their God, in that I caused

פָּנַי מֵהֶם וָאֶתְּנֵם בְּיַד צָרֵיהֶם
וַיִּפְּלוּ בַחֶרֶב כֻּלָם:
24 כְּטֻמְאָתָם וּכְפִשְׁעֵיהֶם עָשִׂיתִי
25 אֹתָם וָאַסְתִּר פָּנַי מֵהֶם: לָכֵן
כֹּה אָמַר אֲדֹנָי יֱהוִֹה עַתָּה
אָשִׁיב אֶת־שְׁבִית יַעֲקֹב
וְרִחַמְתִּי כָּל־בֵּית יִשְׂרָאֵל
26 וְקִנֵּאתִי לְשֵׁם קָדְשִׁי: וְנָשׂוּ
אֶת־כְּלִמָּתָם וְאֶת־כָּל־
מַעֲלָם אֲשֶׁר מָעֲלוּ־בִי
בְּשִׁבְתָּם עַל־אַדְמָתָם לָבֶטַח
27 וְאֵין מַחֲרִיד: בְּשׁוֹבְבִי אוֹתָם
מִן־הָעַמִּים וְקִבַּצְתִּי אֹתָם
מֵאַרְצוֹת אֹיְבֵיהֶם וְנִקְדַּשְׁתִּי
28 בָם לְעֵינֵי הַגּוֹיִם רַבִּים: וְיָדְעוּ
כִּי אֲנִי יֱהוִֹה אֱלֹהֵיהֶם

v. 25. שבות ק'   v. 26. חסר א'

---

all of them. This is a hyperbolical expression. What it means is that a great number of them perished.

25-29 FINAL REASSURANCE OF ISRAEL'S REDEMPTION

25. *now.* The decree of punishment for Israel's sins having been fulfilled, a new and happy era will be inaugurated for the nation.

I will be jealous for My holy name. See on xxxviii. 19.

26. *they shall bear their shame.* Settled securely in his land and enjoying in abundance God's blessing, Israel will feel deeply ashamed of his evil past. The *kethib* apparently intends 'they will forget,' but it does not suit the context

which strikes the note of permanent national fidelity and happiness.

27. *when I have brought them back.* This verse is to be connected with the preceding: *none shall make them afraid, when I have brought them back.*

am sanctified in them. See on verse 7.

many nations. The adjective without the definite article is irregular. The sense may be: 'the nations (who will be) many.'

28. *they shall know that I am the LORD.* God's dealings with Israel will bring home to the nations that He reveals Himself in history no less than in Nature, and there is a Divine plan in human affairs which gradually unfolds itself in time.

them to go into captivity among the
nations, and have gathered them
unto their own land; and I will
leave none of them any more there;
29. neither will I hide My face any
more from them; for I have poured
out My spirit upon the house of
Israel, saith the Lord GOD.'

בְּהַגְלוֹתִי אוֹתָם אֶל־הַגּוֹיִם
וְכִנַּסְתִּים אֶל־אַדְמָתָם וְלֹא־
אוֹתִיר עוֹד מֵהֶם שָׁם: וְלֹא־ 29
אַסְתִּיר עוֹד פָּנַי מֵהֶם אֲשֶׁר
שָׁפַכְתִּי אֶת־רוּחִי עַל־בֵּית
יִשְׂרָאֵל נְאֻם אֲדֹנָי יֱהֹוִה:

40   CHAPTER XL   מ

1. In the five and twentieth year of
our captivity, in the beginning of

בְּעֶשְׂרִים וְחָמֵשׁ שָׁנָה לְגָלוּתֵנוּ 1

there. In foreign lands.

29. *neither will I hide My face any more from them.* My Divine Presence will never again leave them (Targum).

I have poured out My spirit upon the house of Israel. Some Jewish commentators explain that in the Messianic age the spirit of prophecy will be restored to Israel; others that under the benign influence of God's spirit, the nation will not again lapse into evil and so the redeemed state of Israel will endure.

CHAPTER XL

THE TEMPLE OF THE FUTURE

IN the concluding section, chapters xl-xlviii, Ezekiel draws a design of the Temple, the sacrificial worship, the people and the land in the new era which follows the overthrow of Gog. In a vision, the prophet finds himself transported to a very high mountain in Jerusalem where he beholds the Temple in the process of being rebuilt. An angel who measures the outer and inner courts, the buildings of the Temple and their annexes acts as his guide and interpreter. The prophet witnesses the return of the Divine Presence in the *Merkabah* which he saw at the beginning of his career (i) and when he foretold the destruction of the city (ix), and he is instructed to furnish the people with a complete plan of the Temple and its services. He is told the regulations which are to govern the sacrifices, the qualifications of the priests and their duties and privileges, the responsibilities and prerogatives of the prince, and the apportionment of the land to the tribes of Israel.

These closing chapters present almost insuperable difficulties. They contain discrepancies, contradictions with Pentateuchal laws, and terms which do not occur elsewhere. Reference will be made to them in the commentary as they occur in the text. The Rabbis of the Talmud (Men. 45a) remarked that only the prophet Elijah, who will herald the ultimate redemption, will elucidate these chapters. They added the observation that had it not been for Rabbi Chanina ben Hezekiah, who explained several of these difficulties, the Book of Ezekiel would have been excluded from the Scriptural canon.

1-4 INTRODUCTION

1. *in the five and twentieth year of our captivity.* viz. the captivity of Jehoiachin in 597 B.C.E. when Ezekiel had been exiled to Babylon. The date is, accordingly, 572.

the year, in the tenth day of the month, in the fourteenth year after that the city was smitten, in the selfsame day, the hand of the LORD was upon me, and He brought me thither. 2. In the visions of God brought He me into the land of Israel, and set me down upon a very high mountain, whereon was as it were the frame of a city on the south. 3. And He brought me thither, and, behold, there was a man, whose appearance was like the appearance of brass, with a line of

בְּרֹאשׁ הַשָּׁנָה בֶּעָשׂוֹר לַחֹדֶשׁ
בְּאַרְבַּע עֶשְׂרֵה שָׁנָה אַחַר
אֲשֶׁר הֻכְּתָה הָעִיר בְּעֶצֶם
הַיּוֹם הַזֶּה הָיְתָה עָלַי יַד־
יְהוָה וַיָּבֵא אֹתִי שָׁמָּה:
2 בְּמַרְאוֹת אֱלֹהִים הֱבִיאַנִי
אֶל־אֶרֶץ יִשְׂרָאֵל וַיְנִיחֵנִי
אֶל־הַר גָּבֹהַּ מְאֹד וְעָלָיו
3 כְּמִבְנֵה־עִיר מִנֶּגֶב: וַיָּבֵיא
אוֹתִי שָׁמָּה וְהִנֵּה־אִישׁ מַרְאֵהוּ
כְּמַרְאֵה נְחֹשֶׁת וּפְתִיל־־

---

in the beginning of the year, in the tenth day of the month. As already stated on i. 1, the vision concerning the departure of the *Merkabah* came to Ezekiel in the thirtieth year of the last Jubilee celebrated in the Land of Israel before the Babylonian exile, which was the fifth year of Jehoiachin's captivity. Since the vision of this chapter is dated twenty-five years after his captivity, it must have occurred in a Jubilee year. This fact makes the dating of this verse, otherwise very difficult to explain, quite clear. While the Hebrew New Year begins on the first of Tishri, the Jubilee year was inaugurated on the tenth of that month (Lev. xxv. 9f.). The beginning of the Jubilee year, which is also the Day of Atonement when the enslaved regain their freedom and sinners have their transgressions pardoned, was thus a most appropriate day for the vision which portrayed the redemption of Israel and the rebuilding of the Temple (Kimchi).

the hand of the LORD was upon me. See on i. 3.

thither. To *the city that was smitten.*

2. *in the visions of God brought He me.*

The prophet was transported to Jerusalem only in spirit; physically he remained in Babylon.

a very high mountain. The Mount of Zion, or the Temple Mount on which the Sanctuary had stood. It appeared to him *very high* in accordance with the prediction: *And it shall come to pass in the end of days, that the mountain of the LORD'S house shall be established as the top of the mountains, and shall be exalted above the hills* (Isa. ii. 2); cf. also xvii. 22.

whereon was . . . the frame of a city on the south. The Jewish commentators understand this of the site of the new Jerusalem which would be situated to the south of the Temple Mount. On this interpretation *whereon* should be 'by which' as in A.V. Modern expositors explain it as the 'Temple structure which would look like a city' (Lofthouse).

3. *He brought me thither.* i.e. when He had brought me thither.

a man, whose appearance . . . of brass. A Divine messenger of radiant appearance (cf. the description of the *chayyoth* in i. 7, they sparkled like the colour of burnished brass).

flax in his hand, and a measuring
reed; and he stood in the gate.
4. And the man said unto me: 'Son
of man, behold with thine eyes, and
hear with thine ears, and set thy
heart upon all that I shall show thee,
for to the intent that I might show
them unto thee art thou brought
hither; declare all that thou seest to
the house of Israel.'

5. And behold a wall on the outside of the house round about, and
in the man's hand a measuring reed
of six cubits long, of a cubit and a
handbreadth each; so he measured
the breadth of the building, one
reed, and the height, one reed.

6. Then came he unto the gate
which looketh toward the east, and

פִּשְׁתִּים בְּיָדוֹ וּקְנֵה הַמִּדָּה
4 וְהוּא עֹמֵד בַּשָּׁעַר: וַיְדַבֵּר
אֵלַי הָאִישׁ בֶּן־אָדָם רְאֵה
בְעֵינֶיךָ וּבְאָזְנֶיךָ שְׁמָע וְשִׂים
לִבְּךָ לְכֹל אֲשֶׁר־אֲנִי מַרְאֶה
אוֹתָךְ כִּי לְמַעַן הַרְאוֹתְכָה
הֻבָאתָה הֵנָּה הַגֵּד אֶת־כָּל־
אֲשֶׁר־אַתָּה רֹאֶה לְבֵית
5 יִשְׂרָאֵל: וְהִנֵּה חוֹמָה מִחוּץ
לַבַּיִת סָבִיב | סָבִיב וּבְיַד
הָאִישׁ קְנֵה הַמִּדָּה שֵׁשׁ־אַמּוֹת
בָּאַמָּה וָטֹפַח וַיָּמָד אֶת־רֹחַב
הַבִּנְיָן קָנֶה אֶחָד וְקוֹמָה קָנֶה
6 אֶחָד: וַיָּבוֹא אֶל־שַׁעַר
אֲשֶׁר פָּנָיו דֶּרֶךְ הַקָּדִימָה וַיַּעַל

v. 4. קמץ בלא אס״ף

a line of flax . . . a measuring reed. The
former was to be used for large measurements and the latter for small.

he stood in the gate. Probably the east
gate, as appears from verse 6.

4. declare all that thou seest to the house of
Israel. Ezekiel was commanded to con-
centrate all his faculties to grasp the
details of what he is shown and told, so
that he would be able to repeat them to
the people and thereby strengthen their
hope in the final deliverance.

5-16 THE SURROUNDING WALL AND
OUTER GATEWAY ON THE EAST

5. a wall on the outside of the house round
about. The first act of the guide was to
measure the dimensions of the wall
surrounding the whole Temple area,
since it would be erected before any
structure within.

a measuring reed of six cubits long, of a
cubit and a handbreadth. The ordinary
cubit consisted of five handbreadths, but
that used for building the Temple
measured one ordinary cubit and one
handbreadth, i.e. six handbreadths. Cf.
Mishnah Kelim xvii. 10: 'The standard
cubit of the Temple premises was six,
that of the vessels five handbreadths.'
The handbreadth was about three and
a half inches, the cubit twenty-one
inches, and the reed ten and a half feet.
the building. i.e. the surrounding wall;
note its extraordinary thickness.

the height, one reed. Proportionately the
wall was low, so as to afford a better
view of the Temple buildings.

6. came he unto the gate which looketh
toward the east. The guide, who was
outside measuring the wall, now entered
the east gateway which is the main
approach to the Temple.

267

went up the steps thereof; and he measured the jamb of the gate, one reed broad, and the other jamb, one reed broad. 7. And every cell was one reed long, and one reed broad; and the space between the cells was five cubits; and the jambs of the gate by the porch of the gate within were one reed. 8. He measured also the porch of the gate toward the house, one reed. 9. Then measured he the porch of the gate, eight cubits; and the posts thereof, two cubits; and the porch of the gate was inward. 10. And the cells of the gate eastward were three on this side,

בְּמַעֲלוֹתָו֒ וַיָּ֫מָד | אֶת־סַף הַשַּׁעַר קָנֶה אֶחָד רֹחַב וְאֵת סַף אֶחָד קָנֶה אֶחָד רֹחַב׃ 7 וְהַתָּא קָנֶה אֶחָד אֹ֫רֶךְ וְקָנֶה אֶחָד רֹחַב וּבֵין הַתָּאִים חָמֵשׁ אַמּוֹת וְסַף הַשַּׁעַר מֵאֵצֶל אֻלָם הַשַּׁעַר מֵהַבַּ֫יִת קָנֶה אֶחָד׃ 8 וַיָּ֫מָד אֶת־אֻלָם הַשַּׁעַר 9 מֵהַבַּיִת קָנֶה אֶחָד׃ וַיָּ֫מָד אֶת־ אֻלָם הַשַּׁעַר שְׁמֹנֶה אַמּוֹת וְאֵילָו שְׁתַּ֫יִם אַמּוֹת וְאֻלָם 10 הַשַּׁעַר מֵהַבָּ֫יִת׃ וְתָאֵי הַשַּׁעַר

v. 6. ואיליו ק׳   v. 9. במעלותיו ק׳

went up the steps thereof. Before reaching the gateway, he had to ascend some steps on the slope of the Temple Mount, the courts and the Temple being situated higher up the mountain.

he measured the jamb of the gate, one reed broad. The width of the two side-posts of the gateway was the same as that of the wall. The Hebrew *saph* denotes 'door-posts' as well as 'threshold.'

7. *every cell.* There were six cells along the passage of the gateway, three on the north side and three on the south, probably used as guardrooms. Each cell was six cubits square.

the space between the cells was five cubits. A wall five cubits thick separated one cell from the other on each of the two sides.

the jambs of the gate, etc. At the end of both walls of the porch, running from east to west, were two circular posts of the same thickness as the wall, viz. six cubits. The width of these posts from east to west was two cubits, as stated in verse 9. The west end of the porch

from post to post was fitted with closing doors.

8. *the porch of the gate toward the house.* The thickness of the wall of the porch, which lay in the interior of the gateway, was six cubits.

9. *the porch of the gate.* The space of the porch from east to west.

the posts thereof. As already stated on verse 7, the two posts at the end of the two walls of the porch were each two cubits wide. Their thickness was six cubits each to correspond with the thickness of the wall. With the extension of the space of the porch by a post of two cubits, the total length of the porch from east to west measured ten cubits.

the porch of the gate was inward. Only this porch was within and at the end of the gateway, towards the interior; but with the inner gateways the porch was outwards, i.e. away from the Temple.

10. *the cells of the gate eastward.* There were six guardrooms, three on each side,

and three on that side; they three
were of one measure; and the posts
had one measure on this side and
on that side. 11. And he measured
the breadth of the entry of the gate,
ten cubits; and the length of the
gate, thirteen cubits; 12. and a
border before the cells, one cubit
[on this side], and a border, one
cubit on that side; and the cells, six
cubits on this side, and six cubits
on that side. 13. And he measured
the gate from the roof of the one
cell to the roof of the other, a breadth
of five and twenty cubits; door

דֶּרֶךְ הַקָּדִים שְׁלֹשָׁה מִפֹּה
וּשְׁלֹשָׁה מִפֹּה מִזֶּה אָחַת
לִשְׁלָשְׁתָּם וּמִדָּה אַחַת לָאֵילִם
11 מִפֹּה וּמִפֹּו: וַיָּמָד אֶת־רֹחַב
פֶּתַח־הַשַּׁעַר עֶשֶׂר אַמּוֹת
אֹרֶךְ הַשַּׁעַר שְׁלוֹשׁ עֶשְׂרֵה
12 אַמּוֹת: וּגְבוּל לִפְנֵי הַתָּאוֹת
אַמָּה אֶחָת וְאַמָּה־אַחַת
גְּבוּל מִפֹּה וְהַתָּא שֵׁשׁ־אַמּוֹת
13 מִפֹּו וְשֵׁשׁ אַמּוֹת מִפֹּו: וַיָּמָד
אֶת־הַשַּׁעַר מִגַּג הַתָּא לְגַגּוֹ
רֹחַב עֶשְׂרִים וְחָמֵשׁ אַמּוֹת

all of the same size. For the measurements and divisions of these six cells, see
on verse 7.

they three were of one measure. viz. the
three on each side.

the posts had one measure. This refers
either to the posts of the porch mentioned in verse 9, or more probably to
the partitions between the cells.

11. *the breadth of the entry of the gate.*
The open space of the entry on the east
between the two posts was ten cubits.
This was also the measure of all the
other gates in the Temple buildings.

the length of the gate. According to
Rashi, this is the space of the porch, the
west end of the gateway, from north to
south. Ten cubits opposite the space
of the gate, added to one and a half cubits
on each side of the entrance, make a
total of thirteen cubits. This measurement from north to south is here defined
as *the length,* because this space was
longer than that from east to west.
Kimchi, however, understands *the length*
as referring to the width of the wall of
the gate; i.e. the extent of the gate-

structure from east to west comprising
two posts, one outside and the other
inside, each of six cubits and a space of
one cubit between them.

12. *a border before the cells.* A space of
one cubit in width on each side of the
passage-way in front of the six guardrooms was marked off as belonging to the
guardrooms, reducing the width of the
passage by two cubits.

13. *the gate from the roof . . . of the
other.* The breadth of the gateway from
roof to roof of the guardrooms was
twenty-five cubits. In the view of
Rashi, this measurement was taken from
the wall of the cell on the north across
the gateway to the wall of the cell on
the south. The total of twenty-five
cubits was made up of the five cubits'
width of each wall, two and a half cubits
on each side of the entry of the gate, and
ten cubits of the breadth of the entry.
Others take the measurement of twenty-
five cubits as being the entire breadth of
the building from the outside north to
the outside south, assigning ten cubits to
the passage and six for a guardroom on
each side, in all twenty-two, leaving one

against door. 14. He made also posts of threescore cubits; even unto the posts of the court in the gates round about. 15. And from the forefront of the gate of the entrance unto the forefront of the inner porch of the gate were fifty cubits. 16. And there were narrow windows to the cells and to their posts within the gate round about, and likewise to the arches; and windows were round about inward; and upon each post were palm-trees.

14 פֶּתַח נֶגֶד פָּתַח׃ וַיַּעַשׂ אֶת־
אֵילִים שִׁשִּׁים אַמָּה וְאֶל־אַיִל
הֶחָצֵר הַשַּׁעַר סָבִיב | סָבִיב׃
15 וְעַל־פְּנֵי הַשַּׁעַר הָיֹאתוֹן עַל־
לִפְנֵי אֻלָם הַשַּׁעַר הַפְּנִימִי
16 חֲמִשִּׁים אַמָּה׃ וְחַלּוֹנוֹת
אֲטֻמוֹת אֶל־הַתָּאִים וְאֶל
אֵלֵיהֵמָה לִפְנִימָה לַשַּׁעַר
סָבִיב | סָבִיב וְכֵן לָאֵלַמּוֹת
וְחַלּוֹנוֹת סָבִיב | סָבִיב
לִפְנִימָה וְאֶל־אַיִל תִּמֹרִים׃

v. 15. האיתון ק

and a half cubits for each back wall. Kimchi questions the soundness of Rashi's interpretation on several grounds, but offers no alternative. He concludes his comment by remarking that no satisfactory explanation can be given of the measurements of the future Temple, and he quotes the Rabbinic statement that only the prophet Elijah will solve all the problems involved.

door against door. The door of the cell by the gate on the south was opposite the door of the cell by the gate on the north.

14. *he made also posts of threescore cubits.* Rashi, following the Targum, interprets this of the height of the posts.

even unto the posts of the court, etc. Of the same height of sixty cubits were the posts of the other gates of the court.

15. *from the forefront of the gate of the entrance.* The entire length of the gate-building, from the outside front of the gate on the east to the front of the porch at the inner end of the gate on the west, was fifty cubits. The Hebrew noun for *entrance* (*ithon*) occurs nowhere else and

is derived from *athah,* 'to come.' It was the main gate used by the people who entered the Temple area.

16. *there were narrow windows to the cells.* The word *atumim* occurs in 1 Kings vi. 4 in the description of the windows in king Solomon's Temple. The root-meaning being 'shut,' another interpretation is that the windows were fitted with lattice-work (R.V. 'closed').

and to their posts within the gate round about. The reference is probably to the partitions between the cells. Some commentators understand *their posts* as those of the porch at the inner end of the gate. These, too, had windows.

the arches. Many moderns agree with Rashi and Kimchi in translating 'porch.' That is to say, there were also windows in the porches and cells, and in the posts of the other gates in the interior.

windows were round about inward. They were towards the interior and not towards the wall outside (Kimchi).

upon each post were palm-trees. The posts had ornamental tops shaped like palm-trees.

17. Then brought he me into the outer court, and, lo, there were chambers and a pavement, made for the court round about; thirty chambers were upon the pavement. 18. And the pavement was by the side of the gates, corresponding unto the length of the gates, even the lower pavement. 19. Then he measured the breadth from the forefront of the lower gate unto the forefront of the inner court without, a hundred cubits, eastward as also northward.

20. And the gate of the outer court that looked toward the north, he measured the length thereof and the breadth thereof. 21. And the cells thereof were three on this side and three on that side; and the posts thereof and the arches thereof were after the measure of the first gate;

17 וַיְבִיאֵנִי אֶל־הֶחָצֵר הַחִיצוֹנָה
וְהִנֵּה לְשָׁכוֹת וְרִצְפָה עָשׂוּי
לֶחָצֵר סָבִיב | סָבִיב שְׁלֹשִׁים
לְשָׁכוֹת אֶל־הָרִצְפָה:

18 וְהָרִצְפָה אֶל־כֶּתֶף הַשְּׁעָרִים
לְעֻמַּת אֹרֶךְ הַשְּׁעָרִים
19 הָרִצְפָה הַתַּחְתּוֹנָה: וַיָּמָד
רֹחַב מִלִּפְנֵי הַשַּׁעַר הַתַּחְתּוֹנָה
לִפְנֵי הֶחָצֵר הַפְּנִימִי מִחוּץ
מֵאָה אַמָּה הַקָּדִים וְהַצָּפוֹן:

20 וְהַשַּׁעַר אֲשֶׁר פָּנָיו דֶּרֶךְ הַצָּפוֹן
לֶחָצֵר הַחִיצוֹנָה מָדַד אָרְכּוֹ
21 וְרָחְבּוֹ: וְתָאָו שְׁלֹשָׁה מִפֹּה
וּשְׁלֹשָׁה מִפֹּה וְאֵילָו וְאֵלַמּוֹ
הָיָה כְּמִדַּת הַשַּׁעַר הָרִאשׁוֹן

v. 19. מלעיל   v. 21. ותאיו ק   v. 21. ואיליו ק   v. 21. ואלמיו ק

17-27 THE OUTER COURT AND REMAINING GATEWAYS

17. *then brought he me into the outer court.* The prophet, who had hitherto been in the gateway, was then led from there into the outer court, known in Talmudic literature as 'the court of women.' It is called *outer court* because beyond it, but closer to the Temple, was another court. *chambers.* The thirty chambers, built on stone pavements, were situated inside against the surrounding wall, ten on each of the three sides north, east and south, on the west being another building (cf. xli. 12). They were for the use of worshippers (cf. Jer. xxxv. 2, 4).

18. *the pavement was by the side of the gates.* The pavement was laid along the walls on each side of the gates.

corresponding unto the length of the gates. It extended into the court level with the gateway, viz. forty-four cubits, substract-ing six cubits for the thickness of the outer wall.

the lower pavement. It is so-called because it was laid around the outer court, which was on a lower level than the inner court to which one ascended by steps (verse 22).

19. *the lower gate.* viz. in the outer court. The measurement is from the inner front of this gate to the outer front of the gate in the inner court.

eastward as also northward. The same space of a hundred cubits is measured from the gate on the east as well as from the gate on the north.

20. *the length thereof and the breadth thereof.* The dimensions of the north gate were identical with those of the east gate.

21. *were after the measure of the first gate.* The dimensions and details of this gateway were the same as those of the

the length thereof was fifty cubits, and the breadth five and twenty cubits. 22. And the windows thereof, and the arches thereof, and the palm-trees thereof, were after the measure of the gate that looketh toward the east; and it was ascended by seven steps; and the arches thereof were before them. 23. And there was a gate to the inner court over against the other gate, northward as also eastward; and he measured from gate to gate a hundred cubits.

24. And he led me toward the south, and behold a gate toward the south; and he measured the posts thereof and the arches thereof according to these measures. 25. And there were windows in it and in the arches thereof round about, like those windows; the length was fifty cubits, and the breadth five and twenty cubits. 26. And there were seven steps to go up to it, and the arches thereof were before them;

חֲמִשִּׁים אַמָּה אָרְכּוֹ וְרֹחַב

22 חָמֵשׁ וְעֶשְׂרִים בָּאַמָּה: וְחַלּוֹנָו

וְאֵילַמָּו וְתִמֹרָו כְּמִדַּת הַשַּׁעַר

אֲשֶׁר פָּנָיו דֶּרֶךְ הַקָּדִים

וּבְמַעֲלוֹת שֶׁבַע יַעֲלוּ־בוֹ

23 וְאֵילַמָּו לִפְנֵיהֶם: וְשַׁעַר

לֶחָצֵר הַפְּנִימִי נֶגֶד הַשַּׁעַר

לַצָּפוֹן וְלַקָּדִים וַיָּמָד מִשַּׁעַר

אֶל־שַׁעַר מֵאָה אַמָּה:

24 וַיּוֹלִכֵנִי דֶּרֶךְ הַדָּרוֹם וְהִנֵּה־

שַׁעַר דֶּרֶךְ הַדָּרוֹם וּמָדַד אֵילָו

וְאֵילַמָּו כַּמִּדּוֹת הָאֵלֶּה:

25 וְחַלּוֹנִים לוֹ וּלְאֵילַמָּו סָבִיב ׀

סָבִיב כְּהַחֲלֹנוֹת הָאֵלֶּה

חֲמִשִּׁים אַמָּה אֹרֶךְ וְרֹחַב חָמֵשׁ

26 וְעֶשְׂרִים אַמָּה: וּמַעֲלוֹת

שִׁבְעָה עֹלוֹתָו וְאֵילַמָּו

v. 22. וחלוניו ק׳.   v. 22. ואילמיו ק׳.   v. 22. ותמריו ק׳.   v. 22. ואילמיו ק׳.   v. 24. איליו ק׳.

v. 24. ואילמיו ק׳.   v. 25. ולאילמיו ק׳.   v. 26. עלותיו ק׳.   v. 26. ואילמיו ק׳.

eastern gateway on the Temple Mount (verses 7ff.).

22. *it was ascended by seven steps.* The gate lay on a higher level and was reached by seven steps.

the arches thereof were before them. The porch at the end of the gate lay above the seven steps (Rashi, Kimchi). Davidson renders: 'and the porch thereof was to the inside' and comments: i.e. at the inner end of the gate, looking toward the interior of the whole Temple-buildings.

23. *there was a gate to the inner court.* The north and east gates of the inner court were exactly opposite the corresponding gates of the outer court.

24. *toward the south.* From the east of the outer court Ezekiel was taken to the south; there he saw a gateway whose dimensions and other details were the same as in the north and east gates.

25. *and in the arches thereof.* In its porch there were windows.

like those windows. The windows of the guardrooms and of the porch of the south gateway were like those of the east and north.

the length was fifty cubits, etc. See on verses 13, 15.

26. *the arches thereof were before them.* See on verse 22.

and it had palm-trees, one on this side, and another on that side, upon the posts thereof. 27. And there was a gate to the inner court toward the south; and he measured from gate to gate toward the south a hundred cubits.

28. Then he brought me to the inner court by the south gate; and he measured the south gate according to these measures; 29. and the cells thereof, and the posts thereof, and the arches thereof, according to these measures; and there were windows in it and in the arches thereof round about; it was fifty cubits long, and five and twenty cubits broad. 30. And there were arches round about, five and twenty cubits long, and five cubits broad.

לִפְנֵיהֶם וְתִמֹרִים לוֹ אֶחָד מִפּוֹ
27 וְאֶחָד מִפּוֹ אֶל־אֵילָו: וְשַׁעַר
לֶחָצֵר הַפְּנִימִי דֶּרֶךְ הַדָּרוֹם
וַיָּמָד מִשַּׁעַר אֶל־הַשַּׁעַר דֶּרֶךְ
28 הַדָּרוֹם מֵאָה אַמּוֹת: וַיְבִיאֵנִי
אֶל־חָצֵר הַפְּנִימִי בְּשַׁעַר
הַדָּרוֹם וַיָּמָד אֶת־הַשַּׁעַר
הַדָּרוֹם כַּמִּדּוֹת הָאֵלֶּה: וְתָאָו
וְאֵילָו וְאֵלַמָּו כַּמִּדּוֹת הָאֵלֶּה
וְחַלּוֹנוֹת לוֹ וּלְאֵלַמָּו סָבִיב |
סָבִיב חֲמִשִּׁים אַמָּה אֹרֶךְ
וְרֹחַב עֶשְׂרִים וְחָמֵשׁ אַמּוֹת:
30 וְאֵלַמּוֹת סָבִיב | סָבִיב אֹרֶךְ
חָמֵשׁ וְעֶשְׂרִים אַמָּה וְרֹחַב

---

v. 26. אילַו ק׳   v. 29. ואליַו ק׳   v. 29. ותאיַו ק׳   v. 29. ואלמיַו ק׳   v. 29. ולאלמיַו ק׳

---

palm-trees. See on verse 16.

27. *there was a gate to the inner court.* While standing in the south of the outer court, he noticed on the opposite side a gate in the inner court. The distance between the gate of the outer court and that of the inner court on the south was the same as that between the gates of the two courts on the north and the east (verse 23), viz. one hundred cubits.

28-47 THE INNER COURT AND ITS CHAMBERS

28. *he brought me to the inner court by the south gate.* From his position at the south side of the outer court (verse 24), Ezekiel entered the inner court through the south gate. The gates of the inner court and outer court, separated by a distance of one hundred cubits, corresponded to each other in every respect except in the position of the porch. While the porch of the gates of the outer court lay at the inner end of the gateway, that of the inner court was situated at the outer end facing the porch of the outer gates.

29. *according to these measures.* In dimension and every other respect, except in the position of the porch, these gates were exactly like those of the outer court.

in it. In each of the cells.

in the arches thereof. They also had windows in the walls of the porch round about.

fifty cubits long, and five and twenty cubits broad. Cf. verse 25, and see on verses 13, 15.

30. *there were arches round about.* These arches or porches were built either against or into the walls of the inner court, occupying on each side twenty-five cubits in length and five in breadth.

31. And the arches thereof were toward the outer court; and palm-trees were upon the posts thereof; and the going up to it had eight steps.

32. And he brought me into the inner court toward the east; and he measured the gate according to these measures; 33. and the cells thereof, and the posts thereof, and the arches thereof, according to these measures; and there were windows therein and in the arches thereof round about; it was fifty cubits long, and five and twenty cubits broad. 34. And the arches thereof were toward the outer court; and palm-trees were upon the posts thereof, on this side, and on that side; and the going up to it had eight steps.

35. And he brought me to the north gate; and he measured it according to these measures; 36. the cells thereof, the posts thereof, and the arches thereof; and there were windows therein round about; the length was fifty cubits, and the breadth five and twenty cubits.

31 חָמֵשׁ אַמּוֹת: וְאֵילַמּוֹ אֶל־
חָצֵר הַחִצוֹנָה וְתָמֹרִים אֶל־
אֵילָו וּמַעֲלוֹת שְׁמוֹנֶה מַעֲלָו:
32 וַיְבִיאֵנִי אֶל־הֶחָצֵר הַפְּנִימִי
דֶּרֶךְ הַקָּדִים וַיָּמָד אֶת־
33 הַשַּׁעַר כַּמִּדּוֹת הָאֵלֶּה: וְתָאֹו
וְאֵלָו וְאֵלַמּוֹ כַּמִּדּוֹת הָאֵלֶּה
וְחַלּוֹנוֹת לוֹ וּלְאֵלַמּוֹ סָבִיב ׀
סָבִיב אֹרֶךְ חֲמִשִּׁים אַמָּה
וְרֹחַב חָמֵשׁ וְעֶשְׂרִים אַמָּה:
34 וְאֵלַמָּו לֶחָצֵר הַחִיצוֹנָה
וְתִמֹרִים אֶל־אֵילָו מִפּוֹ וּמִפּוֹ
וּשְׁמֹנֶה מַעֲלוֹת מַעֲלָו:
35 וַיְבִיאֵנִי אֶל־שַׁעַר הַצָּפוֹן
36 וּמָדַד כַּמִּדּוֹת הָאֵלֶּה: תָּאֹו
אֵלָו וְאֵלַמּוֹ וְחַלּוֹנוֹת לוֹ סָבִיב
׀ סָבִיב אֹרֶךְ חֲמִשִּׁים אַמָּה
וְרֹחַב חָמֵשׁ וְעֶשְׂרִים אַמָּה:

---

v. 31. ואלמיו ק׳ איליו ק׳ מעליו ק׳   v. 33. ותאיו ק׳ ואליו ק׳ ואלמיו ק׳ ולאלמיו ק׳
v. 34. ואלמיו ק׳ איליו ק׳ מעליו ק׳   v. 36. תאיו ק׳ אליו ק׳ ואלמיו ק׳

31. *the arches thereof were toward the outer court.* In contrast to the porches of the gates of the outer court which lay at the inner end, the porch of the gates of the inner court was at the outer end facing the outer court (see on verse 28). Rashi and Kimchi interpret the clause to mean that, unlike the porch of the outer court, the porch of the inner court protruded outwards and not towards the Temple. The east gate of the inner court would thus have a porch jutting out into the outer court.

the going up to it had eight steps. The inner court lay on a higher level than the outer, and the Temple buildings higher still. The inner gate was reached from the outer court by a flight of eight steps. Kimchi understands this as referring to the ascent from the court of the lay-Israelites to the court of the priests in the inner court, and the mention of seven steps in verse 22 as meaning the ascent from the outer to the inner court.

32. *he brought me into the inner court toward the east.* Ezekiel was conducted through the three gates of the inner court to note their measurements, beginning with the south gate (verse 28) and concluding with the north gate (verse 35). The dimensions and details of these gates were all alike.

37. And the posts thereof were
toward the outer court; and palm-
trees were upon the posts thereof,
on this side, and on that side; and
the going up to it had eight steps.

38. And a chamber with the entry
thereof was by the posts at the gates;
there was the burnt-offering to be
washed.   39. And in the porch of
the gate were two tables on this side,
and two tables on that side, to slay
thereon the burnt-offering and the
sin-offering and the guilt-offering.
40. And on the one side without, as
one goeth up to the entry of the gate
toward the north, were two tables;
and on the other side of the porch
of the gate were two tables. 41. Four
tables were on this side, and four
tables on that side, by the side of
the gate; eight tables, whereupon to

37 וְאֵילָו לֶחָצֵר הַחִיצוֹנָה
וְתִמֹרִים אֶל–אֵילָו מִפּוֹ
וּמִפּוֹ וּשְׁמֹנֶה מַעֲלוֹת מַעֲלָו׃
38 וְלִשְׁכָּה וּפִתְחָה בְּאֵילִים
הַשְּׁעָרִים שָׁם יָדִיחוּ אֶת–
39 הָעֹלָה׃ וּבְאֻלָם הַשַּׁעַר שְׁנַיִם
שֻׁלְחָנוֹת מִפּוֹ וּשְׁנַיִם שֻׁלְחָנוֹת
מִפֹּה לִשְׁחוֹט אֲלֵיהֶם הָעֹלָה
40 וְהַחַטָּאת וְהָאָשָׁם׃ וְאֶל–
הַכָּתֵף מִחוּצָה לָעוֹלֶה לְפֶתַח
הַשַּׁעַר הַצָּפוֹנָה שְׁנַיִם שֻׁלְחָנוֹת
וְאֶל–הַכָּתֵף הָאַחֶרֶת אֲשֶׁר
לְאֻלָם הַשַּׁעַר שְׁנַיִם שֻׁלְחָנוֹת׃
41 אַרְבָּעָה שֻׁלְחָנוֹת מִפֹּה
וְאַרְבָּעָה שֻׁלְחָנוֹת מִפֹּה
לְכֶתֶף הַשָּׁעַר שְׁמוֹנָה שֻׁלְחָנוֹת

v. 37. ואיליו ק׳   v. 37. איליו ק׳   v. 37. מעליו ק׳   v. 39. נ״א עליהם

38. *a chamber with the entry thereof was
by the posts at the gates.* This chamber
was intended for washing the burnt-
offering, but its exact position is not
described. Rashi and Kimchi rightly
assume that this chamber was situated
within the inner court at the north gate.
Their assumption is supported by two
facts, viz. the account of the chamber
immediately follows that of the north
inner gate, and the slaughtering of the
animal for the burnt-offering was performed on the north side before the altar
(Lev. i. 11).

there was the burnt-offering to be washed.
The intestines and legs of the burnt-
offerings had to be washed before being
brought to the altar (Lev. i. 9).

39. *in the porch of the gate were two tables*

. . . and two tables. Within the porch
of the north gate of the inner court were
four tables, two towards the east and
two towards the west, on which the
animals for the most holy sacrifices were
slaughtered.

40. *on the one side without . . . toward
the north.* The reference is still to the
north gate. Four tables also stood
beyond the porch and within the gateway
towards the inner court which was
reached by steps, two to the east and
two to the west.

41. *by the side of the gate.* The position
of these eight tables as here described is
not clear; but it appears that they were
inside the gateway, beyond the four
tables mentioned in verse 40, nearer the
inner court, four on each side.

slay the sacrifices. 42. Moreover there were four tables for the burnt-offering, of hewn stone, a cubit and a half long, and a cubit and a half broad, and one cubit high, whereupon to lay the instruments wherewith the burnt-offering and the sacrifice are slain. 43. And the slabs, a handbreadth long, were fastened within round about; and upon the tables was to be the flesh of the offering. 44. And without the inner gate were chambers for the guard in the inner court, which was at the side of the north gate, and their prospect was toward the south; one at the side of the east

42 אֲלֵיהֶם יִשְׁחָטוּ׃ וְאַרְבָּעָה
שֻׁלְחָנוֹת לָעוֹלָה אַבְנֵי גָזִית
אֹרֶךְ אַמָּה אַחַת וָחֵצִי וְרֹחַב
אַמָּה אַחַת וָחֵצִי וְגֹבַהּ אַמָּה
אֶחָת אֲלֵיהֶם וְיַנִּיחוּ אֶת־
הַכֵּלִים אֲשֶׁר יִשְׁחֲטוּ אֶת־
43 הָעוֹלָה בָּם וְהַזָּבַח׃ וְהַשְׁפַתַּיִם
טֹפַח אֶחָד מוּכָנִים בַּבַּיִת
סָבִיב ׀ סָבִיב וְאֶל־הַשֻּׁלְחָנוֹת
44 בְּשַׂר הַקָּרְבָּן׃ וּמִחוּצָה
לַשַּׁעַר הַפְּנִימִי לִשְׁכוֹת שָׁרִים
בֶּחָצֵר הַפְּנִימִי אֲשֶׁר אֶל־
כֶּתֶף שַׁעַר הַצָּפוֹן וּפְנֵיהֶם
דֶּרֶךְ הַדָּרוֹם אֶחָד אֶל־כֶּתֶף

v. 43. כצ״ל   v. 41. נ״א עליהם

whereupon to slay the sacrifices. This applies to all the tables spoken of in the preceding verses. There were accordingly sixteen tables for the slaughtering of the sacrificial animals.

42. *the instruments.* viz. knives and receptacles for collecting the blood. The position of these four tables is not defined.

43. *slabs.* The meaning of the word *shephattaim* is doubtful. The Targum translates it as 'hooks,' which were fixed on pillars within the chamber round about for the purpose of hanging up the carcasses to be flayed. This rendering has been adopted in the English versions.

upon the tables was to be the flesh of the offering. This is to be connected with the preceding clause: and the tables (which were placed between the hooks) were to be used for the flesh of the offerings. The description in Mishnah

Middoth iii. 5 reads: 'The place of slaughtering lay north of the altar, and there stood eight short pillars. Upon these were square blocks of cedar into which iron hooks were fixed, three rows to each, whereon the carcasses were hung. They were flayed on marble tables between the pillars.'

44. *without the inner gate.* These chambers were not within the gateway but outside it and in the inner court, as distinctly stated later in the verse.

the guard. This rendering is based on the pointing of the Hebrew word as *sarim.* The Targum, followed by all Jewish commentators, point it as *sharim,* 'the singers' (so A.V. and R.V.), i.e. the choir of the Levites who provided a musical accompaniment during the sacrificial rites.

their prospect was toward the south. The entrance of the chambers at both sides of the north gate faced the south.

gate having the prospect toward the
north. 45. And he said unto me:
'This chamber, whose prospect is
toward the south, is for the priests,
the keepers of the charge of the
house. 46. And the chamber whose
prospect is toward the north is for
the priests, the keepers of the charge
of the altar; these are the sons of
Zadok, who from among the sons of
Levi come near to the LORD to
minister unto Him.'

47. And he measured the court, a
hundred cubits long, and a hundred
cubits broad, foursquare; and the
altar was before the house.

48. Then he brought me to the
porch of the house, and measured
each post of the porch, five cubits on

שַׁעַר הַקֹּדִים פְּנֵי דֶּרֶךְ הַצָּפֽוֹן׃

45 וַיְדַבֵּר אֵלַי זֹה הַלִּשְׁכָּה אֲשֶׁר
פָּנֶיהָ דֶּרֶךְ הַדָּרוֹם לַכֹּהֲנִים
שֹׁמְרֵי מִשְׁמֶרֶת הַבָּֽיִת׃

46 וְהַלִּשְׁכָּה אֲשֶׁר פָּנֶיהָ דֶּרֶךְ
הַצָּפוֹן לַכֹּהֲנִים שֹׁמְרֵי
מִשְׁמֶרֶת הַמִּזְבֵּחַ הֵמָּה בְנֵי־
צָדוֹק הַקְּרֵבִים מִבְּנֵי־לֵוִי

47 אֶל־יְהוָה לְשָׁרְתֽוֹ׃ וַיָּמָד
אֶת־הֶחָצֵר אֹרֶךְ ׀ מֵאָה אַמָּה
וְרֹחַב מֵאָה אַמָּה מְרֻבָּעַת

48 וְהַמִּזְבֵּחַ לִפְנֵי הַבָּֽיִת׃ וַיְבִאֵנִי
אֶל־אֻלָם הַבַּיִת וַיָּמָד אֶל

one at the side of the east gate. One
chamber was at the side of the east gate
with its entrance towards the north.

45. he said unto me. The guide explained
to him the purpose of the chambers.

this chamber . . . is for the priests. i.e.
the Levites, the singers and ministers of
the Sanctuary (Rashi). Kimchi, on the
other hand, explains that in addition to
the chambers for the Levites spoken of
in verse 44, another was reserved for the
priests who were in charge of various
duties in the Temple. Malbim offers the
interpretation: since only the priests
descended from Zadok would be worthy
to minister in the future Temple, and the
other priests who had gone astray would
be reduced to the rank of keepers of the
house (xliv. 14f.), the prophet was
informed that the disqualified priests
would occupy the chamber of the singers.

46. the keepers of the charge of the altar.
The priests who are to minister at the
altar; i.e. the sons of Zadok are to occupy

the chamber which opens towards the
north.

these are the sons of Zadok. Zadok, the
High Priest in king Solomon's Temple,
was a descendant of Phinehas upon whom
was conferred the covenant of an everlasting priesthood (Num. xxv. 13).

47. he measured the court. The area of
the inner court, measured along the inner
fronts of the three gates and along the
front of the house, was a square of one
hundred cubits.

the altar was before the house. The altar
stood in the centre of the inner court
opposite the house. The location of the
altar is mentioned here incidentally.

48-49 THE PORCH OF THE TEMPLE
48. to the porch of the house. From the
inner court and its gates the prophet is
conducted to the east front of the
Temple.

each post of the porch. The thickness of
the post from east to west on each side
of the entrance was the same as the wall
of the porch, five cubits.

this side, and five cubits on that side; and the breadth of the gate was three cubits on this side, and three cubits on that side. 49. The length of the porch was twenty cubits, and the breadth eleven cubits; and it was by steps that it was ascended; and there were pillars by the posts, one on this side, and another on that side.

אֵלָם חָמֵשׁ אַמּוֹת מִפֹּה וְחָמֵשׁ אַמּוֹת מִפֹּה וְרֹחַב הַשַּׁעַר שָׁלֹשׁ אַמּוֹת מִפּוֹ וְשָׁלֹשׁ אַמּוֹת מִפּוֹ: אֹרֶךְ הָאֵלָם עֶשְׂרִים אַמָּה ⁴⁹ וְרֹחַב עַשְׁתֵּי עֶשְׂרֵה אַמָּה וּבַמַּעֲלוֹת אֲשֶׁר יַעֲלוּ אֵלָיו וְעַמֻּדִים אֶל־הָאֵילִים אֶחָד מִפֹּה וְאֶחָד מִפֹּה:

41 CHAPTER XLI **מא**

1. And he brought me to the temple, and measured the posts, six cubits broad on the one side, and six cubits broad on the other side,

וַיְבִיאֵנִי אֶל־הַהֵיכָל וַיָּמָד ¹ אֶת־הָאֵילִים שֵׁשׁ־אַמּוֹת רֹחַב מִפּוֹ וְשֵׁשׁ־אַמּוֹת רֹחַב־

the breadth of the gate, etc. The length of the porch from north to south was, as stated in the next verse, twenty cubits; each of the two posts at the entrance from north to south had a width of three cubits, leaving an open space of fourteen cubits. The phrase *the breadth of the gate* does not refer to the number of cubits that follows, but denotes 'the breadth of the gate was such as would allow two posts of three cubits each on either side,' viz. fourteen cubits (Kimchi). Malbim maintains that *sha'ar*, translated *gate*, denotes the solid posts on either side of the gateway, not the space itself. This view is held by several modern expositors.

49. *the length of the porch was twenty cubits.* Length here signifies the longer dimension, from north to south, since the breadth, from east to west, was only eleven cubits. The *length* of the porch, twenty cubits, represented the breadth of the Temple (cf. 1 Kings vi. 3).

it was by steps that it was ascended. The terrace of the Temple, which was on a higher level than the inner court, was reached by steps from the space between the altar and the porch. The measurement of the steps is not given.

there were pillars by the posts. At each side of the posts of the porch a pillar stood, narrowing to some extent the open space of fourteen cubits. These pillars corresponded to Jachin and Boaz of king Solomon's Temple (1 Kings vii. 21).

CHAPTER XLI
THE TEMPLE AND ITS SIDE-CHAMBERS
1-4 THE HOLY OF HOLIES

1. *six cubits broad.* Led out of the porch of the Temple, the prophet sees his guide measuring the two posts of the entrance wall. Each of these, like the wall itself, was six cubits wide from east to west; but the wall of this gate was one cubit thicker than that of the entrance of the porch.

which was the breadth of the tent.
2. And the breadth of the entrance
was ten cubits; and the sides of the
entrance were five cubits on the one
side, and five cubits on the other
side; and he measured the length
thereof, forty cubits, and the
breadth, twenty cubits.

3. Then went he inward, and
measured each post of the entrance,
two cubits; and the entrance, six
cubits; and the breadth of the
entrance, seven cubits. 4. And he
measured the length thereof, twenty
cubits, and the breadth, twenty
cubits, before the temple; and he
said unto me: 'This is the most holy
place.'

2 מִפֹּו לְרֹחַב הָאֹהֶל: וְרֹחַב
הַפֶּתַח עֶשֶׂר אַמֹּות וְכִתְפֹות
הַפֶּתַח חָמֵשׁ אַמֹּות מִפֹּו וְחָמֵשׁ
אַמֹּות מִפֹּו וַיָּמָד אָרְכֹּו
אַרְבָּעִים אַמָּה וְרֹחַב עֶשְׂרִים
3 אַמָּה: וּבָא לִפְנִימָה וַיָּמָד
אֵיל־הַפֶּתַח שְׁתַּיִם אַמֹּות
וְהַפֶּתַח שֵׁשׁ אַמֹּות וְרֹחַב
4 הַפֶּתַח שֶׁבַע אַמֹּות: וַיָּמָד
אֶת־אָרְכֹּו עֶשְׂרִים אַמָּה
וְרֹחַב עֶשְׂרִים אַמָּה אֶל־פְּנֵי
הַהֵיכָל וַיֹּאמֶר אֵלַי זֶה קֹדֶשׁ

the breadth of the tent. The doorway,
six cubits broad, is here called *the tent*
because the posts were shaped like an
arch at the top like a tent.

2. *the breadth of the entrance was ten
cubits.* The open space of the entrance
between the two side-posts was ten
cubits, while the width of each of the
two side-walls of the entrance, including
the width of the two posts, was five
cubits. This makes up the total breadth
of the structure, viz. twenty cubits.

the length thereof, forty cubits. This
refers to the middle section of the Temple
between the porch on the east and the
most holy place on the west.

3. *went he inward.* The angel alone went
inside the most holy place. Ezekiel,
being an ordinary priest, was allowed to
enter the Temple but not the Holy of
Holies. The inner Sanctuary was entered only by the High Priest on the Day
of Atonement (Lev. xvi).

*each post of the entrance, two cubits ; and
the entrance, six cubits.* This statement
presents difficulty. Since the breadth
of the entrance to the most holy place is

said to be seven cubits, the measurement
of *six cubits* must refer to the thickness of
the wall from east to west. If this be so
what is the meaning of *each post of the
entrance, two cubits ?* Does it imply that
the post was only two cubits thick and did
not cover the whole thickness of the
wall? Rashi understands the measurement of two cubits for the post as
referring to the whole width of the
entrance and that of six cubits for the
entrance to its height. Rabbi Elijah of
Wilna explained the text as follows: the
thickness of the side walls between the
Temple and the Holy of Holies from east
to west was four cubits, and a post of two
cubits in thickness was attached to each
end wall towards the outer section,
making a total of six cubits for the whole
width of the entrance. The seven cubits
refers to the passage in-between from
north to south.

4. *before the temple.* i.e. along the whole
breadth of the Temple.

this is the most holy place. The guide
explained to Ezekiel that the area of
twenty cubits square was the site of the
Holy of Holies.

5. Then he measured the wall of the house, six cubits; and the breadth of every side-chamber, four cubits, round about the house on every side. 6. And the side-chambers were one over another, three and thirty times; and there were cornices in the wall which belonged to the house for the side-chambers round about, that they might have hold therein, and not have hold in the wall of the house. 7. And the side-chambers were broader as they wound about higher and higher; for the winding about of the house went higher and higher round about the house; therefore the breadth of the house continued

⁵ הַקְּדָשִׁים : וַיָּמָד קִיר הַבַּיִת
שֵׁשׁ אַמּוֹת וְרֹחַב הַצֵּלָע אַרְבַּע
אַמּוֹת סָבִיב ׀ סָבִיב לַבַּיִת
⁶ סָבִיב : וְהַצְּלָעוֹת צֵלָע אֶל־
צֵלָע שָׁלוֹשׁ וּשְׁלֹשִׁים פְּעָמִים
וּבָאוֹת בַּקִּיר אֲשֶׁר־לַבַּיִת
לַצְּלָעוֹת סָבִיב ׀ סָבִיב לִהְיוֹת
אֲחוּזִים וְלֹא־יִהְיוּ אֲחוּזִים
⁷ בְּקִיר הַבָּיִת : וְרָחֲבָה וְנָסְבָה
לְמַעְלָה לְמַעְלָה לַצְּלָעוֹת
כִּי מוּסַב־הַבַּיִת לְמַעְלָה
לְמַעְלָה סָבִיב ׀ סָבִיב לַבַּיִת
עַל־כֵּן רֹחַב לַבַּיִת לְמָעְלָה

5–11 THE SIDE-CHAMBERS

5. *the wall of the house, six cubits.* The wall of the Temple around the north, west and south sides was six cubits thick at its base.

the breadth of every side-chamber, four cubits. Attached to the wall of the Temple on the north, west and south sides were side-chambers in three stories. Only the chamber on the ground floor, referred to in this verse, was four cubits wide; the chambers in the upper stories were larger owing to the rebatements in the wall of the Temple as it ascended.

6. *the side-chambers . . . three and thirty times.* The side-chambers numbered thirty-three in all. There were five on the north, five on the south and one along the whole of the west wall. This number was trebled by building two upper stories over the ground floor.

cornices in the wall . . . that they might have hold therein. The wall of the Temple, which was six cubits thick at the base, diminished in thickness as it

ascended at three points, to serve as supports for the beams of the three stories of the side-chambers (cf. 1 Kings vi. 6).

not have hold in the wall of the house. The wall was built with rebatements for the purpose of avoiding holes being made in the wall to let in the beams.

7. *the side-chambers were broader,* etc. As one ascended by a spiral staircase from the ground floor to the middle and from the middle to the upper story, the side-chambers round about the Temple widened in proportion to the rebatements in the wall.

for the winding . . . went higher and higher. i.e. the winding or spiral staircase went higher and higher (Kimchi).

therefore the breadth of the house continued upward. Better, 'therefore the breadth (of the side-chambers) towards the house continued upward'; i.e. because of the narrowing of the wall on which the chambers were built, the side-chambers

upward; and so one went up from
the lowest row to the highest by the
middle.   8. I saw also that the house
had a raised basement round about;
the foundations of the side-chambers
were a full reed of six cubits to the
joining. 9. The breadth of the
outer wall which belonged to the
side-chambers was five cubits; and
so that which was left by the
structure of the side-chambers that
belonged to the house. 10. And
between the chambers was a breadth
of twenty cubits round about the
house on every side. 11. And the

וְכֵן הַתַּחְתֹּנָה יַעֲלֶה עַל־
8 הָעֶלְיוֹנָה לַתִּיכוֹנָה: וְרָאִיתִי
לַבַּיִת גֹּבַהּ סָבִיב | סָבִיב
מִיסְדוֹת הַצְּלָעוֹת מְלוֹ הַקָּנֶה
9 שֵׁשׁ אַמּוֹת אַצִּילָה: רֹחַב
הַקִּיר אֲשֶׁר־לַצֵּלָע אֶל־
הַחוּץ חָמֵשׁ אַמּוֹת וַאֲשֶׁר מֻנָּח
10 בֵּית צְלָעוֹת אֲשֶׁר לַבָּיִת: וּבֵין
הַלְּשָׁכוֹת רֹחַב עֶשְׂרִים אַמָּה
סָבִיב לַבַּיִת סָבִיב | סָבִיב:

v. 8. מוסדות ק׳   v. 8. כצ״ל

in the two upper stories became so much
broader towards the house, but there was
no widening on the opposite side where
the whole wall appeared to be of the same
thickness.

one went up from the lowest row, etc.
The topmost story was reached by a
staircase from the ground floor which
passed through the middle floor.

8. *the house had a raised basement* (gobah).
The Temple stood on a platform six
cubits above the level of the inner court
and was reached by steps (cf. xl. 49).
Rashi and Kimchi understand *gobah*
to denote the height of the Temple.
That is to say, Ezekiel noticed that the
structure was lofty in comparison with
the adjoining side-chambers, without
giving its measurement. On their interpretation, the mention of the foundations of the side-chambers being a full
reed of six cubits (cf. xl. 5) relates to the
width of the foundations below the
surface, while the wall above the ground
was, as stated in the next verse, five cubits
thick.

to the joining. The meaning of the
Hebrew *atstsilah* is not clear. The
Targum, followed by Rashi and Kimchi,
translated as 'large,' i.e. the larger cubits
consisting of six handbreadths each (so

A.V. and R.V.). A.J. defines it as an
architectural term as does R.V. margin,
'to the joint,' which Davidson explains as
the point where the vertical line of the
height of the platform cut the level of the
court.

9. *the breadth of the outer wall.* viz. the
outer wall of the side-chambers around
the Temple.

*and so that which was left by the structure
of the side-chambers.* Outside the side-
chambers, on the north and south sides,
there was a free space (*munnach*) of five
cubits, as described in verse 11. The
connection between the two parts of the
verse is in respect of the measurement.
As the width of the outside wall of the
side-chambers was five cubits, so was
the width of the free space outside them.
According to Rashi, the *munnach* was not
outside and along the whole length of the
walls of the side-chambers north and
south, but the term refers to the two
corners, north-east and south-east, where
there were no side-chambers.

10. *between the chambers was a breadth of
twenty cubits.* Between the wall of the
side-chambers and the wall of the cells
in the inner court, on the north and
south, was a space of twenty cubits.

doors of the side-chambers were toward the place that was left, one door toward the north, and another door toward the south; and the breadth of the place that was left was five cubits round about.

12. And the building that was before the separate place at the side toward the west was seventy cubits broad; and the wall of the building was five cubits thick round about, and the length thereof ninety cubits.

13. And he measured the house, a hundred cubits long; and the separate place, and the building, with the walls thereof, a hundred

11 וּפֶ֙תַח הַצֵּלָ֜ע לַמֻּנָּ֗ח פֶּ֤תַח אֶחָד֙ דֶּ֣רֶךְ הַצָּפ֔וֹן וּפֶ֥תַח אֶחָ֖ד לַדָּר֑וֹם וְרֹ֙חַב֙ מְק֣וֹם הַמֻּנָּ֔ח חָמֵ֥שׁ אַמּ֛וֹת סָבִ֖יב ׀ סָבִֽיב׃

12 וְהַבִּנְיָ֡ן אֲשֶׁר֩ אֶל־פְּנֵ֨י הַגִּזְרָ֜ה פְּאַ֣ת דֶּֽרֶךְ־הַיָּ֗ם רֹ֚חַב שִׁבְעִ֣ים אַמָּ֔ה וְקִ֧יר הַבִּנְיָ֛ן חָֽמֵשׁ־אַמּ֥וֹת רֹ֛חַב סָבִ֖יב ׀ סָבִ֑יב וְאָרְכּ֖וֹ תִּשְׁעִ֥ים אַמָּֽה׃

13 וּמָדַ֣ד אֶת־הַבַּ֔יִת אֹ֖רֶךְ מֵאָ֣ה אַמָּ֑ה וְהַגִּזְרָ֧ה וְהַבִּנְיָ֛ה וְקִירוֹתֶ֖יהָ

---

11. the doors of the side-chambers . . . that was left. The only entrance to the side-chambers was from the *munnach*, the free space of five cubits outside the side-chambers, one door on the north and another on the south. According to Rashi's view that the *munnach* was at the north-east and south-east corners, the doors of the side-chambers were situated there. Wherever the doors were located, there were only two, one on the north and the other on the south side, and all the separate chambers were made accessible by communicating doors leading from one to the other.

round about. i.e. on the north and south.

12 THE HINDER BUILDING

the building that was before the separate place. The Jewish commentators offer different interpretations of the meaning and situation of *binyan* (*building*) and *gizrah* (*separate place*). Rashi takes *binyan* to be the side-chambers adjoining the Temple, and *gizrah* the Temple structure; and he explains the verse as follows: the Temple with its side-chambers on both sides measured seventy cubits from north to south at the west end, the wall of the side-chambers round

about was five cubits wide, and the length of the Temple and its chambers up to the porch ninety cubits. The total length, including the porch, was one-hundred cubits, while the breadth of the whole structure at the east end was a hundred cubits. It was thirty cubits more at the west end because there were two structures, each fifteen cubits wide, on the sides of the porch. These dimensions follow the order of the First Temple as given in Mishnah Middoth iv. 7. Another interpretation, followed by A.J., is that the *gizrah* refers to a passage, twenty cubits in width, which ran along the Temple terrace on the three sides, north, west and south, and that the *binyan* was a separate building behind the Temple westwards in front of the *gizrah*, seventy cubits in breadth from east to west, and ninety in length from north to south, its walls being five cubits in thickness.

13-15a THE TOTAL DIMENSIONS

13. *the house, a hundred cubits long.* According to Rashi, quoted on verse 12, this signifies the total measurement of the Temple from the extreme east to the west, including the side-chamber behind the west wall. This measurement agrees

cubits long; 14. also the breadth of the face of the house and of the separate place toward the east, a hundred cubits. 15. And he measured the length of the building before the separate place which was at the back thereof, and the galleries thereof on the one side and on the other side, a hundred cubits.

Now the temple, and the inner place, and the porches of the court,

14 אֹרֶךְ מֵאָה אַמָּה: וְרֹחַב פְּנֵי
הַבַּיִת וְהַגִּזְרָה לַקָּדִים מֵאָה
15 אַמָּה: וּמָדַד אֹרֶךְ־הַבִּנְיָן
אֶל־פְּנֵי הַגִּזְרָה אֲשֶׁר עַל־
אַחֲרֶיהָ וְאַתִּקֶיהָא מִפּוֹ וּמִפּוֹ
מֵאָה אַמָּה וְהַהֵיכָל הַפְּנִימִי
16 וְאֻלַמֵּי הֶחָצֵר: הַסִּפִּים

v. 15. ואתיקיהא ק'

with that given in Middoth iv. 7 of the First Temple; and the latter part of the verse, which speaks of *the separate place, and the building, with the walls thereof, a hundred cubits long*, must then be taken as explanatory of the first part of the verse. But on the other interpretation, two different measurements of a hundred cubits are intended. The Temple from east to west, extending from the wall of the porch to the wall of the side-chambers of the west end inclusive, was one hundred cubits. Similarly, from the wall of the side-chamber of the Temple to the outer wall of the *binyan* on the extreme west, measured a hundred cubits, viz. *the separate place* twenty, the interior of the *binyan* seventy, and the two walls of the *binyan* five each. Apparently, on this interpretation, the *raised basement* five cubits wide, spoken of in verse 8, existed on two sides, north and south, but not on the west. Or, perhaps, *the separate place* on the west included the breadth of the *raised basement*, whereas on the north and south its breadth measured twenty cubits apart from the *raised basement*.

14. *the breadth . . . a hundred cubits.* This total, in the opinion of Rashi, is made up of the breadth of the Temple with the side-chambers on both sides being seventy cubits (see on verse 12) and of two structures fifteen cubits each on either side of the porch. Kimchi contends that the mode of expression of the present verse is against Rashi's interpretation which assumes that the *gizrah*

is identical with *house*, whereas *house* and *gizrah* are differentiated. According to the alternative explanation cited on verse 12, this measurement of a hundred cubits from north to south is made up as follows: the two *gizroth* forty, the two *raised basements* ten, the two outer walls of the side-chambers ten, the two side-chambers eight, the two walls of the *house* on the north and south twelve and the interior of the *house* twenty: one hundred cubits in all.

15. *the length of the building.* As he measured the length of the *house* on the north (verse 12), so did he measure its length on the south, walking back from east to west (Rashi). On the alternative interpretation, the reference is to the building behind the Temple westwards which was in front of the *gizrah*, described here as being *at the back thereof.* Its total length from north to south was a hundred cubits; its interior was ninety, as stated in verse 12, and the two side walls were ten cubits.

the galleries. The Hebrew term *attik* (again in verse 16, xlii. 3, 5) is of uncertain meaning. Rashi, following the Targum, renders: 'the structures in both corners or sides of the porch.' Kimchi suggests 'cells and chambers,' while others understand it to mean a system of galleries or balconies along the wall outside.

15b-26. THE INTERIOR OF THE TEMPLE *now the temple, and the inner place, and the porches of the court.* These words are

16. the jambs, and the narrow windows, and the galleries, that they three had round about, over against the jambs there was a veneering of wood round about, and from the ground up to the windows; and the windows were covered; 17. to the space above the door, even unto the inner house, and without, and on all the wall round about within and without, by measure. 18. And it was made with cherubim and palm-trees; and a palm-tree was between cherub and cherub, and every cherub had two faces; 19. so that there was the face of a man toward the palm-tree on the one side, and the face of a young lion toward the palm-tree on the other side; thus was it made through all the house

וְהַחַלּוֹנִים הָאֲטֻמוֹת
וְהָאַתִּיקִים ׀ סָבִיב לִשְׁלָשְׁתָּם
נֶגֶד הַסַּף שָׂחִיף עֵץ סָבִיב ׀
סָבִיב וְהָאָרֶץ עַד־הַחַלֹּנוֹת
17 וְהַחַלֹּנוֹת מְכֻסּוֹת: עַל־מֵעַל
הַפֶּתַח וְעַד־הַבַּיִת הַפְּנִימִי
וְלַחוּץ וְאֶל־כָּל־הַקִּיר
סָבִיב ׀ סָבִיב בַּפְּנִימִי וּבַחִיצוֹן
18 מִדּוֹת: וְעָשׂוּי כְּרוּבִים
וְתִמֹרִים וְתִמֹרָה בֵּין־כְּרוּב
לִכְרוּב וּשְׁנַיִם פָּנִים לַכְּרוּב:
19 וּפְנֵי אָדָם אֶל־הַתִּמֹרָה מִפּוֹ
וּפְנֵי־כְפִיר אֶל־הַתִּמֹרָה
מִפּוֹ עָשׂוּי אֶל־כָּל־הַבַּיִת

נ״א שָׂחִיף v. 16.

to be connected with the next verse. That is to say, the Temple, the most holy place and the porches of the court, all had jambs, narrow windows and galleries (Rashi). In the view of Kimchi, *by measure* at the end of verse 17 is the predicate of all the subjects enumerated in the latter part of verse 15, as well as in verses 16f., meaning: all these, too, had separate measurements. Though he measured the total length and breadth of the Temple, he also made separate measurements of its three sections, the porches, jambs, windows, etc.

16. *narrow windows.* See on xl. 16.

they three had round about. See on verse 15.

over against the jambs . . . round about. This is a new sentence describing the ornamentation of the stone walls. The walls round about on both sides of the door-posts were covered with panels.

from the ground up to the windows. The walls, beginning from the floor, up to the windows and also above them (*the windows were covered*) were panelled.

17. *to the space above the door . . . by measure.* This is to be connected with *from the ground up to the windows* in the preceding verse. The veneering of wood covered the walls from the ground, above the door and all the walls of the most holy place and the Temple.

18. *it was made with cherubim and palm-trees.* On the wooden panels were carved figures of cherubim and palm-trees as in Solomon's Temple (1 Kings vi. 29).

two faces. One of a man and the other of a young lion.

19. *the face of a man*, etc. The two faces of each cherub were turned in opposite directions, so that each palm-tree was between the human face of one cherub and the lion's face of another cherub.

round about. 20. From the ground unto above the door were cherubim and palm-trees made; and so on the wall of the temple. 21. As for the temple, the jambs were squared; and the face of the sanctuary had an appearance such as is the appearance.

22. The altar, three cubits high, and the length thereof two cubits, was of wood, and so the corners thereof; the length thereof, and the walls thereof, were also of wood; and he said unto me: 'This is the table that is before the LORD.'

23. And the temple and the sanctuary had two doors. 24. And

20 סָבִיב ׀ סָבִיב: מֵהָאָ֫רֶץ
עַד־מֵעַל הַפֶּ֫תַח הַכְּרוּבִ֑ים
וְהַתִּמֹרִ֖ים עֲשׂוּיִ֑ם וְקִ֣יר
21 הַהֵיכָ֑ל: הַהֵיכָ֖ל מְזוּזַ֣ת
רְבֻעָ֑ה וּפְנֵ֣י הַקֹּ֫דֶשׁ הַמַּרְאֶ֖ה
22 כַּמַּרְאֶֽה: הַמִּזְבֵּ֙חַ עֵ֣ץ שָׁל֣וֹשׁ
אַמּוֹת֩ גָּבֹ֨הַ וְאׇרְכּ֜וֹ שְׁתַּֽיִם־אַמּ֗וֹת
וּמִקְצֹֽעוֹתָיו֙ ל֔וֹ וְאׇרְכּ֥וֹ
וְקִֽירֹתָ֖יו עֵ֑ץ וַיְדַבֵּ֣ר אֵלַ֔י זֶ֚ה
הַשֻּׁלְחָ֔ן אֲשֶׁ֖ר לִפְנֵ֥י יְהוָֽה:
23 וּשְׁתַּ֛יִם דְּלָת֖וֹת לַהֵיכָ֑ל

v. 20. נקוד עליו

---

20. *from the ground unto above the door.* The figures of cherubim and palm-trees covered the walls from the floor to the top.

and so on the wall of the temple. The clause seems superfluous since *all the house* has already been included in these decorations (verse 19). Perhaps the dots over the word *hechal* (*temple*), Kimchi remarks, have some connection with the difficulty. It is worthy of note that Kimchi's comment agrees with the theory of some modern scholars that the dots signify words meant to be deleted ; cf. *The Soncino Chumash* on Deut. xxix. 28, and Fisch, *Midrash Haggadol, Numbers*, p. 196, note e. Some Hebrew MSS. omit the word, connecting *the wall of* with the next verse: 'as for the wall of the temple.'

21. *the jambs were squared.* The doorposts of the Temple were not round but four-cornered.

the face of the sanctuary, etc. The doorposts of the most holy place were square in shape like those of the Temple. Rashi quotes the rendering of the Targum: 'in the Holy of Holies there was a vision of the Divine chariot with a

flashing fire such as I saw by the river Chebar.'

22. *the altar.* i.e. the altar of incense, also called the altar of the interior, which stood in the Temple. The Targum understands it as referring to the table of showbread, mentioned at the end of the verse, and interprets *the altar* as meaning that opposite the altar was a table three cubits high.

the corners thereof. There were four projecting corners on the four sides of the altar, the whole construction of which was of wood.

this is the table that is before the LORD. If the reference is to the altar, it is here called *table* to indicate that at a time when the Temple is not in existence, the table in a man's house can become a substitute for the altar in regard to the expiation of sin (Ber. 55a). The Talmudic statement is explained as having the poor as guests at one's table; or, the food is prepared strictly according to the dietary laws.

23. *the temple and the sanctuary had two doors.* The Temple and Holy of Holies each had a double door: one towards the

the doors had two leaves [apiece], two turning leaves; two leaves for the one door, and two leaves for the other. 25. And there were made on them, on the doors of the temple, cherubim and palm-trees, like as were made upon the walls; and there were thick beams of wood upon the face of the porch without. 26. And there were narrow windows and palm-trees on the one side and on the other side, on the sides of the porch; there were also the brackets of the house, and the thick beams.

24 וְלַקֹּדֶשׁ וּשְׁתַּיִם דְּלָתוֹת לַדְּלָתוֹת שְׁתַּיִם מוּסַבּוֹת דְּלָתוֹת שְׁתַּיִם לְדֶלֶת אֶחָת וּשְׁתֵּי דְלָתוֹת לָאַחֶרֶת:

25 וַעֲשׂוּיָה אֲלֵיהֶן אֶל־דַּלְתוֹת הַהֵיכָל כְּרוּבִים וְתִמֹרִים כַּאֲשֶׁר עֲשׂוּיִם לַקִּירוֹת וְעָב עֵץ אֶל־פְּנֵי הָאוּלָם מֵהַחוּץ:

26 וְחַלּוֹנִים אֲטֻמוֹת וְתִמֹרִים מִפּוֹ וּמִפּוֹ אֶל־כִּתְפוֹת הָאוּלָם וְצַלְעוֹת הַבַּיִת וְהָעֻבִּים:

---

42   **CHAPTER XLII**   מב

1. Then he brought me forth into the outer court, the way toward the north; and he brought me into the

1 וַיּוֹצִאֵנִי אֶל־הֶחָצֵר הַחִיצוֹנָה הַדֶּרֶךְ דֶּרֶךְ הַצָּפוֹן וַיְבִאֵנִי

---

outside and the other towards the inside of the door-posts, the space between the two doors being the width of the door-posts, viz. six cubits.

24. *the doors had two leaves.* Each of the two doors spoken of in the preceding verse had two main leaves, one to the north and the other to the south, while each leaf had two leaves, so that each door consisted of four leaves.

two leaves for the one door. i.e. two smaller leaves for each half of the door.

25. *there were made.* The feminine form of the Hebrew is explained by Kimchi as governed by the word 'figure' to be understood.

thick beams of wood upon the face of the porch without. Beams served to hold the wall of the Temple and that of the porch together, as in Solomon's Temple (1 Kings vii. 6). These protruded through both sides of the porch towards

the exterior (Rashi). There was a beam in the wall of the porch without, opposite the altar (Kimchi).

26. *there were narrow windows . . . on the sides of the porch.* Windows and palm-trees were on both side walls of the porch entrance.

there were also the brackets of the house, and the thick beams. The Talmud defines *tsal'oth* (*brackets*) as beams along the top of walls upon which the cross-beams rest, and *'ubbim* (*thick beams*) as the cross-beams which form the basis of the ceiling (B.K. 67a).

CHAPTER XLII
1-12   THE PRIESTS' CHAMBERS

1. *he brought me forth into the outer court.* From the porch where the prophet was standing (xli. 25f.), he was led to the outer court via the inner court, through the northern gate.

chamber that was over against the
separate place, and which was over
against the building, toward the
north, 2. even to the front of the
length of a hundred cubits, with the
door on the north, and the breadth
of fifty cubits, 3. over against the
twenty cubits which belonged to the
inner court, and over against the
pavement which belonged to the
outer court; with gallery against
gallery in three stories. 4. And
before the chambers was a walk of
ten cubits breadth inward, a way of

אֶל־הַלִּשְׁכָּה אֲשֶׁר נֶגֶד הַגִּזְרָה
וַאֲשֶׁר־נֶגֶד הַבִּנְיָן אֶל־
2 הַצָּפוֹן: אֶל־פְּנֵי אֹרֶךְ אַמּוֹת
הַמֵּאָה פֶּתַח הַצָּפוֹן וְהָרֹחַב
3 חֲמִשִּׁים אַמּוֹת: נֶגֶד הָעֶשְׂרִים
אֲשֶׁר לֶחָצֵר הַפְּנִימִי וְנֶגֶד
רִצְפָה אֲשֶׁר לֶחָצֵר הַחִיצוֹנָה
אַתִּיק אֶל־פְּנֵי־אַתִּיק
4 בַּשְּׁלִשִׁים: וְלִפְנֵי הַלְּשָׁכוֹת
מַהֲלַךְ עֶשֶׂר אַמּוֹת רֹחַב אֶל־

into the chamber. i.e. the block of
chambers.

that was over against the separate place.
For the meaning and situation of the
Gizrah, see on xli. 12. The chambers
spoken of here are those referred to in
xli. 10. Alongside the *Gizrah* which
was twenty cubits wide, north and south
of the Temple, blocks of chambers were
erected. The construction and use of
the chambers are described later in the
chapter. The only entrance to these
chambers, as well as to the *Gizrah*
between them and the side-chambers
along the Temple walls, was from the
outer court, since the inner court at the
east end was completely shut off by the
width of the Temple which it immediately adjoined (Rashi).

*and which was over against the building,
toward the north.* The reference is
either to the Temple-building, or to the
surrounding wall of the outer court with
its cells on the opposite side which is
also called *building* in xl. 5. Though the
outer wall of the Temple area was a
distance away from the block of
chambers, they are described as being
over against the other because there was
no intervening structure.

2. *the front of the length of a hundred
cubits . . . the breadth of fifty cubits.*

Since this block was one hundred cubits
long and fifty wide, it follows that the
open space in the outer court between
the chambers and the wall of the outer
court on the north was fifty cubits and
its length from east to west one hundred
cubits (Rashi). Others understand the
text as merely giving the length of the
block as one hundred cubits, corresponding to the length of the Temple proper,
and its breadth from north to south as
fifty cubits.

3. *over against the twenty cubits . . . to
the inner court, and over against the
pavement . . . to the outer court.* The
situation of the block mentioned in
verse 1 is here defined more precisely.
It lay between the twenty cubits wide
Gizrah on the south and the *pavement*
running along the wall of the outer
court on the north.

with gallery against gallery in three stories.
For the Hebrew term rendered *gallery,*
see on xli. 15. Kimchi understands the
phrase as 'chamber above chamber in
three stories.'

4. *before the chambers was a walk of ten
cubits breadth inward.* The chambers
occupied two blocks divided by a passage
ten cubits broad (Kimchi). The length

one cubit; and their doors were toward the north. 5. Now the upper chambers were shorter; for the galleries took away from these, more than from the lower and the middlemost, in the building. 6. For they were in three stories, and they had not pillars as the pillars of the courts; therefore room was taken away from the lowest and the middlemost, in comparison with the ground. 7. And the wall that was without by the side of the chambers,

הַפְּנִימִית דֶּרֶךְ אַמָּה אֶחָת
5 וּפִתְחֵיהֶם לַצָּפוֹן: וְהַלְּשָׁכוֹת
הָעֶלְיוֹנֹת קְצֻרוֹת כִּי־יוֹכְלוּ
אֲתִיקִים מֵהֵנָּה מֵהַתַּחְתֹּנוֹת
6 וּמֵהַתִּיכֹנוֹת בִּנְיָן: כִּי
מְשֻׁלָּשׁוֹת הֵנָּה וְאֵין לָהֶן
עַמּוּדִים כְּעַמּוּדֵי הַחֲצֵרוֹת
עַל־כֵּן נֶאֱצַל מֵהַתַּחְתֹּנוֹת
7 וּמֵהַתִּיכֹנוֹת מֵהָאָרֶץ: וְגָדֵר
אֲשֶׁר־לַחוּץ לְעֻמַּת הַלְּשָׁכוֹת

of the passage or *walk* was, according to some authorities, the same as that of the block, viz. one hundred cubits.

a way of one cubit. The meaning of the phrase is obscure. Rashi, who interprets *a walk of ten cubits breadth* as referring to a passage leading to the *Gizrah*, explains it as 'a narrow entrance one cubit wide at the corner of the north-eastern wall of the inner court,' leading to a narrow passage which is described in the text as being *of ten cubits breadth*, because it ran alongside the breadth of the projecting structure on the side of the porch, which was eleven cubits from east to west and fifteen long from north to south.

their doors were toward the north. According to Rashi, the entrances of the chambers opened on the north into the outer court. Some suggest that if the *walk of ten cubits breadth* refers to a passage between two blocks of chambers, the description of the doors as *toward the north* means that they opened on to this passage.

5. *the upper chambers were shorter.* Rashi and Kimchi confess their inability to understand this verse and the next. If, however, *attikim* is defined as 'gal-

leries,' the meaning of the text becomes clear. The chambers on the top story were smaller than those of the lower stories, because the outer wall of the upper story was inward as compared with the lower wall in order to leave room for the galleries which did not protrude beyond the front lower wall.

6. *for they were in three stories,* etc. Because the galleries of the upper story did not, as other galleries in the courts, project from the front wall with supporting pillars, but were built within the chambers and rested on the wall on the story below, the chambers of the upper story were perforce shortened to the extent of the space taken up by the galleries.

7. *the wall that was without.* As is evident from verse 4, the chambers on the north and south of the inner court were in two blocks divided by a passage ten cubits in breadth. The situation of these two blocks is further explained in this verse and the next. The block of cells along the *Gizrah* was one hundred cubits long like the Temple itself, while the second wing of cells, which was opposite and facing the outer court, measured fifty cubits from west to east.

toward the outer court in front of the
chambers, the length thereof was
fifty cubits. 8. For the length of
the chambers that were toward the
outer court was fifty cubits; and, lo,
before the temple were a hundred
cubits. 9. And from under these
chambers was the entry on the east
side, as one goeth into them from
the outer court. 10. In the breadth
of the wall of the court toward the
east, before the separate place, and
before the building, there were
chambers, 11. with a way before
them; like the appearance of the
chambers which were toward the

דֶּרֶךְ הֶחָצֵר הַחִיצוֹנָה אֶל־
פְּנֵי הַלְּשָׁכוֹת אָרְכּוֹ חֲמִשִּׁים
8 אַמָּה: כִּי־אֹרֶךְ הַלְּשָׁכוֹת
אֲשֶׁר לֶחָצֵר הַחִיצוֹנָה חֲמִשִּׁים
אַמָּה וְהִנֵּה עַל־פְּנֵי הַהֵיכָל
9 מֵאָה אַמָּה: וּמִתַּחְתָּה לְשָׁכוֹת
הָאֵלֶּה הַמָּבוֹא מֵהַקָּדִים
בְּבֹאוֹ לָהֵנָּה מֵהֶחָצֵר הַחִיצֹנָה:
10 בְּרֹחַב ׀ גֶּדֶר הֶחָצֵר דֶּרֶךְ
הַקָּדִים אֶל־פְּנֵי הַגִּזְרָה וְאֶל־
11 פְּנֵי הַבִּנְיָן לְשָׁכוֹת: וְדֶרֶךְ
לִפְנֵיהֶם כְּמַרְאֵה הַלְּשָׁכוֹת

v. 9. ומתחת הלשכות ק׳ v. 9. המביא ק׳

The outer wall of this block formed part
of the boundary between the inner and
outer courts. It is with the remaining
length of fifty cubits, running from the
end of the shorter block to a point
opposite the end of the Temple proper,
that this verse deals. This space, fifty
cubits in length, was closed by a *wall*,
literally 'a fence,' running in a line with
the outer wall of the block.

by the side of the chambers. The wall is
described as being at the extreme end of
the inner court, towards the outer court
and opposite to and in front of the
chambers of the longer block.

the length thereof was fifty cubits. The
portion of the wall which ran parallel to
the longer block was fifty cubits long,
but from there it continued up to the
northern gate of the inner court.
Chambers, similar in every respect, were
erected opposite on the south side.

8. *the length of the chambers,* etc. This
refers to the shorter block of chambers
lying towards the outer court.

and, lo, before the temple were a hundred

cubits. The block of chambers alongside
the *Gizrah* facing the Temple was one
hundred cubits long.

9. *from under these chambers was the entry
on the east side.* From the outer court,
there was an entrance to the chambers
at the east end of the shorter block.
A flight of steps, which faced eastward,
ran parallel to the wall of the inner court.
The preposition *under* is used because
the outer court was on a lower level than
the inner court upon which the chambers
stood.

10. *in the breadth of the wall of the court
toward the east.* Ezekiel also saw on the
east side of the wall of the inner court
chambers similar in some respects to
those on the north side. The exact
location of these chambers is not stated.
Rashi suggests that they were in the
outer court alongside the eastern wall of
the inner court.

11. *with a way before them.* The
reference is to the *walk* or passage ten
cubits wide in front of the chambers
(Elijah of Wilna).

north, as long as they, and as
broad as they, with all their goings
out, and according to their fashions;
and as their doors, 12. so were also
the doors of the chambers that were
toward the south, there was a door
in the head of the way, even the way
directly before the wall, toward the
way from the east, as one entereth
into them.

13. Then said he unto me: 'The
north chambers and the south
chambers, which are before the
separate place, they are the holy
chambers, where the priests that are
near unto the LORD shall eat the most
holy things; there shall they lay the
most holy things, and the meal-
offering, and the sin-offering, and

אֲשֶׁר דֶּרֶךְ הַצָּפוֹן כְּאָרְכָּן כֵּן
רָחְבָּן וְכֹל מוֹצָאֵיהֶן
וּכְמִשְׁפְּטֵיהֶן וּכְפִתְחֵיהֶן:
12 וּכְפִתְחֵי הַלְּשָׁכוֹת אֲשֶׁר דֶּרֶךְ
הַדָּרוֹם פֶּתַח בְּרֹאשׁ דָּרֶךְ
דֶּרֶךְ בִּפְנֵי הַגְּדֶרֶת הֲגִינָה דֶּרֶךְ
13 הַקָּדִים בְּבוֹאָן: וַיֹּאמֶר אֵלַי
לִשְׁכוֹת הַצָּפוֹן לִשְׁכוֹת
הַדָּרוֹם אֲשֶׁר אֶל־פְּנֵי הַגִּזְרָה
הֵנָּה | לִשְׁכוֹת הַקֹּדֶשׁ אֲשֶׁר
יֹאכְלוּ־שָׁם הַכֹּהֲנִים אֲשֶׁר־
קְרוֹבִים לַיהֹוָה קָדְשֵׁי
הַקֳּדָשִׁים שָׁם יַנִּיחוּ | קָדְשֵׁי
הַקֳּדָשִׁים וְהַמִּנְחָה וְהַחַטָּאת

---

as long as they, and as broad as they.
Elijah of Wilna renders this phrase:
'as was their length, so was their breadth.'
That is to say, in every respect these
chambers were similar to those on the
north side, except for their dimensions,
since these were built in square fashion.
12. *so were also the doors of the chambers
that were toward the south.* This implies
that Ezekiel also saw on the south side
chambers similar to those on the north
side.
*a door in the head of the way, even the way
directly before the wall.* The construction of this clause is very difficult and of
uncertain meaning. Some explain it as
referring to an entrance to the southern
block of chambers at the eastern end of
the outer set corresponding to the
entrance to the northern block, described
in verse 9. Rashi and Kimchi, following
the Targum, understand the words
translated *even the way directly before
the wall* as indicating the platform on

which the choir of Levites stood. The
meaning of the text will then be that
Ezekiel saw a door on the east side where
this platform was located.

13-14 THE PURPOSE OF THE CHAMBERS

13. *said he unto me.* The angel who
accompanied the prophet explained to
him the uses to which the chambers were
to be put.

the north chambers, etc. i.e. those in the
longer blocks which extended for a
hundred cubits in front of either side of
the *Gizrah.*

the priests that are near unto the LORD.
The descendants of Zadok who alone
would be found worthy to minister in
the future Temple (cf. xl. 46, xliv. 15f.).

the most holy things, and the meal-offering,
etc. The general statement, *the most
holy things,* is defined by three types of
offerings. The portions of these sac-

the guilt-offering; for the place is holy. 14. When the priests enter in, then shall they not go out of the holy place into the outer court, but there they shall lay their garments wherein they minister, for they are holy; and they shall put on other garments, and shall approach to that which pertaineth to the people.'

15. Now when he had made an end of measuring the inner house, he brought me forth by the way of the gate whose prospect is toward the east, and measured it round about. 16. He measured the east side with the measuring reed, five hundred reeds, with the measuring reed

וְהָאָשָׁם כִּי הַמָּקוֹם קָדֹשׁ׃
14 בְּבֹאָם הַכֹּהֲנִים וְלֹא־יֵצְאוּ
מֵהַקֹּדֶשׁ אֶל־הֶחָצֵר הַחִיצוֹנָה
וְשָׁם יַנִּיחוּ בִגְדֵיהֶם אֲשֶׁר־
יְשָׁרְתוּ בָהֶן כִּי־קֹדֶשׁ הֵנָּה
וְלָבְשׁוּ בְּגָדִים אֲחֵרִים וְקָרְבוּ
15 אֶל־אֲשֶׁר לָעָם׃ וְכִלָּה אֶת־
מִדּוֹת הַבַּיִת הַפְּנִימִי וְהוֹצִיאַנִי
דֶּרֶךְ הַשַּׁעַר אֲשֶׁר פָּנָיו דֶּרֶךְ
הַקָּדִים וּמְדָדוֹ סָבִיב ׀ סָבִיב׃
16 מָדַד רוּחַ הַקָּדִים בִּקְנֵה
הַמִּדָּה חֲמֵשׁ־אֵמוֹת קָנִים

v. 14. ולבשו ק׳ v. 16. מאות ק׳

rifices, which the priests received as their dues, were to be eaten in these chambers.

14. *when the priests enter in.* When the priests enter these chambers to eat the portions which were their due.

but there they shall lay their garments. Besides being used by the priests as a place wherein to eat their dues from the offerings, these chambers were also to be their vestry. The priests were not allowed to mingle with the laity while wearing their vestments; they had to deposit them in these chambers and put on their ordinary clothes before leaving the priests' enclosure.

15-20 TOTAL MEASUREMENTS OF THE TEMPLE BUILDINGS

15. *he had made an end of measuring the inner house.* The subject is the angel whom Ezekiel accompanied. The *inner house* includes the courts with all the subsidiary chambers.

the gate whose prospect is toward the east. i.e. the gate of the wall of the Temple Mount on the east, mentioned in xl. 6 as the point from which they had started.

measured it round about. After completing the measurements of the outer court, inner court, the house and chambers, the angel measured the entire area outside the surrounding wall.

16. *five hundred reeds.* Two views are held about the dimensions of the total area of the Temple buildings on the outside. Rashi understands *reeds* in this and the following verses as being each six cubits long (cf. xl. 5). On this hypothesis, the Temple buildings measured three thousand cubits on each side. He quotes in support a passage from the liturgy of the Second Day of Tabernacles which is based on the same interpretation. Praying for the restoration of the Temple, the liturgist (Kalir) states that the future Temple would be thirty-six times the size of the old Temple. The old was only five hundred cubits square, whereas the future Temple would measure three thousand cubits square. Kimchi, on the other hand, basing himself probably on xlv. 2, holds that the total measurement of the Temple buildings was five hundred *cubits* on

round about. 17. He measured the north side, five hundred reeds, with the measuring reed round about. 18. He measured the south side, five hundred reeds, with the measuring reed. 19. He turned about to the west side, and measured five hundred reeds with the measuring reed. 20. He measured it by the four sides; it had a wall round about, the length five hundred, and the breadth five hundred, to make a separation between that which was holy and that which was common.

17 בְּקָנֶה הַמִּדָּה סָבִיב: מָדַד רוּחַ הַצָּפוֹן חֲמֵשׁ־מֵאוֹת קָנִים
18 בְּקָנֶה הַמִּדָּה סָבִיב: אֶת רוּחַ הַדָּרוֹם מָדָד חֲמֵשׁ־מֵאוֹת
19 קָנִים בִּקְנֵה הַמִּדָּה: סָבַב אֶל־רוּחַ הַיָּם מָדַד חֲמֵשׁ־ מֵאוֹת קָנִים בִּקְנֵה הַמִּדָּה:
20 לְאַרְבַּע רוּחוֹת מְדָדוֹ חוֹמָה לוֹ סָבִיב ׀ סָבִיב אֹרֶךְ חֲמֵשׁ מֵאוֹת וְרֹחַב חֲמֵשׁ מֵאוֹת לְהַבְדִּיל בֵּין הַקֹּדֶשׁ לְחֹל:

43   CHAPTER XLIII   מג

1. Afterward he brought me to the gate, even the gate that looketh

1 וַיּוֹלִכֵנִי אֶל־הַשַּׁעַר שַׁעַר

---

each side. But he does not indicate how he explains the term *reeds* instead of 'cubits' in this connection. Perhaps he renders the text: 'he measured . . . five hundred (cubits) with the reeds, the standard measure of six cubits,' as distinctly stated in the clause that follows. Kimchi's explanation, which allows only a square of five hundred cubits for the Temple area, is accounted for by the measurements given in the text to the various structures. For instance, on the east side, from north to south: fifty cubits the northern outer gate-house, one hundred between the outer and inner courts, fifty the northern inner gate-house, one hundred the inner court, fifty the southern inner gate-house, one hundred the outer court on the south, and fifty the southern outer gate-house—making a total of five hundred cubits.

round about. i.e. the whole length of the east side (Kimchi).

19. *he turned about to the west side.* The verb *turned about* is used here because, with the wall on the west side, the measurement of the *surrounding* wall was completed (Kimchi).

20. *to make a separation . . . that which was common.* In comparison with the area surrounded by the wall on the Temple Mount, the city of Jerusalem was considered unholy. But the entire area of the Land of Israel up to the Holy of Holies was classified by the Rabbis under ten degrees of holiness (cf. Mishnah Kelim i. 6-9, and *Midrash Haggadol*, ed. Fisch, *Numbers*, pp. 229-232).

CHAPTER XLIII

1-9 RETURN OF THE DIVINE PRESENCE TO THE TEMPLE

1. *afterward he brought me . . . toward the east.* Having been shown the measurements of the surrounding wall, Ezekiel was brought back to the east gate

toward the east; 2. and, behold, the glory of the God of Israel came from the way of the east; and His voice was like the sound of many waters; and the earth did shine with His glory. 3. And the appearance of the vision which I saw was like the vision that I saw when I came to destroy the city; and the visions were like the vision that I saw by the river Chebar; and I fell upon my face. 4. And the glory of the LORD came into the house by the way of the gate whose prospect is toward the east. 5. And a spirit took me up, and brought me into

2 אֲשֶׁר פֹּנֶה דֶּרֶךְ הַקָּדִים: וְהִנֵּה
כְּבוֹד אֱלֹהֵי יִשְׂרָאֵל בָּא
מִדֶּרֶךְ הַקָּדִים וְקוֹלוֹ כְּקוֹל
מַיִם רַבִּים וְהָאָרֶץ הֵאִירָה
3 מִכְּבֹדוֹ: וּכְמַרְאֵה הַמַּרְאֶה
אֲשֶׁר רָאִיתִי כַּמַּרְאֶה אֲשֶׁר־
רָאִיתִי בְּבֹאִי לְשַׁחֵת אֶת־
הָעִיר וּמַרְאוֹת כַּמַּרְאֶה אֲשֶׁר
רָאִיתִי אֶל־נְהַר כְּבָר וָאֶפֹּל
4 אֶל־פָּנָי: וּכְבוֹד יְהוָה בָּא
אֶל־הַבָּיִת דֶּרֶךְ שַׁעַר אֲשֶׁר
5 פָּנָיו דֶּרֶךְ הַקָּדִים: וַתִּשָּׂאֵנִי

---

which he had left (xlii. 15), to witness the return of the Divine glory.

2. *from the way of the east.* It was by the east gate that the Divine Presence had departed from the Temple (x. 19) and gone up to the mountain, remaining there on *the east side of the city* (xi. 23). Consequently the return was from the direction of the east and the entrance by the east gate (verse 4).

His voice was like the sound of many waters. The allusion is to the sound made by the cherubim in their flight (cf. i. 24). The Targum renders the phrase: 'the voice of those who praise His name.'

the earth did shine with His glory. The splendour of the Divine Presence illumined the earth.

3. *like the vision that I saw when I came to destroy the city.* The vision in which God manifested His entry into the restored Temple was that of the *Merkabah* which Ezekiel had seen on two previous occasions: in the first vision of his prophetic career by the river Chebar (i), and in the vision of the destruction of

the city (viii-xi). Although the prophet had taken no part in the destruction of Jerusalem, he attributes the destruction to himself because he had prophesied it (Targum). Commenting on this verse, the Rabbis remarked that the word *vision* is repeated nine times (where the plural occurs it is counted as two), and it intimates that, except for Moses who was privileged to see a vision clearly, all other prophets, including Ezekiel, were allowed to behold it only after it had undergone a process of ninefold obscuration. In allusion to this Rabbinic teaching, the liturgist of the second day of Tabernacles wrote, 'They shall behold the Divine glory on His throne in visions through nine shining visions', i.e. unobscured.

4. *the glory of the LORD came into the house.* Standing outside the east gate, Ezekiel witnessed the entry of the Divine glory into the Temple by that gate, from which it had previously departed (see on verse 2).

5. *a spirit took me up, and brought me into the inner court.* Hitherto the prophet was led from one place to another by the

the inner court; and, behold, the glory of the Lord filled the house. 6. And I heard one speaking unto me out of the house; and a man stood by me. 7. And He said unto me: 'Son of man, this is the place of My throne, and the place of the soles of My feet, where I will dwell in the midst of the children of Israel for ever; and the house of Israel shall no more defile My holy name, neither they, nor their kings, by their harlotry, and by the carcasses of their kings in their high places; 8. in their setting of their threshold by My threshold, and their door-post beside My door-post, and there

רוּחַ וַתְּבִאֵנִי אֶל־הֶחָצֵר הַפְּנִימִי וְהִנֵּה מָלֵא כְבוֹד־
6 יְהֹוָה הַבָּיִת: וָאֶשְׁמַע מִדַּבֵּר אֵלַי מֵהַבַּיִת וְאִישׁ הָיָה עֹמֵד
7 אֶצְלִי: וַיֹּאמֶר אֵלַי בֶּן־אָדָם אֶת־מְקוֹם כִּסְאִי וְאֶת־מְקוֹם כַּפּוֹת רַגְלַי אֲשֶׁר אֶשְׁכָּן־שָׁם בְּתוֹךְ בְּנֵי־יִשְׂרָאֵל לְעוֹלָם וְלֹא יְטַמְּאוּ עוֹד בֵּית־יִשְׂרָאֵל שֵׁם קָדְשִׁי הֵמָּה וּמַלְכֵיהֶם בִּזְנוּתָם וּבְפִגְרֵי מַלְכֵיהֶם
8 בְּמוֹתָם: בְּתִתָּם סִפָּם אֶת־ סִפִּי וּמְזוּזָתָם אֵצֶל מְזוּזָתִי

accompanying angel; but now that he beheld the *Merkabah*, he was transported by the *spirit* as in his first vision of it (cf. ii. 2, viii. 3).

6. *I heard one speaking unto me out of the house.* The form of the verb, *middabber*, is reflexive, denoting 'speaking to one-self.' This construction is used for communicating the word of God to man to euphemize the direct relationship between man and God. Cf. Num. vii. 89 where the same form occurs in the transmission of the Divine word to Moses.

a man stood by me. It is not clear whether he was the same angel who appeared to Ezekiel at the beginning of the vision of the future Temple or another. He did not enter the Temple whence issued the Divine voice, but remained with the prophet in the inner court.

7. *the place of My throne, and the place of the soles of My feet.* In contrast to the

former Temple which was only God's *footstool*, His throne being in heaven (Isa. lx. 13; Ps. cxxxii. 7; Lam. ii. 1; 1 Chron. xxviii. 2), the new Temple will become in a complete sense the abode of the Divine Presence, indicated by the combination of *throne* and *soles of My feet.*

harlotry. i.e. the idolatrous worship described in viii. 6ff.

the carcasses of their kings. The allusion is to some Judean kings who were buried in the grounds of their palace which was in close proximity of the Temple (cf. 2 Kings xxi. 18, 26). Such defilement of the Sanctuary would not be tolerated in the ideal Temple.

in their high places. Which were erected on their sepulchres for idol-worship. Several Hebrew MSS. read *bemotham*, 'in their death,' instead of *bamotham*, 'their high places.' Apparently this was the reading of the Targum and Elijah of Wilna.

was but the wall between Me and them; and they have defiled My holy name by their abominations which they have committed; wherefore I have consumed them in Mine anger. 9. Now let them put away their harlotry, and the carcasses of their kings, far from Me, and I will dwell in the midst of them for ever.

10. Thou, son of man, show the house to the house of Israel, that they may be ashamed of their iniquities; and let them measure accurately. 11. And if they be ashamed of all that they have done, make known unto them the form of

וְהִקִּיר בֵּינִי וּבֵינֵיהֶם וְטִמְּאוּ ׀
אֶת־שֵׁם קָדְשִׁי בְּתוֹעֲבוֹתָם
אֲשֶׁר עָשׂוּ וָאֲכַל אֹתָם בְּאַפִּי ׃
9 עַתָּה יְרַחֲקוּ אֶת־זְנוּתָם וּפִגְרֵי
מַלְכֵיהֶם מִמֶּנִּי וְשָׁכַנְתִּי
10 בְתוֹכָם לְעוֹלָם ׃ אַתָּה בֶן־
אָדָם הַגֵּד אֶת־בֵּית־יִשְׂרָאֵל
אֶת־הַבַּיִת וְיִכָּלְמוּ
מֵעֲוֹנוֹתֵיהֶם וּמָדְדוּ אֶת־
11 תָּכְנִית ׃ וְאִם־נִכְלְמוּ מִכֹּל
אֲשֶׁר־עָשׂוּ צוּרַת הַבַּיִת

v. 10. הפטרת תצוה

8. *there was but the wall between Me and them.* The reference is to king Solomon's palace, one side of which was virtually enclosed by the south wall of the Temple court (cf. 1 Kings vii. 8). To safeguard the purity and holiness of the future Temple, a large area around it was to be set apart for outer and inner courts and settlements for the priests and Levites (cf. xlv. 2ff.).

9. *now let them put away their harlotry.* Rashi and Kimchi render: 'now they shall put away their harlotry'; either because there will be a separating place between the Temple of the future and private dwellings, or more probably because the people will be dominated by a new spirit.

far from Me. i.e. far from My Sanctuary.

I will dwell in the midst of them for ever. The new spirit of purification and regeneration will render Israel worthy of being as a nation and as individuals the abode of the Divine Presence.

10-12 A COMMAND TO EZEKIEL

The prophet is commanded to reveal to Israel the plan of the future Temple,

explain it to them in detail, and acquaint them with the use to which all its sections were to be put.

10. *show the house to the house of Israel.* Having seen in his vision the entire plan of the Temple, Ezekiel is instructed to describe it in all its particulars to his fellow-exiles, with the assurance that the new Sanctuary will be of permanent duration because the new age will be free from sin.

that they may be ashamed of their iniquities. The plan of the future Temple would recall the loss of the former Sanctuary brought about by their sins, and induce in them a feeling of remorse and contrition.

let them measure accurately. Let them pay attention to all the minute details and exact measurements of the buildings as delineated in the plan.

11. *if they be ashamed of all that they have done,* etc. If the plan moves them to shame and remorse for their former sins, then give them a detailed account of it in writing and they will be found worthy to behold the new Temple.

the form of the house. The general out-

the house, and the fashion thereof, and the goings out thereof, and the comings in thereof, and all the forms thereof, and all the ordinances thereof, and all the forms thereof, and all the laws thereof, and write it in their sight; that they may keep the whole form thereof, and all the ordinances thereof, and do them.

12. This is the law of the house: upon the top of the mountain the whole limit thereof round about shall be most holy. Behold, this is the law of the house.

13. And these are the measures of the altar by cubits—the cubit is a

וּתְכוּנָתוֹ וּמוֹצָאָיו וּמוֹבָאָיו
וְכָל־צוּרֹתָו וְאֵת כָּל־חֻקֹּתָיו
וְכָל־צוּרֹתָו וְכָל־תּוֹרֹתָו
הוֹדַע אוֹתָם וּכְתֹב לְעֵינֵיהֶם
וְיִשְׁמְרוּ אֶת־כָּל־צוּרָתוֹ
וְאֶת־כָּל־חֻקֹּתָיו וְעָשׂוּ
אוֹתָם: זֹאת תּוֹרַת הַבָּיִת עַל־ 12
רֹאשׁ הָהָר כָּל־גְּבֻלוֹ סָבִיב ׀
סָבִיב קֹדֶשׁ קָדָשִׁים הִנֵּה־
זֹאת תּוֹרַת הַבָּיִת: וְאֵלֶּה 13
מִדּוֹת הַמִּזְבֵּחַ בָּאַמּוֹת אַמָּה

v. 11. צורתיו ק׳   v. 11. צורתיו ק׳   v. 11. תורתיו ק׳

---

line of the Temple area within the surrounding wall.

the fashion thereof. The various sections, chambers and cells.

the goings out . . . the comings in. The gates and entrances.

all the forms thereof. The shape and form of the various departments.

all the ordinances thereof. The use to which the sections and fixtures were to be put.

all the forms thereof. The ornaments, such as the cherubim and palms.

all the laws thereof. Regulating the departments assigned to the priests, the laity and women (Kimchi).

that they may keep the whole form thereof . . . and do them. Their belief in the restoration of the Temple in all its features outlined in the plan will render them worthy to put it into operation. The allusion is to the final deliverance of Israel and the restoration of the Temple in the Messianic age (Kimchi).

12. *this is the law of the house.* Referring to the plan set out in detail above (xl-xlii) and here in general terms.

upon the top of the mountain. The Temple of the future is to be erected on the summit, not like the former on the slope of the mountain (Kimchi)

the whole limit thereof . . . shall be most holy. The expression *most holy* is used in a relative sense. In contrast to Jerusalem which is considered 'holy,' the Temple area within the surrounding wall is *most holy.* But the Temple area comprised different degrees of holiness, the west part of which is called *most holy* (see on xlii. 20).

13-17 THE ALTAR OF
BURNT-OFFERING

13. *these are the measures of the altar.* viz. the altar of the burnt-offering which stood in the centre of the inner court opposite the entrance of the Temple, previously mentioned in xl. 47. The obscurity of the terminology used in this verse has given rise to a variety of interpretations as to the dimensions and shape of the altar. The most convincing is that of Malbim based on the Talmud: the altar built in square fashion, probably of stone, was ten cubits high and consisted of three blocks formed by two

cubit and a handbreadth: the bottom shall be a cubit, and the breadth a cubit, and the border thereof by the edge thereof round about a span; and this shall be the base of the altar. 14. And from the bottom upon the ground to the lower settle shall be two cubits, and the breadth one cubit; and from the lesser settle to the greater settle shall be four cubits, and the breadth a cubit. 15. And the hearth shall be four

אַמָּה וָטֹפַח וְחֵיק הָאַמָּה
וְאַמָּה־רֹחַב וּגְבוּלָהּ אֶל־
שְׂפָתָהּ סָבִיב זֶרֶת הָאֶחָד וְזֶה
14 גַּב הַמִּזְבֵּחַ: וּמֵחֵיק הָאָרֶץ
עַד־הָעֲזָרָה הַתַּחְתּוֹנָה שְׁתַּיִם
אַמּוֹת וְרֹחַב אַמָּה אֶחָת
וּמֵהָעֲזָרָה הַקְּטַנָּה עַד־
הָעֲזָרָה הַגְּדוֹלָה אַרְבַּע אַמּוֹת
15 וְרֹחַב הָאַמָּה: וְהָהַרְאֵל

indents or contractions. The base (*bottom*) was thirty-two cubits wide and two cubits high (that of the Second Temple was only one cubit high). Indented one cubit on each side rose the second block of the altar to a height of four cubits, reducing its width to thirty cubits. This second block was called *the lesser settle*. On top of it was the third block also four cubits in height, but reduced now to twenty-eight cubits in width, called *the greater settle*. Finally the platform, where the sacrifices were burnt, is named *the hearth*. This is the explanation of the text which is adopted in the following comments.

by cubits—the cubit is a cubit and a handbreadth. Malbim renders: 'by two kinds of cubits: an ordinary cubit (of five handbreadths) and a larger cubit consisting of a cubit and a handbreadth.' That is to say, some of the dimensions of the altar were measured according to the smaller and others according to the larger cubit.

the bottom shall be a cubit, and the breadth a cubit. The height of the base as well as its breadth formed by the contraction was measured according to the standard cubit of five handbreadths.

the border thereof by the edge . . . a span. This refers to a kind of belt in the middle of the altar projecting half a cubit as a dividing-line between the blood of

sacrifices which was to be sprinkled above and the blood of others which was to be sprinkled below. This corresponded to the *grating of network of brass* in the portable altar of the wilderness (Exod. xxvii. 4) and the 'red line' of the altar in the Second Temple (Malbim). Others understand the text as referring to a moulded edge or close screen around the ledge of the base one cubit in breadth.

this shall be the base of the altar. Unconsciously agreeing with the LXX, Malbim renders the clause: 'this is the height of the altar,' and understands it as the heading of the next verse.

14. *from the bottom . . . shall be two cubits.* The height of the base from the ground to the indent was two cubits, and the ledge around the altar on its four sides was one cubit. Both dimensions were to be measured by the standard cubit of five handbreadths. The block above the first indent is called *the lower settle* because the height of its base was only two cubits, whereas the topmost was four cubits high.

and the breadth. This refers to the second indent at the end of the second block.

15. *the hearth shall be four cubits.* The topmost of the three blocks was four cubits in height and upon its upper surface the sacrifices were burnt. The

cubits; and from the hearth and upward there shall be four horns. 16. And the hearth shall be twelve cubits long by twelve broad, square in the four sides thereof. 17. And the settle shall be fourteen cubits long by fourteen broad in the four sides thereof; and the border about it shall be half a cubit; and the bottom thereof shall be a cubit about; and the steps thereof shall look toward the east.'

18. And He said unto me: 'Son of man, thus saith the Lord GOD:

אַרְבַּע אַמּוֹת וּמֵהָאֲרִאֵיל 15
וּלְמַעְלָה הַקְּרָנוֹת אַרְבַּע:
וְהָאֲרִיאֵל שְׁתֵּים עֶשְׂרֵה אֹרֶךְ 16
בִּשְׁתֵּים עֶשְׂרֵה רֹחַב רָבוּעַ
אֶל אַרְבַּעַת רְבָעָיו: וְהָעֲזָרָה 17
אַרְבַּע עֶשְׂרֵה אֹרֶךְ בְּאַרְבַּע
עֶשְׂרֵה רֹחַב אֶל אַרְבַּעַת
רְבָעֶיהָ וְהַגְּבוּל סָבִיב אוֹתָהּ
חֲצִי הָאַמָּה וְהַחֵיק־לָהּ אַמָּה
סָבִיב וּמַעֲלֹתֵהוּ פְּנוֹת קָדִים: 18
וַיֹּאמֶר אֵלַי בֶּן־אָדָם כֹּה אָמַר

v. 15. ומהאריאל ק׳   v. 16. והאריאל ק׳

Hebrew name is *ariel*, applied in Isa. xxix. 1 to Jerusalem.

from the hearth and upward there shall be four horns. The four cubits, mentioned as being the height of the top block, includes the projecting four corners, the length of which was one cubit. This gives the total height for the altar as ten cubits.

16. *the hearth shall be twelve cubits*, etc. This describes the area of the platform or topmost surface of the altar. According to the Mishnah (Middoth iii. 1), the measurement of twelve cubits is to be taken from the centre of the hearth towards each side, as implied in the concluding words of the verse. This would bring the area of the hearth to twenty-four cubits square. The actual area, however, was twenty-eight cubits (see on verse 13), but two cubits on each side were used for other purposes: the outside cubit was taken up by the four corners or horns, and the inner cubit, bordering on the hearth, served as a path for the priests to walk round.

17. *the settle shall be fourteen cubits . . . in the four sides thereof.* While the exact area reserved for the burning of the

sacrifices is stated in the preceding verse, this measurement of fourteen cubits towards each side (twenty-eight cubits square) refers to the entire area, including the two cubits on the sides taken up by the horns and the ledge used by the priests. The third block above the second indent, *the greater settle*, is mentioned here and in verse 20 simply as *the settle*.

the border about it. See on verse 12.

the bottom thereof shall be a cubit about. This is repeated from verse 13 to intimate that the width of one cubit of the base was measured from the second block above it and not from the border which protruded half a cubit from the wall of the block.

the steps thereof shall look toward the east. The approach to the altar was on the east side. As steps were forbidden on the altar (Exod. xx. 23), it is probable that a sloping path is intended.

18-27 DEDICATION OF THE ALTAR

18. *He said unto me.* The speaker is God Who, as stated in verse 6, revealed Himself to Ezekiel.

These are the ordinances of the altar in the day when they shall make it, to offer burnt-offerings thereon, and to dash blood against it. 19. Thou shalt give to the priests the Levites that are of the seed of Zadok, who are near unto Me, to minister unto Me, saith the Lord GOD, a young bullock for a sin-offering. 20. And thou shalt take of the blood thereof, and put it on the four horns of it, and on the four corners of the settle, and upon the border round about; thus shalt thou purify it and make atonement for it. 21. Thou shalt also take the bullock of

אֲדֹנָי יֱהֹוִה אֵלֶּה חֻקּוֹת הַמִּזְבֵּחַ
בְּיוֹם הֵעָשׂוֹתוֹ לְהַעֲלוֹת עָלָיו
עוֹלָה וְלִזְרֹק עָלָיו דָּם:
19 וְנָתַתָּה אֶל־הַכֹּהֲנִים הַלְוִיִּם
אֲשֶׁר הֵם מִזֶּרַע צָדוֹק
הַקְּרֹבִים אֵלַי נְאֻם אֲדֹנָי יֱהֹוִה
לְשָׁרְתֵנִי פַּר בֶּן־בָּקָר
20 לְחַטָּאת: וְלָקַחְתָּ מִדָּמוֹ
וְנָתַתָּה עַל־אַרְבַּע קַרְנוֹתָיו
וְאֶל־אַרְבַּע פִּנּוֹת הָעֲזָרָה
וְאֶל־הַגְּבוּל סָבִיב וְחִטֵּאתָ
21 אוֹתוֹ וְכִפַּרְתָּהוּ: וְלָקַחְתָּ אֵת

in the day when they shall make it. On the day the altar is completed it is to be dedicated by the offering of sacrifices, as was done on the eighth day of the consecration of the Tabernacle in the wilderness (Lev. ix).

to offer burnt-offerings thereon, and to dash blood against it. The purpose of consecrating the altar is to purify it and make it usable for the two functions here enumerated

19. *thou shalt give.* Ezekiel, being a priest, is to officiate in the restored Temple at the consecration service as High Priest and assign some of the rites to the other priests.

the priests the Levites. The priests who originate from the tribe of Levi.

that are of the seed of Zadok. Zadok, the first High Priest in king Solomon's Temple, was a descendant of Phinehas who was rewarded with *the covenant of an everlasting priesthood* (Num. xxv. 13). Only his descendants would be found worthy to minister in the Temple of the future (see on xl. 46).

a young bullock for a sin-offering. To be connected with the verb *thou shalt give* at the beginning of the verse. The same kind of sacrifice was offered by Moses at the consecration of the Tabernacle.

20. *thou shalt take of the blood thereof.* The priestly function at the sacrificial service began with collecting the blood in a vessel, the slaughtering of the animal being permitted by a layman. This first priestly function and those subsequent to it at the dedication sacrifices were to be performed by Ezekiel.

the settle. i.e. the greater settle (verse 14).

upon the border round about. i.e. the projecting belt of a half a cubit wide in the middle of the altar (see on verse 13).

shalt thou purify it and make atonement for it. The dedicatory sacrifices were intended to purify and elevate the altar from a secular to a sacred status fit for its sacrificial purpose (Rashi).

the sin-offering, and it shall be
burnt in the appointed place of the
house, without the sanctuary.
22. And on the second day thou
shalt offer a he-goat without blemish
for a sin-offering; and they shall
purify the altar, as they did purify it
with the bullock. 23. When thou
hast made an end of purifying it,
thou shalt offer a young bullock
without blemish, and a ram out of
the flock without blemish. 24. And
thou shalt present them before the
LORD, and the priests shall cast salt
upon them, and they shall offer them
up for a burnt-offering unto the
LORD. 25. Seven days shalt thou
prepare every day a goat for a sin-
offering; they shall also prepare a

הַפָּר הַחַטָּאת וּשְׂרָפוֹ בְּמִפְקַד
22 הַבַּיִת מִחוּץ לַמִּקְדָּשׁ: וּבַיּוֹם
הַשֵּׁנִי תַּקְרִיב שְׂעִיר־עִזִּים
תָּמִים לְחַטָּאת וְחִטְּאוּ אֶת־
הַמִּזְבֵּחַ כַּאֲשֶׁר חִטְּאוּ בַּפָּר:
23 בְּכַלּוֹתְךָ מֵחַטֵּא תַּקְרִיב פַּר
בֶּן־בָּקָר תָּמִים וְאַיִל מִן־
24 הַצֹּאן תָּמִים: וְהִקְרַבְתָּם
לִפְנֵי יְהֹוָה וְהִשְׁלִיכוּ הַכֹּהֲנִים
עֲלֵיהֶם מֶלַח וְהֶעֱלוּ אוֹתָם
25 עֹלָה לַיהֹוָה: שִׁבְעַת יָמִים
תַּעֲשֶׂה שְׂעִיר־חַטָּאת לַיּוֹם

---

21. *it shall be burnt.* lit. 'he shall burn
it,' a common impersonal construction
in Hebrew.

*in the appointed place of the house, without
the sanctuary.* The exact spot where the
carcass of the sin-offering was to be
burnt is not specified, but it had to be
within the wall of the Temple Mount and
outside the inner court. Like the
bullock at the consecration of the
Tabernacle in the wilderness and the bull-
calf offered by Aaron on the eighth day
of the consecration and other public
burnt-offerings, this dedicatory sin-
offering was to be burnt wholly after its
blood had been sprinkled on the altar.

22. *a he-goat . . . for a sin-offering.*
An innovation, since no such sacrifice
was offered at the consecration of the
Tabernacle.

as they did purify it with the bullock. The
blood of the he-goat is to be sprinkled
on the altar as was done with the blood
of the bullock.

23. *when thou hast made an end of
purifying it.* After the he-goat of the
sin-offering had been sacrificed, a young

bullock and a ram were to be brought
as a burnt-offering.

24. *thou shalt present them.* i.e. burn
them on the altar.

the priests shall cast salt upon them. In
accordance with the law of Lev. ii. 13:
With all thine offerings thou shalt offer salt.
Salt, as a preservative, is the symbol of
the everlasting covenant between God
and Israel.

25. *seven days.* i.e. till the end of seven
days. That is to say, the sacrifices
which were offered on the second day
(verse 22), differing from those brought
on the first day, are to be repeated daily
for a period of six days, making a total
of seven days inclusive of the first.
Elijah of Wilna and Malbim hold that
seven days are to be counted in addition
to the first day on which the sin-offering
of one bullock was brought; and that on
the eighth day referred to in verse 27, the
offerings enjoined in verse 25 would still
be brought in addition to the further
offerings mentioned in verse 27.

every day a goat. This is to be a special
feature of the Temple of the future.

young bullock, and a ram out of the flock, without blemish. 26. Seven days shall they make atonement for the altar and cleanse it; so shall they consecrate it. 27. And when they have accomplished the days, it shall be that upon the eighth day, and forward, the priests shall make your burnt-offerings upon the altar, and your peace-offerings; and I will accept you, saith the Lord God.'

וּפַר בֶּן־בָּקָר וְאַיִל מִן־הַצֹּאן
26 תְּמִימִים יַעֲשׂוּ: שִׁבְעַת יָמִים
יְכַפְּרוּ אֶת־הַמִּזְבֵּחַ וְטִהֲרוּ
27 אֹתוֹ וּמִלְאוּ יָדָו: וִיכַלּוּ אֶת־
הַיָּמִים וְהָיָה בַיּוֹם הַשְּׁמִינִי
וָהָלְאָה יַעֲשׂוּ הַכֹּהֲנִים עַל־
הַמִּזְבֵּחַ אֶת־עוֹלוֹתֵיכֶם
וְאֶת־שַׁלְמֵיכֶם וְרָצִאתִי
אֶתְכֶם נְאֻם אֲדֹנָי יֱהֹוִה: *

<hr/>

44 CHAPTER XLIV מד

1. Then he brought me back the way of the outer gate of the sanctuary, which looketh toward the east; and it was shut. 2. And the Lord said unto me: 'This gate shall

1 וַיָּשֶׁב אֹתִי דֶּרֶךְ שַׁעַר הַמִּקְדָּשׁ
הַחִיצוֹן הַפֹּנֶה קָדִים וְהוּא
2 סָגוּר: וַיֹּאמֶר אֵלַי יְהֹוָה

<hr/>

v. 26. למדנחאי וכפרו כתיב יכפרו ק' v. 26. ידיו ק' v. 27. א' במקום י' v. 27. עד כאן

No parallel can be found in any previous consecration rite (see on verse 22).

a young bullock, and a ram. For a burnt-offering.

26. *shall they make atonement for the altar.* See on verse 20.

and cleanse it. To render it fit for its holy purpose.

consecrate it. lit. 'fill its hands.' The idiom is commonly used for the initiation or consecration of the priests. Here it is applied to the altar.

27. *when they have accomplished the days.* After the priests had performed the rites of consecration for seven days.

the eighth day, etc. When the consecration ritual is completed, the regular sacrificial service will begin.

I will accept you. God will accept their offerings, because their conduct will be pleasing to Him (Kimchi).

CHAPTER XLIV

EZEKIEL is now instructed in the order of service in the restored Temple (xliv-xlvi). Only the priests and Levites who had preserved their religious integrity and moral purity would be deemed worthy to act as its ministers. Their maintenance would be a charge on the nation in the form of various dues, since they will receive no portion in the land.

1-3 THE OUTER EAST GATE AND THE PRINCE

1. *he brought me back.* The subject of the verb is the angel who acted as guide. Standing in the inner court (xliii. 5), Ezekiel was brought back in the direction of the outer east gate by which he had previously entered (xliii. 1); but he found it shut after the glory of God had entered by it.

2. *this gate shall be shut,* etc. The gate

be shut, it shall not be opened,
neither shall any man enter in by it,
for the LORD, the God of Israel,
hath entered in by it; therefore it
shall be shut.   3. As for the prince,
being a prince, he shall sit therein to
eat bread before the LORD; he shall
enter by the way of the porch of the
gate, and shall go out by the way of
the same.'

4. Then he brought me the way of
the north gate before the house; and
I looked, and, behold, the glory of
the LORD filled the house of the
LORD; and I fell upon my face.
5. And the LORD said unto me: 'Son
of man, mark well, and behold with

הַשַּׁעַר הַזֶּה סָגוּר יִהְיֶה לֹא
יִפָּתֵחַ וְאִישׁ לֹא־יָבֹא בוֹ כִּי
יְהוָה אֱלֹהֵי־יִשְׂרָאֵל בָּא בוֹ
וְהָיָה סָגוּר: אֶת־הַנָּשִׂיא 3
נָשִׂיא־הוּא יֵשֶׁב־בּוֹ לֶאֱכָל־
לֶחֶם לִפְנֵי יְהוָה מִדֶּרֶךְ אוּלָם
הַשַּׁעַר יָבוֹא וּמִדַּרְכּוֹ יֵצֵא:
וַיְבִיאֵנִי דֶּרֶךְ־שַׁעַר הַצָּפוֹן 4
אֶל־פְּנֵי הַבַּיִת וָאֵרֶא וְהִנֵּה
מָלֵא כְבוֹד־יְהוָה אֶת־בֵּית
יְהוָה וָאֶפֹּל אֶל־פָּנָי: וַיֹּאמֶר 5
אֵלַי יְהוָה בֶּן־אָדָם שִׂים לִבְּךָ

v. 3. יתיר ו' כצ״ל v. 3.

by which God's glory had entered is to
be closed and never again opened, an
indication that the Divine Presence
would never again depart from the
Sanctuary (Malbim).

3. *being a prince* (nasi). The rank of
the future ruler will not be *melech* (king)
but *nasi*, as it was said, *David My
servant shall be their prince for ever*
(xxxvii. 25) (Kimchi).

he shall sit therein to eat bread. Only the
nasi, by reason of his exalted office, is
permitted to use the interior of the
outer east gateway to partake of the
sacrificial meal.   But even he is not to
enter through the east gate from the
outside, but is to pass into the outer
court either through the north or the
south gateway, and then enter the porch
from the court.

he shall enter by the way of the porch, etc.
He enters the interior of the porch for
his sacrificial meal from the way of the
porch the interior of which faces the
outer court, and leaves by the same way,
passing into the outer court and from

thence through the open gates to the
exterior of the Temple area.

4-14 QUALIFICATIONS OF THE TEMPLE MINISTERS

4. *then he brought me the way of the north
gate.*   Standing in the outer court in
front of the east gateway (verse 1), the
prophet is now led into the inner court
to the front of the house, not through
the inner east gate opposite, which is to
be kept closed on week-days (xlvi. 1),
but by the way of the north gate of the
inner court.

*the glory of the LORD filled the house of
the LORD.*   After the gate had been shut
(verse 1), Ezekiel is shown a second time
the glory of the LORD filling the house,
lest he mistook the closing of the entrance
as an indication of the departure of the
Divine Presence (see on verse 2)
(Malbim).

5. *mark well.*   He is to pay close attention to and thoroughly grasp all the
ordinances in connection with the service
of the Temple.

thine eyes, and hear with thine ears all that I say unto thee concerning all the ordinances of the house of the LORD, and all the laws thereof; and mark well the entering in of the house, with every going forth of the sanctuary. 6. And thou shalt say to the rebellious, even to the house of Israel: Thus saith the Lord GOD: O ye house of Israel, let it suffice you of all your abominations, 7. in that ye have brought in aliens, uncircumcised in heart and uncircumcised in flesh, to be in My sanctuary, to profane it, even My house, when ye offer My bread, the fat and the blood, and they have broken My covenant, to add unto all your abominations. 8. And ye have not

וּרְאֵה בְעֵינֶיךָ וּבְאָזְנֶיךָ שְׁמָע
אֵת כָּל־אֲשֶׁר אֲנִי מְדַבֵּר אֹתָךְ
לְכָל־חֻקּוֹת בֵּית־יְהוָה
וּלְכָל־תּוֹרֹתָו וְשַׂמְתָּ לִבְּךָ
לִמְבוֹא הַבַּיִת בְּכֹל מוֹצָאֵי
6 הַמִּקְדָּשׁ׃ וְאָמַרְתָּ אֶל־מֶרִי
אֶל־בֵּית יִשְׂרָאֵל כֹּה אָמַר
אֲדֹנָי יֱהוִה רַב־לָכֶם מִכָּל־
תּוֹעֲבוֹתֵיכֶם בֵּית יִשְׂרָאֵל׃
7 בַּהֲבִיאֲכֶם בְּנֵי־נֵכָר עַרְלֵי־
לֵב וְעַרְלֵי בָשָׂר לִהְיוֹת
בְּמִקְדָּשִׁי לְחַלְּלוֹ אֶת־בֵּיתִי
בְּהַקְרִיבְכֶם אֶת־לַחְמִי חֵלֶב
וָדָם וַיָּפֵרוּ אֶת־בְּרִיתִי אֶל
8 כָּל־תּוֹעֲבוֹתֵיכֶם׃ וְלֹא

v. 5. קמץ בלא אתנ"ף v. 5. תורתיו ק׳

---

behold with thine eyes. The exact measurements.

hear with thine ears. The verbal instructions given to him.

and mark well the entering in of the house, etc. He is further to notice the various gates for entering and leaving, each of which is to be used by a particular section of the people according to its grade, since there were departments of varying degrees of holiness within the Temple area (Kimchi).

6. *the rebellious.* An abbreviation of *rebellious house,* a phrase frequently used in the earlier part of the Book (e.g. ii. 5, iii. 9, xii. 2).

let it suffice you of all your abominations. In permitting unauthorized persons to discharge priestly functions, as indicated

in the next verse. That practice must be strictly avoided in the new Temple.

7. *aliens, uncircumcised in heart and uncircumcised in flesh.* Rabbinic interpretation explains this to mean priests who were estranged from God by their evil deeds and those who were disqualified from service in the house of God through not having been circumcised for reasons of health. But the Targum takes the phrase literally and renders *benë nechar* (*aliens*) as 'heathen persons.' The allusion is probably to prisoners of war who were employed for menial service in the Temple (cf. Josh. ix. 27) and were subsequently assigned some of the ministerial duties.

My bread. The sacrifices are so described in Lev. xxi. 6.

they have broken My covenant. Which was limited to Israel.

kept the charge of My holy things;
but ye have set keepers of My
charge in My sanctuary to please
yourselves.

9. Thus saith the Lord GOD: No
alien, uncircumcised in heart and
uncircumcised in flesh, shall enter
into My sanctuary, even any alien
that is among the children of Israel.

10. But the Levites, that went far
from Me, when Israel went astray,
that went astray from Me after their
idols, they shall bear their iniquity;
11. and they shall be ministers in
My sanctuary, having charge at the
gates of the house, and ministering in
the house: they shall slay the burnt-
offering and the sacrifice for the
people, and they shall stand before
them to minister unto them. 12. Because they ministered unto them
before their idols, and became a

שְׁמַרְתֶּם מִשְׁמֶרֶת קָדָשָׁי
וַתְּשִׂימוּן לְשֹׁמְרֵי מִשְׁמַרְתִּי
בְּמִקְדָּשִׁי לָכֶם: כֹּה־אָמַר 9
אֲדֹנָי יֱהֹוִה כָּל־בֶּן־נֵכָר עֶרֶל
לֵב וְעֶרֶל בָּשָׂר לֹא יָבוֹא אֶל־
מִקְדָּשִׁי לְכָל־בֶּן־נֵכָר אֲשֶׁר
בְּתוֹךְ בְּנֵי יִשְׂרָאֵל: כִּי אִם־ 10
הַלְוִיִּם אֲשֶׁר רָחֲקוּ מֵעָלַי
בִּתְעוֹת יִשְׂרָאֵל אֲשֶׁר תָּעוּ
מֵעָלַי אַחֲרֵי גִּלּוּלֵיהֶם וְנָשְׂאוּ
עֲוֹנָם: וְהָיוּ בְמִקְדָּשִׁי מְשָׁרְתִים 11
פְּקֻדּוֹת אֶל־שַׁעֲרֵי הַבַּיִת
וּמְשָׁרְתִים אֶת־הַבָּיִת הֵמָּה
יִשְׁחֲטוּ אֶת־הָעֹלָה וְאֶת־
הַזֶּבַח לָעָם וְהֵמָּה יַעַמְדוּ
לִפְנֵיהֶם לְשָׁרְתָם: יַעַן אֲשֶׁר 12
יְשָׁרְתוּ אוֹתָם לִפְנֵי גִלּוּלֵיהֶם

v. 9. סבירין יבואו

8. *to please yourselves.* Not the qualifications demanded by God were the test for
the appointment of the men to serve in
the Temple, and the selection was made
not for the Divine approval but their
own.

9. *any alien that is among the children of
Israel.* See on verse 27. Non-Israelites
were forbidden to come within certain
parts of the Temple area. A stone with
a Greek inscription, warning Gentiles
against penetrating within the inner
Temple walls, was discovered in 1870.
It dates from the time of Herod and is
now in the Museum at Constantinople.

10. *but the Levites . . . they shall bear
their iniquity.* All the menial work in
the Temple hitherto done by strangers
is to be performed by Levites who,

because of their past sins, would be
deprived of their higher offices and
reduced to subordinate rank. The term
Levites here denotes priests other than
the Zadokites (cf. verse 15).

11. *they shall be ministers,* etc. Their
functions will be to guard the gateways
and do service of lesser importance in
the Sanctuary, as detailed below.

they shall slay the burnt-offering. In fact,
the slaughtering of the animal for
sacrifice was not a priestly function and
might be performed by a layman (see on
xliii. 20).

stand before them to minister unto them.
They will serve the people in preparing
their sacrificial meals.

12. *unto them.* viz. the people.

stumblingblock of iniquity unto the house of Israel; therefore have I lifted up My hand against them, saith the Lord GOD, and they shall bear their iniquity. 13. And they shall not come near unto Me, to minister unto Me in the priest's office, nor to come near to any of My holy things, unto the things that are most holy; but they shall bear their shame, and their abominations which they have committed. 14. And I will make them keepers of the charge of the house, for all the service thereof, and for all that shall be done therein.

15. But the priests the Levites, the sons of Zadok, that kept the charge of My sanctuary when the children of Israel went astray from Me, they shall come near to Me to minister unto Me; and they shall stand before Me to offer unto Me the fat and the blood, saith the Lord GOD; 16. they shall enter into My sanctuary, and they shall come near to My table, to minister unto Me, and they shall

וְהָיוּ לְבֵית־יִשְׂרָאֵל לְמִכְשׁוֹל
עָוֹן עַל־כֵּן נָשָׂאתִי יָדִי עֲלֵיהֶם
נְאֻם אֲדֹנָי יְהוִֹה וְנָשְׂאוּ עֲוֹנָם׃
13 וְלֹא־יִגְּשׁוּ אֵלַי לְכַהֵן לִי
וְלָגֶשֶׁת עַל־כָּל־קָדָשַׁי אֶל־
קָדְשֵׁי הַקֳּדָשִׁים וְנָשְׂאוּ
כְּלִמָּתָם וְתוֹעֲבוֹתָם אֲשֶׁר
14 עָשׂוּ׃ וְנָתַתִּי אוֹתָם שֹׁמְרֵי
מִשְׁמֶרֶת הַבַּיִת לְכֹל עֲבֹדָתוֹ
וּלְכֹל אֲשֶׁר יֵעָשֶׂה בּוֹ׃
15 וְהַכֹּהֲנִים הַלְוִיִּם בְּנֵי צָדוֹק
אֲשֶׁר שָׁמְרוּ אֶת־מִשְׁמֶרֶת
מִקְדָּשִׁי בִּתְעוֹת בְּנֵי־יִשְׂרָאֵל
מֵעָלַי הֵמָּה יִקְרְבוּ אֵלַי
לְשָׁרְתֵנִי וְעָמְדוּ לְפָנַי
לְהַקְרִיב לִי חֵלֶב וָדָם נְאֻם
16 אֲדֹנָי יְהוִֹה׃ הֵמָּה יָבֹאוּ אֶל־
מִקְדָּשִׁי וְהֵמָּה יִקְרְבוּ אֶל־
שֻׁלְחָנִי לְשָׁרְתֵנִי וְשָׁמְרוּ אֶת־

v. 15. הפטרת אמור

became a stumblingblock of iniquity. By ministering to their idols, the Levites spread idolatry among the people.

I lifted up My hand. See on xx. 5.

they shall bear their iniquity. The penalty being their reduction in status to that of lay servants in the Temple.

13. *nor to come near to any of My holy things.* They are not even to be permitted to keep watch in the inner court (Elijah of Wilna).

unto the things that are most holy. Nor will they be allowed to minister at the sacrificial service (Elijah of Wilna).

14. *keepers of the charge of the house.* They will be restricted to functions in the outer court of the Temple (Elijah of Wilna).

15-27 REGULATIONS FOR THE ZADOKITE PRIESTS

15. *the sons of Zadok.* See on xliii. 19.

16. *to My table.* To partake of the sacrificial flesh, *table* being figurative of the altar (cf. xli. 22). The Targum interprets the word in its literal sense and refers it to the table of showbread (cf. Exod. xxv. 23ff.).

keep My charge. 17. And it shall be that when they enter in at the gates of the inner court, they shall be clothed with linen garments; and no wool shall come upon them, while they minister in the gates of the inner court, and within. 18. They shall have linen tires upon their heads, and shall have linen breeches upon their loins; they shall not gird themselves with any thing that causeth sweat. 19. And when they go forth into the outer court, even into the outer court to the people, they shall put off their garments wherein they minister, and lay them in the holy chambers, and they shall put on other garments, that they sanctify not the people

17 מִשְׁמַרְתִּי : וְהָיָה בְּבוֹאָם אֶל־
שַׁעֲרֵי הֶחָצֵר הַפְּנִימִית בִּגְדֵי
פִשְׁתִּים יִלְבָּשׁוּ וְלֹא־יַעֲלֶה
עֲלֵיהֶם צֶמֶר בְּשָׁרְתָם בְּשַׁעֲרֵי
הֶחָצֵר הַפְּנִימִית וָבָיְתָה :
18 פַּאֲרֵי פִשְׁתִּים יִהְיוּ עַל־
רֹאשָׁם וּמִכְנְסֵי פִשְׁתִּים יִהְיוּ
עַל־מָתְנֵיהֶם לֹא יַחְגְּרוּ
19 בַּיָּזַע : וּבְצֵאתָם אֶל־הֶחָצֵר
הַחִיצוֹנָה אֶל־הֶחָצֵר
הַחִיצוֹנָה אֶל־הָעָם יִפְשְׁטוּ
אֶת־בִּגְדֵיהֶם אֲשֶׁר־הֵמָּה
מְשָׁרְתִם בָּם וְהִנִּיחוּ אוֹתָם
בְּלִשְׁכֹת הַקֹּדֶשׁ וְלָבְשׁוּ בְּגָדִים
אֲחֵרִים וְלֹא־יְקַדְּשׁוּ אֶת־

they shall keep My charge. This is in contrast to *the charge of the house* (verse 14) which will be assigned to the disqualified priests.

17. *they shall be clothed with linen garments.* This regulation constitutes a new feature in the Temple. The garments of the priests will not be, as in the former Temple, partly of wool but only of linen. It cannot be interpreted, Kimchi points out, of the linen vestments worn by the High Priest on the Day of Atonement when he entered the Holy of Holies, because *the inner court* is distinct from the Holy of Holies, and also the use of the plural implies priests generally.

and within. i.e. the interior of the Temple.

18. *with any thing that causeth sweat.* e.g. a woollen girdle (Rashi). The

Rabbis explain: They shall not gird themselves in the part of the body which causes sweat, i.e. not as high as the armpits nor as low as the loins, but at the height of the elbows (Zeb. 18b).

19. *even into the outer court to the people.* The repetition emphasizes that the outer court referred to is really the laymen's section, and it is called *outer court* in contrast to the priests' section (Kimchi). According to Elijah of Wilna, the purpose of the repetition is to make it clear that only when the priests go out to mingle with the people are they to remove their vestments, but not if they go out and return immediately.

lay them in the holy chambers. Cf. xlii. 14.

that they sanctify not the people with their garments. The Targum renders: 'that they shall not mingle with the people in their vestments'; i.e. the priests shall

306

with their garments. 20. Neither shall they shave their heads, nor suffer their locks to grow long; they shall only poll their heads. 21. Neither shall any priest drink wine, when they enter into the inner court. 22. Neither shall they take for their wives a widow, nor her that is put away; but they shall take virgins of the seed of the house of Israel, or a widow that is the widow of a priest. 23. And they shall teach My people the difference between the holy and the common, and cause them to discern between the unclean and the clean. 24. And in a controversy they shall stand to

20 הָעָם בְּבִגְדֵיהֶם׃ וְרֹאשָׁם לֹא
יְגַלֵּחוּ וּפֶרַע לֹא יְשַׁלֵּחוּ כָּסוֹם
21 יִכְסְמוּ אֶת־רָאשֵׁיהֶם׃ וְיַיִן
לֹא־יִשְׁתּוּ כָּל־כֹּהֵן בְּבוֹאָם
אֶל־־הֶחָצֵר הַפְּנִימִית׃
22 וְאַלְמָנָה וּגְרוּשָׁה לֹא־יִקְחוּ
לָהֶם לְנָשִׁים כִּי אִם־בְּתוּלֹת
מִזֶּרַע בֵּית יִשְׂרָאֵל וְהָאַלְמָנָה
אֲשֶׁר־תִּהְיֶה אַלְמָנָה מִכֹּהֵן
23 יִקָּחוּ׃ וְאֶת־עַמִּי יוֹרוּ בֵּין
קֹדֶשׁ לְחֹל וּבֵין־טָמֵא לְטָהוֹר
24 יוֹדִעֻם׃ וְעַל־רִיב הֵמָּה

not give the erroneous impression that the laity are subject to the same rules of holiness as they, which might happen as the effect of contact with them while still wearing the holy garments. But this regulation may only be part of the general rule that 'holiness' was communicated by means of actual contact (cf. Exod. xxix. 37; Lev. vi. 20).

20. *neither shall they shave their heads*, etc. Both making the head bald by shaving and letting the hair grow long appear to have been a heathen practice and were forbidden to the Israelite priests (Lev. xxi. 5, 10).

they shall only poll their heads. Both extremes are to be avoided, and the hair should be worn at medium length. The Talmud deduced from this text that the priests should cut their hair once in thirty days (Sanh. 22b).

21. *when they enter into the inner court*. i.e. into the Temple (Rashi). More precisely, what is meant is the area from the altar inwards to the Sanctuary. Although this (cf. x. 9) and other laws had been enjoined in the Torah, they are reaffirmed among the new

regulations which applied in the ideal Temple.

22. *but they shall take virgins*. The Jewish commentators understand this of the High Priests, in conformity with Lev. xxi. 13f.

or a widow, etc. On the hypothesis that the first clause relates only to the High Priest, these words are taken to mean: but as for a widow, an ordnary priest may marry her, and the repetition of *widow* implies that a divorcee or a woman who had undergone the rite of *chalitsah* (cf. Deut. xxv. 5ff.) is forbidden to an ordinary priest. In addition to this interpretation, Kimchi offers the alternative that all priests who serve in the ideal Temple would not be allowed to marry widows, although hitherto permitted, unless their former husbands had been priests. On this reading of the text, it has to be assumed that the law was made stricter for the possible reason that 'when the moral standards had lowered, it was found necessary to do so in order to protect the purity of the priestly families' (Hertz).

23. *they shall teach My people*. An important function of the priests was to

judge; according to Mine ordinances shall they judge it; and they shall keep My laws and My statutes in all My appointed seasons, and they shall hallow My sabbaths. 25. And they shall come near no dead person to defile themselves; but for father, or for mother, or for son, or for daughter, for brother, or for sister that hath had no husband, they may defile themselves. 26. And after he is cleansed, they shall reckon unto him seven days. 27. And in the day that he goeth into the sanctuary, into the inner court, to minister in

יַעֲמְדוּ לְ ' שְׁפֹּט בְּמִשְׁפָּטַי
וּשְׁפָטֻהוּ וְאֶת־תּוֹרֹתַי וְאֶת־
חֻקֹּתַי בְּכָל־מוֹעֲדַי יִשְׁמֹרוּ
וְאֶת־שַׁבְּתוֹתַי יְקַדֵּשׁוּ:

25 וְאֶל־מֵת אָדָם לֹא יָבוֹא
לְטָמְאָה כִּי אִם־לְאָב וּלְאֵם
וּלְבֵן וּלְבַת לְאָח וּלְאָחוֹת
אֲשֶׁר־לֹא־הָיְתָה לְאִישׁ

26 יִטַּמָּאוּ: וְאַחֲרֵי טׇהֳרָתוֹ שִׁבְעַת

27 יָמִים יִסְפְּרוּ־לוֹ: וּבְיוֹם בֹּאוֹ
אֶל־הַקֹּדֶשׁ אֶל־הֶחָצֵר
הַפְּנִימִית לְשָׁרֵת בַּקֹּדֶשׁ

v. 24. למשפט ק'   v. 24. ישפטהו ק'

---

instruct the people in all religious matters (cf. Deut. xxxiii. 10; Mal. ii. 7).

24. *according to Mine ordinances shall they judge it.* The priests should also act as judges in civil cases (cf. Deut. xvii. 8ff., xix. 17, xxi. 5). Their decisions must not be arbitrary, but based on the law of God.

My laws and My statutes . . . appointed seasons . . . sabbaths. They are strictly to observe the laws and regulations concerning the sacrifices to be offered on festivals and Sabbaths (Kimchi). Elijah of Wilna comments that the priests are charged with the task of instructing the people in the whole range of Jewish jurisprudence as later classified in the six Orders of the Mishnah and Talmud: *between the holy and the common* (verse 23) signifies the Order of *Kodashim* (hallowed things); *between the unclean and the clean* the Order *Tohoroth* (cleannesses); *to judge* (verse 24) the Order of *Nezikin* (torts); *My laws* the Order of *Nashim* (women); *My statutes* the Order of *Zeraïm* (seeds); *My appointed seasons* the Order of *Moed* (festivals).

25. *they may defile themselves.* This refers to ordinary priests; but the High Priest is forbidden to go near any dead body (cf. Lev. xxi. 1ff., 11).

26. *after he is cleansed.* After the separation caused by contact with the dead (Rashi, quoting M.K. 15b). After becoming clean at the end of seven days, he shall count a further period of seven days before entering the Sanctuary. This is an additional regulation for the ideal Temple to heighten its sanctity (Kimchi and Malbim).

they shall reckon unto him seven days. His fellow-priests are to count seven days for him. Should he forget, it is their duty to prevent him from entering the Sanctuary until he is again clean (Kimchi).

27. *in the day that he goeth into the sanctuary.* This verse has no connection with the preceding. It refers to the offering of a tenth of an ephah brought by all priests at their consecration when they officiated for the first time (Lev. vi. 13) (Rashi, quoting M.K. 15b, 16a). Kimchi, on the other hand, interprets: When the priest resumes his ministry

the sanctuary, he shall offer his sin-
offering, saith the Lord GOD.
28. And it shall be unto them for
an inheritance: I am their inheritance; and ye shall give them no
possession in Israel: I am their
possession. 29. The meal-offering,
and the sin-offering, and the guilt-
offering, they, even they, shall eat;
and every devoted thing in Israel
shall be theirs. 30. And the first of
all the first-fruits of every thing,
and every heave-offering of every
thing, of all your offerings, shall be
for the priests; ye shall also give unto
the priest the first of your dough, to
cause a blessing to rest on thy house.

יַקְרִיב חַטָּאתוֹ נְאֻם אֲדֹנָי
יֱהֹוִה: וְהָיְתָה לָהֶם לְנַחֲלָה 28
אֲנִי נַחֲלָתָם וַאֲחֻזָּה לֹא־תִתְּנוּ
לָהֶם בְּיִשְׂרָאֵל אֲנִי אֲחֻזָּתָם:
הַמִּנְחָה וְהַחַטָּאת וְהָאָשָׁם 29
הֵמָּה יֹאכְלוּם וְכָל־חֵרֶם
בְּיִשְׂרָאֵל לָהֶם יִהְיֶה:
וְרֵאשִׁית כָּל־בִּכּוּרֵי כֹל 30
וְכָל־תְּרוּמַת כֹּל מִכֹּל
תְּרוּמוֹתֵיכֶם לַכֹּהֲנִים יִהְיֶה
וְרֵאשִׁית עֲרִיסוֹתֵיכֶם תִּתְּנוּ
לַכֹּהֵן לְהָנִיחַ בְּרָכָה אֶל־
בֵּיתֶךָ: כָּל־נְבֵלָה וּטְרֵפָה 31

after he had undergone ritual purification, he is to offer a sin-offering for his
defilement. This, too, would be an
innovation in the new Temple. Kimchi
questions the Talmudic view quoted by
Rashi, because he understands the verse
to refer to an offering brought by the
priest on the resumption of his duties
and not the consecration offering brought
by him when he first enters the sacerdotal
service.

28-31 MAINTENANCE OF THE PRIESTS

28. *it shall be unto them for an inheritance.*
The priesthood is their inheritance, and
they receive no allotment in the land (cf.
Deut. xviii. 1f.).

29. *meal-offering . . . sin-offering . . .
guilt-offering.* viz. the residue of the
meal-offering. Likewise, a share of the
sin- and guilt-offering was given to the
priest after the fat had been offered on
the altar.

every devoted thing. The term *cherem*
as here employed denotes all kinds of

property consecrated to God which
could not be redeemed and had to be
given to the priests (cf. Lev. xxvii. 28;
Num. xviii. 14).

30. *the first of all the first-fruits of every
thing.* The first of all fruits for which
the Holy Land is distinguished, i.e. the
seven species enumerated in Deut.
viii. 8, in accordance with the injunction
of Num. xviii. 13 (Kimchi). See further,
Soncino Chumash on Deut. xxvi. 2.

heave-offering of every thing. Of all
products which are subject to the law of
Terumah (cf. Num. xv. 19, xviii. 19).
The reference is to what is called the
Terumah Gedolah (the great heave-
offering).

of all your offerings. The allusion is to
the heave-offering of the Levite's tithe,
in accordance with the law of Num.
xviii. 26ff.

the first of your dough. Cf. Num. xv. 20.

to cause a blessing to rest on thy house.
Cf. Mal. iii. 10; Prov. iii. 9f.

31. The priests shall not eat of any thing that dieth of itself, or is torn, whether it be fowl or beast.

מִן־הָעוֹף וּמִן־הַבְּהֵמָה לֹא
יֹאכְלוּ הַכֹּהֲנִים׃ ∗

45   CHAPTER XLV   מה

1. Moreover, when ye shall divide by lot the land for inheritance, ye shall set apart an offering unto the LORD, a holy portion of the land; the length shall be the length of five and twenty thousand reeds, and the breadth shall be ten thousand; it shall be holy in all the border thereof round about. 2. Of this

וּבְהַפִּילְכֶם אֶת־הָאָרֶץ 1
בְּנַחֲלָה תָּרִימוּ תְרוּמָה לַיהֹוָה
קֹדֶשׁ מִן־הָאָרֶץ אֹרֶךְ חֲמִשָּׁה
וְעֶשְׂרִים אֶלֶף אֹרֶךְ וְרֹחַב
עֲשָׂרָה אָלֶף קֹדֶשׁ־הוּא
בְּכָל־גְּבוּלָהּ סָבִיב׃ יִהְיֶה 2

עד כאן v. 31.

31. *the priests shall not eat*, etc. Though the prohibition applies to all Israelites (cf. Exod. xxii. 30; Lev. vii. 24; Deut. xiv. 21), a special warning is addressed to the priests because these forbidden objects communicate uncleanness to the consumer, and the priests are under special obligation to guard against defilement (Kimchi). Because the priests were permitted to eat the flesh of the sin-offering which was a bird whose head had been pinched off (Lev. v. 8), though this is forbidden to laymen, they were in need of a special warning to observe the dietary laws in all other respects (Rashi, quoting Men. 45a).

CHAPTER XLV

AFTER being instructed in the plan of the Temple and its consecration, the ministering priests and regulations concerning their vestments, personal conduct and functions, Ezekiel receives a command about the division of the Land of Israel among the tribes. In Jerusalem territory is to be allocated to the priests, Levites and the *Nasi*, as well as a section for the lay Israelites. Having assigned to the *Nasi* an estate ample for his maintenance, the prophet in God's name exhorts him and his successors to practise strict justice, placing upon them the responsibility to see that righteousness prevails

in the land and accurate standards of weights, measures and coinage are used. The *Nasi* is to receive the prescribed dues from the people and it is his obligation to provide what is necessary for the upkeep of the sacrificial service.

1-8 ALLOCATION OF LAND

1. *when ye shall divide . . . the land for inheritance.* The whole land is to be divided afresh among the tribes (cf. xlvii. 13ff.). The area of the holy city is dealt with in this section. The Jerusalem of the future is to be divided into three parts, assigned respectively to the priests (the Temple being in the centre), the Levites and the lay Israelites.

an offering unto the LORD. i.e. the allocation of a portion of land as a site for the Temple.

reeds. The Hebrew is simply *five and twenty thousand.* The addition of *reeds* (each six cubits long, cf. xl. 5) agrees with Rashi, but Kimchi understands the measurements to be in cubits (see on xlii. 16).

holy in all the border thereof round about. This area which is reserved for the priests and includes the Temple, is invested with a degree of holiness higher than that of the other portions.

there shall be for the holy place five hundred in length by five hundred in breadth, square round about; and fifty cubits for the open land round about it. 3. And of this measure shalt thou measure a length of five and twenty thousand, and a breadth of ten thousand; and in it shall be the sanctuary, which is most holy. 4. It is a holy portion of the land; it shall be for the priests, the ministers of the sanctuary, that come near to minister unto the LORD; and it shall be a place for their houses, and a place consecrated for the sanctuary. 5. And five and twenty thousand in length, and ten thousand in breadth, which shall be unto the Levites, the

מִזֶּה אֶל־הַקֹּדֶשׁ חֲמֵשׁ מֵאוֹת
בַּחֲמֵשׁ מֵאוֹת מְרֻבָּע סָבִיב
וַחֲמִשִּׁים אַמָּה מִגְרָשׁ לוֹ
3 סָבִיב: וּמִן־הַמִּדָּה הַזֹּאת
תָּמוֹד אֹרֶךְ חֲמִשָּׁה וְעֶשְׂרִים
אֶלֶף וְרֹחַב עֲשֶׂרֶת אֲלָפִים
וּבוֹ־יִהְיֶה הַמִּקְדָּשׁ קֹדֶשׁ
4 קָדָשִׁים: קֹדֶשׁ מִן־הָאָרֶץ
הוּא לַכֹּהֲנִים מְשָׁרְתֵי הַמִּקְדָּשׁ
יִהְיֶה הַקְּרֵבִים לְשָׁרֵת אֶת־
יְהֹוָה וְהָיָה לָהֶם מָקוֹם לְבָתִּים
5 וּמִקְדָּשׁ לַמִּקְדָּשׁ: וַחֲמִשָּׁה
וְעֶשְׂרִים אֶלֶף אֹרֶךְ וַעֲשֶׂרֶת
אֲלָפִים רֹחַב יִהְיֶה לַלְוִיִּם

v. 3. חמשה ק' v. 5. והיה ק'

2. *of this there shall be for the holy place.* In the centre of the priests' allocation, mentioned in the previous verse, was to be the site of the Temple, measuring five hundred (reeds or cubits) square.

fifty cubits for the open land round about it. An open space of fifty cubits is to surround the Temple area on all sides to separate it from the dwellings of the priests.

3. *of this measure shalt thou measure.* Kimchi interprets the verse as indicating that within the allotment 25,000 by 10,000 assigned to the priests is the Temple area 500 cubits square. But Rashi understands the intention as being to equalize the measurement of the priests' portion with that allotted for the Temple: as the latter was measured in *reeds* (cf. xlii. 16), this must also apply to the former.

in it shall be the sanctuary, which is most holy. In the holy area of the Temple Mount is to be erected the Sanctuary which is in the degree of *most holy.*

4. *it is a holy portion of the land; it shall be for the priests.* The area defined in verse 1 is to be assigned entirely to the priests.

that come near to minister unto the LORD. viz. the descendants of Zadōk the High Priest (see on xliii. 19).

it shall be a place for their houses, etc. After setting aside 500 (cubits or reeds) square in the centre for the Temple, the rest of the land, i.e. 24,000 along the east and west and 9,500 along the north and south, is to be used for settlement by the priests. This is inclusive of the fifty cubits around the Temple area (verse 2) which is to be left as an open space.

5. *which shall be unto the Levites.* A portion of land, equal in extent to that of the priests and close to it, is to be

ministers of the house, for a possession unto themselves, for twenty chambers. 6. And ye shall appoint the possession of the city five thousand broad, and five and twenty thousand long, side by side with the offering of the holy portion; it shall be for the whole house of Israel. 7. And for the prince, on the one side and on the other side of the holy offering and of the possession of the city, in front of the holy offering and in front of the possession of the city, on the west side westward, and on the east side eastward; and in length answerable unto one of the portions, from the west border unto the east border 8. of the land; it shall be to him for a posses-

מְשָׁרְתֵי הַבַּיִת לָהֶם לַאֲחֻזָּה
6 עֶשְׂרִים לְשָׁכֹת׃ וַאֲחֻזַּת הָעִיר
תִּתְּנוּ חֲמֵשֶׁת אֲלָפִים רֹחַב
וְאֹרֶךְ חֲמִשָּׁה וְעֶשְׂרִים אֶלֶף
לְעֻמַּת תְּרוּמַת הַקֹּדֶשׁ לְכָל־
7 בֵּית יִשְׂרָאֵל יִהְיֶה׃ וְלַנָּשִׂיא
מִזֶּה וּמִזֶּה לִתְרוּמַת הַקֹּדֶשׁ
וְלַאֲחֻזַּת הָעִיר אֶל־פְּנֵי
תְרוּמַת הַקֹּדֶשׁ וְאֶל־פְּנֵי
אֲחֻזַּת הָעִיר מִפְּאַת יָם יָמָּה
וּמִפְּאַת קֵדְמָה קָדִימָה וְאֹרֶךְ
לְעֻמּוֹת אַחַד הַחֲלָקִים מִגְּבוּל
8 יָם אֶל־גְּבוּל קָדִימָה׃ לָאָרֶץ

---

assigned to the Levites for their settlement. According to Rashi, it was situated to the south of the priests' portion; others hold that it was to the north of it.

the ministers of the house. In contrast to the priests who are described as ministering *unto the LORD* (verse 4), performing the sacrificial rites, the Levites are only *ministers of the house*, acting as watchers, gate-keepers, etc. (see on xliv. 11).

for twenty chambers. At the extreme end of their territory and close to the priests' portion, twenty chambers are to be built for the gate-keepers, so that they would be near the Temple. The rest of the land is to be used for the Levites' dwellings.

6. *the possession of the city.* The area assigned to the laity is a tract of land 25,000 long and 5,000 broad, running alongside the portion of the priests to the south. The whole territory allocated for the holy city, comprising the domains of the priests, Levites and laymen would

therefore total 25,000 (cubits or reeds) square.

it shall be for the whole house of Israel. This section of Jerusalem is to be free for any Israelite to dwell in and not assigned to one tribe only.

7. *on the one side,* etc. The land of the *Nasi* is situated on either side of the holy territory allocated to the priests, Levites and the city. That is to say, the width of his domain from north to south is to be 25,000 over against the holy area, and its length run parallel to the portions of the tribes to the Jordan on the extreme east and to the Mediterranean on the extreme west. The portion of the *Nasi* is to be equal to that of a whole tribe, i.e. 25,000 broad across the whole country from east to west, except for the 25,000 square tract in the centre assigned to the priests, Levites and the city (cf. xlviii. 21).

unto one of the portions. i.e. parallel to one of the portions of the tribes.

8. *of the land.* A.J. connects this with the preceding verse; but A.V. and R.V.

sion in Israel, and My princes shall
no more wrong My people; but they
shall give the land to the house of
Israel according to their tribes.

9. Thus saith the Lord GOD: Let
it suffice you, O princes of Israel;
remove violence and spoil, and
execute justice and righteousness;
take away your exactions from My
people, saith the Lord GOD.

10. Ye shall have just balances,
and a just ephah, and a just bath.
11. The ephah and the bath shall be
of one measure, that the bath may
contain the tenth part of a homer,
and the ephah the tenth part of a

יִהְיֶה־לּוֹ לַאֲחֻזָּה בְּיִשְׂרָאֵל
וְלֹא־יוֹנוּ עוֹד נְשִׂיאַי אֶת־
עַמִּי וְהָאָרֶץ יִתְּנוּ לְבֵית־
יִשְׂרָאֵל לְשִׁבְטֵיהֶם: כֹּה־ 9
אָמַר אֲדֹנָי יֱהֹוִה רַב־לָכֶם
נְשִׂיאֵי יִשְׂרָאֵל חָמָס וָשֹׁד
הָסִירוּ וּמִשְׁפָּט וּצְדָקָה עֲשׂוּ
הָרִימוּ גְרֻשֹׁתֵיכֶם מֵעַל עַמִּי
נְאֻם אֲדֹנָי יֱהֹוִה: מֹאזְנֵי־צֶדֶק 10
וְאֵיפַת־צֶדֶק וּבַת־צֶדֶק יְהִי
לָכֶם: הָאֵיפָה וְהַבַּת תֹּכֶן 11
אֶחָד יִהְיֶה לָשֵׂאת מַעְשַׂר
הַחֹמֶר הַבָּת וַעֲשִׂירִת הַחֹמֶר

begin a new sentence and render: 'in the
land,' following Kimchi.
My princes shall no more wrong My people.
As did the kings before the destruction
of the two Kingdoms; because they will
have sufficient land for their personal
needs and also for the reason that the
new era is to be dominated by reverence
of God (Kimchi).

9-17 RIGHTS AND DUTIES OF THE NASI

9. *let it suffice you, O princes of Israel.*
Kimchi interprets the words as spoken
in connection with the former kings of
Israel and Judah: 'let there be an end
to your exactions and oppressions.'
Other Jewish commentators with greater
probability understand them as an
exhortation to the rulers in the reorganized land: 'your allowance is large
enough, and you have no need to acquire
more by unjust demands upon the
people.'
take away your exactions. The noun

gerushah is derived from the root *garash*,
'eject,' and is used of the unjust displace-
ment of an owner from his property;
cf. *the women of My people ye cast out
from their pleasant houses* (Mic. ii. 9).

10. *just balances.* Hitherto inaccurate
weights and measures were in use (cf. the
denunciations in Amos viii. 5; Mic. vi.
11). It will be the duty of the future
rulers to eliminate this evil and enforce
the use of just weights and measures in
accordance with the injunction of the
Torah (Lev. xix. 35f.; Deut. xxv. 13ff.).
ephah . . . bath. A dry and liquid
measure.

11. *shall be of one measure.* The capacity
of the *ephah* and *bath* is the same, viz.
one tenth of a *homer*.

*that the bath may contain the tenth part
of a homer.* Following the Targum,
Kimchi comments: 'in respect of the
tithe one *bath* shall be taken from a
(liquid) *homer*,' and similarly with the
next clause.

homer; the measure thereof shall be after the homer. 12. And the shekel shall be twenty gerahs; twenty shekels, five and twenty shekels, ten, and five shekels, shall be your maneh.

13. This is the offering that ye shall set apart: the sixth part of an ephah out of a homer of wheat, and ye shall give the sixth part of an ephah out of a homer of barley; 14. and the set portion of oil, the bath of oil, shall be the tithe of the bath out of the cor, which is ten baths, even a homer; for ten baths

הָאֵיפָה אֶל־הַחֹמֶר יִהְיֶה
12 מַתְכֻּנְתּוֹ: וְהַשֶּׁקֶל עֶשְׂרִים
גֵּרָה עֶשְׂרִים שְׁקָלִים חֲמִשָּׁה
וְעֶשְׂרִים שְׁקָלִים עֲשָׂרָה
וַחֲמִשָּׁה שֶׁקֶל הַמָּנֶה יִהְיֶה
13 לָכֶם: זֹאת הַתְּרוּמָה אֲשֶׁר
תָּרִימוּ שִׁשִּׁית הָאֵיפָה מֵחֹמֶר
הַחִטִּים וְשִׁשִּׁיתֶם הָאֵיפָה
14 מֵחֹמֶר הַשְּׂעֹרִים: וְחֹק הַשֶּׁמֶן
הַבַּת הַשֶּׁמֶן מַעְשַׂר הַבַּת מִן־
הַכֹּר עֲשֶׂרֶת הַבַּתִּים חֹמֶר
כִּי־עֲשֶׂרֶת הַבַּתִּים חֹמֶר:

the measure thereof shall be after the homer. To whatever size the *homer* may be altered, its tenth part—the *bath* and *ephah*—has to be adjusted accordingly and become the standard measure for the allocation of the tithe (Rashi).

12. *twenty shekels . . . shall be your maneh.* The Alexandrine version of the LXX reads: 'fifty shekels shall be your mina' instead of *five shekels shall be your maneh*, and accordingly modern commentators emend *chamishshah* (five) into *chamishshim* (fifty). They apparently misunderstand the text as stating that the *maneh* equals sixty shekels. It is possible that the Greek version reflects the tradition which is found in the Talmud (Bekh. 50a, b) which interprets the verse as follows: The original value of the shekel in the time of Moses was twenty gerahs (cf. Exod. xxx. 13; Lev. xxvii. 25). In Ezekiel's period the value of the shekel was increased by a fifth to twenty-four gerahs, and the shekel of the Torah was made equal to the Tyrian sela. Therefore it is here pointed out that of the original shekel (of twenty gerahs) there shall be pieces of twenty, twenty-five, ten and five shekels (sixty

in all) in the new sacred *maneh;* but of the new shekel (consisting of twenty-four gerahs) there will only be fifty in the sacred and twenty-five in the common *maneh* (cf. *Midrash Haggadol, Numbers,* ed. Fisch, p. 200). The reason why four different units are enumerated in the verse is that they were in use in those denominations.

13. *the sixth part of an ephah out of a homer of wheat.* The various contributions which are enumerated were made to the *Nasi*, from which he had the duty to supply the needs of the Temple service. The Rabbis point out that the proportion of one-sixtieth is the minimum which even the illiberal person is not to decrease.

14. *the set portion of oil.* Required for the meal-offering.

the tithe of the bath out of the cor, etc. The *cor* is identical with the *homer*, consisting of ten *baths*. From a *cor* of oil the due is one tenth of a *bath*, i.e. one hundredth part of a *cor*.

for ten baths are a homer. i.e. the standard of this measure remains unchanged in the new era (Kimchi).

are a homer; 15. and one lamb of
the flock, out of two hundred, from
the well-watered pastures of Israel;
for a meal-offering, and for a burnt-
offering, and for peace-offerings, to
make atonement for them, saith the
Lord God.

16. All the people of the land shall
give this offering for the prince in
Israel. 17. And it shall be the
prince's part to give the burnt-
offerings, and the meal-offerings,
and the drink-offerings, in the feasts,
and in the new moons, and in the
sabbaths, in all the appointed
seasons of the house of Israel; he
shall prepare the sin-offering, and
the meal-offering, and the burnt-
offering, and the peace-offerings, to
make atonement for the house of
Israel.

18. Thus saith the Lord God: In
the first month, in the first day of
the month, thou shalt take a young
bullock without blemish; and thou

15 וְשֶׂה־אַחַת מִן־הַצֹּאן מִן־
הַמָּאתַיִם מִמַּשְׁקֵה יִשְׂרָאֵל
לְמִנְחָה וּלְעוֹלָה וְלִשְׁלָמִים
לְכַפֵּר עֲלֵיהֶם נְאֻם אֲדֹנָי
16 יֱהֹוִה: כָּל־הָעָם הָאָרֶץ יִהְיוּ
אֶל־הַתְּרוּמָה הַזֹּאת לַנָּשִׂיא
17 בְּיִשְׂרָאֵל: וְעַל־הַנָּשִׂיא יִהְיֶה
הָעוֹלוֹת וְהַמִּנְחָה וְהַנֵּסֶךְ
בַּחַגִּים וּבֶחֳדָשִׁים וּבַשַּׁבָּתוֹת
בְּכָל־מוֹעֲדֵי בֵּית יִשְׂרָאֵל
הוּא־יַעֲשֶׂה אֶת־הַחַטָּאת
וְאֶת־הַמִּנְחָה וְאֶת־הָעוֹלָה
וְאֶת־הַשְּׁלָמִים לְכַפֵּר בְּעַד
18 בֵּית־יִשְׂרָאֵל: כֹּה־אָמַר
אֲדֹנָי יֱהֹוִה בָּרִאשׁוֹן בְּאֶחָד
לַחֹדֶשׁ תִּקַּח פַּר־בֶּן־בָּקָר
תָּמִים וְחִטֵּאתָ אֶת־הַמִּקְדָּשׁ:

v. 16. הפטרת פרשת החדש והספרדים מתחילין כה אמר אדני (v. 18)

15. *one lamb . . . out of two hundred.*
From a flock of two hundred sheep one
is to be donated.

from the well-watered pastures of Israel.
i.e. well-fed and developed sheep.

for a meal-offering, etc. Referring to
the dues of grain and oil spoken of in
verses 13f.

to make atonement for them. In respect
of the sins which they had committed in
exile (Kimchi).

16. *this offering.* The offerings spoken
of above.

for the prince in Israel. All the dues are
to be given to the *Nasi* who is responsible
for providing all the necessary sacrifices.

17. *the burnt-offerings . . . drink-offerings.* This refers to the communal
sacrifices during the whole year
(Malbim).

he shall prepare. i.e. he shall supply the
sacrifices for public worship out of the
dues he had received from the people, so
that every Israelite may have a share in
the offerings (Malbim).

18-25   THE FESTIVAL OFFERINGS
18. *the first month.* viz. Nisan, as is
clear from verse 21.

thou shalt take a young bullock. Some of
the sacrifices prescribed for certain
seasons in this and the next chapter are
quite new in the Temple ritual; with

shalt purify the sanctuary. 19. And the priest shall take of the blood of the sin-offering, and put it upon the doorposts of the house, and upon the four corners of the settle of the altar, and upon the posts of the gate of the inner court. 20. And so thou shalt do on the seventh day of the month for every one that erreth, and for him that is simple; so shall ye make atonement for the house. 21. In the first month, in the fourteenth day of the month, ye shall have the passover; a feast of seven days; unleavened bread shall be eaten. 22. And upon that day shall the prince prepare for himself and for all the people of the land a

19 וְלָקַח הַכֹּהֵן מִדַּם הַחַטָּאת
וְנָתַן אֶל־מְזוּזַת הַבַּיִת וְאֶל־
אַרְבַּע פִּנּוֹת הָעֲזָרָה לַמִּזְבֵּחַ
וְעַל־מְזוּזַת שַׁעַר הֶחָצֵר
20 הַפְּנִימִית: וְכֵן תַּעֲשֶׂה בְּשִׁבְעָה
בַחֹדֶשׁ מֵאִישׁ שֹׁגֶה וּמִפֶּתִי
וְכִפַּרְתֶּם אֶת־הַבָּיִת:
21 בָּרִאשׁוֹן בְּאַרְבָּעָה עָשָׂר יוֹם
לַחֹדֶשׁ יִהְיֶה לָכֶם הַפָּסַח חָג
שְׁבֻעוֹת יָמִים מַצּוֹת יֵאָכֵל:
22 וְעָשָׂה הַנָּשִׂיא בַּיּוֹם הַהוּא
בַּעֲדוֹ וּבְעַד כָּל־עַם הָאָרֶץ

others the type and numbers are in contradiction with those enjoined in the Mosaic law. This disagreement gave rise to two different views recorded in the Talmud (Men. 45a). Some Rabbis held that these sacrifices were specially ordained as an innovation for the new Temple, and only Elijah, who is destined to herald the Messianic era, will be able to explain it all satisfactorily. Others were of the opinion that the sacrifices detailed here are not connected with the ritual of the festivals, but constitute a series of dedicatory offerings in the new Temple, the consecration of which began, as with the Tabernacle in the wilderness (Exod. xl. 2), on the first of Nisan. Accordingly, the sacrifice referred to here is identical with that mentioned in xliii. 19ff.

19. *doorposts.* In the Hebrew the noun is singular. On the hypothesis that this sacrifice and that of xliii. 19 are identical, Kimchi remarks that the various applications of the blood commanded in the two passages are complementary.

the four corners of the settle of the altar. viz. of *the greater settle* of the altar (see on xliii. 20).

upon the posts of the gate of the inner court. This refers either to the men's section in the Temple court or the priests' section (Kimchi). *Gate* is used in a collective sense and denotes the three gates of the inner court (Malbim).

20. *so thou shalt do on the seventh day of the month.* viz. the seventh day of the consecration of the altar (xliii. 26). When that was accomplished, atonement was to be made for those who may have entered forbidden ground in the Temple area by error or ignorance during the festive days of dedication. This sacrifice is special for the occasion (Kimchi).

21. *the passover.* The slaughtering of the paschal lamb.

22. *that day.* This may be understood either as the fourteenth of Nisan or the fifteenth, the first day of Passover (Kimchi).

shall the prince prepare. See on verse **17.**

bullock for a sin-offering. 23. And the seven days of the feast he shall prepare a burnt-offering to the LORD, seven bullocks and seven rams without blemish daily the seven days; and a he-goat daily for a sin-offering. 24. And he shall prepare a meal-offering, an ephah for a bullock, and an ephah for a ram, and a hin of oil to an ephah. 25. In the seventh month, in the fifteenth day of the month, in the feast, shall he do the like the seven days; to the sin-offering as well as the burnt-offering, and the meal-offering as well as the oil.

23 פַּר חַטָּאת׃ וְשִׁבְעַ֖ת יְמֵֽי־הֶחָ֑ג יַעֲשֶׂ֨ה עוֹלָ֤ה לַֽיהוָֹה֙ שִׁבְעַ֤ת פָּרִים֙ וְשִׁבְעַ֣ת אֵילִ֣ים תְּמִימִ֔ם לַיּ֖וֹם שִׁבְעַ֣ת הַיָּמִ֑ים וְחַטָּ֛את 24 שְׂעִ֥יר עִזִּ֖ים לַיּֽוֹם׃ וּמִנְחָ֗ה אֵיפָ֥ה לַפָּ֛ר וְאֵיפָ֥ה לָאַ֖יִל יַעֲשֶׂ֑ה וְשֶׁ֖מֶן הִ֥ין לָאֵיפָֽה׃ 25 בַּשְּׁבִיעִ֡י בַּחֲמִשָּׁה֩ עָשָׂ֨ר י֤וֹם לַחֹ֙דֶשׁ֙ בֶּחָ֔ג יַעֲשֶׂ֖ה כָּאֵ֑לֶּה שִׁבְעַ֣ת הַיָּמִ֗ים כַּֽחַטָּאת֙ כָּֽעֹלָ֔ה וְכַמִּנְחָ֖ה וְכַשָּֽׁמֶן׃

46   CHAPTER XLVI   מו

1. Thus saith the Lord GOD: The gate of the inner court that looketh

1 כֹּֽה־אָמַ֞ר אֲדֹנָ֣י יְהוִֹ֗ה שַׁ֣עַר

---

a bullock for a sin-offering. This and all the other sacrifices specified for the festivals of Passover and Tabernacles and other days mentioned later are not identical with the sacrifices ordered in the Mosaic law for those occasions. The Jewish commentators maintain that they were special offerings in connection with the dedication of the Temple.

23. *the seven days of the feast,* etc. In addition to the sacrifices normally offered during the Passover (Num. xxviii. 19) the following are to be brought.

24. *meal-offering.* The amount of this offering is different from that ordinarily required on the Passover (Num. xxviii. 20) and supplemented it.

25. *the seventh month.* Tishri.

in the feast. viz. Tabernacles which is frequently called simply *the feast.*

shall he do the like the seven days. The Nasi shall provide the same offerings on the seven days of Tabernacles as he was required to do for the seven days of Passover (verse 23). As stated on verse 22, these sacrifices were to be brought in addition to the usual festival offerings as special during the period of consecrating the Temple. No additional sacrifices were required for the eighth day of Tabernacles, because the rites of dedication were completed on the seventh day.

CHAPTER XLVI

1-7 OFFERINGS ON THE SABBATH AND NEW MOON

1. *the gate of the inner court.* While the outer east gate is always to be kept shut (xliv. 2), the inner east gate of the priests' section, which opened into the men's section, is to be closed during the six working days and opened only on the Sabbath and new moon when many worshippers visit the Temple. This regulation did not apply in the former Temple.

toward the east shall be shut the six working days; but on the sabbath day it shall be opened, and in the day of the new moon it shall be opened. 2. And the prince shall enter by the way of the porch of the gate without, and shall stand by the post of the gate, and the priests shall prepare his burnt-offering and his peace-offerings, and he shall worship at the threshold of the gate; then he shall go forth; but the gate shall not be shut until the evening. 3. Likewise the people of the land shall worship at the door of that gate before the LORD in the sabbaths and in the new moons. 4. And the burnt-offering that the prince shall offer unto the LORD shall be in the sabbath day six lambs without blemish and a ram without blemish; 5. and the meal-offering shall be an ephah for the ram, and the meal-offering for the lambs as he is able to give, and a hin of oil to an

הֶחָצֵר הַפְּנִימִית הַפֹּנֶה קָדִים
יִהְיֶה סָגוּר שֵׁשֶׁת יְמֵי הַמַּעֲשֶׂה
וּבְיוֹם הַשַּׁבָּת יִפָּתֵחַ וּבְיוֹם
2 הַחֹדֶשׁ יִפָּתֵחַ: וּבָא הַנָּשִׂיא
דֶּרֶךְ אוּלָם הַשַּׁעַר מִחוּץ
וְעָמַד עַל־מְזוּזַת הַשַּׁעַר וְעָשׂוּ
הַכֹּהֲנִים אֶת־עוֹלָתוֹ וְאֶת־
שְׁלָמָיו וְהִשְׁתַּחֲוָה עַל־מִפְתַּן
הַשַּׁעַר וְיָצָא וְהַשַּׁעַר לֹא־
3 יִסָּגֵר עַד־הָעָרֶב: וְהִשְׁתַּחֲווּ
עַם־הָאָרֶץ פֶּתַח הַשַּׁעַר
הַהוּא בַּשַּׁבָּתוֹת וּבֶחֳדָשִׁים
4 לִפְנֵי יְהוָה: וְהָעֹלָה אֲשֶׁר־
יַקְרִב הַנָּשִׂיא לַיהוָה בְּיוֹם
הַשַּׁבָּת שִׁשָּׁה כְבָשִׂים תְּמִימִם
5 וְאַיִל תָּמִים: וּמִנְחָה אֵיפָה
לָאַיִל וְלַכְּבָשִׂים מִנְחָה מַתַּת

2. *by the way of the porch of the gate without.* From the outer court, the *Nasi* enters the east inner gateway by its porch which opened outwards into the outer court (xl. 34).

shall stand by the post of the gate. Having entered the east inner gateway, he is to proceed to its west end from which point he is able to witness the sacrificial service at the altar.

the priests shall prepare his burnt-offering. The *Nasi*, as the representative of the nation and therefore regarded as the offerer, is to stand at the east gateway opposite the altar and watch the sacrificial rite.

the gate shall not be shut until the evening.

After his departure, the gate is to be left open for others who come to worship at all times of the day.

3. *the people of the land.* i.e. the ordinary Israelite as distinct from the *Nasi*.

in the sabbaths and in the new moons. Cf. Isa. lxvi. 23.

4. *six lambs . . . and a ram.* These sacrifices, which differ from those prescribed for the Sabbath (Num. xxviii. 9), are a new institution; unless, as Metsudath David suggests, the Sabbaths are those which occur during the period of dedication.

5. *the meal-offering for the lambs as he is able to give.* While the quantity of the meal-offering in respect of the ram is

ephah. 6. And in the day of the new moon it shall be a young bullock without blemish; and six lambs, and a ram; they shall be without blemish; 7. and he shall prepare a meal-offering, an ephah for the bullock, and an ephah for the ram, and for the lambs according as his means suffice, and a hin of oil to an ephah. 8. And when the prince shall enter, he shall go in by the way of the porch of the gate, and he shall go forth by the way thereof. 9. But when the people of the land shall come before the LORD in the appointed seasons, he that entereth by the way of the north gate to worship shall go forth by the way of the south gate; and he that entereth by the way of the south gate shall go forth by the way of the north gate; he shall not return by the way of the gate whereby he came in, but shall go forth straight before him. 10. And the prince, when they go in, shall go in in the midst of them; and when they go forth, they shall go forth

6 יָדוֹ וְשֶׁמֶן הִין לָאֵיפָה: וּבְיוֹם
הַחֹדֶשׁ פַּר בֶּן־בָּקָר תְּמִימָם
וְשֵׁשֶׁת כְּבָשִׂים וָאַיִל תְּמִימִם
7 יִהְיוּ: וְאֵיפָה לַפָּר וְאֵיפָה
לָאַיִל יַעֲשֶׂה מִנְחָה וְלַכְּבָשִׂים
כַּאֲשֶׁר תַּשִּׂיג יָדוֹ וְשֶׁמֶן הִין
8 לָאֵיפָה: וּבְבוֹא הַנָּשִׂיא דֶּרֶךְ
אוּלָם הַשַּׁעַר יָבוֹא וּבְדַרְכּוֹ
9 יֵצֵא: וּבְבוֹא עַם־הָאָרֶץ
לִפְנֵי יְהֹוָה בַּמּוֹעֲדִים הַבָּא
דֶּרֶךְ שַׁעַר צָפוֹן לְהִשְׁתַּחֲוֹת
יֵצֵא דֶּרֶךְ־שַׁעַר נֶגֶב וְהַבָּא
דֶּרֶךְ־שַׁעַר נֶגֶב יֵצֵא דֶּרֶךְ־
שַׁעַר צָפוֹנָה לֹא יָשׁוּב דֶּרֶךְ
הַשַּׁעַר אֲשֶׁר־בָּא בוֹ כִּי נִכְחוֹ
10 יֵצֵאוּ: וְהַנָּשִׂיא בְּתוֹכָם
בְּבוֹאָם יָבוֹא וּבְצֵאתָם יֵצֵאוּ:

v. 9. יצא ק'

specified, that of the meal-offering in respect of the lambs is to be voluntary in its quantity.

6. *in the day of the new moon.* Contrast Num. xxviii. 11ff. The comment on verse 4 applies also here.

7. *for the lambs according as his means suffice.* See on verse 5.

8-10 ENTRANCE AND EXIT OF THE WORSHIPPERS

8. *when the prince shall enter.* On a Sabbath and new moon.

he shall go forth by the way thereof. Only on a Sabbath and new moon is the *Nasi* to enter by the porch of the east gateway and leave by the same way. On

festivals, when the worshippers were many, both he and they were to enter either by the south or north gate and leave by the opposite gate, as stated in verse 10.

9. *the appointed seasons.* viz. the three pilgrim festivals, Passover, Pentecost and Tabernacles, when every male in Israel had to visit the Temple.

shall go forth straight before him. On the festivals, owing to the throng in the Temple court, they are to enter by one of the side gates, either north or south, worship at the east gate towards the Temple and leave by the opposite gate.

10. *the prince . . . shall go in in the midst of them.* On these festival occasions, the *Nasi* is to enter and leave by

together. 11. And in the feasts and in the appointed seasons the meal-offering shall be an ephah for a bullock, and an ephah for a ram, and for the lambs as he is able to give, and a hin of oil to an ephah.

12. And when the prince shall prepare a freewill-offering, a burnt-offering or peace-offerings as a freewill-offering unto the LORD, one shall open for him the gate that looketh toward the east, and he shall prepare his burnt-offering and his peace-offerings, as he doth on the sabbath day; then he shall go forth; and after his going forth one shall shut the gate.

13. And thou shalt prepare a lamb of the first year without blemish for a burnt-offering unto the LORD daily; morning by morning shalt thou prepare it. 14. And thou shalt prepare a meal-offering with it morning by morning, the sixth part of an ephah, and the third part of a hin of oil, to moisten the fine flour: a meal-offering unto the LORD continually by a perpetual ordinance.

15. Thus shall they prepare the lamb, and the meal-offering, and

11 וּבַחַגִּים וּבַמּוֹעֲדִים תִּהְיֶה
הַמִּנְחָה אֵיפָה לַפָּר וְאֵיפָה
לָאַיִל וְלַכְּבָשִׂים מַתַּת יָדוֹ
12 וְשֶׁמֶן הִין לָאֵיפָה: וְכִי־יַעֲשֶׂה
הַנָּשִׂיא נְדָבָה עוֹלָה אוֹ־
שְׁלָמִים נְדָבָה לַיהֹוָה וּפָתַח
לוֹ אֶת־הַשַּׁעַר הַפֹּנֶה קָדִים
וְעָשָׂה אֶת־עֹלָתוֹ וְאֶת־
שְׁלָמָיו כַּאֲשֶׁר יַעֲשֶׂה בְּיוֹם
הַשַּׁבָּת וְיָצָא וְסָגַר אֶת־הַשַּׁעַר
13 אַחֲרֵי צֵאתוֹ: וְכֶבֶשׂ בֶּן־שְׁנָתוֹ
תָּמִים תַּעֲשֶׂה עוֹלָה לַיּוֹם
לַיהֹוָה בַּבֹּקֶר בַּבֹּקֶר תַּעֲשֶׂה
14 אֹתוֹ: וּמִנְחָה תַעֲשֶׂה עָלָיו
בַּבֹּקֶר בַּבֹּקֶר שִׁשִּׁית הָאֵיפָה
וְשֶׁמֶן שְׁלִישִׁית הַהִין לָרֹס אֶת־
הַסֹּלֶת מִנְחָה לַיהֹוָה חֻקּוֹת
15 עוֹלָם תָּמִיד: וְעָשׂוּ אֶת־
הַכֶּבֶשׂ וְאֶת־הַמִּנְחָה וְאֶת־

---

v. 15. ‏יעשו ק׳

the same gate as the worshippers, because, as Kimchi remarks, it accords with the honour and dignity of a ruler to be among his people.

11-15 FURTHER REGULATIONS CONCERNING OFFERINGS

11. Cf. verse 7. Some Jewish commentators define *feasts* as Pentecost and *appointed seasons* as the New Year and Day of Atonement.

12. *when the prince shall prepare a freewill-offering.* If the *Nasi* happen to bring a freewill-offering on a week-day, when

the east inner gate is closed, it is to be opened for him and closed immediately after his departure. Only on the Sabbaths and new moon, when people were free from work and came to worship in the Temple in considerable numbers, the gate remained open until the evening.

13. *thou shalt prepare a lamb . . . daily.* This is identical with the daily or continual offering ordained in Num. xxviii. 4f.; but this sacrifice differs from that in *Numbers* in the amount of its meal-offering and in the omission of the evening sacrifice.

the oil, morning by morning, for a
continual burnt-offering.

16. Thus saith the Lord GOD: If
the prince give a gift unto any of his
sons, it is his inheritance, it shall
belong to his sons; it is their
possession by inheritance. 17. But
if he give of his inheritance a gift to
one of his servants, it shall be his to
the year of liberty; then it shall
return to the prince; but as for his
inheritance, it shall be for his sons.
18. Moreover the prince shall not
take of the people's inheritance, to
thrust them wrongfully out of their
possession; he shall give inheritance
to his sons out of his own possession;
that My people be not scattered
every man from his possession.'

19. Then he brought me through
the entry, which was at the side of
the gate, into the holy chambers for

הַשֶּׁמֶן בַּבֹּקֶר בַּבֹּקֶר עֹלַת

16 תָּמִיד׃׃ כֹּה־אָמַר אֲדֹנָי

יֱהֹוִה כִּי־יִתֵּן הַנָּשִׂיא מַתָּנָה

לְאִישׁ מִבָּנָיו נַחֲלָתוֹ הִיא לְבָנָיו

תִּהְיֶה אֲחֻזָּתָם הִיא בְּנַחֲלָה׃

17 וְכִי־יִתֵּן מַתָּנָה מִנַּחֲלָתוֹ

לְאַחַד מֵעֲבָדָיו וְהָיְתָה לּוֹ

עַד־שְׁנַת הַדְּרוֹר וְשָׁבַת

לַנָּשִׂיא אַךְ נַחֲלָתוֹ בָּנָיו לָהֶם

18 תִּהְיֶה׃ וְלֹא־יִקַּח הַנָּשִׂיא

מִנַּחֲלַת הָעָם לְהוֹנֹתָם

מֵאֲחֻזָּתָם מֵאֲחֻזָּתוֹ יַנְחִל אֶת־

בָּנָיו לְמַעַן אֲשֶׁר לֹא־יָפֻצוּ

19 עַמִּי אִישׁ מֵאֲחֻזָּתוֹ׃׃ וַיְבִיאֵנִי

בַמָּבוֹא אֲשֶׁר עַל־כֶּתֶף

הַשַּׁעַר אֶל־הַלִּשְׁכוֹת הַקֹּדֶשׁ

v. 15.   v. 18. ע״כ לספרדים   ע״כ לאשכנזים

16-18 LIMITED RIGHTS OF THE
NASI OVER HIS LAND

16. *it is his inheritance, it shall belong to
his sons.* A gift of landed property given
by the *Nasi* to one of his sons is not
regarded as a gift which reverts to its
original owner in the Jubilee Year. It
is rather a possession by inheritance and
is therefore transmitted to the sons of the
recipient.

17. *the year of liberty.* The Jubilee Year,
occurring every fiftieth year (Lev. xxv.
10ff.).

*as for his inheritance, it shall be for his
sons.* Kimchi construes: 'his inheritance
is exclusively the inheritance of his sons,
it shall be theirs,' understanding the word

inheritance as virtually repeated before
his sons.

18. *the prince shall not take of the people's
inheritance.* Such an incident as Ahab's
seizure of Naboth's vineyard (1 Kings
xxi) is to be strictly prohibited in the
new era.

19-24 SUPPLEMENT TO THE
DESCRIPTION OF THE TEMPLE

19. *he brought me.* The subject is
Ezekiel's guide.

*through the entry, which was at the side
of the gate.* The reference is probably
to the entrance described in xlii. 9, at
the side of the north gate.

the holy chambers for the priests. They
ran parallel to the Temple on either side,
described in xlii. 1ff.

the priests, which looked toward the north; and, behold, there was a place on the hinder part westward. 20. And he said unto me: 'This is the place where the priests shall boil the guilt-offering and the sin-offering, where they shall bake the meal-offering; that they bring them not forth into the outer court, to sanctify the people.'

21. Then he brought me forth into the outer court, and caused me to pass by the four corners of the court; and, behold, in every corner of the court there was a court. 22. In the four corners of the court there were courts inclosed, forty cubits long and thirty broad; these four in the corners were of one measure. 23. And there was a row

אֶל־הַכֹּהֲנִים הַפֹּנוֹת צָפוֹנָה
וְהִנֵּה־שָׁם מָקוֹם בַּיַּרְכָתָ֫ם
20 יָמָּה: וַיֹּאמֶר אֵלַי זֶה הַמָּקוֹם
אֲשֶׁר יְבַשְּׁלוּ־שָׁם הַכֹּהֲנִים
אֶת־הָאָשָׁם וְאֶת־הַחַטָּאת
אֲשֶׁר יֹאפוּ אֶת־הַמִּנְחָה
לְבִלְתִּי הוֹצִיא אֶל־הֶחָצֵר
הַחִיצוֹנָה לְקַדֵּשׁ אֶת־הָעָם:
21 וַיּוֹצִיאֵנִי אֶל־הֶחָצֵר הַחִיצוֹנָה
וַיַּעֲבִרֵנִי אֶל־־אַרְבַּעַת
מִקְצוֹעֵי הֶחָצֵר וְהִנֵּה חָצֵר
בְּמִקְצֹעַ הֶחָצֵר חָצֵר בְּמִקְצֹעַ
22 הֶחָצֵר: בְּאַרְבַּעַת מִקְצֹעֹת
הֶחָצֵר חֲצֵרוֹת קְטֻרוֹת
אַרְבָּעִים אֹרֶךְ וּשְׁלֹשִׁים רֹחַב
מִדָּה אַחַת לְאַרְבַּעְתָּם
23 מְהֻקְצָעוֹת: וְטוּר סָבִיב בָּהֶם

v. 19. בירכתים ק׳   v. 22. נקוד עליו

which looked toward the north. i.e. they opened towards the outer court northwards.

there was a place on the hinder part westward. At the extreme west end of the longer block of chambers.

20. *the guilt-offering,* etc. The flesh of these sacrifices and the residue of the meal-offering may only be eaten by priests.

to sanctify the people. See on xliv. 19.

21. *in every corner of the court there was a court.* The prophet is now taken from the inner into the outer court where he is shown four enclosures or small courts located at the four corners of the court.

22. *courts inclosed.* The Hebrew word *keturoth,* rendered *inclosed,* is of uncertain meaning. The Rabbis (Middoth 35a) understood it as 'uncovered,' i.e. the enclosures in the four corners were roofless to allow the smoke to pass out freely.

long . . . broad. Length from east to west and breadth from north to south.

in the corners. The Hebrew word for this is placed at the end of the verse and the letters are marked with dots. This is an indication by the Masoretes that the word is doubtful and perhaps to be deleted. It is not found in most of the ancient versions.

of masonry round about in them, round about the four, and it was made with boiling-places under the rows round about. 24. Then said he unto me: 'These are the boiling-places, where the ministers of the house shall boil the sacrifice of the people.'

סָבִיב לְאַרְבַּעְתָּם וּמְבַשְּׁלוֹת עָשׂוּי מִתַּחַת הַטִּירוֹת סָבִיב:

24 וַיֹּאמֶר אֵלַי אֵלֶּה בֵּית הַמְבַשְּׁלִים אֲשֶׁר יְבַשְּׁלוּ־שָׁם מְשָׁרְתֵי הַבַּיִת אֶת־זֶבַח הָעָם:

| 47 | CHAPTER XLVII | מז |

1. And he brought me back unto the door of the house; and, behold, waters issued out from under the threshold of the house eastward, for the forefront of the house looked toward the east; and the waters came down from under, from the right side of the house, on the south of the altar. 2. Then brought he

1 וַיְשִׁבֵנִי אֶל־פֶּתַח הַבַּיִת וְהִנֵּה־מַיִם יֹצְאִים מִתַּחַת מִפְתַּן הַבַּיִת קָדִימָה כִּי־פְנֵי הַבַּיִת קָדִים וְהַמַּיִם יֹרְדִים מִתַּחַת מִכֶּתֶף הַבַּיִת הַיְמָנִית 2 מִנֶּגֶב לַמִּזְבֵּחַ: וַיּוֹצִאֵנִי

23. *of masonry.* Not in the Hebrew text and to be understood.

it was made with boiling-places under the rows. Round about, within the four courts, low recesses were constructed, hollow within for fire-places and openings on top for placing pots over the fire.

24. *ministers of the house.* This more strictly denotes the Levites (cf. xliv. 11), but here it may possibly include the priests.

shall boil the sacrifice of the people. The allusion is to the peace-offerings, the flesh of which is permitted to the offerers. The flesh of such offerings, including the parts belonging to the priests, may be consumed outside the inner court. Hence the installation of cooking facilities for this type of sacrifice in the outer court.

CHAPTER XLVII

IN a final vision Ezekiel is shown the abundance of blessing which the new Temple will bring to the people of Israel. Standing in front of the Sanctuary, he beholds a stream issuing from its threshold, gradually growing into a river, fertilizing the surrounding land, producing fruit and leaves which possess supernatural powers of healing, and sweetening the salt water of the Dead Sea into which it flows. He then draws a plan of the frontiers of the country and describes the boundaries of the portions to be allotted as an everlasting possession to the twelve tribes.

1-12 THE STREAM FROM THE TEMPLE

1. *he brought me back.* Ezekiel is led from the outer court where he was standing (xlvi. 21) back to the inner court where he had previously been.

waters issued out from under the threshold of the house. The abnormal character of this stream is thus made evident.

the waters came down . . . on the south of the altar. The stream flowed in a south-easterly direction passing the altar on the south side and emerged into the open on the south side of the outer east gate.

me out by the way of the gate northward, and led me round by the way without unto the outer gate, by the way of the gate that looketh toward the east; and, behold, there trickled forth waters on the right side.

3. When the man went forth eastward with the line in his hand, he measured a thousand cubits, and he caused me to pass through the waters, waters that were to the ankles. 4. Again he measured a thousand, and caused me to pass through the waters, waters that were to the knees. Again he measured a thousand, and caused me to pass through waters that were to the loins. 5. Afterward he measured a thousand; and it was a river that I could not pass through; for the waters were risen, waters to swim in, a river that could not be passed through. 6. And he said unto me: 'Hast thou seen this, O son of man?' Then he led me, and caused me to return to the bank of the river.

7. Now when I had been brought back, behold, upon the bank of the

דֶּרֶךְ־שַׁעַר צָפוֹנָה וַיְסִבֵּנִי
דֶּרֶךְ חוּץ אֶל־שַׁעַר הַחוּץ
דֶּרֶךְ הַפּוֹנֶה קָדִים וְהִנֵּה־מַיִם
מְפַכִּים מִן־הַכָּתֵף הַיְמָנִית:

3 בְּצֵאת־הָאִישׁ קָדִים וְקָו בְּיָדוֹ
וַיָּמָד אֶלֶף בָּאַמָּה וַיַּעֲבִרֵנִי
4 בַמַּיִם מֵי אָפְסָיִם: וַיָּמָד אֶלֶף
וַיַּעֲבִרֵנִי בַמַּיִם מַיִם בִּרְכָּיִם
וַיָּמָד אֶלֶף וַיַּעֲבִרֵנִי מֵי מָתְנָיִם:

5 וַיָּמָד אֶלֶף נַחַל אֲשֶׁר לֹא־
אוּכַל לַעֲבֹר כִּי־גָאוּ הַמַּיִם
מֵי שָׂחוּ נַחַל אֲשֶׁר לֹא־יֵעָבֵר:

6 וַיֹּאמֶר אֵלַי הֲרָאִיתָ בֶן־אָדָם
וַיּוֹלִכֵנִי וַיְשִׁבֵנִי עַל־שְׂפַת

7 הַנָּחַל: בְּשׁוּבֵנִי וְהִנֵּה אֶל־

---

v. 3. ‎נ״א עַל‎ v. 6. ‎כצ״ל‎ v. 7. ‎נ״א לֹא נמצא מלה עַל נ״א עַל‎

2. *by the way of the gate northward.* Since the inner and outer east gates were closed (xliv. 2, xlvi. 1), the prophet had to be led from the Temple area by the north gate.

led me round by the way without unto the outer gate. From the north outer gate he was conducted outside the wall of the Temple Mount to the east gate.

trickled. The root *pachach* does not occur elsewhere in the Bible. It is evidently the root from which the noun *pach*, 'jar' with a narrow mouth, is derived.

on the right side. i.e. at the south side of the east gate.

3. *when the man went forth eastward.* viz. Ezekiel's guide who led him to the east gate.

the line. Identical with the *line of flax*

in xl. 3, although a different word is used there.

waters that were to the ankles. After a distance of a thousand cubits from the east outer gate, the stream had grown to the depth of a man's ankles.

4. *again he measured a thousand.* After a distance of a second thousand cubits to the east, the depth of the waters reached the knees, and after a third thousand cubits the loins.

5. *waters to swim in.* After the fourth thousand cubits, the depth was such that the stream was impassable except by swimming across.

6. *hast thou seen this?* viz. the increasing depth of the water.

caused me to return to the bank of the river. Having been conducted a distance of

river were very many trees on the
one side and on the other.   8. Then
said he unto me: 'These waters
issue forth toward the eastern
region, and shall go down into the
Arabah; and when they shall enter
into the sea, into the sea of the
putrid waters, the waters shall be
healed.   9. And it shall come to
pass, that every living creature
wherewith it swarmeth, whithersoever the rivers shall come, shall live;
and there shall be a very great
multitude of fish; for these waters
are come thither, that all things be
healed and may live whithersoever
the river cometh.   10. And it shall

שְׂפַת הַנַּחַל עֵץ רַב מְאֹד מִזֶּה
8 וּמִזֶּה: וַיֹּאמֶר אֵלַי הַמַּיִם
הָאֵלֶּה יוֹצְאִים אֶל־הַגְּלִילָה
הַקַּדְמוֹנָה וְיָרְדוּ עַל־הָעֲרָבָה
וּבָאוּ הַיָּמָּה אֶל־הַיָּמָּה
הַמּוּצָאִים וְנִרְפְּאוּ הַמָּיִם:
9 וְהָיָה כָל־נֶפֶשׁ חַיָּה | אֲשֶׁר־
יִשְׁרֹץ אֶל כָּל־אֲשֶׁר יָבוֹא
שָׁם נַחֲלַיִם יִחְיֶה וְהָיָה הַדָּגָה
רַבָּה מְאֹד כִּי בָאוּ שָׁמָּה הַמַּיִם
הָאֵלֶּה וְיֵרָפְאוּ וָחָי כֹּל אֲשֶׁר־
10 יָבוֹא שָׁמָּה הַנָּחַל: וְהָיָה

קמץ בז״ק   v. 9. נחת הא'   v. 8.

four thousand cubits, about a mile and
a third, Ezekiel was brought back to the
bank of the river that he might obtain
a view of the extraordinary fertility
which it had produced throughout the
region.

7. *very many trees.* Both banks, which
presumably had been bare when Ezekiel
set out, were now covered with trees.

8. *these waters issue forth toward the
eastern region.* The prophet is informed
that the river, of which he had only seen
a part, extends over a great area eastward.

the Arabah. 'A term still used for what
is now known as the "Ghor," the deep
trench below the sea-level through which
the Jordan flows from the Lake of
Gennesaret to the Dead Sea, and
extending to the steppes between the
Dead Sea and the Gulf of Akabah at the
head of the Red Sea' (Lofthouse).

into the sea. i.e. the Dead Sea.

the putrid waters. A.J. apparently follows the Peshitta which has 'the bitter
waters.' A.V. renders: 'which being

brought forth into the sea' and R.V.:
'into the sea (shall the waters go) which
were made to issue forth.'   The Hebrew
word *mutsaim* cannot mean 'putrid.'
The Rabbis (quoted by Rashi and
Kimchi) interpret that the river divided
into two separate streams, one flowing
east to the Dead Sea and the other west
to the Mediterranean, as probably
indicated in Zech. xiv. 8.   They explain
the first clause, *they shall enter into the
sea,* as referring to the Dead Sea and the
following clause to the Mediterranean,
understanding the latter as: into the sea
'which is brought out' (so lit.) from the
inhabited world to compass the globe.

the waters shall be healed. Its waters will
sweeten the salty and foul water of the
Dead Sea.   The verb is used similarly in
2 Kings ii. 21f.

9. *every living creature . . . shall live.*
Wherever the river in its two branches
(the Hebrew noun has the dual forma-
tion) flows, the waters of the sea will be
made fresh, and where previously no
aquatic creatures could exist will now
swarm with them.

come to pass, that fishers shall stand by it from En-gedi even unto En-eglaim; there shall be a place for the spreading of nets; their fish shall be after their kinds, as the fish of the Great Sea, exceeding many. 11. But the miry places thereof, and the marshes thereof, shall not be healed; they shall be given for salt. 12. And by the river upon the bank thereof, on this side and on that side, shall grow every tree for food, whose leaf shall not wither, neither shall the fruit thereof fail; it shall bring forth new fruit every month, because the waters thereof issue out of the sanctuary; and the fruit thereof shall be for food, and the leaf thereof for healing.'

13. Thus saith the Lord GOD: 'This shall be the border, whereby ye shall divide the land for inheritance according to the twelve tribes of Israel, Joseph receiving two portions. 14. And ye shall inherit it, one as well as another, concerning

יַעַמְדוּ עָלָיו דַּוָּגִים מֵעֵין גֶּדִי
וְעַד־עֵין עֶגְלַיִם מִשְׁטוֹחַ
לַחֲרָמִים יִהְיוּ לְמִינָה תִּהְיֶה
דְנָתָם כִּדְגַת הַיָּם הַגָּדוֹל רַבָּה
מְאֹד: בִּצֹּאתָו וּגְבָאָיו וְלֹא 11
יֵרָפְאוּ לְמֶלַח נִתָּנוּ: וְעַל־ 12
הַנַּחַל יַעֲלֶה עַל־שְׂפָתוֹ מִזֶּה |
וּמִזֶּה | כָּל־עֵץ־מַאֲכָל לֹא־
יִבּוֹל עָלֵהוּ וְלֹא־יִתֹּם פִּרְיוֹ
לָחֳדָשָׁיו יְבַכֵּר כִּי מֵימָיו מִן־
הַמִּקְדָּשׁ הֵמָּה יוֹצְאִים וְהָיוּ
פִרְיוֹ לְמַאֲכָל וְעָלֵהוּ
לִתְרוּפָה: כֹּה אָמַר אֲדֹנָי 13
יֱהוִֹה גֵּה גְבוּל אֲשֶׁר תִּתְנַחֲלוּ
אֶת־הָאָרֶץ לִשְׁנֵי עָשָׂר שִׁבְטֵי
יִשְׂרָאֵל יוֹסֵף חֲבָלִים:
וּנְחַלְתֶּם אוֹתָהּ אִישׁ כְּאָחִיו 14

---

10. *En-gedi.* lit. 'the well of the kid,' the modern Ain Jidi, located about the centre of the western shore of the Dead Sea.

En-eglaim. 'Perhaps the village of Ain-el-feshkah at the northwest end of the Dead Sea' (Lofthouse).

the Great Sea. The Mediterranean.

11. *they shall be given for salt.* The marshy land around the Dead Sea will remain in its former state to supply the needs of the people for salt.

12. *by the river . . . shall grow every tree for food.* The fertility of the banks along the river, referred to in verse 7, is here described in detail. The trees will not only produce fruit in abundance,

bearing a new crop every month, but their leaves will be possessed of curative powers. Apart from its literal meaning, the image of the river also indicates the moral regeneration which would be effected by the existence of the Temple and the spiritual bliss which will ensue.

13-23 THE NEW FRONTIERS OF THE HOLY LAND

13. *Joseph receiving two portions.* Manasseh and Ephraim are reckoned as two tribes. This explains the number *twelve tribes* given in the preceding clause, seeing that the tribe of Levi received no portion.

14. *one as well as another.* This means that each tribe will receive an equal tract,

326

which I lifted up My hand to give it unto your fathers; and this land shall fall unto you for inheritance. 15. And this shall be the border of the land: on the north side, from the Great Sea, by the way of Hethlon, unto the entrance of Zedad; 16. Hamath, Berothah, Sibraim, which is between the border of Damascus and the border of Hamath; Hazer-hatticon, which is by the border of Hauran. 17. And the border from the sea shall be Hazar-enon at the border of Damascus, and on the north northward is the border of Hamath. This is the

אֲשֶׁר נָשָׂאתִי אֶת־יָדִי לְתִתָּהּ לַאֲבֹתֵיכֶם וְנָפְלָה הָאָרֶץ
15 הַזֹּאת לָכֶם בְּנַחֲלָה: וְזֶה־גְּבוּל הָאָרֶץ לִפְאַת צָפוֹנָה מִן־הַיָּם הַגָּדוֹל הַדֶּרֶךְ חֶתְלֹן לְבוֹא
16 צְדָדָה: חֲמָת | בֵּרוֹתָה סִבְרַיִם אֲשֶׁר בֵּין־גְּבוּל דַּמֶּשֶׂק וּבֵין גְּבוּל חֲמָת חָצֵר הַתִּיכוֹן אֲשֶׁר אֶל־גְּבוּל חַוְרָן:
17 וְהָיָה גְבוּל מִן־הַיָּם חֲצַר עֵינוֹן גְּבוּל דַּמֶּשֶׂק וְצָפוֹן | צָפוֹנָה וּגְבוּל חֲמָת וְאֵת פְּאַת צָפוֹן:

in contrast to the first division of the land when the numerical strength of the tribes was taken into consideration (cf. Num. xxvi. 54).

I lifted up My hand. A gesture when taking an oath.

15. *the land.* i.e. the land of Israel on the western side of the Jordan.

on the north side, etc. The northern boundary starts from the Mediterranean on the west; its eastern end is Hazar-enon (verse 17), and it borders on the territory of Hamath and Damascus.

Hethlon. 'Either Heitela, six miles from the coast north of Tripoli, or Adlun, on the coast north of the mouth of the Kasimiye, between Zarephath and Tyre' (Lofthouse).

Zedad. Usually identified with Sadad, south-east of Homs.

16. *Hamath.* This is not the same as the Hamath mentioned in Num. xxxiv. 8, but is to be identified with *Hamath the great* in Amos vi. 2. This region will be included in the territory of the future

Land of Israel, as stated in Zech. ix. 2 (Kimchi). The modern view is that the same town is intended. It was a Hittite stronghold situated on the Orontes.

Berothah. Probably the Berothai of 2 Sam. viii. 8, a city belonging to the king of Zobah. Some identify it with Beraitan near Baalbek.

Sibraim. It may be the Ziphron of Num. xxxiv. 9, between Hamath and Homs.

Hazer-hatticon. i.e. 'central Hazer,' which is considered by some authorities to be identical with Hazar-enon in the next verse.

Hauran. A region east of the Jordan.

17. *Hazar-enon.* Cf. Num. xxxiv. 9f. The sea on the west and Hazar-enan on the east are given in *Numbers* as the limits of the northern frontier. This boundary will be extended in the Holy Land of the future, running along Damascus, Hamath and beyond, to other places not specified here (Kimchi, Malbim).

north side. 18. And the east side, between Hauran and Damascus and Gilead, and the land of Israel, by the Jordan, from the border unto the east sea shall ye measure. This is the east side. 19. And the south side southward shall be from Tamar as far as the waters of Meriboth-kadesh, to the Brook, unto the Great Sea. This is the south side southward. 20. And the west side shall be the Great Sea, from the border as far as over against the entrance of Hamath. This is the west side.

21. So shall ye divide this land unto you according to the tribes of Israel. 22. And it shall come to pass, that ye shall divide it by lot for an inheritance unto you and to the strangers that sojourn among

18 וּפְאַת קָדִים מִבֵּין חַוְרָן וּמִבֵּין
דַּמֶּשֶׂק וּמִבֵּין הַגִּלְעָד וּמִבֵּין
אֶרֶץ יִשְׂרָאֵל הַיַּרְדֵּן מִגְּבוּל
עַל־הַיָּם הַקַּדְמוֹנִי תָּמֹדּוּ וְאֵת
פְּאַת קָדִימָה: 19 וּפְאַת נֶגֶב
תֵּימָנָה מִתָּמָר עַד־מֵי
מְרִיבוֹת קָדֵשׁ נַחֲלָה אֶל־
הַיָּם הַגָּדוֹל וְאֵת פְּאַת־תֵּימָנָה
נֶגְבָּה: 20 וּפְאַת־יָם הַיָּם הַגָּדוֹל
מִגְּבוּל עַד־נֹכַח לְבוֹא חֲמָת
זֹאת פְּאַת־יָם: 21 וְחִלַּקְתֶּם
אֶת־הָאָרֶץ הַזֹּאת לָכֶם
לְשִׁבְטֵי יִשְׂרָאֵל: 22 וְהָיָה תַּפִּלוּ
אוֹתָהּ בְּנַחֲלָה לָכֶם וּלְהַגֵּרִים
הַגָּרִים בְּתוֹכְכֶם אֲשֶׁר־

18. *between Hauran and Damascus and Gilead, and the land of Israel.* The first two are the starting-point of the eastern boundary at the northern end, while the last two are referred to as being separated by the eastern border, viz. the Jordan, running from north to south.

by the Jordan, from the border unto the east sea shall ye measure. Rashi explains: The Jordan forms the eastern frontier from the north-east corner and extends to the Dead Sea. Transjordan is therefore not included.

19. *Tamar.* The name means 'palm-tree' and the Targum identifies it with Jericho which is called *the city of palm-trees* (Deut. xxxiv. 3); others consider it to be Hazazon-tamar (Gen. xiv. 7), another name of En-gedi (cf. 2 Chron. xx. 2 and see on verse 10).

the waters of Meriboth-kadesh. Cf. Num. xxvii. 14. Kadesh is the modern Ain

Kadis in the desert between Egypt and Canaan.

to the Brook. i.e. the Brook of Egypt (cf. Num. xxxiv. 5), now called Wadi-el-Arish.

20. *from the border as far as over against the entrance of Hamath.* The western frontier is the Mediterranean starting from the Brook of Egypt, the extreme point in the south, and extending as far as the entrance to Hamath (see on verse 16) in the north-west.

21. *this land.* The land west of the Jordan, the borders of which were described in the preceding verses.

22. *the strangers that sojourn among you.* Jewish commentators explain the allusion to be to aliens who were resident among the Israelites in exile, embraced Judaism, and brought up families there. They are to receive an equal allotment of land with

you, who shall beget children among
you; and they shall be unto you as
the home-born among the children
of Israel; they shall have inheritance
with you among the tribes of Israel.
23. And it shall come to pass, that in
what tribe the stranger sojourneth,
there shall ye give him his inheritance, saith the Lord GOD.

הוֹלִדוּ בָנִים בְּתוֹכְכֶם וְהָיוּ
לָכֶם כְּאֶזְרָח בִּבְנֵי יִשְׂרָאֵל
אִתְּכֶם יִפְּלוּ בְנַחֲלָה בְּתוֹךְ
שִׁבְטֵי יִשְׂרָאֵל : וְהָיָה בַשֵּׁבֶט 23
אֲשֶׁר־גָּר הַגֵּר אִתּוֹ שָׁם תִּתְּנוּ
נַחֲלָתוֹ נְאֻם אֲדֹנָי יֱהֹוִה:

48 CHAPTER XLVIII מח

1. Now these are the names of the
tribes: from the north end, beside
the way of Hethlon to the entrance
of Hamath, Hazar-enan, at the
border of Damascus, northward
beside Hamath; and they shall have
their sides east and west: Dan, one

וְאֵלֶּה שְׁמוֹת הַשְּׁבָטִים מִקְצֵה 1
צָפוֹנָה אֶל־יַד דֶּרֶךְ־חֶתְלֹן |
לְבוֹא חֲמָת חֲצַר עֵינָן גְּבוּל
דַּמֶּשֶׂק צָפוֹנָה אֶל־יַד חֲמָת
וְהָיוּ־לוֹ פְאַת־קָדִים הַיָּם הֵן

---

the Israelites. This interpretation is
apparently based on the Talmudic
dictum (Yeb. 24b) that no proselytes will
be accepted in the Messanic age. On the
modern view, this law applies to aliens
who, by begetting children in the Land of
Israel, gave evidence of their intention of
residing there permanently.

23. *there shall ye give him his inheritance.*
A portion of land is to be assigned to him
in the territory of the tribe among which
he lived.

CHAPTER XLVIII
APPORTIONMENT OF THE LAND

THE boundaries of the land being
determined, the prophet deals finally
with its division among the tribes. The
whole territory west of the Jordan is to
be divided into twelve parallel portions
running from east to west, each tribe
receiving an equal share in the following
order from north to south: Dan, Asher,
Naphtali, Manasseh, Ephraim, Reuben,
Judah, Benjamin, Simeon, Issachar,
Zebulun and Gad. Between the ter-

ritories of Judah and Benjamin is
situated *the holy portion of the land,* i.e.
Jerusalem, comprising the Temple area,
the domains of the priests, Levites and
the *Nasi,* as well as a city for lay-
Israelites. It is noteworthy that the
tribes descended from the handmaids,
Bilhah and Zilpah, are placed at the
extreme ends, farthest from the Sanctuary.

1-7 TERRITORIES OF THE SEVEN TRIBES
NORTH OF THE SANCTIFIED PORTION

1. *these are the names of the tribes.*
Among whom the land of the northern
zone is to be divided.

from the north end. As with the boundaries of the land, so here the description
of the tribal territories begins with the
northern end.

beside the way of Hethlon, etc. The
northern frontier is described from west
to east along the way of Hethlon, the
entrance of Hamath, Hazar-enan, etc.

and they shall have. Kimchi renders:
'and they shall be his,' i.e. the frontier

portion. 2. And by the border of Dan, from the east side unto the west side: Asher, one portion. 3. And by the border of Asher, from the east side even unto the west side: Naphtali, one portion. 4. And by the border of Naphtali, from the east side unto the west side: Manasseh, one portion. 5. And by the border of Manasseh, from the east side unto the west side: Ephraim, one portion. 6. And by the border of Ephraim, from the east side even unto the west side: Reuben, one portion. 7. And by the border of Reuben, from the east side unto the west side: Judah, one portion.

8. And by the border of Judah, from the east side unto the west side, shall be the offering which ye shall set aside, five and twenty thousand reeds in breadth, and in length as one of the portions, from the east side unto the west side; and the sanctuary shall be in the midst

2 אֶחָד : וְעַל ׀ גְּבוּל דָּן מִפְּאַת
קָדִים עַד־פְּאַת יָמָּה אָשֵׁר
3 אֶחָד : וְעַל ׀ גְּבוּל אָשֵׁר מִפְּאַת
קָדִימָה וְעַד־פְּאַת־יָמָּה
4 נַפְתָּלִי אֶחָד : וְעַל ׀ גְּבוּל
נַפְתָּלִי מִפְּאַת קָדְמָה עַד־
5 פְּאַת יָמָּה מְנַשֶּׁה אֶחָד : וְעַל ׀
גְּבוּל מְנַשֶּׁה מִפְּאַת קָדְמָה
עַד־פְּאַת יָמָּה אֶפְרַיִם אֶחָד :
6 וְעַל ׀ גְּבוּל אֶפְרַיִם מִפְּאַת
קָדִים וְעַד־פְּאַת־יָמָּה
7 רְאוּבֵן אֶחָד : וְעַל ׀ גְּבוּל
רְאוּבֵן מִפְּאַת קָדִים עַד־
8 פְּאַת יָמָּה יְהוּדָה אֶחָד : וְעַל
גְּבוּל יְהוּדָה מִפְּאַת קָדִים
עַד־פְּאַת יָמָּה תִּהְיֶה
הַתְּרוּמָה אֲשֶׁר־תָּרִימוּ חֲמִשָּׁה
וְעֶשְׂרִים אֶלֶף רֹחַב וְאֹרֶךְ
כְּאַחַד הַחֲלָקִים מִפְּאַת
קָדִימָה עַד־פְּאַת־יָמָּה
וְהָיָה הַמִּקְדָּשׁ בְּתוֹכוֹ :

כצ"ל v. 8.

places just mentioned, along the whole length from west to east, shall be apportioned to Dan (so A.V., 'these are his sides'). No mention is made of the width of these tribal tracts. But the Rabbis (*Siphrë, Deuteronomy*, section 315, quoted by Rashi) give the width as 25,000 reeds. Apparently the Rabbis derived this from the clause *in breadth, and in length as one of the portions* (verse 8), which equated the dimensions

of *the sanctified portion* with those of a tribal tract.

2. *by the border of Dan.* Next to Dan to the south is the territory of Asher, and similarly with what follows.

8-22 THE SANCTIFIED PORTION
8. *by the border of Judah*, etc. Bordering on Judah's territory to the south, a tract 25,000 cubits from north to south and the

ot it. 9. The offering that ye shall set apart unto the LORD shall be five and twenty thousand reeds in length, and ten thousand in breadth. 10. And for these, even for the priests, shall be the holy offering; toward the north five and twenty thousand [in length], and toward the west ten thousand in breadth, and toward the east ten thousand in breadth, and toward the south five and twenty thousand in length; and the sanctuary of the LORD shall be in the midst thereof. 11. The sanctified portion shall be for the priests of the sons of Zadok, that have kept My charge, that went not astray when the children of Israel went astray, as the Levites went astray. 12. And it shall be unto them a portion set apart from the offering of the land, a thing most holy, by the border of the Levites.

9 הַתְּרוּמָ֞ה אֲשֶׁ֧ר תָּרִ֛ימוּ לַֽיהוָ֖ה אֹ֗רֶךְ חֲמִשָּׁ֤ה וְעֶשְׂרִים֙ אֶ֔לֶף וְרֹ֖חַב עֲשֶׂ֥רֶת אֲלָפִֽים׃

10 וּ֠לְאֵ֜לֶּה תִּהְיֶ֣ה תְרֽוּמַת־הַקֹּ֗דֶשׁ לַכֹּהֲנִים֩ צָפ֨וֹנָה חֲמִשָּׁ֧ה וְעֶשְׂרִ֣ים אֶ֗לֶף וְיָ֙מָּה֙ רֹ֚חַב עֲשֶׂ֣רֶת אֲלָפִ֔ים וְקָדִ֗ימָה רֹ֚חַב עֲשֶׂ֣רֶת אֲלָפִ֔ים וְנֶ֕גְבָּה אֹ֕רֶךְ חֲמִשָּׁ֥ה וְעֶשְׂרִ֖ים אָ֑לֶף וְהָיָ֥ה מִקְדַּשׁ־יְהוָ֖ה בְּתוֹכֽוֹ׃

11 לַכֹּהֲנִ֤ים הַֽמְקֻדָּשׁ֙ מִבְּנֵ֣י צָד֔וֹק אֲשֶׁ֥ר שָׁמְר֖וּ מִשְׁמַרְתִּ֑י אֲשֶׁ֣ר לֹֽא־תָע֗וּ בִּתְעוֹת֙ בְּנֵ֣י יִשְׂרָאֵ֔ל כַּאֲשֶׁ֥ר תָּע֖וּ הַלְוִיִּֽם׃

12 וְהָ֥יְתָה לָהֶ֛ם תְּרֽוּמִיָּ֖ה מִתְּרוּמַ֣ת הָאָ֑רֶץ קֹ֥דֶשׁ קָדָשִׁ֖ים אֶל־

v. 10. ב׳ טעמים

---

whole length of the land from east to west, is to be set aside for special settlements which are detailed (cf. xlv. 1ff.).

9. *the offering* (terumah) . . . *unto the LORD.* viz. a tract to be inhabited by the priests, and in its centre space allocated as the area of the Temple.

10. *for the priests, shall be the holy offering.* This explains the preceding verse. The *offering* within the larger *offering* is the priests' domain with the Temple in the centre.

toward the north, etc. The northern and southern extent of the priests' domain measured 25,000 long from east to west, and the eastern and western 10,000 from north to south.

11. *the sanctified portion shall be for the priests.* So also Rashi; but Kimchi, following the Targum, renders: '(this portion) shall be for the sanctified priests' (similarly A.V. and R.V.: 'it shall be for the priests that are sanctified'). Grammatically the former is preferable.

the sons of Zadok. Cf. xliv. 15.

12. *a portion . . . from the offering of the land, a thing most holy.* While the larger tract, set apart as an *offering of the land* for the priests, Levites, the *Nasi* and the city, is holy in contrast to the land in general, the smaller strip measuring 25,000 by 10,000 reserved for the priests and the Temple, is *most holy* (cf. xlv. 3).

by the border of the Levites. See on the next verse.

13. And answerable unto the border of the priests, the Levites shall have five and twenty thousand in length, and ten thousand in breadth; all the length shall be five and twenty thousand, and the breadth ten thousand. 14. And they shall not sell of it, nor exchange, nor alienate the first portion of the land; for it is holy unto the LORD.

15. And the five thousand that are left in the breadth, in front of the five and twenty thousand, shall be for common use, for the city, for dwelling and for open land; and the city shall be in the midst thereof.

16. And these shall be the measures

13 גְּבוּל הַלְוִיִּם: וְהַלְוִיִּם לְעֻמַּת
גְּבוּל הַכֹּהֲנִים חֲמִשָּׁה וְעֶשְׂרִים
אֶלֶף אֹרֶךְ וְרֹחַב עֲשֶׂרֶת
אֲלָפִים כָּל־אֹרֶךְ חֲמִשָּׁה
וְעֶשְׂרִים אֶלֶף וְרֹחַב עֲשֶׂרֶת
14 אֲלָפִים: וְלֹא־יִמְכְּרוּ מִמֶּנּוּ
וְלֹא יָמֵר וְלֹא יַעֲבוֹר רֵאשִׁית
הָאָרֶץ כִּי־קֹדֶשׁ לַיהוָה:
15 וַחֲמֵשֶׁת אֲלָפִים הַנּוֹתָר בָּרֹחַב
עַל־פְּנֵי חֲמִשָּׁה וְעֶשְׂרִים אֶלֶף
חֹל־הוּא לָעִיר לְמוֹשָׁב
וּלְמִגְרָשׁ וְהָיְתָה הָעִיר
16 בְּתוֹכֹה: וְאֵלֶּה מִדּוֹתֶיהָ פְּאַת

v. 14. יעביר ק׳   v. 15. בתוכו ק׳

13. *answerable unto the border of the priests,* etc. The portion assigned to the Levites within *the offering set apart* is of the same dimension as that of the priests, viz. 25,000 long east to west by 10,000 broad north to south, and runs close to it. According to Rashi, it was situated to the south of the priests' portion; others are of the opinion that it was to the north of it.

all the length . . . and the breadth. Whereas the priests did not have the whole portion for their own use, since an area of 500 square was set aside for the Sanctuary, the Levites had the use of all their portion.

14. *they shall not sell of it.* This regulation applies to the territories of the priests and Levites. Their possessions are holy like the *terumah* and therefore inalienable.

the first portion (reshith). *Terumah,* the priestly dues from the crops, is called *reshith, first-fruits,* in Deut. xviii. 4.

Similarly, the portions of the priests and Levites in the land are designated *terumah* (verse 9) and *reshith,* and the same law holds good of both.

15. *the five thousand that are left in the breadth.* The whole tract set aside as an *offering* measured 25,000 cubits (or reeds) square. Of this, the domains of the priests and Levites occupied the entire length from east to west and 20,000 of the breadth from north to south. There was accordingly a narrow strip left 25,000 long by 5,000 wide. This portion was to be used for the city and its surrounding fields.

16. *these shall be the measures thereof.* viz. of the city. In the centre of the strip of land, measuring 25,000 by 5,000, the city is to be located. It would occupy an area of 4,500 square, surrounded by an open space measuring 250 on each side, making a total of 5,000 square. This left two unoccupied strips of 10,000 by 5,000 to the east and west.

thereof: the north side four thousand and five hundred, and the south side four thousand and five hundred, and on the east side four thousand and five hundred, and the west side four thousand and five hundred. 17. And the city shall have open land: toward the north two hundred and fifty, and toward the south two hundred and fifty, and toward the east two hundred and fifty, and toward the west two hundred and fifty. 18. And the residue in the length, answerable unto the holy offering, shall be ten thousand eastward, and ten thousand westward; and it shall be answerable unto the holy offering; and the increase thereof shall be for food unto them that serve the city. 19. And they that serve the city, out of all the tribes of Israel, shall till it. 20. All the offering shall be five and twenty thousand by five and twenty

צָפֹ֗ון חֲמֵ֤שׁ מֵאֹות֙ וְאַרְבַּ֣עַת
אֲלָפִ֔ים וּפְאַת־נֶ֙גֶב֙ חֲמֵ֣שׁ חֲמֵ֣שׁ
מֵאֹ֔ות וְאַרְבַּ֖עַת אֲלָפִ֑ים
וּמִפְּאַ֣ת קָדִ֗ים חֲמֵ֤שׁ מֵאֹות֙
וְאַרְבַּ֣עַת אֲלָפִ֔ים וּפְאַת־יָ֖מָּה
חֲמֵ֣שׁ מֵאֹ֔ות וְאַרְבַּ֖עַת אֲלָפִֽים׃
17 וְהָיָ֨ה מִגְרָ֤שׁ לָעִיר֙ צָפֹ֔ונָה
חֲמִשִּׁ֥ים וּמָאתַ֖יִם וְנֶ֑גְבָּה
חֲמִשִּׁ֥ים וּמָאתַ֖יִם וְקָדִ֕ימָה
חֲמִשִּׁ֥ים וּמָאתַ֖יִם וְיָ֖מָּה חֲמִשִּׁ֥ים
18 וּמָאתָֽיִם׃ וְהַנֹּותָ֨ר בָּאֹ֜רֶךְ
לְעֻמַּ֣ת ׀ תְּרוּמַ֣ת הַקֹּ֗דֶשׁ עֲשֶׂ֤רֶת
אֲלָפִים֙ קָדִ֔ימָה וַעֲשֶׂ֣רֶת
אֲלָפִים֙ יָ֔מָּה וְהָיָ֗ה לְעֻמַּת֙
תְּרוּמַ֣ת הַקֹּ֔דֶשׁ וְהָיְתָ֤ה
תְבוּאָתֹה֙ לְלֶ֔חֶם לְעֹבְדֵ֖י
19 הָעִֽיר׃ וְהָעֹבֵ֖ד הָעִ֑יר
יַֽעַבְד֕וּהוּ מִכֹּ֖ל שִׁבְטֵ֥י יִשְׂרָאֵֽל׃
20 כָּל־הַתְּרוּמָ֗ה חֲמִשָּׁ֤ה
וְעֶשְׂרִים֙ אֶ֔לֶף בַּחֲמִשָּׁ֖ה

v. 16. חמש כתיב ולא קרי v. 18. תבואתו ק׳

---

17. open land. Which must neither be built upon nor cultivated.

18. the residue in the length, answerable unto the holy offering. Since the city with its surrounding open spaces occupied a square of 5,000 in the centre, there remained of the 25,000 in length assigned to the city area a portion 10,000 long on the east and west, running along the south of the *holy offering* allotted to the priests. This residue on either side of the city is to be cultivated and the produce used for the needs of its population.

19. out of all the tribes of Israel. The city is the possession of the whole nation. Therefore all its inhabitants, regardless of their tribal descent, have to work in it for the common good.

20. all the offering. The total area, comprising the domains of the priests, Levites and city, formed a square of 25,000 by 25,000 cubits (Kimchi) or reeds (Rashi).

thousand; ye shall set apart the holy offering foursquare, with the possession of the city.

21. And the residue shall be for the prince, on the one side and on the other of the holy offering and of the possession of the city, in front of the five and twenty thousand of the offering toward the east border, and westward in front of the five and twenty thousand toward the west border, answerable unto the portions, it shall be for the prince; and the holy offering and the sanctuary of the house shall be in the midst thereof. 22. Thus the possession of the Levites, and the possession of the city, shall be in the midst of that which is the prince's; between the border of Judah and the border of Benjamin shall be the prince's.

23. And as for the rest of the tribes: from the east side unto the west side: Benjamin, one portion.

24. And by the border of Benjamin, from the east side unto the west side:

וְעֶשְׂרִים אֶלֶף רְבִיעִית תָּרִימוּ
אֶת־תְּרוּמַת הַקֹּדֶשׁ אֶל־
21 אֲחֻזַּת הָעִיר: וְהַנּוֹתָר לַנָּשִׂיא
מִזֶּה וּמִזֶּה ׀ לִתְרוּמַת־הַקֹּדֶשׁ
וְלַאֲחֻזַּת הָעִיר אֶל־פְּנֵי
חֲמִשָּׁה וְעֶשְׂרִים אֶלֶף ׀ תְּרוּמָה
עַד־גְּבוּל קָדִימָה וְיָמָּה עַל־
פְּנֵי חֲמִשָּׁה וְעֶשְׂרִים אֶלֶף עַל־
גְּבוּל יָמָּה לְעֻמַּת חֲלָקִים
לַנָּשִׂיא וְהָיְתָה תְּרוּמַת הַקֹּדֶשׁ
וּמִקְדַּשׁ הַבַּיִת בְּתוֹכֹה:
22 וּמֵאֲחֻזַּת הַלְוִיִּם וּמֵאֲחֻזַּת
הָעִיר בְּתוֹךְ אֲשֶׁר לַנָּשִׂיא יִהְיֶה
בֵּין ׀ גְּבוּל יְהוּדָה וּבֵין גְּבוּל
23 בִּנְיָמִן לַנָּשִׂיא יִהְיֶה: וְיֶתֶר
הַשְּׁבָטִים מִפְּאַת קָדִימָה עַד־
24 פְּאַת־יָמָּה בִּנְיָמִן אֶחָד: וְעַל ׀
גְּבוּל בִּנְיָמִן מִפְּאַת קָדִימָה

v. 21. בתוכו ק'

21. the residue shall be for the prince. The territory assigned to the priests, Levites and city formed a square of 25,000 in the centre of a strip 25,000 broad extending across the whole country from the Jordan to the Mediterranean, and situated between the portions of Judah and Benjamin. The domain of the Nasi is made up of the remainder of this strip on both sides extending to the Jordan on the east and the Mediterranean on the west.

answerable unto the portions. The territory of the Nasi ran alongside the portion of Judah on the north and of Benjamin on the south.

the holy offering and the sanctuary, etc. The portion of the priests with the Temple in the centre is situated between the two halves of the domain of the Nasi.

22. the possession of the Levites. This is to be connected with the preceding verse. The domain of the Levites also lay between the land assigned to the Nasi.

23-29 THE PORTIONS OF THE OTHER FIVE TRIBES

23. as for the rest of the tribes. The remaining five tribes received their land to the south of *the sanctified portion.*

334

Simeon, one portion. 25. And by the border of Simeon, from the east side unto the west side: Issachar, one portion. 26. And by the border of Issachar, from the east side unto the west side: Zebulun, one portion. 27. And by the border of Zebulun, from the east side unto the west side: Gad, one portion. 28. And by the border of Gad, at the south side southward, the border shall be even from Tamar unto the waters of Meribath-kadesh, to the Brook, unto the Great Sea. 29. This is the land which ye shall divide by lot unto the tribes of Israel for inheritance, and these are their portions, saith the Lord God.

30. And these are the goings out of the city: on the north side four thousand and five hundred reeds by measure; 31. and the gates of the city shall be after the names of the tribes of Israel; three gates

עַד־פְּאַת־יָמָּה שִׁמְעֹון
25 אֶחָד: וְעַל | גְּבוּל שִׁמְעֹון
מִפְּאַת קָדִימָה עַד־פְּאַת־
26 יָמָּה יִשָּׂשכָר אֶחָד: וְעַל |
גְּבוּל יִשָּׂשכָר מִפְּאַת קָדִימָה
עַד־פְּאַת־יָמָּה זְבוּלֻן אֶחָד:
27 וְעַל | גְּבוּל זְבוּלֻן מִפְּאַת
קָדִמָה עַד־פְּאַת־יָמָּה גָּד
28 אֶחָד: וְעַל גְּבוּל גָּד אֶל־פְּאַת
נֶגֶב תֵּימָנָה וְהָיָה גְבוּל מִתָּמָר
מֵי מְרִיבַת קָדֵשׁ נַחֲלָה עַל־
29 הַיָּם הַגָּדֹול: זֹאת הָאָרֶץ
אֲשֶׁר־תַּפִּילוּ מִנַּחֲלָה לְשִׁבְטֵי
יִשְׂרָאֵל וְאֵלֶּה מַחְלְקֹתָם נְאֻם
30 אֲדֹנָי יְהֹוִה: וְאֵלֶּה תֹּוצְאֹת
הָעִיר מִפְּאַת צָפֹון חֲמֵשׁ מֵאֹות
וְאַרְבַּעַת אֲלָפִים מִדָּה:
31 וְשַׁעֲרֵי הָעִיר עַל־שְׁמֹות
שִׁבְטֵי יִשְׂרָאֵל שְׁעָרִים שְׁלֹושָׁה

28. *from Tamar unto the . . . Great Sea.* The territory of Gad at the southern extremity runs along the border of the whole land (cf. xlvii. 19).

29. *this is the land . . . and these are their portions.* This is the extent of the land to be occupied by Israel in the restoration, larger than in former days, and this is the plan of its division among the tribes, which varies from the former plan (Malbim).

30-35 THE GATES AND THE CITY'S NEW NAME
30. *these are the goings out of the city.*

The gates of the city; there are twelve in all, three on each side, named after the twelve tribes.

on the north side . . . by measure. The dimensions of the city are repeated here because of the mention of its gates (Kimchi).

31. *the gates of the city . . . tribes of Israel.* The gates on the north and south are named after the sons of Leah; two of the east gates after the sons of Rachel, and the third after the son of her handmaid Bilhah; two of the west gates after the sons of Zilpah, the handmaid

northward: the gate of Reuben, one; the gate of Judah, one; the gate of Levi, one; 32. and at the east side four thousand and five hundred reeds; and three gates: even the gate of Joseph, one; the gate of Benjamin, one; the gate of Dan, one; 33. and at the south side four thousand and five hundred reeds by measure; and three gates: the gate of Simeon, one; the gate of Issachar, one; the gate of Zebulun, one; 34. at the west side four thousand and five hundred reeds, with their three gates: the gate of Gad, one; the gate of Asher, one; the gate of Naphtali, one. 35. It shall be eighteen thousand reeds round about. And the name of the city from that day shall be The LORD is there.'

צְפוֹנָה שַׁעַר רְאוּבֵן אֶחָד שַׁעַר יְהוּדָה אֶחָד שַׁעַר לֵוִי אֶחָד:

32 וְאֶל־פְּאַת קָדִימָה חֲמֵשׁ מֵאוֹת וְאַרְבַּעַת אֲלָפִים וּשְׁעָרִים שְׁלֹשָׁה וְשַׁעַר יוֹסֵף אֶחָד שַׁעַר בִּנְיָמִן אֶחָד שַׁעַר

33 דָּן אֶחָד: וּפְאַת־נֶגְבָּה חֲמֵשׁ מֵאוֹת וְאַרְבַּעַת אֲלָפִים מִדָּה וּשְׁעָרִים שְׁלֹשָׁה שַׁעַר שִׁמְעוֹן אֶחָד שַׁעַר יִשָּׂשכָר אֶחָד שַׁעַר

34 זְבוּלֻן אֶחָד: פְּאַת־יָמָּה חֲמֵשׁ מֵאוֹת וְאַרְבַּעַת אֲלָפִים שְׁעָרֵיהֶם שְׁלֹשָׁה שַׁעַר גָּד אֶחָד שַׁעַר אָשֵׁר אֶחָד שַׁעַר נַפְתָּלִי

35 אֶחָד: סָבִיב שְׁמֹנָה עָשָׂר אָלֶף וְשֵׁם־הָעִיר מִיּוֹם יְהוָה | שָׁמָּה:

חזק

סכום הפסוקים של יחזקאל אלף ומאתים ושבעים ושלשה· כאיל תערג על אפיקי מים כן נפשי תערג אליך אלהים סימן· וחציו· ויהי בעשתי עשרה שנה באחד לחדש· וסדריו תשעה ועשרים· ותרא אתו כי טוב הוא סימן:

of Leah, and the third after Naphtali, the second son of Bilhah.

32. the gate of Joseph. To include Levi in the number twelve, Ephraim and Manasseh are united under the designation of Joseph.

35. eighteen thousand reeds round about. The circumference of the city is about 18,000 cubits (Kimchi) or reeds (Rashi).
the name of the city . . . The LORD is

there. The Jerusalem of the future will receive a new name, symbolizing the permanence of the Divine Presence in the new city. Ezekiel saw in a vision the departure of God's glory from the former Temple and city (xf.); he also beheld the return to the new Temple (xliii). He now concludes with the assurance that the Divine glory will never again depart from the Temple and the new Jerusalem (see on xliv. 2).

AUTHORITIES QUOTED
TERMS AND ABBREVIATIONS

AUTHORITIES QUOTED

Abarbanel, Isaac (1437-1509, Jewish Commentator).

Barnes, W. E. (Christian Hebraist), *Ezekiel* in *A New Commentary on Holy Scripture*, ed. Gore, etc.

Benjamin of Tudela (Jewish Traveller, 12th century), *Itinerary*.

Biur—Hebrew Commentary on the Pentateuch by Moses Mendelssohn (1729-1786) and collaborators.

Cooke, G. A. (Christian Hebraist), *Ezekiel* (International Critical Commentary).

Davidson, A. B. (Christian Hebraist), *Ezekiel* (Cambridge Bible).

Ehrlich, A. B. (Bible Exegete), *Randglossen zur hebräischen Bibel*.

Eitan, I. (Jewish Orientalist), *A Contribution to Biblical Lexicography*.

Elijah of Wilna (1720-1797, Annotator on the Bible and Talmud).

Franck, A. (Jewish Scholar), *The Kabbalah*.

Geiger, A. (Jewish Exegete), *Urschrift und Uebersetzungen der Bibel*.

Ginzberg, L. (Jewish Scholar), *Ginze Schechter*.

Hertz, J. H. (late Chief Rabbi), *The Pentateuch with Haftorahs*.

Ibn Ezra, Abraham (1092-1167, Jewish Commentator).

Jehudah Halevi (*c.* 1085-*c.* 1142, Jewish Poet and Philosopher), *Kuzari*.

Jellinek, A. (Jewish Scholar), *Beth ha-Midrash*.

Kimchi, David (1160-1235, Jewish Commentator).

Kirkpatrick, A. F. (Christian Hebraist), *The Doctrine of the Prophets*.

Lofthouse, W. F. (Christian Hebraist), *Ezekiel* (Century Bible).

Maimonides, Moses (1135-1204, Jewish Philosopher), *Guide for the Perplexed*.

Malbim, M. L. (1809-1879, Jewish Commentator).

McFadyen, J. E. (Christian Hebraist), *Ezekiel* in Peake's *Commentary on the Bible*.

Mechilta—Ancient Rabbinical Commentary on *Exodus*.

Metsudath David ('Tower of David'), Hebrew Commentary on Books of the Bible by David Altschul (17th century).

Midrash—Rabbinical Homilies on the Pentateuch, etc.

Mishnah—Codification of Jewish law (*c.* 200 C.E.).

Nachmanides, Moses (1194-*c.* 1270, Jewish Commentator).

Peshitta—Syriac Translation of the Bible (2nd century C.E.).

Pesikta Rabbathi—Midrashic Homilies (*c.* 9th century).

Pirkë d'R. Eliezer—A Midrashic collection (9th century).

Rabbinowitz, J. (Anglo-Jewish Scholar), *Mishnah Megillah*.

Rashi (Rabbi Solomon ben Isaac, 1040-1105, Jewish Commentator).

Robinson, Wheeler (Christian Hebraist), *Two Hebrew Prophets*).

AUTHORITIES QUOTED—*continued.*

Scholem, G. (Jewish Scholar), *Major Trends in Jewish Mysticism.*

Seder Olam—Early Jewish Chronicle.

Septuagint—Greek Translation of the Bible, begun in the third century B.C.E.

Shulchan Aruch—Compendium of Jewish law (16th century).

Siphra—Ancient Rabbinical Commentary on *Leviticus.*

Siphrë—Ancient Rabbinical Commentary on *Numbers* and *Deuteronomy.*

Smith, W. R. (Christian Orientalist), *The Prophets of Israel.*

Stanley, A. P. (English Ecclesiastical Scholar), *Sinai and Palestine.*

Strabo (*c.* 63 B.C.E.-21 C.E., Greek Geographer).

Sulzberger, M. (American-Jewish Scholar), *The Ancient Hebrew Parliament.*

Talmud—Corpus of Jewish Law and Thought, compiled at the end of the fifth century C.E.

Tanchuma—Midrashic Commentary on the Pentateuch (original version 4th century C.E.).

Targum—Aramaic Translation of the Bible (1st and 2nd centuries C.E.).

Thomson, W. M. (Christian Traveller), *The Land and the Book.*

Tosephta—A Codification of Jewish law, parallel to the Mishnah.

Tristram, H. B. (Natural Scientist), *The Natural History of the Bible.*

Ad. loc. At that place.

A.J. American-Jewish Translation of the Scriptures.

A.V. Authorized Version.

A.Z. *Abodah Zarah*, Talmudical tractate.

B.B. *Baba Bathra*, Talmudical tractate.

B.C.E. Before the Christian era.

B.D.B. *Hebrew and English Lexicon*, ed. Brown, Driver and Briggs.

Bech. *Bechoroth*, Talmudical tractate.

Ber. *Berachoth*, Talmudical tractate.

Ber. R. *Bereshith Rabbah*, Midrashic Commentary on *Genesis*.

B.K. *Baba Kamma*, Talmudical tractate.

c. About

C.E. Common era.

Cf. Compare, refer to.

Chag. *Chagigah*, Talmudical tractate.

ed. Edition, or edited by.

e.g. For example.

etc. And so forth.

f. Following verse or chapter (plural ff.).

Git. *Gittin*, Talmudical tractate.

i.e. That is

kerẽ. The Hebrew as it is read according to the Masoretes.

Kerith. *Kerithoth*, Talmudical tractate.

kethib. The Hebrew as it is written according to tradition.

Kidd. *Kiddushin*, Talmudical tractate.

lit. Literally.

LXX. Septuagint (see Authorities Quoted).

Makk. *Makkoth*, Talmudical tractate.

Meg. *Megillah*, Talmudical tractate.

Men. *Menachoth*, Talmudical tractate.

Merkabah. The Divine Chariot in Ezekiel's **visions**:

M.K. *Moed Katon*, Talmudical tractate.

MS. Manuscript (plural MSS.).

M.T. Masoretic text.

Nasi. 'Prince', the ruler of the reorganized Israel State

R.H. *Rosh Hashanah*, Talmudical tractate.

R.V. Revised version.

Sanh. *Sanhedrin*, Talmudical tractate.

Shab. *Shabbath*, Talmudical tractate.

Shebi. *Shebiith*, Talmudical tractate.

Suk. *Sukkah*, Talmudical tractate.

Taan. *Taanith*, Talmudical tractate.

T.B. Talmud of Babylon.

viz. Namely.

Yeb. *Yebamoth*, Talmudical tractate.

Zeb. *Zebachim*, Talmudical tractate.

Nasi. Prince, the ruler of the reorganized Israel State

R.H. Rosh Hashanah, Talmudical tractate.

R.V. Revised version.

Sanh. Sanhedrin, Talmudical tractate.

Shab. Shabbath, Talmudical tractate.

Shebi. Shebiith, Talmudical tractate.

Suk. Sukkah, Talmudical tractate.

Taan. Taanith, Talmudical tractate.

T.B. Talmud of Babylon.

viz. Namely.

Yeb. Yebamoth, Talmudical tractate.

Zeb. Zebachim, Talmudical tractate.

INDEX

I. NAMES AND SUBJECTS

INDEX

I. NAMES AND SUBJECTS

A

Abraham, 226

Adulteress, punishment of a, 94, 155

Alexander the Great, 254

Aliens, allotment of land to, 328f.

Altars, idolatrous, 30

Ammon, 138, 141f.; prophecy against, 168f., 170

Amorite, 84, 95

Angels, of destruction, 47

Anthropomorphisms, 8, 25

Antimony, 158

Arabah, the, 325

Arabia, 184

Aram, 98, 183

Arrows, used in divination, 138, 139

Arvad, 180, 181

Asher, allotment to, 329; the gate of, 336

Asshur, 184

Assyria, former greatness of, 208f.; invasion by, 154f.; Israel's alliance with, 91, 152; overthrow of, 210f., 218; Samaria's advances to, 150f.

Aven (Heliopolis), 205

B

Baal, worship of, in Samaria, 109

Baal-meon, 170

Babylon, arrogance of, 35; desecrated the Temple, 39; exile to, foretold, 66; invasion of Judea by, 2f., 132, 154f.; Israel's rebellion against, denounced, 2, 57; Judea's advances to, 152f.; 'worst of the nations,' 39

Balances, accurate, enjoined, 313

Baldness, artificial, mark of mourning, 38, 187

Balm, traffic in, 183

Balsam, traffic in, 183

Bamah, 127

Barber's razor, 24

Barley, 73

Bashan, fatlings of, 263; oaks of, 179

Bath (measure), 313f.

Battering rams, 19, 139, 174

Benjamin, allocation to, 334; the gate of, 336

Benjamin of Tudela, *quoted*, ix

Berothah, 327

Beryl, 5, 53, 191

Beth-jeshimoth, 170

Blaspheme, meaning of, 126

Blood, 'eating with the,' 226

Bones, vision of the dry, 246ff.

Branch, put to the nose (pagan rite), 46

Bread, 'of men,' eating the, 165; 'staff of,' 23, 28, 78

Bribery, in Jerusalem, 145

Brier, pricking, 194

Brook (of Egypt), the, 328, 335

Burnt-offering, 275f., 299f., 301, 304, 315, 317, 318, 320

C

Calamus, traffic in, 183

Canaan, meaning 'merchant,' 91, 101

Canneh, 184

Cannibalism, 27

Carbuncles, 191; traffic in, 183

Carnelian, 191

Cassia, traffic in, 183

Cedar, of Lebanon, 179; symbol of Jerusalem, 101

Chaldea, images painted on walls in, 152; Israel's alliance with, 91

'Chambers of imagery,' 44

Chebar, the river, 2, 15, 18, 54, 55f., 293

Cherethites, the, 172

Cherub(im), the, 48, 50ff., 62, 192, 284f., 286

Child, treatment of a newborn, 84

Conduits, 208

Cor (measure), 314

Coral, traffic in, 183

Corpse, defilement by a, 49, 308

Covenant, new, with Israel, 233

Crete, 171

Crocodile, the, symbol of Egypt, 196, 213

Cub (land), 202

Cubit, dimension of a, 267

Cush, 254

Cushions, 'sewn upon elbows,' 73f.

Cypress-trees, 179, 209

Cyprus, 180

Cyrus, king, 201

D

Damascus, 183, 327, 328

Dan, allotment to, 329; the gate of, 336

Daniel, piety of, 78, 80; wisdom of, 189

Davidic dynasty, to be restored, 107, 233, 251f.

Dedan, 171, 182, 184, 255

Diblah, the wilderness of, 33

Divination, 75, 138, 148

Dough, first portion of the, 309

INDEX

Doves, of the valleys, 37
Drink-offerings, 127, 315
Dung, used as fuel, 22f.

E

Eagle, parable of the, 100ff.
Earrings, 87
Eden, 184; the garden of, 191, 210, 212, 245
Edom, prophecy against, 170f., 235ff.
Egypt, destruction of, by Babylon, 216; doom of, 201ff.; experience of Israel in, 84f.; Israel's alliance with, 90, 104; Judea's advances to, 153f.; linen produced in, 180; promises of help unreliable, 105, 197; prophecy against, 196ff., 212
Elam, 218
Elders, council will perish from the, 39f.
Electrum, the colour of, 3, 8, 41
Elishah, the isles of, 180
Emerald, 191
En-eglaim, 326
En-gedi, 326
Enoch, the Books of, *quoted*, 5, 9
Ephah (measure), 313f.
Ephraim, allocation to, 330; name for the Northern Kingdom, 250
Ethiopia, 198, 202, 203
Exile, 'stuff for,' 63
Ezekiel, appointed 'watchman' to Israel, 16, 222; assumes rôle of a refugee, 63ff.; attitude of exiles towards, 227f.; Book of, xiiif.; call to, xiii, 1f.; characteristics as prophet, ixf.; comforts the exiles, 60f.; commanded to lie on his sides, 20f.; denounced rebellion against Babylon, 57ff.; eats 'roll of a book,' 11f.; foretells the doom of Jerusalem, 161ff.; hair shaven, 24f.; intercedes in vain for Jerusalem, 49f.; messages to exiles in Babylon, 14, 62; mission of, 9ff.; mysticism of, xiff.; ordered an austere diet, 66f.; personal life of, ix; priestly element in, xf.; receives news of Jerusalem's fall, 225f.; sees the vision of dry bones, 246ff.; silence imposed by God, 18; style of, x; Temple of the future revealed to, 265ff.; to sigh over destruction of the Temple, 134f.; traditional sepulchre of, ix; visions of, 1ff., 12, 40ff., 46ff., 50ff., 246ff., 265ff. ; wife dies, 164f.

F

Face, covering the, 64
Foot, stamping the, gesture of gloating, 169; of grief, 32
Foxes, in ruins, 69
Freewill offering, 320
Fruits, first-ripe, offered in the Temple, 130, 309

G

Gabriel (archangel), 47, 48
Gad, allocation to, 335; the gate of, 336
Gammadim, the, 181
Gebal, 180
Gerah (coin), 314
Gilead, 328
God, anger of, 28, 32, 34, 35, 37, 46, 72, 79, 93f., 123, 128, 137, 142, 147, 149, 242, 257, 295; covenant of, with Israel, 86, 99, 233; delights not in death of the wicked, 112, 115, 223; entices false prophets, 77; forgives Israel, 100; glory of, manifested, 8, 14f., 17f., 42, 55, 263, 293f., 302f.; holiness of, xvf.; Holy One of Israel, 260, 'jealousy,' meaning of, xv, 41f., 155, 239, 257; Judge, 114, 232f.; justice of, xivf., 34; love for Israel, 83ff.; 'married' Israel, 86; mindful of covenant with Israel, 99; name of, profaned, 73, 130, 148, 242f., 260; pitiless towards sinful Israel, 34, 35, 50; promises Israel's restoration, 61, 99, 106f., 128f., 131, 192, 231ff., 238ff., 264f.; redeemed Israel from Egypt, 121; sanctified by Israel, 130f., 264; 'Shepherd' of Israel, 230ff.; will profane the Temple, 166; will sanctify His name, 243
Gog, war against, 253ff.
Golden calves, in Beth-el and Dan, 109
Gomer, 254
Grapes, sour, 108
Griddle, 20
Guilt-offering, 275, 291, 309, 322

H

Hailstones, 71
Hamath, 327ff.
Hamonah, 262
Hamon-gog, 261f.
Hands, clapping the, gesture of grief, 32
Hands, smiting together, 136, 137, 169
Haran, 184
Hauran, 327, 328
Hazar-enon, 327, 329
Hazer-hatticon, 327
Heart, a new, 114, 243; of flesh, 61, 243; stony, 61, 243
Heave-offering, 130, 309
Helbon, wine of, 183
Helech, 181
Herodotus, *quoted*, 175, 182, 199
Hethlon, 327, 329
High places, idolatrous, 30, 88, 90, 127, 238, 294
Hills, scene of idolatry, 29, 32, 127
Hin, quantity of a, 22
Hittite, 84, 95
Holiness, Ezekiel's concept of, xvf.
Homer (measure), 313f.
Honey, used in idolatrous rites, 89

INDEX

II. Hebrew Words.

349